THE OFFICIAL HORSE BREEDS STANDARDS BOOK

The Complete
Guide to the Standards of all
North American
Equine Breed Associations

FRAN LYNGHAUG

Voyageur Press

Dedication

To the Maker of all horses, Who enjoys them tremendously and will come at the end of the ages, mounted on His horse. It was by His grace that this book was inspired and accomplished.

First published in 2009 by Voyageur Press, an imprint of MBI Publishing Company, 400 First Avenue North, Suite 300, Minneapolis, MN 55401 USA

Voyageur Press titles are also available at discounts in bulk quantity for industrial or sales–promotional use. For details write to Special Sales Manager at MBI Publishing Company, 400 First Avenue North, Suite 300, Minneapolis, MN 55401 USA.

To find out more about our books, visit us online at www.voyageurpress.com.

Library of Congress Cataloging-in-Publication Data

Lynghaug, F.
The official horse breeds standards guide : the complete guide to the standards of all North American equine breed associations / Fran Lynghaug.
p. cm.
Includes bibliographical references and index.
ISBN 978-0-7603-3499-7 (plc : alk. paper)
1. Horse breeds—Standards—North America. 2. Horse breeds—North America—Societies, etc. I. Title.
SF290.N7L964 2009
636.1002'187—dc22

2009006684

Editor: Michael Dregni

Printed in China

On the front cover, top and bottom left: Arabian stallions. *Shutterstock*
Bottom right: Gypsy Vanner horse. *Mark J. Barrett / WR Ranch*

On the title page: Mangalarga Marchador mare and foal. *Kay Holloway*

On the back cover, top: Andalusian stallion. *Richard Beard*
Bottom: Mangalarga Marchador mare and foal. *Kay Holloway*

CONTENTS

Part 4 Draft Breeds: Powerhouse Horses

Part 5 Ponies and Small Horses: Small Size, Big Heart

Part 6 The Classics: Warmbloods and Performance Horses

INTRODUCTION

This book is a reference to the many equine breeds found in North America. It is for anyone interested in horses or ponies who would like to become better acquainted with the qualifications and structure of a breed. It contains descriptions, histories, and official standards of what each horse and pony should be, as presented by their registry. As well as a guide for registering purebreds, it is also a surprising revelation on the many different kinds of equines.

As much as possible, all North American equine breeds with a national registry or representative organization were included. For accuracy's sake, it was important to use registry information because breed facts and standards originate from them. It was attempted not to change their wording or meanings in any way. Contributing registries were either parent societies, or those affiliated with the foreign parent societies and are representatives of them in North America.

It is hoped that a new understanding of the breeds and clarity of the differences among them will bring light to all of the wonderful and interesting horses and ponies.

A NOTE ABOUT THE EXPERTS

The importance of implementing the expertise of national breed organizations and registries for this book cannot be overstated. They are the best recognizable authorities and encyclopedias on equines, as well as the best sources to interpret or expound on equine standards. In most cases, they have facts and insights not accessible anywhere else. Their concern for the breed is the basis for a consistent group effort that endures over time with the purpose of advancing breed purity and understanding.

They provide guidelines for accepted conformation through careful study and by utilizing the knowledge of respected professionals. Having an acute interest in the betterment of their individual breed, they work diligently toward that end. After researching the facts, pooling their sources, and giving much thought and deliberation, they institute breed standards to be as correct and exact as possible. Usually this is done without pay or reward of any kind, yet oftentimes at the risk of criticism and disregard of others. Yet they do it because they love their breed.

Consequently, what they have to say is received as a serious definition. When entering a horse show or registering a horse, their qualifications are all that should matter.

It was through their extraordinary group cooperation and patience that this book was made possible. I am deeply grateful for the privilege and honor of working with them. They win the blue ribbon in the arena of selflessness for caring enough to share the intricacies and many facets of their beloved equines with others.

—*Fran Lynghaug*

ACKNOWLEDGMENTS

Without a doubt, this book was made possible only with the help of a great number of professional horse people who participated with their time and effort to provide a true representation of their breeds, either with articles, advice, research, reviews, or photographs. I regret that space inhibits me from naming each one, but they did a remarkable job. I wouldn't have been able to do this book without these sources and am deeply grateful to them all.

Especially crucial and worthy of special mention were the contributions and professional advice from the Equus Survival Trust and Victoria Tollman. More than a few breeds in this book would not have been included or they wouldn't have been accurately presented without her.

I am particularly grateful to Michael Dregni at Voyageur Press, who understood the vision for this book and was willing to undertake it.

I appreciate the input from my good friend, Theresa Williams, whom I bounced many ideas off and whose input was invaluable.

My husband, Dick, is at the top of the list for his patience while I worked on this project. My kids—Ameé, Tara, Rick, Cat, and Josh—all contributed in some way. My mom and sisters—Karen, Cathy, and Sue—all provided their support in one way or another. My granddaughter, Haley, was particularly patient and lent a hand with the illustrated diagrams.

Thank you all from the bottom of my heart.

—*Fran Lynghaug*

"I can do all things through Christ Jesus which strengtheneth me."

—Phil. 4:13, KJV

DISCLAIMER

Some horse experts may contend that not all of the equine breeds presented in this book are true breeds. Genetically speaking, that may be true, yet in general equine social circles, they have been accepted as breeds.

According to the U.S. Department of Agriculture, Handbook No. 394, "A breed of horse may be defined as a group of horses of common origin and possessing certain, well-defined, distinctive, uniformly transmitted characteristics that are not common to other horses. . . ."

The purpose of this book is to honestly depict the traits usually common to a particular kind of equine. For that reason, it is attempted to give equal attention to all the breeds as represented by the breed organizations and to take each one seriously. There are no presumptions as to which breeds are "authentic" and which are not.

It may also seem that there are several representations of the same breed. If attention is focused on the breed standards, it will be evident that there are differences.

The hope is to define the various breeds or types as accurately as possible, for they are so wonderfully diverse and beautiful in their own unique ways.

THE BREED STANDARD

What are breed standards and why are they important?

Webster defines a standard as "an accepted measure of comparison for quantitative or qualitative value; criterion." Criterion is a standard on which a judgment is based. In other words, a standard is the epitome of a person's or group's intelligent deduction of what the ultimate object is; what it contains, what it looks like, how it acts, and the measure of its worth. A standard is the ideal of what something should be.

Purebreds are supposed to look and behave the way their standards describe. The quality of a horse is directly related to how closely it resembles its breed standards. Observers who marvel at the beauty of a particular horse are, in essence, agreeing with the standards of that breed.

Standards differ from breed to breed. Due to the differences in background and uses, what is an asset in one can be a serious fault in another. Therefore, equine registries have found it necessary to define their own individual breed standards. A knowledgeable breeder is familiar with his or her breed's particular standards and is constantly attempting to achieve them.

In dealing with the genetic nature of animals, physical perfection can never be attained, but the ideal standard is held up as the comparison of how close a horse can be to this ultimate goal. In the show ring, equines are judged by comparing them to their standards. Those that deviate greatly from their breed standards, such as having an unacceptable color, are not considered in any way to be better because they are unique or are different from others in the breed. Instead, they are considerably distanced from what their breed is supposed to be. Individuals that adhere closely to their standards are typically regarded as more desirable for showing and breeding. They hold a higher prestigious position and have much to offer their breed. They are considered more valuable, being appreciated for their better quality.

The difficulty is not in producing a unique horse, but in producing many horses that closely resemble their standards. When this is achieved, it is a sign of a stabilized, recognizable type and good professional breeding. Overall, the purest breeds typically contain many horses with common characteristics, for their gene base is proven and consistent. When a breed like this is mentioned, an immediate mental picture of what it looks like easily comes to mind. An observer is assured of what kind of equine he or she is seeing because it looks the same as others in the breed.

The ironic twist is that an individual horse that carries most of the attributes of its breed to the highest degree is, in fact, unique because of the difficulty in producing this kind of quality. Gene combinations of sire and dam are always a gamble. Not until eleven months later will it be evident if the result mirrors what the pedigree says is there. It is a wonderful challenge attempting to produce the perfect equine.

It can be easy for breeders to be blinded to the faults in their breed lines, due to seeing their own horses on a daily basis. Anything different may look wrong to them, until the quality of their own stock is proven in the show ring under the (hopefully) unbiased opinion of a judge familiar with the breed standards, or the performance ring where the better individuals naturally surface. A horse's worth can also be tested in day-to-day riding or work. These are the defining elements that prove the true quality in a horse or pony and are the reasons why adhesion to standards is so important.

Webster's first definition of a standard is a flag, and that is what the standards in this book are, brilliant flags waving for all to see.

Part 1

Horses of the Range

Breeds of North America's Wild Regions

These are horses that came from wild American ranges, often with foundations that go back even further. Some came from the eastern ranges and are the last remnants of once vast hordes that populated the sea coast. Some are fresh off the panorama of the wide open West. Others have expanded far beyond their original ranges and have become the most popular horse in the world. Still others wait quietly in the recesses of America, rare treasures yet to be discovered. All have something to contribute to the horse world.

They hale distinctly from a time and place where a pioneering workforce was actively establishing a new nation. They are the ancient Spanish breeds, the Indian mounts, or the cow horses filling the need for skill and endurance. They raced, drove cattle, or delivered the mail. Some were America's first warhorses. Many existed for centuries, defying nature and humans in remote areas where their purity could continue.

Their hardiness is profound and popular beyond American borders. With them, the West was won, civilizations were transported, battles were fought, and livestock was moved to feed a nation. Nature instilled them with the strength and survival capabilities that far surpass others.

Independent and devoted, agile and careful, intelligent and agreeable, they are a paradox. They uniquely personify the American way of life.

ABACO BARB

Relaxing in the tropical heat, Abaco Barbs stand in the shade of Caribbean pines to stay cool. *Milanne Rehor*

Arkwild, Inc.
2829 Bird Avenue, Suite 5, PMB 170
Miami, FL 33133
www.arkwild.org

On a small island situated about 150 miles off the southeastern shore of Florida and just north of Nassau in the Bahamas, there lives a herd of rare Spanish horses. The island is called Great Abaco, and it is the only place where these special Spanish horses exist. They have possibly lived here for centuries. They are the Abaco Barbs, wild and romantic Spanish Barb horses. (Abaco is pronounced A´-ba-co, with the accent on the "A.")

The Abaco Barb is considered by some experts as the rarest breed of horse on the planet. DNA tests show that the Abacos are definitely related to the Puerto Rican Paso Fino and are probably the best representative of Spanish Barbs in this region.

They originate from hardy Spanish stock that could endure appalling conditions. When first brought to the New World aboard ships, they survived the journey of six or more weeks, often with little food or water. The horses were either shipwrecked (there are many Spanish shipwrecks on the island's reefs) or abandoned on Great Abaco. Another possibility is that their ancestors were brought from Cuba to help in logging the forests of Grand Abaco and were abandoned when the lumber company switched to tractors.

At one time, there were around two hundred Abaco Barb horses on Great Abaco. Few people would have expected domesticated horses to survive for centuries unattended in this isolated island unlike any other horse county. But the Abaco Barbs did. They aren't the typical scruffy little horses, hard pressed to survive, that are sometimes found on western American frontiers. Instead, they are healthy horses of Barb size, 13 to 13.2 hands, and they are beautiful, bright-coated animals in an assortment of colors, including bays, pintos, and roans. If approached by people, they are cautious, but not spooky, simply turning and walking away or hiding in small, discreet places. They are tough enough to survive on their own, with their only predators being the occasional wild dog that attacks their young, and humans.

Due to the Abaco Barb's endangered status, they are not captured and used for riding or work as other wild horses have been, but are kept in their natural habitat. None of the survivors today has ever had so much as a halter or rope guiding it. They remain rather quiet and confident in their surroundings, unlike wild mainland bands on open plains that find it necessary to move extreme distances. They are curious and intelligent, drifting in and out of the forests with noble grace and dignity. They live on thousands of acres of pine forests on the island, as free as the island winds.

History

There are two competing theories concerning the origins of the Abaco Barb. The first is that they were brought to the New World by Christopher Columbus, or other Spanish explorers, and were either shipwrecked or abandoned on Great Abaco. Columbus did have two horse farms in Cuba, but horses in Cuba today bear no resemblance to the Abaco Barbs.

The second theory holds that the horses were brought to the island from Cuba around the turn of the twentieth century by an American company, Owens-Illinois, when it established logging operations there. According to local sources, these horses were abandoned when tractors came into use; however, it has not been possible to trace the manifests or other documents showing what types the horses were or how many were brought in. Additionally, it seems odd that stallions and mares would both be used for work. If this is the horses' true origin, it is possible that they have only been on Abaco for more than a century.

The logging camps were abandoned in the early 1900s. Little can be found of the logging settlements or industry anymore, except for old logging roads. One notable settlement was called Norman Castle, which was abandoned in 1929 and became the site where the horses found refuge many years later. Regardless of how long the horses lived on the island, they survived more than half of the last century without human interference. Left alone on the island, the horses thrived.

Trees remain of the utmost importance to the Abaco Barb. Caribbean pines (*Pinus caribaea*) exist only on Grand Bahama, Andros, Great Abaco, and New Providence islands. These pine forests have for millennia sheltered flocks of wild parrots and migrating birds, as well as wild hogs abandoned by the early settlers; scores of species of orchids, and other plants, and thousands of insects live there. The forests have also provided a home for the horses, giving shade and protecting them from the burning sun. Without the forests, there was a danger that the pinto spotted horses would become sunburned.

The horses tramp out networks of pathways among the grazing places and sloughs where they water. Even in the worst droughts, the horses have water. The limey outcroppings keep their hooves pared down and naturally trimmed.

Originally the horses had enough room to roam and graze, and they grew sleek. Only an occasional horse was lost to people who captured them for work on sugar cane mills on the island. Bred to survive harsh conditions, they flourished.

In the 1960s, however, disaster struck the horses. It wasn't a hurricane, catastrophic drought, tidal wave, fire, flood, or disease. Instead, it was a road. A simple road was built on Great Abaco running from one end of the island to the other. The Owens-Illinois company had returned and built the road to harvest the remaining forests for pulpwood. The shelter of the pines was gone.

Suddenly, there was access to logging roads left a century ago that had been abandoned but were still passable. The island had been sparsely populated, but now there was a jump in the human population, and some islanders found it great sport to harass and kill the horses. At times they ran the horses down old narrow logging roads until they were close enough to rope them out a vehicle window or until the horses dropped from exhaustion. Many of these victims became legends for the vicious cruelty visited on them and their gruesome ends. After an accident resulting in the death of a child trying to climb unattended on a horse owned by an island resident, there were attempts to wipe out every wild horse on the island by local residents. Wholesale slaughter ensued. These attacks to eliminate all the island horses almost succeeded.

With the slaughter, the horses nearly became extinct by the early 1970s. Around that time, however, three horses were brought out of captivity to a farm being developed near the original herd area. That effort resulted in a herd of about thirty-five head, but their survival is threatened again.

Breed Survival

In 1992, Milanne Rehor, an avid sailor, was planning a vacation to the Bahamas; in preparation, she read two lines in the *Yachtman's Guide to the Bahamas* about the wild horses on Great Abaco. She decided to visit New Plymouth in Green Turtle Cay, an island lying about two miles north of Abaco, where she inquired about the horses. There, she was told the horses had all been killed, and there were not any more wild horses on Abaco.

Sources said, "The horses all died of pesticide poisoning." "I've been going to Abaco for twenty years and I never heard of any horses." "There were horses here, but when the big road went in, some

man tried to capture one by throwing a spear at it. It died." "They all died." This was amazing news, considering that Abaco is a significant island with thousands of acres and only two miles away. No one knew anything about the horses.

Rehor contacted Lynn Key and her husband, Henry, manager of a citrus farm in the Norman Castle area. The Keys took her to the farm and forest area where the horses roamed. Rehor was stunned to find such stately and mysterious horses. They were a healthy, energetic herd of about thirty head that had survived the slaughter of the 1960s. They had beautiful, bright coats in an assortment of colors, including bays, pintos, and roans. Rehor was determined to find out everything about them.

Senator Edison Key, Henry's father, gave her more background information: "When we were clearing the land for a [cattle ranch] project in the early 1970s, we found [horse] carcasses and bones all over. I thought it just wasn't right." That cattle business had ended when Owens-Illinois left.

At that time, the Keys and others decided to help re-establish the native stock of wild horses on Great Abaco. Edison Key and his brother-in-law, Morton Sawyer, were partners in developing the farm and provided the site and resources to create a haven for the horses.

Morton Sawyer's son, Floyd, already had two native Abaco Barb wild horses at the farm, mares named Liz and Jingo. Jingo may have been Liz's foal and may have been named after the horse in the classic 1959 children's story, *Jingo: Wild Horse of Abaco*, written by Jocelyn Arundel and illustrated by Wesley Dennis. The bays in the herd today are from Liz and Jingo, and some of them bear the delicate features that mirror the image of Jingo in Dennis' drawings.

A pinto stallion named Castle, which descended from the native wild Abaco herd, was brought to the farm from Marsh Harbour on Great Abaco, and every pinto in today's growing herd is stamped with his unmistakable look. Castle died a natural death around 1989, when he was close to thirty years old.

The Roman nose and obvious depth of body are Spanish traits, making this Abaco Barb look much larger than the typical 13-hand Abaco. *Milanne Rehor*

Castle, Liz, and Jingo were lucky. Since they had been in captivity, they had escaped the 1970s slaughter. As far as anyone can tell, they were the last surviving native island stock in existence. They shared buildings, shelter, feed, grass, and grain with the cattle on the farm. When a vet came to check the cattle, the vet also checked the horses. One farm hand was assigned to the horses full time, until the herd reached twelve head and were released. All the wild Abaco Barbs on the island today are descendants of these three horses.

By 1992, when Rehor first observed the horses, the future seemed bright for them. By 1997, however, the herd had dropped from more than thirty to sixteen head. Individuals identified by sight had vanished; corpses and skeletons were found, but the reasons for death were not known. To reverse this trend, Rehor started the Abaco Wild Horse Fund (now Arkwild) in the United States and the Wild Horses of Abaco Preservation Society (WHOA) in the Bahamas. These organizations helped the plight of the horses, and with the birth of four fillies in one year, the herd grew to twenty-one.

DNA Testing

Work began in 1992 to identify the origins of the Abaco Barbs, but the horses' background remained unclear until 1998, when a few people recognized traits that hinted the horses probably were pure Spanish Barbs. The horses were eventually tested in 2002. After three separate DNA analyses, it was discovered that they were in fact descendents of

A beautiful splash white pinto Abaco Barb running. Sunshine can be especially detrimental to horses like these who need the protection of pine trees, many of which have been harvested for pulpwood.

Spanish Barb horses brought to the New World during the time of Columbus and other Spanish explorers. One genetic analyst stated that the horses share some mitochondrial DNA with the Sulphur Spring mustangs of Utah. These mustangs were tested to have some of the highest similarities to Spanish-type horses of any of the wild-type horses tested in the United States. Based on this—as well as photo and video records—the Great Abaco Island horses were accepted in 2002 by the Horse of the Americas Registry as the Abaco Barb, a new strain of the Spanish Barb breed.

Due to their Spanish Barb ancestry, Abacos have unique traits and may be the only breed capable of contributing these traits back to the Spanish Barb population, which is also recognized throughout the world as critically endangered. This makes the Abacos equally rare and extremely valuable in the equine world. There are no other Spanish types quite like them.

Victoria Tollman, executive director of the Equus Survival Trust, stated: "Initial DNA studies show that Abacos show a high degree of Spanish Barb traits, including the very unusual splash white

gene. Abacos, perhaps even more so than the other Colonial Spanish breeds, are very significant to conservation because they represent a time capsule of genetics of the first era Iberian horses to reach the New World—genetics that were present during the Golden Age of Spain at the time the New World was being settled. More . . . studies are needed to better understand how the Abacos fit into the general Colonial Spanish family and what unique traits they alone may be able to contribute back to the world." But she warned, "We are running out of time. With so few left, they are the most critically endangered breed on the planet."

Today, there is a handful of remaining Abaco Barb horses battling for their lives. Hurricane Floyd caused enough damage to the forests for the horses to stay full time on the farm after 1999. They grew obese, many individuals developed laminitis, and they stopped reproducing. Possible pesticide and herbicide residue from the farm may also have been causing problems.

The government of the Bahamas designated a preserve and conservation area established for the horses in 2003. The preserve was granted more than six hundred acres of fenced forest to return the horses to their natural habitat and wean them off the over-rich grass on the farm.

Since the horses cannot be taken off the farm food completely (they spent too many years subsisting on it exclusively), they are given access to limited miniature pastures that are rotated frequently. Thus, the remaining mares and stallion have been returned to their natural habitat. The other stallions live beyond the controlled pastures, waiting for the next expansion of the fenced areas to include them. All the horses are descended from the last stallion of the original wild herd.

Great Abaco Island has some ten thousand full-time residents, but this is increasing rapidly. In the winter, the population swells with tourists as well as second-home owners and their guests. Since the horses are protected and reside in a remote area, the only way to reach them is to take a guided tour. The horses are proving to be of historical and cultural interest, part of the flavor and mystery of the tropical atmosphere of Great Abaco. As Rehor observed, "You have to see them to believe them."

The horses have a wide range of reactions to strangers and visitors. If people are relaxed and comfortable with them, the horses are equally so. At other times, people who have been pushy or brash have been rewarded with only glimpses of the horses as they run off.

Great Abaco's horses—as well as its wild boar and parrots—still survive. They are struggling symbols of a future where beautiful wild things still exist and are appreciated.

Characteristics

Abaco Barbs have compact bodies and strong legs, beautiful long tails, flowing manes, and gleaming coats. As with all Barb horses, they have convex, or Roman, noses. Eyes are large and ears are quite large and pointed, being slightly hooked in at the tips. Tails are low-set and long, often touching the ground. Chestnuts on the inside of the front legs are small and, on the rear legs, are nonexistent.

Abaco Barbs closely resemble Spanish horses, especially the Puerto Rican Paso Fino. All skeletons found so far have the unique five-lumbar vertebrae. Similarly, all have shown the fuller structure of the Wing of Atlas—the first cervical vertebra behind the skull. The side wings of this vertebra are rounded and fuller. This diversity is found only in Spanish Mustangs or Barb types.

Colors are bay, strawberry roan, and three different color arrangements of pintos: war bonnet, medicine hat, and a pattern sometimes referred to as splash white. Splash white is unique in that the color is only on the forequarters, or on the forequarters, back, and a bit on the rump (which may also extend down a leg), while the rest of the horse is white.

The horses appear to be quite large; it is only after approaching them when the viewer realizes they are only a bit more than 13 hands. They have never been precisely measured, but their size looks to be about 13 to 13.2 hands. Their size has not changed significantly in the past sixteen years or so.

Their surefootedness is phenomenal. Rehor stated, "You wouldn't believe your eyes if you saw them running through the rocky forest, jumping logs, scrambling up the hills. Amazing, considering how lame they used to be [when restricted to the farm and contracting laminitis]."

There have been questions about inbreeding concerns, but Rehor found all horses to be healthy when she first observed them in 1992, and they have continued to be robust-looking since. "In an environment like this, flawed animals die fast. The herd of thirty-five when I first came here was beautiful—not a messed-up animal in the bunch."

Once the herd is back up to something resembling normal numbers, they will be given as much freedom as possible. The horses flourished without outside intervention for so many centuries that it seems likely they will return to the same healthy numbers if given a chance.

Credit: Milanne Rehor and Wild Horses of Abaco Preservation Society

AMERICAN INDIAN HORSE

American Indian Horses have a variety of colors. *Chris Hurd*

The American Indian Horse Registry
9028 State Park Road
Lockhart, Texas 78644
www.indianhorse.com

It is difficult to describe how different and special American Indian Horses are. First impressions of them are of beauty and elegance, then gentleness and love for attention. Most of all, they transmit an underlying current of pervasive and mysterious energy. It is in their stance, the tilt of their head, or flick of an ear, but mostly it's in their eyes. It's a look that misses nothing and gauges everything.

Indian Horses emit a certain sense of knowing that goes beyond the ordinary. They size up a situation, discerning between friend and foe. More than

anything, they *think* and make sensible deductions. Their trust must be won. Once that is established, they are the most loyal, brave, and wonderful creatures that ever befriended humans.

It is this survival attitude and perception that has enabled American Indian Horses to retain their intelligence and common-sense nature and allowed them to continue for so long under such extreme and diverse conditions that would have destroyed other animals. And it is what attracts and endears them to their owners.

America's Living Legend
The ancestry of the American Indian Horse traces all the way back to fleet Arabian horses that were brought to Spain, where they were bred with Barb

and Andalusian stock, resulting in what was widely known as the best horse in the world of that time. Magnificent Spanish riding horses were used as a mighty force in various military campaigns.

In the late 1400s and early 1500s, Columbus, and then Spanish conquistadors, brought these horses to the New World. For the next five hundred years, Spanish horses influenced both North and South America. They helped establish modern development of both these continents in multiple ways, and in the process they became precursors to American Indian Horses.

In the decades after the Spanish conquered Mexico and the southern and western parts of what is now the United States, some horses escaped, multiplied, and migrated north. They thrived on the North American plains, and were used extensively by the Plains Indians, who retain their tribal names today—Apache, Comanche, Lakota, Kiowa, Nez Perce, Omaha, Ute, and many more. Due to their association with the various tribes, wild Spanish horses eventually became known as American Indian Horses.

They became an integral part of tribal life, transforming the Plains Indians from nomads surviving on foot to effective hunters and warriors. Most tribes counted their wealth in horses, using them extensively for barter and gifts and even paid for their brides with them. Tribal shamans often kept unusually colored horses as "great medicine" and

Buckskin overo American Indian Horse. This is a well balanced horse with clean legs, nicely angled shoulder and pleasant head. Excessive muscling is not desirable. *Chris Hurd*

used them for ceremonies. Those who owned buffalo and hunting horses prized them so much that the horses were tethered to their owner's wrist at night to prevent theft by other tribes.

For more than two centuries, Native Americans with horses kept their territory free from the greater numbers and technology of European intruders. This was due primarily to their horses, which were far better than anything the U.S. Calvary had. Indian Horses proved their superiority and toughness by continually outmaneuvering and outrunning the cavalry's European warmbloods.

Eventually, the U.S. Army attempted to conquer Native Americans the only way possible—by depriving them of their quick, hardy horses. The army repeatedly massacred complete Indian Horse herds because they were such a threat. This fact more than anything else proves the superiority of Indian Horses over other horses of the time.

The toughness of the Indian Horse was also appreciated by cowboys. One of the most colorful episodes in the history of Indian Horses was when they were used to gather millions of wild longhorn cattle off the Texas range after the War Between the States. To do this, Indian Horses swam every river from Texas to Canada and endured stampedes, tornadoes, hailstorms, and freezing blizzards. They did it all while foraging on grass and brush without grain, and they came through it ready for more. Most of them were not much larger than the longhorns they drove. A lesser breed would never have survived such adversities.

Since that time, the American Indian Horse has been owned and admired by every culture of the Americas. They have been called a multitude of names: cow pony, buffalo horse, mustang, Indian Horse, Cayuse, Chickasaw, or Spanish pony, but they are all the same animal with the same roots.

American Indian Horses and Colonial Spanish Horses

The American Indian Horse Registry also accepts Colonial Spanish Horses, not to be confused with wild Indian Horses. Colonial Spanish Horses are often selectively bred and were never wild, although their foundation goes back to wild herds from the North American plains.

Colonial Spanish Horses that are accepted in the registry retain some of the same attributes that separates wild mustangs from other horses, but not to the same extent as the mustangs.

About one-fourth of today's American Indian Horses were once wild mustangs taken off Bureau of Land Management (BLM) ranges and adopted by new owners.

After five hundred years of concentrated and exclusive living on western American open ranges, the original Indian Horse types show definite, proven traits. They existed under the most exacting and unrelenting breeding criteria—only the strongest survived. They lived by their wits, instincts, and sturdy physiques.

Today, wild mustangs remain on the same plains, living a tough existence in wild herds without outside influences. Government roundups and adoptions always leave some on the plains, where they continue to be naturally honed by nature.

American Indian Horses are athletic and attractive horses that come in virtually every equine color; they can be appaloosa spotted, paint spotted, or solid colored with every variation imaginable occurring. They are known for their common sense, savvy on the trail, intelligence, and ability to size up a situation. Some have been known to save their owners' lives on more than one occasion. Their loyalty is as legendary as their beauty and toughness. They exude a noble presence, these magnificent, strong, and trainable horses. Anyone fortunate enough to share their life with an Indian Horse knows how truly special it is.

Unique Character

Mustang Indian Horses captured from the BLM plains areas are much more expressive than domestic horses. One owner, Karen Nowak, tells of an Indian Horse Mustang she worked with, saying that he "was one of the coolest horses I have ever seen and has taught me more about horse behavior

This buckskin youngster's head is wide between the eyes and tapers to a fine muzzle. Ears are nicely set and the mane is coarse. Blue eyes are acceptable. *Chris Hurd*

than any other horse I have been around."

Without a doubt, Indian Horses read body language better than the average horse because their safety depended on such judgments when in the wild. For them, instantly responding to the small and silent nuances of herd warnings is a necessity for survival. Few people are aware of this kind of language that Indian Horses know and speak so well. The horses are so in tune to the world around them, they can pick up on the most minute thing—not only subtle body language, but also hidden emotions in others.

"I have no doubts about this," states Lona Patton, long-time Indian Horse owner and trainer. "I also think that is part of the reason people either hate and distrust them, or totally love them. People tend to fear what they cannot control, and you can't *control* a Mustang, not like you can a domestic [horse]. But you can use their innate instincts to gain their undying trust and [establish a] loyal bond that goes

above and beyond any domestic I've ever known. Most people tend to fear and dislike animals that prove to be smarter than them, calling them stupid and bullheaded, when in reality it is merely a lack of trust and partnership."

Patton experienced that kind of closeness when she got her Indian Horse, Metawa. On his first ride out of the pasture, she took him down the road, but he refused to go any farther. Knowing about and trusting the instincts of Indian Horses, Patton turned back. She found out the next day there were two mountain lions in the area that killed her neighbor's two llamas. Metawa also saved her another time when Patton was suddenly attacked by a horse that had been abused by a previous owner. Metawa raced from two pastures away to drive away the attacking horse. This goes far beyond the typical relationship most people have with their horses.

Patton laughs at the suggestion that her horse might run away if she released him in a park. "I'd

A varnish roan American Indian Horse with white eye sclera common to appaloosa colored horses. *Chris Hurd*

have to really work hard to do that! I have 110 percent trust in him, and I know he loves me. Even in wide open spaces, he comes to me instead of running off. I couldn't lose him if I tried!"

Comments about bonding with Indian Horses are numerous from owners: "The connection between my horse and me is so strong that it goes beyond words." "When an Indian Horse accepts you, there is a closeness that's not equal to anything else." "They take you into their heart. It's a forever thing." "I learned more from them than they did from me. They caused me to believe in God." "I am truly one with my horse, and that feeling can't be described unless you experience it yourself."

"Not just anyone can partner with an Indian Horse," says Nanci Falley, president of the American Indian Horse Registry, "[and] those who do, have that rarest of combinations, which is unlike anything else I've ever seen in the horse world. I call it respectful tolerance and an innate joy in the relationship. The horses are simply amazing!"

Once accepted, an owner has the complete and unique trust of the Indian Horse. Such acceptance is unparalleled with most other horses. It means an absolute and total giving of themselves.

The American Indian Horse Legacy

Indian Horses have contributed to the making of a number of American breeds—the Morgan, Quarter Horse, American Saddlebred, and the Tennessee Walking Horse are only a few. Most of the color breeds can trace their ancestry back to Indian Horses—the Paint, Palomino, Appaloosa, and Buckskin to name some. All horse breeds native to America began with at least a little Indian Horse ancestry, which has been on the North and South American continents for two centuries.

Modern-day American Indian Horses are as beautiful and useful now as they were to the Plains people. These are not scrubby individuals with scraggly coats and wild eyes. It should be remembered what the conditions under which Native Americans and their horses were forced to exist. The lifestyle and hazardous terrain took its toll on

human and animal in equal measure. With outside forces pushing into their territories, Native nations and their herds existed on whatever meager rations were available. The horses decreased in size, but this was not deterioration; it was the efficiency of survival. They became stronger and hardier and learned to exist on what nature provided, often having to travel long distances to find enough food and water to sustain them. Their very existence depended upon their intelligence and cunning, and they became masters at the art of eluding those who pursued them.

When the U. S. Army killed thousands of Indian Horses and forced the Native Americans onto reservations, Indian Horses for the most part disappeared, except for a few bands. Those remaining were preserved by people who had a vision and realized the importance of keeping links to the past alive. Many camps hid their finest Spanish stallions and mares and continued to raise them; consequently, some Indian Horse herds were kept pure over the years.

In the late 1950s, several collectors of these horses formed an organization to preserve what they called Spanish Mustangs. A Native American in California, however, felt that the Native influence was being ignored and founded a separate registry in 1961 named the American Indian Horse Registry, which continues to this day. Its purpose is to preserve the American Indian Horse and its history. The AIHR sustains the original dream of its founder and holds great pride that through its registry, today's owners of American Indian Horses in the Original Class can point to the various tribal names associated with the pedigrees of their horses.

Standards

As the original mount of the Plains Indians, the American Indian Horse has come far yet has changed little over the years. Better care and herd management may have added a little to its size and general condition, but nothing has altered its great heart and spirit.

The American Indian Horse carries Spanish Barb, Arabian, Mustang, and/or Foundation

Appaloosa blood in its veins. It shows the litheness, agility, endurance, and load-carrying capabilities of these bloodlines. It is strongly built, has excellent feet and legs, and possesses as much savvy as any horse that ever lived.

Indian Horses can work cattle, herd sheep, or rock a baby to sleep with their easy gait (many Indian Horses are naturally gaited with what is sometimes called the Indian shuffle). Additionally, they can do all this on less feed and less pampering than most horse people would ever believe.

They are highly intelligent, capable of learning and excelling in nearly every capacity for which the Native Americans valued their mounts: hardiness, stamina, and the fortitude to withstand great odds, along with a willing attitude, love for human companionship, and a desire to please.

It is with this in mind that the American Indian Horse Registry pursues the goal of perpetuating and promoting the original type of horse used by the Native American nations, as well as their hybrid and modern-day descendants. To this end, the American Indian Horse Registry has five classifications of registration:

Class O (Original) includes horses whose ancestry can be traced to Native American herds and that otherwise fit the Original status criteria. Class O horses are not bred to conform to popular modern horse breed standards, but are bred with the objective to preserve original bloodlines of Native American Indian nations. Class O horses registered since 1979 have bloodlines that trace back to various American Indian tribes and families.

Class AA includes horses that have one parent registered in Class O and also may include BLM mustangs, as well as other horses that can claim a line containing American Indian heritage.

Class A horses have unknown bloodlines, but are definitely Indian Horse type. Most horses with combined characteristics of Class M and A qualify for Class A registration as well as many so-called grade or backyard horses.

Class M (Modern) horses include breeding of Modern type. Moderns are considered descendants of the Original Indian Horses and are respected as such. They may have parents registered with the Quarter, Paint, Palomino, Pinto, Appaloosa, and similar associations.

Class P is for ponies of Indian Horse type. Eligible ponies include those with Galiceno or Pony of the Americas (POA) in their pedigrees. Ponies of unknown ancestry may also qualify.

No horse or pony exhibiting draft horse breeding can be registered. By not adhering to cookie-cutter standards, the original American Indian Horse comes in many sizes and types. Emphasis is not placed on modern conformation type (of any breed), but rather on soundness and body types, leaning toward strength and stamina.

The American Indian Horse Registry has no height requirements. The Indian Horse is generally a smaller, compact animal, normally 15 hands or less, although their height can range from 13 to 16 hands, with larger and smaller sizes being common. They weigh 700 to 1,000 pounds, with a few individuals over or under this.

American Indian Horses display virtually every color that can be seen in horses, thus the American Indian Horse Registry has no color requirements. Colored Appaloosas of the Foundation type are common, as are the various paints, pintos, and mixtures of colors. Often there are rare colors, such as lilac roan, peacock spotted leopard, or sabino paint. Unusual markings, such as lightning marks, leg striping, line-backing, or varnish marks, are much more common due to the Spanish Barb influence. Normally the varnish roans are fairly light colored on the body with varnish looking marks in varying stages of darker colors. (Sometimes Appaloosas or their crosses have these varnish markings on their facial bones, knees, hocks, and lower legs.)

No particular head shape is preferred. The dished face of the Arabian, the Roman nose of the Barb, or the more modern straight profile may be found in the Indian Horse, but large, wide-set eyes, full nostrils, and alert ears are desired. Overall, the Indian Horse should have an alert and interested appearance.

Indian Horses especially enjoy companionship. These two are grooming each other. *Chris Hurd*

Indian Horses are well made and have excellent feet and legs. Straight legs are not to be placed over serviceably sound legs. Defects causing unsoundness are to be heavily penalized in the breeding pen, as well as the show ring. Modern breed conformation criteria that causes or contributes to soundness problems—such as small feet, heavy, bunchy muscling, excessive fat, and an excessively wide (as opposed to deep) barrel—should be penalized as not desirable in Indian Horses. They don't have the overly muscled or fat body style of the modern breeds.

Their hooves are hard and healthy. They do not have small feet in comparison to body structure, overly straight legs, or overly defined conformation. They also do not have many of the digestive, nervous, and muscular problems associated with more modern breeds.

Indian Horses often have a lot of fetlock and body hair (if it is allowed to grow out), which protects them from the elements. They are naturally highly prepared to survive hot summers in arid deserts, or frigid cold in bitter winters, and the sloppy conditions in between, doing so on less feed and with less care than other horses. They can be ridden long distances with fewer injuries, perform heavy ranch and range work with more power, and generally provide better "horsepower" than horses much larger.

They are intelligent, independent, flexible, and competent when it comes to taking care of themselves. They still have what could be called a wild streak, which allows them to respond well to danger, yet American Indian Horses are friendly and courageous, and easily trusted around children and pets.

Credit: The American Indian Horse Registry

AMERICAN QUARTER HORSE

Muscling in the Quarter Horse, as on this stallion, is evident over the entire body, but especially on the rear quarters.
Caryl Chrisman

American Quarter Horse Association
P.O. Box 200
Amarillo, Texas 79168
www.aqha.com

The American Quarter Horse—there's nothing else is like it. Durable, quick, willing to please, it is the king of the American West. None can challenge its status as an equine leader. From the backwoods of a new nation, it rose to surpass all others in popularity. It mirrors what the United States is all about. Starting from a mixed foundation, it developed into a determined and reliable breed, a force to be reckoned with, excelling at almost anything put in front of it. From breaking new frontiers to performing dressage, it has proven its right to the title as the very best, earning the status of number one in the world. The American Quarter Horse truly epitomizes the American spirit.

Virtually everyone has heard about, or seen, an American Quarter Horse. It is most familiar in mounted events at rodeos, working on ranches, or being ridden in Western movies. Its reputation for quick speed, agility, trainability, and cow sense has solidly established it among professionals and amateurs alike. It has the widest range of devoted fans and the largest single-breed equine registry in the world. Its popularity continues to soar as its talents are appreciated, whether for ever-expanding competitions or just pleasure riding.

History

The American Quarter Horse is the first breed of horse native to what is now the United States. Former American Quarter Horse Association (AQHA) President J. D. Blondin once wrote, "Since colonial Williamsburg, the American Quarter Horse has served as an icon of the American West. It has secured a place in history as the versatile breed of choice for early Americans who pioneered across this great nation and settled into untamed land. It greatly benefited those who owned it then and it remains just as popular today."

The history of the Quarter Horse began when early Spanish explorers first brought their horses to Florida. Later, in the 1600s, other various breeds were brought to the English colonies. A distinct strain resulted from crossing the Spanish horses with the colonists' English breeding stock, which was recorded as early as 1611.

By the time the American Revolutionary War began, the colonists had grown greatly attached to horse racing. In colonial Virginia and the Carolinas, riding horses evolved to fill the colonists' passion for short-distance racing. Their horses gained fame for running in quarter-mile races, a favorite pastime of the colonists. Any unsown field or thoroughfare served as a racetrack (which probably accounts for the evolution of dirt racetracks in America). One-on-one match races were run down village streets, country lanes, and level pastures. This sprint racing in the early colonies was the earliest known example of horse racing in the United States.

The first recorded American Quarter Horse races were held at Enrico County (now Henrico County), Virginia, in 1674. Reports from that time show that by 1690, substantial purses were being offered at races, proving their popularity. Racing was a serious sport, and it was not uncommon for large plantations to change hands on the outcome of one of those sprints.

The heavily muscled, compact horses could run short distances over a straightaway faster than any other. Thoroughbred stock of similar conformation from England was then introduced, and later during westward expansion, wild mustang broodmares of the American frontier were added to the gene pool. This produced a distinct strain of horses with its own unique conformation, athletic ability, and wonderful disposition.

Word about the versatile new horses soon spread across the country, as respect and appreciation for them grew. Their inherent agility and disposition proved to be ideally suited for both recreation and work on developing western frontiers. They still plowed fields and served as saddle horses, but as westward expansion grew, so did their uses. They explored vast woodlands, broke sod for new farms, and drove cattle up the trails from Texas. This latter duty gained them the greatest fame—that of being natural cow horses.

These horses did not have an official breed name at that time, but the fastest in racing were the first to be recorded as "Celebrated American Quarter Running Horses." Prior to 1940, American Quarter Horses were most commonly known as Steeldusts, after a famous quarter-mile racing stallion of the century, or less frequently as Billys, after a horse sired by Shiloh that was out of a daughter of Steeldust. Over the years, there were different variations of names. Collectively they were called Quarter Horses by a group of horsemen and ranchers from the southwestern United States who became dedicated to preserving the pedigrees. These ranch horses were selectively bred for both speed in quarter-mile races and cow sense on the open range.

William Anson was the first person to try to define the Quarter Horse as a distinct breed. Anson was from England, but came to the United States when he was twenty-one and established a ranch near Christoval, Texas. He published the first information that linked the Quarter Horse to its colonial beginnings. Horse shows began to appear where horsemen brought their Quarter Horses to be judged. Anson sponsored and judged this type of show in 1908 at the Northside Coliseum in conjunction with the Southwestern Exposition and Fat Stock Show.

Early Quarter Horse Breeding

In the early 1900s, Richard M. Kleberg Sr., Robert J. Kleberg Jr., and Caesar Kleberg began developing a superior ranch horse type that had speed, athletic ability, intelligence, and cow sense. In 1916, they intensified that effort after they purchased a yearling colt from famed American Quarter Horse breeder George Clegg. They found this horse not only possessed all of the desired traits, but more importantly, he also could pass them on to future generations. This stallion, later named Old Sorrel, became the founding sire for the King Ranch American Quarter Horses.

Old Sorrel was sired by Hickory Bill whose sire was Peter McCue. Old Sorrel went on to sire many great stallions, including Little Richard and Tomate Laureles, which were designated AQHA foundation sires based on desirable American Quarter Horse qualities. Old Sorrel also sired other foundation stallions, such as Solis, Macanudo, and Hired Hand. Solis went on to sire Wimpy, the stallion that was later named Grand Champion at the 1941 Southwestern Exposition and Fat Stock Show and given the number "1" in the registry of the newly formed American Quarter Horse Association (AQHA). Old Sorrel and his grandson, Wimpy, stand out as two important foundation sires, not only for the King Ranch type, but for the Quarter Horse breed in general.

Peter McCue was another foundation stallion and one of the greatest sires of the American Quarter

Horse breed. Sired by Dan Tucker out of Nora M, he was foaled at Samuel Watkins' Little Grove Stock Farm in 1895. The 16-hand bay horse had tremendous speed, so Watkins often raced him.

As a sire, Peter McCue was legendary, stamping offspring with his speed and physical characteristics of the early American Quarter Horse breed. His influence as a sire spread west when he was purchased by breeders in Texas, Oklahoma, and Colorado. He sired Chief and Sheik, American Quarter Horse foundation sires, as well as Harmon Baker, Badger, and Hickory Bill, the great grand sire of Wimpy. Peter McCue died in 1923 at age twenty-eight.

Other Foundation Sires

After 1940, the King Ranch American Quarter Horse breeding program continued under the supervision of Richard M. Kleberg Jr. Both he and Robert J. Kleberg Jr. continued to make the King Ranch a leader in the American Quarter Horse industry, establishing a dynasty of champion cutting horses led by its stallions Mr. San Peppy and Peppy San Badger (also known as Little Peppy). Both Richard and Robert Kleberg Jr. are honored in the American Quarter Horse Hall of Fame for their involvement with the breed.

Leo, a 1940 stallion sired by Joe Reed II (who was sired by Joe Reed) was bred by John W. House. Leo's dam was Little Fanny, who was also sired by Joe Reed. While Leo displayed considerable speed, reportedly winning twenty of his twenty-two starts, it was his reputation as a sire that made him famous. An all-time leading sire of broodmares, Leo's daughters produced fourteen champions. In addition to speed, Leo's foals displayed excellent conformation, athletic ability, quiet dispositions, and cow sense. He died in 1967.

Three Bars, the most influential Thoroughbred in American Quarter Horse history, was foaled in

Opposite: The pleasant head and extensive muscling is apparent in this Quarter Horse stallion. *Midge Ames/ courtesy Caryl Chrisman*

1940 near Lexington, Kentucky. Despite severe circulatory problems in a hind leg, Three Bars won races as a three-, four-, and five-year-old. As a six-year-old in 1946, he set a 0:57 3/5 track record over 5 furlongs at the Phoenix fairgrounds in Arizona. The chestnut stallion possessed not only speed, but also excellent conformation and disposition, which he passed on to 558 American Quarter Horse offspring. A legendary sire of almost transcendental genetics, Three Bars sired champions in all facets of the American Quarter Horse breed, with four AQHA Supreme Champions, twenty-nine AQHA Champions, fourteen racing champions, and sixty-four racing stakes winners. His impact still weighs heavily on the breed today, as even now he figures prominently in the pedigree of virtually every champion, from racing to cutting to showing. He died in 1968 at the age of twenty-eight.

Since 1991, First Down Dash has been one of the leading racing sires. His ability to pass flawless conformation and an exemplary attitude to his offspring has resulted in progeny earnings exceeding $64.3 million.

Quarter Horse Racing

Organized American Quarter Horse racing got its start in Tucson, Arizona, at a racetrack called Hacienda Moltacqua. The track boasted a card of races that included not only American Quarter Horses, but also trotters, Thoroughbreds, and even some steeplechasers. Soon, however, American Quarter Horse racing outgrew its stage-sharing position with the other racing breeds at Hacienda Moltacqua. Thus in 1943, a new racetrack was built and designed especially for the sport of American Quarter Horse racing. That track was Rillito Park Racetrack in Tucson.

Today, horse racing ranks among the top spectator sports in America. American Quarter Horses continue to excel at racing at more than one hundred racetracks throughout North America, with total purses reaching some $95 million. In 2007, the total starters in American Quarter Horse races numbered 16,607. It is interesting to note that the quarter-mile is still the most popular distance for racing, and the best blaze the 440 yards in 21 seconds or less.

American Quarter Horses Today

Throughout its history, the breed has also been known for its calm disposition and cow sense, or the ability to outmaneuver cattle. Today, the heavy muscling and sprinter's speed remain characteristic traits, but horses within the breed have been bred to specialize in particular events. There are American Quarter Horses competing in every discipline imaginable, from traditional rodeo events such as roping and barrel racing, to the refined English classes of dressage and show jumping. They compete in horse shows around the world.

American Quarter Horses have always been appreciated for their racing ability, ranch work, and rodeo activities, among many other attributes, yet the number one interest of their owners remains riding "America's Horse" for recreation.

American Quarter Horse Association

Enthusiasts such as William Anson, Dan Casement, and Robert Denhardt recognized that the horses famous for their quarter-mile sprints also had specific physical characteristics that set them apart from other horses. Denhardt wanted to form a breed registry to preserve the bloodlines of these horses, whose ancestry traced back to the English colonies. He held a meeting at the Fort Worth Club in Texas that coincided with the 1940 Southwestern Exposition and Fat Stock Show. This marked the founding of the American Quarter Horse Association (AQHA) and when the breed officially became the American Quarter Horse.

AQHA is now the world's largest equine single-breed registry. It has 2,700 approved shows and 9,300 sanctioned races held each year, and recognizes a whole slew of outstanding athletes. Competition options are nearly unlimited—pleasure driving, jumping, halter, cutting, reining, and roping. Besides the United States, Canada, and Mexico, American Quarter Horses can be found

This Quarter Horse stallion has a wonderful head with prominent jaws, clean-cut throatlatch, powerful build, and trim legs, all characteristics of a good Quarter Horse. *Midyett Ranch*

in eighty-three other countries. The American Quarter Horse Association leads the equine industry with a record 3,500 members and more than 5 million registered horses worldwide. Horses that earn a certain number of points in a particular class are invited to the AQHA World Championship Show. The invitational show draws more than 3,500 open and amateur exhibitors from around the globe. These exhibitors compete for award purses valued at nearly $2.5 million, making it the largest and richest world championship horse show in existence.

Although the athletic prowess of the American Quarter Horse carries many riders to the winner's circle, it is the breed's versatility and gentle nature that have made it the world's most popular horse. Both a novice rider of any age and a seasoned professional can find an American Quarter Horse that will provide a pleasurable ride.

Standards

Of course, beyond its appearance, a registered American Quarter Horse foal is the product of a registered American Quarter Horse dam and sire.

The AQHA also offers an Appendix registry for foals with one American Quarter Horse parent and one Thoroughbred parent registered with the Jockey Club.

The American Quarter Horse is characterized by a short, broad head topped by small, active ears, large eyes set wide apart, sensitive nostrils over a shallow muzzle, and a firm mouth. Well-developed jaws imply great strength.

The medium length neck joins the sloping shoulders at a near-45-degree angle with a distinct throatlatch. The chest is deep and broad with wide-set forelegs that blend well into the shoulders.

The powerful, muscled forearm extends to the knee, whether viewed from the front or side. The back is close-coupled, is especially full and powerful across the kidneys, and is full through the thigh, stifle, gaskin, and down the hock.

The rear quarters are broad, deep, and heavy when viewed from either side or rear. The hind leg is muscled inside and out. The hocks are wide, deep, straight, and clean, with the foot that is well-rounded and roomy and has an especially deep, open heel.

The generally acceptable height of the American Quarter Horse ranges from 14.3 to 15.1 hands, with weight ranging from 1,100 to 1,300 pounds.

The AQHA recognizes sixteen colors, with sorrel being the most prominent. Other colors are bay, black, brown, buckskin, chestnut, dun, red dun, gray, grullo, palomino, perlino, cremello, and red, blue, and bay roan. It is interesting to note that the official gray coloring is what newcomers often call white, but there are no white American Quarter Horses. White markings, including white above the knee, are allowed if both parents are registered. Horses with excessive white are now allowed to be registered, but it is considered an undesirable trait.

The parentage requirements for Appendix and regular AQH registration are as follows:

- A numbered registered AQH parent plus a Thoroughbred parent—Appendix registration
- A numbered registered AQH parent plus an Appendix AQH parent—Appendix registration
- A numbered registered AQH parent plus a numbered registered AQH—numbered registered AQH
- An Appendix registered parent plus an Appendix registered parent—not eligible for registration
- An Appendix registered parent plus a Thoroughbred—not eligible for registration

The American Quarter Horse Association strives to keep the American Quarter Horse as the powerful athlete it always has been. American Quarter Horses born after January 1, 2007, that are a descendants of the American Quarter Horse Impressive (AQHA registration number 0767246) must be tested for hyperkalemic periodic paralysis (HYPP) to be eligible for registration. Any horse testing positive (H/H) will not be eligible for registration. HYPP is a muscular disease caused by a hereditary genetic defect leading to uncontrolled muscle twitching and weakness, and in severe cases can lead to death.

Credit: American Quarter Horse Association

Opposite: Pronounced forearm muscling is clearly seen here, as is rear muscling. This is a solidly built breed.
Caryl Chrisman

AMERICAN SORRAIA MUSTANG

Young bay Sorraia stallion and mares. Note the dark trim on the ears, intelligent expression, and dorsal stripe. *Lucia Roda*

American Heritage Horse Association
26232 Shirttail Canyon Road
PO Box 27, Pringle
South Dakota 57773-0027
www.americanheritagehorse.org

The American Sorraia Mustang is a rare type of Spanish Mustang, which is on the critical list of rare breeds. American Sorraia Mustangs contain a special genetic history: they are the proven descendants of the endangered Sorraia Horse of Portugal, showing the genetic markers and physical characteristics of their Portuguese ancestors.

The Sorraia (pronounced sore-AA´-ya) gained a reputation as the horse of Columbus and Hernando Cortés, but originally it was an unwanted horse. When Columbus bought the first horses for his voyage, he purchased Spanish bloodstock and was expecting a shipload of only those horses; however a portion of the actual shipment included Sorraia horses instead.

Sorraia horses are primitive wild horses originating in the basin of the Rio Sorraia in Portugal, which was not far from the Atlantic Ocean. Sorraia horses of Columbus's time were much more plentiful and retained the dubious description of being

This young stallion has exotic Iberian facial features, desirable in Sorraia Mustangs.
Lucia Roda

wild, just as the American Sorraia Mustangs were regarded centuries later.

Sorraias ended up in the New World as a result of that con by a horse broker of the time. The tide was going out, Columbus' ships needed to set sail right away or they would miss favorable weather. Nobody wanted to be caught at sea during hurricane season, so off they went.

What they discovered was that Sorraia horses could handle the climate of the New World in ways that other horses could not; in fact, they survived and thrived. The Mediterranean climate from which Sorraias originated was similar to Mexico or California. They were also able to endure any number of extreme climate changes—from the deserts and mountains of Peru, to the North American high deserts and prairies.

There is no dispute that the conquistadors brought many types of Iberian bloodstock with them to the New World. Conquer, convert, and expand was the nature of the Spanish empire, and it quickly became apparent that the Sorraia was suitable for the grueling tasks of these tough

expeditions. They soon earned a reputation as hardy, resilient horses, eminently suitable for expansion efforts in the New World.

These tough Sorraias horses of the 1400s and 1500s were direct ancestors of the American Sorraia Mustangs of the twenty-first century. The Sorraia Horse and the American Sorraia Mustang have survived for hundreds of years, populating from southern Mexico to colonial California. Over the centuries, their endurance has been greatly valued. They were the horses of the Pony Express, the *vaqueros* (cowboys) of Mexico, and the Native Americans. Much of North America was built on their backs.

The Sorraia breed of Portugal eventually died out in America, but Sorraia Mustangs have continued on, living in the most remote areas of North America, which includes the Book Cliffs region of Utah as well as populations in several other small regional pockets. The fact that they have proliferated in the same kind of environment as the original Sorraia has kept them so characteristically like their Portuguese ancestors.

Sorraia colt and mares show uniformity of type and color, signs of consistent and strong genetic inheritance. *Lucia Roda*

Characteristics

Sorraia Mustangs are brave, loyal, and fierce. They are a family horse that will go the distance for their human partner. Longtime breeder Lucia Roda has found them to be horses that bond exceptionally well with humans. "I wonder sometimes how I ever got so lucky to have these horses," she says. "They have become an integral part of my family for me and my children."

Sorraia Mustangs are willing and intelligent, but "these are not push-button horses and will not abide abuse," Roda says. "They are, however, always willing to try. They like to learn and like having a job."

The American Sorraia Mustang is a tough, hardy horse able to excel athletically in many disciplines. There are Sorraia Mustangs competing in dressage, eventing, carriage driving, jumping, team penning, rodeo, endurance, polo, and gymkhana.

There are only about 250 living American Sorraias in the U.S. registry today. The registry tries to preserve all that the horses are and have been, while still promoting them for all they can be. The Sorraia horse of Portugal is also an endangered breed, which puts added value on the American Sorraia Mustang.

Conformation

The American Sorraia Mustang is a slim, leggy horse with a long elegant head and large, expressive deep-set eyes that do not have the bulge of pony eyes. The head profile is convex in nature and no less than straight in profile. They have medium to long ears.

The neck can be quite slim in horses that are lean, but conversely can be well crested in horses that enjoy a more fat condition. The neck tie-in is lower to the chest, like most Iberian breeds.

The heart girth is deep, while the chest is narrow and more A-shaped as opposed to the chest of other horses that is shaped like an "H" in front.

Hips are rafter shaped. The tail set is moderate to low and should fit smoothly into the curve of the hip. They have excellent bone, feet, and gaits. Muscling is smooth and flat without the heavy look found in some modern breeds.

The hair coat is fine, and they have little fetlock hair, even in individuals living in colder winter climates. Chestnuts are smaller or missing all together, and ergots are rarely seen.

They are uphill structured horses, which enables them to move with collection more easily than many other breeds. They keep their feet up under them at all times and are always alert to their surroundings.

Some individuals may have a four-beat lateral gait. Historically among old cowboys of the West, these mounts were called the $40 horses because they were such a smooth ride. The average horse of

that time went for $10.

The colors of the horse reflect their primitive ancestry. American Sorraia Mustangs are either dun or grullo. Roans of those base colors are allowed with appropriate pedigree documentation, but red dun is not admitted at all. Excessive white markings are faulted and not allowed in breeding stock.

Most striking, however, are the primitive markings on the horses. A dorsal stripe is always present. They can have shoulder crosses, leg barring, or stripes, facial cobwebbing, and chest or rib hair stripes. Highly prized are the bi-colored mane and tail that look frosted with a lighter color.

Standards

The American Sorraia Mustang is registered with the American Heritage Horse Association under the umbrella organization named the Windcross Conservancy. Horses within this registry are qualified by pedigree, history, genotype, and phenotype. No horses found in the wild are accepted; therefore

American Sorraia Mustang stallion. *Lucia Roda*

horses of modern herd management areas do not qualify for registration.

The Sorraia Mustang comes from the foundation blood of the Spanish Mustang. The original horses were in the majority of Sorraia-like Spanish Mustang descendants from southern Mexico, Alta in California, and what is now the Book Cliffs region of Utah.

All stallions and breeding mares are required to submit hair samples for DNA parentage testing. This is to verify parents and ancestors that would otherwise be lost with the current management of wild herd populations. Basic parentage of the horse is investigated, and then the mitochondrial DNA of the horse is searched, along with the haplotype groupings of the horse. Horses of the American Sorraia Mustang breed share haplotype groupings with their Portuguese cousins, the Sorraia. Currently, the information and populations that have been tracked are in the majority of parentage testing.

A great deal of effort is being made to document, record, and store information and stories about the very first Sorraia Mustang horses. The genealogy of the horses is tracked not only by blood, but also by the written history of its ancestors. Through science, they can be traced back to Portugal's Sorraias and the genes or lines remaining there. Through written and some oral traditions, most can be tracked back to the late nineteenth and early twentieth centuries.

Interestingly, when the Sorraia Mustangs are in a wild environment, they show a continuing progression back to the wild horse of their Portuguese ancestors. The genetics remain quite dominant.

To register a Sorraia Mustang, the conformation should meet the list provided in this section, and a dorsal stripe should be present. The added bonuses of bi-coloring, leg barring, or hair stripes are prized, but the lack of dynamic leg barring, for instance, on an otherwise correct horse with registered parents would not prevent it from being registered. It would probably not make the first choice for reproduction, but a good breeding horse that produces breed type better than itself, but lacks some other desirable trait (such as dark leg coloration), is still considered a good breeding Sorraia Mustang.

Like any breed, the goal is to breed for the standard and hope to get close to the ideal by definition. The traits of the American Sorraia Mustang are as follows:

- Convex profiles: no less than straight
- No dished faces
- Long narrow face
- Smooth muscling
- Moderate to low tailset
- Rafter hip (preferable)
- Lower neck set than modern horses
- Square horse built uphill
- Sound legs and feet
- Medium round canon bones
- Good hoof wall in proportion to the horse
- Long, elegant neck with clean throatlatch
- Well laid back shoulder
- Narrow chest with deep heart girth
- Ears medium long, rimmed, tipped, and sometimes striped
- No overt jowls (as seen on Quarter Horses and some warmbloods)
- Medium to short back with well defined withers
- Bi-coloring in mane and tail (very desirable, but not required)
- Leg barring
- Dorsal stripe (necessary)
- Cobwebbing
- Hair stripes
- May have brindling
- Sooty faces and legs darker than body
- Dun or grulla colors; no red duns allowed.
- Roans of the base colors—dun or grulla—are allowed
- No overo or tobiano color patterns; no appaloosa snowflakes, blankets, or leopard spots

Credit: Lucia Roda and American Heritage Horse Association

BANKER HORSE

Spanish characteristics of this Shackleford stallion include depth in the body, and sloped croup. *Carolyn S. Mason*

Corolla Wild Horse Fund, Inc.
P.O. Box 361
1126 Old Schoolhouse Lane
Corolla, North Carolina 27927
www.corollawildhorses.com

Foundation for Shackleford Horses, Inc.
306 Gold Farm Road
Beaufort, North Carolina 28516
www.shacklefordhorses.org

Off the shores of North Carolina, there is a string of barrier islands called the Outer Banks that run along the entire coastline. On some of these sandbar islands, wild mustangs have been living for some five hundred years. They are the last remnants of once-numerous herds of Spanish stock that roamed freely on the islands. Native Outer Banks residents refer to them as Banker, or Banks, ponies, although genetically they are small horses. They are some of the last remaining Spanish mustangs—and one of the purest herds—living wild on the East Coast.

Wild Banker Horses truly represent the Outer Banks spirit—untamed and rugged. They have survived centuries of fierce nor'easter winds and hurricanes. Their wild mystique has become an integral part of what draws hundreds of thousands of visitors to these barrier island beaches every year. Nowhere else can free-roaming mustangs be seen walking along the beach.

Historical data lead to the conclusion that their ancestors were left on the islands in the early sixteenth century. It is believed that they arrived via shipwrecks, failed attempts at colonization, and purposeful seeding by Spanish explorers prior to colonization efforts. For hundreds of years, colonists and wild Spanish mustangs lived together on the islands.

As true descendents of Spanish mustangs, Banker Horses carry certain physiological and distinguishing features of ancient Spanish horses, such as the Iberian Barb. Their consistent size, even temperament, great endurance, and startling beauty all point to their dramatic history.

In 1982, members of the Spanish Mustang Registry came to the Outer Banks to observe the remaining horses. They found small bands of Banker Horses still existing in their natural state, as they had been for centuries, on the portions of the Outer Banks that are part of the North Carolina counties of Currituck, Hyde, and Carteret. One of the members is Emmett Brislawn, son of the founder of the Spanish Mustang Registry. He remarked, at the time, that it was difficult at first to picture such a western horse in such an eastern setting. Another cowboy in the group said, "People don't know how rare this little horse is and how hard it is to come by."

The isolated Outer Banks were ideal to find horses pure enough to qualify for registration. As a pure breed, they were registered with the Spanish Mustang Registry until founder Bob Brislawn's death.

Home on the Outer Banks

In order to understand Banker Horses, it is important to understand the location and environment where they live. The Outer Banks range three to eight miles from North Carolina's shoreline. They descend southward along the entire North Carolina coastline, separated from the mainland by large sounds of water. They span a length of some 175 miles from the Virginia border in the north, to Cape Lookout, and continuing southward for miles. Most of the islands are one-half to two miles wide.

The North Carolina Outer Banks are islands located in the remote eastern areas of three counties mentioned previously. Currituck County borders Dare County in the north and Hyde County in the south. The horses live at the extreme northern end of Corolla Island, part of Currituck County.

More horses live on Shackleford Banks. This island is part of Cape Lookout National Seashore, located 175 miles to the south near Beaufort and Morehead City. It is roughly nine miles long and three thousand acres and can only be reached by ferries carrying people, but not vehicles.

Ocracoke Island is the farthest distance off the mainland shore, around twenty miles from Hyde County. Only nineteen ponies remain there in a fenced enclosure, and they are no longer considered wild. The herd is managed by the Cape Hatteras National Seashore and can only be reached by ferry.

Centuries ago, the Outer Banks were known as "the sand banks." Perhaps the islands are best described by the name a Native American tribe that lived there gave them; the tribe called the islands *Hatterasil*, an Algonquin word meaning "there is less vegetation." Until recently, these were some of the most isolated and undeveloped areas in the nation, functioning mostly as protection for the North Carolina shoreline against the Atlantic Ocean. There was no electricity in Corolla until 1964, no telephone until the mid 1970s, and the only paved road stopped fifteen miles south of Corolla until 1985. When the road was paved from Duck to Corolla, the tiny fishing village suddenly exploded with the development of upscale oceanfront vacation homes.

The waters surrounding the Outer Banks are some of the most dangerous in the world; they are referred to as the Graveyard of the Atlantic. The islands' sand banks are always shifting, which has caused numerous shipwrecks in times past. Many early Spanish ships carrying horses, as well as other livestock, were wrecked on these shores.

Weather on the islands is hot, balmy, and windy; oftentimes hurricanes strike. The islands can also get cold; there can be freezing temperatures in winter with rare instances of sleet and snow.

All of the horses on the Outer Banks are Banker Horses, of which there are the individual, isolated

Bachelor band on Shackleford grazing on the coarse salt grasses of the marshes. *Carolyn S. Mason*

Banker horses wade past Cape Lookout lighthouse. *Carolyn S. Mason*

herds: the Corolla horses, Shackleford horses, and Ocracoke horses.

The horses used to roam freely from Beaufort Inlet in Carteret County, to the Virginia state line. Today, the northern Banks Horses' range has been reduced to an area north of Corolla that is accessible only by four-wheel-drive vehicles. The horses here freely roam the beaches, marshes, maritime forests, Currituck Banks Wildlife Refuge, North Carolina Estuarine Research Reserve, and populated areas of Swan Beach, North Swan Beach, and Carova. The Corolla wild horses have numerous ponds as well as the Currituck Sound as their sources of fresh water. They graze on saltmeadow cordgrass, sea oats, dune grass, and American beach grass.

Shackleford Banks is an uninhabited barrier island where horses roam the dunes, marshes, and maritime forest. They swim in the small channels between the island and the nearby tidal flats. The tidal flats ebb out on the low tides and disappear again with the next high tide. The tide rises and falls every eight hours, and foals born on the flats must swim back to the island before the tide comes in. At high tide, some mudflats on Shackleford are under two feet of water.

The horses on Shackleford Banks feed entirely on the coarse salt grasses of the marshes and islands. When not near a spring or waterhole, they get fresh water by pawing deep enough in the sand to reach fresh water that seeps into the excavation. These reservoirs serve for their drinking use while they remain open.

The fenced in horses on Ocracoke have their needs cared for by the National Park Service.

An incredibly hardy breed, Bankers have survived on their own through centuries of hurricanes, nor'easters, droughts, heavy winds, insects, and intentional shootings by humans.

History

Accounts of Spanish explorations and colonization attempts in the early 1500s along the North Carolina coast noted that Spanish Barb and Iberian horses were imported there. One colony's records in particular, the failed d'Allyon colony, provided a description of its circumstances that proved a combination of events occurred to help establish feral horse herds along the barrier islands.

Spanish ships also traded livestock and other supplies with English colonists. An English captain, Richard Greenville, reported in his ship's log from 1584 to 1590 that the ship traded goods for "mares and male horses" from Spaniards in Hispaniola before coming to the North Carolina area.

Much later, proof that wild horses existed in North Carolina was recorded by English historian John Lawson, who explored and documented the southeastern part of the state from 1700 until 1711. Attesting to the horses' superb quality and hardiness, Lawson wrote, "The horses are well shaped and swift. The best of them would sell for ten or twelve pounds in England. They prove excellent drudges, and will travel incredible journeys. They are troubled with very few distempers. . . . As for sprains, splints and ringbones, they are here never met withal, as I can learn."

In 1856, historian Edmund Ruffin visited the Outer Banks. He was famous as an authority on agriculture and as an editor, but more often remembered and credited with firing the first shot in the American Civil War. He wrote, "Twice a year on the Banks, the stock owners hold a wild horse penning, at which time all of the wild horses on the island were corralled and the colts branded. The horse pennings are much attended, and are very interesting festivals for all the residents of the neighboring mainland. There are few adults residing within a day's sailing of the horse pen[ning] that have not attended one or more of these exciting scenes."

Fighting Corolla Banker stallions. Continuity of color and type is apparent. *Corolla Wild Horse Fund*

Ruffin noted that all of the horses in use on the reef and on many of the nearest farms on the mainland were from the wild "banks" horse herds. He described them as "all of small size with rough shaggy coats, and long manes: their hoofs in many cases grow to unusual lengths, they are capable of great endurance of labor and hardship, and live so roughly that any others from abroad seldom live a year on such food and other such great exposure. By the same token . . . when the banks horses were removed to the mainland, away from the salt marshes, many die before learning to eat grain . . ."

Conserving Banker Horses

According to *National Geographic* magazine, in 1926 there were an estimated five thousand to six thousand wild horses throughout the Outer Banks. Now, there are fewer than 210 of these rare horses left in the wild. With the development of areas, such as Nags Head, into resorts for the wealthy, their numbers soon became an issue for developers. In 1938 on Cape Hatteras, Dare County placed a bounty on the few remaining wild horses, effectively eliminating the horses there. Only a few privately owned horses remain today.

With increased interest in the development of the other islands, along with the decreased value of the horses to the island residents, the issue of the horses has been pushed to the forefront. Now only two herds remain wild and free-roaming on the Outer Banks: the Corolla herd, which numbers less than 90 head, and the Shackleford herd, maintained by federal law at 110 to 130 horses.

Around 2006, some Shackleford horses were relocated to Cedar Island, which is at the eastern tip of the Carteret County mainland and inside, or west of, the Outer Banks. (Cedar Island is not truly part of the Outer Banks.) With the 35 horses there and the 117 on Shackleford, about 152 Shackleford horses still exist as free-roaming wild horses.

There are only nineteen horses left on Ocracoke Island. The National Park Service manages the Ocracoke horses, but these horses are confined, are not considered wild, and recently have experienced interbreeding from outside horses.

Survival on Corolla

The Corolla Wild Horse Fund was established in 1989 to heighten awareness concerning the wild horses in the area. As the Currituck Outer Banks became more developed, twenty horses were killed or injured by vehicles on the highway. Volunteers mobilized the community to find a solution.

In 1996, the remaining horses on Corolla were relocated behind two sound-to-sea fences, one that separated them from the highly populated areas of Corolla, and another located at the Virginia state line. Access to this area is only by four-wheel-drive vehicles along the beach and sand cartways. Although there is far less development in this area when compared to the southern portions of the county, construction is occurring at an alarming rate. With each new home comes a reduction of indigenous vegetation and grasses that are not always replaced. The continued destruction of this major food source for the horses increases their dependence on the endangered and fragile vegetation left in the refuge area.

The northernmost beaches, where the horses are, cover eleven miles or twelve-thousand-plus acres. Although this land is designated as the Corolla horses' sanctuary area, 80 percent of the land is privately owned and subject to development. There are 3,100 platted lots in the area and nearly half of those are built out. The remaining 20 percent is government owned.

The only known impact the horses have for certain is their draw to tourists—they are the number one tourist attraction. Some sixty thousand tourists come to the islands each week in the summer months.

Investors want to develop the Outer Banks, but the horses stand in their way. Though they add value by providing a cultural heritage to the area, the issue of where they are to live, or if they should live at all, has become controversial. Seven horses were shot and killed between 2001 and 2007.

Corolla Banker herd. *Corolla Wild Horse Fund*

One of the ways in which the Corolla Wild Horse Fund manages the Corolla herd size is by making horses available through an adoption program. Select numbers of horses are removed regularly from the Outer Banks for adoption purposes. Generally, yearlings or younger fillies and gelded colts are available, as younger animals have a much easier time transitioning to a domestic lifestyle, and the gene pool is less affected by their removal. Stallions are available on a case-by-case basis. The horse population is also controlled by non-hormonal contraception delivered by dart.

All adoption horses are tested for equine infectious anemia, vaccinated, wormed, halter broke, and qualified for registration with the Horse of the Americas Registry as Colonial Spanish Mustangs.

Survival on Shackleford

The Shackleford horses are the largest genetically viable group of North Carolina Banker Horses remaining. In 1996, Dr. Jay Kirkpatrick, director of Science and Conservation Biology, Zoo Montana, wrote, "The Shackleford wild horses are the oldest documented population in North America and they should be managed with the utmost care. . . . The wild horse is one of America's most valuable wildlife species . . . and the Shackleford horses are one of our oldest legacies."

At that time, people all over North Carolina supported protective legislation for the Shackleford horses. The Foundation for Shackleford Horses was founded in 1997 to protect and preserve Shackleford horses. The resulting Shackleford Banks Wild Horse Protection Act of 1998 was supported by Governor James Hunt and the entire North Carolina Delegation, and was signed into law by President Bill Clinton. Due to this legislation and the fact that Shackleford is not populated by people, the Shackleford horses have experienced a more protected life than those on Corolla.

The American Livestock Breeds Conservancy has moved the status of the Banker Horse from the threatened list to the critical list. The Banker strain is also on the critical breeds list of the Equus Survival Trust. Conservation of these horses is vitally important as they are a genetically ancient strain of Colonial Spanish Mustangs. There are less than five hundred breeding mares left in the world.

Characteristics

When members of the Spanish Mustang Registry came to the Outer Banks in 1982, they were satisfied that the Banker Horses, in particular the Corolla strain, were as lineally pure to sixteenth century Spanish importations as could be found in North America. Banker Horses compare closely to the selectively bred South American Spanish derivative equine stock. Around the 1980s, two Shackleford horses were registered with the Spanish Mustang Registry.

More recent historical research and genetic testing indicates that Banker Horses descended from a core group of an old type of Spanish horse. One genetic variant found in the Shackleford horses, the blood variant Q-ac, is believed to have been contributed by the Spanish horses of four hundred years ago. This genetic marker has been found only in descendents of those ancient types of Spanish horses. Easily lost through genetic drift, Q-ac has been documented in the Puerto Rican Paso Finos, the isolated mustang population of Montana's Pryor Mountains, and the horses of Shackleford Banks.

In 2007, representatives from the Horse of the Americas, the American Livestock Breeds Conservancy, and the American Indian Horse Registry inspected the wild Banker Horses. They noted, in particular, definitive evidence of the traditional balance and conformation of Colonial Spanish Horses in the Banker Horses. They were so amazed at the consistently strong Spanish traits they saw in each horse that they decided any horse from Corolla and Shackleford Islands would be registered as pure in their registries.

Colors of Banker Horses are bay, chestnut, black, and sorrel, and they can have flaxen manes and tails as well as the paint spotting pattern.

The Corollas stand about 14 hands tall. The Shacklefords average about 13 hands.

The Corolla horses have both convex and concave facial profiles with crescent-shaped nostrils, graceful Iberian necks, base-wide build, and Spanish action at the walk, trot, and canter. The Shackleford horses also have both concave and convex facial profiles with crescent-shaped nostrils. They too have smooth movement.

One striking similarity they have to the Arabian and Iberian ancestry is the number of vertebra, as Bank Horses have a five-lumbar vertebrae instead of six—one less than most breeds. Other typical Spanish Horse traits include a low tailset and no chestnuts on rear legs.

Natural selection has culled out all unhealthy characteristics. These are hardy and tough little horses, capable of surviving great deprivations.

General Observations

One of the members in the 2007 inspection group was Steve Edwards, who trained wild mustangs captured from the western ranges. Edwards was allowed to adopt a young Corolla stallion, a wild colt that was removed from the herd for emergency surgery. Later, it became the only Corolla stallion in captivity available for breeding.

Edwards was quickly taken with the colt. "He was completely halter trained in forty-five minutes. Within twenty-four hours he comfortably wore a saddle and took a child on his back." Edwards also adopted a three-year-old mare that went from wild horse to gentled trail mount in a little over three weeks. A few weeks later, Edwards was asked to take a mature stallion that had to be removed from the herd because it had learned how to escape the sanctuary and enter the town of Corolla. A week later, the stallion was carrying a rider.

Edwards marveled at the gentle nature of the horses compared to their western cousins. "So far it appears that they are much easier to train than any domestic horses I have run into."

Edwards was not the only member of the inspection team impressed with the wild horses of the Outer Banks. Vickie Ives, one of the top breeders of Colonial Spanish horses, adopted several Banker Horses. "We are proud to add the Corolla horses to our breeding program. . . . These little Corolla horses have a wonderful Colonial Spanish type in a compact size with tremendous trainability, real Spanish action, and a unique desire to please. They will make excellent mounts for our younger riders and for our senior clients."

The captive horses owned by Edwards and Ives may become part of the foundation stock of Corolla horses of the future. The current management plan for the wild herd at Corolla requires the herd to be maintained at a level of only sixty horses or less. According to Edwards, sixty horses are not enough to provide the genetic diversity to keep the breed alive. "Most experts agree that at least one hundred horses is the minimum number to provide a healthy breeding program."

Ives agrees: "They are already fairly closely related with only twenty-seven alleles found in the Corolla herd, according to genetic testing done by Dr. Gus Cothran of Texas A&M [University], one of the nation's premier researchers in the genotype of domestic horses. Reducing the herd size to only sixty horses limits the genetic diversity tremendously. I would hate to see such a wonderful strain of Colonial Spanish horses threatened by extensive inbreeding."

The concern is about a genetic collapse of the Corolla Bankers because of their diminishing numbers. All who know these great historic Spanish purebreds hope their herd will be allowed to increase in numbers.

"Once the Corolla wild horses are gone, they are gone forever," states Karen McCalpin, executive director of the Corolla Wild Horse Fund. "They are the last remaining herd of wild horses on the northern Outer Banks. They are an important part of the nation's history and the history of North Carolina."

A majestic Banker strides on the beach, as free as the waves behind him. *Corolla Wild Horse Fund*

Carolyn Mason from the Foundation for Shackleford Horses says, "These fascinating animals are a source of fondness and pride to the local residents, of delight and interest among visitors . . . and a national treasure and living history of the United States."

Credit: Corolla Wild Horse Fund, Inc. and Foundation for Shackleford Horses, Inc.

CAROLINA MARSH TACKY

Carolina Marsh Tacky Association
6685 Quarter Hoss Lane
Hollywood, South Carolina 29449
www.marshtacky.org

Tough, beautiful, and full of history, the Carolina Marsh Tacky is one of America's best-kept secrets. Few know of this exquisite little breed, and those who do cannot understand how such a wonderful riding horse has passed through recent decades almost unnoticed and is now slipping into threatened oblivion. It is an unpretentious horse, full of steady endurance and shining personality. It is surefooted and swamp savvy. As a trail and hunting horse, it cannot be beat.

According to the Gullah culture, preserved by the descendants of the South Carolina island plantation slaves, the word "tacky" means little. Tagged onto the word "marsh," the name means little marsh horse. Marsh Tackys were as common as sparrows at one time, and thus were not as highly valued compared to blooded horses brought to the eastern colonies. So "tacky" also became synonymous with meaning something cheap or common to the colonists. This, however did not reflect the value the Gullah people placed on their Marsh Tackys, who used them for everything from plowing to racing. Every Gullah family had at least one Marsh Tacky and depended on them for their livelihood. Marsh Tackys were plucky, enduring, and thrifty horses.

Once plentiful in the Carolinas, Virginia, and Georgia, the Marsh Tacky has now dwindled to dangerously low numbers, taking their last stand in South Carolina. It is one of the rarest and most endangered horse breeds on the planet.

The Tacky is an eastern member of the Colonial Spanish equine group and is thought to be most closely related to the Florida Cracker Horses from the same group. It is likely that both also share some

Carolina Marsh Tackys are naturally beautiful. This one has the desirable chiseled head. *Dwain Snyder*

close genetic heritage with the Banker Horses that exist wild in North Carolina's Outer Banks.

The Carolina Marsh Tacky was one of the first colonial breeds developed in America, primarily from horses brought to this continent some five hundred years ago. Its rootstock began with Spanish horses transported during the exploration and colonization of America. These historic horses were tough, surviving terrible ocean voyages often with insufficient forage. From this foundation and down through the centuries, the Tacky basically has not changed much in all. It remains an easy keeper in extreme circumstances and continues to display classic Colonial Spanish traits of that era, unlike other evolved types of Spanish horses that are popular today.

DNA and visual evidence suggests that there are a few Tackys that have retained a high degree of the Iberian type—another time capsule of genetic material from colonial times. Most of these Tackys have stayed small, as their heritage would dictate. They average 13 hands and weigh under 700 pounds.

History

Two hundred years ago, free-roaming Tackys were so plentiful on the Carolinas and Georgia coast that they were almost considered a nuisance. Still, to the original colonists, they were a reliable form of transportation and the farm tractor of that time. They were also important mounts for the original cattle drives of America. No doubt the Native Americans along the southeastern seaboard prized these hearty, savvy horses too; the Chickasaw, Cherokee, Seminole, and Choctaw all likely came into contact with the little horses.

When the settlers began importing blooded horses—Thoroughbreds, Arabians, and other oriental horses—from overseas, portions of the hearty little Spanish horse populations managed to remain pure. Tackys thrived particularly well in feral and semi-feral states in the South Carolina Lowcountry marshlands, where other animals would have perished. They were often captured, tamed, and made into reliable mounts for children. Many worked the fields or pulled buggies and carts.

They were also used for crossbreeding. It is theorized that Tackys were used early in the development of the foundation bloodlines of the Quarter Horse and the Kentucky Mountain Saddle Horses.

Tackys were probably America's first warhorses. They were used in a military capacity as the mounts of Francis Marion and his militia to lead raids in South Carolina against the British during the American Revolutionary War. Marion and his mounted men darted out of the Carolina marshes to attack, then withdrew quickly back into the waters where the British horses had difficulty following. This is how Marion earned his famed nickname, "the Swamp Fox." With little ammunition, Marion was successful with his lightening-quick ambushes and raids, a feat for which the Marsh Tacky was particularly adept.

Throughout the 1800s, Tackys were reported as far north as Myrtle Beach, South Carolina, and as far south as St. Simons Island, Georgia, almost to the Florida border. The first recorded documentation of horses on the islands came during the American Civil War. Union troops stormed Hilton Head Island, South Carolina, and when the slaves there were set free, they were offered "forty acres and a Marsh Tacky" to begin their new lives. For these people, Tacky horses were instrumental toward establishing new homes in the United States.

In the years following the American Civil War, Tackys continued to be useful. Their ability to navigate safely through the marshy swamps made them exceptional saddle and hunting horses. They were part of everyday life, pulling plows, hauling firewood, and drawing wagons to market, as well as mounts for hunting wild game and transporters that hauled the family carriage to church. They carried the mail, pulled the doctor's buggy, and got the teacher to the schoolhouse. For the Gullah farmers, the Marsh Tacky was as indispensable as the tractor is today.

Recent History

Modern history, both documented and anecdotal, indicates Tackys still roamed freely by the hundreds in the early twentieth century on the islands off South Carolina, including Hilton Head. In those days, Tackys were a way of life for both Gullah families and whites; everyone on Hilton Head, at one time or another, had a Marsh Tacky—or two or three. Racing derbies were often held on Hilton

Head until the 1960s, with Tackys running on a stretch of beach, rounding a turn, and returning to the finish.

Native islanders continued to breed and use the Tackys until the 1950s, when developers started paving roads and buying up real estate. By 1974, one lone Tacky survivor was left cropping grass on the lawn of a local island restaurant.

A few dedicated breeders elsewhere quietly hung on. Precious few Marsh Tacky breeders have doggedly persevered through to the present time, and now few Tackys can be found beyond those preserved by these breeders. The most recent band was only "discovered" in the late 1990s.

Today, the Marsh Tacky's range has been reduced to South Carolina, where they are critically endangered and number somewhere between 125 to 175 individuals. The Equus Survival Trust lists them as extremely critical.

Only a handful of breeders and conservationists stand between extinction of the Tacky and its continuance. Concerted efforts have been made to save the last remaining bands. Additionally, DNA testing has been done to determine the Spanish connection and to establish a breeding management plan to keep the gene pool genetically diverse and healthy. Toward this end, the Carolina Marsh Tacky Association and its breeders are striving to document and process records.

The largest surviving herd is with the Lowther family in South Carolina. This family has bred Tackys for three generations, tracing the original herd all the way back to the American Civil War in South Carolina. D. P. Lowther now has more than one hundred pure Tacky horses. They are divided into several breeding groups and display a wide variety of solid colors, including grullas, duns, and roans, as well as primitive markings and patterns. Yet all have the same distinctive and related Tacky look: a straight or convex Iberian profile with wide foreheads; deep, powerful chests, though often narrow in width; and hindquarters that slope steeply, all evidence of the Barbary blood. Hooves are typically flinty

and durable; none seem to require anything but proper trimming.

Standards

Marsh Tackies should be surefooted in wooded and swampy lands, and have the ability to get out of boggy areas calmly, safely, and effectively. The ideal temperament is alert but calm, levelheaded, and not prone to panic.

Defects include horses that are nervous and flighty, as well as ones that are dull with little alertness.

General Appearance: Marsh Tacky horses have traditionally been balanced and athletic. They are also known for being easy keepers on forages with little supplemental feeding.

Gait: Most Tacky horses have a fluid, smooth trot. A few in the past have been gaited, and this tendency is not penalized should it reappear in the breed. A short, rough, choppy trot is to be avoided.

Height: The usual height is from 14 to 14.2 hands high at the withers. The usual range in height is from 13 to 15 hands, with few being below or above this range. At the extremes of the range, horses tend to lose overall typeness. A tall or short typey horse is acceptable, but horses that are too short or too tall without strong overall type should not be chosen as breeding animals.

Head: The head is important as it relates to breed type. Outside breeding shows up readily in the head conformation. The profile of the head is usually flat or slightly concave, but becomes slightly convex from the nasal region to the top of the muzzle. Some are more uniformly convex, while others are nearly straight. To be avoided are fine heads that are markedly dished, like the Arabian's, or heads that are markedly convex from poll to muzzle.

From the front view, the head has a characteristic shape. It is wide between the eyes, then tapers and is finely chiseled, or defined, through the mid region. Most typical heads flare back out at the region of the nostrils and then taper to a fine muzzle.

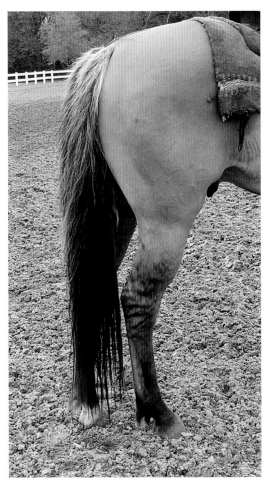

An example of primitive leg stripes are quite noticeable on this Tacky, as is the bi-colored, long tail. *Equus Survival Trust*

The most usual off-type is wider through the mid region, and coarser, thicker, and rounder through the muzzle.

The nostrils are usually fine and crescent shaped at rest. They flare larger and more open when excited or under exertion. To be avoided are large, coarse, round, open nostrils.

The ears are usually short to medium length, and most have a distinctive inward pointing notch at the tips. To be avoided are long, straight, thick, wide, or boxy ears with no inward notch at the tip.

The eyes are usually large and bold, though some have smaller eyes, which are acceptable. The eyes are high on the head. To be avoided are large, bold eyes that are low on the head.

The profile of the muzzle from the side is refined, with the top lip usually longer than the bottom lip. Avoid coarse and thick lower lips that are loose, large, and project beyond the upper lip.

Neck: The neck is usually wide from the side, though it is still typical to have a slight ewe neck. The neck is attached lower on the chest than most other breeds. Avoid necks that are thin, long, and set high on the chest.

Withers: The withers are usually pronounced and obvious, or even sharp. Avoid thick, low, meaty withers.

Back: The back is usually short and strong. Some have a longer back, but weak, long backs that are weakly tied into croup and withers should be avoided.

Rear: The croup and hip are important indicators of type. The usual conformation is angled from the top of the croup to the tail base at a 30-degree slope, although some are steeper than this. Flat, high croups are not typical.

The tail is usually set on low so that it appears to fall off the croup smoothly. A high tailset above the angle of the croup is not typical.

The rear end usually has a distinct break at the point of the hip, so that the line from the top of croup to point of hip is one line or curve. Then this line breaks and continues as a different curve from the point of the hip to the back of the gaskin. Avoid a smooth, round curve from top of croup to the gaskin, as seen in Quarter Horses. Overly conditioned horses may be difficult to evaluate on this detail, as fat can obscure the true conformation here.

From the rear view, the spine is usually at the top of the rear, and the muscles taper down off of this (rafter-hipped). This is a combination of the type and amount of muscling, as well as the location of the hip joint. To be avoided is thicker muscling and higher hips that result in a distinct deep crease

This bay roan Tacky mare has the proper conformation, including a wide neck, short, strong back, and deep chest.
Equus Survival Trust

down the middle, so that the midpoint is lower rather than higher.

From the side, the hips should be long and well angled, rather than steep and short.

Front: From the side, the chest is deep and usually accounts for about half the height of the horse. From the front, the chest is narrow and the legs usually point up to an "A" shape at the chest, rather than a broader flatter appearance. This aspect varies in the breed, and historic photos show more narrowness here than can be seen on many modern horses. Expect variation in this aspect, but very wide chests are penalized. These usually accompany heads that are off-type from the front view.

The shoulder is ideally long and has a 45- to 55-degree angle. Short shoulders that are steeper than 55 degrees are not desirable.

From the front view, the limbs should fall straight from the shoulder to the ground.

Rear Limbs: From the rear view, the rear limbs are usually straight or turned slightly inward at the

hocks, but then straight from there to the ground. The legs are flexible, and at the trot, the hind track can land past the front track. The muscling is long and tapering. Avoid excessive cow hocks as well as heavy, bunchy muscling (most obvious in the gaskin) or tight tendons.

There is usually no feathering on the fetlocks. Avoid coarse, abundant feathering.

Feet are balanced and of the size to fit the overall weight of the horse. Hooves are tough and wear well.

Chestnuts: These vary from small and nearly nonexistent, to larger and more obvious. The most typical are the small, flat ones, and some horses lack rear chestnuts entirely. Very large and thick chestnuts should be penalized.

Color: Any color is permissible, but some colors are more common. The most common colors include bay, black, grullo, dun, blue roan, and bay roan. Chestnut, red dun, and strawberry roan are also common. Some of them have primitive markings, like dorsal stripes and zebra leg stripes. Many horses have little or no white markings on them, while some have extensive white on the legs and heads. Other colors are no indication by themselves of crossbreeding. Mating of individuals with the most white on them could produce foals with enough white to have body spots.

Most of the manes and tails are long, also indicating their Spanish heritage. No doubt the longer hair was retained in the New World as a useful trait, protecting them against flies and mosquitoes rampant in the South Carolina Lowcountry. Some of them have primitive markings, like dorsal stripes and zebra leg stripes.

Temperament: Temperament is one of the most important aspects of a Marsh Tacky, and unfortunately is impossible to observe by just looking at the horse.

For all its ruggedness, the Carolina Marsh Tacky is a gentle, good-natured horse, full of curiosity and, when trained, becomes a trusted, intelligent partner. During most of its existence, the Tacky had to survive by foraging on its own and managed to thrive; it has retained this trait and remained a thrifty easy-keeper.

Tackies are excellent on trails, surefooted, and efficient in water situations. Those who have ridden them rave about their uncanny ability to negotiate swamps without panic or fuss, including rolling over to get out when they get stuck. Tackys seem to have a built-in "woods sense" and a natural ability for negotiating water and mud. "If a horse panics in the water, then it is not a Marsh Tacky," boasts one breeder. Another claims that Tacky horses "know how to wear their feet," attesting to their surefootedness, smooth ride, and thoughtful approach to rough terrain. They are smart, calmly taking in unfamiliar situations, and

this innate intelligence helps with their training. They don't have the panic and flight attitude of other breeds, and their gentleness is appreciated especially by women and children, yet they are bold when used for hunting or working cattle. They show great promise for endurance, competitive trail, barrel racing, dressage, or event competitions.

Tacky horse owner David Grant states:

> You can have the prettiest horse in the world, but if it doesn't have enough sense or hardiness to survive, what do you have? The Tacky has an innate sense of self-preservation. I have ridden my grulla stud for one year now, and he has pulled me out of some pretty tough situations, and he is only three years old. On one hunt, we fell into a hole large enough for him to roll down into. He just rolled out from under me and literally crawled out. The most amazing thing is that he came back to get me. He has already developed an ear for the dogs baying and will pick his own way to them. Tackies are very easy keepers. I have fifteen and have had very few problems. They stay fat on grass and hay, their feet require very little if any trimming, their resistance to insects is astounding, and the list of their many attributes goes on and on.

The Carolina Marsh Tacky is an honored historic breed that has survived more than four hundred years virtually intact. It is a national treasure forever stamped on the hearts of those who know it.

Credit: Victoria Tollman and Equus Survival Trust

CERBAT

Bay Cerbat stallion with outstanding conformation, consistent with its Spanish ancestry. *Apache Trail Ranch*

Apple Tree Ranch
4970 South Kansas Settlement Road
Willcox, Arizona 85643
www.angelfire.com/az/xochitl

In the Cerbat Mountain area of northwestern Arizona, there is a small yet distinct herd of Spanish Mustangs that is one of the purest Spanish horse descendants in the United States. Documentation obtained from a pioneer rancher family in 1966, and published in a national magazine that same year, stated the herd was present when the family settled in the area in the 1860s. To their knowledge, no outside blood had ever been introduced. The

local Native Americans made no claim upon the horses, stating they had "always been there."

The most plausible explanation for the presence of the Cerbat herd is the prevailing theory that their ancestors either escaped from, or were lost by, early Spaniards. A study into the history of the area reveals that a number of Spanish expeditions ranged into Arizona, New Mexico, and California. Loss, escape, theft by Apaches, and other means would easily supply the seed stock into the Cerbat area. Blood testing of these horses shows without a doubt that they carry Spanish markers.

Living in an extremely inhospitable environment at an altitude ranging from five to seven thousand feet, the original herd evolved into exceptionally tough, agile horses with extraordinary endurance and survival ability. Their day-to-day lives involved navigating around and through rough boulders, rocks, and brush.

Due to drought conditions in the area in 1971, ranchers began eliminating these historic animals to preserve more water for range cattle, not realizing wild horses will dig for water and thereby open up waterholes for the cattle as well. Much of Arizona land was owned by the Bureau of Land Management (BLM), which leased it to the ranchers, who did what they wanted with the horses.

At about that time, a local rancher who apparently regretted the destruction of the horses gave permission to a friend, a veteran Arizona cowboy by the name of Ira Wakefield, to capture and keep the last surviving herd. This small band of horses lived in total isolation at an altitude of seven thousand feet in an exceptionally rough section of the mountains. The land they ran on was owned by the BLM, which at that time had not yet begun the business of adopting out wild horses or managing herds.

Wakefield's plans for the roundup progressed slowly due to the extreme difficulty in getting vehicles into the rough terrain of the area, but he eventually managed to build an enclosure around the main source of the horses' water. Less than twenty animals were captured and marked with Wakefield's brand on the capture site. Then they were brought down to the flatlands where they were issued the required Arizona paperwork. The group was divided among several people with a number of animals going to Washington State.

One stallion and three mares were released by Wakefield into an adjacent mountain range some miles distant from the original capture site. The remaining horses were taken to the Phoenix area and later were moved to Colorado, except for one stallion. He was placed on the Cayuse Ranch in Oshoto, Wyoming, the home of Robert E. Brislawn, founder of the Spanish Mustang Registry.

A year later, the small herd that had been turned loose was water trapped, and the foals were removed and brought to Phoenix. The herd consisted of a

Distinctive and beautiful Cerbat mare. Some Cerbats are gaited. *Apache Trail Ranch*

Regal looking five-year-old Cerbat stallion that is a rare seal brown. *Apache Trail Ranch*

yearling colt, two yearling fillies, and one weanling filly. All except one yearling filly were purchased by Apache Trail Ranch, which then was located north of Phoenix. Realizing the rarity of these horses, the ranch decided to preserve the genetics by producing a pure breeding herd of Cerbat horses. With just the one colt and the two young fillies, the future was not bright, but with the acquisition of two mares from the Colorado group, the genetic variation was improved.

For many reasons, it is highly probable that this Cerbat herd was one of the purest groups of feral Spanish-descended horses in existence. The area in which the group lived is remote with extremely rough terrain, making the introduction of outside gene sources difficult at best. There is documentation of the horses' presence prior to the settling of the area by white settlers more than 130 years earlier. There is lack of a Native American claim, and there was an extremely heavy Spanish influx into the Arizona area for hundreds of years.

Genetic blood testing by the University of Kentucky proved the Cerbat horses to be of Spanish descent. Further evidence of their Spanish connection was the fact that a number of these Cerbat horses were laterally gaited, doing a credible "paso"

gait, though without the extreme action of their cousins, the Paso breeds. This is not at all surprising, as they carry genes similar to the Peruvian Paso, indicating a common ancestor.

Although the Cerbat's blood testing showed them to be heavily inbred and from a closed herd situation, like many wild animals in similar situations, apparently all defective genetic material had been bred out. This means that any animals possessing abnormal or imperfect genes were culled naturally, leaving only those with superior qualities designed for survival and reproduction. Additionally, their physical size decreased to adjust to reduced food supply.

In 1990, surprising news arrived: A small herd of horses believed to be descended from the handful of Cerbat horses left behind in 1971 were found in the same Arizona area. A group of eight was water trapped, and blood samples were taken and sent to the University of Kentucky for comparison with those taken from the horses captured in 1971. Although they were even more inbred, they did indeed match up with the 1971 group. It is probable that this newly captured group had no more than five ancestors and no less than three, according to the blood test, therefore making the horses extremely inbred.

The condition of the horses disproved there were any detrimental effects commonly associated with inbreeding. The new Cerbats were healthy, strong, and actually a bit larger than the original group. Lateral gaits were evident in these horses as well, and though undeniably related to the 1971 group, the addition of the new horses to the breeding program was a welcome asset.

Characteristics

Though the 1971 horses were small in size, with only one individual reaching more than 13.2 hands, the succeeding generation leaped in size by more than a hand. This substantiated the theory that their small size was caused by the inhospitable environment in the mountains. Horses that survived the first year of their lives in the mountains remained small, but were extremely healthy and strong. The weanling filly that had been caught and then acquired by Apache Trail Ranch grew to almost 15 hands due to better feed.

Cerbats do not come in any exotic colors. Only bay and chestnut, with an occasional seal brown, seem to be consistent in their genetic inheritance, however, at least 50 percent of these bays and chestnuts are also roans. A rather odd occurrence in the Cerbats is that roan foals are born roan, whereas in many other breeds, roan foals show their roan color only after the shedding of the foal coat.

Cerbat ears are small and curved. The eyes are rather high set. A definite relationship to the old-type Andalusian can be seen in the facial profile.

The chest is not flat between the legs, but is rather narrow in comparison to American breeds and is well "veed" up (inverted V-shaped). Shoulders are laid back, and the heart girth is deep.

Due perhaps to centuries of mountain living or simply their genetic inheritance, their legs and feet are excellent with well-boned legs and thick-walled feet. Backs are short, and hindquarters are sturdy, deep, and powerful. Chestnuts on forelegs are small and smooth, and are extremely small or nonexistent on the rear legs. Ergots are tiny or nonexistent.

Cerbat horses demonstrate outstanding disposition. They are quick to learn, intelligent, and willing, with a penchant for association with humans. Marye Ann Thompson, owner of Apache Trail Ranch, says, "They have the best dispositions of any horses I ever worked with. They are virtually spook-proof and totally sensible. Plus they have more bone than most of the other Spanish Mustangs and seem to pass on their good qualities to their offspring, regardless of what they are bred to, which is really nice."

As a product of their Spanish inheritance, plus their more recent feral environment, Cerbat horses are tough, hardy, extremely durable animals. One interesting fact is that the resting pulse rate per minute in all individuals tested is rather low— in the thirties—which should be of value in any type of endurance competition. In fact, one-half Cerbat and five-eighths Cerbat horses have proven their capabilities by doing well in competitive and endurance rides as well as in three-day eventing.

Cerbat horses are extremely consistent in reproduction, which is not surprising considering they are so closely akin in genetic makeup. The mares have no difficulty in foaling. The Cerbat mares captured in 1971 produced well into their twenties. Foals are strong at birth and are usually on their feet and nursing within fifteen to twenty minutes, a necessity when living in predator country for generations.

Currently, there are less than fifty purebred Cerbats. Though still limited in numbers in the pure state, the herd has been preserved, and with future expected growth being high, a small number have been made available to a few select owners who wish to continue to breed them.

All Cerbats that are shown are registered with the Spanish Mustang Registry and can also be registered with the Horse of the Americas Registry.

The future looks bright for this distinct Spanish herd that was doomed to extinction more than thirty years ago.

Credit: Marye Ann Thompson

COLONIAL SPANISH

Horse of the Americas, Inc.
202 Forest Trail Road
Marshall, Texas 75670
www.horseoftheamericas.com

The broad list of Colonial Spanish horses includes a tiny Havapai Pony from a small genetic base of less than forty horses; a Sulphur Springs or Pryor Mustang, which is occasionally offered for adoption by the Bureau of Land Management (BLM); or a tribal original like a Cherokee or Choctaw horse. All of these horses descended from ancient Spanish stock first brought to America around the time of its colonization. The registry for them is Horse of the Americas (HOA), which is open to all Colonial Spanish horses.

These historical horses are America's first horses and should be preserved for future generations. Each one carries its own bit of history. Some have been selectively bred for certain uses. Others were selected naturally for certain traits, like hooves that could handle the hardest terrain or for being easy keepers for survival in severe northern winters. These strengths make each subgroup unique and worthy of preservation in their own right. They have come a long way via diverse routes to reach the twenty-first century.

Colonial Spanish horses stand as a unique collection among horse breeds. Their history and breeding make them a genetic resource of great value. They are also distinct from most other breeds and ancestral to many, but their uniqueness is one of the major impediments to conservation. As the general horse-owning public has gone to the Arabian, Thoroughbred, warmblood, and stock horse types, the other less popular types have become rarer. International horse breeding is now very homogeneous, and the more unique types are clearly being left behind.

The current Colonial Spanish horse comes to us because previous generations of breeders cared enough to assure its survival. As with any

Bob Brislawn stands on his Cayuse Ranch with a Colonial Spanish 100 percent Brislawn Foundation grulla stallion. *Courtesy Gretchen L. Patterson*

Colonial Spanish 100 percent Wilbur–Cruce horse with an overo pattern. *Courtesy Gretchen L. Patterson*

conservation effort, each breeder had slightly different ideas and goals. Past breeding has resulted in a variety of strains and subgroups, each of which being slightly different by ancestry and type. These differences are in some cases minor, in others distinctive. The differences have been a source of disagreements as to what is pure and what is not within the Colonial Spanish horse spectrum and has been one cause of the multiple registries. Each registry designates a slightly different group of horses as pure. This can contribute to conservation, but likewise can contribute to divisions, which defeats the purpose of their continued existence. The Colonials deserve better. They are indeed important, because they possess most of the basic components of the present breed.

Horse of the Americas Registry is a unified registry for America's first horse, the Colonial Spanish, a historic horse group that contains, among others, the Spanish Mustang, Barb, Original Indian Horse, and Cayuse. Horse of the Americas has registered more than seven hundred horses to date, and the number of applications increases almost daily. Approved strains include:

- Brislawn foundation
- Original Horse of the Americas foundation
- Book Cliffs
- Tribal
- Havapai Pony
- Belsky
- Romero/McKinley
- Romero/Gonzalez/Marques
- Gilbert Jones foundation
- Wilbur-Cruce
- Yates

Other Colonial Spanish strains registered with Horse of the Americas—such as the Abaco Barb, Banker Horse, Carolina Marsh Tacky, Cerbat, Florida Cracker, Kiger, Nokota, Pryor Mountain Mustang, Spanish Barb, and Sulphur Springs Horse—have their own registries as well. (They are presented elsewhere in this book.)

The value of the various strains is that each one is a survivor from a earlier time when the Colonial Spanish horse was *the* horse in North America. Each has a portion of the overall genetic mix that was brought here during Spanish exploration. Each has a role to play toward the conservation of the Colonial Spanish horse.

History

The original horses brought to America from Spain were relatively unselected. They first came to the Caribbean islands where their populations were increased before being exported either north or south to the mainland continents. In the case of North America, most went to Mexico first, thereby populating the southeastern United States through Mexico, rather than more directly from the Caribbean. The North American horses ultimately came from this somewhat indiscriminate and early imported base.

South American horses, in contrast, originally tended to derive about half their genetics from the Caribbean horses and half from direct imports of highly selected horses from Spain. These later imports changed the average type of horses in South America.

This difference in foundation blood is one reason for the current dissimilarity between the North American and South American horses today. Other disparities were fostered by the diverse selection goals in South America. Both factors resulted in related, but different, types of horses. In addition, the South American horses have become popular and common in several countries within the continent, with some becoming the national horse, such as the Puerto Rican Paso Fino and Peruvian Paso.

The lack of popularity of the Colonial Spanish horse subtypes in North America has been a mixed blessing, as their breeders have tended to be loyal to them, yet have tended to work very much outside the mainstream of horse breeders and users in North America. This has kept Colonials obscure from general horse circles longer than intended. Their isolation has resulted in constant pressure to increase their size and harmonize their conformation to more popular North American breeds. The danger of this trend is that it could result in homogenizing out what traits are left of the Colonial Spanish horse, which was a purebred longer than some of today's popular breeds.

In the early 1700s, the purely Spanish horse could be found in an arc from the Carolinas to Florida, west through Tennessee, and then throughout all of the western mountains and the Great Plains. In the Northeast and Central East, the colonists were from northwestern Europe and the horses they brought were more draft or Thoroughbred types, rather than the Colonial Spanish type. Even in these non-Spanish areas, the Colonial Spanish horse was highly valued and still contributed to the overall mix of American horses. Due to their wide geographic distribution of pure populations, as well as their contribution to other crossbred types, Colonial Spanish horses were the most common of all horses throughout North America at that time and were widely used for riding as well as draft. In addition to being the common mount of Native American tribes and white colonists, there were also immense herds of feral animals that were descended from escaped or strayed animals from the owned herds.

Colonial Spanish horses came to be considered to be too small for cavalry use by the colonists and were slowly supplanted by taller and heavier types from the Northeast as integral parts of colonial expansion in North America. In the final stages, this process was fairly rapid, expedited by the extermination of the horse herds of Native Americans during the latter's subjection in the late 1800s.

The close association of the Spanish horse with both Native American and Mexican cultures also caused the popularity of these horses to diminish, in contrast to the highly favored, larger horses of the dominant Anglo-American culture, whose horses tended to be more northern European types. The end result was that by the twentieth century, only a handful of Colonial Spanish horses were left of the once-vast herds.

Colonial Spanish silver dun Choctaw mare. *Courtesy Gretchen L. Patterson*

Brislawn and the Original Horse of the Americas Foundation

Many of the pure Spanish horses in North America remained in isolated feral herds and became rare fairly early in the twentieth century due to the practice of shooting the Spanish stallions and replacing them with draft, or blooded, stallions (generally Thoroughbred or coach) in an attempt to "improve," or breed up, the feral herds as sources of draft or remount stock.

The relatively small handful of western Colonial Spanish horses that survived through these lean years founded the present Brislawn strain, and so is the horse of interest when considering the history of the current breed. These Colonial Spanish horses that persisted through that period of low herd numbers will forever stamp the resulting breed in more important ways than the millions of horses that once roamed the continent but failed to survive.

Bob Brislawn, who founded the Spanish Mustang Registry in 1957, used many feral horses in his herd. He obtained several of his foundation horses from an Apache named Monty Holbrook, who lived in Utah and was an excellent mustanger (capturer of feral horses). Thus most of the feral components of the Brislawn horses originated from Utah horses, although isolated horses from other herds contributed as well.

Brislawn also selected some of the ranch's finest Colonial Spanish horses to begin the Horse of the Americas herd, bringing the first "stud bunch" to the Wild Horse Research Farm in California in 1971. Jeff Edwards, the other original Horse of the Americas founder, later wrote, "In 1972 the Department of Agriculture recognized Bob Brislawn as the founder of the Spanish Barb Mustang horse. Now with the horses on the Research Farm being personally selected by Bob Brislawn they are 'authenticated.' " Thus, the Brislawn horses contributed widely to the present breed.

Book Cliffs

A later major source of feral Colonial Spanish type horses were the herds in the Book Cliffs of Utah. This area has an interesting geological formation that looks like sheer walls of rock. The valleys in between are where Monty Holbrook captured wild horses for the Brislawns. These horses figured prominently in the Brislawn herds as well as others. In some herds, Book Cliffs horses are still present and unique, but their main impact has been their use for other horse breeds. While today's Book Cliff horses are generally no longer considered pure, the neighboring Sand Wash area is reputed to still be home to some typical Spanish Colonial horses.

Tribal

Feral horses were not the only group to contribute to the Colonial Spanish horse of today. Many foundation horses came from the horse herds of Native Americans. The original Spanish horses were obtained at first from a chain of missions across the south in early Spanish colonial days, and their breed continued on in the tribes.

The Native herds were especially important in the early twentieth century. Most of these tribal horses have only influenced the present breed through individual horses and not through groups that continue to be bred pure within the strain. Tribes contributing to the continuation of tribal horses include Cheyenne, Lakota, Paiute, Navajo, and a few others. Horses from the northern tribes contributed heavily to the Brislawn herd along with the feral stock they used. The search is always on for breeders or families that have kept the original type pure, but these have become increasingly rare as the years go by.

A few tribal types have continued to be bred as distinct strains. The Choctaw and Cherokee horses are among these. Both of these tribes, in addition to the Chickasaw and Creek, were avid horse breeders in their original homes in the southeast. The quality of their horses was specifically mentioned as being excellent in various travel journals from the late 1700s and early 1800s. Some of these horses have unique Iberian blood types, which provide evidence of the accuracy of the oral history about isolation surrounding the herds.

These horses were brought from the Southeast to what is now Oklahoma on the Trail of Tears. This was a forced relocation by the U.S. government in

Colonial Spanish 50 percent Havapai Pony black stallion. *Courtesy Gretchen L. Patterson*

the 1830s of seventy thousand Native Americas from eastern tribes that were moved westward across the Mississippi River to areas that the white European settlers did not want. These tribes became important mediators between several of the western tribes and the government, and it is likely that exchanges of horses between tribes occurred during the many meetings that were held. No doubt some western horses were added to the eastern tribal herds in this way.

Some individual families were important in preserving the tribal horses. The Whitmire line, which also includes horses from the Corntassle family, is a Cherokee line that can be traced back to the American Indian removal from Etocha, Georgia, in 1835. It probably goes back even further, as court records from 1775 indicate that these families had herds of horses at that time. A few Mexican stallions, which had leopard-type color patterns, were also used in the Whitmire line of Cherokee horses, but the exact source of the stallions is unknown.

The Whitmire horses were always kept within the line of the female side, although outside stallions were occasionally introduced. The stallions were of Mexican, Choctaw, or Comanche breeding, and were therefore also Colonial Spanish. Some of the Comanche stallions came from the Black Moon Comanche of Oklahoma and bore leopard color patterns; at least one Mexican stallion was a buckskin leopard. The outside stallions were carefully and specifically selected to be as similar to the Cherokee strain as possible and to be Colonial Spanish in type. Many of the Cherokee horses that remain today are gaited, and many have unusual color patterns including several Medicine Hat Paint horses.

The major families that preserved the Choctaw horses until recently were the Brame, Crisp, Locke, Self, Helms, Thurman, and Carter families. Horses were run on the open range in areas where other types of horses were not kept. These families had hundreds of horses of consistent Spanish type and widely varying colors, including the "Spanish roan" sabino type, leopard and blanketed, and others such as overo paints.

The Choctaw horses are occasionally gaited. They are also quick. Hal Brame was noted for taking his little Paint horse to parties and dances, and wagering on races of more than fifty yards. He took a lot of money from cowboys with Quarter Horses and Thoroughbreds who went away with increased respect for small Paint Indian horses.

From the hundreds of Choctaw and Cherokee horses that were available as recently as 1975, there are now only a few survivors. This is due to the dispersal of many large herds following the deaths of some of the elder breeders. Probably only fifty-nine pure Choctaw and Cherokee horses could be assembled in 1988, but a few breeders are trying to assure that this type continues into the future as a part of the overall breeding of Spanish horses. Most of the present Choctaw and Cherokee horses are in the herds of Bryant and Darlene Rickman. Many horses in the various registries are of partial Choctaw breeding, confirming that the Choctaw horses have made a wide impact on the general Colonial Spanish horse breed of today. The stallions Choctaw, Choctaw Sundance, and Chief Pushmataha had an especially great influence on the horse of the Spanish Mustang Registry, the Society for the Preservation of the Barb Horse (SPBH), and the Southwest Spanish Mustang Association.

Havapai Pony

These ponies once lived in the Havapai region of the Grand Canyon. Their history is still being explored. The first mention of them occurred at the beginning of the twentieth century and ran through the late 1960s. There are accounts and lore that were circulated about sightings of small Grand Canyon horses, and many early twentieth century photographs exist of these tiny Colonial Spanish type horses in the Grand Canyon. They lived both as wild herds and as a part of Havasupai Indian life. The Havasupai were the native residents of the Grand Canyon who rode and used the small horses for generations.

The National Park Service was given a mandate to remove non-native species from National Parks, which may have been the main factor in the loss of the wild Havapai Pony bands. Also, there was uncertainty concerning the impact on the Grand Canyon with construction of the 1960 dam on the Colorado River that created Lake Powell. There was growing public criticism regarding the forty-year practice of killing wild burros and horses. Perhaps due to this criticism, removal of wild horses for preservation became a greater concern for the National Park Service.

Regardless of how it was accomplished and whatever the chain of events that followed, the accepted conclusion is that there was an authentic Havapai Pony mare, Grand Canyon I. She and her daughter made their way into Colonial Spanish breeding programs in the 1970s. Their history begins with their owner, Robert Brislawn, who took Grand Canyon I to the Wild Horse Research Farm (later called the Horse of the Americas Research Farm) in Porterville, California, where she produced three foals. They all were later transported to Texas when the largest breeding group of the remaining herd was purchased in 1988. Another small group was moved to California.

Grand Canyon I was a Havapai Pony of typical size. She was originally selected by Brislawn for a study on genetic size. Once at the Wild Horse Research Farm, she produced several foals by Snipper, a small, black Book Cliffs stallion.

During the mid to late 1980s, breeders of the existing Horse of the Americas stock incorporated some of their finest Colonial Spanish stallions into the Havapai Pony program. The strain was expanded, adding both paint and appaloosa color patterns and occasional lateral gaits, while preserving the small size characteristic. Other breeders have now joined that effort.

The Havapai Ponies are a re-creation of the horses of the Havasupai Indians. Using the blood of the little mare, Grand Canyon I, and stallions of recorded Colonial Spanish ancestry, the Havapai Pony breeders are attempting to preserve a smaller Colonial Spanish horse.

Havapai Ponies generally stand 13.2 hands or under, which is called Classic size. Those standing over or under 13.2 hands are termed Standard size. Even Standard Havapai Ponies rarely stand over 14 hands. They are a Colonial Spanish pony that utilizes the flexion, endurance, and trainability of the Colonial Spanish horse, yet sized for those who have use for a smaller mount of Barb type. They are naturally sound and amicable, which makes them well suited as mounts for children.

Belsky

Other important subtypes of Colonial Spanish horses are the rancher strains. Some of these, such as breeder Tom Waggoner's horses, figure not only in the background of the Colonial Spanish horses, but also in the makeup of the American Quarter Horse. Most of the old ranch strains were Spanish in the 1800s, with the later addition of horses from the Northeast. One rancher who kept the original Spanish type was Ilo Belsky. He ranched in Nebraska, and his herd began from horses that accompanied cattle driven from Texas in the late 1800s. He kept the best horses, and then selectively bred them back mostly to those in his own herd.

Early in the history of their conservation, Belsky popularized his horses as good for ranching. They tended, on average, to be heavier and more thickly made than some of the other strains, although some were the lighter type. His horses were commonly roan, gray, dun, or dark colors.

Belsky horses are now rare, considered a unique western group of Spanish horse, and figure in the background of many Spanish Barbs. They are especially prominent in Spanish Barb Breeders Association (SBBA) horses and, to a lesser degree, in Spanish Mustang Registry and Southwest Spanish Mustang Association horses.

Romero/McKinley and Romero/Gonzalez/Marques

Another important rancher strain is the Romero strain. Horses of this strain are from a ranch near Cebolla, New Mexico, where Spanish horses were raised for generations. The Romero ranch passed to the McKinley family, which still maintains a few horses of the original strain. These horses figure heavily in some lines of Spanish Barb horses.

Another independent New Mexico line confusingly also involves a family named Romero, but is also associated with the Gonzalez and Marques families in Rio Arriba County, New Mexico. They were all involved in the active trade that New Mexicans had with the Comanche tribe for a period covering several centuries, but most were active in the 1800s. Some of these Romero/Gonzalez/Marques horses were gaited and also had flashy calico/paint patterns. This influence persists in some horses raised by Bob Ele and Gilbert Jones, who preserved another rancher strain of the Colonial Spanish breed.

Gilbert Jones

Gilbert Jones of Finley, Oklahoma, was also crucial in maintaining Spanish horses of rancher strains. Due to his moving from Texas to New Mexico and then to Oklahoma, his herd had influences from a wide variety of sources. Many early horses that he included in his breeding program were those from Kiowa, Comanche, and Chickasaw tribes, as well as some from Anglo ranchers such as Tom Waggoner. Some of the tribal horses were from strains of buffalo runners once frequently used on the Llano Estacado, a geographical region in West Texas and eastern New Mexico where many wild mustangs once roamed and lived. Many of the Waggoner horses came from the Llano Estacado, as did some of Gilbert Jones's stock.

These horses were all blended into a single strain. When Brislawn spent a few years in Oklahoma, there was an exchange of Brislawn and Jones horses. Later in the development of the strain, many Choctaw and Cherokee horses were included and now represent a high proportion of the breeding of several Jones horses today. His herd is one of the few sources of Waggoner, Tom East, Kiowa, and Comanche breeding left today.

Other individual Mexican horses that came into the Jones and Choctaw lines were horses from the Huasteca tribe. Two Huasteca horses were imported from Yucatan in southeast Mexico and are responsible for many of the leopard-type markings in some strains today.

Wilbur-Cruce

Father Eusebio Kino was one of the Catholic priests who established missions in Mexico during the sixteenth and seventeenth centuries. Reputed to be an excellent horseman and breeder of horses, Kino ran a breeding operation for original Spanish horses and other livestock. His little horses carried missionaries, native people, and settlers for thousands of miles through the rugged West with comparatively little feed, water, or care.

Some of his horses ended up in Arizona, where they were bred and used as working horses on Dr. Reuben Wilbur's ranch beginning in 1885. Wilbur kept his horses intact and untouched from other outcrosses. His horses were highly praised and treasured for their quickness, surefootedness, hard feet, intelligence, and courage.

The horses ran free on the ranch, fending for themselves. The rugged environment influenced the selection process; only horses used for work were rounded up and trained. Their strength was amazing: an 800-pound Wilbur horse could hold a 1,000-pound bull while carrying a 200-pound man and an enormous saddle.

Wilbur's family name became the Wilbur-Cruce family through marriage. Their herd lived in isolation on the ranch for more than one hundred years until 1989, when Miss Eva Cruce dispersed the livestock due to her old age. Some eighty horses were sold, and from these horses came the Wilbur-Cruce strain of horses. They came to the attention of the Spanish Barb Breeders Association, Spanish Mustang Registry, and Gilbert Jones. A few breeders continue the line of horses, both purebred and outcrosses.

Yates

In addition to the feral, tribal, and rancher horses, there were some Spanish Colonial horses from

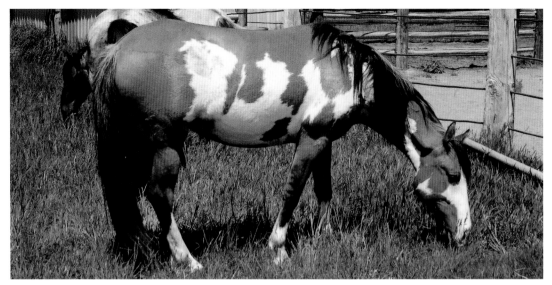

Brislawn Foundation and Book Cliffs dun overo mare. *Courtesy Gretchen L. Patterson*

Mexico. These Mexican horses usually were single horses and not a strain. One exception was a group assembled by Ira Yates, who also figures prominently in the history of the Texas Longhorn. The Yates horses are small, of dun, or grulla color, and still exist in the care of Tally Johnson in Oklahoma. Originally from 150 miles southwest of Mexico City, the first group was assembled in 1950 and the line still continues today.

Registries

Most of the Colonial Spanish horses today can be traced to the previously mentioned sources and came either as individual horses, or as contributions of distinct strains. These distinct strains include feral (Brislawn/Holbrook, Cerbat, Pryor Mountain, and Kiger), native tribe (Choctaw and Cherokee), rancher (Belsky, Romero, Jones, and Wilber-Cruce), and Mexican (Yates and Huasteca) horses. These are all generally western or southwestern subgroups. A few other sources have contributed strains from the southeast United States that are of special interest due to their location and history.

The situation with the numerous registries for the Colonial Spanish horse can be confusing.

Each registry is slightly different in history and outlook from the others. The Horse of the Americas Registry acts as umbrella for all of the other groups in the sense that it will accept horses that are accepted by other registries, as well as horses submitted for inspection and possible inclusion in its own.

Foundation horses for breeds such as the Brislawn foundation, Book Cliffs foundation, Belsky, and Havapai Pony lines may be named with some accuracy today. Establishing foundation lines for some breeds, such as the accepted feral lines, is an ongoing process and many overlap. Good examples are the many breeds that primarily owe their original conservation to Robert Brislawn, such as the Book Cliffs foundation, the Horse of the Americas foundation, and the Havapai Ponies. Others originally preserved by Gilbert Jones and Jewel Whitmire make up both the Jones foundation and the Tribal foundation horses.

The breeds are preserved in several groups for a reason. For example, the Jones foundation horses are not all tribal horses and not all Brislawn foundation horses are Book Cliffs, but all Book Cliffs seem to owe their preservation to the Brislawns.

Characteristics

Today's average Colonial Spanish Horse stands between 13.1 and 14.2 hands and weighs between 750 and 1,000 pounds, although the tiny Havapai Ponies from the Grand Canyon can be much smaller. With modern feeding methods and good care, some of these horses can reach up to nearly 16 hands and may weigh up to some 1,100 pounds.

Horses from lines that have been allowed to run on open ranges for generations often grow larger than their ancestors, if acquired when young and put on feed with a good parasite-control program. The next generation born from such horses may be larger yet, as the horses are simply being allowed to reach their genetic potential. (After all, the conquistadors did not come to America dragging their stirrups on the ground!) As they are descended from Spanish horses brought to the New World during the colonization of the Americas, they do not conform to many of the standards used later by western horse registries that promoted sprinter-type conformation.

Bred for beauty and endurance, the Colonial Spanish horse quickly adapted to the challenging environments of the American frontier—the heat of the Southwest, the wetlands of the Southeast, and the near-arctic winters of the High Plains and Northwest. These radically different climatic conditions forged their different physical adaptations, which must be taken into consideration in judging Colonial Spanish horses. It is a much more physically variable breed than the more homozygous modern western horse breeds.

Three distinct Colonial Spanish horse types, with intermediate types that fall somewhere between, are the following:

- Southwestern type: The lighter-bodied and leggy Spanish Mustang is called the light, or Southwestern, type.
- Northern type: The heavy, or Northern, type is a more blocky horse, like the Spanish Ginete.
- Andalusian type: The third resembles the Andalusian, the classic Spanish horse seen in Renaissance art. This third type is the only one included in certain other Colonial Spanish registries. Some consider it a fusion of heavy and light, a median type. However, it may be the true prototype.

Extremes of climate shaped the lighter and heavier horses in North America—or at least selected the survival of certain types in demanding geographical areas. Even though these three types, and the combinations resulting from crossing them, may appear quite different from one another, they have many physical characteristics in common.

A physical description of the Colonial Spanish Horse, including similarities and differences in the types, follows:

Head: There are three possible head profiles: concave, straight, and convex. In general, the Northerns have a broader jaw and blunter muzzle than the Southwesterns. The head of the Southwestern types is often narrow and more triangular shaped when viewed from the front.

Ears: The ears are medium to short, alert, often deeply hooked, and also called "fox ears." Many have a darker coat color on the rims of the ears than the horse's base coat; this is termed "rimmed." The inner ear hair has natural protection in the form of thick, wooly hair, usually lighter in color than the base coat.

Southwesterns have much less inner ear hair than Northerns. Neither inner nor outer ear hair is trimmed in the Colonial Spanish horse. However, horses with ears trimmed for other equine events that may require it are not to be penalized.

Eyes: Colonial Spanish horses include those with the most unique eye colorations of any breed in the world. Their eyes may be dark, tan, golden, gray, hazel, green, navy, blue, and parti-colored; any of these may also include the sclera. Some of the purest have blue, "glass," or parti-colored eyes; these unique colors are not penalized at halter or in judged performance classes. The Colonial Spanish horse has a medium to large, wide-set eye with a prominent arch. The eyes are alert, and the horse shows interest in all activity around it. Some have heavy bone protruding over the eyes.

Muzzle: The muzzle is refined and small, the mouth is shallow, and the lips are firm. Many wear a four-inch-wide bit, and some have moustaches. The most primitively marked horses will usually show a lighter-colored muzzle, or "mealy nose." Parrot mouth is rarely seen in the Colonial Spanish horse, but since it may cause grazing problems and inefficient chewing and is highly inheritable, such animals should be seriously penalized at halter, especially if they are breeding stock. The nostril is crescent shaped and will close tightly.

An unusual trait is that the Colonial Spanish horse produces a strange, rattling type of snort when it confronts a questionable situation or object. This sound has been referred to as the horse having "rollers in the nose," and is unlike the snort of most other types of horses. It is part of herd behavior and is used to alert other herd members to possible danger. Since the Spanish Mustang is a more natural breed than the human-made ones, its herd behaviors, such as this one, are often more pronounced.

Neck: The neck is strong and moderate in length—about the same length as from the withers to the croup—and not heavily muscled. The throatlatch is deep with a strong, gracefully curved bottom line. The hollow between the jaws is well defined. The Northern type carries more crest than the Southwestern, with the Andalusian type generally having the most graceful necks of the three physiological types. All show shorter and more powerful necks in proportion to the rest of their body than modern breeds of Thoroughbred descent. While excessive crest is not desired, a strong crest is often noted and not to be penalized.

Mane and Tail: The forelock and mane are not to be trimmed, pulled, or clipped in any way, unless the exhibitor is required to trim them for other equine events (such as open shows or drill team competitions). The mane and tail may be very long and is often quite dense, especially in the Andalusian and Northern types.

A double mane, or a mane parting to fall on alternate sides of the neck, is common, and exhibitors are not required to train a mane to fall on one side for showing at halter. Some Colonial Spanish horses have a scanty mane and tail, especially some appaloosas and duns. Although the long mane is generally considered desirable in the Colonial Spanish horse, the thin mane and "rat tail" are not to be penalized at halter.

Shoulder: The shoulder is long, sloping, and laid back with smooth muscling. The forward point of the shoulder is prominent. The horse is often heavier on the forequarters than the hindquarters.

Chest: The chest is medium to narrow. The Southwestern type is narrower than the other types, but in all types there is a well-defined inverted "V" between the front legs. The chest is well muscled, but not bulgy and never broad or flat.

Barrel: The barrel is slightly tapering. It has well-sprung ribs; in all types, when looking at the horse from the front, the barrel should be plainly visible on both sides. The heart girth is deep (as opposed to wide) with good heart and lung space in front of a full abdomen. It should be short-coupled. The underline is longer than the topline, with a more rounded underline on the Andalusian and Northern types. The flank space behind the ribs is short.

Legs: The legs are strong and of medium bone with long, smooth muscling that carries down well into the knees and hocks. They are uniquely flexible with stretchy but strong tendons that are well defined from the bone. The joints also allow great flexibility of motion and are rather large. The length of the cannon is short to medium with round and dense bone, but never heavy in appearance.

An outward rotation of the fetlock joint may look similar to, but less obvious than, the *termino* of the Paso Fino and Peruvian Paso. This is seen most often at the trot or in the movements of the gaited variety. Called "winging" or "paddling" in breeds in which it is undesirable, such action is not a fault in the Colonial Spanish horse, unless it interferes with movement and/or clips opposing hooves.

Colonial Spanish champagne overo stallion. *Courtesy Gretchen L. Patterson*

Otherwise, this action can add to the smoothness of the gait.

The hind legs should be strong with hocks well defined, but without excessive flesh. Tendons and suspensor ligaments are well defined. The rear legs may also be set slightly under the body, allowing the forward reach of the hind stride to land just beneath the rider's stirrup. The hind legs are straight to slightly turned out. Any leg deviation that causes interference is to be heavily penalized.

The pasterns are of medium length and sloping under a strong fetlock. In most horses, the hind pasterns may be somewhat shorter and straighter than the front, but all are long and angular enough to give a springy, smooth ride. The angle should be approximately the same as the shoulder and hoof wall.

Hoof: The hooves are small, but adequate for the horse's size and body weight. Most wear 00 or 0 shoes, if they are shod at all. The hoof is hard and dense, so many never require shoeing. The hooves are generally more egg-shaped than round with a distinct point at the toe, especially on the hind feet. The circumference is smaller at the coronary band than at the ground surface. Hoof color may be black, gray, white, or striped (laminated).

Back: The back is well-defined, and withers are not too pronounced, but blend nicely into the neck and back. The back is short, strong, and well proportioned, stout but never flat. The withers should be higher than the top of the hip.

Hindquarters: The croup is short and sloping with a slightly low tailset; the hips are well rounded. The Southwesterns have narrower hips than the Andalusian or Northern types, but none have bulgy, excessively heavy hip muscling or much width between the hip bones. The tail is set medium low to low. The tail is usually long and may be heavy.

Gait: The heritage of the Colonial Spanish horse includes virtually all so-called saddle gaits, including varieties of the pace and broken pace, the trot and the broken trot, the running walk and the fox trot. Since most gaited Colonial Spanish horses have some of the outward rotation of the fetlock joint called *termino*, they are often referred to as having Paso gaits, similar to, but not as animated as, the gaits of the Peruvian Paso and Paso

Fino. Colonial Spanish horses do not show excessive *termino*; it is certainly not as pronounced as in Pasos.

All gaits are acceptable in this breed, and no particular gait is preferred over another, so long as they do not interfere with sound movement and show good endurance. The gaits are not choppy, but have a good degree of smoothness and are comfortable for the rider, even on those horses that are not gaited, performing only at the walk, trot, and canter.

Ground-covering ability is an important characteristic and extreme collection is not desired; the horse should have ability to cover ground well and have smoothness of gait.

Temperament: The Colonial Spanish horse is bold, yet calm, alert, curious, proud, and trainable. The horse is expected to perform with energy, but without foolishness.

General Comments: Emphasis in judging at halter should first be on soundness and stamina, then on ground-covering ability. The judge should place horses according to how he or she believes they would perform on a full day's ride over challenging terrain, and then consider their potential readiness to do the same day after day. Modern breed conformation criteria that may potentially cause soundness problems in long-distance riding—such as feet too small for the horse's body weight, heavy, bunchy muscling, or excessive fat—should be penalized. Endurance qualities are more important to Colonial Spanish horses than sprinting ability, but many are reasonably fast over short distances and still have good stamina.

What a Colonial Spanish horse is supposed to look like has been the subject of many debates. One of the purposes of the Horse of the Americas Registry is to advocate a certain heterozygous nature inherent to the various subgroups of these horses.

All Colonial Spanish horses have these characteristics (among others) in common:

- Neck, back, shoulder, heart girth, and hip are approximately the same length.

- Bone over the eye is heavier and more protruding than in modern horses.
- Back often has one less lumbar vertebra. If the sixth is present, the fifth and sixth lumbar vertebrae are usually fused. Often the shorter-backed horse will have one less pair of ribs.
- Tailset will be low and hip more deeply angled than most modern horses. This "Spanish hip" allows for more flexion and extension so that at the trot, the horse's rear foot will land just below, or only slightly behind, a line drawn from the back of the stirrup to the ground.
- Gaits will be smooth and comfortable, whether lateral or diagonal. The Colonial Spanish usually has an overstride, with the hind foot landing in front of the front hoof.
- Structurally, bone will be dense, hoof wall thick, and cannon bone round rather than oval.
- Chestnuts will be small or often missing entirely, especially on the hind legs.
- Nostrils will be strongly crescent shaped and able to close up tightly.
- Shoulders will be strongly angled and well laid back.
- Ears are fine and narrow. They range from the short fox ear to the longer narrow ear of the Southwestern, but are not blunt or wide. A pronounced hook inward at the tips is noted in many Colonials.
- Necks have a strong crest when the horse is in good condition. The head is attached to the neck with a cleanly arched throatlatch.

Horses can be registered if already recorded as Spanish Mustangs, original Indian Horses, and Barbs, and the Horse of the Americas Registry will inspect Colonial Spanish type feral horses for possible inclusion.

Credit: Horse of the Americas, Inc.

Wilbur-Cruce credit: Silke Schneider and Gretchen Patterson

Colonial Spanish horse. Ears are hooked in slightly and the muzzle is refined with tight lips. *Courtesy Gretchen L. Patterson*

COLORADO RANGER

Colorado Ranger Horse Association
1510 Greenhouse Lane
Wampum, Pennsylvania 16157
www.coloradoranger.com

In 1878, the former president of the United States, Ulysses S. Grant, developed a friendship with the Sultan Hamid of the Ottoman Empire during a world tour. Before Grant left Turkey, the sultan presented him with two horses, whose descendants continue to make an impact today. One was a desert Arabian named Leopard, the other a Barb named Linden Tree. Both of these stallions are listed in studbooks of two major American breed registries, the Arabian Horse Association and the Jockey Club. Their influence on the horse world touches almost every breed in the United States today.

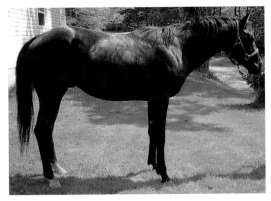

Colorado Ranger stud—a well-balanced horse with long neck, nice shoulder, and overall quality. *Sherry Byrd*

History

The two stallions arrived in 1879 in Virginia, where they spent several years with breeder Randolph Huntington. By using these horses, Huntington hoped to perfect what would become a new breed of light harness horses that he called the Americo/Arab Trotting horse. Financial troubles, however, contributed to the demise of the project.

Around the turn of the century, Leopard and Linden Tree moved west to the ranch holdings of General George Colby in Beatrice, Nebraska. Here, the two desert stallions left strong, desirable traits on their foals from the native range mares on the Colby ranch. Some of these mares were, in fact, horses from the western Indian tribes that had been forced onto reservations in the Nebraska area. When the two stallions were crossed with the mares, it resulted in a new type of versatile using horse with a lot of cow sense, or cattle-working ability. Their reputation soon spread.

The Ira J. Whipple family introduced the horses to Colorado with the purchase of an outstanding group of young mares the family bought from

General Colby. All the mares had been sired by either Leopard or Linden Tree. To head the band of mares, Whipple selected Tony, a double-bred grandson of Leopard.

Early in the 1900s, Mike Ruby, one of the greatest horsemen of the plains, developed an interest in this line because of the horses' reputation for working cows, their good disposition, and their stamina. He began breeding them by acquiring as his herd sires Patches, a son of Tony from the Colby Ranch, and Max, the Barb stallion from the ranch of Colorado Governor Oliver Shoupe. Max was halo-spotted, meaning he had spots with faded halo outlines around them. He was sired by a renowned horse called the Waldron Leopard and out of an Arabian mare.

Ruby was different in many ways than many of the ranchers of his day. Well before most of the prominent registries were founded, he maintained accurate written records of his mares, stallions, and their offspring, which was an unusual practice at that time. His handwritten records included foaling dates, colors, and complete pedigrees and were important to establishing a breed. They have been preserved as part of the Colorado Ranger Horse Association's corporate records, and Ruby is recognized as the founder of the Colorado Ranger breed.

Ruby continued to enlarge his herd, and in 1934 he was invited to display two of his stallions at the National Western Stock Show in Denver. His leopard-patterned stallions, Leopard No. 3 and Fox No. 10, were seen by thousands of visitors. Encouraged by the faculty members of Colorado Agricultural College (now Colorado State University), the new breed of horse was officially named the Colorado Ranger, because it was originally bred and raised in Colorado under range conditions. Verbal references to those "rangerbred" horses eventually led to their being more commonly known as Rangerbreds, although the official name of Colorado Ranger remains.

With the naming of the breed came a breed registry. Ruby founded the Colorado Ranger Horse Association (CRHA) in 1935, and the state of Colorado granted him a corporate charter in 1938. Patches and Max were named foundation sires of the breed and listed first in the CRHA association's studbook.

The majority of Rangerbreds were often much louder colored, or more patterned, than other early Appaloosas, which were mostly roans. Due to registrations being available only to CRHA members and there being a fifty-member limit, many horses with a Rangerbred heritage were not able to be registered at that time. (Those with color patterns were, however, accepted by the Appaloosa Horse Club Registry that came into being several months later.) This was the beginning of establishing the Colorado Ranger as a breed.

The breed took a setback when the drought years in the mid 1930s took its toll on the horses, as grass and water were hard to come by. Now an aging horseman, Ruby drove his horses from the plains to save them. Refusing to see a lifetime's endeavor destroyed, he made a trail herd and drove his J Bar horses from eastern Colorado to new leases on the western slopes of the Rockies. This was a distance of more than three hundred miles over which he drove a substantial herd through rough Rocky Mountain terrain.

Ruby made horse history on that drive. This man could face adversity without flinching, but he had tears in his eyes as he told of a drought-stricken mare on the drive and her newborn foal that died due to lack of its mother's milk. Four months later in the lush mountain meadows, the mare began producing milk for her colt that lay dead three hundred miles back on the prairies. Two years later, the rains began, and Ruby made another long, historic drive back to the home range, testifying to the toughness and bravery of not only himself, but also his horses.

Impact of Rangerbreds

As time went on, the Ruby family's herd grew to several hundred head of horses, and the family supplied many other ranches throughout Colorado and other western states with its horses. Sometimes the horses were sold, while other times they were leased.

This is verified by people who knew the Rubys and lived around them. Mike Ruby often leased groups of horses to various ranchers throughout Colorado and other western states. These ranchers were simply looking to improve their own breeding herds, or just wanted new blood. Some may have been breeding for a specific type, like what evolved into the Quarter Horse or Appaloosas. Even though there were noticeable appaloosa-colored/patterned horses in the Ruby herds, there were the muted roan patterns and solid-colored animals as well. A rancher might come to the Ruby ranch to lease some mares, pick out a group of roan or solid-colored ones, and take them home to breed with Appaloosas. Later, the leased group would be returned, and maybe the next time this same group (or portions of it) would be leased by a rancher breeding for the Quarter Horse type, who would take the mares home to breed with Quarter Horses.

In this way, the Rangerbred greatly influenced and was affected by the Quarter Horse and

Appaloosa breeding of that time and area. All these breeds were particularly noted for their athletic ability and were primarily bred for ranches. They were in demand as working cow horses.

There is no doubt that some Rangerbred bloodlines were in some of these early Quarter and Appaloosa horses. Research has found CRHA-registered lines in the old National Quarter Horse Breeders' Association registry and in various Appaloosa lines.

Registry

In 1964, the CRHA lifted the fifty-member limit, and registration was opened to all horses meeting pedigree requirements, regardless of owner membership status. Since then, the CRHA has registered many Appaloosas with a Rangerbred heritage that were lost to the organization for so many years.

Additional Appaloosa bloodlines with Rangerbred connections are still being recognized through continued pedigree research. The most recent research indicates that one out of every five Appaloosas is eligible for registry with the CRHA. Appaloosa pedigrees are checked for Rangerbred heritage by the organization at no charge to the owner. About 90 percent of all registered Rangerbreds are also registered Appaloosas.

The CRHA is the oldest of the western horse breed registries in the United States. It is not a color registry; founder Mike Ruby wisely decided that a horse's ability has nothing to do with his "hide." Due to this, Rangerbreds come in a wide variety of color patterns: from solid bays, classic blacks, grays, and roans, all the way to colorful blankets and leopards. All Rangerbreds carry equal registration status regardless of color. This is a breed that traces its purity through known bloodlines only. The registry still uses the bloodline grading system developed by Ruby to denote bloodline concentration.

To meet requirements for registration, a horse must show a direct descent from one of the foundation stallions, Patches No. 1 and/or Max No. 2. Rangerbreds may be outcrossed on horses of other recognized breed registries, including the Jockey Club, American Quarter Horse Association, Appaloosa registries (U.S., Canadian, and foreign), Arabian Horse Association, AraAppaloosa, and Foundation Breeders' International. With certain reservations, they may also be outcrossed to horses registered with the Appaloosa Color Breeders Association, American Appaloosa Association, and International Colored Appaloosa Association. No Paint, Pinto, or pony outcrosses are approved. Outcrossed mares must be registered with one of these registries, or show positive proof of parentage tracing to one of or a combination of the accepted registries, with approval.

Characteristics

Rangerbreds are basically stock horses, yet just like most stock breeds now, some Rangerbreds will do well in English riding and dressage. They also do well in competitive and endurance distance riding.

They range in size from 14 to 15 or more hands. Small, foxy ears are desired. They come in all colors with the appaloosa spotting being the only approved color pattern.

Generally speaking, Rangerbreds are people friendly, attention loving horses.

There are several different types of Rangerbreds; those bred with a higher percentage of Quarter Horse will favor the Quarter Horse traits. Likewise, those with higher Thoroughbred percentage up close will favor the Thoroughbred or sport horse type of look. Some can have thinning manes and tails with summer shedding like some Appaloosas.

CRHA board member Sherry Byrd states, "I like the breed because they have the added dimension of that long traceable pedigree going back into history: being connected with Ulysses S. Grant—and of course the Turkey/Middle East angle [Barb and Arab], as well. The Rangerbred has more of an exotic touch to it."

Credit: Sherry Byrd, Colorado Ranger Horse Association

FLORIDA CRACKER HORSE

This Florida Cracker is calm and trusting as it strolls in a parade. Note the light build. *James Levy*

Florida Cracker Horse Association, Inc.
2992 Lake Bradford Road South
Tallahassee, Florida 32310
www.floridacrackerhorses.com

Most people, even in Florida, do not have a good idea what a Cracker Horse is, yet it has played a huge part in Florida's long historic past, particularly in connection with the cattle industry. Owners like to call it a heritage horse. It has displayed consistent Spanish traits for nearly five hundred years through various circumstances.

Florida Cracker Horses are descendents of the first horses to set foot in North America that were originally brought to Florida by the Spanish during the colonial period, when the active cattle industry was founded. Florida cowboys who managed the cows were known locally as cow hunters and nicknamed "crackers," because of the sound made by cracking the air with their cow whips. This name was also given to the small, agile Spanish horses they rode extensively to work the cattle.

Florida Cracker Horses are wonderful little riding horses that have endurance, strength, and an easy ride, traits that have been lost in some other breeds. They have a lot of heart, giving their utmost beyond normal limitations, and do not tire as quickly as others. They are still going at the end of a long work day, when other horses have been resting from the morning's work. Their forte is their tough resilience, durability, easy ride, and strong herding instinct.

Their genetic heritage is derived from the Iberian horse of early Spain, tracing their ancestry to stock brought in the 1500s when Florida was discovered by the Spaniards. The horses' genetic base is generally the same as that of the Spanish Mustang, Paso Fino, Peruivian Paso, Criollo, and other breeds developed from horses originally introduced by the Spanish into the Caribbean Islands, Cuba, and the continents of North and South America.

From the early 1500s and continuing well into the twentieth century, the Cracker Horse served many Florida residents, including Spanish conquistadors, settlers, Christian missionaries, and at least seven Native American tribes. It also served those who were drawn there to settle under the flags of Spain, France, England, the Confederate States of America, and the United States. Today, there is a dedicated group of owners who still use the rare Cracker Horse.

History

As early as Columbus's second voyage to the Caribbean in 1493, Spanish horses were brought to the island of Hispaniola (now part of Haiti). Here, they formed the basis of the first of the famed Caribbean Islands breeding herds. The first horses to set foot on Florida soil were acquired from a variety of these island herds.

In 1521, Ponce de León brought some of them on his second Florida trip. He used them as mounts for ranking members of his party, the expedition's scouts, and those riders who were responsible for herding the livestock that was their food supply. Other conquistadors also brought horses to Florida. Pánfilo de Narváez came in 1528 and is said to have lost many horses by either accidental or deliberate release. He is also credited with setting 213 horses ashore at the mouth of Charlotte Harbor from ships that were drawing too much water. In 1539, Hernando De Soto brought many horses to southeastern Florida to support his search for gold. In 1540, Diego Maldonado brought many cattle for De Soto and presumably a sufficient number of horses for herding them to the area of what is now Santa Rosa County. Unable to rendezvous with De Soto, much of his stock was lost or abandoned.

It is presumed that up until this point, all of the horses landing in Florida had come from the Caribbean Islands. In 1559, though, Tristan de Luna brought a great number of horses from Mexico for the purpose of founding a colony in an area that is now Pensacola. His project failed, and once again livestock was lost or abandoned.

Still, the primary sources were the Caribbean Islands breeding farms that supplied the horses needed by conquistadors for their exploits in the New World. Most of the horses that were brought to the Caribbean Islands for breed stock came from the Spanish province of Cordova. They were the result of a mixture, over a long period of time, of the North African Barb, the Spanish Gararo Pony, the Sorraia, and other horses of the Iberian Peninsula. Some people refer to these horses as Spanish Jennets, while others call them Spanish Barbs.

These Spanish horses ranged in size from 13.2 to 15 hands. Their general description included a short back, sloping rump, low tailset, good limbs and hooves, wide forehead, beautiful eyes, delicately formed nostrils, and sloping shoulders. (More could be said about their physical characteristics, as the writers of that period used lengthy and glowing descriptive phrases.) Based on that description, Cracker Horses of today obviously share many of the same characteristics as those brought to the Caribbean Islands, and then to Florida, well over four hundred years ago.

There is much speculation that the strays and escapees of the animals brought by the conquistadors to sustain their explorations were the start of large numbers of feral horses and cattle found in Florida. It is likely that it was not until the early 1600s when there were sufficient numbers to have served as the base for the populations of Spanish livestock when Florida became part of the United States in 1821.

The free-roaming Cracker Horses evolved over a long period of time by natural selection. They were molded and tempered by nature and a challenging environment into the horse that ultimately had a large part in the emergence of Florida as a ranching and agriculture state. They were well adapted to the environment and were useful in

Ever the cowhorse, this Florida Cracker demonstrates what the breed does naturally.
James Levy

working the local Spanish-derived Cracker cattle. The horses also played a major role in the Seminole tribe's culture.

During the early 1600s, the Spaniards made a modest start of cattle ranching in north Florida, and by the midpoint of that century, cattle and horse numbers had increased significantly. By the end of the seventeeth century, the Florida cattle industry was enjoying some success, as there were thirty-four *ranchos* across northern Florida. An example would be the rancho De La Chua in the area of what is now Alachua County, which is reported to have had as many as one thousand cows and horses. Historical data like this demonstrates that the Cracker Horse is undoubtedly a remnant of Spanish horses.

Recent History

Until the early part of the twentieth century, Cracker Horses were numerous in Florida. Many of them were roaming free on open ranges, while others were used by frontier cattlemen and settlers. Over the years, they were known by a variety of names: Chickasaw pony, Seminole pony, Marsh Tacky, Prairie pony, Florida horse, Florida cow pony, Grass Gut, Woods pony, and others.

Florida was considered an open-range state until about 1949. There was a lot of resistance to fencing, and any cow that was run over by an automobile or train had to be paid for by the driver. Up until this time, cattle, horses, and swine could run most anywhere that was not fenced. Horses that lived in the wild were pretty much like deer and just as quick, because their lives depended on their instincts.

The Cracker breed suffered a reversal of fortune in the 1930s, when a serious decline in their numbers began. The Great Depression led to the creation of a number of relief programs, one of which encouraged the movement of cattle from the Dust Bowl states into Florida. Cattle from the western Dust Bowl regions were moved in, and with them came the screwworm. This, in turn, led to changes in cattle ranching.

Before the screwworm, cowmen used Cracker Horses to herd and drive the free-roaming scrub cows and Cracker cattle. With the arrival of the screwworm came fencing, dipping vats, and a need to rope cattle and hold them for treatment. This radically changed the sort of horse needed to work cattle out on the range. As a result, ranchers turned to the larger, stronger horses, like the Quarter Horse. The Florida Cracker Horse lost its demand and became quite rare. Therefore, the influx of western cattle was a threat to both the Cracker Horse and Cracker cattle, and although both persist to the present day, they are only remnants of once-numerous types.

The Cracker Horse's survival over the next fifty years resulted from the work of a few families, which continued to breed it for their own use. It was these ranching families and individuals whose perseverance and preservation of distinct blood-lines kept the horses from disappearing entirely. They include the Ayers, Harvey, Bronson, Matchett, Partin, and Whaley families.

In 1984, John Law Ayers of Brooksville, Florida, donated a group of his Cracker Horses to the state. Ayers had maintained a herd of pure Cracker Horse stock, resisting temptations to cross them with other breeds. This group started the state-owned herds in Tallahassee and in the Withlacoochee State Forest. In the Paynes Prairie Preserve State Park, where free-roaming Spanish horses were once quite numerous, a herd was started in 1985, also with the Ayers line of horses donated to the pre-serve by a citizen's support organization.

By 1989, however, Cracker Horses appeared to be near extinction. The state had three small herds. The rest of them, about one hundred head, were owned by several cattle and ranching families that continued to breed them. These pioneering families and their unique horses spanned many generations and kept the Cracker Horse from becoming extinct. They appreciated the Cracker Horse's stamina, intelligence, quickness, endurance, and easy ride. They preserved many excellent examples of classic, old-style Spanish type in their horses.

Registry

Fearing that Cracker Horses might become extinct, Florida cattlemen contacted others in the 1980s who owned or shared an interest in the breed. The Florida Cracker Horse Association (FCHA) was founded in 1989 and the registry in 1991. Immediately, seventy-five Foundation horses and fourteen of their offspring were registered. The Foundation registry was only for animals that were considered by expert evaluation teams to be pure. These horses had to have a verifiable and direct line back to known herds. There was no provision for breeding up; percentage horses were not allowed to be registered. Foundation horses came primarily from four different Cracker lines

that had been bred continuously for more than seventy years by different ranches. Since that time, there have been nine hundred horses registered as Florida Cracker Horses.

The FCHA is succeeding in preserving the Cracker Horse as a distinct and unique Colonial Spanish breed. The Cracker Horse is promoted as a vital part of Florida's heritage and is gaining in popularity, though it is still quite rare. In 2008, it was made the official horse of the state of Florida, which has brought this little heritage horse the honor it deserves and more public interest in its future.

There are three main family lines of Crackers today with a few smaller groups. The state's Department of Agriculture and Consumer Services oversees two small Ayers-line Cracker herds—one in Tallahassee inside the city limits and one on the Withlacoochee State Forest near Brooksville. (The Paynes Prairie Preserve horses are for display only in a historical and natural savannah grassland on the prairie.) Buck Mitchell in Trenton raises Bronson-line Crackers. The Harvey-line Crackers are in Okeechobee with Jim Harvey on the Harvey Ranch. There are small groups of Partin, Whaley, Matchett, and Thrasher lines.

Both state-owned horse herds live at locations that are managed like fenced farm areas, and the horses exist most of the time on natural grass pas-tures. State-owned horses are transferred between the herds to keep the genetic base broad while maintaining the pure lines. Stallions of the Ayers bloodline have been added from other herds to broaden the genetic base.

Although Crackers are believed to be parasite and disease resistant, the state has them vaccinated and dewormed regularly because they are in rela-tively small areas of around sixty-five acres. The horses have some interaction with people, but are not consistently trained like most other horses; they are only imprinted at birth and some halter training is done. They are not considered wild like western Bureau of Land Management horses, but as one owner remarked, "When you purchase horses from these herds, they are about as wild as a June hare!"

Once a year at public auction, the state sells surplus stock from its herds of Cracker cattle and Cracker Horses, and individual breeders are invited to consign theirs to the sale also. Those wishing to own a living, tangible link to Florida's past can purchase Cracker Horses or cattle there.

Characteristics

During the frontier years and on into the mid twentieth century, the Cracker Horse was used for just about anything for which horses were used: pulling wagons, buggies, sleds, plows, and cane mills or taking kids to school. Most of all, they were appreciated as cow ponies.

Today, although still used primarily as cow ponies, they are finding a place in other activities for which horses in Florida are being used, such as team penning, team roping, trail riding, endurance riding, and as mounts for historical reenactments.

Like their ancestors, Cracker Horses range in size from 13.2 to 15 hands, with short backs, sloping rumps, and other Spanish characteristics. Their weight ranges from 750 to 1,000 pounds.

They are known for their unusual strength, endurance, strong herding instinct, quickness, and fast walking gait. Though not considered to be a gaited breed, many Crackers do have a single-foot or running walk gait.

Cracker Horses can be any color that is common to the horse; however, solid colors and grays are dominant in the Crackers of today. Being gaited and having black-based colors are common traits in Spanish horses of other regions, too.

Although the Cracker Horse is considered to be small in comparison to other breeds, its endurance, strength, toughness, easy ride, and versatility make it just as much a horse for today as it was during the years of the conquest. The Cracker has never been subjected to a single purpose or fad breeding. It demonstrates a gene pool that could be an asset to restore qualities that might be lost or weakened in other breeds.

Perhaps the most enduring quality of Cracker Horses seems to be their tendency to bond with

This Florida Cracker stallion has an exquisite head and intelligent expression. The breed is a nice size for easy mounting. *James Levy*

one person. They may do whatever any rider asks, but for that special person, they respond with a willingness that can be noticed in their eyes and body. It is not reluctance to work for another person; they just seem less enthusiastic. They also seem to have a sense of humor and keen interest in their owner when interacting with them.

Their common sense is extraordinary. One owner remarked how his Cracker Horse would not do anything to hurt him. If something startled her, she would always move away from her owner, even if the cause of the start was on the off side. One month after this mare was first ridden, she and her rider got hung up in barbwire in the scrub forest. The mare went down, and her rider got the wind knocked out of him. While he lay on the ground, she got up and, rather than running away, she came over to him and checked to make sure he was okay.

Standards

Head: The head is refined and intelligent in appearance. The profile is straight or slightly concave. A Roman nose is not characteristic of Cracker Horses. The throatlatch is deeper than other breeds, such as the Quarter Horse, for more proficient air intake. The jaw is short and well defined. The eyes are keen with an alert expression, and there is a reasonable width between them. The protruding bone above the eye is not pronounced. The eye colors are dark, dark with a white rim (sclera), gray, or blue.

The muzzle is small or tapering. The mouth is shallow and may be fairly narrow. The nostrils are crescent shaped, and the horse may frequently exhibit a peculiar snort, or "rollers in the nose." The ears are short to medium, alert in appearance, and do not show excessive width between them.

Neck: The neck is well defined, fairly narrow, without excessive crest, and is about the same length as the distance from the withers to the croup.

Mane and Tail: The mane and forelock are medium heavy and may be long, although a sparse mane and tail may be seen on some Cracker Horses.

Chest: The chest is medium to narrow in width with a good inverted "V" shape. Broad, flat chests are not characteristic of Cracker Horses.

Shoulders: The shoulders are long and sloping with a 40- to 50-degree angle. A well-laid-back shoulder with smooth muscling is preferred. The withers are pronounced, but not prominent.

Back: The back is short, narrow, and strong with well-sprung ribs. The point of the withers and the point of the croup are equal in height. The underline is longer than the topline. The belly is trim with a fairly straight belly line.

Hindquarters: The croup is sloping and short. The hips are round and usually not wide between the hip bones. The tail is set medium low, is medium thick, and on some horses may be quite long.

Legs: The forearms have light, long muscling. The cannon bones are round and medium short. The pasterns are medium and springy. The gaskins have light, smooth muscling. Feathering is none to light. Chestnuts are small or nonexistent. Front legs are straight with a fairly large knee. Back legs are strong, have moderate angulation, well-defined hock without excess flesh, and are straight when viewed from the rear. They are not sickle hocked, post legged, or cow hocked.

Hoof: The hoof is round and of a hard, dense texture. Hoof colors may be black, striped, or white.

Size: Small to medium in size, from 13 to 15.2 hands in height and generally weighing less than 1,000 pounds.

Color: The Cracker Horse includes all colors known to the horse, however, solid colors, roans, and grays are most common.

Gait or Action: A variety of gaits are found in Cracker Horses. They include the flatfoot walk, running walk, ambling, single-foot, pacing, four-beat gait, and Paso-type gaits, as well as regular gaits.

While the Cracker's external type is distinctive, breed proponents insist that the best way to tell a Cracker Horse is to ride one. The gaits found in these horses are easy and ground covering.

Cracker Horses are willing workers whose action shows spirit, not laziness, and they have amazing stamina and endurance. Crackers have been used for trail and pleasure riding, reining, team roping, team penning, pulling wagons, and always as working cow horses.

Preservation of the Cracker Horse is succeeding. Some new breeding herds have been started, and the numbers are slowly increasing. Demand for the Cracker Horse is continuing to rise, and once again it is gaining usage for activities other than cow-pony work. It is demonstrating its diverse capabilities for the twenty-first century, just as it did for Florida's Spanish and frontier eras.

An important factor that engenders hope for the breed is that the Cracker Horse can be used by any family member. At a recent FCHA fall weekend ride, the age span of attendees ranged from one year to more than eighty years old. Several families in attendance represented three generations. The youngest rider was a seven-year-old girl who completed the twelve-mile ride on her Cracker mare.

Credits: Florida Cracker Horse Association; and Stephen Monroe, Florida Department of Agriculture and Consumer Services, Division of Animal Industry

FOUNDATION QUARTER HORSE

Foundation Quarter Horse Registry
P.O. Box 230
Sterling, Colorado 80751
www.fqhr.net

The Quarter cow horse has been known in song, legend, and fact as the hard-working partner most frequently used to tame the American West. It has earned its place in history. Would there have been a cowboy or a rancher without the Quarter Horse? How would the history of the cattle industry read without it? There are many things that define the United States and that are especially American, one being the Foundation Quarter Horse.

The breed's origin now is more than two hundred years old, coming from oriental, Chickasaw, Quarter Running stock, mustang, and Thoroughbred blood. After two centuries of breeding, the result today is the Foundation Quarter Horse—the cowboy's horse on the ranch and show, and the rodeo horse in the arena. This breed has proven to be the quintessential working horse, excelling in performance as well as riding enjoyment for all the family. As America's all-around horse, the Foundation Quarter Horse has paid its dues, earning the accolade, "The greatest cow horse to ever look through a bridle."

The term "quarter horse" originated in colonial times, with such names as the Celebrated American Running Quarter Horse, the Quarter Mile Running Horse, or simply the Quarter Horse. They were a product of the times in early American history, when short-speed match racing was popular and breeding for this was in style.

They were first called Quarter Horses because of their speed. J. F. D. Smith, who toured America in 1773, wrote, "In the southern part of the colony 'Virginia' they are much attached to quarter racing; they have a breed that performs it with astonishing

Built low to the ground, the Foundation Quarter Horse packs more horse for its height than other breeds. Every part of his body is adorned in muscle. *Ritz Ranch*

velocity, beating every other for that distance at ease." He also wrote, "I'm confident that there is not a horse in England, nor perhaps in the whole world, that can excel them in rapid speed." Smith noted at that time that "the Quarter Horse was a breed." Other writers used the term Quarter Horse several years before him.

Down through the centuries, quarter-mile running horses continued to be popular. In the first book published on Quarter Horses entitled *The Quarter Horse* by H. T. Fletcher (published in 1941 and edited by Bob Denhardt), he wrote:

> To this good day no county fair or Fourth of July celebration is complete without the quarter-of-a-mile race; every community in Southwest Texas has a 'Billy' [quarter-mile-running] horse that is worth its money. The Billy horses became popular over Texas and even spread to other states. Mr. Fleming bred Billy horses for more than 40 years. In 1875 he and John King, a neighbor, started a Billy Stud book. As Fleming and King have been dead many years, I can learn nothing of its whereabouts. (Denhardt, "He Was Called Billy," *The Quarter Horse*, vol. 1 [Fort Worth: The American Quarter Horse Association, 1941])

What was needed then, possibly more than today, was the all-around horse. The early colonists desired short speed for sport and respectability, but their lifestyle and vocation required a horse that could race, work, drive, and ride—a truly versatile family horse.

Foundation Traits

Match racing not only required speed and ability, but also the foundation of a docile disposition and an abundance of intelligence. The original Quarter Horses were built upon what most true breeders and experienced horsemen today consider priorities in a breeding program: first, intelligence; second, disposition; third, ability; and fourth, conformation.

Besides intelligence, disposition, and ability, early Quarter Horses had to have the body type to work cattle. Colonial history records describe early Quarter Horses as being 14 to 15 hands in height, stout, and heavily muscled when compared to other horses of that day.

When the Quarter Horse was first used, it was recognized that at least half the area of the entire nation could produce beef on its natural forage. To manage cattle, there was no better means than the Quarter Horse, which was qualified and endowed naturally with the necessary endurance, agility, substance, and cow sense.

The largest contributing reason for the popularity and growth of the Foundation Quarter Horse Registry is its return to these roots, unlike the modern breeders who have other priorities in their breeding programs. These more modern breeders strive for a different type of Quarter Horse, citing that now the need, expectation, and use of the Quarter Horse has changed since colonial times.

Registry

Breeder Bill Anson desired to establish a Quarter Horse studbook in the early 1900s. He stated in *The Quarter Horse* that he felt the Quarter Horse was a definite breed prior to the English Thoroughbred. The English Thoroughbred Studbook was established in 1827 to register purebreds, while the American Thoroughbred Studbook was not established until 1868. That was nearly one hundred years after the Quarter Horse was called a breed.

It was long overdue for the Quarter Horse to have a registry when the American Quarter Horse Association (AQHA) was established in 1940. Horses were registered by a threefold standard: bloodlines (pedigree), conformation (inspection and produce), and performance (ability and versatility); these were, and still are, worthy requirements. This was the desire of the first directors of the AQHA.

If the cowboys and ranchers wanted to run short horses as they had always done, this was accepted, but the intent of the registry at the beginning was to register and preserve the "bulldog or ranch

With a beautiful head, clean legs, and an athlete's body, this chestnut stallion is an outstanding example of the King family of working Foundation Quarter Horses. *Black River Quarter Horse Ranch*

type" Quarter Horse. This did include some Thoroughbreds of worthy type and ability; however the Thoroughbreds of the early foundation horses are not the same as Thoroughbred horses of today.

Bill Anson described the Quarter Horse in these terms: "The immense breast and chest, enormous forearm, loin and thighs, the heavy layers of muscle are not found in the same proportion in any other breed."

Many of the Thoroughbreds entered in the Quarter Horse shows were rejects from the racetracks. The height of these horses was much greater than that of the original Quarter Horse. The difference in conformation was easy to recognize.

The first Western Pleasure classes with these racetrack Thoroughbreds turned into runaway classes. The lucky winner was the one who could hold on long enough to be the last one still in the saddle. Something had to be done about this, so the horses were trained to alter their natural free movement and head carriage, until the end result was a horse that could not run away because it had its nose lower to the ground.

The old-time master Quarter Horse breeders had an eye for good horses. This, plus the fact that the horses were used on a daily ranch routine, gave breeders a chance to see the results of their program. The Quarter Horse as it was known then was the ranch horse that did everything, being used in whatever task needed to be done. It was medium sized, neither too big or too small for the many everyday ranch jobs. It could pull the light wagon or buggy, drive cows, rope calves and drag them to the branding crew, go to town for supplies, or take the kids safely to school.

This type of horse must have a certain kind of mind. It could not be flighty, nervous, short tempered, or sulky. The big, wide-set, soft eyes showed trust and intelligence. The short foxy ears displayed interest and alertness. The nicely refined muzzle and large jaw showed good Quarter Horse breeding. The quiet, willing disposition was another defining quality, but this was quickly lost with the addition of too much Thoroughbred blood or by abusive, quick training.

The disagreement over type and the addition of Thoroughbred blood were bitterly fought. The old National Quarter Horse Breeders Association at Hockley, Texas, was founded in 1945, but lasted only four or five years before it merged with AQHA. By 1949, there were many requests from members to close the books and keep the breed intact. This was contested, and the struggle went on through the 1950s. The elected officials favored growth over preservation, and by 1960 it was clear the conservative breeders were outnumbered.

Yet there were many articles written in defense of keeping the original Quarter Horse by great old-time breeders who knew the true value of their horses. These conservative foundation breeders were a quieter type who could not see the need for lots of high-priced advertising, and they continued to breed and use their own horses in the cattle business.

In 1961, Bob Denhardt, the first secretary of AQHA, put forth a motion for a compromise to unify the association. He wanted to form a group

This sorrel gelding's compact body style is typical of the working lines of his lineage used for ranch and cattle work as well as the show pen. *Black River Quarter Horse Ranch*

within the AQHA that would list and preserve the foundation blood and close that group to any further addition of Thoroughbred blood. It was not approved.

Many years passed in which no foundation stallion was advertised, because the majority of people now preferred the new type and considered it as the real Quarter Horse. By now there were only a few breeders who doggedly preserved their own breeding programs and refused to add Thoroughbred blood. In working ranch situations, the cattle had to carry horse expenses so the ranch could have usable working cow horses. These hard-headed breeders sacrificed financial gain and popularity to retain the type of horses that was best suited for daily ranch work.

Finally, but slowly, a few people became interested in the foundation horses and began to appreciate their dispositions and ability. Foundation-bred Quarter Horses were excelling in rodeo and other athletic events, and people were beginning to notice. By the early 1990s, a few of the "old-timers" began talking once again about recording and preserving these foundation families, thinking

there would be at least a small amount of interest. Instead, they found that interest in foundation horses had skyrocketed. This was the last chance to save the foundation lines.

In 1994, the Foundation Quarter Horse Registry was incorporated in Colorado. Its purpose was to perpetuate and continue the hopes and dreams of Billy Fleming, Billy Anson, Bob Denhardt, Dan Casement, Coke Roberds, and so many other Quarter Horse people.

Purpose of Foundation Breeding

When the Quarter Horse came into its own, it had to work for a living, thus the term "the working horse" was born. Over time, the Quarter Horse built and established a reputation that was true to this term. Its owner depended on it for a living, as did the cowboy, rancher, farmer, circuit-riding preacher, and short match-race folks. Since so much was expected from those early working Quarter cow horses, it was necessary and expedient to breed not only for physical ability, but also for that quiet, unique disposition and intelligence that had given these horses the reputation of dependability.

Red dun stallion with prominent Quarter Horse features carries the wonderful family oriented disposition of the Poco Bueno/ King foundation breeding. *Black River Quarter Horse Ranch*

The modern horse show arena has affected much change in so many aspects of today's horse world. It has thrust the refinement of the horses into the spotlight, accepting the judge's concept of what is considered pretty, and has made specialization the norm, rather than the all-around horse type. Most show horses are limited, specializing only in their events and having only certain abilities.

Since many top breeders are so focused on the traits necessary to win, they can fail to add athletic ability and the mindset to work. Without this, the non-winners are a waste and an overload to the market. For example, when the race Quarter Horse breeders fail to include disposition and structure in their programs, these kinds of horses benefit neither the breeder nor the breed. There is more to performance than the ability to run. Many horses have more than enough speed, but there is danger in losing that elite foundation disposition that is the throttle and steering of their versatility.

Once in a while, breeders can produce a top show horse, top roping horse, or some super event winner. Truthfully, however, the all-around breeder is the one who can supply a horse that will satisfy

first-time horse owners, or those who simply need a horse that is safe for all the family to ride. The breeder who produces all-around versatile horses has a 100 percent saleable crop and does not have to worry about his or her non-winners.

The Foundation Quarter Horse was bred to work and does this work better than any other breed. It has proven and made its mark as the most usable, dependable, versatile athlete of the equine world. This horse will satisfy the need of the young novice rider, or the professional by being the best roping or cutting horse one could hope for. A horse that is gentle and safe for everyone to handle is an asset to the breed. The Foundation Quarter Horse is the all-around horse. No other breed fits in so many places.

Foundation of the Foundation

The AQHA was originally organized with the intent of preserving and perpetuating the working cow horse bloodlines. Therefore, the Foundation Quarter Horse Registry recognizes those horses listed in the first five studbooks of AQHA as Foundation bred.

The Foundation Quarter Horse is not promoted as the modern Halter or Western Pleasure horse. It is a breed that returns to the concept and purpose of the "do it all" horse. Many are owner bred, owner raised, owner trained, and owner shown Foundation Quarter Horses.

This breed can display and present not only what the Quarter Horse is, but also what it can do. There is no specialization in the breed for one particular aspect of showing; rather, it is a "do everything" working horse.

The Foundation Quarter Horse is bred for soundness and a level-headed disposition. It is trained to fit the needs of the corporate cattleman or weekend rider quite nicely. Proclaimed and known to be the most versatile horse of the century, this is the horse that has won the hearts and loyalty of many.

To the great breeders of the past, and now to the Foundation Quarter Horse Registry, the priority is usability and versatility found in the foundation blood.

Criteria for Registration

The Foundation Quarter Horse Registry recognizes the first twenty-seven thousand horses registered in the Quarter Horse registry as foundation bred. Most individuals carrying 75 percent foundation blood are eligible for registration. The fourth generation is critical (great grandsires and great grand dams); of that generation 75 percent should descend from, or run to, foundation blood.

No registered Thoroughbred may be closer than the fourth generation. The 75-percent foundation percentage program encourages the perpetuation of foundation blood, while limiting or eliminating Thoroughbred blood. There is also a limit to white on the horse, rather than a promotion toward white coloring.

Those families known to carry hyperkalemic periodic paralysis (HYPP) disease are not eligible for registration, regardless of generation or testing. The Foundation Quarter Horse Registry has taken a stand against it since 1994.

Sharon J. Spier, DVM, PhD, from the University of California, Davis School of Veterinary Medicine, states of HYPP:

This is a hereditary muscular disease that produces unpredictable attacks of paralysis which can lead to collapse and sudden death. A horse carrying the defective gene but showing minimal signs has the same chance of passing the gene to future generations as does the affected horse with severe signs. It became widespread when breeders sought to produce horses with heavy musculature, but not necessarily all those with heavy musculature [inherit it]. It is more inherited from a specific Quarter Horse line whose descendents are so numerous that the genetic mutation in the bloodline is widespread. It is inherited from generation to generation with equal frequency; it does not get "diluted" out. Breeding an affected heterozygous horse to a normal horse will result in about 50 percent normal offspring, while 50 percent will carry the defective gene. Breeding an affected homozygote horse will result in all offspring carrying the gene regardless of the status of the other parent.

Selective breeding to normal horses could entirely eliminate the disease. As it is inherited as a dominant condition, it can and is being spread to other breeds. It is to everyone's benefit to take the necessary steps to selectively breed HYPP out of existence before it becomes so widespread that this is impossible. This can be done with DNA testing, which is accurate and reliable.

Characteristics

The Foundation Quarter Horse is easily recognized by the body shape and unique conformation. It is more horse for the height than is found in any other breed. Built low to the ground, much of the time it does not exceed 15 hands but, due to the build, will often weigh 1,200 pounds or more. The pattern of the muscle adorns nearly every part of the body.

Ever the athlete, Foundation Quarter Horses are up to anything needing quick movement and a steady mind. *Daniel Johnson*

The horse has small alert ears and wide-set, honest, bright eyes that window its great intelligence and kindness. It has a bulging jaw and a neck of moderate length that is joined low into the sloping shoulder and topped by a well-defined wither. The back is short with strong loins, a deep barrel with long underline, and well sprung ribs with great heart girth.

The space between the forelegs is ample to supply a wide, well-developed chest. The forearms, gaskins, and hindquarters carry the type of muscle that separates the Foundation Quarter Horse from all others. Seen from the rear, the power-filled stifles are wider than the croup.

The bones of the Foundation Quarter Horse are trim, dense, and sturdy. A rugged frame is necessary to support the bulk that provides the horse's strength. The cannon bones are short and flat, set above strong pasterns. The foot is deep with an open heel and well rounded with sufficient size.

This is the horse to ride, enjoy, and be proud of. To ride and use this horse is to love it. The Foundation Quarter Horse is the best all-around horse known to humans. It has proven itself in rodeos, roping, team penning, cutting, reining, barrels, trail riding, and more. Its gentle disposition makes it the ideal horse for the entire family. It is an easy keeper, thrifty, surefooted, balanced, and intelligent. Adding these up, the Foundation Quarter Horse is the greatest equine athlete in the world. It can do more things better than any breed known, and still be a delight to all the family.

Of no other breed can it be said that it is "the greatest cow horse to ever look through a bridle."

Credit: Foundation Quarter Horse Registry

KIGER MESTEÑO

Kiger Mesteño stallion. Dorsal stripe is mandatory and leg stripes are desirable as well as a noticeable neck crest.
Dave and Annette Farnsworth

Kiger Mesteño Association
11124 NE Halsey, Suite 591
Portland, Oregon 97220
www.kigermustangs.org

No other horse today is quite like the Kiger Mesteño in legend or reality. Stunning beauty and spirit, primitive markings, beautiful dun factor coloring, dense bone, compact hooves, and a well-crested neck round out this unique and tough horse. The Kiger Mesteños are agile, remarkably intelligent, courageous, and bold; renowned for their athletic ability, stamina, endurance, and sure-footedness. These traits are combined with their gentleness, calm temperament, and willingness to please. Truly standing out in a crowd, they have a regal carriage and a high step fit for royalty. Pleasure, trail, performance, endurance, driving, packing, cutting—they can do it all!

The Kiger Mesteños were discovered in Kiger Gorge in Oregon's Steens Mountain. After a roundup in 1971, it was first noticed they were a particular kind of horse. Their striking beauty and similar color and conformation made a great impression. Since then, they have been separated from other wild mustangs and valued for their unique characteristics.

Their exact history is unknown prior to 1971, when the Wild Free-Roaming Horse and Burro Act was passed by the U.S. Congress to protect, manage, and control the wild equine populations. In order to keep the herds at manageable levels, roundups or gatherings were, and still are, held periodically, during which the horses are counted, branded, and examined. Excess animals are offered for adoption to the public, and the rest are returned to the range.

Kiger Mesteños were first separated in 1977 after one of these gatherings in the remote area of Beatty's

Butte, Oregon. Bureau of Land Management (BLM) Wild Horse Specialist E. Ron Harding noticed them while inspecting the herd. A number of the horses were unusually similar both in type and quality. Upon closer observation, he determined that they carried the primitive markings of the Spanish mustangs. Harding arranged for these horses to be separated from the rest and held at the Burns District facility in Oregon. Then, a suitable area was chosen to release them. To prevent losing all the horses to a natural catastrophe, two Herd Management Areas (HMA) were selected in southeastern Oregon. Twenty of the horses were released in the Kiger HMA and seven in the Riddle HMA.

It was soon decided that these Kiger Mesteños should become an established, registered breed. Spanish markers were found in their blood during genetic testing by the University of Kentucky. Thus, the Kiger Mesteños were set aside and saved for future concerns. With growing interest in this exceptional breed, their continued survival is assured.

The Kiger Mesteño Association was founded in 1988 to help protect and preserve these rare remaining wild mustangs and their captive counterparts. A registry and standard of perfection were established for Kiger and half-Kiger horses. To be eligible for registration today, a horse needs to have been rounded up from either the Kiger or Riddle HMA in southeast Oregon or have parents that traced back to one of these areas.

The association took its name from the famous stallion, Mesteño. A legendary foundation stallion captured along with his mares in the original roundup of Beatty's Butte, many of today's Kigers are descended from Mesteño. The name means "wild" or "unclaimed" horse in Spanish. Upon seeing this stallion, BLM officials knew he should never be put up for adoption, but instead become the lead sire for the Kiger Mustangs. They named him Mesteño and released him into the Kiger HMA. He was last seen alive in 1996 at the approximate age of twenty-seven. To this day, Mesteño's fate is unknown, but for all who know the Kigers,

The Iberian features on this Kiger Mesteño leave no doubt about its Spanish forebears. *Canyon Creek Kigers L.L.C.*

Mesteño will always roam free and watch over the herds on Steens Mountain.

Famous Kigers

The life of Mesteño, the outstanding Kiger foundation stallion, is captured in a Breyer Horse Series. The series depicts the life of Mesteño from a colt to his older years, and marked the first time Breyer introduced a series depicting the life of one horse.

Another famous Kiger is Cougar. His story begins with Bobby Ingersoll, a professional horse trainer who became interested in the idea of training a wild horse for reining and cow horse competition. In 1990, while he was judging the Bell A Ranch cutting competition in Burns, Oregon, he met two BLM employees. They introduced him to a small local band of wild horses running in the Kiger Gorge in Steens Mountain. The horses exhibited similar characteristics to Spanish Barb horses, including the dun factor coloring, black points, and zebra stripes on their legs.

Ingersoll accepted the invitation to visit the BLM corrals just outside of town. It was there where he first saw Cougar, a two-year-old colt.

Striking Kiger Mesteño stallion with excellent conformation and beautiful head. *Canyon Creek Kigers L.L.C.*

Cougar was turned out in a large corral with two other mustangs about the same age. He captured Ingersoll's interest by the way he began to herd one of the other colts by putting that colt through the same type of controlled movements found in the performance arena. Just like in a cow horse contest or cutting exhibition, Cougar boxed the black colt on the end of the corral and then ran him down the fence, turning several times in each direction. He ended his play by circling up the colt in the middle of the pen.

At this point, Ingersoll was impressed with Cougar because of his obvious natural herding instinct (cowboys call it "cow instinct") and became interested in training this real, born-on-the-mountain wild horse to be a show horse in reining competition. He adopted him and called him Kiger Cougar.

Cougar's training began under Ingersoll, who used a program to which the mustang could relate. Time, patience, and understanding of the natural habits, instincts, and ways of the horse were the disciplines used. Cougar showed Ingersoll from the beginning that he was an individual that liked to please and, most importantly, had the ability to accept training. After Cougar had been handled for a time, he became gentle and everyone loved the kind and bright little stallion. He was a joy to be around and would lick salt off anyone's hand if it was offered.

Cougar was brought along slowly in the beginning, but soon he reached the pace of any other horse. He was ridden only sixty days in preparation for the reining work. Next, he was put on cattle to expand his natural ability to herd and match the action of the cow. His training lasted until near the end of his third year.

When he was two and three years old, Cougar performed in several exhibitions in California, Oregon, and Nevada. There was a great amount of interest in the Kiger Mustang stallion that year.

It was Ingersoll's intent to train and show Cougar in the 1992 Snaffle Bit Futurities. In August 1992, Cougar was shown at the Paso Robles County Fair. He won first place over all the other breeds in the Snaffle Bit Class. The following month, Cougar was shown at the World Championship Snaffle Bit Futurity in Reno, Nevada. He placed twenty-first out of 150 horses of mostly registered American Quarter Horses. In 1993, he was retired to stud, breeding a limited number of Kiger mares.

In 1994, Ingersoll was asked to consider sending Cougar to the Kentucky Horse Park in Lexington, Kentucky. Although it was hard to let him go, Ingersoll did and Couger lives there today. He is in a beautiful spot where he is on permanent display representing his Kiger Mesteño heritage. Every day he is carefully groomed and shown under saddle to the delight of hundreds of park visitors.★

Standards

Kiger Mesteños carry the dominant genes that code for the primitive dun factor coloration and markings. Dun factor horses are most commonly identified as duns and grullas. Kigers have variations of the dun color factor, which include dun, red

When Kigers are born, their legs are cream in color. As they mature, they shed out to their dark leg color and leg bars. *Canyon Creek Kigers L.L.C.*

dun, grulla, bay, black, claybank (diluted pale cream color), and roan. Dun factor markings include dorsal stripe, jack (shoulder) stripe, zebra stripes on legs, arm bars, bi-colored mane and tail, ears with dark outline and fawn-colored interior, facial mask, and cobwebbing (distinctive line markings).

On Kiger Mesteños, the dorsal stripe is mandatory, with herringbone stripes being desirable. Stripes on the lower legs are highly desirable.

The Kiger Mesteño should have good saddle conformation. In general, it should be compact, light to moderately muscled, smooth and stylish in appearance. It should have clean, dense bone with sufficient substance, well-developed joints and tendons, and exhibit a fine coat. It averages about 13.2 to 15.2 hands in height.

The head should be medium in size, clean cut, and should taper slightly from jaw to muzzle. The profile side view can be straight, concave, or slightly bulged, like the Tarpan. The lower jaw is wide and clean cut, with medium fine muzzle and small, firm lips with medium nostrils. Ears should be medium in length, finely pointed, slightly hooked at the tips on the inside, set wide apart, and carried alertly. Eyes are prominent. Cobwebbing and masking are highly desirable.

An elegant Kiger Mesteño. *Joan Gross*

Neck is medium length, well crested, clean cut at the throatlatch, smoothly joined to the shoulder, and deep at the point of the shoulder. Mane and foretop are full and bi-colored. Some may tend to have upright manes of Tarpan type.

The body conformation of the Kiger Mesteño is distinctive, with chest of good depth and a short back that is broad and moderately muscled. The barrel should be oval, with well-sprung ribs and full flank. The sternum should not protrude.

Shoulders should be long in length and at 45- to 50-degree slope, blending into smooth,

Note the bi-colored mane and tail, leg barring, short level back, and slope to the croup. *Joan Gross*

well-defined, but not too high withers. The withers should be slightly higher than the point of the hip and well defined, but not prominent. Wither stripes, crosses, shadows, bars, and stripes on chest and legs are highly desirable.

When viewed from the front, forelegs should be moderately spaced with an inverted "V" appearance where they connect to the chest, and the legs should be thin and must be straight. Legs should be wide and sinewy when viewed from the side. Cannons are short to medium, wide, flat, and free from muscling. Fetlock joint should not be round, but rather wide. Pasterns should be clean, strong, and of medium length, with the slope to correlate with the slope of the shoulder. The hoof should be of medium size, round to oblong, with thick walls. Kiger horses tend to be mule footed.

The hind legs should be squarely set and placed so that the horse turns on its hindquarters with the legs under it. The hips should be well rounded. Croup should be rounded gently, with medium- to low-set tail, and well carried. The tail is to be full

with light-colored guard hair. Muscles in the hip and thigh should be long and sinewy, not heavy as characterized in draft horses. The rear hocks should be wide, deep, and clean. Viewed from the rear, the hind legs are usually closer at the hocks than at the fetlocks. Hind cannons are short to medium, wide, and flat, with tendons standing well out from the bone and being well defined.

The hind feet should resemble the forefeet and should be medium in size, smooth, and dense. The feet are compact with recessed sole and frog, tending to be oblong or mule footed.

The Kiger should be tractable, but with good spirit. The horse should be lively and light, tending toward higher-than-average front leg action.

Credit: Randy Billinger, Tornado Alley Kigers, and Kiger Mesteño Association.

★"The Kiger Cougar Story," originally published in the April 2000 *Kiger Focus*, written by Jeanne Daly and Bobby Ingersoll

LAC LA CROIX INDIAN PONY

Lac La Croix Indian Pony Society
1–341 Clarkson Road
Castleton, Ontario K0K 1M0, Canada
www.rarebreedscanada.ca

Lac La Croix Indian Ponies are extremely hardy, enduring, and athletic animals that hold a special historical significance to Canada. Their use goes back to before Canada became a country. With their sturdy constitution and versatility, they contributed much to the development of northern Ontario. The ponies have been around a long time, and have been shaped and honed by nature to be survivors.

Also known as the Lac La Croix, or just Indian, Pony, the breed is believed to have descended from the Colonial Spanish horse and the Canadian horse. Its numbers used to be in the thousands, but now the breed's survival is threatened, while the few remaining horses attempt a comeback.

The Lac La Croix Indian Pony was originally located in the Nett Lake, Lake Vermillion, and Lac La Croix areas bordering Minnesota and Canada. The breed was developed over time by the Boise Forte Band of Ojibwe. The village in which the ponies last lived was located on the Canadian side of Lac La Croix, a relatively large lake bordering Ontario that is almost directly north and slightly east of Lake Vermillion. In 1873, the village became a reservation when a treaty was negotiated by Chief Blackstone.

These ponies had been living with the Boise Forte Ojibwe since before the 1800s, until they were removed in 1977. From the thousands of ponies that used to live there, now there are only about 110 known ponies, and not all are breeding stock—some are geldings and foals. Also the ponies no longer live in that area. Today, there are a number owned by individuals scattered in various areas.

Beautiful black Lac La Croix stallion with his mares. The breed comes in many colorful variations. *Bob Walker*

History

The Lac La Croix Ponies were early on used for hauling lumber, running trap lines, and transportation. The last remaining animals in existence were eventually turned loose to fend for themselves.

The population was almost decimated during the mid twentieth century. Around the 1960s, any pockets of known ponies left in Minnesota were gone. The remaining population lived on the Canadian side of the border and was small, only being used by the native people of Lac La Croix First Nation. The ponies were on the Neguaguon Lake Chippewa Reserve on the north side of Lac La Croix and east of Fort Frances, Ontario, near the Ontario–Manitoba border and the U.S. border.

In past years, the reserve was an isolated location accessible only by water in the summer and over roads made on the ice in winter. There was an island nearby, called Pony Island by the locals, where the ponies were herded by their Ojibwe keepers over the ice just before spring. They stayed on the island all summer, foaling and breeding again for the next year and foraging for food. In the winter, when the ice covered the lakes, they were herded back to be used for hauling, logging, or any work as required until spring was imminent and the cycle began again.

The ponies had been allowed to wander free, living in the woods and foraging for food like other wildlife. By the 1960s, they were seldom used, being largely replaced by machines, yet they were considered part of the landscape by the Native Americans.

In 1965–1967, the village was visited by a researcher and writer named Lester Bower. Thinking an animal he saw was a young moose, Bower shot the last young male pony while in the bush. There remained a much older stallion that lived into the 1970s, but he eventually died of old age. Population numbers were extremely low during this period.

A group of people eventually formed the Lac La Croix Indian Pony Society and were fortunate enough to obtain photos from some Lac La Croix residents of approximately seven different animals, including two of the four mares later rescued in 1977. Three of the ponies in the photos had died from causes unknown. The four remaining mares had been turned loose in the woods to forage for themselves in the early 1970s.

Unfortunately, Canada's Health Department officials apparently deemed the ponies a health threat and unwanted pests wandering free, thus it was only a matter of time before the ponies would be destroyed.

In February 1977, following the Health Department's plan to eliminate the breed, four Minnesota men responded to the plight of these four known descendents of the original Indian Ponies and went to rescue them. One of these men, Fred Isham, lived on Minnesota's Nett Lake reservation, though he was originally from the Lac La Croix reservation. He was pivotal in encouraging the owners of the ponies to allow them to be taken to Minnesota. Isham visited the Lac La Croix First Nation Reserve every summer, and was aware of the ponies' imminent demise.

The men were able to load the ponies on a trailer for transport across the lake to Minnesota. Although they had not been handled by humans for a number of years, the ponies were still gentle. The older mares reportedly accepted the halters easily, and the younger ones also did after a bit of a struggle. The mares appeared to be in good shape, with full coats and good feet, and were well nourished. Two of them were twenty-five to thirty years old, while the other two were approximately eleven years old. They were the last known representatives of the breed. None of the four mares were bred when they were rescued.

According to the research of the time, Lac La Croix Indian Ponies were believed to be descendents of Spanish Mustangs, which was true in part. Once settled in their new home in Minnesota, the ponies were bred to a Spanish Mustang stallion off the North Dakota plains. It is unclear exactly how much was known about the details of the breed at the time., but the choice of stallion was apparently accurate enough. With the introduction of a male line, the breed survived.

Lac La Croix Ponies have sturdy builds and iron hard hooves. *Equilore*

Walter Saatela, another one of the four men who rescued the ponies, kept and bred them on his farm for many years. When the job became too much for him, another volunteer, Bob Walker, kept and bred the ponies at his place. Walker tried to keep them in the same manner that they had been managed by Saatela, and encouraged others to join the cause, selling off some stock as the numbers grew. The ponies had free range and little human intervention. They roamed Walker's large, wooded property, continuing to forage largely for themselves, with only hay as they needed it, water, and a run-in shelter.

In the early 1990s, Walker contacted the Rare Breeds Canada (RBC) organization. He believed that these Indian Ponies had historical significance, and that their country of origin could have an important role in their care and survival. In 1993, Jy Chiperzak of RBC initiated the research and visited Walker. Satisfied there was sufficient historical data to support the possibilities, negotiations began and a repatriation project was launched. RBC purchased one stallion and three mares (descendents of the original four mares) and transported them from Minnesota back to Canada. These four ponies formed the first foundation

breeding group in Canada, set up to increase the pony's numbers once again. In 1996, a second breeding group was purchased, and in 1999, the third breeding group was repatriated.

The Ponies' Plight

Today, the ponies numbers are slowly growing. None of the remaining ponies live on the Lac La Croix or any other reservation, but are scattered in other parts of Ontario and Minnesota.

The Lac La Croix Indian Ponies still face a real danger of extinction. Total breeding population is approximately twenty-seven males (of which six are under age two), forty-nine females (of which twelve are fillies), and nineteen that are geldings and/or barren stock. Eighty-nine percent of the horses are in Ontario, while 11 percent are in Minnesota.

The population trends of the breed vary significantly, initially due to lack of documentation and differing management styles or economic and geographic factors, but also due to lack of numbers. A seemingly exceptional high rate of mortality was documented.

It is quite clear that with the controlled breeding program now in place, the population is growing steadily and exponentially. As more of the young female stock mature, the population growth rate should climb sharper. With insufficient data, however, further conclusions for their future are not yet possible.

A lot of foaling information is absent between the years 1977 and 1999. It is believed that the mortality rate had consistently been extremely high due to the type of management of the animals, including free-range foraging and little or no human intervention for most herds. Since the involvement of RBC, there is accurate record-keeping from 1999 onward.

With numbers as low as this, there is always the risk of losing the breed. Nature plays a role in the availability and spread of diseases, such as the West Nile virus. Nature also plays a role in the genetic stabilization of the breed where a small gene pool is present. Due to the lack of a broader breeding stock, all animals are utilized, almost regardless of their own conformity, and necessary culling (removal of substandard animals from the breeding program) is done sparingly or not at all.

Humans have also proven to be unstable as caregivers for rare breeds, with the vast majority of owners in general only keeping animals in times of interest, stable family situation, convenience, good health, and low costs. Records indicate that at least twice in Minnesota, Lac La Croix Ponies were brought to meat plants. One time was reportedly during the mid 1900s as part of a roundup of ponies living wild, which contributed to them becoming extinct in the United States. It also happened once again since their rescue in more recent years.

Currently in Minnesota, the ponies are located in Gheen and Winton, with a few others sporadically located in northern Minnesota areas, all of which not being too far from their original rescuers. In Canada, the RBC has concentrated on spreading the population across distances as part of their preservation plan to reduce risk of local disease and threat. There are ponies in parts of Ontario and Alberta.

Testing

RBC and the Lac La Croix Indian Pony Society have done a heritage genome blood typing project with the assistance of America's renowned equine geneticist, Dr. Gus Cothran. He conducts a study of genetic variation in domestic horses, with particular interest in breeds with small population sizes, such as the Lac La Croix Indian Pony. The Lac La Croix project was done primarily to determine the scope of the genetic base and genetic history of the breed and to ensure that the breeding program was potentially sustainable without outside bloodlines. It also provided animal identification, parentage conformation, and a method of initializing a "herd book" for future registration purposes.

All ponies at the end of the study, with the exception of approximately sixteen, had blood sample DNA performed. The purpose was to determine if the genetic analysis was consistent with the written documentation and verbal records purporting that

this breed is a Spanish Mustang and Canadian horse descendant. Results are pending.

Currently there are two different male lines; Keokuk, a black pony born in 1980; and Nimkii, also a black born in 1985.

Characteristics

The Lac La Croix Indian Ponies are sturdy animals, more disease resistant and hardier than any current domestic breed. They are better mothers and "birthers" than most other breeds. While being slower to mature, when they do start producing offspring, they out-produce the modern equine types yet still have a more extended lifespan.

They are extremely strong for their size, versatile, and athletic. Low maintenance and cost effective for their output, they are suited to any purpose, from lumber hauling, buggy driving, pleasure riding, and competition, to eventing and jumping. They are stable and trustworthy enough to participate in programs for the riding disabled.

They are intelligent thinkers and have often gone from point A to point B with no human companion giving orders, just their load. They tend to avoid self-injury and are able to get themselves out of situations that would otherwise result in injury and require treatment. They possess a common sense that is unequalled in the modern horse world. This characteristic is perhaps the most difficult one to show people or describe, but for anybody who has worked with a Lac La Croix Pony, this will be the first trait he or she will mention about the ponies.

These personality traits alone make them invaluable and worth saving regardless of the historical significance or their abilities.

This is an animal of extreme curiosity, intelligence, and kindness. They possess intuitive thinking and, in stale, passive environments, require "entertainment" to keep them occupied to prevent them from finding their own entertainment and getting into trouble. They will problem-solve difficult situations and are generally agreeable to anything asked of them, if they are allowed first to assess the situation for themselves.

Beautiful herd of Lac La Croix Ponies in various colors, but all are the same size and type. *Equilore*

Physical maturity is slow and takes place well into the fifth, sixth, or seventh year of life, although they are used for breeding prior to that, generally at two to three years of age (fillies bred at three years, studs used at two years). They produce one foal per successful breeding. There are no records of twins being born, although it is believed possible, but rare.

Without being a breed that exists for a single purpose (such as a draft horse, Hackney, or Thoroughbred), the strength, nature, size, and amiability of the Lac La Croix Indian Pony make it a perfect all-around horse for the average horse owner and any day-to-day activity. These ponies can get into and out of dense bush more easily than a draft horse and do not balk at being asked to push their way through trees, breaking off branches as they go and making their own paths.

Pound for pound, they are capable of just as much hauling work as a draft horse. With their extremely durable feet and legs and amazing stamina, they can pull a cart all day long over various rough terrain without damaging or bruising their feet. They have a cannon bone of approximately 7 to 7.5 inches thick, and therefore can easily carry the average adult, regardless of the person's size.

They are not a gaited horse, although they have a smooth, natural rhythm that makes it look like they float over the ground. They have nice leg action, and at the trot their topline does not appear to move at all.

Conformation details include:
- Straight back (topline)
- Low withers
- Sloping croup
- Low-set tail
- Small, iron-hard hooves and legs, but with a relatively thick and strong cannon bone
- Small ears, profusely haired and set wide apart
- Kind, gentle eyes
- Broad forehead tapering toward the muzzle
- Average height of 12.2 to 13.2 hands, with mares averaging 12 to13 hands and stallions 13 to 14.2 hands
- Any solid color except white or cream; small white markings are permitted on the face and lower legs
- No patterned colors (appaloosa, pinto, etc.)

Today, Lac La Croix Indian Ponies are used for pleasure riding, event riding, and driving carts.

Credit: Wayne and Jane Mullen, Equilore Farm; Lac La Croix Indian Pony Society

NOKOTA

Nokota Horse Conservancy
208 NW 1st Street
Linton, North Dakota 58552
www.nokotahorse.org

The Nokotas are naturally beautiful and athletic horses that developed on the North American plains during the nineteenth century. They are descended from an enclave of wild horses that inhabited the Little Missouri Badlands in southwestern North Dakota for at least one hundred years. President Theodore Roosevelt lived and ranched in the these badlands as a young man, and he wrote about the horses, noting that they were "as wild as the antelope of whose domain they have intruded."

This blue roan Nokota herd stallion is quiet and friendly yet very competitive. *Shawn Hamilton CLiX Photography/ courtesy Nokota Horse Conservancy*

History

Roosevelt observed that the wild bands developed from renegade ranch and Indian horses, a process that was uncontrollable during the open range era of the 1880s. Some of the ranch horses of that time were brought into North Dakota by cattlemen from Texas and the Southwest who were expanding their operations to the northern plains. Others were Cayuse-based stock from Montana and other points west.

The Marquis de Mores, a wealthy Frenchman who was a contemporary of Roosevelt's and founded the town of Medora, North Dakota (now the location of Theodore Roosevelt National Park), bred horses in the badlands. He used Sioux mares that he purchased after they were confiscated from Sitting Bull's people and other Lakota bands when they surrendered at Fort Buford, North Dakota, in 1881. Some of these mares still had visible bullet wounds from life with the Hunkpapa Lakota, who used them when they fought in the Battle at Little Big Horn and other battles. De Mores admired the durability and stamina of the Indian horses, as well as their exotic heritage. Like other ranchers of that time, he let his horses loose on the open range and complained of loss to wild stallions and thieves.

Thus, the Sioux horses are believed to have influenced the wild herds and saddle stock of local ranchers, as recorded by historians such as J. Frank Dobie and in the oral and written accounts of early ranchers. Other evidence of the influence of Sioux horses points to the seemingly minimal phenotypic changes of the horses over the past century.

De Mores sold some of the Sioux mares to A. C. Huidekoper, who developed the immense HT Ranch and Little Missouri Horse Company some twenty miles to the southeast of Medora. Huidekoper crossed his Sioux mares with a Thoroughbred stallion and a Percheron stallion to produce polo ponies, cow ponies, and all-purpose saddle and harness horses. The practice of breeding local and Indian pony mares to Thoroughbred, draft, early Quarter Horse, and driving stallions in order to produce an agile and tough all-purpose horse continued well into the twentieth century.

Crossbred Indian horses were the standard ranch mount for many years, and they in turn contributed to the wild herds in the Little Missouri Badlands. When homesteaders and small-scale ranchers replaced open-range ranchers during the early 1900s, they continued to lose some of their horses to the wild herds. However, the transition from large-scale, open ranching to more intensive, controlled livestock production resulted in less tolerance for wild horses and less interest in their merits as saddle stock.

During the twentieth century, federal and state agencies eradicated most wild bands from public grazing lands. At the same time, ranchers increasingly developed a preference for Quarter Horses and other emerging modern breeds, while disparaging of the presence of wild and Indian horses. Ranchers continued to chase wild horses in the Little Missouri Badlands for sport, admiring their indomitable spirit and evasion abilities. Captured animals were increasingly sold for profit, many to slaughter buyers. Over the years, many of the draftier animals that became wild must have been removed in roundups, probably because they were easier to capture and were more valuable by weight.

The social and physical conditions of life in the badlands seem to have encouraged the retention of Spanish and Indian pony characteristics in the animals that survived. Only the hardiest and most intelligent horses were able to withstand the long, frigid winters of western North Dakota and escape capture in the rugged, steep terrain. As a result, the Nokota horses of today retain many of the best features of their early ancestors. Photographs of the De Mores and HT Ranch Sioux horses show individuals that look strikingly similar to today's Nokotas.

Much of the Little Missouri Badlands remained as unfenced public grazing land until the creation of Theodore Roosevelt National Park during the

Although energetic and alert, this traditional Nokota lead mare is level-headed and affable. *Shawn Hamilton CLiX Photography/courtesy Nokota Horse Conservancy*

Unusual historic color patterns are one of the Nokota's most striking characteristics. This youngster is a beautiful overo. *Nokota Horse Conservancy*

1950s. At that time, some of the remaining wild harem bands—the last surviving wild horses in North Dakota—were inadvertently enclosed into the fifty-thousand-acre south unit of the park. For twenty years, the park sought to eradicate the horses despite local support for their presence. During the 1970s, park policy was amended to preserve a small number of horses as an "historic demonstration herd," yet, in 1973, the National Park Service (NSP) was granted legal exemption from the Wild and Free-Roaming Horse and Burro Act of 1971, as well as other legislation governing the management of feral equines on public lands.

In the following decade, the park decided to remove the original wild horses and replace them with representatives of contemporary breeds, including Quarter Horses and an Arabian stallion. The motive for this decision was to increase revenue from the sale of horses following the periodic roundups held to control population size. Park managers cited phenotypic conformity among the horses and a preponderance of blue roans, blacks, and grays as undesirable characteristics of the park herd.

Preservation

In 1979, brothers Leo and Frank Kuntz of Linton, North Dakota, began buying individual horses removed from the park for use in competitive cross-country racing. They quickly became impressed with the strength, stamina, and intelligence of the horses. When old-time ranchers began commenting on the Kuntz horses' resemblance to turn-of-the century ranch and Indian horses, the brothers began investigating their horses' history. By the mid-1980s, they had committed to preserving these types of horses and began buying as many as they could from park roundups, which had become increasingly focused on eliminating the original wild horses.

In 1986, the Kuntz brothers purchased fifty-one horses after a park roundup, including many animals now regarded as important foundation stock. In the same year, anthropologist Castle McLaughlin began compiling a comprehensive social, cultural, and management history of the horses for the NPS. Medora-area rancher Tom Tescher, who began observing the wild horses about 1950 and often managed roundups for the park, contributed valuable documentation of the herd's social and genealogical history.

During the 1980s and 1990s, the Kuntz brothers and McLaughlin waged a vigorous campaign to have the NPS reinstate the animals they named "Nokota" horses back in the park. Their efforts garnered widespread media coverage and the support of several wild-horse experts, Native Americans, and other concerned citizens.

In 1993, the state of North Dakota passed legislation declaring the Nokota as the state's "honorary equine," in recognition of its role in North Dakota history. Yet despite increasing pressure from historians and wild-horse experts, the NPS has persistently

The indomitable and free spirit of a Nokota herd on a North Dakota range. *Nokota Horse Conservancy*

refused to consider managing a historically accurate wild-horse herd in Theodore Roosevelt National Park. Today, virtually all of the horses in the park are the offspring of recently introduced domestic stock.

Failing to make headway with the NPS, the Kuntz brothers promoted the value of the horses among riders interested in sound, athletic animals. While working at a ranch in Montana, Leo Kuntz met Pennsylvanians Blair and Charlie Fleischmann, an active couple in the steeplechase and fox-hunting community. Impressed and intrigued by the Kuntz brothers' horses, the Fleischmanns began introducing Nokotas to fellow equestrians in Virginia and Pennsylvania. Other individuals successfully introduced them into equestrian communities in California, the Pacific Northwest, and elsewhere.

The horses demonstrated their versatility by excelling at ranch work, fox hunting, stadium jumping, timed events, endurance rides, and even dressage. Thus, a community of interested owners and riders began to develop.

Galvanized by Blair Fleischmann, the non-profit Nokota Horse Conservancy was organized in 1999 to preserve the horses and maintain a registry. In concert with Frank and Leo Kuntz, the conservancy struggles to maintain a core breeding herd of 125 animals that are descendants from stock removed from the Little Missouri Badlands, relying solely on donations from the Kuntz family and other devotees to keep the herd alive. In 2000, the Kuntz brothers received the Rio Vista award for outstanding animal rescue and welfare work.

Several preservation breeders have also emerged, including Dale and Holly Offermann who stand their Nakota stud, Chief, on their Rocking Bar Ranch in Arlington, Washington. Chief is one of the best-known ambassadors for the breed; he is a nationally known gray liberty stallion whose sire and dam were wild and removed from the park. (Liberty horses are trained in the liberty arts, that is, performing stunts without the use of tack, both under saddle and on the ground.) Chief freely and easily performs Lipizzaner-type exercises on command.

Blue Moon Rising, a Nokota gelding that was the first Nokota to be accepted into the Horse of the Americas Registry, represents the new breed at the Kentucky Horse Park in Lexington.

In 2007, Nokota horses were selected as the annual Benefit Model by the Breyer Model Horse Company. Considering the number of model horses that Breyer has done, this is quite an honor.

Nokota horses are now owned by both professional and amateur riders in a number of both western and English disciplines, and have been warmly received as field hunters, jumpers, and all-around youth horses.

A ranch-type Nokota stallion, undeniably athletic and relentless, and one of the Conservancy's most dominant stallions. *Shawn Hamilton CLiX Photography/courtesy Nokota Horse Conservancy*

A traditional Nokota stallion, standing only 14.2 hands, but compact, powerful, and "old-line." *Dominique Braud/courtesy Nokota Horse Conservancy*

A colorful ranch-type Nokota stallion, athletic with good bone. This is a stunning foundation stallion in a Nokota herd. *Shelly Hauge/ courtesy Nokota Horse Conservancy*

Characteristics

Characteristics of the Nokota breed include great intelligence, hardiness, a square-set stance, thick, dark hooves, and unusual, intrinsic color patterns.

Like other wild horses, they also have extremely strong legs and feet. Researchers have become increasingly interested in this characteristic; farriers and horse owners are beginning to utilize what they learn about wild-horse legs and hooves to promote soundness in domestic horses.

One of the most striking Nokota characteristic is the preservation of the coat patterns often associated with horses of Iberian descent. Roans, frame overos, and sabinos dominate the breed, and Medicine Hat markings are not uncommon. Blue roan is the predominant color and is, to some extent, a hallmark of the breed. Some of the horses also exhibit a strong dun factor, and many of the roans are grullo at birth and into their first year. Black, the base color for roan, is common, as is gray. Bay, brown, and chestnut occur with less frequency.

Nokota horses are strikingly athletic and most demonstrate a natural jumping ability. Some owners have reported Nokotas with unusual gaits, such as an amble or "Indian shuffle." Professional trainers who have worked with Nokota horses have remarked on their capacity for rapid learning, independent thinking, and problem-solving capabilities—qualities that were imperative to their survival in the wild.

There are an estimated 150 foundation and foundation-bred horses that descend wholly from animals removed from the park, and they are the focus of conservation efforts. The registry also tracks crossbred horses that are at least one-quarter of foundation descent. Since the 1980s, the Kuntz family has bred many park horses with their own ranch stock, including running Quarter Horses, horses obtained from the Standing Rock Sioux Reservation, Thoroughbreds, and ponies. The resulting crossbred Nokotas have enjoyed widespread success as using horses in a variety of activities.

The registry recognizes two somewhat distinct phenotypes of Nokota horses, Traditionals and Ranch Stock, although individual horses often exhibit traits associated with both types.

Traditional Nokotas share many phenotypic characteristics with Spanish Mustangs. They are small, sturdy, and refined, seldom reaching 15 hands in height, with large eyes, delicate, inward-curving ears, well-defined shoulders, short backs, sloped croups, and low-set tails. Many have exceptionally long manes and tails, while some have hair around their fetlocks.

In 1994, Dr. Phillip Sponenberg evaluated both the park and the Kuntz horses, and concluded that the latter owned about twenty individual animals (while the park had none left) that were phenotypically consistent with conformation standards for Colonial Spanish horses such as Spanish Mustangs. Since that time, Leo Kuntz has selectively bred those animals to maintain and concentrate these Spanish characteristics. Known as traditionals, their preservation is a priority to the conservancy.

While it is clear that horses of Colonial Spanish breeding were important to the foundation of early Indian and ranch herds on the northern plains, they were always less numerous than in the Southwest and far west, where they were concentrated near Spanish settlements. The artist Frederic Remington and other nineteenth-century observers often remarked on a distinction between mustang horses of the Southwest and Indian and ranch stock on the northern ranges, which were somewhat larger and rangier. These differences were probably due to both environmental conditions and crossbreeding.

Contrary to popular belief, most Native Americans did not selectively breed to preserve mustang or Spanish traits in their horses. During the nineteenth century, Euro-American notions of animal husbandry increasingly focused on the appearance and purity of descent, ideas that were critical to the project of creating animal "breeds." In contrast, with the partial exception of coat pattern and color, Plains Indians (and early Anglo settlers) overwhelmingly valued performance characteristics, such as speed, stamina, and durability. While this focus served to encourage the retention of hardy Iberian traits, it did not preclude the use of other influences, as Native Americans creatively adapted to the changing conditions of life on the plains and mounted warfare.

Ranch Stock Nokotas are larger and more robust, showing the effects of past crossbreeding, especially to draft horses. These horses reflect an early and sustained history of interbreeding between Spanish and Indian animals, as well as other early ranch strains of both saddle and utility types.

The expanding cattle industry, progressing settlements, and the U.S. Cavalry introduced larger, heavier-boned horses to the northern plains after the American Civil War. These bigger horses were well received by Native Americans, who crossed them with their ponies. Horses of this type often appear in photographs taken on Indian reservations in the Dakotas and Montana before 1900. Sitting Bull's autobiographical ledger drawings depict him riding to war on a large, stout, blue roan with feathered fetlocks.

Such crossbreds were useful for a variety of purposes and were sometimes called Dakota Stouts. They were the backbone of the ranching industry in North Dakota between 1880 and 1950. Even though they were replaced by Quarter Horses and other specialized saddle stock, they continued in service as dray animals and rodeo broncs. Today, these ranch types are finding new favor as field hunters, dressage horses, and show jumpers.

Genetic analysis of the Nokotas has suggested descent from a wide range of both Iberian and western European horses, with no significant relationship to any contemporary recognized breed. A century or longer of living wild in a harsh environment with constant threat from humans has molded their heritage into a constellation of set phenotypic characteristics that remain observable over several generations of out-breeding.

While their history and coat patterns are colorful, it is the Nokotas horses' balance, athleticism, soundness, and thoughtfulness that have stirred a genuine interest among serious riders. Nokota horses have survived thus far on the merit of their abilities and through the intervention of appreciative individuals, such as the Marquis De Mores, the Kuntz brothers, and the Fleischmanns. Their future will depend on the same factors.

Credit: Castle McLaughlin, Ph.D., vice president of the Nokota Horse Conservancy and associate curator of North American Ethnography, Peabody Museum of Archaeology and Ethnology, Harvard University and Nokota Horse Conservancy

PRYOR MOUNTAIN MUSTANG

Pryor Mountain stallion with distinctive leg barring and back lining. Pryors have short, hooked ears, short backs, low tail sets, depth of neck and body, and overall balance. The sloped hip here is rounded off with muscle. *Daphne Hartman*

Pryor Mountain Mustang Breeders Association
P.O. Box 884
Lovell, Wyoming 82431
www.pryorhorses.com

The Pryor Mountains border Montana and Wyoming and are extremely rugged with high terrain elevations from 3,900 to 8,000 feet. The landscape includes arid desert, high grass meadows, and timberland. The climate is cold in winter, and hot and dry in the summer. Ranging on this contrasting wilderness is a small herd of wild horses known as the Pryor Mountain Mustangs. They are colorful horses that often have barring on their shoulders and legs—primitive markings handed down from their Spanish ancestors. People from all over the world have come to study, photograph, and write about these unique equines.

History

Spanish horses in North America were hardy animals, prized for their capabilities to endure adverse conditions and remain tractable. They could carry heavy loads and were surefooted. They remained entrenched in American history, helping to establish the new nation.

Their ancestors were brought by Spanish explorers in the sixteenth century and used extensively to establish colonies in the unpopulated areas of the New World. Some of these early Spanish horses retained characteristics from ancient breeds, such as Barbs, Tarpans, Arabians, Andalusians, and Sorraias. The combination of these breeds produced certain definable traits. Barbs were quick, could carry heavy loads, boasted great endurance, and were easy keepers. Tarpans were small primitive horses from Eastern Europe that were mostly grullo with a dorsal strip and had black manes and tails. Arabians were renowned for their stamina and refined beauty. Andalusians were agile with great riding compatibility and strength. Sorraias were small, hardy Portuguese horses that could thrive in poor environments. They had a dorsal stripe and leg stripes, and were always either grullo or dun in color.

Eventually America's Spanish horses were replaced with the more popular draft or racing horses brought to the East Coast. Some managed to escape before being bred with the new European horses that were pressing westward. These wild Spanish horses, referred to as mustangs, thrived on the western plains for which they were especially adapted. Eventually, there were millions of Spanish mustangs roaming America.

Their numbers, however, began to dwindle over the centuries due to competition with cattle and sheep for food and water, as the West became more populated. Mustangs were hunted and killed to remove them from valuable grazing land. By the middle of the twentieth century, there only remained pockets of horses that managed to escape and thrive in the more inaccessible places, which included the remote area of the Pryor Mountain. It is possible that the Crow Indians had a hand in the initial introduction of horses to that area. Regardless of how they got there, some Spanish horses managed to survive in this mountain range for more than two hundred years.

Nature took over from the initial Spanish breeding that produced such beautiful and useful horses. The Pryor Mountain Mustangs were isolated from outside influences, preventing little deviation from the original type. They remained small and compact animals, with heavy manes and tails, and were hardy enough to survive on their own.

Spanish Ancestry

Evidence of the Pryor Mountain horses' Spanish ancestry has been proven by genetic studies and blood type tests. Dr. Gus Cothran, an invaluable authority on equine genetics, tested them and concluded they were "primarily derived from horses with Spanish ancestry."

D. Phillip Sponenberg, DVM, PhD, stated in his article, "North American Colonial Spanish Horse," that most Pryor Mountain Mustangs "have Spanish conformation. They are found along a major Crow and Shoshone migration route, and they probably have an origin in tribal horses. . . . They are an interesting group since colors include bay, black, roan, chestnut, dun, grullo, and a few buckskins and minimally expressed calico paints. This array of colors, especially the relatively high proportion of black and black based colors, is also consistent with a Spanish origin."

In 1968, Secretary of the Interior Stewart Udall announced the creation of the Wild Horse Refuge in the Pryor Mountains to preserve this unique breed of Colonial Spanish Mustang. The refuge was the first of its kind in the country, as it was land set aside specifically for the preservation of mustangs.

Dr. Sponenberg emphasized that the Pryor Mountain Mustangs are an important resource for Spanish horse conservation in North America:

The Pryor Mountain Mustangs are fortunate in inhabiting the first wild horse refuge that is specifically set up to conserve mustangs. That they are Spanish is an added bonus and private individuals are now becoming interested in conserving this type. The Bureau of Land Management (BLM) has recently been acknowledging the uniqueness of this herd and is working to preserve the Spanish type on this range. This herd is one of the most accessible feral horse herds and seeing these horses in their home environment is well worth the trip to this range.

The Tillett Ranch was another source that was instrumental in saving the Pryor Mountain horses.

Barring on this filly will be similar to her dam's. *Darlene Wohlart/equinephotography.com*

When the Pryor Mountain Mustang range was started, a fence was put up between the horse range and the Tillett Ranch, and there were Pryor horses on each side of the fence. The Tilletts kept their Pryor horses separate from the rest of their horses and began adopting them out.

Today, tourists can still observe the Pryor Mountain Mustang in its natural surroundings on the range. Mustangs have also been put up for adoption, which is held every two to four years, depending on the condition of the range and number of adult horses. To ensure the viability of the herd, between 120 and 150 horses need to be maintained on the range to protect the gene pool. Until recent years, the "pretty" horses were adopted out; this left the majority of the horses on the range to be blacks or bays. Around 1994, the theory changed to adopt out horses of various colors to maintain a diversity of colors of horses on the range. Now there are plenty of duns and grullos, as well as blacks, bays, and others.

Registry

The Pryor Mountain Mustang Breeders Association (PMMBA) was founded in 1992 to preserve the gene pool of Colonial Spanish horses, as found in the wild herd of the Pryor Mountain Mustangs, and to establish a registry for their progeny. It cooperates with the BLM to protect, preserve, promote, and enhance the wild herd of mustangs that currently inhabit the Pryor Mountain Wild Horse Refuge.

To be eligible for registration, a horse born in captivity must have a dam and sire already registered. An adopted horse must have a copy of the BLM adoption certificate, or a statement from the Tillett Ranch stating it is a Pryor horse, and a certificate of blood typing from the University of Kentucky. The first three horses that were registered with the

PMMBA came from the Tillett Ranch.

As of April 2008, the PMMBA had registered 209 horses. Pryors now are located in sixteen states: California, Florida, Idaho, Illinois, Indiana, Maryland, Massachusetts, Missouri, Montana, Oregon, South Dakota, Texas, Utah, Washington, Virginia, and Wyoming, plus one in Canada. This is quite an accomplishment considering there are so few Pryor horses.

Characteristics

Pryor horses can be any color, but the majority are dun or grullo and include red or blue roan. Most carry the markings of ancient primitive horses. These markings include the dorsal stripe down the back, stripes on the withers, and distinctive tiger stripes on the legs. The colors of the horses are usually vibrant and clear.

Their average size is about 14 hands high, and they weigh 700 to 800 pounds when maturing under feral conditions. Horses raised by people can grow larger. Due to their size, Pryor horses make great mountain horses and are easy to mount and dismount. Though small, they are durable, intelligent, and surefooted with great stamina.

They have fairly heavy bodies with good bones and medium-length necks. Their manes and tails are usually quite long, and they have thick, sometimes curly winter coats.

Pryors have fine, neat heads with wide-set, intelligent eyes and small hooked ears. The head profile is either convex or straight. The broad forehead tapers to the muzzle. The teeth meet evenly, but the upper lip is usually longer than the bottom, which helps when grazing on short grass. The nostrils are usually small and crescent shaped when the horses are at rest, but flare open when alert or during exertion.

Sloped croups and low tailsets are common. The shoulders are sloping and long. Withers are prominent. Chests are a medium to narrow width.

Leg chestnuts are either small or nonexistent: sometimes this happens on only two legs, while other times it happens on all four. They have hard hooves and rarely do they need to be shod; hooves

are an ample size to accommodate their weight.

Some have a distinctive five-lumbar vertebrae, or the fifth and sixth vertebrae are fused, characteristics atypical of other horses, which have six and no fused vertebrae.

Many exhibit paso gaits, and genetic testing has proven they are closely related to the Puerto Rican Paso Fino, a definite Spanish breed. Pryors are intelligent, strong, and exhibit true Colonial Spanish type.

The disposition of the Pryor horse is quite different than domestic horses. Once the horse gets to know and depend on a person, it becomes social, wanting to be around people, much like a dog, and to be petted. Most Pryor horses are calm, having an easygoing temperament, as well as smart and willing to learn. When trail riding, they are extremely alert to their surroundings and make great trail horses, because of their stamina and surefootedness.

The PMMBA recognizes the unique genetics of this important breed and attempts to preserve it by selectively breeding adopted Pryor Mountain Mustangs. The number of PMMBA horses has been recognized by the American Livestock Breeds Conservancy as critical, with fewer than two hundred registrations each year in the United States and an estimated global population of less than two thousand. The Pryor horses are on the critical list along with nine other Colonial Spanish strains.

There currently are four PMMBA members, located in Wyoming, Missouri, and Massachusetts, who are raising registered Pryor horses to preserve the bloodlines of the Pryor Mountain Mustang. Since the establishment of the PMMBA, the members have promoted the horses by riding them in parades, horse shows, endurance riding, trail riding, herding cattle, and roping. The Pryor Mountain Mustangs can be trained to do anything other domestic horses can do.

Credit: Dale Hartman, Pryor Mountaiin Mustang Breeders Association; and Dr. D. Phillip Sponenberg, DVM, PhD

SPANISH BARB

Spanish Barb Breeders Association
P.O. Box 1628
Silver City, New Mexico 88062
www.spanishbarb.com

Spanish Barbs are historic horses with an aura of legend surrounding them. They are an ageless and world-renowned breed. Paintings from the old masters depict Spanish kings and nobility mounted on what appear to be large, full-bodied, Barb-type horses of exceptional beauty.

Barbs were the first horses to populate the New World, predating all other breeds. These graceful, agile, and fleet horses were undeniably rugged, surefooted, willing, and enduring—all much-needed and sought-after traits in frontier times. Throughout the five centuries the Spanish Barb has survived in North America, valuable characteristics and abilities first established in the breed long ago in Spain by the Moors have remained intact today.

History

The Spanish Barb's unusual history begins, not in Spain, but in the scrub-brush mountains and the dry plains of North Africa. There, the Zenata, an extraordinary horse-warrior tribe of Berbers, joined with the Muslims, and in 711 AD, seven thousand of these superb horsemen made up the initial force that first invaded Iberia. The seven-hundred-year occupation of Spain by the Moors brought about monumental changes in the lives of the people and, especially, in the breeding of horses.

The agile, desert-bred African Barb was crossed with the existing stock of Spain, creating a new horse type that was bred throughout the entire southern half of Spain. Spanish horses had already received an infusion of Barb blood during the earlier rule of Carthage. The superior horses of Al-Andalus (Iberian Peninsula) developed from this cross and became world famous by the Middle Ages. They were much sought after by the royal stud farms of all Europe.

An elegant Spanish Barb stallion: refined head, short, level back, and wonderful shoulder layback. *Spanish Barb Breeders Association*

An exquisite Spanish Barb mare. *Joe Cardinal*

In the year 1492, the Spanish had regained possession of their country and began their own invasion force—the conquistadors. The Spanish exploration and settlement in the Americas depended, in large part, on the livestock initially brought over from Spain, and none proved more necessary than their horses. By royal edict, horses were transported to the New World, and breeding farms were established.

Thus, the Spanish Barb was introduced into North America by Spanish adventurers who brought the breed first to the Caribbean Islands. Later, the horses were brought into Mexico, Central and South America, and eventually to the vast southwest of what is now the United States.

During the sixteenth and seventeenth centuries, the Spaniards established settlements in northern Florida and the areas along the Gulf of Mexico and the southeastern Atlantic. The Chickasaw and Choctaw Indians, as well as the Creeks, acquired many Spanish horses. It was mainly from trading with these eastern Native American tribes and capturing strays that the English colonists acquired Spanish horses.

The English, for the most part, appeared unaware that the horse of the Spaniards had been the first of such animals on the continent. They apparently believed the finely bred horses they purchased from, or traded with, the Indians, or caught running in wild herds to be "native" horses. The English utilized these horses under saddle or for plowing, as well as raced them at every available opportunity.

The eventual importation of English racers, which at the time were line-bred Oriental Barbs with a liberal dash of Irish blood, led to the crossing of the Spanish/Indian horses to the English imports—basically Spanish Barb to Oriental Barb. This union created the Colonial Short Horse, later known as the celebrated American Quarter-of-a-Mile Running Horse. All of those deep-bodied horses averaging 14 hands carried the same prepotent genes of the Spanish Barb.

Spanish horses were later raised on the lands granted to the missions and ranches in the vast territory between the Arkansas River and Mexico. They not only populated the entire western area of North America, but were transferred east, providing most of the broodmares for the imported English stallions of the eastern colonists. Whether they were called Spanish, Chickasaw, Colonial, Western, or Plantation horses, their heritage remained Spanish Barb.

The blood of Spanish horses can be found in the foundation stock of the early Thoroughbred, Standardbred, Morgan, Quarter Horse, and Plantation horse (known today as the Tennessee Walking Horse) of the early southern states. Many of the color registries in the United States today (Palomino, Buckskin/Dun, Paint, and Appaloosa) can thank the horses bred by the early Spaniards in North America for the outstanding coat-color inheritance of their horses.

Until the time of the U.S. acquisition of the Spanish-held western territories in 1803, the blood of the Spanish Barb flowed in the veins of more early American horses than anyone had imagined—and with good reason. These horses had the courage and sturdiness especially suited for exploration and ranching. Yet the ancient bloodlines of the Spanish Barb were nearly annihilated during the nineteenth century.

Americans at that time knew little to nothing of the long history of the ancient Spanish breed, nor of its contributions in creating the early English "thoroughly bred" horse, or the Lipizzan, Andalusian, Lusitano, and various European crossbred horses. Even so, the new settlers heading west appreciated these horses' unequalled working ability, stamina, versatility, and temperament.

Outcrosses

Despite the many attributes retained by the breed during their two hundred rugged years of existence in western America, harsh environments and careless breeding practices had diminished the remaining Spanish Barb in size and beauty. As a result, the descendants of the once-renowned Spanish breed were considered much too small to suit the rugged Westerners' tastes of that day and age.

Wanting to create an exclusively American breed, yet one that would incorporate all of the abilities genetically carried by the pure Spanish Barb, western ranches brought about a flurry of experimental crossbreeding. Larger eastern stallions of a variety of types and breeds were brought to the West and crossed with mares from the old, disbanded Spanish ranches of the southwest, as well as on mares purchased cheaply and brought up from Mexico. The Steeldust and Copperbottom bloodlines that are still found in the Quarter Horse were created at that time when the predominantly Oriental Barb bloodlines—carried by the Thoroughbred stallion Sir Archy—were crossed on Spanish mares.

The contribution made by the Spanish horse to both history and other breeds of the world will never be diminished. At one time in America's past, the Spanish horse could be found from the Atlantic Seaboard to the Pacific Coast, and from the borders of Canada to the tip of Mexico, but time, humans, and circumstances brought many changes, including the culling of this once plenteous breed.

This proud Spanish Barb stallion is solid with good straight legs. *Dragoon Mountain Spanish Barbs*

Foundation Breeders

Slaughter and extensive crossbreeding nearly destroyed the pure old-time Spanish Barb by the latter part of the nineteenth century. Had it not been for the regard and foresight of a few western ranchers who valued and admired the traits and unmatched abilities of the pure Spanish Barb, this historic breed would have remained only a legend in North America.

At the beginning of the twentieth century, when Bob and Ferdinand Brislawn acquired several Spanish Barb horses from the remote Book Cliffs area of Utah, the few survivors of this all-but-forgotten breed appeared on the brink of extinction. During this same time, Ilo Belsky searched out individual horses and began raising a small herd of dun and grullo Spanish Barbs on his Sand Hills ranch in Nebraska.

These were the only Spanish Barb horses known to exist in North America until the McKinley family purchased the thirty-thousand-acre D. D. Romero ranch west of Los Lunas, New Mexico. This was an original Spanish land grant awarded

These Spanish Barb geldings show the convex Iberian profile and great depth of body and neck. Prominent bone structure above the eye is typical. *Don MacCarter*

to the Romero family and later purchased by their descendants when New Mexico became a state in 1848. Señor Romero was in his eighties at the time of the sale to the McKinleys, and part of the purchase agreement was the condition that the McKinleys would look after and protect the remaining Romero horses. Romero was extremely proud of his heritage and that of his horses, and boasted of the fact that no *gringo* horses had ever been crossed on any of his stock.

Selected horses from these three small groups—descendants of a few Book Cliffs horses, several of the Belsky horses, and a number of the Romero/McKinley horses, in addition to one medicine hat Paint stallion whose sire came from San Domingo pueblo in northern New Mexico—became the foundation for the restoration of the Spanish Barb in North America.

Registry

Undertaking the challenge of restoring and preserving a nearly decimated, but valuable and historic, breed of horse is an unusual and difficult endeavor, and one that had never been successfully achieved by American horse breeders before. The genetic and historic research involved was painstaking and time consuming. Only the most serious and dedicated individuals would commit. Breeding had to be approached with extreme care, as the surviving bloodlines represented a small gene pool. If prudent, knowledgeable methods were not utilized, there would be serious genetic problems.

In 1972, the Spanish Barb Breeders Association (SBBA) began with some thirty breeding horses. In order to ensure the continuation of the breed whose nucleus was so small, elective, intelligent line-breeding and inbreeding played a vital part in the early years. The successful use of close breeding programs became evident in the quality of the resulting foals and the stabilization of the desired attributes of the breed.

In 1996, the registry created a separate division to track a strain of the Colonial Spanish horse, known as the Wilbur-Cruce Mission horse, as a possible addition to the registry. Wilbur-Cruce horses trace their descent from horses bred by Father Eusebio Kino of Mission Dolores in Mexico. The reintroduction of some of the original blood that created the Spanish Barb served to strengthen the gene pool and, at the same time, ensured the complete

Cruce
-year
con-
lard.
sions:
nent
enta-
n has
grade
tered
reed-
e the
that

ration
mea-
ts are
ccep-
verall
n the
iation

n the
some
s pro-
vious
curate
ing its
t rests
ed by
in its

direct link with the past.

Related Breeds

Nearly five centuries have passed since the landing of the first Spanish horses in the New World, and presently there are several breeds descending from those original Spanish Barb horses residing in South America that are rarely seen outside of their respective countries. The Argentine Criollo, Brazilian Criollo, and Chilean Criollo are among some of those descendants. Specialized breeding for purely gaited horses in South America and the Caribbean has resulted in the beautiful Peruvian Paso and the Paso Fino, both of which are now bred in the United States. These attractive horses were conceived and raised exclusively for the smoothness of their gaits and the comfort of their ride. Due to that selectivity, they are no longer suited to the wide diversity of performance for which the original Spanish Barb horses were developed by the Moors eleven centuries ago.

The remaining descendants of Spanish Barb horses in North America have been purposely bred by the SBBA to retain all of the characteristics of their ancestors. Occasionally, a pacer has occurred among these descendants of the originals, a genetic reminder of their close relationship to the Spanish/Moorish horses of the ancient past, as well as to their more specialized relatives in the present.

Standards

The breed standard for the Spanish Barb horse serves as a criterion by which the individuals are judged. It also provides a basis of comparison by which horses are measured for acceptance, placement, or rejection, in relation to being numbered within the registry. Every aspect of the breed standard has been designed to promote the *ideal* for the breed, with the goal of attaining complete restoration in quality and excellence.

The overall appearance of the Spanish Barb is one of balance and smoothness, with depth of neck and body, roundness of hip, short, clean legs and a well-set, distinctively refined head.

Spanish Barbs stand at 13.3 to 14.3 hands in height. A few individuals may mature slightly under or over, but they do not represent the norm. The ancient horses of Spain were deceptively portrayed to be larger than their actual size due to their erect carriage and great depth of body. The Spanish Barb of today continues to give the impression of being a larger horse than it actually is. The breed is also slow to mature.

All colors are found within the breed. Due to the heritage of the African Barb, a variety of unusual coat colors are found, such paints—overo, tobiano, and sabino, and blanket roans. The traditional chestnut, bay, and black, in addition to the predominant colors endowed by the various phases of dun, are inherited from the ancient Iberian horses.

The head is distinctly Iberian Barb in type: lean and refined with a straight or slightly convex profile. The ears are short to medium, curved inward, and slightly back at the tips. The eyes are set well forward on the head and are primarily brown; blue eyes occur occasionally. A prominent bone structure above the eye is characteristic. The muzzle is refined, short, and tapered, being set off by a shallow mouth and firm lips. The nostrils are crescent shaped and of ample size for air intake when enlarged during exertion.

There is great depth of both neck and body. The chest is strong, medium in width, and sufficiently muscled inside the forearm to form an arch. The ribs are well sprung, never slab-sided, and the heart girth is deep, depending on the height and overall size of the horse. The shoulder is well angled and in balance with the back and heart girth.

The back is short and strong, in proportion to the length of the shoulder, forelegs, and depth of girth. The loin is powerful. The croup is round and sufficiently full in width and length to be in balance with the body. The hindquarters are not heavily muscled, and the flank is deep. The tailset is medium to low.

The legs are straight, strong, and well formed with long muscling in the forearms and thighs, and short, clean cannons. The bone is dense, with the circumference of the front cannons averaging 7.5 to 7.875 inches. The joints are well developed, strong, and free of excess flesh. The pasterns are strong, medium in length and slope, and have good flexibility that contributes to the smoothness of the gaits. The hooves are ample and well shaped, with an excellent frog formation and thick walls that are extremely hard. During the summer, the feathering is either lacking or curled tightly against the lower leg.

Chestnuts on the front legs should be small, smooth, and non-protruding. When they appear on the hind legs, they should be extremely small and flush with the leg. Ergots are either lacking, small, or appear to be more like a callous.

Under normal conditions the mane, forelock, and tail are quite long and full. An exceptionally full mane will sometimes fall naturally on both sides of the neck.

The classical-style characteristic to the Spanish Barb and all Iberian Barb descended breeds is displayed by their natural carriage, action, intelligence, and temperament under saddle. These somewhat elusive traits remain an important part of their heritage and appeal, and are basic to the breed's successful restoration.

Their large, deep girth houses the heart and lungs, and it is the size of these organs of circulation and respiration in relationship to the overall size of the horses that endows them with the stamina and weight-carrying abilities. For this reason, the Spanish Barb is a natural when it comes to endurance and competitive trail events. With proper conditioning, this breed may be the endurance horse of the future, exactly as its ancestors were centuries ago. The well-proportioned skeletal structure of the breed, the long, smooth muscling, and the natural movement may be adapted to the graceful, controlled actions required by dressage. It could also be trained for the quick, darting moves of the cutting horse, or the efficient strides of strenuous cross-country eventing. The skeletal strucure and the accompanying muscle formation are made for optimum performance, and the deep heart girth is part of the engine that provides the power.

The well-balanced body, stamina, and range for extension and hock action of the Spanish Barb allow the horse to perform such movements as quick turns off the hind quarters and sliding stops.

While their natural physical ability is unquestionably among the best to be found, ability alone does not always produce a winner. Disposition and intelligence are also required in order to achieve responsive handling and peak performance. In this area, the Spanish Barb again proves to be exceptional, displaying a cooperative willingness in

Spanish Barb in mounted shooting competition. Most Spanish Barbs are less than 15 hands. The breed's cooperative temperament blends this horse with its rider to make an unbeatable team. *Dragoon Mountain Spanish Barbs*

response to correct handling and schooling, which blends horse and rider into an unbeatable team. The Spanish Barb's conformation, ability, and exceptional temperament combine to produce an attractive horse suited to whatever area of performance a rider desires to pursue.

While these horses are hot-bloods, displaying all of the *brio* under saddle for which the Spanish breeds have always been noted, their body metabolism is extremely efficient. They recover quickly from physical exertion when properly conditioned, and their pulse and respiration rates are normally lower than those of other breeds. They are easy keepers, needing smaller portions of a nutritional diet in order to maintain a high level of energy and a proper body weight.

During the early years of the SBBA's existence, only geldings and non-breeding stock were sold (unless a buyer had both the means and the land necessary to become a breeder). There were simply not enough breeding horses available to allow any of them to be lost to the restoration program. Now that the breed has been safely brought back to a sufficient population to ensure its survival, owners in various sections of the country have gradually begun to train for a wide range of performance: endurance, reining, jumping, timed events, gymkhana, dressage, combined eventing, mounted shooting, and pleasure.

Many individuals from any number of breeds can attain performance greatness, but the Spanish Barbs have the added dimension of temperament and personality that makes them very special indeed.

Credit: Silke Schneider, Spanish Barb Breeders Association

SPANISH MUSTANG

Natural Spanish movement and Iberian profile are both evident in this beautiful Spanish Mustang. *Jane K. Greenwood*

Spanish Mustang Registry, Inc.
323 County Road 419
Chilton, Texas 76632
www.spanishmustang.org

Spanish Mustangs are a living part of American history, descending from horses brought to North America around five hundred years ago. They are direct descendants of the first horses brought by early Spanish conquistadors. These Spanish wonders were considered the finest horses in the known world at the time of the conquest of the New World. They left a legacy in their tough, beautiful, hardy descendants that endure to this day—the Spanish Mustang.

Spanish Mustangs have often been confused with the feral horses currently managed by the Bureau of Land Management (BLM), but there is a vast difference in both appearance and ancestry. Spanish Mustangs carry in their veins the blood of warhorses ridden by men who explored and conquered a new land, forever changing the history of the Americas.

History

As ordered from the Spanish throne, Columbus brought the first Spanish horses to the New World on his second voyage. Thereafter, each succeeding ship carried choice Spanish stock, and breeding farms were set up in the Caribbean and then in Mexico. Breeding farms such as the one operated by Father Eusebio Kino, a Jesuit priest in Sonora, Mexico, placed their horses with each group of converted Christian Indians, as Kino and others expanded their efforts farther and farther north.

The Apaches ravaged and pillaged these little *visitas*, taking stock at will. They also plundered deep into Mexico, allegedly as far as Mexico City. Their goal was often to acquire well-bred and trained Spanish horses from the Mexican *estancias*. By trading these valuable horses northward to other tribes, the Apaches became the primary promoters of spreading Spanish horses throughout the West.

Over the years, horses escaped or were lost or stolen, and many became feral, roaming all over the West. Eventually, they numbered in the hundreds of thousands. They were closely related to—and indeed, basically the same breed as—the horses maintained by some of the Native American tribes. They spread across the plains, changing the lives of Native Americans and playing an important role as mounts for trappers, cowboys, pony express riders, homesteaders, and all those who settled the West.

Thousands of Spanish Mustangs were used as cow horses and for ranch work. When fighting Indians were riding Spanish Mustangs, the U.S. Cavalry opted to "fight fire with fire" and adopted hundreds of Spanish Mustangs. This was a necessary tactic, as the American-bred horses of the cavalry were no match for the Spanish-descended war ponies in the inhospitable and barren mountains and plains of the West.

Founding of a Breed

Spanish Mustangs lived on western plains until the early part of the twentieth century, when they came to the brink of extinction. Their salvation can be attributed primarily to Bob Brislawn of Oshoto, Wyoming. Born in the Palouse country in 1890, he made his own way at an early age, working on ranches, mining, or freighting. During his years in the West, his horses of choice were mustangs of Spanish descent. His respect for them was enormous, as they thrived on forage that could not support other breeds and never seemed to tire. He never hobbled or tied his Spanish Mustangs in camp because they stayed with him, much like pet dogs. He was impressed with their speed, agility, and, above all, their will to survive.

As Brislawn roamed the West, he realized the authentic Spanish Mustang was being methodically exterminated. Thus, he commenced his search for horses of essentially pure Spanish blood, desiring to preserve those few remaining. Vast herds

This striking roan stallion has a medicine hat spotting pattern, which was highly valued to the American Indians. *Many Ponies*

of mustangs still roamed the land, but in only a few of the most isolated herds could he find pure Spanish horses descended from the horses of the conquistadors. Brislawn dedicated his life to finding and preserving these last few remnants of the true Spanish Mustang.

He started his preservation project in 1925 and acquired two full brothers, Buckshot and Ute, which became his first foundation stallions. They were sired by a buckskin stallion named Monty, which was captured later in Utah in 1927, and out of a dam from the Ute Indian reservation. Brislawn's founding stock was chosen originally by type as well as history, as it had no known infusion of other breeds. He kept this stock on his ranch, breeding and culling out those offspring that did not throw "true." It took him from about 1925 until 1957 before he felt he had true Spanish Mustang representatives.

Brislawn bred his few mares for years with the assistance of his brother, Ferdinand, and was unaware that others shared his dream of preserving this unique, rare breed. The work spread, and in 1957 (long before the advent of the BLM Adopt-A-Horse program), a group headed up by Bob Brislawn incorporated the Spanish Mustang Registry (SMR), which became the first and oldest mustang registry in the country.

The first horses in the registry were from Native American tribes or ranches that could prove only pure Spanish horses had been bred there. Twenty animals were initially registered at that time.

As a registry, the SMR is now more than fifty years old, but the foundation stock started much longer ago than that. Today, with more than 3,700 registrations, Brislawn's goal is closer to being realized.

In Competition

The modern Spanish Mustang has lost none of the traits found in the Great Plains horses of yesteryear. Today's Spanish Mustangs retain their ancestors' stamina and ability to travel long distances without undue stress. Although conditioning is necessary for the longer rides, practically any range-raised Spanish Mustang can complete in a sanctioned novice ride of twenty-five miles in less than five hours with no undue stress.

Emmett Brislawn, son of the founder of the SMR, entered his sixteen-year-old stallion Yellow Fox (SMR 3) in the Bitterroot ride in 1966. Coming out of retirement, in which he had spent his days on the Cayuse Ranch with his herd of mares, this Cheyenne-bred buckskin stallion won championships for Heavyweight, All-Around Horse, and Best Out-of-State Horse, carrying more than two hundred pounds. This is not at all unusual when considering that Yellow Fox had been trained in his younger years to run down wild horses. They say that when he ran for the finish line, the old horse would throw up his head, still looking for the wild horses.

In 1989, Kim Kingsley, riding Chief Yellow Fox, a grandson of Yellow Fox, was awarded the coveted Jim Jones Award in the sanctioned American Endurance Ride Conference (AERC). Kingsley rode Chief Yellow Fox for 1,550 miles in one season, all in 50- or 100-mile rides and carried approximately 250 pounds the entire season. Chief Half Moon, another stallion owned by Kingsley, was second nationally with 1,250 endurance miles.

Martha Gresham of Auburn, Alabama, riding Cholla Bay, accumulated one thousand miles a year in AERC-sanctioned endurance rides for three consecutive years.

Steve Huffman of Mississippi, riding his Brislawn-bred gelding, Dutch Pete, has done extremely well in endurance rides. In the one-hundred-mile 1990 Tallahala Marathon, the team of Huffman and Dutch Pete tied with two Arabians with a time of 13 hours, 45 minutes—7 hours faster than the next two competitors, which were Arabians.

Huffman and Dutch Pete also qualified and rode in the National Championship Endurance Race series in 1991, earning seventh place nationally. They won the first of the three required races and

These Spanish Mustangs have straight head profiles and their muscle coupling is smooth. Many in the breed are gaited. *Jane K. Greenwood*

took the red ribbon in the second race by completing the one hundred miles in just over ten hours. Holding first place in the nation going into the third and final race, all was going well until a runaway horse crashed into Dutch Pete, injuring his shoulder and forcing him from the race. Regardless of the fact that only two of the three races were completed, Huffman and Dutch Pete still placed in the top ten horse-rider teams in the nation, winning over teams that had completed all three races!

More recently, Don Funk on his Spanish Mustang stallion, Geronimo's Warrior (SMR 2006), won first place in the National Mileage Championship in 2000 with 2,240 miles, and again in 2001 with 2,075 miles. They were top in the nation from 2000 through 2003 in mileage overall. Additionally, this team won the Jim Jones stallion award (stallion ridden with the most miles completed during the ride season) in 2000 through 2004. Winning first place in the Heavyweight division for the Midwest Region in both 2000 and 2001, they also took second place in the Heavyweight division for the Easyboot Award (completing fifty miles per day for a minimum of three consecutive days).

Characteristics

The Spanish Mustang is a medium-sized horse, ranging from 13.2 to 15 hands, with an average size of approximately 14.2 hands and with proportional weight. It is smooth muscled with a short back, rounded rump, and low-set tail. Its coupling is smooth and the overall appearance is of a well-balanced, smoothly built horse. The girth is deep, with well-laid-back shoulders and fairly pronounced withers.

The horse possesses the classic Spanish-type head with a straight or concave forehead and a convex nose, contrasting to the straight forehead and nose of most breeds. Ears are medium to short and usually notched or curved toward each other. The neck is well crested in mares and geldings, and heavily crested in mature stallions.

The chest is narrow but deep, with the front legs joining the chest in an "A" shape rather than straight across. Chestnuts are small or missing altogether, particularly on the rear legs. Feet are extremely sound with thick walls. Many Spanish Mustangs have what is typically known as a mule foot, which resists bruising due to the concave sole. Upper forelegs are long and cannons are short, with the cannon bones having a larger circumference than other breeds of comparable size and weight.

Characteristically having a long stride, many are gaited with a comfortable four-beat gait, such as the amble, running walk, or single foot. Some individuals are laterally gaited and do a credible paso gait, though without extreme knee action.

They are hardy animals and tend to be less prone to injury, particularly of the legs and feet, than other breeds. They have a different mentality than domesticated horses. They are not "push-button" horses and will not abide abuse. However, they bond well with their owners and, once bonded, become attached to that person.

Highly intelligent with an innate sense of self-preservation, they are not prone to putting themselves into any situation that may be dangerous. Compared to other domesticated breeds, they retain a great many of the instincts that helped them survive in the feral state.

Colors are extremely varied. Coat inheritance from early Spanish horses transmitted many colors and patterns, including dun, grullo, buckskin, appaloosa, overo, and sabino paint, as well as the more common colors of bay, chestnut, black, and white.

Some Spanish Mustangs have the rare and unique medicine hat spotting pattern, which is mostly white with color down the dorsal area, on the ears, and on top of the head that resembles a bonnet, and markings on the chest resembling a shield. Horses with the medicine hat pattern were prized in Native American culture, as the chest shield was believed to protect the "sacred" horses with that pattern. Medicine hat horses were used as ceremonial animals, buffalo runners, and warhorses. The spotted war bonnet is another similar pattern on a horse, as it is one step further in the removal of pigment than the medicine hat pattern. Horses with the spotted war bonnet pattern have only the "bonnet" and very little color, if any, on other areas of their body. All spots in both the medicine hat and war bonnet are roan—white hairs mixed with the predominant color.

Strengths: Environmental conditions must have certainly had a role in the development of these horses over the many generations in a feral state. Wild Spanish Mustangs developed in response to their environment, with nature culling out those less suited to the locale. Although the Spanish horse was not a feral animal when it arrived on American soil, once turned loose it managed not only to survive, but also to thrive in the New World, which attests to the versatility and strength of the breed. Genetic imperfections, if any, were culled by the most critical judge of all—Nature.

The end result is an extremely hardy and sturdy Spanish-type horse exhibiting the aptitude to perform—and perform well—in almost any equine field. The staying power and endurance of these Spanish Mustang descendants is legendary. They are demonstrating to the world the attributes they have inherited from their Spanish progenitors, as well as traits developed through centuries of the cruelest and most selective of breeding programs—that only the strongest survive in the wild.

Frank Hopkins, the renowned endurance rider in the latter part of the last century and a rider of Spanish Mustangs, is quoted as saying "You can't beat mustang intelligence in the entire equine race. These animals have had to shift for themselves for generations. They had to work out their own destiny or be destroyed. Those that survived were animals of superior intelligence." The legend of Frank Hopkins' historic three-thousand-mile ride on his Spanish Mustang stallion across the Arabian Desert in 1890 was the basis for the Disney movie *Hidalgo*.

Temperament: Spanish Mustangs are exceptionally different than other breeds in more than just physical appearance. They are intelligent and bold, even when strangers to new circumstances. Some, when ridden for the first time on the trail, have been known to lead others and then be used for work on trails the next day.

They are one of the strongest and most intelligent breeds, not "hot" like other high-strung horses can be. They can come up to whatever action level they need to be amazingly fast, yet as

Spanish Mustangs have well-crested necks and come in various colors. This one has some Appaloosa characteristics. *Free Spirit Spanish Mustangs*

fast as they come up to a higher level, their energy can go down. They are horses that do not waste energy: when they need it, it is there; when they do not, it is conserved. Perhaps this is one reason why they can go and go and go. Their endurance has astounded riders of other breeds. They can work six days a week in a stockyard herding cattle, or ride day after day in steep mountain terrain carrying a two-hundred-pound rider, and not lose condition or attitude.

That attitude is another reason why they stand apart from other breeds. Once they bond with someone, they will do just about anything asked of them and do everything they can to keep that person safe. There are instances of Spanish Mustangs standing their ground and attacking dogs, and even a bear, to keep their owners from harm. These horses do not always choose flight in the typical equine "fight or flight" response. More than one professional trainer has learned this after being chased from a round pen for putting too much pressure on a Spanish Mustang, or not adjusting the training methods to the horse's superior intelligence level. These horses cannot be bullied with training. Creating a bond with them works the best and makes them a partner for life, proving

them to be "All the horse you'll ever need—and then some!"

The Spanish Mustang is a "using horse" and is versatile and well equipped to compete in various fields. Though eager to acquaint the public with this fine breed, the primary aim of SMR is to ensure the retention of the qualities that allowed this distinctive horse to survive under adverse conditions over the centuries. It is with a great deal of pride that the breeders and owners of Spanish Mustangs can honestly state that the preservation of their horse has been accomplished without compromising the historical value or uniqueness of the breed.

Spanish Mustangs are now as they have always been, and the principal registry tenet is that there will be no attempt to crossbreed or otherwise change these magnificent animals. With the trend toward conforming breeds to satisfy various show standards, this rare breed is among the few that has not lost many of its characteristics due to more popular whims.

Now that its preservation has been ensured, the current focus is on the promotion of this special breed—one that changed the face of a continent.

Credit: Spanish Mustang Registry

STEENS MOUNTAIN KIGER

Steens Mountain Kiger claybank mare. *Annette Croul*

Steens Mountain Kiger Registry

26450 Horsell Road
Bend, Oregon 97701
www.kigers.com

Kiger horses (pronounced Kye´-grr) have become a phenomenon among mustang populations. Spanish characteristics, plus a heavy dose of dun factoring, have gained these horses nationwide attention. As a result, Kigers have stepped beyond mustang status to become a popular domestic breed. Noted for their intelligence and stamina, they are strikingly Spanish in phenotype, and it is believed that their ancestry dates back to the conquistadors who brought Spanish horses with them to the New World.

Discovered by the Bureau of Land Management (BLM) in 1977, these wild horses were found on the high desert of southeastern Oregon. Rumors had circulated for years in Oregon about the line-backed mustangs called "Oreanas" and their similarity to Spanish horses. Government officials agreed that here was a special horse. Individuals in the herd were strikingly similar in color and conformation, and had distinct dun markings (stripes on legs, for example). For preservation's sake, they moved the small band of horses to the north end of Steens Mountain near Kiger Gorge, from where the breed takes its name. This group of horses became pivotal to the Kiger program.

The majority of these horses, around nineteen, were placed at what today is called Kiger Herd

Management Area (HMA) on Steens Mountain. At the time, this area's known capacity was twenty to thirty head, so it is likely it was cleared of previous livestock. The known exceptions were two resident mares that were retained.

The value of the band was that its type was so distinctly Spanish. The herd's link to ancient Spanish bloodlines was proven in the 1990s, when blood testing was performed by Dr. Gus Cothran, the renowned equine geneticist. The DNA clearly proved the horses had a strong Spanish connection: while genetically diverse, they had a higher degree of relatedness to Spanish domestic breeds than most other wild populations.

History

In 1979, the small band of Spanish-looking horses were moved to two separate areas on Steens Mountain—Kiger HMA and Riddle Mountain, just a few miles east of Kiger HMA. It was decided they would be grouped and managed differently in each area according to distinct characteristics, with the dun and grullo colors being in one group, while dorsal stripes and dark borders on the ears were in another. The BLM retained as much as possible the dun and grullo coloring of the horse, but did allow a margin for white markings, off coloration, and a variety in body color.

The BLM modified its plans in the late 1980s to create uniformity between the Kiger and Riddle areas. Many horses that had non-dun coloration or white markings, or were dun in phenotype but varied in color genotype, were made available to the public. Horses of non-conforming colors have continued to surface in the herds occasionally and are also made available at adoptions. When these horses are offered for adoption, they are represented as Kiger/Riddle livestock by the government.

Steens Mountain Kigers, such as this dun gelding, are not only durable mounts, but also affectionate and trustworthy.
Annette Croul

Steens Mountain Kiger dun mare with three-week-old filly. *Annette Croul*

Therefore, the Steens Mountain Kiger Registry accepts any color horse, as long as it can be traced to one of these two herds.

In 1988, two dun mares from the nearby Sheepshead HMA were added to the population at Kiger HMA. BLM officials have denied adding any other horses to the Kiger or Riddle herds since then. Thus these horses have been restricted from any additional outside types.

In the opinion of the Steens Mountain Kiger Registry, this management history does not justify the claim that Kigers "come from all over." Horses from Sand Springs, Warm Springs, Potholes, Palomino Butte, and even from Nevada and Utah have been labeled "Kigers," but the Steens Mountain Kiger Registry considers them to be from their respective areas and not qualified for its registry. The Burns District BLM stated that there are no future plans to add outside horses to the Kiger herds.

By limiting registration to horses directly connected to the Kiger or Riddle Mountain HMAs, the Steens Mountain Kiger Registry has incorporated a closed studbook, believing it is the only way to preserve the integrity of the Kiger breed.

Today, wild Kigers continue to be protected on both these HMAs in southeastern Oregon. Kiger HMA covers nearly 37,000 acres and has an Appropriate Management Level of fifty-one to eighty-two horses, while Riddle Mountain contains nearly 28,000 acres and has an Appropriate Management of thirty-three to fifty-six horses. When populations exceed the levels, wild Kigers are gathered and offered for adoption. This event generally occurs every four years, depending on range conditions, predators, and the reproduction rate of the wild horses.

The competition is fierce for wild Kiger adoptions. For this reason alone, more breeders are raising Kigers on private farms and ranches.

Domestic Kigers have the advantage of being readily available as well as being accustomed to human contact.

The BLM has made significant progress in the management of the wild horse herds in Oregon. Until recently, adoptable Kiger mustangs have been in short supply. There were less than 20 horses at the first Kiger adoptions, whereas in 2007 there were more than 160. The demand was at its highest in 1995, when 1,358 people were vying to adopt only 83 available Kigers. Thanks to outside pressure from land interest groups, however, and the soon-to-be implemented use of birth control for feral Kiger populations, it is anticipated that the numbers of horses available for adoption will again return to a level where demand exceeds the supply. A current rough estimate of Kigers in the general population is still well under 2,500.

Registry

Since the Steens Mountain Kiger Registry's inception in 1996, more than eight hundred horses have been registered. Kigers are now represented in thirty-one states, as well as overseas.

To qualify for registration, a horse must originate from one of two herds on Steens Mountain in Oregon, or be the descendant of horses that qualify. Horses that are not from either the Kiger or Riddle Mountain HMAs, or domestic-raised horses that do not have ancestors from those areas, are not accepted. There is, however, a half-Kiger division in the registry for horses with one qualifying parent. The Steens Mountain Kiger Registry recommends that breeders have DNA parentage testing performed on their Kigers.

The breeding goal is to achieve a balanced using horse that retains the Spanish appearance.

Steens Mountain Kiger claybank stallion. The phenotype is that of a quality Spanish horse. *Annette Croul*

Majestic red dun stallion with refined head and vibrant color. *Rancho Bayo*

This should be accomplished by exclusively using stock originating from Kiger or Riddle Mountain HMAs and/or direct descendants. While some have embraced other dun mustangs as "Kigers," the government itself is specific on the subject. The BLM states that the name "Kiger Mustang" is given only to the horses maintained on the two designated HMAs in southeastern Oregon. Conscientious breeders maintain that integrity.

In a general sense, the term "Kiger Mustang" is used to describe a government-managed wild Kiger, while "Kiger Horse" is applied to one bred in captivity and is a descendent of horses from those areas. The entire Steens Mountain Kiger Registry population is inclusively known as Steens Mountain Kigers.

Although there is pride in owning a mustang, most breeders own the captive-bred Kiger Horses, which are not mustangs. The BLM states that horses not born in a feral environment are not mustangs. As of 2001, only 26 percent of the horses registered in the Steens Mountain Kiger Registry are freeze-branded horses. The majority have been born and raised in captivity.

Life With Kigers

Avid Kiger breeder Bettye Roberts states in an interview what true Kiger temperament is like:

"I'm a lifelong horse person. I have owned everything from Shetlands to drafts . . . but when I got my first Kigers, I immediately noticed a difference in how they think compared to other horses. Maybe it's only that they are more expressive. . . . They seem to analyze situations better, they know how to keep themselves out of trouble better, and most of them have a can-do attitude. Of course in some of them, as with any mustang, the survival instincts are so strong that you don't always get that kind of receptivity . . . but if you've got a good one, you know it. This kind of horse will go to the mat for you. It's the reason I will never go back to [other horses]. These Kigers are not only intelligent, they are personable, sometimes phenomenally so. . . .

"The receptive ones kind of spoil you, and then you have the expectation that they should all be that sharp, [but] they are not. In truth, sometimes you have one that will go the 'other way.' As near as I can tell, it's all about how they decide to use their inherited survival mechanisms. Fortunately, most Kigers are curious and give you the benefit of the doubt. They are a social breed, and many of them will extend their society to include their owners. In some cases, that would be an understatement.

"They will soak their own hay if it is stemmy. They'll steal your car keys right out of your pocket if you aren't careful. They aren't big on being ignored. . . . One mare showed up on my back porch to be cared for when injured. I had two Kiger geldings run up from the field to protect a girl who was thrown to the ground by another [breed of] horse; they chased away the curious [horses], and never left her side until help arrived.

"And then there was my Kiger gelding, who followed me out to pasture, saw me digging a hole, and started digging, too . . . and subsequently stomped the nest of snakes that I had unintentionally uncovered. While I am sure that other breeds have representatives in them that react similarly, I haven't seen it to the frequency and the extent that I've seen in the Kigers. . . . They are very unpretentious horses. While I've known a few of them that lacked confidence, most of them are the other way around. They just assume that they *can*.

"Now as a breed, they aren't all a piece of cake . . . . It's all because they *think for themselves*. But when that intelligence gets channeled in the right direction, you can end up with a horse that you'll never part with, a horse with good common sense and a ton of try.

"I think that is what keeps people interested in the Kiger breed. It certainly isn't because they can run faster or jump higher, because they can't. Nature didn't make them to excel at any specific athletic task; nature honed them for survival. And survival requires just a few things, namely, a conservative metabolism, the ability to sprint, and a good brain. I had owned horses for forty-five years before I got into Kigers, but observing them was a completely new experience. Just when I thought I knew a lot about horses, I found out I didn't know so much after all.

"Thanks to coloration and a lot of mane and tail, they have a visual attraction. But then you get one and find out that there is so much more underneath. As a breed they probably have a couple of decades to go yet in terms of refinement. And they are not the horse to have if you are planning on competing in timed events. But the right Kiger can be perfect for the average owner who wants a relationship with [his or her] horse."

Kigers in the Public Eye

The Steens Mountain Kiger Registry's best-known son is Donner of Steens Mountain. He was purchased by DreamWorks SKG to be used as a representative and model for the 2002 animated film, *Spirit: Stallion of the Cimarron*.

Kiger Sundance was a model for one of the No More Nightmares plush animals, and Kiger Hawk's image graced the packaging of Equerry's, Inc., products.

The first horse admitted to the Steens Mountain Kiger Registry studbook, the notable Steens Kiger, sired both Donner and Sundance. His photo is easily recognized worldwide, as he is an icon of the breed. "He is truly one of the most majestic horses I have ever seen," one devotee remarked. "His disposition, willingness, versatility, conformation, beauty, and brains place him above most."

The Kiger breed has also been well represented by such stallions as Kiger Cougar, a reining horse exhibited at the 1992 World Championship Snaffle Bit Futurity in Reno, Nevada, by Bobby Ingersoll. In 2006, Bobby Elliott competed against two hundred Quarter Horses on the Kiger stallion, Spirit of Casey Tibbs.

The Associated Press surprised the public in 1999 with an article about that year's wild Kiger adoption held in Burns, Oregon. The record sum of $19,000 was paid to adopt a Kiger mustang filly, the highest amount ever paid to adopt a mustang of any type or strain. Another horse adopted in that year, Goodfield's Kiger Sombra, has represented the Kiger breed annually at the Kentucky Horse Park.

Kigers have been featured in media shows on the Discovery Channel, Public Broadcasting Service (PBS), and Horseworld, as well as Mamba Productions of Europe. Three Kigers have

Proud claybank stallion. Kigers are ideally short coupled, but not heavily muscled. *Bettye Roberts*

participated in the Tevis Cup, a one-day, 100-hundred-mile race held annually in California that is probably the most popular U. S. endurance event.

Standards

The domestic Kiger should be bred for conformation, disposition, and color, in that order. The phenotype is that of a Spanish horse.

Breeders of dun-factored horses are encouraged to concentrate on producing horses with dun factor, but the horses that do not possess this color are not penalized. Currently 70 percent of Kigers are dun, but they can also be other colors, including bay, grullo, red dun, claybank, gray, and black.

The typical zebra-type stripes usually associated with dun coloring fits almost like hand and glove with Kigers. Many have these types of stripes, or barring, on their legs as well as a dorsal stripe, shoulder stripe, and dark ear trim. Manes and tails can be bi-colored. Some Kigers have white markings, but excessive white is discouraged.

The head profile is straight or slightly convex, not dished. Kigers have hook-shaped ears.

The neck is set rather low to the shoulder and is never a "pencil," or thin, neck. Spanish breeds have a thicker neck and ideally with more arch than that of a Quarter Horse.

Kigers have abundant manes and tails. They have short cannons and heavy-walled hooves, which are exceptionally rugged and rarely need shoes.

Ideally, the hindquarters should be well rounded and squarely set. Their tail set is low. Kigers are preferably short-coupled, but not heavily muscled. While most Kigers exhibit an ambling trot, the Kiger is not a gaited breed.

Kigers range from 13.3 to 16 hands, with an average height of 14.3 hands. Owner/breeder preference ranges from the small Sorraia (pronounced sore-eye´-a) types of Kigers—considered by some to represent the horses of antiquity—to a taller, more-modern Kiger suited for dressage.

Kigers are not timed-event horses, generally lacking the speed necessary to compete with horses bred for such events. They are agile and suitable for general-purpose ranch work, and a few rare individuals have shown enough cow sense to compete on a world level. Kigers have also been used for driving, packing, endurance riding, and trail.

In temperament, Kigers are known for their trainability, with stallions and geldings generally proving to be more tractable than mares. As with all mustangs, trust issues must be overcome first when working with horses that have been born in the wild. Kigers have been proven not only to be durable mounts, but also affectionate and trustworthy companions.

Steens Mountain Kigers are attempting to secure a position within the mainstream of equine society while at the same time preserving their mustang heritage. More people are beginning to ride and use Kigers, discovering the benefits of owning horses that offer the best of both worlds—horses with style, intelligence, and good temperament complemented by the mustang hardiness. Most individuals who purchase a Kiger add another one to their barn shortly thereafter. This is a testament to the nature of the Kiger.

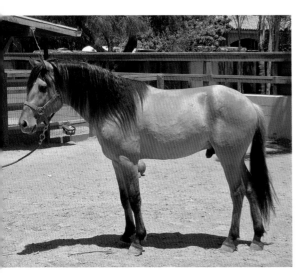

This stallion is the taller, more modern type of Kiger with elegant neck, head, and good bone. *Annette Croul*

Credit: Steens Mountain Kiger Registry

SULPHUR SPRINGS HORSE

The barring on this Sulphur Springs stallion is unmistakable, including the rump and possible shadowing on the neck.
Ken Benefril

SulphurSprings Horse Registry, Inc.
1245 South 6300 West
Cedar City, Utah 84720
www.sulphurspringshorseregistry.com

In the southwest corner of Utah lies a mountain range that is home to a special wild horse. Descended from ancient Iberian horses brought from Spain, they have remained in the Mountain Home Range area, where they managed to survive for two centuries. While the large herds of wild horses in the valleys and lower foothills were caught or killed off, the wild horses of the Mountain Home Range remained isolated and free. They apparently did not mix extensively with the domestic horses in the valleys and managed to escape all attempts to capture them. Mustangers were not able to catch them because of the rocky terrain and heavy stands of pinyon-juniper woodlands on the range.

The Bureau of Land Management (BLM) recognized the special characteristics of the wild horses and named them after the Sulphur Springs area from which they came, located in the Mountain Home Range, the north half of the Herd Management Area (HMA), where it regulates the herd.

Sulphurs are a small population of horses, the last remnant group of Southern California Spanish horses. Spanish horses were considered to be the finest horses in the world at the time of the conquest, and they left a living legacy in these tough, hardy, extremely beautiful horses of the Sulphur Spring herd.

As noted equine expert Dr. Gus Cothran states, "What I can tell you is that the Sulphur horses have the highest similarity to Spanish-type horses of any wild horse population in the U.S. that I have tested. There is more to learn, but they definitely have Spanish ancestry and possibly are primarily derived from Spanish horses."

History

Archaeological evidence in the Iberian Peninsula of modern-day Spain and Portugal indicates that the origin of the Spanish horse dates back to at least 25,000 BC in the form of its primitive ancestor, the Sorraia breed. The oldest reference to the horse in Portugal is its portrayal in the cave paintings and engravings of Escorial, in the Alentejo area. These show the convex head and arched neck of the true Iberian horse, rather than the pony-like sketches of the Lascaux cave paintings in France.

The Sorraia remained isolated for several millennia in the southern part of Iberia in the Alentejo and Andalusian regions, where modern Portugal and Spain are now. Around 3000 BC, Iberian tribes from North Africa invaded the peninsula, which would later be named after them, and there was an influx of oriental horse breeds from Libya, Egypt, and Syria.

The warriors of the Iberian Peninsula were superior horsemen. In historic times, it is well documented that the Iberian cavalry had achieved fame as an effective and fearless foe, with much of its success due to its fine mounts. The cavalry's warfare consisted of individual horse charges with fast starts, stops, and pirouettes, followed by retreats and renewed attacks. It was a form of riding made possible by the use of stirrups, curb bits, and incredibly agile horses. In further invasions, the Carthaginians and Romans recognized the superiority of the Iberian horses and horsemanship. This acknowledgment led the Romans to adopt the Iberian equestrian style of warfare and set up stud farms in the conquered Iberian territories. Most of the horses for these studs came from the present-day Andalusian region.

In 711 AD, Moorish Muslims invaded the Iberian Peninsula, at the time being ruled by Visigoths. In varying degrees, the Muslims occupied the peninsula until the end of the fifteenth century. These people brought some of their native Berber (or Barb) horses with them, which were interbred with the Iberian horses. The exchange of Barb and Iberian blood was mutually beneficial and produced many similarities between the two breeds.

During the almost eight hundred years for which Spain and Portugal were in constant war with the Moors, horses and horsemanship had become finely attuned to the war exercises. By the seventeenth century, the Iberian warhorse—or Jennet, as it was beginning to be called—had become important not only in the battlefield, but also in the riding academies founded in France, Germany, Italy, and Austria. The turbulent history of the Iberian Peninsula and the later explorations of the seagoing Spaniards had much to do with the distribution of the Spanish horse to all parts of the then-known world.

No breed has had more influence on the modern horse than the Iberian horse. Welsh Mountain Ponies, Lipizzaner, German, Danish, and Dutch Warmbloods, Irish Connemara Ponies, Hackney, Cleveland Bay, Kladruber, Peruvian Paso, and even the American Quarter Horse—all find their roots in the Iberian horse. Certainly, that Iberian blood lives on today in the Sulphurs.

Columbus brought Iberian-type horses on his voyages, and their hardiness helped them withstand the rigors and poor conditions of the journey better than others. Every ship arriving to the New World carried some of Spain's choice breeding stock, including their superb Iberian warhorses. The conquistadors introduced and dispersed them throughout the New World. Herman Cortes proclaimed, "After God, we owed our victory to the horses." Spanish horses were eventually used in almost every facet of progress in North America.

Trade caravans were established along the Old Spanish Trail that linked Los Angeles, California, to Santa Fe, New Mexico. From 1830 to 1855, these routes became the most notorious for horse thievery in the history of the Southwest. Virtually thousands of Spanish horses were driven across the Old Spanish Trail into Utah, where they escaped or were purchased or stolen during numerous raids by Ute Chief Walkara. Many of these horses escaped into the mountains of southwestern Utah, where they survived on their own.

BLM and the Sulphur Herd

Many of the wild horses in the western states were killed or captured before the U. S. Congress passed legislation in 1971 to protect, manage, and control wild horses and burros on public lands. The Wild Free-Roaming Horse and Burro Act declared these animals to be "living symbols of the historic and pioneer spirit of the West." Congress further declared that "wild free-roaming horses and burros shall be protected from capture, branding, harassment, or death" and that they were "an integral part of the natural system of the public lands." BLM regulations now required that wild horses and burros be considered along with other resource values within the area.

The BLM now maintains and manages wild horses and burros in HMAs. In the ten states in which the BLM manages horses, there are 270 herd areas. In Utah, about 3,600 horses are found among twenty-three different herds scattered across the state.

The Sulphur herd roams a vast, unpopulated region of alternating high desert basins and expansive mountain ranges. In some spots, the range rises to nearly ten thousand feet in elevation. Their home, the Needle Range, is a starkly beautiful mountain block that lies about forty-five miles west of Milford, Utah, along the Nevada state line.

Sulphur horses are rounded up every few years, depending on the number of horses on the HMA. The BLM likes to maintain a population of around two hundred to three hundred head. They turn back horses that exhibit Iberian traits and markings, attempting to preserve the bloodline.

None of the other herds are as distinctive as those in the Sulphur HMA. It is evident the Sulphurs have an influence from the ancient Iberian horse in their genetic makeup. This is expressed by the prominence of their primitive dun factor coloration, their ability to survive in a harsh environment, and their willingness to inhabit such a rocky, mountainous area as the Mountain Home Range.

Over the years, the Sulphur herds bred with escaped ranch livestock, but most still retain many of the Spanish Barb traits. Like the original Colonial Spanish horse of America, which had displayed some characteristics of the extinct wild Tarpan horse, the Sulphur horses exhibit many of those ancient traits. Dominant colors include dun, buckskin, and grullo. Physical characteristics include ears that curve in like a bird beak, dorsal stripe, bi-colored mane and tail, tiger-striped legs, and occasional chest barring. Sulphurs are deep-bodied, but narrow-chested, and have Iberian-type heads.

Remoteness and seclusion preserved this large herd of Spanish-type horses on the Mountain Home Range. There is historical importance for these Spanish horses, which have become increasingly rare, and they are subsequently in need of conservation. The horse currently in Spain, through centuries of divergent selection, is distinct from America's Colonial Spanish horse, which is more old-type Iberian. The result is that these New World remnants are important to overall conservation since their varieties are closer in type to the historic horse of the Spanish Golden

Age than are the current horses in the Iberia Peninsula.

"Colonial Spanish horses are of great historic importance in the New World," states Dr. Phillip Sponenberg, DVM, PhD. "These horses are a direct remnant of the horses of the Golden Age of Spain, which type is now mostly or wholly extinct in Spain. The Colonial Spanish horses are therefore a treasure chest of genetic wealth from a time long gone. In addition, they are capable and durable mounts for a wide variety of equine pursuits, and their abilities [had] been vastly undervalued for most of the 1900s."

The Portuguese are interested in doing more genetic testing, and local genetic testing is also in progress. Sulphurs are genetically almost identical to the Chilean Criollo, the oldest and purest of the Criollo breeds. Their highest individual similarity values also include the Paso Fino. Genetic studies done on the Sulphur mitochondrial DNA (mtDNA) pattern has shown that they may in fact be an ancestral horse breed.

Genetically, Sulphurs are completely different from any other herd in the United States. Their DNA blood markers show that not only do they cluster within the Iberian breeds, but also their mtDNA shows the Sulphur Iberian pattern is carried in every horse tested in the Sulphur herd. This is sufficient evidence of their Spanish roots. They all seem to carry that one pattern, with no other outside pattern having been found yet, which is extremely significant, once again pointing to their primitiveness. They may prove to be an intact herd of ancestral horses, a genetic type that represents the ancestral wild populations.

These horses may be the last true wild Spanish Mustangs left, and their future should be protected. If they are not protected, they could become extinct and the bloodline could be lost forever.

Registry

In 1998, the Sulphur Horse Registry (now the SulphurSprings Horse Registry) began to keep track of Sulphur horses in private hands. All Sulphur horses either captured in the Sulphur HMA or descended from those horses are eligible for registration regardless of sex, color, markings, or type. Adopted wild horses from the BLM must have documentation stating that they were from the Sulphur range. The registry works with the BLM at adoptions to support the horses and answer questions that potential owners may have. Roundups occur whenever herd numbers exceed the allotted herd size of two hundred to three hundred head on the HMA. The ones that exhibit Iberian traits, markings, and color are turned back to the range.

There also is an Appendix division for Sulphur crosses. Horses registered must have a direct connection with the Sulphur horses—either they were born on the HMA or they are the offspring of horses from there. As of 2008, there were 241 registered horses, but the registry is growing. People from all around the world are starting to recognize the breed.

Characteristics

While it is the SulphurSprings Horse Registry's stance not to tell breeders how they should breed, there is a need to breed for the Colonial Spanish type found in the Sulphur herd, which is vitally important as there are differences in type.

These horses are of an ancient breed that does not conform to many of the standards used by registries preserving western horse breeds based on short sprinter-type conformation. Bred for beauty and endurance, they are a much more physically variable breed than the more homozygous modern western horse breeds. Yet the distinctive type of these horses sets them apart from other breeds and other origins.

Size and Weight: Generally, it is a medium-sized horse, although size is increasing with improved nutrition and some selection among breeders. The usual height is 14.2 to 15.2 hands. Some exceptional horses are up to 16 hands high or slightly more. Weight varies with height, but most are around 800 to 900 pounds.

Head: The head is of medium length, with a tendency to be long and fairly narrow with a

Young, nice-looking stallion with leg barring and bi-colored mane and tail. Some Sulphurs have long, dense manes and tails.
Ken Benefril

convex profile. Forehead is broad, but face and muzzle are narrow from a frontal view.

Ears: Fairly long and of medium shape, the ears tend to hook toward each other at the tip.

Eyes: The eyes are elliptic and almond-shaped.

Muzzle: The muzzle is refined and small. The mouth is shallow and the lips firm. From the side, the upper lip is usually longer than the lower one, although the teeth meet evenly. Nostrils are usually small and crescent shaped when the horse is resting and can close tightly, but do flare with alertness or exertion. Many horses wear a 4-inch-wide bit, and some have "mustaches." Many of the most primitively marked horses will show a lighter muzzle or "mealy nose." Parrot mouth is rarely seen in the Sulphur, but since it may cause grazing problems and inefficient chewing and is highly inheritable, such animals should be seriously penalized at halter, especially if they are breeding stock.

An unusual note is that the Sulphur horse produces a strange, rattling type of snort when the animal confronts a questionable situation or object. This sound has been referred to as having "rollers in the nose," and is unlike the snort of most other types of horses. This sound is part of the horse's herd behavior and is used to alert other herd members to possible danger. Since this is a more natural breed than the "manmade" ones, its herd behaviors, such as this one, are often more pronounced.

Neck: The neck is comparatively long and flexible.

Mane and Tail: Both may be long and often quite dense; some have distinct bi-coloring. Tails typically are not raised when animated, as with Arabians, but are low set.

Shoulder: The long, well angulated shoulders have smooth muscling. The forward point of the shoulder is prominent. The horse is often heavier on the forequarters than the hindquarters.

Chest: The chest is narrow, but deep, with the front legs leaving the body fairly close together. There is a well-defined inverted "V" shape between the front legs. The chest is well muscled, but not bulgy, and never broad and flat. It is deeper from the side view and usually accounts for about half of the height of the horse from the ground to the withers.

Barrel: The barrel is slightly tapering with well-sprung ribs. When looking at the horse from the front, the barrel should be plainly visible on both sides. The heart girth is deep (as opposed to wide) with good heart and lung space in front of a full abdomen. The horse is short coupled, and the underline is longer than the topline. The flank space behind the ribs is short.

Legs: They are rather long with long cannon bones, but strong and of medium-dense bone. Smooth muscling carries down well into the knees and hocks. They are uniquely flexible with stretchy but strong tendons, which are well defined from the bone. The joints also allow great flexibility of motion and are rather large. The rear legs may be set slightly under the body, allowing the forward reach of the hind stride to land just beneath the rider's stirrup. The hind legs are straight to slightly turned out. The pasterns are of medium length and sloping under a strong fetlock. The hind pasterns may be somewhat shorter and straighter than the front, but all are long and angular enough to give a springy, smooth ride. The angle should be approximately the same as the shoulder and hoof wall.

The chestnuts (especially rear ones) and ergots are small or missing altogether.

Hooves: They are small and upright rather than flat, but adequate for the horse's size and body weight. Most wear 00 or 0 shoes. They are generally more egg-shaped than round with a distinct point at the toe, especially on the hind feet. The hooves are hard and dense, with many never requiring shoeing. Their circumference is smaller at the coronary band than at the ground surface. Hoof color may be black, gray, white, or striped (laminated).

Back: Prominent withers and a medium-long, straight back are present in this breed.

Hindquarters: The horse has sloping, rafter-shaped hips that do not drop steeply. The muscling is characteristically long and tapering, even in the heavily muscled individuals, rather than the short

and bunchy muscling characteristic of bulldog-like stock and draft breeds.

Gait: Long, fluent strides mark the breed's gait, which has considerable knee action due to the longer cannon bones. The horse flexes easily at the poll and has a natural ability to collect itself. Many of the horses have gaits other than the usual trot of most breeds, which can include a running walk, single foot, amble, pace, and the paso gaits of other more southerly Spanish strains, such as the Peruvian Paso and Paso Fino. It is important to note that these gaits refer to the pattern of the footfall and not to any sideward, or lateral, tendency of the path of the foot. While both are typical of some of the Paso breeds, only the pattern of footfalls is the actual gait.

Color and Coat Type: Dorsal stripe, tiger-striped legs, and occasional chest barring are desirable markings for the horse to have. There are minimal variations for color, and this restricted variation should be maintained. Dominant colors include dun, buckskin, and grullo. Other colors found throughout the region include bay, black, sorrel, palomino, and various roans, including blue, red, strawberry, etc. Occasionally some can be found with curly coats, manes, and tails.

Temperament: Mellow and dependable, they settle in nicely after adoption once they learn to trust their new owners. Trust is everything to them. Once that is established, they give their all.

They are quite hardy. Heat and humidity do not seem to bother them too much. They are easy keepers, for the most part. Their hooves are hard and do not have to be shod for normal riding.

Says Naylene Nield, president of the Sulphur Spring Horse Registry, "I find them to be very smart and easy to teach, as they are very eager to learn and willing to please. They are very mellow and affectionate toward people as well as each other. They are constantly grooming each other and playing together to keep themselves occupied in between feedings. You would think they were all very young when you watch them as they enjoy teasing and romping and jumping around [like] young foals."

Sulphurs have longer cannon bones; withers are typically prominent.
Ken Benefril

Nield observes that Suphurs, as well as most mustangs, are a hearty animal. They have a wonderfully pleasant disposition and temperament and are generally loving and passionate toward their owners. Once someone has earned their trust, they are loyal and affectionate, usually much more so than other horses. They are surefooted and strong, and they love riding in the mountains and on trails. As such, they would make great prospects for endurance horses.

"I have watched other owners with their Sulphur Springs horses in various shows and competitions and I am not surprised when I see them take home first- and second-place ribbons regularly," Nield says. "I have seen these horses perform very well in just about every area of show and competition." The accomplishments they have achieved are impressive. They also make good trail-riding mounts due to their surefootedness. "They constantly remind me as to the reasons that I chose to have these wonderful horses as my loyal companions and friends." For an all-around good horse, they are the best.

Ken Benefiel, vice president of the registry, says, "I have been astounded by how smart they are and how fast they learn. They are not aggressive towards people or other horses, for the most part. . . . I learn something new from them every day . . . they like as much attention as I can give. We show one of our mares at the Kansas Equifest every year, and people really make a fuss over her and cannot believe that she is a wild mustang. [Sulphurs] can hold up to weather, disease, terrain, and they are capable of traveling long distances with little effect on their well being."

Suphur Spring horses are a great genetic resource from a time long ago and need to be preserved for the future. Once they are gone, there is no replacement.

Credit: SulphurSprings Horse Registry; Ron Roubidoux, Mantua, Utah; Vickie Ives, Karma Farms, Marshall, Texas; Dr. Gus Cothran; Dr. D. Phillip Sponenberg; and Ken Benefiel, Burrton, Kansas

PART 2

RIDING HORSES OF DISTINCTION

STARS OF THE PLEASURE BREEDS

These are light riding horses possessing outstanding traits that even a novice is able to pick out. They are spectacular and unique individuals, which display special features and discriminating characteristics particular only to them. They may have a distinctive coat or coat color. Some have certain head properties or a tail carriage that is exclusively theirs. Others have a flashy presence, displaying their own kind of animated glitz and glamour.

They project a special flare and pizzazz that is all their own. Belonging in the spotlight, they create that "Hey, look at me!" impression. Some sparkle in the show ring, some prance in parades, but all have noticeably visual attributes that allow them to stand out from other light breeds. Their very appearance draws attention and sets them apart from other equines. No other horses are quite like them.

They are horses of distinction.

AKHAL-TEKE

The Akhal-Teke's lithe athleticism can be compared to a greyhound's. *Shah'Zadeh Akhal-Tekes*

The Akhal-Teke Society of America, Inc.
P.O. Box 207
Sanford, North Carolina 27331
www.akhaltekesocietyofamerica.com

The magnificent Akhal-Teke (pronounced ah call tek ee) comes to us intact in all its glory after 10,000 generations of breeding on the central Asian steppes. Since the earliest time of horse domestication, this "Golden Horse" of central Asia has been prized before all other breeds. Bejeweled and decorated in gold and silk, it was ridden into battle by nomads and emperors and buried with honor in the tombs of kings, shamans, and warriors. In Chinese legends, it was known as the "Heavenly Horse" because of the unusually distinctive radiance in its coat. The Han Chinese felt it well worth 80,000 soldiers to obtain just twenty of these brilliant horses, such was its reputation.

The Akhal-Teke retains every quality of endurance, speed, economy, intelligence, and beauty that has been so prized throughout the centuries by so many different societies. Being of such an ancient lineage and due to its geographical isolation (precluding any infusions of pony or draft blood), the Akhal-Teke retains the features of its earliest ancestors.

In a fast-paced world where a horse is often thought to be little more than a living vehicle or a piece of sports equipment, the Akhal-Teke offers a refreshing change.

History

Akhal-Tekes originated in southern Turkmenistan as the chief mounts of Turkmen warriors. At the Akhal oasis, a distance from the main trade routes, the Teke tribe first bred them. Living in the desert, Akhal-Teke horses developed endless stamina and the ability to withstand extremes in temperature and deprivation.

Five successive empires—the Scythians, Parthians, Ywati, Huns, and Turkmen—invaded the area, laying waste to everything before them, yet they carefully preserved these magnificent horses and trained them with the utmost care. In time, the beautiful Akhal-Teke became the central figure in every culture into whose hands it came.

There were excellent reasons for the horse's many stewards to carefully preserve it. No other horse could run faster or travel greater distances on such little, or even total lack of, food and water for days on end, nor was there a horse more intelligent or more devoted to its rider. It was also the only horse that had the glittering colors that helped earn it the nickname "Heavenly Horse."

For three millennia, the Turkmen bred their horses to be more than transportation and included them as a part of their families. Their horses lived tied to their tents and were ridden often in search of a living. The reactions of Akhal-Tekes were used for testing would-be suitors for the daughters of a family. They were hand-fed by the entire family and were included in the count of the family's wealth.

Thus, the Akhal-Teke became sensitive, sensible, and intelligent, learning quickly and with much enthusiasm. It is a horse that seeks to bond with a person of its own, forming a lasting partnership. While most Tekes are friendly to everyone, they tend to respond best to their regular rider, often performing better for "their" person than for a casual rider, even one with better skills. One may start out owning an Akhal-Teke, but in the end, this horse will own the owner. Memories of a first experience with them remain for a lifetime.

Akhal-Tekes glide along effortlessly in the breed's characteristic movement. *Shah'Zadeh Akhal-Tekes*

Today, the role of a Teke has changed from war horse to sport horse, and its unique character suits it well for a variety of disciplines. Akhal-Tekes have won Olympic gold and silver medals in dressage and have been jumping champions throughout Europe.

In Germany, Akhal-Tekes are used for fox hunting and compete in reining. In Russia they are used in youth rodeos. Akhal-Tekes of Canada are making their mark in the sport of Competitive Trail where their legendary fearlessness and trust in the rider makes them the perfect team player. In the United States they are used for eventing, jumping, ranch work and endurance riding.

All over the world, Akhal-Tekes show their ancient prepotency through their purebred and part-bred foals with their exceptional ability, strength, soundness, and beauty. The United States is fortunate to have an ever-increasing number of breeders dedicated to preserving the best of this ancient and valuable horse. Nowadays, it is possible to see examples of the marvelous Teke all across the country in competitions and on breeding farms. Best of all, with a wide choice of superior stallions available at reasonable fees, Teke blood is now available to everyone.

Registry

The Akhal-Teke Society of America oversees two registries: the Akhal-Teke Purebred Registry and the Akhal-Teke Sport Horse Registry for crosses with one half or more Akhal-Teke blood. The Akhal-Teke Sport Horse Registry is not for the creation of a new breed, but to record sport horses whose breeders have utilized the Akhal-Teke gene pool in their bloodlines. Akhal-Tekes are registered on the basis of parentage only.

Characteristics

The Akhal-Teke is a true desert-bred horse with a light, elegant build and distinctive conformation. Its body is long, lean, and typically narrow through the chest, making for an extremely comfortable ride. A characteristic feature is the sparse, short mane and forelock and the absence of feather on the legs.

Perhaps the most amazing feature of the Akhal-Teke is that its coat literally glows like shining metal. Its hair has a unique structure that refracts light, providing a dazzling display of colors from blazing palomino to electric black with glittering gold as the prevailing color.

If the Akhal-Teke was bred over the centuries for any particular purpose, it was to get riders between waterholes quickly and comfortably. Typically these waterholes were 80 miles or farther apart from each other. This use resulted in a comfortable, swift, sleek horse quite different from the more-fashionable breeds common today.

The Akhal-Teke is an intelligent, hot-blooded horse that develops a dog-like devotion to its rider. It has a quiet temperament, but is easily aroused. It is bold, tenacious, tough, resilient, and genetically conditioned to endure extreme heat and cold. The Akhal-Teke can withstand great privation and comes back into form readily when conditions improve. Its exceptionally efficient heart and lungs help with the "equine radiator" effect; it has some of the quickest cardiac recovery scores of any breed at vet checks on endurance rides.

The overall impression is one of an exotic animal exuding grace, power, and athleticism. The comparison in appearance to a cheetah or fine greyhound is not inaccurate.

While degrees in type are allowed and even encouraged, all examples of the breed should carry the distinct characteristics that differentiate the Akhal-Teke from other horses. In judging or grading, basic soundness is of primary importance, followed by the presence of type. Severe faults in conformation are heavily penalized even in the presence of outstanding type. Brilliance in type, conformation, and/or movement—even accompanied by *minor* faults or shortcomings—are recognized and highly rewarded.

General Conformation

The Akhal-Teke is meant to be a medium-sized horse, ranging from 14.3 to 16 hands. Extremes in either direction are not desirable. In general, the

The shimmering metallic glow of the Akhal-Teke coat is a striking feature. *Shah'Zadeh Akhal-Tekes*

Akhal-Teke gives the impression of length without showing weakness or frailty. The horse should be longer than it is tall, with a rectangular silhouette.

The back is long but strong, with a level topline. Withers are high and prominent and attached to a well set-in shoulder. Shoulders should be long, nicely sloped, and exceptionally free-moving. The wither height, combined with the relative narrowness of the chest at the shoulders, makes for an enormous range of motion at the shoulder, giving the Akhal-Teke even greater scope and power.

Although the chest is narrow when viewed from the front, the heart girth is deep. The barrel widens smoothly out to the hips with little curvature of the

ribs, and the hip angle is wide, giving the appearance of strength. Tailset is low.

Faults: Extreme heaviness or reediness; excessively long back, especially when coupled with weak loin connection; extreme downhill conformation; monorchidism or cryptorchidism; thick, coarse, or overly muscular appearance; a square outline, the horse being taller than it is long.

Head and Neck

The Akhal-Teke's head is long and narrow, with most of the length being between the eyes and the muzzle, and the profile is straight or slightly dished. Overall, the head is dry (finely made and without

Akhal-Tekes have a lean, elegant build. *Shah'Zadeh Akhal-Tekes*

excess flesh), with large nostrils and thin lips. Eyes are large, expressive, and often hooded, or oriental, in appearance. Ears are long, slim, mobile, set forward, and alert. The throatlatch is refined, the poll is flexible, and the long, slim neck is set high out of the shoulder.

Faults: Severe overshot or undershot jaw, common or coarse head, thick throatlatch, thick neck, low neck set.

Legs and Feet

The Akhal-Teke is a true desert horse, and thus should possess extreme stamina and hardiness. The presence of adequately dense bone is one such indicator of these traits. Akhal-Tekes have short cannon bones and low-set hocks, while the forearm and gaskins are long and smoothly muscled. Legs are dry with well defined tendons. Joints are large, yet the knees should be flat. Pasterns should be long and display an identical angle to the hoof and shoulder. Hooves are small, round, and extremely hard.

Faults: Any and all limb formations that could contribute to future unsoundness include, but are not limited to, bench knees, calf knees, off-set cannon bones, sickle hocks, wide at the hocks, lack of bone, small joints, pigeon-toes or toed-in stance, and dished hooves. Horses are penalized according to the severity of the fault.

Movement

While not truly gaited, the Akhal-Teke has a highly distinctive fashion of moving. Because it is today what it always was—a horse bred to go very long distances—it does not have the spectacular movement that seems to be currently popular in many other horses. Yet its gaits are one of the most unique and desirable characteristics of the breed. It has magnificent action, liberal and flexible with soft, gliding, fluid strides, utilizing a sweeping motion without the unnecessary elevation of knees and hocks. The action is quite forward in all three gaits, displaying long, energetic strides that float just above the ground at the trot and sweep flat to the ground at the canter with little swing or knee action. The low moving trot and sweeping canter provide for an extremely comfortable ride. All movement is free-flowing and elastic as if the horse is sliding or skimming just above the ground.

The Akhal-Teke should give the impression of lithe athleticism without excessive musculature. Overall, the effect is that of a fine greyhound.

Due to the Teke's characteristically high head carriage, it is naturally more balanced toward its hindquarters. Impulsion is not something to strive for in a Teke, but comes naturally in the breed.

The Akhal-Teke has a different style of jumping than other breeds of horses. It jumps more like a deer, with head and knees up rather than out. Thus its center of balance is over the heart rather than the withers or shoulders. The Akhal-Teke is a naturally careful jumper, keen to leave a good deal of daylight between itself and any rail. It is talented and agile when jumping, and its fearlessness and endurance is unmatched in any other breed.

Faults: Winging, paddling, excessive knee action, heavy or ponderous gaits, lack of forward drive.

Coat

The Akhal-Teke typically has a marvelous metallic gleam to its coat, a feature that is a desirable characteristic and mostly noticed on buckskins, palominos, and duns. This glowing shine in the coat is created by the structure of the hair; its opaque core is greatly reduced in size and may, in areas, be altogether absent. The transparent part of the hair (the medulla) takes up this space and acts like a light-pipe, bending light through one side of the hair and refracting it out the other side, often with a golden cast. This effect produces a bright glitter that is a definitive coat characteristic of the breed.

The skin of the Akhal-Teke is very thin, with its coat and hair being quite fine and silky. In summer the skin around the eyes and nostrils may be bare. It often has a sparse mane and tail, little or no forelock, and no feathering on the fetlocks.

Any color is acceptable in the breed, as is any combination of white markings, which are common, and some sport a great deal of chrome. Sabino pinto markings are not at all unusual. Although all colors occur, golden buckskins and duns are the most prominent.

Few breeds of horse can claim the diversity of coloration to be found in the Akhal-Teke. While some breeders prefer certain colors over others, there are no disallowed colors or markings in the Akhal-Teke breed.

Color Variations

Dominant black, also called "electric black" and "raven black," is quite common for the breed. Combined with the famous Akhal-Teke glow, these horses literally glitter with a blue or purple sheen. This color is so special that it has its own name, *voronaya*, in Russian. This is the color of five-time Olympic medalist (two gold, two silver, one bronze), Absent, and is found in many of his descendants.

Palomino Tekes are truly stunning and usually display plenty of "chrome" (white markings.)

Light palomino in Akhal-Tekes is strikingly brilliant and is a color often seen in the United States. A famous light palomino is Kambar, the world record holder for racing distances of 4,000 to 8,000 meters. He generated interest and the start of Teke-love for many an American.

Akhal-Tekes have long heads, oriental eyes, and long ears.
Kelly Anderson

Mahogany bay has the "sooty" factor, as the hairs have a black tip producing many lovely variations in horse color. Astrachan is a gorgeous mahogany bay and the number one–rated elite Akhal-Teke stallion in North America.

Golden, called *bulanaya* in Russian, is an archetypical color of the Akhal-Teke horse. These horses are sometimes purely buckskin (without a spinal stripe), or dunskin (with a spinal stripe a few shades lighter than the mane and tail, but darker than the coat and plainly visible). Due to the unique structure of the hairs, these horses may be quite dark in color and may even be confused with bay; however, when bred together they can produce perlinos and cremellos.

Dark golden dun (along with similar colors of golden bay, golden buckskin, and golden dun) is another of the archetypical Akhal-Teke colors. In sunlight, the coat glitters with gold in a way that a camera simply cannot capture. This color (actually a form of olive grulla) is so dark that it is often mistaken for a non-red bay, but the stripe down the spine and zebra striping on the legs show that this is a dun.

Bay can be quite spectacular with coats that glitter with red and golden highlights.

Dunskin on the Akhal-Teke can combine dun and cream factors in some striking ways. Usually these horses have black manes and tails, but they can also have bi-colored manes and tails.

Liver chestnut, while not as common in the Teke as it is in other breeds like the Morgan, is still found quite often. In fact, this is the color of the line-founding stallion, 828 Fakirpelvan, sire of the famous European jumper, Penteli.

Chestnut tends to be more golden than red, but there are a fair share of lovely red chestnuts.

Cremello (also known as isabella in Europe) and perlino are found quite commonly in Akhal-Tekes. The glow of the coat on these blue-eyed wonders is so strong that it is visible even in a darkened barn.

Perlino differs from cremello when there is some reddish or brownish color to the tail and often in the hocks, knees, and legs as well. As with the cremello, the eyes are blue.

Claybank or red dun is a rarity among Tekes.

Cream grulla is a combination of grullo or dark golden dun and perlino. In this color, the eyes may be blue, gray, or hazel.

Grays are actually fairly common in Tekes. Those with this color are often beautifully dappled and many turn completely white.

Grullo among Tekes are of the olive variety and are usually called dark golden dun. Grullo can be distinguished from gray by the head being dark and the fact that the color does not change with age.

Rabicano is also seen in the breed. It is a form of roan that shows white only where the skin is thin or particularly stretchy: on the flanks, over the ribs, or on the throatlatch. When it is on the ribs, it is usually in the form of vertical stripes, but generally it is seen only on the flanks, sometimes only on the little flap of skin just over the stifle.

Older stud books list roan as an Akhal-Teke color, although this line seems to have died out.

Credit: The Akhal-Teke Society of America

AMERICAN AZTECA

American Azteca Horse International Association
P.O. Box 1577
Rapid City, South Dakota 57709
www.americanazteca.com

The American Azteca breed inherits beauty, temperament, pride, and spirit from their Andalusian blood, and its strength, heart, and speed from the Quarter Horse. The possibility of paint coloring also brings added flashiness to an already spectacular horse. This combination creates a horse many are proud to own.

The Azteca breed originated in 1972 when the Mexican *charros* (cowboys) began a quest to produce a horse to represent Mexico as their contribution to the equine world. They required a horse with agility, quickness, and cow sense to work on their cattle ranches, yet it needed to retain the elegance needed for exhibition, rodeos, and parades. For this, they chose the Andalusian to cross with their Quarter Horses and Criollo mares.

The results were astounding. The horse that emerged was gifted with athleticism, a willing attitude, speed, heart, stamina, grace, riveting beauty, harmony of form, outstanding disposition, and a great talent to learn. Not only did it possess the ability to work on cattle ranches, but it also had the versatility for many other uses. The Azteca was born and, in the years following, acquired so much recognition it earned the title as the National Horse of Mexico.

It became such a popular horse that inevitably it was noticed by other countries. Horse lovers in the United States were among the first to appreciate the Azteca. It was here that the breed took an interesting turn and developed in a slightly different manner. Although its bloodlines continued to be based on the original Azteca of Mexico—a combination of Quarter Horse and Andalusian—the American Azteca breeders also allowed "Quarter Horses with color"—Paint Horses—in their breeding program. Since the Paint Horse is derived from the Quarter Horse, it is essentially a Quarter

American Azteca D mare.
Diana Allison/ courtesy Rita Greslin Ricard

Horse with color. Thus it could be used to produce American Aztecas, provided their bloodlines are Quarter Horse and don't have more than 25 percent Thoroughbred blood.

Foundation Breeds

Quarter Horses and Paint Horses are popular breeds originating in the United States and known for their great athletic ability. Most are used as pleasure horses, but both breeds are especially renowned as working ranch horses. They are quick, maneuverable, and even tempered, having natural cow sense and often working cattle without much guidance from the rider. Attractive and compactly built, they feature large powerful hindquarters, strong shoulders, and short muscular backs. Quarter Horses were named for their quick burst of speed at quarter-mile races, while Paint Horses were named for their colorful markings.

Andalusians are an ancient and rare breed with great strength, long sloping shoulders, natural collection, and sturdy legs and hooves. Sought after for their quiet temperament and extreme intelligence, they are easily handled, yet have a reserve of energy available when called upon. Throughout history, Andalusians were revered for their abilities as warhorses. These same skills were used in Spain and Portugal to work cattle and the notorious fighting bulls. Andalusians are still used in those capacities today, carrying their riders in the bullring with unimaginable grace and speed.

The Andalusian is the working ranch horse of Spain and Portugal, just as the Quarter Horse is in the United States. Today, 80 percent of all modern breeds trace back to Spain and Portugal's illustrious Andalusian, including the Quarter Horse and Paint Horse. Thus utilizing Andalusian blood is not something new, but a reintroduction of a bloodline that is already present in the Quarter Horse.

The Registry

Although the Azteca began as a breed in Mexico, the culture and tastes in the United States called for a little different type of horse to fit its needs. The American Azteca Horse International Association (AAHIA) takes into consideration the demands, requirements, market, and abilities of breeders and owners of Aztecas in the United States and throughout the world.

With a respectful non-interference attitude toward Mexico's national breed, the AAHIA registry has named Aztecas outside of Mexico as American Aztecas. This signifies that they are the American version of the fabulous Azteca originally created in Mexico.

The AAHIA horses, however, are modeled closely after their Mexican cousins in type. The organization still bases the breed on the combination of Quarter Horse and Andalusian blood and promotes a high quality horse. It does not allow more than 25 percent Thoroughbred blood in any Quarter or Paint Horse used to produce an Azteca. The AAHIA traces back four generations, not including the horse itself, for Thoroughbred blood. If any of those generations have more than 25 percent Thoroughbred blood, that horse is not allowed for breeding an Azteca. The registry reserves the right to research further generations if more Thoroughbred blood is suspected.

Additionally, horses applying for registration have to be tested for hyperkalemic periodic paralysis (HYPP) disease if they have the Quarter Horse "Impressive" bloodline, and they won't qualify unless the test is negative. Tests results may be: (a) positive, meaning the horse has it; (b) negative, meaning the horse does not have it; or (c) negative/positive, meaning the horse may or may not develop it, but may be a carrier, in which case the horse won't qualify for registration either.

Standards

The American Azteca combines characteristics of the Old World breed type in the Andalusian and New World breed type with the Quarter Horse, resulting in a noble, docile, agile, proud, and spectacular horse. It should have a good balance between the two breeds and possess qualities of both. The intention is to create a new type of horse, a new breed that exhibits the best of both ancestor breeds.

With some allowance for variations, the recommended characteristics of the American Azteca are as follows:

Size: The size ranges from 14.2 to 16.0 hands.

Color: Both Quarter Horse and Paint Horse markings and colors are acceptable.

Head: The head is of medium size with a straight, slightly convex or slightly concave profile. It has a broad forehead, expressive eyes, and medium ears, which are mobile and well placed.

Neck: The neck is well muscled, shapely, and slightly arched with a medium crest. It is broad at its base, where it joins onto a long, sloping shoulder.

Body: The withers are broad and slightly muscled, yet defined. The haunches are strong and well muscled, leading to a medium- to low-set tail. A long flowing mane and tail are often present.

Legs: The legs are well muscled with dense bone, good joints, and strong hooves.

Movement: Retained from the Andalusian are free and mobile shoulders and hips, which allow the Azteca to be incredibly athletic and smooth to ride. The movement is naturally collected with a variance of knee action from high and brilliant, to long and flowing.

The American Azteca responds exceptionally well to the different equine High School disciplines requiring suspended and elevated gaits. Qualities passed on from both parent breeds also make it a skillful working cow horse or western horse. It excels at many events, making it an extremely versatile horse. The breed is very easy to train and once taught, never forgets.

Breeding Basics

The goal of breeding American Aztecas is to arrive at a point where a new breed is created. To achieve this, several generations must be bred. The first generation of an American Azteca is an Andalusian bred to a Quarter Horse or Paint Horse; that offspring is given the notation of an American Azteca D. When the American Azteca D is then crossed

American Azteca A mare. *Diana Allison/courtesy Rita Greslin Ricard*

back to an Andalusian, the offspring is labeled as an American Azteca B, or second generation. If an Azteca D is bred to a Quarter Horse, that foal is an American Azteca C offspring. When both an American Azteca D and B are bred, the offspring is an American Azteca A. This generation then has been produced by breeding American Azteca to American Azteca and is not a cross of the two ancestor breeds—thus a new breed has begun. Since the breed comes in A, B, C, or D, the A is significant because it is the third generation or a result of breeding Azteca to Azteca.

There are other combinations that can be used to arrive at an American Azteca A, but this method is the fastest and can still take twelve to fifteen years to achieve. It also gives a great blood percentage to the A, that being five-eighths Andalusian and three-eighths Quarter Horse. A breeding chart is available to show the different letters of an American Azteca and how to get them, or in other words, what crosses are allowed. The letters of A, B, C, and D are not indicative of quality, as there are quality horses at all levels, which are all considered American Aztecas.

It took noted American Azteca breeder, Rita Ricard, about fifteen years of breeding American Aztecas to produce a level A Azteca. This level of Aztecas are very rare, with probably less than fifteen of them of any sex in the United States, and of those, less than five are American Azteca A stallions. Ricard counts it as a real privilege to be one of the first to have bred and raised her American Azteca A stallion, Primero Viento, which is registered as number one in the registry. Primero Viento was produced from an American Azteca B stallion and a D mare, so he has the coveted five-eighths Andalusian, three-eighths Quarter Horse percentage.

Azteca Excellence

Ricard has been an Andalusian breeder since 1980 and has tried many Andalusian crosses with other breeds. She states, "I can honestly say that I have yet to find an Andalusian cross that I don't like, but the American Azteca definitely stood out to me. They are just the perfect type of horse for any purpose. They are wonderful to be around, kind, sensitive, talented, and willing are words that come to mind. They're *easy* to own."

She believes the future of the breed is promising. "They have everything that anyone could desire. The Quarter Horse started from crossing different breeds. It also started out small and blossomed into the huge influence it is today because of its talents. I believe that the American Azteca has even more talents. I expect to see great things with this breed in the future."

Ricard's American Azteca stallion, Vaquero, which is the sire of Primero Viento, was the National Champion Western Pleasure and Reserve National Champion Hunt Seat, and was in the top five for the Dressage Suitability category at the Andalusian National Show. In classes where he competed against both Andalusians and part-bred Andalusians, he won first place in both Doma Vaquera (Spanish reining, which is a combination of reining and dressage) and Trail Class. He also won several West Coast championships and a bronze medal in dressage at a U.S. Dressage Federation show. Another American Azteca, Oro Blanco S.E.R., won Grand National Champion, Reserve Half-Andalusian Senior Stallion, Amateur. "That tells just how versatile and talented this breed is," Ricard says. "You can do it all with one horse!"

So whether the need is for English or western, graceful dancer or working ranch horse, jumper, dressage competitor, western cutting, reining, penning, or just a great companion for trail riding, the American Azteca is a wonderful choice. This horse can do it all and do it well!

Credit: American Azteca Horse International Association

AMERICAN BASHKIR CURLY

Curls of the Bashkir Curly are especially evident in the winter. *Greg Oakes*

American Bashkir Curly Registry
857 Beaver Road
Walton, Kentucky 41094
www.abcregistry.org

The Bashkir Curly is a rare breed of horse that is totally different from all others because it's covered with curls, drawing attention wherever it goes. Crowds are amazed by the horse with curls all over its body. People want to touch the unusual coat, which feels like lamb's wool, and sink their fingers into it instead of petting like they would on a regular horse. Some put their faces up to the curly coated neck to feel it better. The horses seem to understand and are patient with all the attention.

The coat ranges from a crushed velvet look or gentle wave, to tight corkscrew curls. Manes are thick and often wavy, appearing like they had been braided.

A side effect of the Bashkir's unique hair coat is that the hair is hypoallergenic. Most people with horse allergies find that Bashkir Curly horses don't cause an allergic reaction because their hair's genetic design is different from other horse breeds. For people who have allergies to horses, the Bashkir Curly with its special hair coat resolves that problem.

According to one breeder, there is nothing more heartwarming than to see the smile on the face of someone with horse allergies who suddenly realizes that their dream of owning a horse can actually come true when introduced to a Curly.

Others appreciate the breed not only because it's different, but because they have found more in these marvelous horses than their curls. Besides their hypoallergenic coat, other exceptional features of the Curly include versatility, soundness, and a docile temperament which endears them to their owners. The curls are unique and draw attention, yet it's their personality and diversity that sustains their continuing popularity.

History

No one knows for sure the origin of curly horses. Throughout history, there have been various sightings of curly coated horses worldwide. When Napoleon conquered Austria in 1805, he found what he described as "poodle hair horses" at the Vienna Zoo and had some transported back to Paris for his personal enjoyment. In his famous book about evolution, Charles Darwin mentioned curly haired horses in South America in the early 1800s. Various early European horse books mention crisp-haired horses that were also curly.

The celebrated exhibitor of curiosities, P. T. Barnum, purchased a curly coated horse in 1847 from an agent in Cincinnati. Barnum waited for the perfect opportunity to introduce the horse to the public. When noted explorer Colonel John Fremont was lost in the Rocky Mountains and America waited for news of his survival, Barnum took advantage of the situation. As soon as Fremont emerged from the wilderness, Barnum promoted his curly horse as a strange new breed Fremont discovered there. Barnum initially made a small fortune, but his returns became even greater after Fremont sued Barnum for his chicanery. The litigation made national headlines and the free publicity further promoted Barnum's woolly horse exhibit. A few years later when Fremont ran for president, he was lauded as "the Woolly Horse" candidate.

There are many theories as to the Bashkir's origins in North America. Pioneers recorded various sightings of curly haired horses among wild horse herds in the western parts of both Canada and the United States. Canadian pioneer sightings include such diverse places as the Cypress Hills and Aishihik Lake in the Yukon. In America, they were found wild in Nevada and Oregon.

Perhaps the Russians imported the horses when they explored the Pacific Coast of North America, as there is a curly breed of horse in Russia today. The Russians set up various settlements from Sitka in the Aleutian Islands to Fort Ross in California in the late 1700s and early 1800s. This theory was strengthened early in the history of the registry when it was initially believed that the Russian Bashkir horse was curly coated; thus it probably was an ancestor of the American Curly. "Bashkir" refers to a region in Russia, hence the name American Bashkir Curly.

After the fact, it was discovered that it wasn't the Bashkir Russian horse that had a curly coat. It was actually the Lokai, which is a breed in the central and southern regions of Tajikistan. Members of the American Bashkir Curly Registry considered dropping the word "Bashkir" from the name, but after lengthy discussions, they left the name as it was for the sake of public recognition. Many breeders have chosen to refer to their horses as simply American Curlies.

Some people claim that a prominent wealthy Nevada rancher named Tom Dixon imported Curly horses in the 1870s. Research has proven that Dixon purchased a Curly stud and two Curly mares in northern India and imported them to Nevada. He settled in Eureka, Nevada, and used feral herds in his breeding program, which would certainly account for the Curly horses' presence in Nevada.

This theory, however, does not account for their presence in the northwest in the early 1800s when the Crow and Lakota people were capturing and riding Curly horses on the plains of Montana and South Dakota. Proof of this has been found in Native American drawings. Most Indian tribes kept records of important events that occurred during

Bashkir Curly manes can look like they have been braided.
Sonja Oakes

each year with drawings, usually on animal hides, called "winter counts." The Sioux winter count of 1801 drawn by High Dog, a Lakota Indian, depicts the Sioux stealing Curly horses from Crow Indians. There have been several winter counts found that contain the same information.

In 1881, Chief Red Horse, a Minneconjou, was persuaded to create some drawings of the Battle of the Little Bighorn. One of those pictures depicts an Indian riding a curly coated horse.

Descendants of Indian horses are considered to be the Native American line.

Initially, few cowboys bothered with the strange breed; then rough cold weather and temperatures wiped out many wild horses. Only Curlies with their thick winter coats survived, though they were gaunt. Given no choice, ranchers brought in several of these horses for work and quickly discovered their marvelous characteristics. Some were used as ranch saddle horses, while others were crossed with draft horses for heavy farm work.

Peter Damele and his family from Nevada had a history of breeding Curlies after one extremely harsh winter hit the area in 1932. Among the few surviving horses were the Curlies, who were soon discovered to have gentle natures and a certain ease with working cattle. From then on, the Dameles made a concerted effort to capture and breed the Curly horses. Descendents of these horses have come to be known as the Damele line.

Curlies are versatile performance horses, both in English and western classes.
Greg Oakes

Breed Foundation

In 1971, Benny Damele, the son of Peter Damele, joined with a fellow Curly enthusiast, Sunny Martin, and organized the American Bashkir Curly Registry in hopes of preserving the remarkable horse. Due to the small number of horses with which they had to work, inbreeding was a major concern. In an effort to introduce new blood, they chose to cross their Curlies with the following four breeds:

Arabian: This breed shares the same short back as the Curly, indicative of a five-vertebra spine, and is also known for its endurance.

Morgan: Horses whose conformation is similar to that of the Curlies.

Appaloosa: Native American horses bred for endurance that share the unusual Curly trait of shedding mane and tail hair.

Missouri Fox Trotter: A breed that Martin thought shared the smooth gait of the Curly. Today, some people feel that the only "gait" exhibited by the original Curly is actually a running walk, or "Indian shuffle," not the full gait of the Missouri Fox Trotter. This issue has never been proven one way or the other, but the cross produced some beautiful gaited Curly horses.

Many breeders today breed specifically for the "Gaited Curly."

Some of the most notable of these "outside" studs were: Nevada Red (Arabian); Ruby Red King (Morgan); Chocolate Chip D (Appaloosa); and Walkers Prince T (Missouri Fox Trotter).

By the late 1990s, the number of registered Curlies was approaching 3,000. The American Bashkir Curly Registry closed its books in 2000, as many feared that continued crossbreeding would dilute the gene pool to the point where the Curlies unique characteristics would be lost. As a result of that decision, the American Bashkir Curly Registry is now a blood registry as opposed to a coat registry.

Knowing that there were many fine curly coated horses that could no longer be registered, a second registry, the International Curly Horse Organization (ICHO) was founded. ICHO continues to register all horses with a curly coat, regardless of pedigree, which allows the Bureau of Land Management's feral range horses and crossbreds to be tracked. This provides a valuable service to all Curly breeders.

The American Bashkir Curly is now prospering in both North America and Europe. Though used in many disciplines worldwide, the Curly is still a rare breed.

Characteristics

Other than the obvious curly coat, the Bashkir Curly is valued for its gentle disposition, high intelligence, strong bone, soundness, performance versatility, strength, and endurance. As a result of the years of crossbreeding, the Curly can be found in every size and color: mini to draft, solid colored, pinto or appaloosa colored. Only mules are not allowed in the registry.

Among its best traits is the low maintenance for upkeep and it would definitely be classified as an easy keeper, doing well on hay alone. However, it still needs all the care and comforts given to any other horse: to be wormed, vaccinated, and have its feet cared for.

Curlies are famous for their ability to endure hardship. They are able to withstand cold winters and can stay outside year round, which is important to people who get tired of mucking out stalls. Nature has provided Curlies with a unique heating and cooling system. Their thick, curly, winter coat repels rain and snow, and underneath it, air is trapped near the short hair coat next to the body, keeping them warm.

In the spring, they shed their curly coats, which then become straight, wavy, velvety, or turn to marcel or micro curls. Yet they remain hypoallergenic even if their summer coat is straight. Sometimes only portions of their summer coat are straight while other portions remain curly.

As a former feral horse, the Curly has extremely tough hooves, and unlike other breeds, doesn't usually need shoes. The Curly is endowed with tremendous stamina, having a surprising ability to pull and carry.

Naturally gentle, many Curly horses do not have the same flight reaction other breeds have. They don't frighten easily and, in a bad situation, will wait patiently until someone comes to help. They tend to assess, not flee, thus making them safer mounts.

"Curlies seem to bond with people and learn quickly, making them good for children and novice riders," says longtime breeder Sonja Oakes. "Today, when so many people with little or no horse experience are buying horses, it is all the more important that a horse have a well-balanced and gentle nature—qualities Curlies possess. My husband learned to ride as an adult. He was skeptical at first, but the horse seemed to sense he was learning and would stop when he was off balance and wait for him."

Oakes taught her preschool daughters to ride on her Curly horses. "I would be worried about them on any other horse but a Curly." She also trains Curlies for therapeutic riding.

Curlies are suitable for most disciplines, both English and Western. They have performed well in national level dressage, jumping, vaulting, sidesaddle, and endurance riding. Recently there were two Curly horses in the United States that reached high levels in dressage. Curlies excel at anything, including being family-oriented pleasure mounts.

Coat

As for that curly coat—it is not typical horsehair, but more closely resembles mohair; it can even be spun and woven or knit into garments. It is hypoallergenic, so people who are allergic to straight-haired breeds usually will not have a reaction to Curlies.

The winter coat expresses itself in a variety of patterns commonly described as marcel wave, crushed velvet, curl, or micro curl. The summer coat also offers varieties ranging from smooth to wavy. Some horses shed their manes and tail hair every summer, only to grow them back in the winter.

Not all Curlies have curls over their entire body, as some may only have curls over portions of it. A lot depends on the temperature: the colder the weather, the longer the hair and heavier the curl. Genetics no doubt plays a part in this, also.

Standards

The official breed identity standards are as follows:

Size and Weight

Average size is 14 to 16 hands. Average weight is 800 to 1,000 pounds. Some Curlies can weigh up to 1,200 pounds.

Body Conformation

They have a medium-sized head with well-defined jaw and throatlatch, and wide-set eyes with eyelashes that curl up. Ears are short to medium in length with curls inside; the ear hairs do not totally shed out in the summer.

The neck is medium in length and deep at the base of the neck where it joins the shoulder.

The back is noticeably short and Curlies are deep through the girth with a long underline and belly cut high in the flank. They have heavy-boned legs and short cannon bones compared to the forearms.

Forequarters and hindquarters should be supple, yet well muscled. Withers are medium. The croup should be flat or with a shallow slope to the base of the tail.

Curlies should travel easily and smoothly.

- Types of curls on body:
  Fine, soft hair
  Ringlet: can be several inches long
  Marcel wave: deep soft wave in the body coat
  Crushed velvet: soft dense pile of curls in body coat
  Micro curl: really small tight curls that tend to stay all year
  Round: tends to be in the Fox Trotter lines
- Types of curls on mane:
  Extra fine hair
  Kinky: (is preferable)
  Wavy
  Ringlets
- Types of curls on tail:
  Ringlets
  Wavy
- Types of curls on fetlocks:
  Curly (is preferable).
  Wavy
- Mane: Should all or partially be shed in the summer; split mane that hangs on both sides of neck
- Tail: Should shed partially at the head of the tail in the summer; some may shed tail hair completely
- Fetlock hair: Should shed in summer but still retain some long hairs
- Hooves: Almost perfectly round in shape; hard and dense; proportioned to the size of the horse.

Unique Characteristics

Curlies are distinctive in their even-tempered disposition. They also have quick pulse and respiration recovery and very dense bone in the legs. Their noticeably short, strong back indicates a five-lumbar vertebrae. They can completely shed the mane and tail hair in the summer, but their hair will grow back in the fall with the winter coat.

The Curly coat is hypoallergenic. The hairs are

Curlies may not show much of a curly coat in the summer. *Creekside Curlies*

round instead of flat, appear barbed or feathered underneath a microscope, and can be spun and woven. Testing has proven the hair to be closely related to mohair instead of horsehair.

Due to the years of outcrossing, Curlies can be found with differing conformation, sizes, and weights. This influence will probably continue for the next five to ten generations of Curly-to-Curly breeding. However these horses will be registered as long as they meet American Bashkir Curly Registry criteria.

Curly horses have excelled in all disciplines—working cattle, trail riding, endurance, and showing in both English and Western. Therapeutic riding schools have been searching out Curly horses for their programs, as they appreciate their gentleness. Curlies are always a favorite in parades and at equine fairs; every year the Classic Curly Riders can be seen in the Rose Parade in Pasadena, California.

Knowledge of the Curlies now extends beyond the American and Canadian borders, with several having been exported to European countries. Their popularity in Europe is growing by leaps and bounds.

If they sound too good to be true, the only way to truly appreciate Curlies is to see one up close and personal.

Credit: Marni Malet, Bearpaw Ranch

AMERICAN PAINT HORSE

This chestnut tobiano Paint complements the beautiful scenery. *Maria Dryfhout/Shutterstock*

American Paint Horse Association
P.O. Box 961023
Fort Worth, Texas 76161
www.apha.com

The ideal horse's best qualities should be intelligence, willing disposition, sound conformation, versatility, athletic ability, and strength. Add to this some beautiful colors in a seemingly infinite number of distinctive coat patterns, and that is the best description of the American Paint Horse, one of the most popular breeds in the world.

These desirable qualities were first and foremost on the minds of the breed's founders. As a result of the efforts of tens of thousands of people involved with Paints over the past forty-six years, the American Paint Horse has become one of the most favored horses worldwide. Its popularity has grown to include Paint owners in about forty nations and territories, as well as the United States. The breed registry has become one of the fastest-growing in the world, issuing pedigree certificates at a rate of about thirty-five thousand every year.

Paints are colorfully marked, and each is different from any other. *Zuzule/Shutterstock*

History

In 1519 the Spanish explorer Hernando Cortes sailed to the North American continent to find fame and fortune. Along with his entourage of conquistadors, he brought horses to help his men travel across the New World in search of riches. These excursions left behind a profound legacy—the bloodstock that would provide the foundation for a variety of unique, distinct, American-bred horses. According to the Spanish historian Bernal Diaz del Castillo, who traveled with the expedition, there were a few horses among the sixteen warhorses brought on the expedition that had Paint spotting patterns. It is thought that these spotted horses laid the foundation for what is today the American Paint Horse breed.

By the early 1800s, the plains were generously populated by free-ranging horse herds which included the same spotted type horses. Due to their flashy color and performance, they soon became a favorite mount of Native Americans. The Comanche, who were considered to be the finest horsemen on the plains, favored loud colored horses and had many among their immense herds. Evidence of this favoritism is exhibited by drawings of spotted horses found on the painted buffalo robes that served as records for the Comanche.

Throughout the 1800s and late into the 1900s, spotted horses were called by a variety of names: pinto, paint, skewbald, or piebald. In the 1960s, groups began to organize in an effort to preserve these peculiar animals.

A classy-looking mare and foal with beautiful tobiano patterns. *Paula Cobleigh/Shutterstock*

The Registry

Rebecca Tyler Lockhart was one of the admirers of these beautifully colored horses, as well as sound, western stock horse conformation, so she sought the best of both worlds. Overcoming nearly unanimous opposition among breeders, Lockhart forged ahead with her plans for a new stock-type breed that was spotted and a standard to go with it.

In 1962 she called a meeting with a special group of enthusiasts for spotted horses in Gainesville, Texas, which founded the American Paint Stock Horse Association. It was dedicated to preserving horses of color with stock-type conformation. Following a merger with the American Paint Quarter Horse Association in 1965, it became the American Paint Horse Association (APHA).

This group liked the varied, distinct coat patterns of the American Paint Horse, finding them very appealing. Being devotees of western stock-type horses, however, it insisted that stock-type conformation had to be a major criterion for its registry. Western stock horses were appreciated for their talents in working with livestock, as well as their strength, intelligence, speed, and agility. They were typically well-balanced and powerfully built animals.

Lockhart remembered seeing a continuing trend of discrimination against horses with distinctive coat patterns such as Paints. "People looked down on Paints," she remarked. "They just didn't understand. They thought [Paints] were inferior. If a breeder [of solid-colored horses] had a Paint foal, he was ashamed. He thought it was a bad reflection on his herd, that it was connected with inferior blood. He was afraid someone would think there was something wrong with his breeding program. So a lot of ranchers would get rid of them." She recalled that Paints would often be relegated to back pastures, or in some cases suffer a worse fate.

"There were many good Paints that were destroyed back then," agreed Junior Robertson of Waurika, Oklahoma. Robertson was one of the few ranchers in the country who actually admired and owned Paints at the time. One of his most notable horses, even before there was an association for Paints, was Wahoo King. This colorful sorrel Paint set the standard for top competition horses in the 1960s and was well known as a legendary roping horse.

Today, the American Paint Horse breed standard has become widely respected and admired. The breed is now recognized not only for its beautiful coat, but for its sound conformation and musculature as well. It is also highly regarded for its superior intelligence and willing disposition, making it an easily trainable horse.

Standards

While the colorful coat pattern is essential to their identity, American Paint Horses have strict bloodline requirements and a distinctive stock horse body type. To be eligible for the Regular Registry, horses must come from stock horses that are registered with one of three recognized organizations: the APHA, the American Quarter Horse Association, or the Jockey Club (U.S. Thoroughbred Registry). At least one parent must be a registered American Paint Horse.

The APHA also maintains minimum color requirements for registration in the Regular

Paints naturally stand out from solid-colored horses. *Zuzule/Shutterstock*

Registry. Stallions, mares, and geldings that meet the bloodline requirements must have a "qualifying area" of solid white hair (with underlying unpigmented skin) on a non-white horse, or dark hair (with underlying dark skin) on a white horse with unpigmented skin, in order to be included in the Regular Registry. Spots must be on the horse at the time of birth, and Appaloosa spotting is not allowed. Horses with minimal spotting can qualify with a minimum of one spot on the body area that is at least two inches in diameter.

Those horses that do not have sufficient qualifying spotted areas for the Regular Registry, but meet the bloodline requirements, can be considered for the solid Paint-Bred Registry.

Pattern Types

Spotting patterns of Paint Horses have an added attraction over that of most other breeds. They not only have the colors of other breeds, but also superimposed over these colors are a variety of beautifully individualistic spots.

Each Paint Horse has a unique combination of white patches and any background color of the equine spectrum: black, bay, brown, chestnut, dun, red dun, grullo, sorrel, palomino, buckskin, gray, cremello, perlino, and blue, red or bay roan. Markings can be any shape or size and located virtually anywhere on the Paint's body.

Although Paint Horses come in a variety of colors with different markings, there are only three specific coat patterns recognized in the Regular Registry: tobiano, overo, and tovero.

The tobiano pattern may be predominantly dark or white and is distinguished by oval or round spots that extend down the neck and chest of the horse. White often crosses its back between its withers and tail. The tobiano's head markings may be completely solid, or may have a blaze, strip, star, or snip. Generally the legs are fully white, or at least below the knees and hocks. The tail is often two colors.

The overo pattern can be mainly dark or white. Typically, the white will not cross the back of the

horse between its withers and tail. Overos often have bold white head markings, such as a bald face. Also, the body markings will be irregular and scattered, and one or all four legs will be dark. The tail is usually one color.

Overo patterns can also be broken down into three different spotting patterns: frame overo, sabino, and splashed white. Frame overo horses usually have large amounts of white on the head and white spots arranged horizontally on the sides and neck. The feet and legs of these horses are usually dark, although they can have white feet or socks, just as the non-spotted horse can. Frequently frame overos have one or two blue eyes.

Sabino patterns have white on the legs and head, and the white usually creeps up on the body in the form of belly spots. These horses are usually flecked and roaned, although some are crisply spotted. Sometimes sabino horses have blue eyes.

The last pattern, splashed white, is much rarer than the others. Horses with this pattern have white legs and bellies, as well as a great deal of white on the head. The edges of the white are quite crisp. Many splashed white horses have blue eyes.

Since not all coat patterns fit precisely in either the tobiano or overo categories, the APHA expanded its classifications to include the tovero pattern, which has characteristics of both tobiano and overo.

These patterns—tobiano, overo (frame overo, sabino, and splashed white), and tovero are the color patterns that distinguish Paints from other horses. Their colors, markings, and patterns, combined with stock-type conformation, athletic ability, and agreeable dispositions, make the American Paint Horse an investment in quality. Owning an American Paint Horse is an enjoyable, positive experience.

Paints Today

The breed is experiencing an increase in popularity. There are now more than 1,200 approved APHA shows every year around the world. The annual World Championship Paint Horse Show

A beautiful American Paint Horse. *Zuzule/Shutterstock*

can run up to fourteen days with thousands of horses participating.

Paints have a high profile by proving at several venues around the nation that when it comes to intelligence, versatility, and athletic ability, they are at the top of the class. Paints continue to stand out in reining with impressive victories at competitions such as the U.S. Equestrian Team (USET) National Open Reining Championship, the National Reining Horse Association (NRHA) Futurity, and the prestigious U.S. Team Roping Championships. The Pacific Coast Cutting Horse Association Futurity and the National Cutting Horse Association (NCHA) Futurity are other competitions where Paints have proven themselves.

Since 1966, when APHA officially recognized the sport of racing, the Paint racing industry has made major strides forward. In that inaugural year, seventeen starters ran for $1,290 in just two states—Texas and Oklahoma. In 2005, however, more than 600 starters competed in nearly 800 APHA recognized races for purses totaling more than $4.5 million. Today, a total of eighteen states feature Paint racing, including Arizona, California, Colorado, Idaho, Kansas, Louisiana, Michigan, Montana, Nevada, New Mexico, North Dakota, Oklahoma, Oregon, South Dakota, Texas, Utah, Washington, and Wyoming. Paint racing is also offered in Canada.

The American Paint Horse has established itself as an accomplished athlete in and out of the show arena. Whether racing, trail riding, or performing before thousands at worldwide competitions, the American Paint Horse's combination of beauty and performance are unmatched.

Credit: American Paint Horse Association

AMERICAN WHITE HORSE AND AMERICAN CREME HORSE

American White and American Creme Horse Registry

90000 Edwards Road

Naper, Nebraska 68755

http://awachr.com/home

There is nothing so eye catching as white horses. They are like a neon sign flashing for all to see, like an automatic spotlight constantly shining on them. The whiteness of their coats glows like light in the dark, causing other horses to blend into the background by comparison.

Riding a white horse is the dream of almost every young girl or she envisions her hero mounted upon one. White horses are stately and picturesque,

often being mistaken for statues in photos. Their presence is associated with something of definite beauty, honor, or royalty . It does not seem to matter what color tack they wear in a show or parade, they just catch the spectator's eye, irresistibly drawing them in.

Audiences focus automatically on white horses before anything else, and a white horse in motion is positively mesmerizing. Circuses use running or rearing white horses with flowing manes and tails to attract the crowds. Movies and TV programs have featured white horses ridden by the stars to draw more attention to the heroes, as bad guys never rode white horses. Leaders of nations have favored riding white horses, like the first president

American White Horse colt.

of the United States, George Washington, or the emperors of Japan, since white horses are associated with the qualities of goodness and nobility desired in a leader.

Cream colored horses experience the same fame and fascination, as they are often mistaken for white horses. Unless a cream colored horse stands alongside a white horse, the difference cannot be noticed.

America's White Horses

In 1906 a white horse known as Old King was foaled. Owned by Professor Newall of Illinois and used for breeding circus horses, Old King was a snow white, pink-skinned, brown-eyed stallion of unknown breeding. He matured to 15.2 hands and weighed approximately 1,200 pounds. He had a thick neck, stocky build, strong legs, and great intelligence with good disposition. His long, heavy and wavy mane and tail added to his attraction and completed the picture of the perfect kind of horse suitable for such events as a circus.

In 1917, Old King was bought by cattle ranchers Caleb Thompson and his twin brother, Hudson. Crossed with their herd of predominately Morgan mares of various dark colors, Old King produced white foals much like himself. In time, the Thompson ranch established the American White Horse breed and its breeding program. Caleb and his wife, Ruth, eventually bought out Hudson's

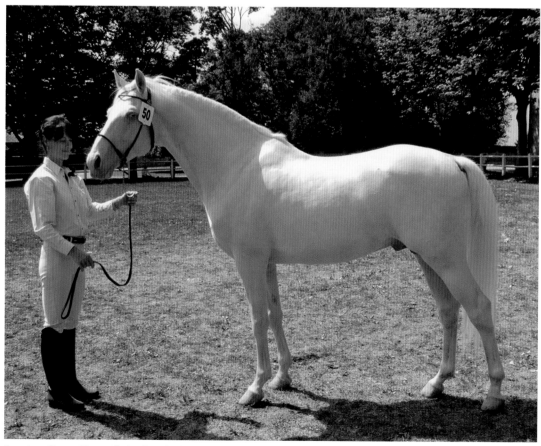

American Creme Horse. *Carley Daugherty*

share of the ranch and began showing their horses at local events.

They originally named their new horse breed the American Albino and organized a breed registry in 1936, registering much of the stock descended from Old King. In 1937 they incorporated the American Albino Horse Club (AAHC), a registry and studbook for white horses. It eventually included a subsidiary, National Recording Club, in which all non-white foals were recorded, including cream colored horses, which were registered as non-white or off-colored. (The American Creme Horse was not officially recognized until about 1980.) The registry eventually moved away from the use of the word "albino" in succeeding title changes, since, genetically, the American White Horse is not a true albino, and neither is its close cousin, the American Creme Horse.

In 1938 the Thompsons moved to a ranch of nearly 2,400 acres in Naper, Nebraska, and named it El Rancho del Caballo Blanco. The local residents, however, called it the White Horse Ranch; this name stuck and a legend began. The Thompsons began a training and riding school for children and started touring with their White Horse Troupe, staging performances that included the children along with the horses from the school. In the 1940s and 1950s the White Horse Troupe became internationally famous and toured all over the United States and Canada. The popularity of the White Horse Ranch also attracted many visitors to its grounds.

In 1945 *Life* magazine visited the ranch and ran an article on it. The White Horse Ranch was subsequently featured in many other magazines, and in 1946, Warner Brothers Studios made a movie short about the ranch. Warner Brothers Studios visited the White Horse Ranch again in 1952 to make another movie short. The two movies, *Ride a White Horse* and *Ranch in White*, are at the Lincoln, Nebraska, state archives and can still be viewed on video there.

Many times the horses the Thompsons used for the entertainment industry were the same ones they used a few years later at their white horse training and riding school. Some of their horses, such as the mare Snow White, served as multipurpose horses. Snow White was a fine jumper and very fast runner. She once raced a stock car on a quarter-mile track and won! She knew a variety of tricks, was used as a driving horse, and in a pinch could be hitched to the plow. Being extremely gentle, she very popular with the training school students and lived into her thirties.

In 1963 Caleb Thompson died, and Ruth had to close down the ranch to tourism and sell the herd. She placed breeding stock horses with friends and white horse breeders to preserve the bloodlines of Old King's descendents. She also continued the studbook and, in 1970, re-incorporated the registry as the American Albino Association, Inc., in Oregon. At that time, the corporation began registering Creme horses in their own registry because a better division between white and cream colored horses was necessary. The apparent confusion as to what a true white color looked like led to the creation of two distinct divisions, the American White Horse Registry and the American Creme Horse Registry (although the "breed" was still registered with the American Albino Association). Additionally, Ruth was now registering horses internationally.

Carley and Dean Daugherty then became involved in the White Horse Ranch. Carley had a history with the Thompsons, as they had been her legal guardians when she was young and had remained close friends. As a little girl, Carley had ridden with the White Horse Troupe. When she was ten years old, she rode and showed the Thompsons' highly schooled stallion, Wings, a horse that knew an awesome number of tricks. Carley directed him through his trick routine for the visitors at the ranch and rode him bareback every morning to bring in the herd of show mares. In 1988, Ruth entered into a contract with Carley and her husband, Dean, to start restoration of the White Horse Ranch.

In 1990 Ruth died and the White Horse Ranch was listed on the National Register of Historic

American White
Horse. *Don and
JoAnn Anderson*

Places. The board of directors of the International American Albino Association voted in 1994 to declare the American White Horse and American Creme Horse two distinct breeds and to promote them as such, rather than using the "American Albino" term. Formerly, they had been promoted as two types within the same breed, but neither the White nor the Creme Horses were true genetic albinos, just horses with light colored skin.

Today, the American White Horse and American Creme Horse Registry continues with many registered Whites and Cremes involved with children or doing ranch activities. This includes 4-H programs, children's parties and other activities. They are especially suited for trained horse trick routines, jumping routines, or similar attractions.

Breed Basics

The "dominant white" and the "dilute cream" are not alike in their genetic makeup, nor, when reproducing, is there any similarity in the effect these two color genes have on the foals produced. The Whites are mostly descendants of Old King, but

only a few Cremes can trace their roots to him. Most Cremes, in fact, are from registered Quarter Horse stock.

White horses are born white and do not change color. They should not be confused with cream colored horses, as they come from a different, dominant white gene, while cream colored horses come from a dilute gene.

White horses will reproduce color as follows: a white horse bred to a colored horse has 50 percent chance of producing a white or colored foal. A white horse bred to a white horse will produce a 75 percent crop of white foals. The off-colored foals of a white horse can be any color, with chestnuts seeming to be in the higher percentage.

The cream color is caused by a recessive gene, meaning that a Creme bred to a horse of color will dilute the color; that is, a Creme bred to a bay will produce a buckskin, and a Creme bred to a chestnut will produce a palomino. A Creme bred to another Creme will produce 100 percent cream colored foals.

Cremes are mostly produced by horses other

than whites: usually buckskins, palominos, duns, or other cream colored horses. The dilute (recessive) gene carried in a palomino, buckskin, dun or cream colored horse is what causes cream color. If two of these horses with the dilute gene are bred to each other and that recessive gene is passed on from both parents, it produces the cream color. Cream color is only produced from two dilute gene carrying parents. A white horse can only produce a Creme if it is bred to a Creme *and* the white horse carries the dilute gene. One of the white horse's parents or ancestors must also have been a dilute gene carrier, from which it had received that gene.

As an example, Carley had an American White mare with blue eyes that she bred to an American White dark-eyed stud whose dam was a cremello that came from several generations of Whites. This pair of White parents produced a Creme foal because the blue-eyed mare (note eye color) had an ancestor with the dilute gene. Both she and the stallion had to each donate a dilute gene in order for the foal to be a Creme Horse. The blue eyes of the White dam indicated a recessive gene in her background and the White stud carried the gene from his dam—thus the Creme foal.

American White Horse

The original American White Horse breed had Old King as a foundation sire, although the studbook is now open to other unrelated horses of like color. The American White Horse is a color breed, thus individuals within the breed will vary in conformation and type according to their background breeding. For example, one from Arabian bloodlines will differ greatly from one with Quarter Horse breeding. The main requirement to be classified as an American White is the horse must have a uniformly, true-white coat and pink skin. No mottling of skin, such as is common with Appaloosas, is acceptable. Since some horses develop a few tiny black spots on their skin in the area of body extremities as they age, these are permitted.

Eye color will vary. White horses have been known to have the following colors of eyes: dark·

brown, dark blue-black, blue, very pale blue, and multicolored (sometimes called parti-eyed). They do not have hazel eyes; only the Cremes do.

The American White Horse is bred not only for white coloring, but also for a good disposition. The breed as a whole is known to be sociable and intelligent with a willing attitude when treated properly. The American White Horse does not go blind or deaf or otherwise is affected adversely, either physically or mentally, because of its coloring, as many preconceived stories have stated.

When given proper care, American Whites live long and useful lives. Many have lived into their late twenties and early thirties. Being pink skinned does require some extra precautions, however. They can be pastured outside, but like the Cremes, it is better if they can be in the shade from 10 a.m. to 4 p.m. and during midday in particular, when ultraviolet rays from the sun are at their strongest. Otherwise they should be handled just like any other colored horse.

White horses are renowned for their temperament and trainability. Carley owned and showed a gelding named White Mystery that was the 1963 Champion Gelding for the White Horse breed. He knew a variety of tricks, was a great jumper, and was used in Roman teams. When Carley was nine years old, she taught him to jump with his eyes covered with a blindfold! That same summer, he was introduced to a saddle for the first time. One week later, Carley was using him for saddle trick riding while on tour. She could ride him bareback with no bridle for performances in which he jumped a four-foot hurdle. He was so gentle that children could learn to ride on him. If he was caught napping in the pasture, children would climb on his back and he would get up and take them for a quiet trip around the pasture. One winter, it snowed so badly that he had to haul a makeshift travois with a fifty-gallon barrel full of water up a hill to the horse pasture, never having been in harness before. He made five more trips up the hill with more barrels without hesitation or trouble.

White horses are beautiful and stunning to

watch. An American White, TWHR Westwind Paris, owned by Don and Jo Ann Anderson of Texas, was cast in three movies. He was featured as the main horse in *Secondhand Lions*, along with four other American White Horses also owned by the Andersons. Paris was featured as the main horse. He was also cast in the 2004 movie, *The Alamo*, starring Dennis Quaid as General Sam Houston, the 2006 movie *Rain*, and several other films.

The American White Horse has proven to be truly versatile and has been used for parades, shows, movies, driving, jumping, gymkhana competition, western and English pleasure, youth camp activities, and handicapped riding programs. It was bred for gentleness, intelligence, beauty, and color. Along with its excellent disposition, the American White has proven to be physically sound and strong, and to have good straight legs. It has no diseases or weaknesses particular to the breed.

American Creme Horse

The American Creme Horse Registry was founded by Ruth Thompson in 1980 to be a registry for cream colored horses with pink skin. As such, the American Creme Horse breed is a color breed, so horses from all major breeds that qualify by color may be registered. If the horse is a product of registered parents, its pedigree is preserved and its bloodline recognized on its registration certificate (such as Quarter Horse, Arabian, or other breeds), as long as documentation of its breeding is provided. In the event that the horse has no proof of its breeding, it may be registered by color without its lineage and it would be identified as to type.

The American Creme Horse must have pink skin. Its skin may be of a darker shade, more like a tan, but must not be gray or black. It cannot have mottling on the skin, such as is common with Appaloosas, nor can it have spots, such as what Paints and Appaloosas have. It must have a solid cream colored coat, which may vary from off white to fairly rich cream, but lighter than palomino. It may be born either nearly white or a darker cream

that looks almost gold, similar to a palomino. This may lighten to near white as it ages, or in rare cases may become a darker cream color. The skin will remain light, however.

The mane and tail may vary from white or cream, to a rich russet coloring. Cremes descending from buckskins or duns may have darker cream points on lower legs. White markings—such as blazes, stars, and socks—are permitted.

Cremes have eyes that can be any color, but most commonly they are pale blue or very pale amber. They can have hazel eyes, which American Whites never have. Cremes never have truly pink or red eyes, but the iris may be such a pale blue that it appears nearly white and the pupil of the eye will reflect pink. This effect, however, is reflected lighting, not eye coloring.

American Cremes have proven to be of good disposition, are intelligent, and perform well according to each horse's particular type. They have been used as jumpers, trail horses, gymkhana competition horses, barrel racers, and driving and ranch horses, as well as pleasure and show horses.

The American Creme has a normal life expectancy if given appropriate care. Like the Whites, their lighter skin is somewhat more sensitive to sun exposure than a dark skinned horse, and it is recommended that shade be provided for them from 10 a.m. to 4 p.m., particularly at midday. This time period may need to be extended for desert or tropical regions. Sun sensitivity varies among different individuals, but only affects the areas where there is no hair covering, such as the end of muzzles and, in some horses, around the eyelids.

Recent research has proven that the light colored hooves of Cremes are just as healthy and durable as dark colored hooves. Cremes do not go blind or deaf or become mentally unstable. Some horse people have stated differently, but this only shows a lack of understanding for these unique horses.

Credit: Carley Daugherty and the American White Horse and Creme Horse Registry

APPALOOSA

Appaloosa Horse Club
2720 West Pullman Road
Moscow, Idaho 83843
www.appaloosa.com

International Colored Appaloosa Association, Inc.
P.O. Box 99
Shipshewana, Indiana 46565
www.icaainc.com

Wherever there are horses, chances are there is an Appaloosa among them. That is because the word is out about this beautiful horse. Not only are Appaloosas different from every other breed, but each one is also different from any other within the breed. It is the handprint of color—what Appaloosa enthusiasts call "the chrome"—that is an intricate part of the breed's mystique. People who own Appaloosas appreciate the difference.

The Appaloosa's distinctive color patterns make it the easiest horse to identify, setting it apart from all others. Its patterns come in an infinite variety—from no spots at all, to more spots than can be counted. Some Appaloosas look as if they have fresh-fallen snow over their backs, loins, and hips. Some Appaloosas are described as "leopards," with Dalmatian-like spots, while others are Appaloosa roans. This is one of the exciting aspects of the Appaloosa: its enormous range of coat colors and patterns. Any number of spotting combinations is possible. The variety and unpredictability is especially intriguing to breeders.

There is even more to the Appaloosa than meets the eye. Breeders have worked hard to preserve the Appaloosa's other special characteristics as well. By

Appaloosa stud horse. *Marybeth Nemec*

selecting for top performance and conformation traits, they have developed a truly extraordinary horse. The Appaloosa has proven his remarkable talents repeatedly by competing in the upper echelons of virtually every sport imaginable—from cutting or reining to racing. While the Appaloosa more than lives up to the athletic demands of today's serious competitions, no other breed can duplicate the quality and characteristics that make the Appaloosa unique. It is the horse Nature destined to be different.

History

The Appaloosa has a bold and colorful heritage, originating some 20,000 years ago. Its coat pattern has fascinated humans since the first hunters recorded its spotted image on their cave walls in what is now France. The peoples of Europe and Asia coveted spotted mounts. Wars were fought with them and over them. They were often presented as gifts of status to the highest rulers, were worshiped in Asia, and were prized mounts of Spanish explorers, Native Americans, and western settlers. Their colorful appearance and unique qualities earned them special recognition. Legends abound about the power, tragedy, and courage of spotted horses, from Persia's Rustam and his spotted mount Rukush to the "blood-sweating" horses (spotted horses) of China and the ghostwind stallion story told by Native American elders.

Though their ancestry can be traced back to earliest recorded time, it is in the melting pot that is America where these spotted horses have established themselves as a true breed. The Nez Perce Indians of the inland northwest deserve much of the credit for the Appaloosa horses of today. With their help, the true beginnings of the Appaloosa as a distinct breed began. The Nez Perce were the only Native Americans known to breed their horses selectively. They were renowned horsemen, and were documented to have had several thousand head of fleet, well-formed horses, with over half estimated to be Appaloosa spotted. Their herds were developed using their own superior

breeding methods and the results were compared by Meriwether Lewis and William Clark to the finest Colonial horses in Virginia.

Up until the association with the Nez Perce, the spotted horses went by various names. Although the Nez Perce never called their horses "Appaloosas," the name indicates the Palouse region in eastern Washington and northern Idaho where the horses were known to be plentiful. White settlers first described the colorful mounts as "a Palouse horse," which was soon slurred to "A Palousey." The term "Appaloosa" is thought to have been a product of this phrase.

The Nez Perce desired only the strongest, fastest, and most sure-footed of mounts and used only the best horses to build their herds. Within their numbers arose a population of horses so distinctive, they inspired early American explorer Meriwether Lewis to describe them in his journal entry, dated February 15, 1806: "Their horses appear to be of an excellent race; they are lofty, elegant formed, active and durable. Some of those horses are pided [sic] with large spots of white irregularly scattered and intermixed with black, brown, bey [sic] or some other dark color . . ."

However, the influx of white settlers to the northwest changed the Nez Perces' destiny and nearly destroyed the legacy of their horse-breeding efforts. When they rebelled against the treaties being imposed upon them, the Nez Perce War of 1877 ensued and they were driven from their homeland by the U.S. Army. The Appaloosa helped them elude the U.S. Cavalry for several months as they traversed more than 1,300 miles of rugged mountain terrain. When Chief Joseph finally surrendered in Montana, the Nez Perce were forced to relinquish their horses. The army quickly disbanded the Indians and their fine horses were dispersed far and wide to soldiers, farmers, army Indian scouts, and even circuses. In their jealous embarrassment over being outsmarted and eluded for so long, the army also ordered many of the Nez Perce horses to be destroyed.

Soon the characteristics so prized by the

Indians were being lost or severely diluted due to indiscriminate breeding, and the Appaloosa breed nearly disappeared. Some that escaped the army or were left behind in the Nez Perce homelands joined the herds of wild horses that roamed the plains. There were also non-treaty Nez Perce people from related tribes who quietly kept on breeding their treasured horses in small communities throughout the Pacific Northwest.

Horse breeders started gathering what they could of the fast-disappearing spotted horses. They began the arduous task of preserving and recreating the animal that had taken the Nez Perce hundreds of years to refine, yet took the army only a few decades to almost wipe out by scattering them to the corners of the country. Breeders used the remnant Appaloosa stock that was bred to each other, and sometimes brought in Arabian blood where necessary and possible to refine and return the Appaloosa to its former glory.

Appaloosa Horse Club

It was Claude Thompson, a wheat farmer from Moro, Oregon, who realized the importance of preserving the spotted-horse breed. He established the Appaloosa Horse Club in 1938 to promote and restore the Appaloosa's position in the horse world. In so doing, the colorful breed began its return from the brink of obscurity. Appaloosa was the name officially adopted when the Appaloosa Horse Club (ApHC) was founded.

Those early years were a period of slow growth for the fledgling registry, as the country was immersed in World War II. After the war ended, however, the registry's growth ascended quickly. In 1947, Thompson appointed 23-year-old George Hatley as executive secretary. Hatley took the shoebox containing the ApHC's records to Moscow, Idaho; there were two hundred registered horses and one hundred ApHC members. The registry quickly outgrew its shoebox.

Today, the ApHC is a major internationally recognized official breed registry. Well over a half million Appaloosas have been entered into the

rolls. It sponsors annual National and World Shows and more than one hundred regional clubs. With 16 percent of registrations stemming from the international market, ApHC recognizes sixteen international affiliates.

The Active Appaloosa

The Appaloosa's color, versatility, willing temperament, and athletic ability make it a popular choice for a number of activities. ApHC classes include roping, jumping, gymkhana events, halter, saddle seat pleasure, and heritage. Many riders have found that Appaloosas have the toughness, resilience, heart, and stamina to travel 25, 50, and even 100 miles in a single day, making them an excellent choice for endurance and competitive riding.

Appaloosas can also race. Fierce competition within the Appaloosa racing industry have produced some of the fastest horses in the world. The breed is recognized as the "middle-distance runner," competing at distances from 220 yards to 8 furlongs. Appaloosa athletes continue to set and break all-breed speed records. Annually more than 450 Appaloosa races pay in excess of $2 million in prize money.

Owners have the luxury of breeding for specific conformation and performance traits—whether selecting for an agile western stock horse or a grand dressage horse. Additionally, the Appaloosa's trustworthy disposition and willingness to please makes it ideal for all ages.

Registration

Breeders may mate Appaloosa to Appaloosa, or may crossbreed with registered American Quarter Horses, Thoroughbreds, or Arabians. Stallions are registered with either the ApHC or an approved breed registry that participates in the ApHC breeding program. They must also be DNA typed.

There are four identifiable characteristics for registration in ApHC, which are:
- Mottled skin
- White eye sclera
- Striped hooves

A beautiful varnish red roan Appaloosa. *Zuzule/Shutterstock*

• Coat pattern

Irregularly pigmented or "mottled" skin is most apparent around the horse's muzzle, eyes, and genitals. Also, many Appaloosas have a distinctly human-looking eye due to the white sclera surrounding the iris (the dark-colored center portion of the eye). Many Appaloosas have vertical stripes on their hooves in the absence of white leg markings. The most widely recognizable characteristic of the breed is the coat pattern.

Mottled or parti-colored skin: The mottled skin characteristic is unique to the Appaloosa horse and is therefore a basic and decisive indicator of the breed. Mottled skin is different from commonly found pink (flesh-colored or non-pigmented) skin because it normally contains dark areas of pigmented skin within the area. The result is a speckled or blotchy pattern of pigmented and non-pigmented skin.

If a horse has mottled skin, it may be found in several places in addition to the muzzle and eye areas. Many other breeds have specks of non-pigmented skin that should not be confused with the Appaloosa's mottled skin.

White sclera: The sclera is the area of the eye that encircles the cornea, which is the colored, or pigmented, portion. The white of the human eye is an example. Although all horses have sclera and can show white around the eye if it is rolled back, up, down, or if the eyelid is lifted, the Appaloosa's white sclera is usually more readily visible than other breeds. This is a distinctive Appaloosa characteristic, provided it is not in combination with a large, white, face marking, such as a bald face.

Striped hooves: Many Appaloosas will have bold, clearly defined, vertical hoof stripes that can be either light or dark striped. But just having striped hooves does not necessarily distinguish Appaloosas from non-Appaloosas. Further identification of other Appaloosa characteristics is necessary in these situations.

Coat patterns: A remarkable aspect of the Appaloosa is the myriad color and pattern combinations they can exhibit. Appaloosa patterns are highly variable, and there are many that may not fit into specific categories easily. Some common terms used to describe coat patterns are:

- Blanket: Solid white commonly over, but not limited to, the hip, with a contrasting base color.
- Spots: White or dark spots over part or all of the body
- Blanket with spots: White blanket that has dark spots within the white
- Roan: Lighter color on parts of the head and over the back, loin, and hips (darker areas may appear along the face frontal bones, above the eye and legs, stifle, point of the hip, and behind the elbow)
- Roan blanket: Roan-colored body with a blanket over, but not limited to, the hip area

Appaloosas are perfect trail horses. This lovely mare is a roan with spots. *Jody and Jori Rafel/Double J Ranch*

Beyond their beautiful color, Appaloosas are great working ranch horses. *Jody and Jori Rafel/Double J Ranch*

- Roan blanket with spots: Roan blanket that has white and/or dark spots within the roan area
- Solid colored horses have a base color with no contrasting color in the form of an Appaloosa coat pattern

Appaloosa patterns should not be confused with overo and tobiano markings of Pintos or Paints, which tend to be larger and of different shape and placement than those of the Appaloosa. Appaloosa spots and spotting patterns can change over the course of the horse's lifetime, but Paint and Pinto spots remain the same.

In order to receive regular registration, a horse must have a recognizable coat pattern or mottled skin and one other characteristic. Horses that receive regular registration are issued numbers (no letters precede the number, but the # symbol does).

Not every Appaloosa is blessed with the easily identifiable characteristics of mottled skin, white eye sclera, striped hooves, and coat pattern. Recognizing this quirk of nature, the ApHC also accepts these non-characteristic horses for registration. They are classified as non-characteristic and their registration numbers are preceded by the letter "N." Non-characteristic Appaloosas can be used for breeding purposes. In order to be shown at ApHC-approved events, however, they must undergo parentage verification and inspection.

Base Coat Colors

The Appaloosa Horse Club recognizes the following thirteen base colors: bay, dark bay or brown, black, buckskin, chestnut, dun, gray, grullo, palomino, red roan, bay roan, blue roan, and white (snow white with pink or light-colored hide; some horses have a white body with dark spots over part or all of their bodies, sometimes referred to as "leopard"). "Varnish marks" are roan markings where the darker color appears in other areas on the body, such as behind the elbows, across the flanks, and other areas.

It's not always easy to predict the color a grown horse will be from the shade it has as a foal. With the exception of gray horses, most foals are born with lighter-colored coats than they will have after they shed later in life.

Disqualifications

No horse shall be registered that has:
- Artificial characteristics or coat patterns
- Draft, pony, albino, Pinto, or Paint breeding
- Continuous leg marking(s) that exceed a line around the throatlatch and behind the ears, and/or
- White marking(s) on the body that are continuous, uninterrupted, longer than six inches, and are separate from an Appaloosa coat pattern, if a pattern is present, and which marking(s) do not blend into the base color
- One parent that is registered with non-breeding stock papers with an approved breed association
- Is less than 14 hands after they are five years old or older.

International Colored Appaloosa Association

Breeders in this association are referred to as "foundation breeders" and the horses referred to as "foundation type" or "blood-breed Appaloosas."

Appaloosa research released in 1994 estimated there were less than 3,000 living registered Appaloosas whose parents, grandparents, and great-grandparents were all registered as Appaloosa rather than another breed. Therefore the International Colored Appaloosa Association (ICAA) was founded in 1991 by several concerned, longtime Appaloosa breeders and owners for the purpose of saving and restoring the Appaloosa as a breed. The ICAA's intent was to preserve the blood-breed (pure) Appaloosa and its heritage, as well as to promote this versatile and athletic horse throughout the world. Its founding board of trustees is concerned, that today's Appaloosa breed teeters on the brink of extinction. Therefore, it has sought to "return the Appaloosa breed registry" to the "purity of the breed."

The ICAA is the first Appaloosa blood-breed registry with its books closed to other breeds, and its registry has classifications based only on pedigrees. The purpose is to preserve the pure equine breed of Appaloosa from undesirable introductions or influences of other breeds. It doesn't accept crossbred horses for registration except geldings showing the Appaloosa coat pattern. The goal is to save all the original Appaloosa's breed traits and to restore it to the admiration and respect it deserves. The ICAA promotes the return of the breed to its original conformation, which would otherwise experience certain extinction. The concept is that there is no such thing as "too much Appaloosa" in a pedigree.

Characteristics

The ideal Appaloosa is most easily described by stating what it obviously is not. It is not a Quarter Horse–, Thoroughbred-, Arabian-, or Morgan-looking horse. Proper breeding practices show that the concept of the big-footed, draft-type "pure Appaloosa" is also inaccurate and not what the original Appaloosa looked like.

A trait to look for in an ICAA-registered Appaloosa is a neck set a bit higher than others due to the breed's use in chasing buffalo, which required seeing higher and moving faster. (A horse sees farther with the head held higher rather than lower, which is its area of close vision.) Also a strong back and deep heart girth, plus good bone on the legs are desirable.

Appaloosas have a variety of head types. Decent-sized ears (for good hearing) and a throatlatch that allows easier breathing are some of the attributes the breed is expected to have. Small feet, small ears, and thin necks are not ideal characteristics for this horse. Appaloosas are renowned for their intelligence and use as a versatile ranch horse.

Currently, it is impossible to be more definitive as to what the conformation of a blood-breed

A beautiful black Appaloosa with blanket and spots. *Zuzule/Shutterstock*

Appaloosa should look like. There are no Appaloosas with eight generations of purebred foundation stock to use as a guide.

Soundness and the physical and mental abilities to perform the skills asked of it are at the top of the list in importance. This is achieved by concentrating the Appaloosa gene pool toward a purebred standard. With each additional generation, the ICAA Appaloosa has a higher concentration of Appaloosa genetics behind it, resulting in a more characteristic Appaloosa. The true Appaloosa is athletic, versatile, and has a family-orientated disposition. It is a distinct breed of horse reminiscent in construction, attitude, and ability of the highly regarded Appaloosa war and buffalo horse of the Pacific Northwest, the world's best rough-country stock horse.

Credit: Appaloosa Horse Club and International Colored Appaloosa Association

ARAAPPALOOSA

AraAppaloosa Foundation Breeders' International

Route 8, Box 317
Fairmont, West Virginia 26554

The AraAppaloosa is a more refined Appaloosa of extraordinary quality—one with color, elegance, performance ability, soundness, stamina, and endurance. It is durable, intelligent, and has a great disposition, yet is capable of great spirit. It displays a combination of the color, personality, and good temperament of the Foundation Appaloosa while retaining the bloodlines and spotlines of the Arabian, which traces back in an unbroken line to the spotted horse of the ages.

Foundation Appaloosa

At its inception in 1938, the Appaloosa Horse Club (ApHC) certified the first 4,932 horses to attain permanent status through inspections as Foundation Appaloosas and gave these horses the "F" prefix before their number. These first horses were considered to be the correct type by the inspectors, who also observed to see if they produced foals of color. Many of these Foundation horses were refined and excellent examples of well-planned breeding programs. They also carried a high percentage of oriental blood, along with the Appaloosa blood tracing to the horses of the Nez Perce, Palouse, and other Native American tribes.

Many of the Foundation horses had distinct characteristics and qualities worth passing on. Additionally, many were genotypes capable of transmitting their color and other attributes to several generations down the line.

Some of the Foundation sire lines known for producing high-performance offspring with refinement are: Apache, Arab Towsirah Alkhar, Bear Paw, Mansfield's Comanche, Freels Chico, Patches, Patchy, Peter K, Red Eagle, Sundance, and Toby.

An elegant, red roan AraAppaloosa stallion. *Claudia and Alexander Kaul*

The AraAppaloosa Foundation Breeders' International (AAFBI) strives to preserve these Foundation lines and welcomes Foundation-bred Appaloosas that carry three or more generations of Appaloosa bloodlines and/or oriental blood.

Spotline Arabian

"Spotline" purebred Arabian horses trace to parti-colored purebreds of the Arabian Desert that had white spots or spotting along with white sclera, some mottled skin, and/or striped hooves—characteristics that make the Appaloosa breed unique. Although some experts do not concede that these characteristics on an Arabian horse are a result of Appaloosa genes, it still is generally agreed that genes producing such color features would certainly complement the Appaloosa.

Many examples of spotted Arabians appear in ancient paintings. The earliest records of Arabian horses are in Egyptian and Middle Eastern artwork, which frequently depicted them with spotted sections on their coats. Since the Arabian has been a distinct breed type for thousands of years, this evidence makes an important statement about what the foundation of the breed looked like. There is no denying that the original Arabian had spotting, and from these ancient artworks, it can be ascertained that spotted Arabians today denote the oldest and purest lines.

There are myriad examples of these markings that appear in breeding logs and early photos, as well as on many modern Arabian horses. Most commonly they are called the "bloody shoulder" or "Kellogg spotted." "Bloody shoulder" refers to red hairs in splotchy patches on one or both shoulders and seen mostly in gray Arabs. Sometimes the red hairs are not visible unless the horse is sweating or being bathed.

"Kellogg spotted" comes from the line of Arabians that were imported by W. K. Kellogg (famous for Kellogg cereals) to America earlier in the twentieth century. These were superb horses from the famous Crabbet Arabian Stud in England. A couple of Kellogg's horses had spots and passed them on to their offspring. The same can be said for other Crabbet and Babson lines.

As well as Arabians, mottled skin and striped hooves are also common on Andalusians and Lipizzaners. Thoroughbreds are another breed that often display spots on their hindquarters, which should not be surprising since they are descendants of oriental horses. The most notable spotted Thoroughbreds are Bend Or, Man O'War, and Candy Spots.

It has been proven that the Arabian spotlines complement and strengthen the Appaloosa spotting gene. The roan gene (not to be confused with the undesirable gray gene) is also useful in attaining optimum color in the AraAppaloosa horse.

History

In 1877 when the Nez Perce failed to escape the U.S. Army, the latter confiscated and destroyed many of the Nez Perce Appaloosas. The horses that survived were crossed with draft animals in an attempt to destroy two centuries of Nez Perce selective breeding.

Claude J. Thompson of Moro, Oregon, founder of the Appaloosa Horse Club, infused the blood of European-bred horses into his native Appaloosas as a way to improve their structure, which the army's draft crosses had altered. He made great strides in restoring the Nez Perce type of Appaloosa by redeveloping its light body with Arabian breeding. Thompson said, "Having some knowledge of the Arabian horse, and knowing that most light breeds were established on Arabian blood, I made a trip to California where I selected and brought home a pure Arabian, Ferras #922, to refine and improve the conformation of my Appaloosa horses."

Ferras' sire and dam were two registered Arabians, Ferdin and Rasima, who were imported from the Crabbet Arabian Stud of England. Thompson most often crossed Ferras to mares of the old Painter Barb line as a way to refine their heavier frames. Seventeen Foundation Appaloosas were sired by Ferras, whose most famous offspring was Red Eagle (ApHC F-209). Claude crossed Ferras with

The AraAppaloosa is a more refined Appaloosa with superb athletic abilities. *Claudia and Alexander Kaul*

Painter's Marvel (ApHC F-47) to produce Red Eagle. Painter's Marvel was a granddaughter of Ferras. Her sire, Painter III, is number F-8, while her dam, Snowflake, is F-2.

Red Eagle represented a turning point for the Appaloosa breed. His coloring was bay and white with bay spots, and he was foaled in 1946. In 1951, Red Eagle won the National Champion stallion title. Later, actor John Derek bought Red Eagle for use in a western film, which never materialized, so Derek sold Red Eagle to Thomas Clay of Caliente, Nevada. While in Nevada, Red Eagle made a name for himself by siring many great horses. Red Eagle's most prominent offspring included American Eagle (F-1472), Simcoes Frosty Eagle, and Hall of Fame stallion Red Eagle's Peacock (F-1476). Red Eagle sired eighty-one registered foals that earned several National Championships and record wins of two Bronze Medallions.

During the 1930s and 1940s, breeders of the Foundation Appaloosas primarily used Arabians and Arabian crosses to refine their spotted horses. More than thirty Arabian stallions are listed as the sires of many Foundation Appaloosas.

The AraAppaloosa

Today, there is a surplus of the heavy, Quarter Horse–type Appaloosa; however, the lighter types infused with Arabian or Thoroughbred blood can still be found. A small percentage of Appaloosa breeders in the United States are determined to keep Claude Thompson's dream alive.

The type of horse needed to continue the breed in the future is the spotted horse of the past, the one the Nez Perce Indians selectively bred and is pictured time and again in paintings throughout history. The AAFBI is a registry that focuses on breeding horses within this heritage, in which the

Arabian breed has had a vital role. Both plans—breeding Appaloosa to Appaloosa, or delving back in the lineage by incorporating oriental/Arabian blood into a breeding program—achieve the same goal: to produce the authentic Appaloosa of the past, the AraAppaloosa.

Owners of valued Appaloosas with Arabian traits are attracted to the breed. In 1997, when Julie and Randy Berghammer found it difficult to obtain registration papers for their Appaloosa mare, they became involved in the AAFBI, which had a hardship clause available for those horses that met the criteria of color and conformation. Their mare was a varnish roan with dark legs and a spot on each hip, commonly referred to as a varnish mark. She also had good conformation and a dished face. She produced a varnish-colored daughter just like herself and a son who also displayed lots of color and a dished face. He was a dark chestnut with a hip blanket, spots, marbling on his barrel, and lightening marks on his legs (common Appaloosa traits). With their beautiful Appaloosa color and obvious Arabian traits, these horses were the type that epitomized the AraAppaloosa. The Berghammers discovered that there were also other horses with Appaloosa/Arabian combined traits that fit the AraAppaloosa description and similarly found their way into the AAFBI.

Registration

When faced with setting up a system to rate horses, the AAFBI decided to highlight known pedigrees and mathematically determine the percentage of blood from these known sources, as well as to emphasize Appaloosa color and characteristics. With use of these pedigrees, breeders can understand which bloodlines help achieve the goal of the perfect AraAppaloosa. The goal is to produce horses that have excellent dispositions, superior athletic conformation, beauty, and Appaloosa color.

A breeding stock certificate is available for solid-colored horses that are produced from qualified parents. A hardship registration is also available for those horses that have no known background.

These horses must display obvious Appaloosa color and characteristics. Conformation must be of the light horse type.

Registration certificates contain a prefix rating, a number, and a suffix rating, such as A 44 ap. From this example, the "A" rating means the horse has at least half Arabian blood; the "44" is the number in the registry; and the "ap" means that the horse has less than half Appaloosa blood. The entire rating list is as follows:

- "a" prefix: at least one-quarter Arabian blood
- "ap" suffix: less than one-half Appaloosa blood
- "A" prefix: at least one-half Arabian blood
- "Ap" suffix: at least one-half Appaloosa blood
- "2A" prefix: at least three-quarters Arabian blood
- "2Ap" suffix: at least three-quarters Appaloosa blood

The AAFBI bloodline rating was established for the express purpose of helping breeders and owners of AraAppaloosas understand what is behind their horses' pedigree. The rating helps determine exactly how much Appaloosa and Arabian blood (which includes Thoroughbred blood) is in the horse being registered. The AAFBI rating is unique because it is based on the most recent four generations. Therefore, as a breeding program continues to focus on restoring the Nez Perce-type Appaloosa, the future foals' rating can improve. (Source: *AraAppaloosa Fact Sheet: The AAFBI Registry and Focused Restoration* by John L. Baker)

Characteristics

With a height varying from 14 to 16 hands, the general appearance of the AraAppaloosa should fit the registry's slogan "tough but elegant." The head must be small and refined. A dished face similar to the Arabian's is desirable but not essential. Eyes should be large and encircled with visible white sclera; ears should be small and curved inward like crescents.

AraAppaloosa. *Claudia and Alexander Kaul*

The neck of the AraAppaloosa should have a natural arch but shouldn't be overly long. Withers are not prominent and the back is short. Although the ideal topline for an Arabian is level, the AraAppaloosa should have a slightly sloping croup and a long, sloping hip, along with deep heart girth and long underline. The overall appearance of the AraAppaloosa should be symmetrical and athletic.

An AraAppaloosa in action is almost unsurpassable in beauty. It has the springy prance, flared nostrils, arched neck, and tail carriage of the Arabian, coupled with the striking contrast of a white blanket and/or spots, striped hooves, and sclera-encircled eyes.

Due to its oriental heritage, an AraAppaloosa foal is likely to inherit loud coloring, although many

AraAppaloosa foals are born with little or no color, then "color out" as they mature. Characteristics such as evident sclera, mottled skin, and striped hooves should be present from birth, even if Appaloosa-type color is not. A variety of patterns exist, but the following are most common:

Spotted blanket: Most breeders prefer this classic pattern. The foreparts of the horse are a solid color, while its rump has a white "blanket" with dark spots. Blankets may vary in size and spots vary in shape, from large egg-shaped spots to halo (roan edged) or teardrop shaped spots.

White blanket: The foreparts are dark and a solid white blanket covers the hindquarters. The blanket may extend to the shoulders.

Marble: The marble pattern comes with maturity. Foals that have this pattern are usually born with a solid color and then roan as they age. Marble AraAppaloosas are often white or roan with speckled spots over their hindquarters. Faces, legs, and necks, however, are often a much darker color. Variations in this pattern are red, strawberry, and blue roans.

Leopard: A marble may seem to be a leopard, but a true leopard AraAppaloosa is foaled snow-white with dark spots over the entire body. A "near leopard" is similar to the true leopard, except the face and upper neck of the horse are a solid color. The legs may be dark with white lightning marks on the cannons. A "fading leopard" is born pure white with loud spots over the coat. If the sire or dam is a gray, however, the owner is sure to see the horse's spots fade with age, resulting in a pure white horse.

Snowflake: This pattern has a dark base color with white spots or flecks sprinkled over the entire body and neck. The snowflake AraAppaloosa is often born solid and then colors with age. There is also a pattern called "snowflake blanket," in which the white spots are concentrated on the rear quarters.

Lace or frosted blanket: The base color of the horse is dark with white "lace" on its rump. Foals that later develop a spotted or white blanket are often born with a muted lace blanket. The blanket may have spots of any size, but the spots are often not too noticeable because there is less contrast.

AraAppaloosas in Action

The future of the AraAppaloosa is moving toward sport horse competition. Many are in endurance racing and several have competed in three-day eventing and dressage.

In Europe, the expanding popularity of the breed is seen in the famous stallion, Congal's Cosmic Sky. He is an AraAppaloosa in Germany that passed the Körung (an advanced breeding suitability test) and is listed in the First Stud Book, which only accepts stallions of the highest perfection with unusually superb conformation and movement. This is a rare and prestigious honor only bestowed on the very best quality stallions, and Sky is the only AraAppaloosa in Germany to have achieved this so far. He also has won his first distance competition, a 36-kilometer race (about 18 miles), competing against sixty-seven horses. He has initiated the excellence of the AraAppaloosa breed to Europe.

AraAppaloosas are great family horses and are quite often used in therapeutic riding programs because of their gentle nature. They make excellent all-around horses, excelling at just about anything for which they are trained, as they are intelligent and pick up training quickly. In the show ring is where they really shine; whether in dressage, hunter/jumper, western pleasure, or saddle seat class, they have a show-ring presence that is breathtaking. AraAppaloosas project the refined elegance of the Arabian and the spotted patterns of the Appaloosa. It is a rare and beautiful breed.

Credit: Randy and Julie Berghammer, Sandy Hollow Farm

ARABIAN

A beautiful Arabian stallion frolicking in the snow. *Pru Critchley*

Arabian Horse Association
10805 E. Bethany Drive
Aurora, Colorado 80014
www.arabianhorses.org

Romance, antiquity, and tradition are integral elements of the Arabian breed's legacy. The Arabian possesses unique qualities that distinguish it from other breeds of horses—their incredible beauty, endurance, and intense affection and loyalty to their owners. Historical figures, such as Napoleon and George Washington, rode Arabians.

The breed is distinctive with their dished head profile; large, lustrous, wide-set eyes on a broad forehead; small, curved ears; and large, efficient nostrils. Known for their deep chest, strong joints, and powerful lungs, Arabians are all-around athletes who can do many things well and love challenges.

History
Authorities are at odds about where the Arabian horse originated. There are certain theories that propose the ancestral Arabian was a wild horse in northern Syria or southern Turkey.

About 3,500 years ago, however, in an area including the valley of the Nile and beyond, the forerunner of the Arabian breed was first noticed when it attained a role alongside kings. Its image appeared on seal rings, stone pillars, and various monuments with regularity after the sixteenth century BC. This ancient horse was observed for many centuries before the term "Arab" was ever used for a race of people or species of horse.

The origin of the word "Arab" is still obscure. Arab is a Semitic word meaning "desert," or the inhabitant thereof, with no reference to nationality. In the Koran, "a'rab" is used for Bedouins (nomadic desert dwellers). Throughout the centuries, the Bedouin tribes that roamed the northern desert in what is now Syria became the most esteemed horse breeders. Their horses reached a zenith of fame as the horse of the "Arabas." The harsh desert environment ensured that only the strongest and keenest horses survived, which passed down many of their resilient physical characteristics that distinguish Arabians to this day.

The Bedouin people bred their horses as war mounts capable of quick forays into enemy camps. The severe desert climate required these nomads to share their food, water, and sometimes even their tents with their horses. Over the millennia, Arabian horses developed a close affinity with humans, as well as a high level of intelligence.

Bedouins zealously maintained the purity of the breed. Even today, the purebred Arabian is virtually the same as the one ridden in ancient Arabia. Due in part to the religious significance attached to this desert horse, as well as its contribution toward the wealth and security of the tribe, the breed flourished in near isolation from other breeds. Traditions of breeding for purity were established so that any mixture of foreign blood from the mountains or the cities surrounding the desert was strictly forbidden. While other desert type breeds developed in North Africa and the periphery of the Great Desert, they were definitely not of the same blood as the Arabian breed and were disdained by the proud Bedouins.

Desert Strains

Arabian mares evolved as the most treasured possession to the Bedouins, who thought no greater gift could be given than an Arabian mare. The value placed upon mares by the Bedouins inevitably led to the practice of tracing of any family of the Arabian horse through the dam. The only requirement of the sire was that he had to be pure. If a dam was a "celebrated" mare of a great mare family, so much the better. Mare families or strains were often named according to the sheik or tribe that bred them.

Bedouins valued purity in a strain of horses above all else, and many tribes owned only one main strain of horse. The five basic families of the breed include Kehilan, Seglawi, Abeyan, Hamdani, and Hadban. Other less choice strains include Managhi (also spelled Muniqi), Jilfan, Shuwayman, and Dahman. Sub-strains developed within each main strain and were named after a celebrated mare or sheik that formed a substantial branch.

A great story of courage, endurance, or speed always accompanied the recitation of the genealogy of the sub-strain, such as the great Kehilet al Krush, the Kehilet Jellabiyat and the Seglawi of Ibn Jedran. Each of these mares carried with it stories of great battles and intrigue. Their daughters were sought after by the most powerful kings, but often remained unattainable. Daughters and granddaughters of these fabled mares changed hands through theft, bribery, and deceit. If any of their descendants were sold, the prices were legendary.

Each strain, when bred pure, developed characteristics that can be recognized and identified. The **Kehilan** (also spelled Kuhailan) strain is noted for depth of chest and masculine power and size. The average pure Kehilan can stand up to 15 hands. Its head is short with a broad forehead and great width in the jowls. Most common colors are gray and chestnut.

The **Seglawi** (also spelled Saqlawi) is known for refinement and almost feminine elegance. This strain is more likely to be fast rather than having great endurance. Seglawi horses display fine bone and longer faces and necks than the Kehilan. The average height is 14.2 hands, and the most common color is bay.

The **Abeyan** (also spelled Abayyan) strain is very similar to the Seglawi. They tend to be refined, and pure Abeyans often have a longer back than that of a typical Arabian. They are small horses, seldom above 14.2 hands, and commonly gray, but carry more white markings than other strains.

Hamdani horses are often considered plain with an athletic, if somewhat masculine, large-boned build. Their heads are more often straight in profile, lacking an extreme *jibbah* (bulging forehead). The Hamdani is one of the largest, standing as tall as 15.2 hands. Common colors are gray and bay.

The **Hadban** strain is a smaller version of the Hamdani, sharing several traits, including a muscular, big-boned build. They are also known for possessing an extremely gentle nature. The average height of a Hadban is 14.3 hands, and the primary color is brown or bay with few, if any, white markings.

Bred in the desert, the Bedouins' remarkable horses evolved like finely tempered steel into the swift, elegant, graceful, and magnificent warhorse with which the Arabs shook the civilized world. Over the centuries, Bedouins zealously maintained the purity of the breed. Due to limited resources, their breeding practices were extremely selective, which eventually established the Arabian as a prized possession throughout the world.

Early Breed Expansion

Europeans had developed bigger horses through the Dark Ages to carry a knight in armor, and their lighter horses were from the pony breeds. Thus, they had nothing with which to compare the smaller, faster horses of the invading Turks. Though very few Arabians accompanied these invaders, an interest in "eastern" horses grew in Europe. To own such a horse would not only allow for the improvement of local stock, but would also endow the fortunate owner with incredible prestige. Such a horse residing in the stable would compare in value to owning a great artistic painting. Europeans of means, primarily aristocracy, went to great lengths to acquire the fabled eastern horses.

Eventually, Europeans began looking to the people of the East for Arabian stock. Soon, European horses had an infusion of Arabian blood, especially as a result of the Christian Crusaders returning from the East between 1099 AD and 1249 AD. With the invention of firearms, heavily armored knights lost their importance, and during the sixteenth century, the handy, light, and speedy horses became more in demand.

As the world slowly shrank due to increasing global travel, the Turkish rulers of the Ottoman Empire began to send gifts of Arabian horses to European heads of state. Thus a revolution in horse breeding occurred when three Arabian stallions were imported to England: the Godolphin Arabian (sometimes called "Barb") imported in 1730, the Byerly Turk (1683), and the Darley Arabian (1703). These three eastern stallions formed the foundation upon which a new breed, the Thoroughbred, was to be built. Today, 93 percent of all modern Thoroughbreds can be traced to these three sires. By direct infusion and through the blood of the Thoroughbred, the Arabian breed has contributed in some degree to all light horse breeds.

The Arabian horse also made inroads into other parts of Europe and even farther east. In France, the Arabian helped to make the famous Percheron and the Limousin (today known as the French Anglo-Arab). Two Arabians were used as foundation sires of the Lipizzaner. In East Prussia, the Arabian was used to create the Trakehner, and in Russia, it contributed extensively to the development of many breeds, including the Orlov Trotter.

In the 1800s, travelers of the Victorian era became enamored with the horse of the desert, and significant Arabian stud farms were founded throughout Europe. The royal families of Poland established notable Arabian studs, as did the kings of Germany and other European nations.

As a result of Lady Anne and Wilfred Blunt's historical sojourns to obtain Egyptian and desert Arabian stock, the world-famous Crabbet Arabian Stud was founded in England. This stud farm eventually provided foundation horses for many countries, including Russia, Poland, Australia, Egypt, and countries across North and South America.

In the United States

The United States was built by utilizing horsepower, and the colonists were quick to realize the value of Arabians. Nathan Harrison of Virginia imported the first Arabian stallion in 1725. This horse reportedly sired three hundred foals from grade mares.

In 1877, President Ulysses S. Grant visited Abdul Hamid II, His Imperial Majesty the Sultan of the Ottoman Empire. There, he was presented with two stallions from the sultan's stable, Leopard and Linden Tree. Leopard was later given to Randolph Huntington, who subsequently imported two mares and two stallions in 1888 from England. This program, limited as it was, is considered as the first purebred Arabian breeding program in the United States.

The Chicago World's Fair (also known as the World's Columbian Exposition) held in 1893 drew widespread

The chiseled head of the Arabian: dished profile, large eyes, and teacup muzzle. *Bridget Lockridge*

public attention and had an important influence on the Arabian horse's foundations in America. While every country in the world was invited to participate, Turkey chose to bring forty-five Arabian horses for a "wild eastern" exhibition. Among the imported Arabians were the mare Nejdme and the stallion Obeyran, which became foundation horses

number one and number two in the Arabian Stud Book of America. Several years later, two mares and one stallion were also registered. Many breeding farms today have horses whose pedigrees can be traced to these nineteenth century Arabians.

One of the most significant imports occurred in 1906, when Homer Davenport received permission

These wide-set eyes reflect the Arabian's intelligence and eloquence.
Pru Critchley

Book by the U.S. Department of Agriculture established the organization as a national registry and the only one for the purebred Arabian breed. Seventy-one purebred Arabians were registered at that point.

Today, the Arabian horse exists in far greater numbers outside of its land of origin than it ever did in the Great Desert. There can be no dispute, however, that the Arabian horse has proven throughout recorded history to be an original breed, of which it remains to this very day. There are now approximately 637,000 purebred Arabians, 340,000 Half Arabians, and 10,000 Anglo-Arabians registered with the Arabian Horse Association.

Egyptian, Polish, and Russian Lines

All Arabians originally came from the Arabian Peninsula, but different countries imported them and set up their own breeding programs. Egyptian, Polish, and Russian Arabians are all examples of different strains of the purebred Arabian that were developed from these early breeding programs.

The Egyptian program focused on hardiness and Arabian type, preserving many of the older desert strains. Many of the homozygous black Arabians, as well as the flaxen-maned chestnut ones, are Egyptian. The term "straight Egyptian" refers to a purebred Arabian's complete sire line, including its sire or grandsires, that goes back to pure Egyptian breeding.

from the sultan of Turkey to export Arabian horses. Davenport, with the backing of then President Theodore Roosevelt, imported twenty-seven horses that became the foundation of the famous Davenport Arabians.

In 1908, the Arabian Horse Club of America (now known as the Arabian Horse Registry of America) was formed and the first studbook was published. Recognition of the Arabian Stud

Polish and Russian Arabian breeding programs were very similar, as their horses were traded, sold, or stolen from each other during wars and invasions. These two programs focused on traits such as stamina and speed; many racing Arabians are products of Russian and Polish breeding.

All these programs have produced National Champion halter and performance horses. There are many breeders in the United States who follow one of these programs and are often referred to as preservationist breeders. Still other breeders concentrate on performance or halter characteristics rather than Arabian strains.

Crabbet Arabians

A Crabbet Arabian is an Arabian whose bloodlines trace back to horses from the once famous Crabbet Park Stud (breeding farm) in England, or the Sheykh Obeyd Stud in Egypt (owned by the same family). These studs were owned by Lady Anne Blunt and her husband, Wilfred Blunt, in the latter half of the nineteenth century. Their purebred Arabian horses were purchased either in Egypt or imported from the Arabian Peninsula.

Crabbet Arabians became world renowned when the Blunts sold their best quality stallions and mares to England and the United States. Most horses that are Crabbet in breeding have lines to the stallions Mesaoud or Raffles. Arabians that trace their heritage in all lines back to horses used in this breeding program are said to be 100 percent Crabbet.

Another term associated with Crabbet Arabians is "CMK" Arabian. CMK breeding stands for Crabbet Maynesboro Kellogg, the names of three Arabian stud farms that used Arabians from desert sources and Crabbet Park in England. All Crabbet Arabians are CMK, but not all CMK Arabians are 100 percent Crabbet.

Arabian Excellence

Given that the Arabian is the original source of quality and speed and remains foremost in the field of endurance and soundness, it has contributed either directly or indirectly to the formation of virtually all the modern breeds of horses. As the oldest of all the light breeds and the foundation stock of most, it is unique in that it does not exist as a result of selective breeding, like other modern light breeds whose breeders found it necessary to establish a registry prior to development. The Arabian is a breed that has been recognized for thousands of years and has been maintained and cherished in its purity as much as is humanly possible. Its influence is commanding to a remarkable degree and invariably dominates all the breeds to which it is introduced, as it contributes superior qualities.

Since the Arabian has been bred and reared in close contact with man from the earliest records and has existed in mutual interdependence, it developed an unequaled ability to bond with humans. It is gentle, affectionate, and familiar, almost to the point of being troublesome. Foals, for example, have no fear of man and are usually indifferent to sudden noises. The Arabian gentleness and tractability, while originally the effect of education, are now inherited, as foals bred in a foreign environment are demonstrating these traits.

Today's purebred Arabian is virtually the same as that ridden in ancient Arabia. Its ancient traits enable it to excel at a variety of activities, displaying athletic talents in disciplines from English to western riding.

Its stamina is legendary as an endurance horse. It is considered the best horse for covering long distances that would exhaust other breeds, and it still has energy for more. Consistently winning competitive trail and endurance rides, the top prizes at endurance events almost always go to riders of Arabians. As an endurance horse, the Arabian has no equal and is the undisputed champion.

The loyal, willing nature of the Arabian makes it the perfect family horse for recreational riding. Its easygoing temperament and smooth gaits are terrific for beginning riders, and its affectionate personality also makes it a great horse for children. Growing up around Arabian horses is an experience that lasts a lifetime.

In the show ring, the Arabian is exceptional, well known for balance and agility. Combined with high intelligence and skillful footwork, it is more than capable in driving and reining events. The Arabian competes in more than four hundred all-Arabian shows, as well as in numerous open shows around the United States and Canada. For speed, agility, and gracefulness, there is nothing like an Arabian.

As the original racehorse, the Arabian is becoming increasingly more popular competing at racetracks throughout the country. Arabians race distances similar to Thoroughbreds, and more than seven hundred all-Arabian races are held throughout the United States annually.

Today's Arabian prices are comparable with other popular breeds; excellent Arabian horses are now accessible to a broad base of horse enthusiasts. With more living Arabian horses in the United States than in all the other countries in the world combined, America has some of the best horses and breeding farms from which to choose.

Standards

The Arabian is a purebred based on pedigree. Horses that only look like Arabians cannot be introduced into the breed. All registered Arabians are validated via DNA to both parents that must be registered as purebred Arabians. A horse conceived and born in the United States or Mexico and whose parents are an eligible stallion and an eligible mare can be registered with the Arabian Horse Association.

Overall appearance: The Arabian can most readily be identified by its dished face, long arching neck, and high tail carriage. When the horse is aroused, it is extremely attentive, and its entire appearance exudes energy, intelligence, courage, and nobility.

Head: The Arabian is especially noted for its delicate head, which has a triangular shape that diminishes rapidly to the small, fine muzzle. Its skull is characterized by its relative shortness, slenderness of the lower jaw, and a larger size brain case.

It features small, tipped-in ears, a tiny teacup muzzle, fine, thin lips, and large, expressive, dark eyes. The nostrils are long, thin, and delicately curled, running upward and outward; their large size assures easy breathing in a hot, dry climate. The eyes are set far apart, nearly at the middle of the head, and are large and lustrous. Long eyelashes were designed to protect the eyes from sand.

The head is frequently enhanced by a slight protrusion over the forehead that extends to just below the eyes. This protrusion, called the *jibbah*, contributes to the Arabian's distinct appearance. The cheek bones are spread wide apart at the throat, enabling the muzzle to be drawn in without compressing the windpipe and permitting the horse to breathe easily when running.

This eloquent, finely chiseled Arabian head has been represented artistically for literally thousands of years. Defined, described, and judged for centuries, the shape and beauty of the Arabian head remains its most unique and sought after quality.

Body: The Arabian's long, arched neck is set high and runs well back into the withers. The withers should be prominent and set well back over a long, sloping shoulder, equal in height with the croup, which has a high tail set.

Many of the Arabian's distinct characteristics proclaim its desert heritage, such as the deep chest, strong joints, and good lungs, which guaranteed its ability to carry riders across large stretches of desert.

In general, Arabians have a short, straight back, a deep chest, well-sprung ribs, deep girth and strong legs of thick density. They have perfect balance and symmetry.

The skeleton is characterized by a relative shortness of skull, a slenderness of the lower jaw and a larger size of brain case. It has fewer vertebrae in the back (usually twenty-three vertebrae as compared to twenty-four in most other equine breeds), as well as in the tail. One of the most distinguishing Arabian characteristics is its naturally high tail carriage sustained by the fewer vertebrae. The pelvic bone has a more horizontal position.

Movement: The Arabian is known for a well coordinated, easy stride with stylish, natural, balanced action. Every time an Arabian moves in its famous floating trot, it announces its proud, graceful nature to the world.

Height: The Arabian horse generally measures 14.1 to 15.1 hands at the withers, although some are above or below this height.

Arched neck, high tail carriage, and alert exuberance are Arabian traits. *Sharon Morris/Shutterstock*

Color: Arabians are bay, gray, chestnut, and black, with an occasional roan. Common markings are stars, strips, snips, or blaze faces, and white feet or white stockings. There are no restrictions about the amount of white on a purebred Arabian.

Today's Arabians are also recognized for their extraordinary intelligence, stamina, and trainability. Although it is the most beautiful of all riding breeds, the Arabian is not just a pretty horse; it is an all-around family horse, competitive sport horse, and work horse. Trail riding, endurance riding, showing, cutting, reining, dressage, jumping, racing, and even ranch work—if a rider is up to it, so is the Arabian.

Credit: Arabian Horse Association

BRINDLE

International Buckskin Horse Association, Inc.
P.O. Box 268
Shelby, Indiana 46377
www.ibha.net

Brindle and Striped Equine International
11819 Pushka
Needville, Texas 77461
www.geocities.com/sbatteate/brindlehos/

The brindle color pattern consists of a watery- or drippy-looking striping, or sometimes just partial striping, over the body of an animal. It is most commonly seen in dogs or cattle, but in horses, the pattern is extremely rare. For this reason, many consider the Brindle horse as a curiosity and quite unique, which is better than the discrimination horses of unusual colors have received in the past.

"I bought my Brindle horse just because the coat pattern was so wild and eye-catching," says Denise Charpilloz of Washington. "I have always been attracted to colorful horses. The brindle pattern is so rare people would approach me to ask, 'What *is* that?' Also, people would point out my Brindle horse to each other, even if they didn't always come up and speak to me directly. More often than not, old-timers will tell me they have been breeding horses for more than thirty years and had *never* seen anything like *that*!"

Expert horse people can live a lifetime and never see a Brindle horse.

Most people say they never knew anything like it existed in horses. After Brindle horse owner J. Sharon Batteate picked up one of her Brindle mares from Texas in an open stock trailer, when she stopped to refuel at various gas stations, people came up and peered in the trailer and exclaimed they had never seen anything like it.

Some Brindles were sold without papers because they were not considered a "correct" color for their

A magnificent Brindle stallion. The stripes look like they are dripping off the horse. *Carole Dunbar*

Brindles stand out from other types of horses and can have various shades of stripes. *Denise Charpilloz*

breed. This happened not only to Brindles, but also to palomino Thoroughbreds, crop-out Paint and Quarter Horses, and others. Fortunately, the climate is much more favorable for unusually colored horses today and the Brindle has experienced much interest.

Brindle coloring has occurred in such diverse breeds as Arabians, Thoroughbreds, mustangs, Quarter Horses, Tennessee Walking Horses, German and Bavarian warmbloods, Russian horses, and Spanish horses, as well as donkeys and mules.

History

The first record of the brindle pattern in horses seems to be by J. A. Lusis in the publication *Genetica*, volume 23, in 1942. In the article entitled, "Striping Patterns in Domestic Horses," he details a brindle Russian cab horse from around the 1800s that was preserved and put in a museum. Reports of brindle or brindle dun patterns from the 1860s to 1870s in the Criollo horses of South America have been documented by writers such as Marrero, Pereyra, Solanet, and Odriozola.

The term "brindle dun" has existed since 1971 as the description for a horse with striping all over its body, and the International Buckskin Horse

Association information booklet used this name as a classification to describe horses with striping in 1977. The booklet described it as "a different and unique body coloration with stripes appearing over the barrel of the body and most, if not all, of the dun factor characteristics. Brindle duns show up in the Netherlands and [is] referred to as an ancient dun color. The peculiar body markings can appear in the form of teardrops or zebra stripes."

In 1988, Mary Jagow of Silver Cliff, Colorado, began organizing the International Striped Horse Association to collect information on various striping patterns. She noticed four basic types of striping: dun factor striping, bay striping (renamed countershading striping), roan striping, and brindle. This organization is no longer in existence.

A website was established for Brindle horses in 1997 by J. Sharon Batteate to provide information on the rare equine brindle coat color, locate other brindle-colored horses, and assemble information on them.

In 1998, Anita Garza began a new registry, the Brindle and Striped Equine International. It accepts horses, ponies, donkeys, zebras, and their hybrids with the brindle pattern. The registry also accepts those with heavy and/or unique dun factor markings and animals with the "netting" pattern.

The February 2006 edition of the *American Quarter Horse Journal*, ran an article on Brindles entitled, "One in a Million," by Christine Hamilton, stating that there finally was verification of the chimera origin (mixed genotypes in the coat from various causes), in two Quarter Horse Brindles. The testing was done at the University of California, Davis. One of the horses was a mare owned by Denise Charpilloz; the other was the stallion, Dunbar's Gold, owned by Carole Dunbar. Thus, it would seem that the brindle pattern is not just some random oddity or abnormality, but before drawing too many conclusions about the pattern, there is a need to locate more examples for study.

Further information about inheritance in Brindle equines was expounded in an article by Tom Moates entitled "Horses of a Different Stripe," Horse Equus magazine, (November of 2006).

Dunbar's Gold was registered in the Brindle and Stiped Equine International as number 1 for Brindle horses in 2000 (he was the first horse entered into the registry). He is a strongly brindled horse—dark red dun with liver chestnut colored stripes, similar to the color of Hershey's chocolate syrup dripping over his coat.

Brindle Basics

Little is currently known about the genetics of the brindle pattern in equines. Previously it was thought to be a random mutation or coat developmental variation that was probably not inheritable, yet examples of Brindles have been found dating back more than one hundred years. Also there are known Brindles that have passed on the pattern to their young, especially with coat texturing.

While dogs are known to have partial brindle patterns, it is not known if the partial striping patterns seen in Brindle equines are the result of partial brindling (as with dogs), or just coat developmental variations that are not inheritable.

Many people confuse the brindle pattern with dun factor markings (stripe down the back, barring on legs, and occasional regular-spaced striping down the ribs). At one time, it was even thought the brindle pattern was just a variation of dun factoring. Indeed, there have been many examples of horses that were probably carrying both dun factoring and brindle coloring. However, numerous photos reveal that many Brindles do not have any dun factor markings whatsoever, indicating the two patterns are probably distinct genetically.

Brindle horses also have texturing in their coat similar to that seen in some Appaloosa horses. Sometimes the pattern seems to be inheritable, especially in terms of coat texturing, but the expression of the darker or more intense pigment that makes the pattern visible is highly variable and changes even with individual horses seasonally and/or yearly. Sometimes the pattern seems to be composed of dark hair (black or brown), or white hair (roan or gray). Stripes on a foal usually grow with it, like spots on a Pinto, but some can shed out a little differently each year.

Information collected since 1990 on Brindle horses is bringing some light on the pattern. It now appears there may be two ways in which a Brindle phenotype (outward appearance) can occur. In some horses, the pattern has not been inheritable, pointing to a possible mosaic or "chimeric" origin, as seen in tortoiseshell cats. In other horses, the pattern has been shown to be inheritable; however, there could be several genes involved in producing similar patterns much the same as pinto/paint spotting can result from several different genes.

Indeterminate patterns are those found in horses, donkeys, or mules with some sort of streaking or texturing that resembles and thus could be the result of brindling, but could also be the result of some other pattern. Some streaking on a brown horse could truly be due to brindling, or it could also have come from dappling breaking up countershading. Another example would be of an animal that supposedly has brindling, but photos do not show the pattern clearly, or it was photographed at a time of year (usually spring) when even normally colored animals will show variations in hair as they shed.

These eye-catching mares have unique-looking, rare brindle striping. *Denise Charpilloz*

Also, it isn't known if some streaking seen on the ribs of a dun horse is actually the result of brindle plus dun, or just extensive dun factor markings.

When looking back at the earliest reports of what is currently called the brindle dun color by the International Buckskin Horse Association, it is speculated that although brindle has often been associated with dun since the first reports of this rare and unusual color, there might actually be two separate components. It now appears to be composed of both factors—brindle and dun—and the combination of both produces the classic brindle dun horse.

However, there is a wide variation in expression of dun factor markings, and some horses considered to be brindle duns might only be the maximum expression of dun factor markings. Others that are "very highly marked" dun factor horses could have resulted from the combination of brindle and dun factors. Additionally, some of the brindle duns are examples of the brindle pattern without any accompanying dun factor markings whatsoever. Since a "heavily marked dun factor" horse, however, would visibly resemble a "brindle plus dun" horse, it will probably always be difficult to distinguish exactly which pattern is shown.

What is known is that chimerism is not the only source of the Brindle pattern in all Brindle horses. Batteate has had two lines in which the pattern was inheritable: her mare Brenda Batty Atty, had three brindled offspring (three brindled out of five total foals), and the mare, Im A Star Moon Bar, had three brindled offspring out of five, plus one carrier. Her son, Ima Star Brindle Bar, sired five brindled foals from seven breedings.

Also Dunbar's Gold has a full brother who has the brindle pattern, his daughter is a Brindle and also his great aunt is a Brindle. Beside these lines, there have also been reports of Brindle offspring from others.

However the brindling occurs, there is much interest in continuing this marvelous and unique color in horses. "I want to try to breed for more Brindles and perhaps restore this ancient coat pattern to the equine world as a viable choice, just like duns or Paints are," says Denise Charpilloz. "I believe this is a potentially important contribution for all horse enthusiasts. I hope others are able to join me in pursuing the Brindle coat pattern."

Credit: J. Sharon Batteate

BUCKSKIN

Buckskins are eye-catching with their distinctive coloring. *Darlene Wohlart/equinephotography.com*

International Buckskin Horse Association, Inc.
P.O. Box 268
Shelby, Indiana 46377
www.ibha.net

The color of a Buckskin horse is an indication of the superior genetic heritage it possesses. Although it is a color, the Buckskin, as well as the grulla or dun horse, is noted for possessing many qualities that are not characteristic of other types of horses. The true Buckskin may be able to trace its lineage through a direct line of dun or buckskin colored ancestors as far back as available recorded history of the animal.

Buckskin is a clear golden color with a black mane and tail. It can be various shades of dark gold to yellow, with dark brown or black points, and sometimes the horse has a dorsal stripe down the spine from the mane to the tail. Buckskins breed true to their own color a large percentage of the time, regardless of the color of their mate.

Among other traits, having a common color is proof of a distinct pure breed. For instance, the Tarpan breed—one of the most unusual in the world today—was a prehistoric wild horse type that became extinct in 1876. Later genetically recreated in 1933, the breed was all mouse dun or grulla in color, typically a sign of original ancient breeds. Another example is the Polish Koniks, a breed preserved today by the Polish government. These small horses are grullo colored and physically identical. They consistently reproduce foals to be of the same height, conformation, and color, so that they are very hard to identify individually since they all look the same.

The proof that the Buckskin is definitely a breed type may be found by viewing its hair under a microscope. When examining the color pigment in the hair shafts of both Buckskin and dun horses, the pigment deposits are arranged very much the same, with the exception that the Buckskin has no concentration of pigment at the tip ends of the hair.

Thus the Buckskin horse is not a mere color, contrary to the popular belief, and is considered to be more than that in the equine world. It has been long noted for its superior qualities and strength. It has more stamina, more determination, harder feet, better bone, and is generally hardier than other horses. A Buckskin with a weak or spavined leg is a rarity. "Tough as wet leather" is a good description of the true Buckskin. Duns, like Buckskins, are also known to have tough hides and durable feet. Early day cowboys often bragged especially about the many good qualities of Buckskin horses as well as duns and grullos. They have long been described as being the toughest horses the West ever had.

History

The registry for Buckskins, the International Buckskin Horse Association (IBHA), also includes dun, red dun, and grullo body colors because all of them trace back to common ancient ancestors.

It is believed that the Spanish Sorraia and the Norwegian Dun are the breeds originating the Buckskin and dun horses of today's light horse industry. The Sorraia was the old original breed of Spain and was a progenitor of Buckskins and duns. The Norwegian Fjord horse (also called the Norwegian Dun) is found today in Norway and other Scandinavian countries and is also a probable contributor. (This breed is so old that its actual origin is lost in antiquity, however, there are many indications that even they obtained their dun coloring from the horses of Spain.) The blood of the Sorraia and the Norwegian Dun filtered into nearly every breed in the world, hence the fact that the Buckskin, dun, or grullo may be found in nearly all breeds today.

Furthermore, it is assumed that the colors as they are known today came from Spanish horses, if for no other reason than that is where the names of the colors originated. The dun terminology is from the *Gateado* name in Spanish, and the Lobo Dun from the Spanish word *lobo*. Grullo (pronounced GREW-yah) is the Spanish name for the Sandhill Crane, a slate colored bird. The word "buckskin" is assumed to have come from an early American settler term describing the color of tanned deer hide.

The Spaniards brought the original Buckskin and dun horses to America when it was first being settled. These horses played an important roll in the making of America and are a part of its heritage.

Color Specifics

Buckskin and grulla colors are both types of dun. Dun is a color that has always been found among horses in the wild. Early wild horses of northwestern America had many dun animals among them. Dun is rarely found in horses bred for racing and showing (i.e. Thoroughbreds and American Saddlebreds), except in Quarter Horses whose background, of course, comes from native-bred horses.

Primitive markings found on horses today are referred to by the IBHA as dun factor points. The term "dun factor" was readily adopted by other

Buckskins are known for their hardiness and tough legs. *Daniel Johnson*

associations in the United States and Australia to refer to the markings. Those markings include the dorsal stripe ("list" or "eel" stripe) down the back of a horse, stripes over the withers, and stripes across the knees and hocks, which are sometimes called zebra stripes. Ventral stripes and chest barring can also be found more in duns and grullas than on Buckskins, but this trait is not considered one of the dun factor markings.

Very rarely a horse will be extensively striped, almost to the extent of a zebra; those of that pattern in the dun color are referred to as "brindle dun" by

IBHA. Such striped horses are known to be found in Siberia, Scandinavia, and Argentina. There are only a few of such horses registered in the IBHA in the United States.

Through natural reproduction in the wild, horses were found to produce the variance of shades within the colors. In the United States when wild horses and domesticated horses ran together with no human interference or control of breeding, dun color variances also occurred.

With the addition of the human element entering the modern day breeding programs, horses of desired pedigrees, show records, conformation, and other attributes are being bred and mixed for certain preferences and body colors. Color is bred for and maintained more truly by those breeders for their choice of color breed registries. Examples are breeders within the registries of Paint, Pinto, Palomino, Buckskin, and Appaloosa, to name a few, who are breeding not only for improved conformation and performance ability, but to maintain the color they like. There are also breeders choosing only to breed for pedigrees, conformation, or performance ability with no regard for color, which sometimes creates undesirable colors, or even undistinguished colors requiring new terminology.

A gray dun can be called just that, although at a later age it would be considered just gray. There is no name for a red dun going gray, but such a horse could appear to be a rose gray in later life. Yellow duns possessing the gray gene might look neither gray nor rose gray and might create some problem in description as they age. Some horses change color or body shade from season to season, but these usually remain within the same color group. Examples would be those Buckskins that appear lighter or darker in winter months. Some grullos also turn almost black in the winter months, but return to their body shade with spring shedding, maintaining the same color from year to year.

Regardless of the variance in shades, Buckskins, duns, and grullas can do almost everything expected of Spanish descended horses: pleasure ride, trail ride, show in hunt seat or western performance, jumping, and dressage are but a few. Cutting cattle, working on ranches, competing in gymkhana, pulling a cart or buggy, and being used in rodeo events (roping, pickup riders, and so on) are other areas of competition, work, and enjoyment in which they can be found. Their color only adds a unique perspective to owning or competing with them.

Registry

The original concept of the international registry was founded as the International Buckskin Horse Registry in California, but in 1971 it was incorporated as the IBHA. Registering Buckskin, dun, red dun, and grullo horses, it has proven to be the largest and most progressive registry in the world for these color types.

IBHA was assisted by Dr. Ben K. Green, an author of horse books who began researching equine colors as a veterinarian in Texas. He worked with IBHA to help develop the understanding and guidelines for registering Buckskin horses. His book, *The Color of Horses*, was the first definitive book on horse colors. His research of thirty years began in West Texas and took him to South America, Europe, and the Middle East.

In 2002, IBHA entered into an alliance with the American Quarter Horse Association, which provided additional exposure for Buckskins and duns and positioned IBHA as the acknowledged authority for those horses. Due to this, the marketability of IBHA registered horses has increased.

The horse industry as a whole continues to grow. A great many people are seeking good breeding stock to add to their herds, thus insisting on registered horses. More people are looking for double registered horses, and many IBHA horses qualify for double registration. Competition has grown in IBHA events, and it is the way to go with the Buckskin, dun, or grulla horses. The value of IBHA registered horses has climbed since the need was created to have such a registry.

IBHA has three registration classifications: Appendix, Tentative, and Permanent. The Appendix registration is for all foals. The Tentative stage is the "proving ground" for stallions and mares. All stallions and mares over one year of age are registered as Tentative, unless both parents are already Permanent. Tentative stallions must sire twelve IBHA registered foals, and Tentative mares must produce three IBHA registered foals to be eligible for advancement to the Permanent stage of registration. Stallions and mares are advanced to Permanent status when they have met the requirements. Geldings are eligible for direct Permanent registration.

Color Standards
Buckskin

A true colored Buckskin should be the color of tanned deer hide with black points. Shades may vary from yellow to dark gold, and points (mane, tail, and legs) are black. Buckskin is a self color (solid color on the main body of the horse) and is clear of any smuttiness that can appear in horses of other body colors. Guard hairs that are buckskin colored grow through the body coat and up over the base of the mane and tail. This is sometimes referred to as "frosted" and can be a lighter shade than buckskin. This trait can be seen in duns also, but not as often.

A Buckskin may or may not have a dorsal stripe. Dappling on the body color is acceptable for registration. Buckskins are not born with dark points, such as black legs, but as their baby hair sheds out, the points become dark. Sometimes dark hairs can be seen in the mane and tail of a foal.

Dun

Dun is an intense color with a hide that has an abundance of pigment in the hairs. It differs from the Buckskin in the respect that the body color is a duller shade and often will have a smutty appearance. Dun horses commonly have dark points of brown to black. Rarely will duns be classified with lighter points or an admixture of light and dark hairs within the points. They sport the dun factor points, which include dorsal stripe and shoulder stripe, and often leg barring will occur as well. Duns vary in body shades and are usually born with their permanent color and dun factor markings, but the latter may develop to be darker later on. The difference between Buckskin and dun, besides the buckskin color, is that dun factor markings, such as barring, are not seen often in Buckskins, but they can still have stripes and dun factoring.

Grullo

Grullo is also considered an intense color. The body color is described as mouse, blue, dove, or slate colored with dark sepia to black points. Grullo has no white hairs mixed in the body hairs. Its hide is comparable to the hide of the dun and is well pigmented to withstand heat and sunlight. It has the dorsal stripe and, in most cases, shoulder stripes and leg barring. The grullo horse is considered one of the most predominant species carrying the dun factor markings (primitive markings, like barring), but the markings are not as prominent as those on the duns. Grullo horses with dun factor markings look like they are a light charcoal color with darker markings over it. They do not look like a gray roan, which has white hairs mixed in, and should not be confused with roan or gray colors.

Red Dun

The red dun will vary in body shades of red, ranging from peach to copper to rich red. In all shades, the accompanying points will be a darker red or chestnut and will be in contrast to a lighter body color. Red dun must have a definite dorsal stripe to be eligible. The dorsal stripe will usually be dark red and predominant. Horses with faint dorsal stripes that do not appear on photos may be denied registration. Leg barring and shoulder stripes are common. The red dun or copper dun is categorized as a self color.

Brindle Dun

Brindle duns have different and unique body coloration with stripes appearing over the barrel of the body. They have most, if not all, of the dun factor characteristics. Brindle duns show up in the Netherlands and are referred to as an ancient dun color. Their peculiar body markings can appear in the form of teardrops or zebra stripes.

White Markings

White markings on the face and lower legs are permissible. Horses having white markings on the body (other than face or lower legs) that do not reflect Paint characteristics will be considered individually. Blue eyes are permissible providing the body color and conformation is acceptable.

A dun stallion. *Stephanie Coffman/Shutterstock*

Interfering white markings are defined as white in an area that would interfere with the dun factor marking. They are not desirable, but are not prohibited either.

Dun Factor Points

These markings can also be on grullos, but are not common in Buckskins.

The dun factor points to be specified for a Dun Factor Class in a horse show shall be as follows:

1. Dorsal stripe
2. Leg barring
3. Ear tips or ears with edging
4. Shoulder stripe or shadowing
5. Neck shadowing
6. Cobwebbing
7. Face masking
8. Mane and/or tail frosting
9. Mottling

The **dorsal stripe** may be black, brown, or red and will vary according to the body color. The stripe will run along the backbone from the withers to the base of the tail, but occasionally, it will not run the full length of the backbone. The width of the stripe

A stunning grulla mare. *Stephanie Coffman/Shutterstock*

will vary. The more pronounced, the better. A dorsal stripe with prongs or barbs extending from the sides is considered better than one without.

Leg barring is horizontal stripes of varying widths that appear across the hocks, on the inside and the front of the hind legs, on the back of forearms, and across the knees.

Ear tips or ears with edging occur when the color on the ends of ears is darker than the body color. Ears are usually outlined on the edges. The most pronounced of ears will have horizontal stripes on the back side.

Shoulder stripe or shadowing is a transverse stripe over the withers running down from them in varying widths and lengths. Occasionally, more than one stripe is seen in different lengths. In some cases, a large shadow effect is seen due to a large area being covered, or stripes close together form the shadow.

Neck shadowing, or neck stripes, are usually dark areas through the neck extending into the hollow of the shoulder. Dark shadows will sometimes appear only on the crest of the neck, or dark lines will point down from the base of the mane.

Cobwebbing originates on the forehead. Lines extend in varying lengths over the forehead resembling a spider web. A few lines extend from the eye in a misplaced "eyebrow" effect. Penciling may occur completely around the eye.

Face masking is black, brown, or red shading on the bridge of the nose, with the same color usually around the eyes. The masking effect may spread to the jaw and muzzle, or can be outlined around the lips and nostrils.

Mane and/or tail frosting is light hairs on either side of the mane or interspersed throughout the mane. In the tail, light hairs appear at the dock of the tail and can run throughout the length of it. The frosted hairs may shed during summer months, in which case they would reappear during the autumn and winter. In some Buckskin horses, the frosting will appear as white hairs mixed through the black mane and tail.

Mottling should not be confused with dapples on a horse's body. Mottling is found on the forearm, gaskins, shoulders, and stifles. It appears as a circular motif in shades darker than the body color. Mottling gives the appearance of "reversed" dapples. It is generally not found on the horse's winter coat.

Conformation

No body color shall be preferred. Conformation is to be considered in judging as not less than 10 percent or more than 20 percent.

The conformation of eligible horses can vary from the Arabian type to the bulldog Quarter Horse type. The ideal type is that of a western or stock saddle horse. There is no preferred type of conformation by IBHA, so owners may breed the type of saddle horse they enjoy most. The horse should be a good representative of its type. Inferior quality horses or ones with undesirable inherent characteristics are not accepted for registration. Horses showing a predominance of draft horse blood are also not eligible.

Ponies are not eligible. The mature horse is to stand at least 14 hands tall.

Disqualifications

Horses appearing to have some dun factor characteristics, but are not of acceptable color, cannot be registered. Palomino horses with a dorsal stripe and line-backed sorrels, chestnuts, grays, and bays will not be accepted as dun horses and are not eligible.

Any horses having albino, Appaloosa, Paint, or Pinto horse characteristics are not eligible for IBHA registration. Mature horses under 14 hands are disqualified for registration, as are horses showing a predominance of gray hairs that become grayer, as well as horses showing roan hairs throughout the body.

Credit: International Buckskin Horse Association, Inc.

HALF ARABIAN AND ANGLO-ARABIAN

This Half Arabian/Saddlebred mare has a pleasant head and trim legs for distance riding. *Henry Gruber*

Arabian Horse Association
10805 E. Bethany Drive
Aurora, Colorado 80014
www.arabianhorses.org

The Arabian horse has captivated people for centuries with its beauty and courageous heart. It was bred to thrive under harsh desert conditions and serve its master with unwavering loyalty. This endearing horse became a treasure and a vital part of the Bedouin family and was cherished above all other possessions. The Arabian's personable nature and innate desire for human companionship have continued as hallmarks of the breed.

As the oldest of all the light breeds and foundation stock for most, the Arabian is unique. It carries bloodlines that trace back a thousand years, making it the purest breed of horse in the world. The purity of its bloodlines enables it to complement any breed with which it is crossed and endows it with prepotency, or genetic strength, to further pass on desirable traits to offspring, such as stamina, refinement, intelligence, and trainability.

Crossing purebred Arabians with other breeds is not a new concept, as this is how all light horse breeds developed. Horsemen through the ages used the Arabian as a fundamental building block in their breeding programs. The tradition of upgrading a breed through the inclusion of Arabian blood has produced some outstanding horses.

Today, Arabian ancestry can be found in many recreational breeds. Lipizzaners, Thoroughbreds, Welsh Ponies, Appaloosas, Quarter Horses, Morgans, Saddlebreds, Tennessee Walking Horses, and many others can trace their origins to the Arabian.

Half Arabian and Anglo-Arabian horses have also proven to be popular. There are 340,000 Half Arabians and 10,000 Anglo-Arabians registered with the Arabian Horse Association (AHA).

The Unique Half Arabian

Horses have increased beauty, endurance, willingness, and intelligence when crossed with an Arabian. They are bred to fulfill a variety of needs, providing riders with unlimited choices for pleasure or performance. The multipurpose Half Arabian is a refined, willing, and able athlete. It can compete and win prize money at local, regional, and national levels, which makes it highly marketable for breeders and owners.

Half Arabians are the result of one registered Arabian parent and a parent of another pure or mixed breed. Grade horses can also be bred to a registered Arabian and produce a foal that can be registered as a Half Arabian.

A wide variety of performance and pleasure Half Arabian horses have evolved. The combinations are as numerous as there are breeds of horses. For a classic saddle-seat equitation horse, the Arabian/Saddlebred is perfect. Besides the Saddlebreds,

English enthusiasts also find exciting horses among the Hackney crosses.

For dressage, there is the expressive Arabian/warmblood. The growth of Dressage, Hunter/Jumper, and Sport Horse divisions makes this cross popular because it is a lighter, elegant, and more responsive horse. The addition of the Sport Horse Nationals to AHA national competitions provides a great showcase for these super athletes.

For a nimble reiner or cutter, the Arabian/Quarter Horse might be the ticket. Avid fans of reining, trail riding, cutting, and working cow events like how Half Arabians can maneuver, respond, learn quickly, and outlast other working western horses. Since the Arabian ranks as the top breed for endurance and other distance riding sports, many Half Arabians compete successfully in these sports also.

When the distinct beauty of the Arabian horse is mixed with one of the color breeds, it produces flashy horses like the Arabian/Pinto, which turns heads wherever it goes. The Arabian adds eye-catching refinement to Buckskin, Palomino, and Appaloosa horses as well.

Whatever the preferred cross is, the Arabian can be counted on to add stamina, intelligence, beauty, and a willing attitude. With more than 300,000 Half Arabians in North America, there is one with the look, way of going, and personality to fit everyone.

Half Arabian Standards

The Half Arabian cross is an effort to infuse the mental and physical attributes of the Arabian with that of another breed. The goal is produce a horse that embodies the positive characteristics of the Arabian along with the positive attributes of the other breed.

Outcrosses to numerous different breeds have been successful. There is no stipulation as to what other breed with which an Arabian must be crossed to produce a Half Arabian. The only criterion is that one parent must be a purebred Arabian.

When crossing the Arabian with a working type

horse, such as a Quarter Horse or Paint, the hope is to achieve a horse that has a strong working type body with a relaxed attitude, perfect for events such as Reining, Western Riding, and Working Cow classes.

The same holds true with other crosses, such as Saddlebred or Dutch Harness crosses for English type mounts, and warmblood or Thoroughbred crosses for hunter or hack type horses. It is important that these horses still retain the attractive Arabian look and trainable disposition. This is not to say, however, that the outcrosses do not have an attractive look or good disposition. It merely means that the desirable look of a Half Arabian horse is similar to a purebred Arabian, but also embodies the positive virtues of the outcross.

A Half Arabian must have one registered purebred Arabian parent, either sire or dam, and the other parent may be a grade horse, a Half Arabian, or a horse registered with another breed. The purebred parent must be registered with either the Arabian Horse Association (AHA), or the Canadian Arabian Horse Registry. A mule, hinny, or any animal other than a horse is not eligible for registration. Horses conceived and born in the United States or Mexico can be registered with the AHA. There are no restrictions regarding height.

The AHA gives Half Arabian and Anglo-Arabian registration numbers from 1A to 9A, depending on how much Arabian blood is present. Horses with one purebred Arabian parent and one non-Arabian parent would be considered Half Arabian (1A). Horses with one purebred Arabian parent and one parent that is Half Arabian are considered three-quarters Arabian (2A). Those from one purebred parent and a three-quarter purebred parent are considered seven-eighths Arabian (3A), and so on up to 9A.

A horse that competes in Half Arabian classes should not be marked down for displaying Arabian characteristics, such as high-set tail carriage. The Half Arabian Halter Division is judged on conformation quality, substance, and Arabian type, in that

order. The horse may show characteristics of any other breed, but the foregoing three qualities take precedence in adjudication of in-hand classes over breed type.

Half Arabian In-Hand Division classes may be divided into Stock/Hunter and Saddle/Pleasure type. This makes it easier to compare apples to apples (so to speak) when judging. In classes that are not divided by discipline, however, no preference should be given to one outcross or the other. The aforementioned judging criteria must always be observed.

The Anglo-Arabian Athlete

A picture of the ultimate sport horse would be one that is substantial, strong, and agile. Add the Arabian's courage, heart, and work ethic, and that is the jumper, eventer, and endurance or dressage horse dreams are made of—the Anglo-Arabian.

The Anglo-Arabian possesses combined traits of two extremely athletic breeds: Arabian and Thoroughbred. The Arabian adds its stamina, intelligence, and refinement, while the Thoroughbred contributes its great racing ability and larger size.

Since the breed is a cross between these two superb light horses, it often expresses great courage and a willing attitude. It has the athleticism, strength, and aptitude for rigorous equestrian events inherited from the Arabian's mental focus and soundness in combination with the Thoroughbred's size and speed. Two great breeds, one extraordinary sport horse!

For a performance potential in a recreational mount, the Anglo-Arabian delivers. Its willing attitude gives active owners a quality horse for everyday riding.

As a true adrenaline delivery machine, the Anglo-Arabian also gives experienced riders the power on demand needed for strenuous equine sports. For the recreational rider who wants quality and a high fitness potential, an Anglo-Arabian is a durable horse with heart, making an excellent choice.

Anglo-Arabians offer a range of capabilities, and each model embodies qualities making them more

The Anglo-Arabian has the capabilities for distance competitions. *Henry Gruber*

than just a horse to ride. They are serious contenders as great sport or show horses, excelling at Olympic events and disciplines that require outstanding ability. They have the speed, heart, and stamina for Federation Equestre Internationale (FEI) disciplines that require superb athletic talent. Worldwide, they make perfect hunter/jumpers and eventers. Anglo-Arabians have the size for long extensions, but remain easily maneuverable. They have the substance and strength for clearing obstacles, but are neither slow nor bulky in their way of going.

Additionally, they have the intelligence and temperament for the painstaking demands of dressage. Anglo-Arabians project a nimble elegance and command attention with their charismatic presence.

They captivate spectators and judges alike with their fluid movement and responsive attitude.

Despite its blue-blooded image, the Anglo-Arabian expresses its true form over long distances. Whether competing in a world-class endurance race over 100 mountainous miles or running 15.5 miles across the flatlands, the Anglo-Arabian is perfect. In distance riding, it is a high-octane horse that is always eager to see what is around the curve or over the next fence.

In England, the Anglo-Arabian is used for fox hunts, steeplechases, and other sporting events. In Spain, riders appreciate the horse's courage in testing the stamina and fighting spirit of bulls destined for the ring. France dedicates a breeding program of Anglo-Arabians to develop finely tuned sport horses that has evolved into the Selle Francais. Many international and Olympic equestrian honors awarded to France for eventing, show jumping, and dressage have been won on famous Anglo-Arabian horses.

In the United States, the Anglo-Arabian has won top awards from national organizations in both endurance and dressage.

Anglo-Arabian History

Early in the history of the Arabian horse in America, directors of the Arabian Horse Registry were sure that the best way to promote Arabians in the United States was to get the U.S. Army interested in using and breeding them. They spent a lot of time, money, and energy proving that Arabians made the best cavalry horses by staging cross-country endurance races. Arabians consistently won the races pitted against the cavalry's Thoroughbreds, which it had been utilizing. This convinced the army of the Arabian's tremendous endurance ability, and in the 1920s, it added Arabian horses to its breeding program. Thus began the first significant introduction of the Arabian/Thoroughbred horse to North America.

Thereafter the Arabian/Thoroughbred cross continued to flourish, producing a superior breed known as the Anglo-Arabian. Serving as both transport and tank, the Anglo-Arabian has the speed and stamina to gallop endless miles across harsh territory and the courage to ride into battle.

Eventually, the army held the studbooks for the Anglo-Arabian. When the army discontinued its horse-mounted cavalry after World War II, it sold the Half Arabian and Anglo-Arabian breed registries to what is now the AHA. The Anglo-Arabian grew from a few hundred horses in 1951 to ten thousand that are now registered.

Anglo-Arabian Standards

An Anglo-Arabian possesses distinct traits of both breeds. The Arabian intelligence, refinement, and stamina mix well with the Thoroughbred's famed size and speed. The ultimate creation is an aristocratic athlete with competitive clout.

Recognized as a separate breed, Anglo-Arabians have their own registry through the AHA. To be eligible in the Anglo-Arabian Registry, the horse must be the result of one of the following crosses:

- Purebred Arabian and Thoroughbred
- Anglo-Arabian and Anglo-Arabian
- Anglo-Arabian and Thoroughbred
- Anglo-Arabian and Arabian

An Anglo-Arabian may be a combination of Arabian and Thoroughbred blood, with no less than 25 percent or more than 75 percent of Arabian blood. Any more would qualify for registration as a Half Arabian, as long as one parent was a purebred Arabian.

Parents must be registered Arabian, Thoroughbred, or Anglo-Arabian horses. The resulting foal must be no less than 25 percent Arabian and no more than 75 percent Arabian. If the foal is more than 75 percent Arabian, it is still eligible for registration within the Half-Arabian Registry, as long as one parent is a purebred Arabian.

The Anglo-Arabian Halter Division is judged on conformation quality, substance, and Arabian type, in that order. The horse also may show characteristics of the Thoroughbred, but the aforementioned three qualities take precedence in adjudication of in-hand classes over breed type.

Height: The Anglo-Arabian is generally 15.2 to 16.3 hands.

Colors: Any solid color is allowed, although several sabino patterned horses are registered.

Disciplines: Anglo-Arabians are eligible for competition in all Half Arabian classes. They excel at jumping, eventing, endurance, dressage, and recreational riding.

Classy Competitors

Why do breeders create hybrid horses such as the Half-Arabian or Anglo-Arabian? It is human nature to try and create something new and different. Some might even call it improving on a breed, although others may say this is not true. Either way, no one can argue about the popularity and interest in Half Arabians. Many Arabian enthusiasts who have purebreds also have Half Arabians and appreciate them both.

Most modern breeds of light horses are derivatives of a cross between an Arabian horse and another breed; this includes the Thoroughbred and the American Quarter Horse. Were it not for innovative breeders, there would not be some of the outstanding breeds of horses enjoyed today.

Although many appreciate their Arabian horse crosses, whether registered or not, there are more recreational and competitive options with a registered horse. Oftentimes it is also easier to sell one that is already registered. A Half Arabian or Anglo-Arabian horse that is registered with another breed can be double registered, thereby adding increased value and marketability for resale.

The AHA continues to administer the Arabian, Anglo-Arabian, and Half Arabian Registries. It offers more opportunities to compete, earn recognition, and win prize money than any other partbred registry or organization. Horses compete in halter, performance, endurance, and competitive trail riding.

There is a world of enjoyment for those involved with the Arabian, Half Arabian, or Anglo-Arabian.

Credit: Arabian Horse Association

MORAB

International Morab Breeders' Association
International Morab Registry
24 Bauneg Beg Road
Sanford, Maine 04073
www.morab.com

Muscular, beautiful, proud, and genuinely loving—that is the Morab. The refined, sculpted beauty of the Arabian, joined with the Morgan's dramatic natural style and stamina, creates an elegantly powerful horse for use in the show ring, as a working horse, or on the trail. Indeed, most Morabs comfortably and quickly switch from any one of these activities to another.

Those who like Arabians or Morgans are often attracted to the Morab because of the unique combination of these two treasured breeds. It expresses the beauty, spirit, and endurance of the Arabian with the strength, power, and common sense of the Morgan. The fusion of these characteristics is genetically complementary and gives the resulting Morab enhanced strength and depth from the Morgan with Arabian refinement and sensitivity. "Muscular, yet refined," best describes the Morab.

It is easy to see why Morab owners treasure their horses and usually keep them for life. They love the Morab disposition and personality; it is eager to please and easy to be around. The combination of its high intelligence with a dependable, affectionate nature is prized by all.

Morabs have excellent conformation that consistently meets the ideal. Even newborn Morab foals are balanced and truly athletic, working naturally off their powerful hindquarters. They are easy keepers and outstanding athletes, performing whatever is asked of them.

Foot and leg problems are a rarity in the breed. Farriers are consistently impressed with the durability of Morab hooves. Most owners choose to leave their Morabs unshod, and their hard hooves require little maintenance. A high percentage of equine

This Morab stallion moves easily and effortlessly.
Pam O'Connell

The sculpted beauty of the Morab head, denoting both strength and refinement. *Pam O'Connell*

veterinarians have chosen to own Morabs, citing the overall perfection of Morab legs and hooves.

Morabs are graceful, free-flowing horses that can conform easily to any type of riding. Many owners report that all they need to do between show classes is to change the gear from English to Western or dressage, and their Morabs transition easily. Mature Morabs seem to welcome the change and stimulation of performing.

The Purebred Morab

Crossbreeding between breeds of horses can produce desirable qualities, but often resulting foals, even from the same breeding, do not always show many consistent traits. This is not true of Morabs. Their qualities are based on foundation lines producing the purebred they are today, answering the question most often asked regarding their status as a breed. Well-bred Morabs have proven over six

generations that they have transmitted their genes with a high degree of certainty to their progeny. In fact, a comparison of first- and fifth-generation foals of the same lines will show almost no changes; Morab breed characteristics remain strong.

One example of this is the Morab's inheritance of the Arabian skeleton, which is unique from other breeds in that it has seventeen ribs (other horses have eighteen), five-lumbar vertebra (others have six), and sixteen tail vertebra (others have eighteen). This skeleton finds its way into the Morab, too, so there are two such breeds with this defining characteristic. It is this ability to transmit like traits to their progeny that makes the Morab a distinct breed, rather than just a nice crossbred horse.

History

The desire to unite the best traits of the Arabian and Morgan into one superlative horse has inspired breeders since the 1800s.

In the 1857 book, *Morgan Horses* by Morgan historian D. C. Linsley, there is a great deal of background information about Arabian outcrossing. A major part of Linsley's book was concerned with perpetuating and improving the Morgan breed, and states that if mares of Morgan blood could not be obtained, mares possessing a strain of racing or Arabian blood could be considered. Linsley specifically recommended one-eighth to one-quarter Arabian blood. Many of these Morgan/Arab crosses (Morabs) were registered in the American Morgan Horse Association prior to the 1948 abolishment of Rule 2 that allowed outcrosses.

Linsley's book contained information about the first volume of the *Morgan Horse Registry*, written by Colonel Joseph Battell, which included an entire chapter devoted to a stallion named Golddust, a horse of great merit. This stallion's bloodlines reveal he was a Morab, registered as #70 in the Morgan registry. He was foaled in 1855 and was bred by Andrew Hoke near Louisville, Kentucky. His sire was Vermont Morgan, and his dam the unregistered Hoke mare. The latter was said to be sired by Zicaaldi, a chestnut Arabian stallion presented by the sultan to the U.S. consul, Mr. Rhind, who imported him to the United States.

Morabs transmit their characteristics with a high rate of certainty. *Clare Plehn*

Golddust became an important sire of the time. He was described as being pure gold in color and 16 hands high. He consistently outperformed any other horse bred before him in Kentucky. He reportedly was never defeated in the show ring at the trot or flat-footed walk; at the flat walk he could do six miles an hour. In 1861, Golddust raced and defeated Iron Duke in a match race, best three out of five heats, for a purse of $10,000.

Besides being an animal of great beauty and refinement, he was noted for endowing his offspring with extreme speed. Although the Civil War and his own untimely death curtailed his stud career, he sired 302 foals and left 44 trotters of record. In "getting" speed (his progeny's racing records), he outranked even the great Hambletonian (foundation sire to racing Standardbreds). In addition to their speed and racing quality, his "get" also illustrated the style and beauty of their Morgan and Arabian lineage. No stallion of his day produced larger, more handsome show-quality horses or more winners in the show ring and trotting races than Golddust.

A search through the International Morab Registry (IMR) records finds more than one hundred of today's Morabs can trace their ancestry back to Golddust.

Early Arabian/Morgan Crosses

Concerning early Arabian statistics with Morgan crossing, *History of the Arabian Horse Club Registry of America*, written in the early 1900s, states a provision for the get of Arabian/Morgan crosses in the early Arabian Horse Club Registry. This reference was discontinued around the time of World War I.

Little more was found until the 1920s when famed publisher William Randolph Hearst had a superior Arabian breeding program as well as a short-lived, but important, Morgan breeding program, which included breeding Morabs. Through the 1930s and 1940s, he bred Morabs by crossing his Arabian stallions of mostly Crabbet- or Davenport-based lines to his Morgan mares and used them for work on the rough mountainous terrain of his ranches. Hearst is credited with having coined the word "Morab," even though some of his Morabs were registered as Morgans in the American Morgan Horse Association (AMHA). To date there have been twenty-five of the IMR-registered Morabs whose ancestry have been traced back to this breeding program.

Another significant early Morab breeding line was also developed by the world-famous SMS Ranch in Texas. The purchase of two Morgan stud colts, along with a band of seven Morgan brood mares just prior to 1920, marked the beginning of the SMS expansion into Morgans. A few years later, three U.S. Remount Arabian stallions were added to the stock, and fine Morab cutting horses evolved.

In 1956, another original program of first-generation Morab breeding was begun by Martha Doyle Fuller of Clovis, California. She wanted to produce a horse that could successfully compete on the open show circuit. After experimenting with several breeds, she found that the Morab was the only one that could consistently fill the bill generation after generation.

It was from her Morab breeding program that the first Morab registry was established. Her daughter and son-in-law, Ilene and James Miller, founded the first Morab association, the American Morab Horse Association, incorporated in 1973, as well as the first Morab registry, the Morab Horse Registry of America (MHRA), often called Clovis for the town where they lived.

Ilene Miller was often referred to as Mrs. Morab for her efforts to locate all existing registered and unregistered Morabs, and for her ongoing, professional promotion of the breed. At the time of her untimely death, it was estimated that she had registered approximately five hundred Morabs in Clovis and sponsored several Morab clubs nationwide. It was due to her efforts and her registry that records of the earliest Morabs were preserved, providing a tie from the past to some of today's Morab breeding programs.

Distinctive Morab characteristics are evident in this foal.

The gentle eye and eloquent head of this mare is inherited in her foal. *Pru Critchley*

The Morab Registry

In 1987, the International Morab Breeders' Association (IMBA) was incorporated, and by 1992, it had instituted the first fully computerized Morab registry, the International Morab Registry (IMR). In an effort to protect breed history and maintain breed continuity, the IMR rules stated that all Morabs registered with a previous Morab registry would be accepted for IMR registration. Thus, bloodlines from the early registry foundations—Golddust, Hearst Morabs, SMS stock, and the Clovis Registry—have been preserved.

In 1978, Ilene Miller and the MHRA established the criteria that a registered Morab cannot exceed the percentages of 25/75 of either Arabian or Morgan bloodlines. This standard is still the rule for today's registered Morabs. All registered first-generation Morabs today are from purebred Morgan and Arabian parents, making them 50 percent Morgan and 50 percent Arabian. Succeeding generations of Morabs can still be bred to one purebred parent Morgan or Arabian, as long as the percentage does not exceed 75 percent of either parent's breed, thus ensuring Morab traits are not lost. Morab-to-Morab breedings are encouraged and there are now third-, fourth-, and even fifth-generation Morab-to-Morab foals recorded and registered in the IMR.

First-generation Morabs and others with one or two purebred parents are eligible for double and triple registrations with the Half-Arabian Registry of the Arabian Horse Association, the Half Morgan Registry in the Archival Morgan Record, and the American Warmblood Registry. Plus, all Morabs have the added possibility of registration with various color and pattern registries, offering many award programs and showing opportunities, in addition to the popular IMBA Lifetime Achievement Award Program (LAAP), which offers incentives and special awards during the entire lifetime of an IMR-registered Morab.

The IMR does not have any marking, color, or pattern restrictions. Morabs can have a rainbow of colors and overo patterns (pinto spotting), as well as gaited movement. IMR is accepted by the Palomino Horse Breeders of America and the International Buckskin Horse Association, and is pending with the Pinto Horse Association of America.

All Morab foals born after January 1, 2003, must be DNA tested and "parent verified." The registry offers these services as well as color testing.

Sport, eventing, combined driving endurance, show, endurance riding, and dressage are events now common to the breed. Morabs qualify for Partners 'N Performance award affiliations with the U.S. Dressage Federation, American Endurance Ride Conference, and U.S. Combined Training Association; others are pending. Recent years have brought a new appreciation of the Morab breed for its own fine qualities. With its great disposition and way of moving, it is also desirable as a family and pleasure riding horse.

Standards

The Morab body should be compact, medium length, well muscled, smooth, and stylish; it should display distinct refinement. The degree of refinement will vary with the breeding, but it should

always be apparent in the head and legs.

Morab refinement isn't the only inherited Arabian influence. The Arabian has often been called the "drinker of winds" for its powerful lungs and endurance capacity. Combining that respiratory makeup with the broad, powerful chest of the Morgan provides the Morab with a naturally superior breathing system.

The Morab possesses a shorter back than that of other breeds (one vertebra less, like the Arabian). This shorter back, combined with the longer croup of the Morgan, endows the Morab with great strength and a smooth, graceful way of moving. It has a natural action or a lower action, depending on the breeding of the animal.

Morabs have a free-flowing gait, working off their powerful hindquarters with natural athletic ability and carry themselves collected. This enables them to excel in competitive and endurance riding, as well as dressage, jumping, and cutting.

Morab hooves and legs hold up well to excessive stress, since the Morgan trait contributes wonderful formation of bone and a medium-length pastern; the Arabian parent adds the broad, hard hoof and lower heel. This accounts for their almost nonexistent foot and leg problems, and many breeders report that their Morabs are never shod, requiring only minimal hoof trimming.

The Morab head may be straight or slightly dished, with a big, powerful jaw that contrasts to the small muzzle, which has large, bold nostrils. The large, dark eyes are set off by a wide forehead. Morabs have thick, luxuriant manes and tails that balance out their muscular build.

Morabs are late to mature, often not reaching their potential until the age of seven, but they remain in top condition for many years.

Despite all the other highly prized Morab traits, most owners and breeders will cite the Morab's intelligent, dependable, and affectionate nature as its most valued quality. When the spirit and people-loving nature of the Arabian is added to the Morgan's compatible character, the resulting breed is a horse that cannot be beat in temperament,

intelligence, and willing attitude. That is why mature Morabs are popular as mounts for children, amateur riders, and senior citizens.

Height: A mature Morab will generally range from 14.3 to 15.3 hands.

Weight: 950 to 1,200 pounds.

Quality: Should have dense bone with sufficient substance, well-developed joints and tendons, and a fine, silky coat. Overall appearance of the Morab is always pleasing, showing great strength, but is never coarse.

Disposition: Calm, affectionate, intelligent, and dependable are the best descriptions of the Morab.

Colors: May be any color and exhibit the white markings typical of a Morgan or Arabian: star, blaze, white stockings, and similar markings.

Eyes: Large, dark, expressive, bright, clear, and wide-set eyes.

Ears: Set wide apart, characteristically curved in at the top, finely pointed and carried alertly.

Mane and Foretop: Full and silky in texture.

Throatlatch: Clean and well defined; never thick.

Neck: Heavy in appearance, but refined and of good length, displaying a natural arched appearance. It should be smoothly joined to the shoulder and deepest at the point of the shoulder. Stallions tend to have a more fully developed crest than either a mare or gelding.

Chest: Has good depth and width. A mature Morab is broad in the chest, which is quite noticeable through the heart and back ribs: also slightly wider through the hip. This room and compaction of body structure gives the Morab stamina, as well as great speed.

Withers: Defined and not too high, but should be slightly higher than the point of the hip.

Shoulders: Muscled and have good length and slope.

Back: Short, broad, and deep in the girth.

Forelegs: Long, sound, with flat bones and large joints; broad forearms; short cannon bones free of meat. Tendons should be squarely set and well apart; when viewed from the front, they should appear thin and must be straight; when viewed from the side, they will appear wide and strong.

Fetlock: Large, not round, but rather wide.

Barrel: Large and round with well-sprung close ribs; deep and full, yet with a trim flank.

Hip: Muscled and of good length with a horizontal pelvic build that endows the Morab with a full, unsloped croup. The shape of the hindquarters and the pelvic angle is the most apparent difference between the Morab and other breeds. Hipbones never show on adults.

Hind Legs: Squarely set and so placed that the Morab turns on its hindquarters with its legs well under it.

Hocks: Neither close together nor wider apart than the fetlocks when viewed from the rear. Should be wide, deep, and clean.

Hooves: Medium sized, nearly round, open at the heel, smooth and dense, but never brittle.

Pasterns: Clean, strong, medium length; should match the slope of the shoulder.

Tail: Set fairly high and carried gaily.

Way of moving: The Morab in action has a free-flowing gait, working off its strong hindquarters, and carries itself collected. A Morab can possess a natural action or a lower action, depending on its breeding.

Credit: International Morab Breeders' Association and the International Morab Registry

Opposite: Muscular, yet refined, describes the ideal Morab. *Pru Critchley*

MORGAN

The American Morgan Horse Association, Inc.
122 Bostwick Road
Shelburne, Vermont 05482
www.morganhorse.com

In 1789, George Washington became the first president of the United States; that same year in southern New England, a small bay colt named Figure was born. Becoming the founding stallion of the Morgan breed, Figure was destined to play a dramatic role in the development of the new nation. As American as apple pie, the Morgan horse was instrumental in forming the United States and continues to be a great horse.

Figure is the horse to which all Morgans are related. He was probably about 15 hands tall, as he was advertised for stud at different times as being a bit more or less at that height. (Measurements were done literally in hands during that period, thus not equated exactly to four inches.) He had a compact, muscular build and was very round in his rear quarters. His stylish way of moving impressed many pioneer farmers and settlers.

He could work hard all day, moving with agility over rocky fields and through dense woods, and still be fresh enough afterwards to win a race. Soon tales of his strength, speed, endurance, and gentle disposition spread throughout the small New England towns. His stud services were offered throughout the Connecticut River Valley, and his ability to stamp progeny with his likeness was astounding. He was ridden by a U.S. president, as well as society ladies who appreciated his calm temperament. Figure

The Morgan's arched neck, depth of body, and trim legs are typical. *Casi Lark*

became a legend in his lifetime and was renamed as the Justin Morgan Horse, after his owner.

It was often speculated as to what type of breeding Figure came from, but facts from the testimony of John Morgan Jr., as written in *The Albany Cultivator* (vol. 9, 1842, p. 110), as well as other evidence, has brought the truth regarding Figure's ancestry and life.

Parentage

Figure was born probably in Massachusetts and was sired by a horse named True Briton, reputed to be the fastest horse in America and originally sold to Colonel James DeLancey for $200, a costly sum even for a purebred at that time. True Briton was then stolen from DeLancey, a Tory during the time of the American Revolution.

True Briton reappeared when he was purchased by Captain Selah Norton, a member of a group who oversaw the defense of the state of Connecticut during the American Revolution. The group met regularly at the War Office on the Green in Lebanon, Connecticut. This was a busy place during the American Revolution, as the French had a huge cavalry that was training horses and troops on the Green, drilling daily in front of the War Office where Norton frequented. It is probable that many horses came and went there at that time.

After the war, Norton apparently had an opportunity to observe True Briton, perhaps through his visits at the War Office, and he bought the horse. Norton changed True Briton's name to Beautiful Bay, which implies what color he was and his quality. He was also known as Traveler. John Morgan Jr. (cousin to Justin Morgan) leased True Briton from Norton in 1788 and 1789, when Figure's dam was bred to him.

Norton also owned Sportsman, a possible great grandsire of Figure on his dam's side. He probably rode Sportsman to the meetings at the War Office. He and Justin Morgan could have been musical friends as they both had an interest in music: Morgan was a reputable composer and both he and Norton wrote musical psalms. Regardless

The Morgan's kind eye and intelligent face denote a true aristocrat. *Linda Konichek*

of the circumstances, Justin Morgan had access to Sportsman, standing him at stud in West Springfield, Massachusetts, in 1778; Norton also advertised Sportsman in other stud seasons during the war.

True Briton was a quality stallion that traced back to the Byerly Turk on his sire's side within five generations. On his dam's side, he traced back to the Godolphin Arabian once within three generations and again in the fourth generation. Also on his dam's side, he had Childers in the fifth generation that was out of the Darley Arabian and the Byerly Turk in the eighth and ninth generations.

Figure's dam was unnamed, but she was sired by a horse named Arabian Ranger who was out of Wildair breeding, going back in the fourth generation to Cade by the famous Godolphin Arabian and Roxana. Also on that side, she had Childers in the sixth generation (by the Darley Arabian). On her dam's side, her grandsire was Sportsman.

Additionally, there were nine other ancestors on both Figure's sire and dam sides that had the word "Arabian" in their names. Figure undoubtedly had Arabian blood, and there was a significant amount of line breeding involving the three most famous and finest stallions of that era: the Godolphin Arabian, the Byerly Turk, and the Darley Arabian,

This stallion's upright neck, compact body, and sheer elegance are Morgan traits. *Bridget Lockridge*

all famous Oriental sires of their time, having great influence on the English Thoroughbred.

It might be said that ancestors coming from further back than a few generations, such as these, could have any noticeable heritable influence. Having the Godolphin Arabian, the Byerly Turk, and the Darley Arabian as ancestors, however, is extremely significant. These are the founding sires of the English Thoroughbred breed and were known to pass their qualities down many generations. A pedigree that included line breeding on all three sires is a well-planned breeding

usually undertaken by knowledgeable horsemen. In other words, Figure's quality was not a happenstance of nature. He was a true aristocrat of the horse world.

Figure's Owners

The man Justin Morgan is most famous in history for his horse, which founded the Morgan breed. He is also less widely known, but equally respected, as a musical composer of notable talent. His family was described as being "substantial yeoman farmers" in Springfield, Massachusetts, and many held town and church offices. In 1771, Morgan was deeded a portion of his father's barn and a small amount of land. A self-described husbandman, or farmer (according to the town's records), Justin Morgan also was a teacher and businessman, but it was his talent as a stallioneer (that is, he maintained stallions and charged stud fees to generate an income) that fixed his reputation in history.

During the American Revolution, Springfield was a cavalry depot for the Patriots, which created a beehive of horse activity in the area. Hartford, Connecticut, the acknowledged horse center of the time, was relatively close by, being just down the river. Morgan had many horse pursuits while in Massachusetts, besides his other endeavors. He owned a few mares and raised foals by the stallions he stood at stud. One of the last mares he owned was bred to True Briton the year he left Springfield in 1788, when he moved his family to Randolph, Vermont.

True Briton was in the possession of Justin's cousin, John Morgan Jr., when this happened. It is unclear who actually owned Figure's dam when she was bred and at the time she had Figure, but when Figure was two years old, he became the property of Justin Morgan.

Figure was then advertised at stud in West Hartford, Connecticut, by Samuel Whitman in 1792, possibly due to a lease agreement, which was common in those times. Figure was apparently taken to Randolph, Vermont, by Justin Morgan late that spring, as he was no longer advertised at stud by Whitman after May 21. Morgan advertised him at stud in 1793, 1794, and 1795. Just when Figure passed out of Morgan's hands is not certain, but it is believed Morgan leased him in the autumn of 1795 to clear land for a Mr. Fisk for $15 a year.

In 1796, Figure was advertised at stud by Jonathan Shepard of Montpelier, Vermont. Shepard often used him in match races with great success. Figure raced against two New York running horses in Brookfield, Vermont, in 1796, defeating both easily. That stretch of road is still known as "Morgan Mile" to this day and is located close to the place Morgan is said to have lived, near the Randolph-Brookfield town line.

Figure switched hands again; in 1797, Jonathan Shepard traded him with a blacksmith shop for a farm. His whereabouts were unknown between 1797 and 1801, but it was possible he was in Canada. He then switched hands several times and ended up with David Goss in 1805. There, he worked on the Goss farm, except for two months in spring when he was on a stallion service circuit, on which he became known as the Goss Horse. In one season, Goss claimed Figure bred 127 mares. Goss sold him in 1811, and Figure was used to haul freight.

The Morgan's expressive head with prominent eyes and small ears. *Bridget Lockridge*

He was part of a six-horse hitch where the horses had to be regularly exchanged for fresh ones—all except for Figure, who outlasted them all.

He spent the balance of his life in and around the state of Vermont. In 1817 he was exhibited at the Randolph, Vermont, fair. The same year, he was the parade mount for President James Monroe in Montpelier, Vermont. In 1821, he was kicked by another horse on the Levi Bean Farm and later died from the injury. He was thirty-two years old.

Founding of a Breed

Figure's style, beauty, intelligence, and good sense guaranteed that he would never be forgotten. During his own lifetime, Figure's versatility as a working horse and prepotency as a sire earned him great respect in colonial New England. In keeping with the custom of the time, he was known by his early owner's name, Justin Morgan, but dedicated fanciers often simply called him "the Justin."

His most respected quality among horsemen was his ability to reproduce foals with his attributes. His descendants were instantly recognizable for their distinctive look (or type) and were revered for their stamina, beauty, willingness to please, and easy-keeping qualities, necessary on Vermont's marginal hillside farms. They played a prominent role in Vermont's history by serving as general purpose horses on farms. Outside markets developed for Morgan horses in the 1830s and 1840s, enabling many Vermont farmers to pay off their mortgages.

Their reputation for strength and endurance quickly spread, and soon early Morgans were invaluable for clearing fields in colonial New England and then beating all comers in trotting, running, pulling, and even walking races *after* a hard day's work. They also fulfilled the role of racehorse on America's early harness racing tracks, with some of Figure's offspring holding racing records.

From this one stallion and three of his get—the stallions Woodbury, Bulrush, and Sherman—emerged a breed of horse that would secure a prominent place in American culture. Morgans were used as light draft and stagecoach horses in

the 1800s and pulled the Concord Coach when it was introduced, leading to the success of stage lines in Vermont.

Morgans became known for their substance and stamina. They distinguished themselves with their strong ground-covering gaits, making them perfect for traveling long distances in the burgeoning country. As their fame spread, the breed moved westward, becoming popular as ranch and Pony Express horses, where their intelligence and ability to work all day were valued.

America's Warhorse

When war divided the nation, the Morgan horse was the U.S. Cavalry's mount of choice. The 1st Vermont Cavalry was mounted entirely on Morgans during the American Civil War, and its troops were so envied that raids were staged to capture the horses for Confederate use. Morgans were smaller than horses from other states, like New York, yet they handled long marches and battles better than larger horses. Many times, the troops and their horses would not have enough to eat, but the powerful Morgans could survive on just about anything. They remained level-headed under fire and could march all day without becoming lame. Some books have even credited the Union victory to the Morgans, because they were quicker in battle than the larger horses ridden by the Confederate troops.

Union General Philip Sheridan rode his black Morgan, Rienzi, into history at the battle of Winchester, which was captured by Thomas Buchanan Read's poem, "Sheridan's Ride." Confederate General Thomas Jonathan "Stonewall" Jackson rode Little Sorrel, a Morgan captured by Confederate troops, until Jackson died from injuries sustained in battle.

So well suited were Morgans to cavalry work that in 1907 the U.S. government established an official Morgan breeding farm in Weybridge, Vermont. From there, Morgans were transferred to remount stallion stations across the nation where they were bred to local mares. This was to improve

Morgans have a distinctive, vigorous, and animated style.

the quality of the offspring and ensure that quality horses would be available in times of war. Morgans were used in both World War I and II.

Gradually after the Civil War, Morgans began to lose favor as they were not fast enough for short distance racing on the tracks and lacked the height desired by many in the city markets. When mounted units were being phased out in the early 1950s, the government farm was deeded to the University of Vermont, where the Morgan

Morgans are up to any athletic challenge.

breeding program has continued. It is the oldest continuous breeding program of any horse breed in the United States today.

In Other Breeds

Morgans have also distinguished themselves by making major contributions to the development of other breeds, including the American Quarter Horse, American Saddlebred, Tennessee Walking Horse, and Standardbred. These breeds have often outstripped the Morgan breed's ability to perform the more specialized tasks.

The Morgan's agility, stamina, beauty, and intelligence are traits that were inherited and valued by the American Quarter Horse. Popular Quarter Horse stallions such as Joe Bailey, Yellow Jacket, Royal King, and Joe Hancock were half- or full-blooded Morgans. Old-timers still tell stories about train cars full of Morgan mares being unloaded on the King Ranch in Kingsville, Texas, to add Morgan characteristics to the ranch's cattle horses.

The Saddlebred world used an abundance of Morgan blood to develop their showy breed, as 90 percent of today's Saddlebreds still carry Morgan ancestry, which contributes to its spirited attitude and flash needed to win in competitions. The Saddlebred foundation stallion, Peavine, was a grandson of the Morgan, Stockbridge Chief, and the well-known Saddlebred, Cabell's Lexington, was a grandson of the Morgan, Black Hawk.

Allen F-1, the foundation sire of the Tennessee Walking Horse, was the offspring of the Morgan mare, Maggie Marshall. Allen F-1 was bred to the mare Gertrude, which is said to have Morgan sires in her pedigree, and produced the influential stallion, Roan Allen F-38. Today's Tennessee Walking Horses still have the looks, endurance, and personality for which Morgans are known.

The American Standardbred also drew on Morgan sons and daughters to add stamina, substance, and purity of gait to their trotting lines.

Each of these breeds has benefited from the Morgan's contributions of sound legs and feet, beauty, intelligence, and endurance, as well as its strong gaits.

The Morgan Today

In bygone days, the Morgan earned its keep by clearing the wooded mountainsides in Vermont. It was developed as a general purpose horse with an ability to perform many tasks well. After a full day of work, it could out-walk, out-trot, and out-run any others under saddle or in harness. Its willingness to take on new challenges established its value with owners who appreciated a good horse.

Its versatility continues to stand the Morgan in good stead today for those who like a horse that can do a little of everything, making it just as valuable to modern owners. The Denver Police Department depends on Morgans to help patrol the streets and control crowds. According to their officers, their Morgans will allow themselves be "talked into" difficult situations and also have an above-average intelligence. They have "the best legs and feet of the entire horse world," says one Denver officer. "They don't have the lumps and bumps like most patrol horses get; they just go, go, go! I believe that my patrol horse should go wherever I say to go, whether it's upstairs, downstairs, whatever—and the Morgan is that kind of horse. If I wanted him to swim the ocean, he would."

The Morgan is neither a fad nor a status symbol, but the sort of prized possession that makes even breeders of other horses take notice and become undying promoters. Its intelligence and good sense make the Morgan a perfect companion. Its willingness and even temperament make it easy for all to enjoy: children or adults, individuals or families, amateurs or professionals. With its soundness, athleticism, and stamina, it is a horse that gets the job done. Its thriftiness and longevity have made this breed a bargain for more than two hundred years. With its proud carriage, upright and graceful neck, intelligent face, and kind eyes, it lifts the heart, is easy to love, and is affordable to own. To please people is the Morgan's heritage.

In the Show Ring

Today's show horses are now asked to be specialists more often than they are asked to perform multiple tasks, but Morgans can still be found winning in every arena of competition, from trail and jumping, to reining and dressage. The versatile Morgan is a breed that can fill any role with the greatest success. Whether used for pleasure riding or competing at the local, national, or international level, the Morgan is the perfect horse. The animated excitement of the park class, the mannerly way of the English Pleasure class, the smoothness of Pleasure Driving or Classic Pleasure riding, the ground-covering action of the Hunter Pleasure riding, or easygoing nature of Western Riding are all accomplished by Morgans with a winning style.

They excel in the Roadster class and are unmatched in Carriage Driving. They have represented the United States in multiple world-class competitions and have come home with numerous honors. Their speed, stamina, and willingness to obey their drivers in demanding situations makes them the most popular breed of carriage horse in the United States.

In the elegant world of dressage, Morgans have earned top honors against all breeds in national competitions. They are naturally balanced and can collect for precise movements with ease. Their medium size makes Morgans especially suitable for riders who want to enjoy all aspects of working with the dressage horse.

This same balance makes the Morgan uniquely qualified for the exciting world of reining. Its agility and power produces winning sliding stops, spins, and reining maneuvers. The Morgan excels at eventing, and its stamina and endurance make it a champion in both combined training and competitive trail rigors. Its ability and power make this horse an exciting mount when faced with the challenges of the jumping arena, where few can match its courage and intelligence. Its compact size allows it to get in and out of tricky jumping combinations safely.

As a Breed

In the late 1800s, D. C. Linsley, a native of Middlebury, Vermont, researched the Morgan breed and compiled an essay on its history and genealogy. Using Linsley's work as a basis, Joseph Battell published the first volume of *The Morgan Horse Register* in 1894.

The Morgan Horse Club, now the American Morgan Horse Association, was organized at the 1909 Vermont State Fair, where the national Morgan horse shows of the early twentieth century were held. In 1948, the American Morgan Horse Register closed its books in order to preserve Morgan type and established a reciprocal agreement for Morgans registered with the Canadian Morgan Horse Association and the British Morgan Horse Society. Today, more than 160,000 Morgan horses have been recorded in the official register.

The Morgan is the first recognized American horse breed in the United States and is the official state animal of both Vermont and Massachusetts. It can trace its roots back to an earlier starting point than any other American breed, most of which identify their foundation stock to horses that were alive at the turn of the twentieth century. This is a full one hundred years after the Morgan breed began. Other American breeds are largely based upon a group of horses chosen for similar traits, such as gait, color, or speed. Morgans are unique in that they can trace their bloodline to one common ancestor over several centuries ago.

Today, twenty generations have passed, and yet the descendents of the phenomenal eighteenth century stallion, Justin Morgan (Figure), still share his remarkable traits. All Morgan horses trace their lineage back to Justin Morgan, the only horse to have a breed named after him.

Standard

The Morgan is best known for its distinctive type, which is still very much reflective of Figure. Morgans can be distinguished from other breeds by their compact, muscular, yet refined bodies, their large expressive eyes, and their chiseled faces. Morgan "upheadedness" (a proud, upright head carriage) and stylish, spirited gaits are also recognizable traits of the breed.

In 1996, the registry removed the "high white rule," which restricted horses with white above the knees and hocks from being registered. The consensus was that any horse that had two registered Morgans for parents should not be restricted from the record books, regardless of it having white above the knees and hocks. Morgans come in all colors and include black, brown, bay, chestnut, palomino, buckskin, smoky black, cremello, perlino, and smoky cream.

The **head** should be expressive with broad forehead; large prominent eyes; straight or slightly dished, short face; firm, fine lips; large nostrils; and well-rounded jowls. The ears should be short and shapely, set rather wide apart, and carried alertly. Mares may have slightly longer ears.

The **throatlatch** is slightly deeper than other breeds and should be refined sufficiently to allow proper flexion at the poll and normal respiration.

The **neck** should come out on top of an extremely well-angulated shoulder, with depth from the top of the withers to the point of the shoulder. It should be slightly arched and should blend with the withers and back. The top line of the neck should be considerably longer than the bottom line. It should be relatively fine in relation to sex, as the stallion should have more crest than the mare or gelding. An animal gelded late in life may resemble the stallion more closely.

The **withers** should be well defined and extend into the back in proportion to the angulation of the shoulder.

The **body** should be compact with a short back, close coupling, broad loins, deep flank, well-sprung ribs, and a long, well muscled croup. A weak, low, or long back is a severe fault. The Morgan should portray good spring of rib and well-rounded buttocks. Slab-sided individuals should be faulted. The stifle should be placed well forward and low in the flank area.

The **legs** should be straight and sound with short cannons, flat bone, and an appearance of overall substance with refinement. The forearm should be relatively long in proportion to the cannon. The pasterns should have sufficient length and angulation to provide a light, springy step.

The extreme angulation of the shoulder can result in the arm being a little more vertical than in other breeds, placing the front legs slightly farther forward on the body, but the front legs should be straight and perpendicular to the ground.

The structure of the **rear legs** is of extreme importance for the selection of a long-lasting equine athlete. The rear cannons should be perpendicular to the ground when the points of hocks and buttocks are in the same vertical lines. Legs should be straight, and the gaskin relatively long in relation to the cannon. Any sign of poor angulation of the hocks, sickle hocks, or cow hocks must be considered a severe fault. Lack of proper flexion of the hock is cause for very close examination of the entire structure of the rear legs and should not be tolerated in breeding stock or show ring winners.

The **feet** should be in proportion to the size of the horse and round, open at the heel, with a concave sole and hoof of dense structure.

Viewed from the front, the **chest** should be well developed. The front legs should be perpendicular to the ground and closely attached to the body.

Viewed from the side, the **top line** should have a gentle curve from the poll to the back, giving the impression of the neck sitting on top of the withers rather than in front of them, then continuing to a short, straight back, and a relatively level croup, and finally rounding into a well muscled thigh.

The **tail** should be attached high and carried well-arched and graceful.

The **underline** should be long and the body deep through the heart girth and flanks.

At maturity, the **croup** should *not* be higher than the withers. Viewed from the rear, the croup should be well rounded and thighs and gaskins well-muscled.

The **height** ranges from 14.1 to 15.2 hands, with some individuals being under or over.

Horses must be serviceably sound—that is, they must not show evidence of lameness, broken wind, or complete loss of sight in either eye.

Stallions two years old and over must have all the fully developed physical characteristics of a stallion. Mature stallions must be masculine in appearance, and likewise, mares must be feminine in appearance.

Other distinctive attributes of the Morgan horse are its presence and personality. These include animation, adaptability, stamina, attitude, vigor, tractability, and alertness.

Correct **way of going** for In-Hand classes is described below:

• The walk should be rapid, flat-footed, and elastic with a four-beat cadence and with the accent on flexion in the pastern.

• The trot should be a two-beat, diagonal gait, animated, elastic, square, and collected. The rear action should be in balance with the front.

• Posing horses must stand squarely on all four feet with the front legs perpendicular to the ground. Rear legs may be placed slightly back. Judges must ask exhibitors to move the hind legs up under the horse for inspection.

Credit: The American Morgan Horse Association, Inc. and Kathy Furr, National Museum of the Morgan Horse

MORIESIAN

Moriesian horse. *Ellie Neerdahls/Twin Artesian Stables*

Moriesian Horse Registry
1001 N. Russell Road
Snohomish, Washington 98290
www.moriesianhorseregistry.com

The Moriesian horse (pronounced "more ree jhin," similar to Polynesian) is the result of a breeding program initiated in the United States to produce horses with the versatility of the Morgan and the elegance and charisma of the Friesian, two breeds from which it takes its name. By blending them together, a combination is produced that cannot be matched.

The famous power of the Friesian in conjunction with the renowned maneuverability of the Morgan creates an exceptional warmblood in the Moriesian. It inherits its size and awesome presence from the Friesian, and refined head and strong hindquarters from the Morgan. The classic beauty of both heritages is vividly displayed. Size and substance with refinement and presence—that is the Moriesian.

Moriesian mare and foal. *Ellie Neerdahls/Twin Artesian Stables*

Friesian Foundation

The Friesian horse reportedly dates back three thousand years, though the breed known today was developed in the twelfth century in northern Europe. Friesians were ridden by the Teutonic Knights and used as warhorses for the crusades. They were always the mount of the aristocrats, owned only by noblemen and knights. Their original breeding and pedigrees were very closely controlled.

Further refinement during the seventeenth century produced a horse that could carry large loads, exist on meager rations, and possessed the agility to be effective in battle. They were heavy bodied, black, upheaded horses with an expressive face, high-set neck, and outstanding crest.

These distinctive trademarks have continued in the modern Friesian breed, with the high-set neck, broad chest, lightly accentuated croup, low-set tail,

and noble face. Equally impressive are the thick, flowing mane, long, luxuriant tail, and feathering from the knees down. They have a rippling, heavier body mass and dense bone, with the average height between 15.2 and 16.3 hands. They are intelligent, graceful, agile, sweet natured, and willing, with a powerful elastic gait. Whether used for jousting, dressage or driving, their beauty projects an awesome presence, leaving a lasting impression.

Crossing Friesians with other breeds has been popular throughout history because of the quality in the resulting foals. They have contributed their outstanding attributes to create the Moriesian breed as well.

Morgan Foundation

The Morgan horse is a distinctly American bred horse. Over two hundred years ago, a legendary horse breeder set out to create the ultimate utility horse. He began with the stallion Figure, later known by his master's name, Justin Morgan. The Morgan breed originated with this dark bay stallion born in 1789 around Springfield, Massachusetts. Justin Morgan was known for his strength, speed, and stamina. He was as adept at clearing land and farm work as he was at challenging racing opponents in colonial New England.

Justin Morgan's ability to stamp his foals with his own traits was also legendary. The Morgan breed grew and spread quickly as thrifty New Englanders recognized the same qualities in his offspring.

This one stallion, Justin Morgan, provided the basis for several of America's native breeds. The Morgan horse has helped establish such breeds as the Standardbred, American Saddlebred, American Quarter Horse, and the Tennessee Walking Horse.

The Morgan is easily recognized by its proud carriage, distinctive and attractive head with expressive eyes, and its upright, graceful neck that is muscular and crested. It is deep bodied and has compact, strongly muscled quarters and short, strong legs. The average height is 14.1 to 15.2 hands.

The Morgan breed exists mainly because of its people-pleasing nature, and because it is also a flexible and maneuverable horse. Morgans are known for their versatility; they excel in park and pleasure riding or driving, dressage, jumping, trail riding, western riding, and cutting. Their stamina also makes them excellent in endurance riding.

The Morgan was instrumental in establishing the Moriesian horse, the same as it as done with many other breeds. Both the Morgan and Friesian are famous for passing on their traits to others and for their trainability, mild manners, and friendly disposition, which have been passed on to the Moriesian.

Breed History

The Moriesian Horse Registry (MHR) was started in 1996 by Betty Pace, owner of Dark Knight Friesians in Utah. Pace saw the Morgan/Friesian cross as taking the best characteristics from each breed to produce a more versatile and lively horse.

Unfortunately, due to illness Pace was unable to maintain the registry and it became dormant for several months. In 1999, Barb Collins made contact with Pace while searching for a way to register a horse and eventually took over the registry. The spelling of the breed changed from Morisian to Moriesian to eliminate mispronunciations. The MHR contracted with the Veterinary Genetics Lab at the University of California, Davis, for DNA testing.

The Moriesian breed has established a reputation as the perfect performance competitor, as well as a quality family horse. Although the breed is young, Moriesians excel in the athletic ability, typically winning both in harness and under saddle. They have the natural capacity to collect into a frame of roundness for classical dressage and carriage driving. The combination of balance and symmetry they portray is truly art in motion.

Moriesians are proving this ability in competition. Breeder Ellie Neerdaels produced an exceptional first-generation registered Moriesian, Opus Black Mikasa, a stallion that has earned Elite Sport Horse status in the registry based on his U.S. Dressage Federation performance. He is also the first foundation stallion in the Moriesian registry and the first to produce second and third generation Moriesians (where both parents are registered Moriesians). With his profound looks, disposition, and talent, he turns many heads.

"My dream evolved to combine the incredible presence and qualities of the Friesian with the versatility of the Morgan, producing more refinement," says Neerdaels. "[This is done by] blending the best to the best to create size and substance, along with refinement and the movement and balance I desired in a sport horse. With selective breeding, my horses turned out to be all of this—plus a pretty face!"

Another Moriesian, Legendary Mars, owned by Susan Solomon, was the yearling American Warmblood Registry (AWR) Halter Champion, plus he took fourth out of all breeds and ages in 1994 at the Royal Dressage Festival in Port Jervis,

Moriesian horse. *Ellie Neerdahls/Twin Artesian Stables*

New York. He showed at Devon, winning fourth in all breed yearling colts. In 1996 he won first in suitability of dressage at the Royal Dressage Festival as a three year old.

Many have shown themselves to excel in combined driving competitions. Dave Wharton, representing Canada with his two Moriesians, competed in the 1993 World Pair Championship in Gladstone, New Jersey, and was one of the select few asked back for a special presentation before the judges. Also, Gloria Austin has won ribbons with her four Moriesians in high level four-in-hand driving competitions.

The variety and high level of these achievements exemplify the Moriesian's beauty and graceful movement.

Characteristics

Moriesians are known to continue to grow and mature until age six, so it is not unusual for them

Moriesian horses. *Ellie Neerdahls/Twin Artesian Stables*

to have a final change of height at that age. Their average size of 15.1 to 16.1 hands makes them comfortable for most riders.

The Moriesian is built for success in all disciplines, with its refined, compact body providing athletic power. It displays a proud, upheaded stature, kind, prominent eyes, expressive face, short back, and dense bone structure. The slope of its shoulder and movement tend to be more Friesian-like, giving it a regal appearance. People admire its luxurious full mane and tail, and some Moriesians exhibit the added bonus of "feathers"—long hair on the lower legs.

Lighter boned than a Friesian, Moriesians have more of the qualities sought after in a sport horse. Their full, upright, sloping neck set into an open shoulder allows for the capability of huge movement. They have the size and bone without being over-bulked—refinement and size without draft coarseness.

They are natural show animals and are magnificent to watch, ride, and drive. Some love to jump and prove to be excellent hunters, expressing great versatility and fluid movement.

As sport horses, Moriesians excel in classical dressage due to their presence and superb ability to come under themselves and propel forward. The trot is up and forward with impulsion from the hindquarters. This comes naturally to the Moriesian, as do collection and the ability to stretch and bend through the haunches, making dressage work seem easy. Their canter is big, forward, and very comfortable. Lateral work seems easy for them.

Moriesians are adaptable and eager to perform. They make wonderful family horses. They love to learn, coming from two breeds known for their heart, mild manners, and friendliness. Their common sense makes people think they are more mature at an early age. The breed is honest, willing to please, and versatile, bringing lasting value to its owner. Its kind, intelligent disposition and easygoing manner makes it a great companion for riders of all ages.

Registry Divisions

MHR Moriesians cannot exceed 75 percent or have less than 25 percent of Friesian or Morgan documented bloodlines to be registered.

The Moriesian Horse Registry has three main divisions and an elite status division:

1. First Generation 'F' (Foundation) Moriesian Horse Registration: This division applies to Moriesians resulting from a Friesian and Morgan cross. DNA typing is required for all mares and stallions.

2. Moriesian 'M' Horse Registration: This division applies to the foal or horse from a Moriesian sire and Moriesian dam. Requirements include DNA proof of parentage.

3. Three Quarter Moriesian Registration: This division applies to the foal or horse resulting from a Moriesian and either a Friesian or Morgan cross, thus it has 75/25 percent of either Morgan or Friesian blood. Requirements include DNA proof of parentage.

4. Elite Moriesian Sport Horse Division: The purpose of this division is to promote the Moriesian breed as sport horses. The horse must be a registered Moriesian and be proven in one of the following tests: In-hand, dressage, combined driving, show jumping (jumpers and hunters), endurance riding, competitive trail riding and performance.

Breed Standard

The head should show a balance of Friesian nobility and Morgan refinement; the eyes are expressive and soft, and the face straight or slightly dished and short. The ears should be small and upright with turned in tips. The neck should rise from a high set on the withers and show a clean arch to an upright headset. The throatlatch should allow flexion. The appearance is regal.

The withers should be defined yet blend into both neck and back cleanly. The powerful shoulders should be a combination of depth from the Morgan and the sloping angle of the Friesian. The back should be strong, well muscled, and short to medium in length, and the barrel round and deep. A long or weak back is a fault. It should blend into broad loins and a well muscled and round croup. The croup should not be higher than the withers.

The legs should be straight, lighter boned than a Friesian but more substantial than a Morgan, with well-defined joints. The front legs should have forearms longer than the cannon bones, and the rear legs should have well muscled gaskins and cannon bones that are perpendicular to the ground. Legs may or may not be feathered, but feathering is preferred. The feet should be size proportionate to leg bone mass and be hard and strong.

The height of the Moriesian should fall between 15.1 and 16.1 hands, though variations are acceptable. Additionally, any color is accepted, though most common are black, bay, and chestnut.

The horse's temperament should be kind, alert, and willing. Both heritages provide the Moriesian a combination of stamina and versatility with calmness and loyalty.

All movement should be free and forward with suspension. The walk should have a distinct four-beat cadence and good length of stride. The trot should have a two-beat cadence, should be balanced and animated, and should show engagement behind and forward reach in front. The canter should have a three-beat cadence and should be well balanced and powerful, with drive from behind.

Credit: Moriesian Horse Registry

PALOMINO

Palomino Horse Association
Route 1, Box 125
Nelson, Missouri 65347
www.palominohorseassoc.com

The Palomino has journeyed down through the pages of history. There are stories about golden horses among the Arabs and the Moors. Crusaders remembered the "Golden Ones" on the battlefield when they fought the desert chiefs of Saladin who rode them. During the crusades, the Muslim leader Saladin presented Richard the Lionheart of England with two splendid war horses; one was a gray, the other a golden Palomino. There are other numerous leaders throughout history that have owned Palominos.

The place of origin of the Palomino probably never will be conclusively determined. Myths and legends of various countries shroud its beginning, which is no modern phenomenon. The golden horse with ivory-colored mane and tail appears in ancient tapestries and paintings of Europe and Asia, as well as in Japanese and Chinese art of past centuries. Nowhere has the first history of the Palomino been recorded, but most horsemen agree that all light-bodied horses have descended from the Arabian and the Barb. There are many Arabian Palominos that are registered with the Palomino Horse Association and they are definitely palomino colored.

These splendid golden horses were favored by Her Majesty Isabella of Bourbon, the beloved queen who pawned her jewels to pay for the expenses of Columbus's first expedition to the New World. In the Remuda Real (royal horse herd) of Spain, Isabella kept a full hundred Palominos. As they were the chosen favorites of the crown, only members of the royal family and nobles of the household were permitted to ride them; a commoner was not allowed to own one. It is on record that Isabella sent a Palomino stallion and five mares to her viceroy in New Spain

Palomino Morab mare. *Bridget Lockridge*

(Mexico) to perpetuate the golden horse in the New World. From this nucleus, Palomino blood spread from the Texas plains to California.

The word "Palomino" is a Spanish surname. Many feel that Palomino is only a color and not a breed, which is true that the color of palomino is apparent in all breeds. Yet the Palomino of Spanish times, the "Golden Dorado," was as close to being a breed as any strain of horse. The Dorado was of Arabic-Moorish-Spanish blood and breeding, closely akin to the Arabian and the Moorish Barb.

The Palomino of Spanish times was not bred by being crossed with sorrels. The Spanish had many shades of golden horses, and when they did use corral breeding (enclosing two horses for definite breeding purposes), a light-colored Palomino mare would be mated with a dark-colored Palomino stallion. This point has been noted in an old book printed in Barcelona in 1774.

Palominos in the Media

The Palomino's flashy gold color and ivory mane and tail attract attention wherever it goes, but it is also a multipurpose horse. Palominos are admired not only for their stunning beauty, but for their versatility, maneuverability, and endurance. They can be found in ranching, racing, rodeos, pleasure riding, parades, shows, fiestas, jumping, trail rides, and all other equine activities. There are even a few Palomino movie stars, including Trigger, Trigger Jr., and Mr. Ed, which were registered with the Palomino Horse Association. Trigger and Trigger Jr. were the faithful mounts of the the famous singing cowboy and movie star, Roy Rogers. Trigger was a half Quarter Horse, half Thoroughbred Palomino. Everyone remembering the 1940s and 1950s knew Trigger. In the 1960s, Mr. Ed, the talking horse, starred in his own eponymous TV series.

Whatever event the Palomino participates in, it draws attention with its colorful glamour. Many Palominos are ridden in parades where their beauty is highlighted and has brought them much popularity. The Palomino Horse Association has had many horses that were ridden in the Tournament of Roses Parade, with some still participating today.

Registry

In the United States, the Original Palomino Registry began in 1935 when Dick Halliday registered the golden stallion El Rey de los Reyes. Halliday researched the golden horse for many years and wrote magazine articles that brought the Palomino to public attention. His articles created a great deal of interest, and within a few years,

Singing cowboy star Roy Rogers poses with his Palomino horse, Trigger, in a 1960s publicity still.

hundreds of breeders were specializing in the propagation of Palomino horses.

Today's Palomino Horse Association is the continuation of the Original Palomino Registry incorporated in 1936. It has many sanctioned shows and members throughout the United States, Canada, and around the world. The registry includes horses from many different countries and does not discriminate against any breed, but recognizes all breeds based on color and conformation. There are horses from every breed registered with the Palomino Horse Association except draft horses and ponies, which cannot be registered, but are issued a Palomino draft or pony certificate under those headings.

Also recognized are unregistered horses with the color that proves to be Palomino. The conformation would depend on the breed of horse, as all breeds differ in their size and other requirements.

Palomino Morab stallion. *Pam O'Connell*

Characteristics

The ideal Palomino color is that of a gold coin, but the shade can vary from light gold to medium or dark gold. The mane and tail should be white, ivory, silver, or flaxen, but 15 percent dark or sorrel hair mixed in is allowed.

In the last few years, cream-colored horses with blue eyes have been accepted. It has been researched and proven that these light-colored Palominos always produce a Palomino and, therefore, are definite breeding stock.

White blazes and white stockings are allowed, but not spots. The body color must be some shade of solid gold. The gold color and flowing white mane and tail are outstanding and outshine most other colors; however, accepted colors can range all the way from cremello to chocolate (dark gold) palomino. The mane and tail should be kept clean and cared for to maintain the white, silver, or flaxen color. Bleaching them white is not allowed.

Credit: Palomino Horse Association

PINTABIAN

Pintabian Horse Registry, Inc.
P.O. Box 360
Karlstad, Minnesota 56732
www.pintabianregistry.com

The Pintabian [pin-TAY´-bee-an] is a horse that has certainly created quite a stir in the horse industry. Known for its timeless beauty, this elegant animal has distinguishing characteristics that set it apart from all other breeds in the equine world. The Pintabian proudly sports the aristocratic class of the Arabian, combined with beautiful spotting.

The Pintabian was originally developed in North America by crossing horses with the tobiano pattern back to Arabians until a strain of tobianos with Arabian type was created. These highly esteemed spotted horses are, in fact, more than 99 percent Arabian in blood. It took dedicated horsemen with fortitude and foresight many years to bring this vivacious breed into existence. The Pintabian's notable physical features and its engaging markings make it impossible to mistake it for a member of any other breed.

Foundation

The Arabian from which the Pintabian so strongly descends is considered the first breed of horse known to humans. Bedouin tribes from the Middle Eastern deserts believed the exquisite Arabian was a gift from God and even included Arabians as members of their households. These horses had their own look. They were prized and guarded zealously by their ancient breeders, who carefully protected the purity of the horses and painstakingly recorded their bloodlines.

The ideal Pintabian, such as this stallion, has impeccable conformation and stunning color.
Pintabian Horse Registry

Beneath the stylish exterior of the Pintabian is a foundation that is ideal for pleasure or show. *Pintabian Horse Registry*

Purebred Arabians, however, did not have the tobiano spotting pattern. Many authorities believe tobiano spotting was introduced to Russia during the Roman Empire, where it became common among the wild horses of the Russian plains. Eventually horses with the same type of spotting spread throughout Europe. Later, tobiano spotting was found among horses brought to North America and was associated with Native Americans, who diligently sought them out for their attractive coloring. Native owners of such horses were regarded as affluent and wealthy.

The historic beauty of the Arabian and the flashy tobiano spotting are now combined in one breed, the Pintabian. The Pintabian Horse Registry, which was officially established in 1992, carries on the traditions of the early Bedouins by keeping accurate records and detailed pedigrees. Its first sanctioned breed show was held in Detroit Lakes, Minnesota,

in 2001 and drew exhibitors from as far away as Alberta, Canada, to compete. Since then, popularity of the Pintabian has spread and it can now be found in Africa, Australia, and Europe, in addition to North America.

Tobiano Pattern

Tobiano is a specific and attractive, non-symmetrical pattern of large irregular markings. The well-defined spots of a tobiano cover the body randomly, but white ordinarily crosses the topline at some point between the ears and the tail. The head is usually colored, but often has the white markings common to those of non-spotted horses (such as a star, strip, blaze, and/or snip). All four legs are generally white. The perfect example of this popular pattern is displayed on the Pintabian.

All tobianos are unique and can range from a largely white horse to one with little white. Most breeders credit the ideal tobiano as being 50 percent colored and 50 percent white.

Due to the simple dominant genetics involved in this spotting pattern, at least one parent must be a tobiano to produce a horse with tobiano markings. A tobiano cannot be produced by two non-tobiano horses.

While tobiano markings are one of its distinguishing characteristics, the Pintabian is not a color breed based solely on this trait.

Arabian Blood

Virtually all modern-day light horse breeds are believed to descend, with varying degrees, from the Arabian. Experts in the field of genetics have known for years that it was possible to augment the captivating tobiano spotting pattern into the Arabian to produce the Pintabian breed.

It is important to note, however, that the Pintabian is not merely a Pinto/Arabian cross. As breeders across the United States and Canada will emphatically explain, these spotted equines do not have 50 percent Arabian blood running through their veins, as the uninitiated may incorrectly believe the name Pintabian indicates. Knowledgeable horse people know that it took devoted breeders a minimum of seven consecutive generations of backcrossing horses with the dominant tobiano trait to pure-bred registered Arabians to achieve their beloved Pintabians. Since the Arabian is considered one of the purest breeds and the Pintabian is more than 99 percent Arabian, the Pintabian is also considered one of the purest breeds in the world today.

The following two-step mathematical equation is used to determine the percentage of Arabian blood of any particular horse:

• Add the percent of Arabian blood of the sire to the percent of Arabian blood of the dam.

• Divide the result by two.

• Crossbred example: If a Pinto stallion with no known Arabian blood is bred to a purebred Arabian mare, the result would be a crossbred that is 50 percent Arabian in blood. (0% + 100% =100; 100/2 = 50% Arabian blood.)

• Pintabian example: If a Pinto stallion that is verifiably 63/64ths Arabian, is bred to a pure-bred registered Arabian mare, the result (provided the offspring has tobiano markings) would be a Pintabian because it would carry over 99 percent Arabian blood. (98.4375% + 100%=198.4375; 198.4375/2=99.21875% Arabian blood.)

The chart below shows the degree and percentage of Arabian blood of each backcrossed generation:

Generation Degree Percentage

First generation=1/2 Arabian=50 percent Arabian blood

Second generation=3/4 Arabian=75 percent Arabian blood

Third generation=7/8 Arabian=87.5 percent Arabian blood

Fourth generation=15/16 Arabian=93.75 percent Arabian blood

Fifth generation=31/32 Arabian=96.875 percent Arabian blood

Sixth generation=63/64 Arabian=98.4375 percent Arabian blood

Seventh generation=127/128 Arabian=99.21875 percent Arabian blood (Pintabian)

A minimum of seven generations of backcrossing tobianos to Arabians results in a relatively pure

Pintabians are born with an innate desire for human companionship. These are lovely foals. *Courtesy Pintabian Horse Registry*

strain of spotted horses with a distinctive appearance. Obviously, this takes dedication and determination on the part of the breeder to breed consistently for seven generations before obtaining a Pintabian, so this makes the breed quite valuable. These parti-colored horses have a standard set of characteristics, unlike crossbred horses, which are hybrids showing the attributes of two separate breeds.

Pintabians consistently produce offspring of similar body type and disposition because of the concentration of their breeding and, like their Arabian counterpart, are one of the purest breeds in existence.

Standards

Each Pintabian is uniquely marked and, quite pre-dictably, physically resembles the Arabian. Traits include a head with a dished face and large, wide-set eyes. The neck is arched, the back is short and strong, the hip is relatively level, and the tail carriage is high.

Pintabians generally stand between 14.2 and 15.2 hands and weigh between 900 and 1,100 pounds.

They come in a variety of colors, which can include black, bay, buckskin, dun, chestnut, gray, grullo, and palomino, along with the contrasting white.

Beneath their stylish external appearance are horses that have the relentless staying power nec-essary for hard work. They are ideal for pleasure, showing, competitive and endurance sports, rac-ing, driving, and they make wonderful youth and family horses. Known for their exceptional gracefulness, stamina, intelligence, versatility, and good disposition, their gentleness, tractability, and willing attitude make them suitable for children as well as adults.

Divisions

Horses that are less than 99 percent Arabian can't be registered as Pintabians, even if they have spots.

Horses that possess the desired tobiano mark-ings and that are more than 99 percent Arabian in blood (but less than 100 percent Arabian, as purebred Arabians do not come in the tobiano pattern), are registered as Pintabians in the Colored Division of the Pintabian Horse Registry. At least one parent must be a tobiano to qualify for reg-istration as a Pintabian.

Horses that are more than 99 percent Arabian in blood (but less than 100 percent Arabian) without the desired tobiano markings may be used to pro-duce Pintabians and are registered in the Breeding Stock Division.

When horses registered in the Breeding Stock Division are bred to Pintabians registered in the Colored Division, the resulting offspring are more than 99 percent Arabian in blood. If the off-spring is tobiano spotted, they can be registered as Pintabians. By continually breeding horses from the Colored Division to either those in the Breeding Division or to another Pintabian, the possibilities of producing a Pintabian are greater because both carry the spotting gene and have the required Arabian blood (as opposed to breeding to another spotted horse or an Arabian with no spotting). In this way, foundation breeding stock is utilized and the breed is progressing more toward the ideal Pintabian. Purebred Arabians may also be used as outcross horses to allow for addi-tional bloodlines and are registered in the Arabian Outcross Division. These horses are of a purebred registered Arabian heritage and are generally solid colored (without spots), but may possess patches of body white.

Pintabian Excellence

After much time and effort, foundation Pintabian breeders have finally seen their hopes and dreams come to fruition. They have successfully attained their goal of producing horses with the ability to perpetually pass on the many fine qualities associ-ated with the Arabian, but with the added dazzle and appeal of spots, to future generations. Pintabians are, to their owners, the most beautiful horses in the world today.

Credit: Pintabian Horse Registry and Rozanne Rector

PINTO HORSE

This tobiano colored Pinto Pleasure type horse shows classic, elevated movement.

Pinto Horse Association of America, Inc.
7330 NW 23rd Street
Bethany, Oklahoma 73008
www.pinto.org

Pinto Horses are a refreshing change of pace from the average horse. It is easy to pick them out in a crowd, as they stand out from all others with their attractive and colorful patterns that are unique and distinctive. Their spots can be seen from a distance, setting them apart from everything else.

Even within the breed, each color pattern is different from all others, with no two looking exactly alike. To have a horse that is so unique that it can never be mistaken for any other, gives a great feeling of pride and appreciation.

Pintos are distinctive in more ways than just their color. They have diverse styles of types, enabling them to exhibit a range of versatile talents. There is a type that fits everyone. Owners are pleased with the differences and the attention their beautiful horses attract.

A Stock type tobiano Pinto in a reining class. This type is associated with the Quarter Horse.

History

Studies of historical art reveal the early existence of what is recognized today as the Pinto Horse. Horses with Pinto markings appeared in ancient art throughout the Middle East. The more dominant tobiano spotting pattern became common among the wild horses of the Russian Steppes, suggesting that the introduction of Pinto coloring spread to Europe possibly as early as during the Roman Empire. For many years, European breeders crossed their native stock to Barb horses, which were introduced there following the Moor invasion of Spain in 711 AD and which also had spotted coat patterns.

European explorers, and especially those that were Spanish, brought their light riding stock, including Pinto spotted horses, to America. In time some of their horses escaped, and eventually spotted mustangs ran wild on the American range. Around the same time period, early Americans imported many of the well-established and stylish European breeds as foundation stock. With the American settlers' migrations to western frontiers, it often became necessary to cross these fancy, but less suitable, breeds of the Eastern seaboard with the wild mustang stock. This was to increase size and attractiveness, as well as availability of horses better suited to the strenuous working conditions of the day. Eventually, great wild herds infused with the flashy spots began to develop across America. They became associated with Native Americans, who domesticated and greatly valued them for their legendary "magical" qualities in battle.

Thus the Western-bred horse became a fixture of America, especially the uniquely marked Pinto, whose colorful presence in parades and films have always added a little extra glamour. Exhibitors crossed their spotted horses with other breeds to produce specific types that also had color patterns.

Registry

The first Pinto organization was the Pinto Horse Society formed in 1941, but it slipped into inactivity. Other attempts at registries for Pintos seemed to fail because they attempted to restrict conformation type, or failed to develop enough publicity to unit Pinto fanciers. Yet some of the breeders with the Pinto Horse Society continued breeding with the principles set down by that organization, even after its demise. The society had created a great deal of interest in the Pinto Horse, particularly in the California area where it was based.

A major problem was that Pintos with cold-blooded ancestry were bred in great numbers, producing poor quality riding horses. As a consequence, the general public and horse show judges associated the word "Pinto" with loudly marked, but poorly conformed, animals. By the early 1950s, this attitude had become so prevalent that even well-built Pintos could not place in a show and had to work twice as hard to warrant even a glance from the judge.

This situation was covered very well in "The Plight of the Pinto," an article by Kay Heikens, which appeared in the December 1954 issue of *Western Horseman*. Heikens was speaking from personal experience of discrimination against the Pinto, as well as citing several episodes involving other Pinto exhibitors. The article inspired others throughout the country to write of similar experiences.

These articles and letters aroused interest in starting a Pinto Horse association and registry. Eventually, the Pinto Horse Association of America (PtHA) was established as a registry and incorporated in 1956 to encourage the promotion of "quality with color" of horses, ponies, and miniatures. There was an astounding response to the PtHA announcement that registration applications for Pintos of all types were now being accepted; more than forty letters per day were being received by PtHA.

Members decided to register Pintos with a wide variety of types so that suitable Pintos could be bred and shown in all areas of horsemanship. PtHA, however, stressed the importance of fineness in the conformation of horses accepted for registration. This emphasis has contributed immeasurably to the improvement of the flashy horses throughout the country. Breeders hoped that the Pinto would be more accepted by the show horse establishment and that all their hard work in selective breeding would pay off.

Their efforts over the years have produced much success. Today, PtHA maintains a registry of more than 135,000 horses, ponies, and miniatures throughout the United States, Canada, Europe, and Asia, and the numbers continue to grow on a daily basis. It registers over five thousand Pintos per year. Cash and prizes from the Pinto World Championship total more than $100,000.

There are a variety of classes for an equally wide variety of Pintos. From Halter, Dressage, Competitive Trail, and Endurance classes, to the vast array of driving and riding disciplines available, Pintos have proven their quality and diversity. With so many different types of Pintos represented in such a wide assortment of classes, it is clear to see the breed offers something for everyone.

Breed Characteristics

Of the many questions posed to the PtHA, the most frequently asked is: What is the difference between Pintos and Paints? The main difference between the Pinto Horse and the Paint Horse (registered by the American Paint Horse Association) is that the Paint Horse must be of documented and registered Paint, Quarter Horse, or Thoroughbred breeding. The difference between the two registries has little to do with color or pattern; only bloodlines matter. Most Paints can also be registered as Stock or Hunter type Pintos. Other breeds as well as Paints can also be registered. PtHA allows for the registration of miniature horses, ponies, and horses derived from other breed crosses, such as Arabian, Morgan, Saddlebred, and Tennessee Walking Horses, to name but a few.

The Pinto Horse is a color breed with documentation of pedigree. "Color breed" means it is a breed with specific color requirements—or in PtHA's case, is a registry with certain colors required of its registered horses. A horse that qualifies as a Pinto must have spots. The accepted spotted pattern must have white areas combined with another basic coat color, making each Pinto unique. Its spots are the kind with which the horse is born and that never change. In other words, Pinto spots are not to be confused with Appaloosa spots, which can change as the horse matures.

Spotting Patterns

There are two recognized Pinto color patterns: tobiano and overo.

Tobiano (toe-bee-ah´-no) appears to be white with large spots of color that often overlap and have a greater percentage of color than white. Spots of color typically originate from the head, chest, flank, and buttock and often include the tail. Legs are generally white, giving the appearance of a white horse with large or flowing spots of color. Generally, the white crosses the center of the back, or topline, of the horse. It is necessary to have a tobiano parent to achieve a tobiano foal.

Overo (o-vair´o) appears to be a colored horse with jagged white markings, usually originating on the horse's side or belly and spreading toward the neck, tail, legs, and back. The color appears to frame the white spots. Thus an overo often has a dark tail, mane, legs, and backline. Bald or white faces often accompany the overo pattern. Some overos show white legs along with splashy white markings, seemingly comprising round, lacy, white spots. White almost never crosses the back, or topline.

Color Requirements for Registration

The color requirement for Pintos to be registered in the Regular Color Division (tobiano or overo) is a minimum of at least four square inches of cumulative white hair with underlying pink skin located on the body, or on certain designated areas of the head (eligible zones). This is compared to Pinto ponies, which must have three square inches of cumulative white, and miniatures, which must have two square inches of cumulative white in eligible areas to qualify for registration. There is no limit to the amount of white a Pinto can have.

The qualifying white does not all have to be in one area; it can be accumulative as long as some white is in one of the eligible areas. Eligible areas include the entire body and upper portion of legs, midway between the point of hock, and the center of the stifle. If the leg white starts below the qualifying line, but extends to or above it, then all connected white below the line will count.

Here is a more detailed description of the eligible areas: The white must be above an imaginary level line drawn around the front legs, midway between the center of the knee and the floor of the chest, or above a line around the back legs, midway between the point of the hock and center of the stifle. If white markings start above these lines and continue down below them, all of the connected white will count. For face white to count, it must be behind a line drawn from the base of the ear to the corner of the mouth, and from the corner of the mouth, under the chin, to the other mouth corner.

Breeding Stock

This is the registry division for Pintos that are solid colored or lack sufficient white to be registered in the regular registry. Animals with insufficient qualifying color necessary for acceptance in the Regular Color Division, but with at least two or more Pinto characteristics, or solid colored animals with documented color (Pinto spotting patterns) within two generations, may be eligible for registration in the Breeding Stock Division.

Pinto characteristics are blue eyes, high leg white above the knee or hock, white hooves, multicolored/striped hooves, pink skin, and collective white in eligible zones, but not enough white to qualify for color.

Pintos registered in the Breeding Stock Division are not allowed to participate in PtHA events, unless the event rules specify that they can. Solid colored mares that are not eligible for Breeding Stock Division, but will be bred to potentially produce Pinto foals, can be registered as Broodmares, but they are not considered Pinto and are not eligible for Pinto shows.

The elegant Pinto Saddle horse is appropriate for driving and saddle seat riding.

Pedigree Requirements and Restrictions

While PtHA accepts animals derived from many different approved breed/registry crosses, it does not accept animals with Appaloosa, draft, or mule breeding or characteristics. Horse stallions must have both sire and dam registered with PtHA or another approved outcross registry. Approved registries include various breeds, from warmbloods and gaited breeds to miniatures, so there are many types accepted for registration. Mares and geldings can be registered on their qualifying color alone. Ponies and both types of miniatures can be registered if their color qualifies, regardless of their sex or the registration of their parents.

Diversity of Divisions

Originally established as primarily a color registry, the association accepts a variety of breeds into its registry. To properly classify the different types, PtHA has established two main methods of classification: size and type.

Size: There are four size classifications of registration: One for horses, one for ponies, one for B miniatures, and one for miniatures.

Classification terms:

Horse: Any equine measuring more than 56 inches (14 hands).

Pony: Any equine measuring over 38 inches and up to 56 inches.

B miniature: Any equine measuring over 34 inches, but not exceeding 38 inches.

Miniature: Any equine measuring 34 inches or less.

Type: Pintos are exhibited and bred according to their type. Each owner decides what type classification his or her Pinto fits best, although types do not apply to miniatures. Basic guidelines for determining types are:

• Hunter: displays the carriage and conformation associated predominantly with Thoroughbred, Connemara or Welsh pony breeding

• Pleasure: displays the carriage and conform-

Miniature Pintos are fun to drive. This is a black tobiano.

This striking Hunter-type stallion is a good example of the lacy patterns overos can have. *Duane and Tammi Vogel*

ation associated predominantly with Arabian or Morgan horse, or Welsh or Shetland pony breeding

• Saddle: gaited horse or pony displaying the carriage, animation, and conformation of Saddlebred, Hackney, Tennessee Walking Horse or modern style Shetland pony breeding

• Stock: displays the carriage and conformation associated with Quarter Horse or Shetland pony breeding

By providing two height divisions for miniature horses and four distinctly different conformation type divisions for horses and ponies, there truly is something for everyone in the Pinto. Each division, having its own rules and standards, allows for exhibition against like conformation and styles.

At some shows, color classes are offered. Tobianos and overos are judged individually on the most ideal markings of the Pinto. Ideal markings are defined as a 50/50 distribution of white and color overall on the Pinto. Classes specifically identified and offered as color classes for these patterns are not judged on conformation, as other normal Halter classes are (in part).

In summary, the Pinto is the breed choice for equine enthusiasts of virtually all disciplines and events. It also can be just for pleasure riding, to get a job done, or when a horse, pony, or miniature with color and eye appeal can be used or shown.

Credit: Pinto Horse Association of America, Inc.

QUARAB

The ideal Straight-type Quarab combines the grace of the Arabian with the strength of the Quarter Horse. *Hans-Peter Marquardt*

International Quarab Horse Association
P.O. Box 263
Hopkins, Michigan 49328
www.quarabs.org

The classy grace of the Arabian horse and the substance of the Quarter Horse or Paint—that is the Quarab. For many years, breeders have been combining this unbeatable mix to produce one of the world's most amazing equines. When the Arabian and Quarter Horse type are brought together, it creates qualities that are the best of both worlds. The Arabian's endurance and spirit uniquely blends with the body, usability, and stability of the Quarter or Paint Horse, producing a superb all-around horse in the Quarab.

Additionally, Quarabs display interesting varieties of coat coloring. The Quarter Horse and Paint side allows breeding for colors like palomino, buckskin, grullo, and pinto, plus all the basic colors.

Quarabs have the typical Arabian intelligence with the Quarter Horse calmness, making a great combination. They are extremely trainable and not "spooky;" they are smart, calm, and easy to handle. As an example, there are instances of Quarabs that were just started under saddle and were already doing figure eights in all three gaits.

Quarabs are talented and versatile in every discipline, in the show ring, on the trail, or on a working ranch. The stamina from the Arabian and the muscling of the Quarter Horse or Paint enables them to excel in reining, cutting, and long distance riding.

Quarabs are compact and athletic, excelling in reining and long-distance riding. *Hans-Peter Marquardt*

Quarabs are always eager to please and willing to keep trying. They are extremely smart, easy to handle, and love to be with people. Owners like to talk about their Quarab's compatibility and willing dispositions. Some Quarabs enjoy trail riding so much that they cry with anticipation whenever they see or hear a horse trailer pulling up to the stable.

One Amish farmer who borrowed a Quarab remarked that it was the best ever for either pulling in harness or riding. Considering all the working horses the Amish are familiar with, this is a significant statement about the Quarab. Long time breeder Ginny Hanks, states, "The breeding of this cross for over forty years gives me the experience to say it is truly the only breed that can do it all!"

History

The breed has been around longer than its registry. American Quarter Horse Association (AQHA) records show that in the 1950s, the Arabian stallion, Indraff, sired two Half Arabians (Quarabs) that were registered as Quarter Horses: Indy Mac and Indy Sue were both out of the Quarter Horse mare Cotton Girl.

Indy Sue was foaled in 1953 and earned forty-four AQHA open performance points in six events, including Western Pleasure, Reining, and Hunter under Saddle. In 1960, she earned an open

Performance Register of Merit and had earnings with the National Cutting Horse Association as well. She was then bred to produce three registered Quarter Horse foals. Her brother, Indy Mac, became a champion on the hunter circuit. There are also reports of a few purebred sabino Arabians that were inspected and registered in the American Paint Horse Association before its book was closed in the early 1980s.

Registry

The United Quarab Registry was the first registry and studbook specifically created to register the offspring of a purebred Arabian and a registered Quarter Horse. Founded in 1984, by 1989 the Painted Quarab Index was added to register those horses having a Paint Horse sire or dam. It was a privately owned studbook that was transferred to another individual and eventually went out of business.

In 1999 a new association, the International Quarab Horse Association (IQHA), was founded by Lisa Striegle, who kept the direction of the original guidelines set in place by the United Quarab Registry in 1984.

Many owners were interested in registering their Half Arabian/Quarter Horse or Paint blend horse with the IQHA because it went beyond the Arabian registry, which only recorded the Arabian half of the pedigree. A registered Quarab had its full heritage recorded, a definite asset for those who appreciated the total breeding of their horse to be recognized.

Since the inception of AQHA, the Quarab's popularity has expanded to new generations as more and more are introduced to, and appreciate, its outstanding characteristics. The registry has spread to international proportions, now including Alaska, Germany, and the Netherlands.

International Stars

An example of the international interest in Quarabs is Tishyno, an IQHA U.S. registered Quarab stallion in Germany that is the most successful in Europe in sport and breed. Having passed Germany's strict stud performance examination, he was registered in the First Stud Book by Zuchtverband fur deutsche Pferde (ZfDP), the breeding association of German horses. (Although Quarabs are registered in the United States, many foreign countries also offer other registry options.) To be registered in Germany's ZfDP First Stud Book, the horse is judged to be a perfect stallion with good bone, hip, movement, and other qualities. If a stallion is judged to be not quite perfect, but still very good, he is registered in the Second Stud Book. So the First Stud Book holds the ultimate prestige for those who qualify, such as Tishyno.

Tishyno's wins include championships in Open Reining and Horsemanship. He has won several distance races, and one victory was in a 60-kilometer distance race (37.28 miles), which he finished in 3 hours and 10 minutes.

He has sired over one hundred foals, many of which are now premium mares, stallions, and geldings, and for eight years in a row they have won at the breed shows. His most famous son, Nahbay Ibn Tishyno, has won many Reining classes and was Arabian-Trophy-Reserve-Champion, Germany, in Reining in 2007, competing against twenty-six Quarter Horses. In Kreuth, Germany, the same year, he won the National Reining Horse Association (NRHA) Jackpot Open with a score of 71.0, along with achieving many other placements.

Tishyno is famous in Germany, has been featured in various magazines, and has established a foundation to the breed in Europe. He and his progeny typify the wonderful diversity of the Quarab and the excitement the breed is creating as its influence continues to spread throughout Europe, as well as North America.

Breed Standard

The Quarab is a breed that has solely Arabian and Quarter Horse or Paint Horse blood. Crosses of one-eighth to seven-eighths of either breed type (Arabian or Quarter Horse stock type) are allowed, but they cannot have any other breed crossed with them.

Quarabs should display the conformation of a good saddle horse. They should appear well muscled, yet smooth and refined, and they are generally compact and of medium length. Quarabs should exhibit a degree of refinement that will vary with their type—Straight, Stock, or Pleasure—however, refinement should always be present in the head and legs.

The overall appearance of the Quarab should be pleasing, never coarse, and exhibit good substance. The body should display good strength with sufficiently dense bone and well developed joints and tendons. The coat should be fine and smooth.

Size: A mature Quarab will generally range from 14.2 to 16 hands, although rare individuals may be slightly shorter or taller depending on the breeding. Weight is generally 900 to 1,200 pounds.

Color: Quarabs may be virtually any color and may exhibit the white markings common to Arabians or Quarter Horses. Recognized colors include: chestnut, black, bay, palomino, buckskin, cremello, perlino, smoky creme (double creme dilution on a black base), red dun, dun, grullo, sorrel, brown, and champagne (of various shades). Roans and grays are designated with their base color: bay gray, black gray, sorrel gray, and so on.

Recognized patterns include: roan, gray, tobiano, overo, and tovero. Roan and gray are uniquely listed as patterns. For example, a Quarab may be described as sorrel gray tobiano, meaning "born sorrel, but turning gray with tobiano superimposed." This is especially helpful to those who are specifically breeding for certain colors. (IQHA has a registered champagne roan horse, the first documented of this color combo in any American breed. They also have black tobianos, black grays, and a black roan [blue roan in Quarter Horses].)

Head: The head should be refined and reflect alert intelligence, and demonstrate quality and beauty. Nostrils should be large and sensitive, and the muzzle should be small with a firm mouth. Well developed jaws give the impression of strength. Quarabs may have a slightly concave, or dished facial structure hinting of their Arabian ancestry, without being extreme; the amount of dish will vary with the type of individual.

Eyes should be large and expressive; they are generally dark, but may be blue (double dilutes or Pintos) or hazel (champagne colored horses). They should appear bright and clear and be set well apart on the head.

Ears should be small, finely pointed, and curve in at the tips. They should be set well apart and carried alertly.

Neck: Manes and forelocks should be full. The throatlatch should be clean and well defined, but never thick, allowing for easy airflow when working. The neck should be smoothly joined to the shoulder and deepest at the point of attachment. It should also be long and refined, but not so much as to appear weak. Thickness of the neck will vary somewhat with the type of individual. The neck should display a natural arch. Stallions tend to have a more fully developed crest than either mares or geldings.

Body: The chest should exhibit good depth and width, with well sprung and close ribs. Heart girth should be wide and solid to allow for ample lung and heart space. The barrel should be large and round, yet trim in the flank. The overall body should be deep and full in the mature Quarab.

Withers should be well defined and of medium height, slightly higher than the point of the hip, and extend well back. This allows them to hold a saddle well. The shoulder should have a deep slope and be strongly muscled and of good length.

The back should be compact, broad, and deep in the girth, as well as close coupled and full and strong across the kidney.

The hip should be quite muscled with a somewhat horizontally built pelvis. When standing with

This Quarab stallion is gentle, quiet, and easy for his young rider to handle. *Hans-Peter Marquardt*

hind legs slightly apart (as in the Halter class), the croup should appear nearly horizontal with little slope, yet should not be extremely flat, as seen in many purebred Arabians. When moving or at work, the croup will appear more sloped, allowing for good engagement of the hindquarters. Overall, the hip and hindquarters should show great strength, with the hind leg being muscled inside and out to provide good driving power.

The tail should be set fairly high with a natural arch and carried gaily, especially at the trot.

Legs: Legs should be long and sound, made up of flat bones and solid, large joints. The forearm should be broad and well muscled, tapering to the knee. The Quarab should possess a short to medium length cannon bone that is free of meatiness. Tendons should lie smoothly over the bone, appearing wide and strong when viewed from the side, yet straight, thin, and set well apart when viewed from the front. The placement of the hind legs should allow the Quarab to turn on its hindquarters with the legs well under its body. Pasterns should be clean, strong, and short to medium in length, and their angle should match that of the shoulder.

The hocks shall be neither close together nor wider apart than the fetlocks when viewed directly from the rear. They should be clean, wide, strong, and straight. Hooves should be medium sized, nearly round, and open at the heel. They should be smooth and dense, but never brittle. Hoof size should be adequate for the size and/or weight of the individual.

Gait: Movement will vary with the individual, depending on its type and breeding, however, all Quarabs should move freely. They should work well off their strong hindquarters and move in a collected manner. While the amount of action will vary with breeding type, extreme Park type action is to be avoided.

Types: Body types may be customized, as there are definite preferences among breeders for the different types. As an example, western ranches tend to prefer the stock type with higher percentages

The Pleasure Quarab more closely displays attributes of the Arabian. *Hans-Peter Marquardt*

of Quarter Horse and Paint traits. Endurance riders prefer the Pleasure type, favoring Arabian traits. The majority of breeders prefer the 50/50 Straight type, which is a blending of the best of both worlds. There is something for everyone with the diversity in types.

Straight or Foundation type Quarabs should be a good blend of both the Arabian and the Quarter Horse or Paint traits. They should not be over-refined, but should exhibit a strong influence from both bloodlines. The Quarab Standard is that of the Straight type Quarab.

Stock types will demonstrate more of the traits commonly associated with the Quarter Horse or Paint, but should retain elegance from the Arabian.

Pleasure types will more closely resemble their Arabian ancestry with more refinement, especially in the head. The body, however, should still show a strong influence from the Quarter Horse or Paint blood.

As for the Quarab's temperament, Tishyno's owner, Hans-Peter Marquardt, comments, "I'm happy to own this unusual horse with a cool mind and a big heart. Tishyno always tries to do his best. He is a perfect all-rounder horse. He can do it all and is now a famous stallion."

Credit: International Quarab Horse Association

PART 3

GAITED
BREEDS

FREE AND EASY MOVERS

From the expanse of green plantations to icy mountain tops, these superlative riding horses have established themselves as the epitome in traveling pleasure. Their marvelous gait gives the rider a sensation of floating along. They are the Cadillacs of horses, being especially talented for incredibly smooth action. Some are small and discreet, while others are tall and flashy. Each has its own unique style of gaiting, whether it is calculated synchronized steps, or huge rhythmical strides that it them swiftly across the ground. All have the characteristic gliding movement that is a treasure to anyone who has ever sat on a horse. They provide the amateur with a comfortable, secure ride, and the expert with the thrill of a lifetime.

AMERICAN SADDLEBRED

American Saddlebred Horse Association
4083 Iron Works Parkway
Lexington, Kentucky 40511
www.asha.net

During the Middle Ages, when traveling within the British Isles was an arduous task, sturdy little horses with a lateral gait offered riders a modicum of comfort while negotiating difficult roads. In Chaucer's *The Canterbury Tales*, they were generically called "palfreys," but in fact the horses were named after the various locations of their supposed sources. Most notable were the Hobby horses from Ireland and the Scottish Galloways.

These hardy horses found their way into other countries. Some were transported to Iceland by the Vikings, who often sailed from the northwestern coasts of England and Ireland around 874 to 930 AD. Today, the horses of Iceland are known as the Icelandic horse, a breed noted for a very fast and pure rack called the tölt.

In the United States, Hobby and Galloway horses brought from the British Isles helped produce what is known today as the American Saddlebred. The Saddlebred has a long and proud history—from the legacy of its service on Gettysburg's battlefield, to the bright lights of Madison Square Garden, it helped establish a nation. The creation of man and nature in concert, the American Saddlebred is truly "the Horse America Made."

Foundation Breeds

When British colonists brought their naturally gaited Hobby and Galloway horses to North America, the horses thrived and became part of the base foundation for the American Saddlebred. Through selective breeding and improved nutrition by breeders in Rhode Island and Virginia, superior animals were developed. Called Narragansett Pacers, after Rhode Island's Narragansett Bay, they became the most popular mounts in the colonies.

(Legend has it that Paul Revere rode a Narragansett Pacer on his famous ride.) As a major commercial product, Narragansett Pacers developed along the eastern seaboard, and thousands were sold to Canada and the Caribbean islands.

At the same time in England, the need for riding horses was reduced when roads began to improve. Horse racing then became a passion with British royalty, who imported Arabian, Barb, and Turkish stallions to cross on native Hobby and Galloway mares, which founded the Thoroughbred breed. The first Thoroughbreds were imported to the American colonies in 1706 and crossed with the native stock, mostly Narragansett Pacers. The prolific use of Narragansetts to produce Thoroughbreds, combined with their heavy export by Spanish colonists to the Caribbean islands, led to the extinction of pure Narragansett Pacers, but they left their remarkable easy gait in their progeny.

By the time of the American Revolutionary War, an all-purpose riding horse, commonly called the "American Horse," was recognized as a definite type. These animals retained the easy gaits and stamina of the Narragansett Pacers, but also had the Thoroughbred's size and quality.

As a Breed

The American Horse was first documented in a 1776 letter to the Continental Congress from a U.S. diplomat in France, who wanted one to give as a gift to Marie Antoinette. Thus the Saddlebred type was recognized as an established breed.

As the United States developed, the American Horse went west with pioneers. In Kentucky, horsemen continued to add Thoroughbred blood to their easy-gaited horses, developing a larger, prettier, all-purpose animal, and initiated the presence of the American Saddlebred as a breed. Kentucky's commercial breeders sold horses throughout the fledgling nation.

The long neck, close-set ears, and expressive eyes all characterize the Saddlebred. *Chris Larson*

In 1839, the Thoroughbred son of imported Hedgeford, (also named Denmark), was foaled in Kentucky. Bred to a naturally gaited mare, he sired Gaines' Denmark, the stallion that established the Denmark family of American Saddlebreds. More than 60 percent of the horses in the first three registry volumes of the American Saddlebred Horse Association can be traced to Gaines' Denmark.

Harrison Chief was designated as a foundation sire along with Denmark. The Chief family had a similar background, with a dominance of blood coming from the Thoroughbred, Messenger, imported in 1788 and considered one of the foundation sires of the Standardbred breed. Crosses of Morgan, Standardbred, and Hackney also contributed to the American Saddlebred.

By the mid nineteenth century, the American Civil War demonstrated the superiority of Saddlebreds on the march and on the battlefield. Most high-ranking officers in both armies rode Saddlebred types: Robert E. Lee had his Traveler, Ulysses S. Grant was on Cincinnati, William Sherman rode Lexington, and Stonewall Jackson was on Little Sorrell. The first three were American types with close Thoroughbred crosses, while the latter was from pacing stock. Generals John Hunt Morgan and Nathan Bedford Forrest rode American Saddlebreds exclusively. So important were the horses that after the surrender, General Grant allowed Confederate veterans to keep the mounts they owned. In peacetime, the great demand for Saddlebreds enabled the horse industry to recover quickly.

At the Shows

An effective marketing tool for the horse industry during the postwar era was the increased popularity of horse shows as public entertainment. They created structured competition and became organized events with an opportunity for owners to show off their horses. The first exhibition was recorded near Lexington, Kentucky, in 1816, and the sport grew over the years. The first National Horse Show was held at the St. Louis Fair in 1856, where gifted Saddlebreds dominated the competition.

In 1888, the rules for showing Saddlebreds were amended to require that horses be shown at the trot in addition to the "saddle gaits" (rack, running walk, fox trot, and/or slow pace). The term "pace" in the context of a saddle gait did not refer to the speedy, flat pace of today's Standardbred racehorses, but to a lateral movement such as an amble or single-foot. Gait was the overriding criteria for the development of the breed, and early registrations were based on the ability of a horse to perform the saddle gaits.

In 1891, the American Saddlebred Horse Association was founded in Louisville, Kentucky, and was the first such organization for an American breed of horse. Its name was changed in 1899 to American Saddle-Horse Breeders' Association, but later was changed back to the former name in 1980 to better describe the association.

Despite the fact that the American Saddlebred was still very much a using animal during the late nineteenth century, the rivalry at horse shows between breeders became intense —especially state pride rivalries between Kentucky and Missouri competitors. Skillful horsemen began making a living at training show horses, and horse shows became the proving ground for quality and type.

Saddlebred Progress

A coal black stallion that was to make a great contribution in status to the shows, but particularly to the Saddlebred breed, burst onto the show scene at St. Louis in 1893. In his illustrious career, the charismatic Rex McDonald was defeated only three times. He was idolized by the public and visited by presidents of the United States.

Another popular Saddlebred was introduced to the breed when an unusual colt of predominantly trotting blood with a dash of Denmark was foaled in 1900 in Kentucky. Bourbon King was sold as a weanling and became a sensation as a five-gaited show stallion, winning the Grand Championship at the old Louisville Horse Show as a three year old. Living to the age of thirty, Bourbon King was the great progenitor of the Chief family.

A Saddlebred is a refined, elegant breed with a distinctively show horse persona. *Darlene Wohlart/equinephotography.com*

In 1917, the Kentucky State Fair offered the first $10,000 Five-Gaited Stake Class and claimed to be the World's Championship Horse Show. There had been no bona fide world's champion since the demise of the old St. Louis Fair around the turn of the century. The American Horse Shows Association (now the U.S. Equestrian Federation) was founded the same year, with a large number of Saddlebred people deeply involved. Through the 1920s, horse shows continued to evolve, with format and rules becoming more standardized.

When motor vehicles diminished the utility of horses, people began looking for another avenue to continue their relationship with the horse. Horse shows fulfilled this need and expanded beyond the southern states to become one of the most popular forms of entertainment, flourishing across the nation. They varied from the high society affairs of

Erect neck, forward ears, and alert attitude distinguish this mare as a quality Saddlebred. *Darlene Wohlart/ equinephotography.com*

New York and Los Angeles, to the great state fairs of the South and the Midwest, to the county fairs that were more athletic contests than society functions. Agriculture was still the mainstay of the United States, and most Americans understood and appreciated the athleticism of Saddlebred horses.

World War II put a damper on recreational activity, but in the second half of the 1940s, horse show excitement was revived. With their exceptional beauty and outstanding abilities, American Saddlebreds dominated the saddle seat classes and elegant, high-action driving disciplines.

Most horse shows featured all breeds, often beginning with a jumping class, and then offered Hackneys, roadsters, and parade horses between the traditional Saddlebred competitions. Spurred by the singing cowboys Roy Rogers and Gene Autry, parade classes were hugely popular and attracted many young men to horse shows. Interest in show horses was evidenced in the 1950s, when the flamboyant fine harness star, the Lemon Drop Kid, emerged as the only Saddlebred ever to grace the cover of *Sports Illustrated*.

An event of note occurred in 1957, when a group of Saddlebred enthusiasts met to form the American Saddlebred Pleasure Horse Association to give stature to English pleasure classes, which had long been a mainstay of the show circuit. This had a tremendous impact on the Saddlebred world over the years, and today the pleasure divisions rival all others in numbers.

In 1959, Charles and Helen Crabtree opened their famous Saddlebred stable in Simpsonville, Kentucky. Success attracts success, and there are now many Saddlebred operations in Shelby County, which currently lays claim to being the "Saddlebred Capital of the World." Despite gasoline shortages and increased competition for the recreational dollar, the Saddlebred world flourished throughout the 1970s and 1980s and has continued in popularity into the twenty-first century.

Standards

The American Saddlebred is the personification of the ultimate show horse. It is well proportioned and presents a beautiful overall picture. The horse carries itself with an attitude; it is alert with neck arched, head up, ears forward, and every movement saying, "Look at me!"

The breed comes in almost all colors. Pinto type spotting patterns are very popular.

It ranges in height from 14 to 17 hands and weighs from 800 to 1,200 pounds.

Large, wide-set, expressive eyes and gracefully shaped ears set close together are positioned on a well-shaped head. The head and eyes of the ideal Saddlebred suggest refinement and intelligence.

The neck is long with a fine, clean throatlatch, and is arched and well-flexed at the poll. The withers are well defined and prominent, while the shoulders are deep and sloping. Well sprung ribs and a strong level back also characterize the breed. The legs are straight with broad flat bones and sharply defined tendons. Long, sloping pasterns give a spring to the stride, making Saddlebreds very comfortable to ride.

Masculinity in stallions and femininity in mares are important qualities to be expressed.

The Saddlebred has clean, rhythmic, and fluid action, which is straight and true. High quality smoothness and balanced proportions complete an overall picture of symmetry and style. Its conformation, personality, and stamina are well suited to accomplish any task requested.

Perhaps the breed's most distinguishing trait is a mental acumen. Happy, alert, and curious, American Saddlebreds possess that people-oriented quality called personality, endearing them to their owners and admirers.

The characteristics that have contributed to the Saddlebred's reputation as the "peacock of the show ring" also make it a versatile horse. Smoothness of gaits and speed, coupled with intelligence and powerful muscling, enable the horse to do whatever is asked of it.

Today, the American Saddlebred is still the ultimate show horse, high-stepping and elegant, from halter to saddle seat classes. A show horse is a spectacle of beauty and grace, but it is also an intense athletic competitor. If conditioned and trained properly, the Saddlebred is capable of almost any task it is asked to perform and does it with style. Outside the traditional saddle seat show arena, the American Saddlebred has been successful in most equine disciplines, from cow horse to jumper and dressage to carriage horse.

Disciplines

In the show ring, American Saddlebreds compete in five primary divisions: Three-Gaited, Five-Gaited, Fine Harness, Park, and Pleasure. Each division has its own look and desired traits; however, all strive to meet the model of an ideal American Saddlebred. Horses are judged on performance, manners, presence, quality, and conformation.

Both the Three- and Five-Gaited classes require horses to display beauty, brilliance, elegance, refinement, and animation. Three-Gaited horses have an animated walk, park trot, and canter. Five-Gaited horses have the animated walk, trot, slow gait, rack, and canter. Protective boots can be worn on the front feet.

Fine Harness horses are elegant, refined, and animated. They are judged on the animated walk, park trot, and "show your horse." Protective boots are sometimes worn on the front feet.

Park Horses are stylish, with finish and quality, and are well mannered. They have animated and graceful gaits.

The Pleasure division has two sections, Show Pleasure and Country Pleasure. Horses in both divisions perform their gaits promptly and in a comfortable manner, giving the distinct impression of an enjoyable ride. Manners are emphasized, and the horses perform a true, flat walk.

The Show Pleasure division horses are alert and responsive to their environment and rider. They show less animation than the Three-Gaited and Fine Harness horses. The class includes Three-Gaited, Five-Gaited, Western, and driving classes.

Country Pleasure horses are typically less showy than the Show Pleasure horse and demonstrate easy, ground-covering action. They are plain shod, suitable for trail riding. Other classes are offered in this division, including Three-Gaited, Five-Gaited, Driving, Western, and Hunter classes.

Other Disciplines

The versatility and athleticism that the American Saddlebred exhibits in the traditional show ring have been translated into successes for the breed in other disciplines as well. The Saddlebred's conformation, personality, durability, and willingness to take on any task make it an elegant athlete for any sport.

Saddlebreds have excelled in dressage, combined driving, eventing, show jumping, and endurance, as well as competitive and recreational trail riding. A Saddlebred is capable of almost any task and will do it with extraordinary talent.

Credit: American Saddlebred Horse Association

GALICENO

The Galiceno is a pleasure to ride. This is a lovely dappled mare. *Galiceno Horse Breeders Association*

Galiceno Horse Breeders
P.O. Box 219
Godley, Texas 76044
www.galiceno.homestead.com

The Galiceno (gal-i-see-no) can best be described as the little horse with the big heart and the illustrious heritage. It takes its name from Galicia, a province in northwestern Spain, where the breed originated. From its earliest times, the region of Galicia was famed throughout Europe for its smooth gaited horses. The modern Galiceno horse is still distinguished by the same swift running walk that was so prized centuries ago. As if it understands its proud heritage, the Galiceno works with the same dignity characteristic of its ancestors.

In the United States, the Galiceno horse is another example of the Spanish legacy. Once the servant of proud conquistadors who brought it to Mexico, the Galiceno now satisfies the most avid rider in the United States. It has been asked to perform myriad tasks and has adapted to each with an innate intelligence, demonstrating the worth that was so valued throughout history. The Galiceno is a joy for pleasure riding and is equally at home as an outstanding working and contest horse.

Although small in stature (less than 14 hands) when compared to the average American horse, the Galiceno is extremely hardy with an abundance of natural courage and stamina. It is nothing for this horse to carry an adult for a day's ride and still be less spent than many larger horses. Its gaits are easy and generally the rider is also less tired at the day's end. With its structural makeup and way of going, it is no wonder that this little horse is becoming more popular every day. It is an ideal mount.

History

Hundreds of years prior to the sailing of the conquistadors, Spanish shepherds used to drive their flocks into the hills while mounted on their favorite breed of horse, the Andalusian. This aristocratic breed originally was a warhorse and the preferred mount of the soldiery. When the shepherds rode their Andalusians up into the hills, they released the horses at night and the stallions often bred with the small, wild mountain Garrano ponies.

Wandering Sorraia stallions from the lower swamplands of the Iberian Peninsula further complicated the cross of Andalusians with the Garrano ponies by contributing their blood as well. Both the Garrano and Sorraia were gaited breeds, meaning that they showed the smooth, rapid, forward Spanish gait once referred to as a running walk.

As a result of the blend of Sorraia, Andalusian, and Garrano heritages, a gaited equine indigenous to the Iberian Peninsula was created—the Galicia mountain ponies. They were unique to that region, exhibiting a more refined head, body, and movement than other wild ponies. They were captured in the mountains of the Galicia area of Spain and were called Galicenos after that region.

The small gaited horses the Spaniards brought to the Caribbean islands were likely to have been descendants of Galicenos. When Hernan Cortez invaded Mexico in 1519, he brought several small framed horses from Cuba, now believed to be Galicenos. It is very probable that these proud, beautiful animals were among the first sixteen horses to land on the mainland of the New World. Cortez brought them to work the mines of Mexico and to carry the wounded and dead from the fields of battle.

Galiceno horses continued to be among those brought by conquistadors from the Caribbean islands to North America in the sixteenth century. Reference to the smaller framed horses is in the original documents relating to the conquistadors. The horses primarily had solid colors and a rapid, smooth forward gait characteristic of Spanish horses that belied their heritage.

The conquistadors eventually released them into the mountainous regions of Mexico's interior, where they remained wild and relatively isolated for several hundred years. There are references to smaller Mexican ponies that resembled the Barb in much of the literature of the time, and now are presumed to have been the Galicenos.

It is impossible to know how much variation occurred in the lines of these original Galicenos, just as it is impossible to determine the entire lineage of mustangs or other horse breeds of that era; records of horse bloodlines were rarely kept back then. Several facts, however, seem to be in agreement concerning the Galiceno: it originated in the mountains of the Galicia region of Spain; it is a small horse with a distinct, smooth, rapid, forward movement unique to Spanish breeds; and the combination of its genetic background is Sorraia, Andalusian, Garrano, and possibly the Barb of Africa. (The inherited foundation from these breeds is currently being studied.)

Occasionally, Galicenos were captured by various groups during the movement into the American frontier during the 1700s and 1800s, or brought in by Spanish missionaries, and many were released in the prairies during conflicts or were lost by their owners. These Galicenos became one of the original Indian ponies, with many references to them, in combination with mustangs, in 1800s literature,

A Galiceno stallion shows good width between the eyes and has Galiceno substance. *Galiceno Horse Breeders Association*

detailing plains horses of the developing West.

Although these small herds of Spanish horses became the ancestors of thousands of mustangs that thrived on the plains of the Southwest, the pure-bred Galiceno remained for centuries in the coastal regions of Mexico, undoubtedly used on ranches, and prized by the natives for its riding ease, courage, endurance, and functional size.

As a Breed

The Galiceno as it is known today was first imported from Mexico in 1958 by several different ranchers. It was officially recognized as a breed when the Galiceno Horse Breeders Association was founded in 1959. Since then, the breed has spread northward through the United States.

Depending upon the individual horse's heritage,

Galicenos may or may not show the smooth Spanish gait, but it is written into the breed's standards because most of the horses originally captured in the Mexican interior in the 1950s showed this Spanish movement.

Blood typing tests of Galicenos were begun to determine the incidence of Spanish markers. A foundation Galiceno stallion, NDs Windfire, has been blood typed by the University of Kentucky to match descendants of a known stallion captured in Mexico. Brought out with an original herd of 135 horses in the mid 1950s, he was later imported to Canada. Windfire's dam was a honey colored buckskin out of a Palomino stallion.

Windfire's DNA shows evidence of Spanish markers, and he has the rapid smooth forward gaiting common to the breed. He is registered with the American Indian Horse Registry, currently designated in Class AA and being considered for Class O (Original), the highest-rated level, based on documentation of his sire's origin.

Registered Galiceno mares are bred for proper coloring, conformation, and height that ranges from 12 to 13.3 hands, and to produce registered Galiceno foals, which can also be registered with the American Indian Horse Registry. Since Galicenos are rare and may be on the endangered breeds list, availability of Galiceno horses is limited.

Characteristics

There are differences between the wild Spanish Galicenos of Galicia and the Galicenos that came out of Mexico. In Spain, the coloring of the horses is more predominantly bay, whereas the ones out of Mexico have a greater variety of solid colors. Otherwise, the head shapes, sizing, body conformation and Spanish forward movement are all similar. Additionally, Galicenos have thick manes and tails on both continents.

In the United States, Galicenos are fast becoming the delight of children and grown-ups alike. They are intelligent, easily trained, and very "aware" animals. They make excellent mounts for youth and small light-framed adults, as they are extremely gentle and easy to handle. They can also be used in harness and as an everyday means of transport. Their good disposition can be counted on, making them the ideal family horse.

They are tough, hardy, tractable, intelligent, versatile, and easy keepers. Famous for their easy gaits, they perform superbly in Western Pleasure classes. Their natural head carriage and way of going make them well suited to this event with a minimum of training. They are also versatile and can make the change from Western to English Pleasure with ease. Their smooth gaits provide a performance that is pleasing to both the judge and the rider.

Despite their size, Galicenos make excellent jumping horses. They enjoy the challenge, and their inbred stamina and willingness to perform allows them to work even the most difficult course cleanly and smoothly.

Their natural ability and speed ensure their continued popularity as competition horses. They have both the speed and quickness to make timed events fun and exciting for the rider. They can run as fast as larger horses, and their size is an advantage for negotiating turns efficiently.

The Galiceno developed cow sense from its years when it was used for ranch work before it was imported to the United States. Combined with their natural agility, this makes them true competitors in cutting. Their native intelligence makes them easily trainable for this event.

Standards

The Galiceno horse has established a type that is distinguishable by many traits. It shows substance, lots of style, beauty, and rhythm. Its natural running walk sets the Galiceno apart from the pony class.

When mature, Galicenos usually stand from 12 to 13.2 hands high, with the majority falling into the 50- to 52-inch height group, and weigh between 625 and 700 pounds. All solid colors prevail, including bays, blacks, sorrels, duns, buckskins, roans, grays, chestnuts, browns, and a few palominos. Their coat is a fine shorthaired type.

The Galiceno head shows lots of character and refinement; there is good width between prominent, kind eyes. Ears are pointed, of medium size (slightly smaller in stallions), and well shaped, with the tips curved inward slightly. The jowls are medium. The neck is slightly arched, with a clear-cut throatlatch, and runs well back into moderate withers.

The body is muscled with a well sprung ribcage. Shoulders slope nicely, showing trim muscle. The chest is medium width, but very full, and the back is short and extremely straight. The croup is not level, but slopes slightly, with tail set moderately high. It is well muscled (though not Quarter Horse style), and rear legs are slightly more under the horse than that of other breeds.

Thighs and gaskins are also well muscled. Joints are strong and well shaped. Forelegs are well structured with smooth muscling. Knees are broad, sloping into the cannons. The sloping pasterns are medium long. The hooves are well proportioned, deep, and open at the heel.

The Galiceno is quick and handy on its feet. The walk is easy with long strides. The trot is well balanced. The natural running walk is very fast and ground covering, providing an easy rhythmical ride.

Credit: Galiceno Horse Breeders

Icelandic

United States Icelandic Horse Congress
4525 Hewitts Point Road
Oconomowoc, Wisconsin 53066
www.icelandics.org

Icelandics should have a cylindrical body and long mane and tail, like this stallion. *Deborah Cook*

The Icelandic is an energetic and powerful little horse. It is a beautiful animal to see as it paces along at a remarkable speed, with its head up and thick mane and tail flying. It's even more exciting to ride. These small horses are a delight as they zoom along at a relaxed tölt or a rolling canter, making trail riding a joy.

Icelandic horses are descendents of European breeds that were brought to Iceland by the Vikings in longboats prior to 910 AD, after which time importation of all animals to the island was banned by the government. This remains true today. No horses can be imported into Iceland, including native horses that were once exported. Thus the Icelandic horse has been purebred from 910 AD to the present. Pedigree trees on the horses can be traced back 150 years.

Most Icelandics have four or five gaits, compared to the three gaits of other breeds. The thrill of their wonderfully smooth tölt and flying pace is fun for riders. The tölt especially is a gait peculiar to Icelandics.

Icelandics are smaller than most American horse breeds (under 14 hands) and are often referred to as ponies by those not familiar with them. They are, however, considered horses by the Icelanders, as physiologically they are, based on bone shape and other determining factors. Although short in stature, they can easily carry grown men on trail rides and in competition. Their size makes mounting easy, yet their attributes are those of a horse.

Icelandics are generally intelligent horses that learn quickly and want to please their rider. Even average Icelandics will tolerate some error on the rider's part without difficulty. They have a positive, dutiful attitude.

Personalities vary from those suitable for children and grandmothers to ride, to those that are for professionals only. Some will carry a child with the utmost care and then show all the power and speed required in the show ring or on the trail. A spirited horse for one may be a runaway horse for another. The power and speed of some horses can be intimidating.

In Iceland

The mountains of Iceland can be dangerous, so Icelandic horses are careful about where they step or they would not have survived for centuries. Until the 1930s, the horses served as the main form of transportation in the mountains, so they were trained to carry riders on the difficult terrain. They also carried freight, plowed fields, pulled wagons, and gave family members a ride to church. With so few bridges, the horses were also expected to be strong swimmers to cross the rivers carrying their loads or riders.

Horses running free in the highlands are barefoot, and thus over the years the breed has developed strong hooves. Horses ridden in Iceland, though, have shoes all around because they are ridden on volcanic soil that would quickly wear down any hoof.

Winters in Iceland are wet, but not terribly cold, although the snow can be deep. In the old days, the horses were turned out for the winter and the hay was reserved for sheep and cows that provided income for the farmers. The horses had to paw down to get the dry grass, and those that could live on that diet and lifestyle survived. Thus most Icelandics today are easy keepers, typically requiring only 11 to 14 pounds of grass hay a day.

Mares, young geldings, and foals less than one year old are still turned out into the highlands in some areas of Iceland, but only for the summer and then they are rounded up in the fall. At the roundup, the horses are identified by their ear-marks, freeze brands, or other distinctive markings and returned to their owners. Often people come to the roundup to buy horses.

Many horse shows in Iceland have the Pace test as part of the shows, which is a pace race usually run as the last event. For this, the horses may run two at a time, although the race is against the clock. At an indoor facility, the horses will pace into the arena and zoom straight through the door at the other end. Competition is open to anyone. There are also pace races in other forms that are held worldwide.

Characteristics

Cold or wet weather in winter is no problem for Icelandics, as they grow long, thick coats in harsh weather. They prefer to be outside even in the worst winter weather, but then shed out to sleek coats in the summer. In hot climates, they probably prefer to be clipped, at least partially.

Although Icelandics can "spook," their reactions even in domestically bred horses seems to be less severe than some other breeds. Horses raised in Iceland tend to look at something that is strange, or even walk toward it to get a better look, before they decide if they should run away. This may be due to a lack of natural predators in Iceland. A quick sidestep or a few quickened steps is the norm with some Icelandics, but there are also those that will take a rider for a hair-raising ride, just as with any other breed.

Icelandic horses have a longer working lifespan than most others; usually they can be ridden into their late twenties and can live much longer than that. They are perfect for endurance rides. John Parke from California has logged over 5,000 trail miles on one of his Icelandics.

Horses raised in Iceland tend to be very sure-footed, and this trait seems to have carried over to the horses born in the United States. Riders new to Icelandics often complain that the horses trip a lot, but this is 99 percent rider error. The change from

Icelandics come in various colors, adding an interesting dimension to their attractiveness. *Hannamariah/ Shutterstock*

the loose rein of western riding, to the collection required to properly ride an Icelandic horse, can be difficult for some riders.

For new owners, taking lessons on Icelandic horses is recommended, and when selecting a horse it is best to attend a professionally taught clinic to learn how to communicate with an Icelandic horse. It may take some time to find the perfect horse for a particular rider. Each Icelandic horse is different in character, training, and gaits. As far as choosing the right horse is concerned, the only important feature is what the back of the ears looks like. That is what a rider looks at when it counts the most.

Some Icelandics are great with kids, and in fact, most like kids. Many Icelandics understand that they must be careful with a child or any person who has trouble balancing on their backs and therefore needs their help. Those same horses can also seem quite spirited for someone who is an experienced rider, but Icelandics are not usually difficult to handle.

Icelandics are usually easy to train, but it is advisable to use a trainer familiar with tölt and pace to refine those gaits. To get the best results from the horses, the riding style and the type of saddle used must be Icelandic. Icelandic saddles look similar to dressage saddles, but are designed to fit Icelandic horses and be comfortable for the rider. Some Icelandics in the United States are trained to ride western and do fine in western gear, as long as it fits them.

World championship shows are held biennially in a host country, and some competitors get heavily involved in them. Horse and rider teams represent their countries in the competition.

Standards

Parentage must be verified by DNA testing when a horse is registered in its new home. In the United States, Icelandic horses are registered with the United States Icelandic Horse Congress. Horses born worldwide are now often microchipped.

Icelandics are bred more selectively now than they were fifty or one hundred years ago. Today, the goal is to produce a more lightly built and athletic horse compared to the draftier type horse produced years ago, yet keep the same healthy, fertile, and durable attributes of the breed.

The size of the Icelandic horse should be 12 to 14 hands, weighing 800 to 1,000 pounds. How much weight a horse can carry depends upon the horse. A 12 or 13 hand Icelandic should be able to easily carry a 250 pound person, and a 14 hand horse would probably be comfortable with a rider up to 300 pounds.

Icelandics have a cylindrical body that should be made up of front, middle, and hind sections that are approximately equal in length. The legs should be about the same length as the depth of the body, with the withers slightly higher than the croup.

Young horses tend to be a bit slab-sided, but by the time they are seven or so they will have muscled out nicely. A mature horse should not be rotund, but a nicely rounded barrel is desirable.

Manes and tails are long and are kept natural in the show ring.

The only consideration given to color is that all varieties should be preserved. Icelandic horses come in all colors except appaloosa patterns.

They are bred to be high energy horses, but they are also expected to be dutiful and obedient. There is very little tolerance for aggressive behavior toward humans.

Gaits

The natural gaits of Icelandic horses are one of their greatest charms (after their wonderful disposition). These are preserved by breeding horses that have strong abilities in the pace and tölt. For all-around use, it is also important that Icelandic horses be able to trot.

Icelandic horses are either four- or five-gaited. The four gaits they all should have are walk, trot, canter (gallop), and tölt, which is an incredibly smooth four-beat gait that lets the rider sit very comfortably while covering ground very quickly.

It is desirable for a tölting horse to bend at the poll and round its back. The faster the horse

The Icelandic horse is a sturdy, natural breed. Manes are not trimmed for the show ring. *Hannamariah/Shutterstock*

goes, the more it is inclined to bring its head up, but usually the horse is also bringing its hind legs further under itself. The horse should not be ventrally flexed.

The fifth gait is the flying pace, which is a two-beat lateral gait that is primarily used on flat open spaces or for racing. With horses reaching up to 35 miles per hour, it is not for the faint of heart.

Head position must be appropriate for the horse's conformation. Some horses tölt with a high head, while others do not. With the flying pace, the horse is quite stiff in the loins and back and up through the body, so the head is held higher, but is still not ventrally flexed.

Evaluations

The United States Icelandic Horse Congress, the national registry, allows some regions to hold evaluations of breeding horses. This is a major undertaking for any group. Horses four years and older can be evaluated in any country with an International Federation for the Icelandic Horse Association (FEIF).

The evaluation is done by two or three certified international breeding judges. Horses are measured for height at the withers, croup, and saddle dip; length from chest to hindquarters; depth and width of chest; width of hips and between thigh bones; width of the front cannon bones; circumference of front knees and around front cannon bones; and hoof length. They are evaluated for conformation and receive scores of 5 to 10 for head, neck, withers and shoulders, back and croup, overall proportions, quality of legs, and correctness of joints and hooves.

The riding portion is evaluated by two or three judges. One judge may be designated as a riding judge and would then ride each horse to measure more accurately its willingness and character. (This is not always done at evaluations.) The horse is shown in a walk, trot, tölt (both slow and fast), slow and fast gallop, and pace (if it has pace). The horse is also scored for its willingness, character, and form under a rider. Scores range from 5 to 10, with 10 being considered ideal. Each score carries a different numerical weight (value); for example, tölt carries a weight of 20, while walk carries a weight of 4.

Once all the calculation is done for conformation and riding abilities, the two scores are combined, giving conformation 40 percent weight and ridden abilities 60 percent.

The goal is to breed a perfect 10. An average horse would score 7.5, while an exceptional horse would score 8 and would be called a First Prize horse.

Evaluations are held by regional riding clubs wherever there are Icelandic horses, usually once a year by each club. All scores are entered into an international database called World Fengur, which is available on the internet by subscription.

Evaluations are serious business, with the horses' scores being recorded for all the world to see. They are entirely different than horse shows, which are usually among friends or riding clubs, and give riders goals to reach while enjoying their horses.

Credit: Flugnir Icelandic Horse Association

KENTUCKY MOUNTAIN SADDLE HORSE

Kentucky Mountain Saddle Horse Association
P.O. Box 1405, 102 Finley Drive, Suite 108
Georgetown, Kentucky 40324
www.kmsha.com

For over two hundred years, the Kentucky Mountain Saddle Horse has lived and flourished in the mountains and valleys of eastern Kentucky. Originally bred for a variety of uses on the family farm, the Kentucky Mountain Saddle Horse quickly became known for more than its versatility and heartiness. Its intelligence, willingness, and, perhaps most notably its smooth, natural four-beat gait drew attention and much appreciation.

How the Kentucky Mountain Saddle Horse got its start is still a great mystery, but it is well known that for centuries, the mountain people of Kentucky bred horses for a smooth, even gait, good temperament, and self sufficiency. These horses were never deemed special by their original owners, who bred them for practical reasons only. Life in the mountains was hard and families were large. Saddle horses were used for a variety of tasks and given little attention for their care. They had to adapt to the environment and be easy keepers. Only the strongest and fittest survived, and this served to make the breed healthy, strong, and highly intelligent.

The breed's other distinguishing feature—its natural four-beat gait—was an easy riding, gentle movement that could be maintained over rough terrain. It had the same footfall pattern as a walk, only quicker, called an amble or rack. The result was that the rider could sit almost motionless while carried at speeds almost as fast as the canter of other horses.

Characteristics

The Kentucky Mountain Saddle Horse is popular as the breed for all reasons. Along with its willing nature and exceptional beauty, the Kentucky Mountain Saddle Horse is admired for its comfortable ride produced by its natural four-beat gait. It frequently sports a dark coat with lighter mane and tail, which is proving to be desirable.

There are no limits with Kentucky Mountain Saddle Horses. They are quiet, forgiving, people-oriented horses. Their willingness and gentleness make them easy to work with and teach almost anything. They love to be with people and constantly want to be part of everything that is happening. Stallions as well as mares will walk up to people in a large pasture, seeking affection and attention.

Many of the soft-gaited horse breeds have so many gaits that a novice can become confused. With Kentucky Mountain Saddle Horses, there are only three gaits to enjoy: the trail walk, the canter, and the saddle gait (known also as a single-foot or amble). These demonstrate several speeds, going from very slow to extremely fast. Some horses are known to rack at over 18 miles per hour. Once the feeling of comfort and exhilaration is achieved, there is less danger that the rider will allow the horse to slip into the bad habit of a pace or trot. Best of all, after a thirty-mile ride, a rider can still walk!

Kentucky Mountain Saddle Horses are impressing crowds at horse events from one end of the United States to the other. This is the experience breeders Mike and Toni Rohm had when they exhibited their stallion. "Folks were just amazed at how calm and quiet he was," says Toni. "I understand that. I've been around horses for a long time, but I'd never seen anything like the Mountain Horses before. It's their disposition that convinced Mike and I to get involved with this wonderful breed. We love the smooth gait and their beauty, but it's the disposition that is really amazing. It's impossible not to love this breed. These guys are just too good to keep a secret."

The Kentucky Mountain Saddle Horse is athletic, compact, and close coupled.

Whether trail or endurance riding, showing, working cattle, or pulling a cart, the Kentucky Mountain Saddle Horse offers its rider intelligence, willingness, versatility, and a smooth natural gait. It's truly a horse for "any reason in any season."

Registry

Although Kentucky's easy-riding saddle horse was well known among the mountain residents of eastern Kentucky, it remained an obscure breed beyond that region until the late 1980s. It was then when a Kentucky resident, Robert Robinson

Jr., envisioned broader recognition for this unique horse. Robinson was raised with mountain horses and found them to be a most unusual breed. "I've been with these horses all my life. They were primarily a workhorse. My father and I worked and used them for all purposes. We pleasure rode them [as well as] worked them; back then we rode a lot."

Robinson had participated in the formation of the other mountain horse registries. There was, however, an area of disagreement that he wished to address: "In the other registries, the smallest horse they would register was 14.2 hands. But we had many good four-beat gaited horses that came in under that size."

Many of the shorter horses seemed to be the most talented in gaiting, such as the horse named Kentucky Goldrush. He stood 14 hands tall and weighed about 1,100 pounds. His neck was set high on his shoulder and his terrific animation and brio (stylish boldness) gave the appearance of a very large horse. A 5-foot 10-inch rider mounted on him still looked good and fit him nicely.

Robinson's decision to embark on the enormous responsibility of forming a registry was sealed when he bred a horse named General Jackson. This gorgeous, strong gaited, flashy stallion stood a sturdy 13 hands tall. Robinson was quick to point out that Jackson was a short horse, not a small horse. This was a horse solid in the tradition of the Narragansett Pacer breed.

In 1989 Robinson founded a registry, the Kentucky Mountain Saddle Horse Association (KMSHA). Careful selection and breeding by the members brought about a rapid base growth, which created a gene pool large enough to accommodate the original breed characteristics without compromising them. Robinson said, "We tried to breed for gentle horses, for good temperament, and a good smooth four-beat gait. If you don't register a good product you're defeating your purpose. We wanted the horse to be the winner."

After Robinson and his volunteers registered the local native mountain horses as foundation stock,

the registry was then opened to receive other horses possessing the same traits. By grouping horses with like characteristics, a gene pool formed from which owners of mares and stallions could review and select compatible breed lines for their horses.

Through this selective breeding of foundation horses with similar approved stock, the smooth gait and gentle disposition was ensured among the horses of the association for generations to come. This approach to breed development has been followed by other important registries. Some of those registries kept their books open (to outside breeds) for more than thirty years to complement the genetics and growth of each breed. Welcoming outside blood that is consistent with the registry usually limits the chance of abnormalities due to lack of variety in breeding options.

Since the KMSHA registry began, the reputation and demand for Kentucky's pleasure riding horses has extended well beyond its mountain area. Today there are over twenty-one thousand registered Kentucky Mountain Saddle Horses throughout the United States, Canada, Germany, France, Switzerland, and Holland. The Kentucky Mountain Saddle Horse is enjoying success as the largest and fastest growing mountain horse breed. Several other breeds of horses also make their claim of establishing their foundation by breeding to the Kentucky Mountain Saddle Horse.

Registration

The KMSHA has now closed its registration books and is working with the University of Kentucky to identify new genetic markers that will further individualize the breed.

All foals are issued temporary papers. Once a horse is under saddle and before it is either bred or reaches the age of four, it must be designated as Certified to Breed (mares or stallions). Before a horse can be certified, its DNA or blood analysis must be on file with the University of Kentucky to establish identity. Temporary registration papers expire on all horses that are not certified by their fourth birth date. Upon satisfactory examination of a horse for conformation and certification of gait under saddle by two examiners or a video of the horse moving, the horse is entered into the permanent registry books. As part of the certification process, a horse must display the following characteristics:

1. Show a gentle, alert, and willing attitude; have a calm, kind demeanor: The evidence of a gentle temperament and willing disposition must be observed by two examiners or shown on a videotape. Any horse that displays temperament that is unruly or unmanageable will not be eligible for certification.

2. Give evidence of a natural, smooth, even, four-beat gait under saddle: The saddle gait is recognized and defined as innate, with four distinct hoof beats. Head bobbing or nodding are not desirable, nor is a stride of more than 24 inches. An 18- to 24-inch stride is acceptable. The horse can lift its front end up and have its back end follow in very quick timing or cadence without jogging its rider in the seat, and the rider experiences little to no vertical motion while in the saddle.

3. Qualify within two class categories: *(a)* Class A is for horses standing at 14 hands or above at maturity; and *(b)* Class B is for horses standing from 11 hands to 13.3 hands at maturity. Measurements are to be taken when the head and neck are raised at the throatlatch, pushing toward the back of the body to produce a tuck in the neck, and should not be taken in a relaxed position. No horse can be registered if it stands less than 11 hands (44 inches) at maturity. There is no upper height limit. Most registered horses average between 13 and 16 hands.

4. Show an above average degree of beauty and refinement: The horse must be of medium bone and substance, reflecting its heritage as an all-around utility breed. It should present an appearance of athleticism

and the ability to perform useful work, having a compact, well muscled, and close coupled frame. Principles of sound conformation relevant to all breeds are applicable; the horse should be well proportioned in the body, neck, hindquarters, and legs.

Registry Limitations

The KMSHA breed registry foundation books are closed for mares and stallions (with some exceptions that include other gaited breed registries). There are, however, still several horses known to exist in the hills of the Appalachians with the exact characteristics that meet the registry requirements and appear from time to time with their owner's intention of getting them registered. Therefore, the KMSHA mare books open for short periods of time to evaluate horses left out of the registry that could enhance the breed "type" for continued genetic improvement. The overall breed numbers are still limited and must be managed wisely in order to preserve the breed's innate qualities.

The Mare Appendix of the KMSHA registry is still open, and consideration is given to outside mares for registry that meet the standard of the breed. These mares are not restricted from showing, but are required to have all male offspring gelded, while female offspring derived from a registered KMSHA stallion may receive full registration.

Foals can be registered with the KMSHA provided that both parents are KMSHA horses. A filly can be registered as an Appendix Mare if she has one parent that is registered KMSHA.

The KMSHA gelding books are still open for registration of geldings that meet the standards of the breed.

Standards

The Kentucky Mountain Saddle Horse is an all-around farm horse, but its primary purpose is for riding. It is valued for its easygoing temperament, intelligence, versatility, and willingness, but especially for its smooth, natural gait.

The head is attractive, cob-sized, not too long

or wide in appearance, and proportional, with a broad flat forehead, well defined jaw, and a profile that is neither severely Roman nor dished. Looking straight at the front of the head, the distance from the middle point between the eyes to the middle point between the nostrils is of medium length. The facial composure overall is pleasing to the observer.

Neck is of medium length and thickness, with the topline of the neck longer than the underline, and meets the back behind the shoulder. The neck should show an ability to flex at the poll and not be tied into the body too low in the chest. Flat, little, or no wither is desirable.

Planes of the legs, when viewed from the front and the rear, should be straight and aligned. Severe cases of sickle hocks, cow hocks, hooves turned in or out, or any other variance from correct structure of the major joints are not desirable.

When viewed from the side, horses should have near equal proportions of the forequarter, body, and hindquarter with proper angulations of the shoulder and humerus. An upright humerus and front legs that are not set too far underneath the body allow for good stride and reach. The horse should have a strong topline, short in the coupling, with a rounded croup. The tailset should be natural.

The horse can be of any solid body color, with white markings accepted only on the face (no bald faces), legs (no excessive amount of white above the knees or hocks), and the area on the belly that is behind the breast bone and under the ends of the ribcage, which should not exceed 36 square inches, or 6 by 6 inches (no bigger than an average sized hand). Otherwise no spots are allowed. Manes and tails can be white. Colors include buckskin, bay, roan, or any combination of solid color with flaxen mane and tail.

Any horse that does not meet the limited amount of white requirement with the KMSHA, but carries significant white markings known as tobiano, overo, and sabino, may be registered with the Spotted Mountain Horse Association (SMHA), a subsidiary of the KMSHA. Although crossbreeding to a Kentucky Mountain Saddle Horse is permissible, the resulting foal is registered with the SMHA only. A foal of either sex with a solid body color and foaled by one or both parents that are Spotted Mountain Horses must be registered with the SMHA. (There is no foolproof genetic test that can determine if a solid colored offspring will throw spots or not.) A solid colored gelding with either one or both parents that are Spotted Mountain Saddle Horses may be registered with either SMHA or KMSHA, but not both.

Credit: Kentucky Mountain Saddle Horse Association

MANGALARGA MARCHADOR

The fluid action of this beautiful Mangalarga Marchador stallion is unmistakable. *Linda Holst*

Mangalarga Marchador Horse Association of America
P.O. Box 770955
Ocala, Florida 34477
www.mmhaa.com

The Mangalarga Marchador is one of the unique breeds of horses in the world. Established for over 180 years in Brazil, Mangalarga Marchador horses are the largest population of horses descending directly from Iberian stock and are considered their national horse breed. Equine professionals have taken note of the Marchador, who fills a need for Americans desiring a larger, naturally gaited horse with a calm temperament. Linda Tellington-Jones, an internationally renowned trainer and clinician known for her "T-touch" methods, enthusiastically states, "One of the great gifts to the horse world is to have the Mangalarga Marchador horse breed introduced at this time for pleasure riders who want an athletic, exotic, magical, yet sensibly personable equine companion. They ride as smooth as a Porsche. With their romantic Iberian heritage, there is no comparison among gaited breeds. This breed is very intelligent and truly a pleasure and joy for all to take part in."

Sturdy and well suited for any terrain, the Mangalarga Marchador flourishes in any climate, whether tropical or cold. They are easy keepers, resistant to disease, and can travel long distances without fatigue. These qualities contributed to an amazing and legendary feat accomplished from May 1991 to June 1993, when three sixty-plus-year-old Brazilian horsemen rode their Mangalarga Marchadors almost 9,000 miles through varied terrains and altitudes from sea level to 15,000 feet in temperatures ranging from 0 to 115 degrees Fahrenheit to prove the breed's stamina. It was the longest horseback endurance ride on record. Their accomplishment was recorded in the 1994 *Guinness Book of World Records* and memorialized by a bronze and marble statue in Brazil.

Mangalarga Marchador horses are bigger than most Peruvians and Paso Finos. Their hind-driven movement is closest to the Peruvian Paso without the *termino*. Built like a Paso in front and a Quarter Horse in the rear, Mangalarga Marchador horses are solid and sturdy with classic Iberian features. They are sure-footed, graceful, intelligent, comfortable to ride, easy to train and have excellent cow sense. Their versatility extends to dressage, cutting, jumping, polo and pleasure riding. They are playful, love people, have docile temperaments and the stallions are unusually easy to handle.

History

In 1751, King D. Joao of Portugal, dedicated to improving the Portuguese national horse breeds, founded the Alter Royal breeding farm, or Coudelaria Alter do Chao, in Portugal. These horses were known as the Alter Royal breed, which was formed from crossing bloodlines of Lusitanos and Spanish Andalusians with selected breeding horses native to the Iberian Peninsula, Madiera, and the Canary Islands. The Alter Royal breed was known for its elegant stature, calm stance, and kind, docile temperament.

In 1808, King Joao and the Royal Family fled with his court to Brazil when Napoleonic armies threatened their homeland. He brought with him his finest Alter Royal stallions and began breeding with Barb mares from Africa and Jennet stallions from Spain that had come with European explorers to Brazil. The Mangalarga Marchador breed as it is known today, was the result of a horse named Sublime being presented as a gift to Gabriel Francisco Junqueira, who was the Baron of Aldenas in 1812, and given by Prince Pedro I, who was later named Emperor of Brazil. The Baron was a famous horse breeder and owner of the established breeding farm Hacienda Campo Alegre, located in the south of the state of Minas Gerais. With the exceptional stallion Sublime, Junqueira began

a breeding program utilizing native Barb mares with a blend of Spanish Jennets. The first animals produced were known as the Sublime Horses, a type of horse known for its rhythmic smooth gaits, gentle character, amazing stamina, and characteristic regal bearing.

Gabriel Junqueria had a nephew, Jose Frausino Junqueria, a deer hunter and sportsman who appreciated the new breed's hardiness and agility on long journeys and became an enthusiastic champion for it. His enthusiasm carried over to a friend and owner of the Mangalarga Farm near Pati do Alferes, Rio de Janeiro. It was not long before the farm bred so many of these horses that the farm name was associated with the breed itself. The horses became known as Mangalarga with the name "Marchador" added to identify the pure, naturally gaited horse. The Mangalarga Marchador horse was classified as a pure breed and later would be easily distinguished from the Mangalarga Paulista breed. (The Mangalarga Paulista is a Brazilian breed created in the 1930s by a group of breeders in the state of Sao Paulo. It was established by crossing the Mangalarga Marchador with an Arabian, Standardbred, or Thoroughbred. A separate registry of Mangalarga Paulista horses was formed in 1934 in Brazil.)

Today, there are hundreds of thousands of registered Mangalarga Marchador horses in Brazil and a number found in several countries outside their Brazilian homeland, including the United States.

Foundation Lines

The traditional breeding of Mangalarga Marchador horses has concentrated on the original pure foundation lines from Hacienda Campo Alegre and famous bloodlines such as Tabatinga, Herdade, Abaiba, Angahy, Favacho, Traituba, and JB. These lines are still in existence today with some of the foundation owner's families continuing to breed Marchadors on their original colonial plantations.

Primary Brazilian breeders cultivate their selection from traditional breeding farms and blended production to compete in numerous exhibitions and national shows. Likewise, for the United States

A regal Mangalarga Marchador stallion has the desirable high-set neck. *Kay Holloway*

to establish a brand new breed of horse and provide for the establishment of bloodlines that will support future generations, there must be thorough analysis and research of the bloodlines by the importers and the breed associations, Mangalarga Marchador Horse Association of America (MMHAA) and the United States Mangalarga Marchador Association (USMMA). A careful selection of imported bloodlines has begun a strong foundation for diversification of the breed in the United States today.

Definitive reference information is presented in the book *Historias Do Cavalo Mangalarga Marchador* by Ricardo Casiuch (Brazil 1997) containing the principle reproduction genealogy and history of the breed. Periodic annuals of the top breeding stock sires and dams with the championship statistics are published by TOP 2000. These books are titled *Garanhoes Mangalarga Marchador* (primary stallions) and *Grandes Femeas Mangalarga Marchador* (elite mares), which provide critical breeding references to the bloodline crosses that produced the national champions.

Top desirable primary bloodlines and origins are Tabatinga, Traituba, Abaiba, Herdade, Sama, Santana, Angahy, Bela Cruz, Caxambu, Campo Lindo–JB, and Favacho. They can be found in the U.S. foundation stallions, such as Batuque Do Regal, who is the son of Tiguara Hypus (Herdade Cadillac), one of two original U.S. foundation stallions imported from Brazil in the early 1990s, and Jallaio de Boa Fe (Festa A. J.), who is a full brother to the "Champion of Champions" Camafeu Da Boa Fe in Brazil with both parents among the top ten sires and dams. Jordao Do Passo Fino (Moleque Tabatinga), Ritmo AJ, and Ninja De Sao Joaquim (Abaiba Gim), are also champion stallions and proven sires of champions.

Top producing mares sired by Famous National Champions have been imported to build ancillary bloodlines. Among them are: Gralha M.U.G., sired by syndicated champion stallion Enigma Scala; Brauna Libertas, sired by syndicated champion stallion Dominio Da Joatinga; Luminosa Da Joatinga, whose bloodlines are from Santana Sorriso and

Mangalarga
Marchador mare and
foal. *Kay Holloway*

Tabatinga Cossaco; Sama Janaina, sired by Grand National Champion Sama Derby; Ibiza Da Boa Fe, sired by Camafeu Da Boa Fe (47 direct and reserve grand championships); Folha da Calciolandia with top picada and Passa Tempo bloodlines; Laponia Trimonte (Tabatinga and Santana); Tapixaba do Vale Vermelho, a top tri-colored pinto; and Mabi do Vale Vermelho with Favacho and Caxambu bloodlines.

Registries

History continues to be written for the Mangalarga Marchador horse breed in the United States. They are regarded as an exotic breed as the first horses were imported from Brazil to Florida in the early 1990s and most people are not familiar with them. The breed had remained in obscurity throughout the decade until it was introduced nationally by the Mangalarga Marchador Horse Association of America (MMHAA) and additional horses were

imported in May of 2001. The MMHAA is the first breed registry to promote and exhibit the Mangalarga Marchador across the nation since its organization in the year 2000. Due to only a small number of horses being exported from their native country of Brazil, Mangalarga Marchador horses have only been added to breed books since 2003.

While there are less than a hundred "foundation" Marchador horses in the United States, they are catching the attention of the horse world. Marketing provided by the Mangalarga Marchador Horse Association of America has included the breed being featured on *Horse Talk* (an independent TV show) and a feature presentation on RFD TV. The Association has also sponsored nine horses marching in the 2002 New Year's Pasadena Rose Parade that was viewed internationally. Since 2000, they have been exhibited at California's Fiesta of the Spanish Horse in Burbank, Western States Horse Expo in Sacramento, Equine Affaire in

Pomona and Massachusetts, EqWest and the Del Mar Nationals in Del Mar, California, Southern National Exposition in Perry, Georgia, Equitana in Lexington, Kentucky, and exhibitions in Oregon. Numerous feature articles in horse publications such as *The Gaited Horse, Conquistador, Western Horseman, Horse Illustrated*, and *Horse and Rider* have also focused on the Mangalarga Marchador.

An imported Mangalarga Marchador is identified with the letter "M" inside a horseshoe brand on the right shoulder if it is registered with the Associacao Brasileira dos Criadores do Cavalo Mangalarga Marchador (ABCCMM) in Brazil. The ABCCMM in Brazil holds annual inspection tests for morphology and national competitions. Gait classes are rigorous and normally last about an hour. The horse is judged for how it executes its gait. A judge will often ask to ride a horse that he is evaluating. Important are carriage, brio and elegance with consistent timing over a wide range of speeds. Horses also participate in functional performance testing including reining competitions, cross country events and endurance tests that can cover distances from 31 to 62 miles.

Each authorized imported horse is also registered with the Mangalarga Marchador Horse Association of America and the United States Mangalarga Marchador Association. The MMHAA is recognized by the American Horse Council and the Brazilian ABCCMM Association (Associacao Brasileira dos Criadores do Cavalo Mangalarga Marchador) and was the founding and original U.S. Mangalarga Marchador breed registration and association. All horses registered with the MMHAA must meet high standards for conformation, natural gait, performance, and temperament.

Breed Standard

The Mangalarga Marchador is considered a medium-built horse that stands strong and well muscled, between 14.2 and 16.2 hands and weighs between 850 and 1,100 pounds. Its coat is fine and silky with a full mane and tail. The dominant color is gray ranging from almost black to pure white.

Other common colors, such as bay, chestnut, and less common, palomino, buckskin, and spotted, can be found along with an exotic burgundy that is peculiar to the breed.

The head of the Mangalarga Marchador is triangular (not concave), with a large flat forehead tapering to a small fine muzzle. It has a straight profile and large dark eyes, which are set wide apart and are extremely vivacious, typical of the Barb horse. The ears are proportional to the head, mobile, parallel, well set and erect with the tips turned inward. The horse has an alert, attentive attitude and upright ears that echo the firm look in the eyes that profess an aptitude equal to any difficult obstacle encountered along the way. The mouth is of medium width and sensitive to the bit. The nostrils are large, dilated, and flexible.

The neck is of medium length, sufficient for the horse to be well balanced for riding and reining. It is pyramidal in shape, light in its general appearance, proportional, oblique, and of strong musculature. It presents flexibility and balance, being harmoniously inserted into the top third of the chest to allow for a proud, high carriage. It is well arched with a possible slight convexity of the dorsal edge. It carries a thin, fine, silky mane.

The withers are well defined and long, offering good direction to the dorsal profile of the neck. The chest is deep, large, muscular, and not overly protrusive. The thorax is deep and allows for great lung capacity, which is one of the reasons for the legendary stamina of the breed. Ribs are long and well arched. The spine is of medium length, straight, well muscled, proportional, and harmoniously joined to the withers and loins. Loins are short, straight, proportional, harmoniously linked to the spine, rump and/or croup, and covered by a strong muscular mass. If the distance from the back to the loins is of less or equal distance to the length of the croup, it is a sign that the horse possesses excellent conformation.

The croup is long, symmetrical, muscular, proportional, and slightly inclined, with a very slightly outstanding sacral bone. It is of a height not superior to that of the withers. The tail is set at a medium height insertion, well planted, with a short base directed downward, and preferably with the tail point slightly turned upward when the animal is in movement. The dock is lightly raised when the animal moves. Tail hair is fine and silky.

Anterior Extremities

The shoulder blades are long, wide, oblique, and muscled with a well delineated implantation, demonstrating a wide range of movement. Arms and forearms are long, well muscled, and well articulated and oblique. The forearms are also straight and vertical. The elbows are wide, well articulated and vertical, equal in direction to the forearm. The shins are straight, short, lean and vertical with strong and well outlined tendons. Hocks are well defined and well articulated. The cannons are of medium length, strong, oblique, and well articulated. The hooves on both front and back are medium sized, solid, dark, and rounded. In Brazil, unless the horse is worked hard every day, it is kept barefoot with only an occasional hoof trim required as it has very thick and tough feet.

Posterior Extremities

The hindquarters are muscular and well implanted, looking similar to a Quarter Horse. Gaskins are strong, long, well articulated, and well positioned. Cannons are lean, firm, well articulated, and well positioned. Pasterns are straight, short, lean, and vertical with strong tendons and well delineated. Coronets are of medium length, strong, oblique, and well articulated. Positioning of both anterior and posterior extremities is correct. The pasterns and hooves are at the slightly lower angle typical of many Spanish horse breeds. This allows the rear legs of the Marchador to overreach without excessive stress to suspensory ligaments because of the triple hoof support of their natural gait.

Evaluation of Movement and Gait

This breed is uniquely different than other four-beat gaited Spanish horses. The Mangalarga Marchador has three of the standard gaits of an non-gaited horse (walk, canter, gallop) and exhibits one or two unique gaits referred to as Picada or Batida that are like the trot. These traits are consistently passed genetically on to offspring.

The walk is a four beat gait with equal integrals between the beats; it is slow, with alternating support between the diagonal and the lateral bipeds always interspersed with triple hoof support. Ideally it must be regular, elastic, and balanced with advance movement tending to the diagonal. There is slight movement of the neck with good flexibility of the joints.

The gallop is a rapid movement of medium speed, asymmetrical, executed in three beats with a sequence of support beginning with the posterior extremity, followed by the collateral diagonal biped (with simultaneous support), and is completed with the opposed anterior extremity. Ideally regular (just with good impulsion and balance), it is executed with crisply neat times of suspension, discreet bascule movement of the neck, and good flexibility of the joints.

The marcha is a marching movement unique to the Mangalarga Marchador that replaces the trot (two diagonal hooves on the ground while two are in the air) of non-gaited breeds. It is symmetrical and performed in a four-beat gait of medium speed with alternating support of lateral and diagonal bipeds with good flexibility of the joints and always is interspersed with solid triple hoof support. Ideally it must be regular, elastic, balanced, with forward movement in a diagonal direction, and with discreet (not exaggerated) movement of the anterior extremities defining a semi-circle when seen from the side.

Support, or the definitive, measurable and consistent presence of triple hoof support between movements, is imperative. Yield, or the ability to cover ground with less movement, is desirable. Attitude, or the position of a semi rigid neck with movement of just the trunk and extremities along with aligned and balanced positioning of the loins, shoulder blades and rump, is desirable. Ideally, a horse in proper attitude should maintain its head at

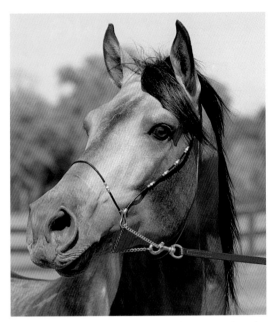

The noble Mangalarga Marchador has large eyes, tipped ears, and a refined muzzle. *Kay Holloway*

about 90 degrees to the neck, which in turn should be obliquely positioned, forming a 45 degree angle relative to the ground.

Style refers to the appearance of elegance, grace, and nobility the horse should maintain while engaged in the marcha. Balance, obviously is desirable while gaiting and addresses the stability of the horse. Consistency during the marcha is important, providing comfort and developing a definable rhythm or beat.

In addition to the walk, canter, and gallop, there are two long reaching, four-beat gaits. While there are similarities with other gaited breeds, it's the four-beat extended reach in front with propelling action from behind stabilized by nano-second, triple hoof support that makes this breed so different. This is the only horse breed in the world that can perform on a lateral and diagonal, making it a joy to work with and a pleasure to ride:

Marcha Picada is a four-beat gait characterized by lateral leg movements with the sequence of the hooves being: right rear, right front, left rear, left front—the hind foot touching the ground a fraction of a second before the front foot. The continuous triple hoof support and the overreach of the hind hoof make the gait very smooth. (This differs from the pace, which is an exclusively lateral movement to the limbs where the two legs on the same side [foreleg and hind leg] go up at the same time as the other side goes down, resulting in only half of the horse's body mass being set on the ground at each time of movement.) At extended picada speed, the head and body lift up like a speedboat in front to create a plane-like sensation that makes the rider feel like he isn't moving. This gait can be likened to the Paso Fino's largo gait or the Peruvian Paso's paso llano without the swinging of the front legs called termino and can be sustained for long periods of time.

Marcha Batida is performed when legs are moving in a diagonal four-beat sequence with moments of triple hoof support. Although in some ways similar, this gait differs from the trot (when there is a brief moment of all the legs suspended in the air) as this horse is always in contact with the ground. The longer and more frequent the moments of triple hoof support, the more comfortable is the gait. The three hooves touching the ground simultaneously is the characteristic picture of these "marching" horses. The horse makes a forward semicircle (not outward as the Peruvian Paso) with the front legs and uses the rear legs as leverage, thus propelling the horse forward. If the horse is marching on level ground at a normal rhythm, the tracks of the two hind feet will cover or pass slightly (overreach) beyond the tracks of the front feet. In movement, the horse executes an alternation of diagonal and lateral supports, which are always softened by an intermediate pause of triple support. It can also be compared to the Columbian Paso Fino's troche and the Missouri Fox Trotter's namesake gait.

Credit: Mangalarga Marchador Horse Association of America and Linda Holst, Rancho Linda Marchadores

MISSOURI FOX TROTTING HORSE

An intelligent head with a deep, strong body typifies the Missouri Fox Trotter. *Daniel Johnson*

Missouri Fox Trotting Horse Breed Association, Inc.
P.O. Box 1027
Ava, Missouri 65608
www.mfthba.com

The Fox Trotting Horse is America's favorite trail riding horse. It is known for its smooth, surefooted ride that is a pleasure for anyone, from young to old, who loves to ride. Its ground-covering gait, called the fox trot, has made it a favorite mount for hunters, forest rangers, and others who travel a lot in the country by horse. Its endurance and surefootedness in rugged terrain is appreciated by ranchers, and its gentle nature and rocking–chair canter can make any Hollywood actor look like a pro. The beauty and classic style of its movement is appreciated in parades and in the show ring.

The Missouri Fox Trotter is naturally gaited. No special shoeing or training is required to make it perform the smooth, flatfoot walk, foxtrot, or rocking-chair canter. Due to its melting-pot background, it may also perform a variety of other smooth saddle gaits.

Its good disposition and trainability are among its many desirable characteristics. It is often described as a horse for all generations because of its gentle attitude, making it easy to handle, easy to train, and easy to ride. It is one of the most versatile and best loved of all the horse breeds, with the intelligence, heart, and stamina to attempt any task asked of it. Its versatility and conformation provide the horse with the ability to pull a surrey, work cattle, or travel endless miles, all performed with true fox trot rhythm and style.

The fox trot is an easy, fluid, four-beat gait that basically is diagonal like the trot, but the horse appears to walk with its front legs and trot with its hind legs. Due to the back feet's sliding action, rather than the hard step of other breeds, the rider experiences little jarring action and is quite comfortable to sit for long periods of time without posting or standing in the saddle.

As pleasure riding continues its rise in popularity, so does the Missouri Fox Trotter. Approximately 90 percent of registered Missouri Fox Trotting Horses are used for family pleasure riding. There is a saying that "to ride one is to own one."

In 2002, the Missouri Fox Trotting Horse received the Missouri State's highest honor when it was officially declared to be the state horse.

History

The breed developed more than a century and a half ago, when pioneers migrated from the hills and plantations of Kentucky, Tennessee, Illinois, Arkansas, and Virginia. They brought their finest possessions, including their best saddle stock, which was largely Arabian, Morgan, and plantation horses from the deep South. Some bloodlines today can still be traced to horses of these states.

Those that settled in the Ozarks found an urgent need for a smooth, quick, easy-traveling horse that was surefooted enough to handle the rocky, hazardous terrain. Horses that were laterally gaited—running walk, pace, stepping pace, or rack—were all very smooth to ride, but the Ozark horsemen found they could not perform their gaits as well under rough riding conditions as the saddle horses that could perform a foxtrot gait.

Thus Ozark horsemen developed the ultimate surefooted, smooth-riding saddle horse by crossing the laterally gaited breeds, such as the American Saddlebred, Standardbred, and Tennessee Walking Horse, with good hard-trotting breeds from that era, such as the Morgan, Thoroughbred, and Arabian horse breeds. Famous families used for foundation stock have been known throughout the Ozarks, and even to this day, the names of Copper Bottom, Diamond, Brimmer, Red Buck, Chief, Steel Dust, Cold Deck, and many others are recognized as foundation stock by fellow U.S. horse breeders and associations.

These efforts resulted in an extremely comfortable, intelligent, and beautiful horse that was hardy enough for the cattle rancher, yet stylish enough to go to town with pride. The ability to travel long distances at a comfortable speed of 5 to 8 miles per hour made it a favorite of the country doctor, sheriff, assessor, and stock raiser. It proved to be capable, adaptable, and dependable for its surefootedness in that mountainous region. It also had the ability to do whatever was needed around the homestead, from plowing to hauling or working cattle, and yet could double as a stylish buggy horse. Old timers called it a people horse because it was gentle, loving, and willing to please. It was known as Missouri's Fox Trotter horse, which eventually became the Missouri Fox Trotting Horse.

Trail Athletes

Due to its stamina, surefootedness, and smooth ground-covering gaits, the Missouri Fox Trotting Horse has also become very popular with field trial competitors and long distance trail riders. It has taken a firm hold as a consistent winner across the nation in the sport of competitive trail riding through the North American Trail Ride Conference (NATRC). The majority of top NATRC competitive horses have historically

The Missouri Fox Trotter appears to walk in front and trot in the rear.
Daniel Johnson

been Arabians and Half Arabians. Within the last decade, however, the Missouri Fox Trotting Horse has gained in popularity. The Rocky Mountain and Midwest sanctioned rides consistently find Missouri Fox Trotters placing in the top six within the Open, Competitive Pleasure, and Novice divisions.

Rock'n EZ Ruby, a six-year-old Missouri Fox Trotting mare, won the title of Grand Champion Horse of the 2002 NATRC Championship Challenge Ride. This is a two-day, eight-mile competitive ride. To qualify for the challenge, horse and rider teams must have won a national championship, logged one thousand competitive trail miles, or finished in the top six in their respective NATRC region. The scoring is based on the horse's conditioning, soundness, manners, trail sense, and ability.

Ruby had only been ridden in Open (most advanced division) for two years, and she won a national championship each year. In her first year as a four-year-old, she won sweepstakes on her first ride and another Fox Trotting gelding won third place at the Championship Challenge. Ruby's rider states, "Our Fox Trotters have spoiled us. They are

tough competitors, but not tough on us after so many miles in the saddle."

Ruby joins top Missouri Fox Trotting NATRC horse, Hickory's Country Gold, a sorrel stallion, as the only Missouri Fox Trotters to win the Grand Champion Championship Challenge title. Hickory's Country Gold is the only NATRC horse to be named grand, national, sweepstakes, and Championship Challenge champion, as well as having been voted as a NATRC Hall of Fame horse.

Another competitor is the Missouri Fox Trotting gelding, Charger's Rampage, of Kentucky. He also is a top NATRC national contender with national championship and national sweepstakes champion titles.

Registry

In the 1940s there was a scramble to abandon saddle horses for automobiles as the main means of transportation. Hoping to preserve the true, all-American Fox Trotting Horse that had been selectively bred for such a long time, a group of interested horse breeders founded an organization in 1948 that eventually became known as the

Missouri Fox Trotting Horse Breed Association (MFTHBA).

The association kept its registry open and accepted horses that could qualify as characteristic foundation stock until 1982, when it required horses to have at least one parent that was permanently registered. Beginning in 1983, the association closed its books so that any horse approved for registration had to have both parents permanently registered.

The organization has enjoyed more consistent growth in recent years, as the reputation of the Missouri Fox Trotting Horse has become better established. Since 1996, MFTHBA has doubled its numbers of horses registered to almost ninety-four thousand. There are horses registered in Canada, the Czech Republic, France, Israel, Switzerland, Scotland, and the United Kingdom, and there are two affiliate organizations in Germany and Austria.

MFTHBA has hundreds of classes at its annual spring and fall shows. World Grand and Reserve Champions have been crowned since 1960. The annual show lasts one full week in September, when the best of the best from across the nation come to compete, trail ride, and visit with fellow Fox Trotting enthusiasts.

Standards

Horses applying for registration must have DNA parentage verification and have both its parents registered.

Size: The Missouri Fox Trotting Horse should stand 14 to 16 hands in height.

Color: All colors are recognized, except for appaloosa coat patterns.

Conformation: The Missouri Fox Trotting Horse should be of good conformation and be able to carry weight. The animal should stand well on its feet and be erect, wide awake, and alert.

The horse should have a neat, clean, intelligently shaped head, pointed ears that are well-shaped, good, large, bright eyes, and a tapered muzzle.

The neck should be graceful, in proportion to length of body, and well-joined to the body.

The back should be reasonably short and strong;

The Missouri Fox Trotter's head has large eyes and tapers to a fine muzzle. *Daniel Johnson*

the body is deep and well-ribbed. The flank should be full, and the chest deep and full. The shoulders should be properly sloped at a 45- to 50-degree angle and well-muscled.

The legs should be muscular and well-tapered. The foot should be well-made, strong, and in proper proportion to the size of the horse.

Gait: The Fox Trotting Horse is not a high-stepping horse, but an extremely surefooted one. The head and tail are slightly elevated, giving the animal a graceful carriage. The rhythmic beat of the hooves and the nodding action of the head give the animal an appearance of relaxation and poise.

Horses are judged on balance, conformation, structure, feet, legs, gait, and conditioning.

Flat foot walk: The walk should be a long and easygoing, flat, four-beat gait performed in a square, stylish manner. The horse reaches in each stride (front and rear) while overstriding the front track. This gait is done with rhythmic motion in time with the feet, and the head and tail should also indicate the natural rhythm.

Fox trot: This is basically a diagonal gait. The

Missouri Fox Trotters have various colors. They aren't high stepping, but are sure-footed. *Daniel Johnson*

horse will perform the fox trot by walking in front and trotting behind, with reach in each stride (front and rear). It may overstep its track, provided it travels straight on all four legs and does a true fox trot. The back feet must exhibit a sliding action in order to keep beat to the gait. Due to the sliding action of the rear feet, rather than the hard step of other breeds, the rider experiences little jarring and is quite comfortable in the saddle for long periods of time.

The horse carries its head slightly elevated, with it having as much rhythmic head motion as possible. This head motion should always be in time with the movement of the feet, and the ears should be relaxed. The tail is carried naturally elevated and should be in rhythm to the foxtrot beat. The natural rhythm of the horse starts at the tip of the nose and goes back to the tip of the tail in one continuous motion.

The ideal characteristics of the fox trot are for the animal to travel with animation, style, and true fox trot rhythm. The horse is to travel in a collected manner.

The head should nod, the ears should indicate the step, and the tail should be part of the rhythm. The step should be springy, consistent, and smooth. The up and down motion should not be noticeable, but rather it should display a smooth, gliding gait without swinging. Swinging out of the legs, or

paddling, is an undesirable trait in the Fox Trotter.

Canter: The canter should be performed in a straight, collected manner with the head and tail slightly elevated. It is often referred to as the rocking-chair canter because it feels like sitting in a rocking chair. The horse should travel with a rolling motion while on the correct lead both front and rear. Excessive pumping of the horse by the rider will be penalized by lowering the horse's placing when being judged.

Judging: When judging, 40 percent shall be allowed for the fox trot gait, 20 percent for the flat foot walk, 20 percent for the canter, 10 percent for conformation, and 10 percent for equitation/horsemanship. The exception to this rule are two- and three-year-old horses and four-year-old amateur horses, which will be judged 50 percent for the fox trot, 25 percent for flat foot walk, 15 percent for conformation, and 10 percent for equitation/horsemanship.

Horses shown must be serviceably sound, and judges shall disqualify any horse with evidence of broken wind or blemishes that judges might deem disqualifying. No special shoeing or training is required for the horses to perform their gaits.

Fox Trotting Horses are shown in a browband type bridle with or without a caveson. Colored browbands and show ribbons for a strip of mane and the forelock are popular show accessories. Horses are shown in western saddles with a horn. No cruel or inhumane bits or other devices are permitted.

Judges shall also disqualify any horse shown with any artificial appliances, such as tie downs, set tails, false tails, switches, or braces. Also any horse having raw or bleeding sores around the coronet or legs are disqualified. The MFTHBA adheres to the U.S. Department of Agriculture (USDA) Horse Protection Act and implements all necessary regulations at affiliated horse shows to ensure the safety of the horses.

Credits: Missouri Fox Trotting Horse Breed Association, Inc., and Stacy Bowman, MFTHBA promotional committee member

MOUNTAIN PLEASURE HORSE

Mountain Pleasure Horse Association
P.O. Box 112
Mount Olivet, Kentucky 41064
www.mtn-pleasure-horse.org

A particular type of horse was bred on the steep hillsides of eastern Kentucky to work the fields and "ride the best." The Mountain Pleasure Horse lived quietly there in the mountains, where breeders maintained the breed by selecting a pleasant gait and disposition as the basic criteria. Throughout generations, these qualities were solidly fixed with focused and discriminate breeding.

For more than 160 years, eastern Kentuckians enjoyed their homegrown product of the Mountain Pleasure Horse. Each generation of Kentuckians told stories of their easy gaited, hardworking, good natured, and reliable horses, which for years were called Mountain Horses or Country Saddle horses. Mountain Pleasure Horses were the old-time gaited horse from which breeders selectively developed the Tennessee Walking Horse, American Saddlebred Horse, and more recently the Rocky Mountain Horse. Long before these, other gaited breeds were in existence.

The Mountain Pleasure Horse has a natural, easy-riding gait, allowing it to cover a lot of ground with minimum effort for both horse and rider. The gait is an evenly spaced, four-beat lateral gait with moderate forward speed and extension, and without exaggerated knee or hock action. Each beat can be distinctly counted, producing a cadence of near equal rhythm. No action devices, aids, or harsh training methods are necessary, or allowed, on Mountain Pleasure Horses.

The disposition and trainability of Mountain Pleasure Horses may be the most appreciated characteristics for novice horse owners. They are very

Mountain Pleasure Horses are tall and graceful with a bold eye. *Jerry Murphy*

intelligent horses that love attention. Veteran trainers of other breeds are amazed at how fast they learn. It is not uncommon to see two- and three-year-olds competing effectively with older horses at area horse shows or on challenging trail rides. Once Mountain Pleasure Horses have been trained, they remember their lessons well. This is an asset to those who do not have the time to ride a horse every day. The Mountain Pleasure Horse is waiting, with its natural gait and willing disposition, whether it is ridden once a week or once a month.

Differences with Rocky Mountain Horses
Some Mountain Pleasure Horses are double registered with the Rocky Mountain Horse Association, and many are also registered with the Kentucky

A naturally arched neck and deep chest typify the Mountain Pleasure Horse. *Daniel Johnson*

Mountain Saddle Horse Association (KMSHA). Consequently, there have been questions about the differences between the Mountain Pleasure Horse and these other breeds.

Some forty-five to fifty years ago, a breeder named Sam Tuttle tapped into the Mountain Horse heritage by crossing native Mountain Pleasure stock with Tobe, his chocolate colored stallion. The popularity of Tobe's descendants eventually led to the founding of the Rocky Mountain Horse Association (RMHA) breed registry.

The key difference between the Mountain Pleasure Horse Association (MPHA) and the RMHA is the genetic foundation. Fewer than 17 percent of the foundation horses of the Mountain Pleasure Horse Association carry any trace of the Tobe bloodline. Quite simply, the Mountain Pleasure Horse breed existed some one hundred years before the existence of the Rocky Mountain Horse, though the MPHA itself was not established until 1989.

In the MPHA, color is not a criteria of quality, while in RMHA, the chocolate color is generally preferred. Besides the chocolate color, there are (to those who study closely) various physical characteristics and slight variations in gait among horses descended from Tobe bloodlines that generally are not present in the Mountain Pleasure Horses.

Generally speaking, Mountain Pleasure Horses tend to be a bit larger (taller), longer bodied, and cover more ground with their gait than the horses from Tobe bloodlines. There is pride that the Mountain Pleasure Horse's genetic heritage helped produce the horses of the Rocky Mountain bloodlines, whose results and color are preferred by some horsemen. For those, however, who want the old-fashioned, smooth ride, and wonderful disposition that over 160 years of Kentucky heritage provides, the Mountain Pleasure Horses may be a better option. The MPHA registry backs the integrity of the breed with blood typing and stringent scrutiny.

Differences with Kentucky Mountain Saddle Horses

Horses registered in the KMSHA are often referred to as Kentucky Mountain Saddle Horses. Several gaited breeds of horses are included in the KMSHA registry, with the Mountain Pleasure Horse being one of them. Whereas the Mountain Pleasure Horse and the Rocky Mountain Horse registries are closed to outside breeds, the Kentucky Mountain Saddle Horse Association registry can admit certain other kinds of gaited horses. As previously mentioned, many horses registered with the MPHA are also double registered with the KMSHA.

The Mountain Pleasure Horse has a natural, easy gait without exaggerated hock or knee action. *Daniel Johnson*

Blood typing has proven that the Mountain Pleasure Horse is the foundation for all other gaited American horses. In fact, Kentucky governor Brereton C. Jones, in September of 1994 at Frankfort, the capital of Kentucky, recognized this in his official proclamation:

1. "The Horsemen of Eastern Kentucky developed a type of horse, known as the Mountain Pleasure Horse, to be smooth of gait, gentle of disposition, willing to work and surefooted as necessary for mountain terrain; and

2. "This Mountain Pleasure Horse has been carefully and closely bred for over 160 traceable years along the original Kentucky mountain bloodlines; and

3. "Blood typing research by the University of Kentucky has shown the Mountain Pleasure Horse to be the parent stock of all the American gaited horse breeds" (including the Rocky Mountain Horse and Tennessee Walking Horse).

Governor Jones recognized the horses "registered by the Mountain Pleasure Horse Association to be the oldest gaited American breed of horse and to be the parent stock of all other American gaited horse breeds."

Registration

The MPHA registration books are now closed and only offspring of registered stallions and mares are eligible for registration. There are no provisions for grade mares. The MPHA registration process requires that all horses submitted for permanent registration must be videotaped demonstrating gait, and the board of directors of the MPHA must approve each horse. The MPHA requires that all its horses be blood typed by the University of Kentucky for absolute identification of parentage before papers are issued.

Standards

The general conformation requirements for the Mountain Pleasure Horse are given as follows:

• The head should be medium sized and in proportion to the body, with medium sized jaws.

• The horse should have bold eyes, well shaped ears, and a face that is neither dished nor protruding.

• The neck should be gracefully arched, medium in length, and set in at an angle to allow a natural carriage, with a break at the poll.

• The horse should have a wide and deep chest.

• The fore and hind legs should be free of any noticeable deformity.

• The shoulders should be sloping, ideally with an angle of 45 degrees.

• Any body color is acceptable, however, spotted Mountain Pleasure Horses are not encouraged by the association for breeding or showing. Standard recognized colors of the Mountain Pleasure Horse include, but are not limited to, bay, black, chestnut, sorrel, roan, gray, cremello, buckskin, palomino, and chocolate.

• Size is from 14.2 to 16 hands, and weight is from 900 to 1,100 pounds.

Credit: Mountain Pleasure Horse Association

NATIONAL SHOW HORSE

National Show Horse Registry
10368 Bluegrass Parkway
Louisville, Kentucky 40299
www.nshregistry.org

By combining the beauty of the Arabian with the high-stepping action of the American Saddlebred, a magnificent horse called the National Show Horse is born. It harmonizes these two distinct horses by projecting grace, stamina, agility, and charisma. Its character and flowing athleticism enthrall show ring crowds wherever it competes.

The grounds for the breed's inception was to meet a growing need within the equine industry for beautiful show horses with athletic ability, new excitement and incentives in the show ring, and a broader base for the show horse world. The National Show Horse Registry (NSHR) has proven since it was founded in 1982 that the combination of Arabian and Saddlebred is perfect to meet that need, creating a breed with classic show ring style and presence. These two basic breeds, bred through a variety of bloodline combinations, have produced a show horse that continues to surpass even its own standards.

The NSHR was established in the best interest of the show horse industry for promotion of the English-type horse. Founders were not satisfied just to have a registry for their new breed. They also wanted to generate broader public appeal and encourage the amateur equestrian athlete. by creating a new atmosphere in the show ring reflecting the excitement produced by the horses themselves.

The National Show Horse is also appealing as a horse the whole family can become involved with,

A magnificent National Show Horse with high-stepping action. *Courtesy Cindy Clinton*

as its versatility underlies its popularity. Whether devoted exclusively to exhibiting the breed, or including it as part of an overall horse program, producing National Show Horses can be an exciting and profitable venture.

Outstanding Competitors

The evolution of the National Show Horse is evidenced in the show records of today's champions. One of the greatest nominated National Show Horse sires was Night of Roses, a World Champion three-gaited Saddlebred stallion that won his championship in the walk/trot division for junior horses. He consistently passed on his personality, carriage, and structure to his foals that were winners in nearly every division at National Show Horse Finals. Of the 123 registered foals he sired, 49 won ribbons in National Show Horse classes—nearly 40 percent. Collectively, they won over $209,000 in prize money, making Roses the National Show Horse High Point Sire from 1995 to 2001, and again in 2007.

Two of the most successful National Show Horses in NSHR history are Power of Love and Second Editions Debut. Power of Love, a black bay National Show Horse gelding foaled in 1989, competed in almost every division the NSHR offered at the time. Frequently, he was a champion in the Five-Gaited, Three-Gaited, English Pleasure, Fine Harness, Pleasure Driving, and Halter classes, and he did this not only in the open divisions, but the amateur division as well. This fantastic animal has show ring winnings of over $136,000.

Second Editions Debut is an elegant gray mare that was foaled in 1993. She competed in the amateur and open divisions throughout her career. Many times a champion in English Pleasure, Pleasure Driving, and Halter, she accumulated over $71,000 in NSHR winnings.

These are just a few of the outstanding representatives about which the National Show Horse breed can brag. National Show Horses are bred to be the ultimate show horse, with the talent and stamina not only to compete at the open level, but

also to have enough tenacity to successfully compete with children in the amateur classes.

Eligibility

Once originating as a cross between registered Arabians and American Saddlebreds, offspring can now be the result of registered National Show Horse parents, or a combination of registered parents from those three breeds. National Show Horse stallions that are registered Arabians or American Saddlebreds must be nominated to qualify for breeding use. The resultant foal is eligible for registration if it is a minimum of 25 percent Arabian, but no more than 99 percent Arabian.

Beside the walk, trot, and canter, there are specific classes for five-gaited horses that can slow gait and rack. All the classes a National Show Horse can compete in include Halter, Five-Gaited, Three-Gaited, Fine Harness, Pleasure Driving, Equitation, English Pleasure, Country and Classic Country Pleasure, Show Hack, Ladies Side Saddle, Hunter Pleasure, Western Pleasure, Walk/Trot 10 and Under, and Lead-Line. Horses can also compete in sport horse events including, but not limited to, Dressage, Eventing, Hunter Over Fences, Endurance/Competitive Trail, and Working Western.

In response to the recent explosion in popularity of horse events based on discipline, the NSHR has formed the Show Horse Alliance, which promotes the Saddle Seat English type horse as a discipline. The emphasis is placed more on phenotype than on genotype. One of the goals is to encourage breeders to create an extreme saddle seat type of horse relatively free of blood content restrictions.

There are no shoeing regulations except that soundness of the horse is required. Artificial tails are not allowed, only natural flowing tails.

Standards

The National Show Horse is an athletic horse that contains size, beauty, and refinement. When observed at rest or in motion, the horse must exhibit a natural presence, and when animated, an extreme brilliance. The horse must exhibit high

The very long, high-set neck adds to the refinement of this National Show Horse stallion. *Stuart Vesty*

carriage when showing or relaxed.

The National Show Horse comes in a variety of colors, including pinto and palomino.

Specifically, the following traits are desirable:

- Motion: balanced with obvious power from the hindquarters flowing into an elevated front end, and the front legs showing both flexion and extension. Proper movement is paramount
- Head: relatively small, short, and refined with large eyes and small, well placed ears, and a straight or slightly concave profile (Roman nose or convex profile not desirable)
- Neck: very long, set high on the shoulder, relatively upright with fine throatlatch, and should be shapely, but without a pronounced crest
- Withers: pronounced withers and a very deep and well laid-back shoulder
- Back: proportionately short back closely coupled, with a long hip and relatively level topline (moderately sloping croup not to be penalized)
- Legs: correct from all angles with long forearms and short cannon bones in front, as well as long, well angled pasterns front and rear
- Bone: refinement of bone, but not lacking in substance, especially in the chest, girth, shoulder and hip
- Tail: a relatively high set tail, natural and flowing
- Height: 14.3 to 16.2 hands tall, with some individuals under or over this.

Credit: National Show Horse Registry

NATIONAL SPOTTED SADDLE HORSE

National Spotted Saddle Horse
Association, Inc.
P.O. Box 898
Murfreesboro, Tennessee 37133
www.nssha.com

While presented as a naturally gaited saddle horse, the National Spotted Saddle Horse exhibits "a coat of many colors." A more beautiful or useful animal cannot be found.

The Spotted Saddle Horse originated in central Tennessee. Spanish American type spotted ponies, prized for their gentle disposition and attractive color and markings, were crossed with other established gaited breeds, mainly Tennessee Walking Horses. This produced naturally gaited riding horses that were large enough for adult riders. They had longer legs, bodies, and necks, yet still retained the gentleness and charm of the spotted pony.

The original purpose of the Spotted Saddle Horse was for a family riding horse used for general pleasure and trail riding. It increased steadily in popularity as more adult riders found they could have a full-sized horse with all the qualities they so admired in the spotted ponies they had as children.

The National Spotted Saddle Horse was bred to excel and is now found in the show ring in various classes from Halter to Driving, including the always exciting Stake (championship) classes. It has been appearing at Bird Dog Field Trials throughout the southern states and is fast becoming a requested mount for similar sporting events.

As the breed has steadfastly gained in demand and popularity as both a pleasure and show horse, many breeding barns have added a training facility as one of their services. Horses are being trained in the areas of show, trail, field trial, or purely backyard pleasure.

The Spotted Saddle Horse resembles a stockier Tennessee Walking Horse. *Amy Dean*

Registry and Eligibility

The National Spotted Saddle Horse Association (NSSHA) was formed in 1979 in Murfreesboro, Tennessee. It established a uniform breed of saddle horse that was naturally gaited and performed without the use of punishing training aids or substances.

The association grew with a steady increase each year in numbers of new horses being registered. Until its formation as a breed registry, many excellent spotted horses were virtually ignored because they were less than 15 hands and thus considered youth horses, not fit mounts for adults. Small horses of this type now form a part of the NSSHA registry, where their excellent qualities are preserved in the new breed.

In order to qualify for registration, a horse must be spotted and exhibit a saddle gait, which may be a flat walk, running walk, pace, rack, or a combination of all gaits, but the horse cannot trot. Any horse, regardless of background, may be registered provided the horse is spotted and exhibits these gaits (unless applying for I-D or Breeding Stock papers).

Horses complying with color and gait requirements and with either a sire or dam registered with NSSHA may be registered in their calendar year of foaling. Geldings that meet the color and gait requirements can also be registered, even those with unknown parentage. Those of unknown and/or unregistered background are assessed at a higher fee. (This applies to mares and stallions that are considered Breeding Stock.) Any horse that is found to have unnatural markings will be rejected from registration.

Solid colored foals that have either a NSSHA registered sire or dam (or both) are accepted for identification registration only. This provides the owner with the background for the possible spotted offspring that these horses may produce. Many owners choose to keep their solid colored foals for use in their breeding program.

Solid colored mares or stallions can qualify by gait as Breeding Stock, including those that do not have a spotted sire or dam, provided they have a NSSHA registered sire or dam. These horses must be gaited; they cannot trot. Horses already registered as Racking Horses, Tennessee Walking Horses, Missouri Fox Trotters, or other gaited

The National Spotted Saddle Horse is distinct from other gaited breeds with its beautiful color. *Daniel Johnson*

horses, as well as good gaited country horses (that have no verifiable pedigree, but produce great spotted offspring when crossed with NSSHA horses) are accepted.

Solid colored horses are not allowed to compete in Spotted Saddle Horse shows, unless the class sheet specifies a solid color class.

Standards

Overall Considerations: The Spotted Saddle Horse most closely resembles the heavier Tennessee Walking Horse than any other breed, due to its predominant influence. There is some variation in characteristics, however, due to activities carried on by a number of different breeders. Some breeders are crossing with Missouri Fox Trotters and Racking Horses. In reality, this is less odd than it may seem, as all these breeds share a common heritage: the old Tennessee Pacer (the original Tennessee Walking Horse).

Some horses show more of the spotted pony type, with heavier heads, legs, and shorter necks. The NSSHA is trying to remedy this by breeding for a larger horse with a longer, finer neck and legs, while still retaining the true spotted color and gentle disposition of the pony.

Conformation: Structure and build closely resembles a smaller, slightly stockier Tennessee Walking Horse.

Height and weight: Most horses range from 13.3 hands to 15.2 hands, with the average being 15 hands. Weight is proportionate to height. NSSHA is aiming toward the larger individual as ideal, but does not discriminate because of size.

Color: Any recognized horse color with white in a spotted pinto type pattern is acceptable. The horse must exhibit color or spotting above the hocks other than on the face. It must possess one spot above a level line, midway between the center of the knee and the floor of the chest, and midway between the point of the hock and the center point of the stifle. A spot two inches or more in diameter must be present, with underlying contrasting skin in that area or in the tail. Facial markings, mixed

tails, and/or high stockings alone do not qualify as a spot.

Markings: These are standard Pinto/Paint type markings, but can be tobiano, overo, or tovero. Many horses exhibit tobiano type markings, yet with bald or bonnet faces as on an overo or sabino. Some also show ragged edges and isolated nondescript spots on basically tobiano type markings. Horses must show spotted coloration.

Head: The head is moderate length and refined, with a soft, gentle expression. Other features include:
- Profile: straight to slightly convex
- Eyes: wide set, soft expression
- Ears: moderately long, set well up on the head, inner tips "hooked," carried alertly
- Jaw: moderate development, tapering to a relatively fine muzzle with a slight rounding off of the end over the nostrils that are average sized; firm lips

Neck: The neck is very slightly arched, is muscular but trim, has moderate length, and is carried high with fairly good head carriage.

Shoulders: The shoulders are long, sloping, and well muscled. Withers are high, fine and extending well into the back.

Chest: The chest is of moderate width and well muscled.

Legs: The legs have the following features:
- Forearms: well muscled, with forelegs set a little under body
- Gaskin: well muscled, but not bulgy
- Knees: wide with clean bone
- Hocks: wide and deep, with clean joints
- Cannons: quite short in front, slightly longer in rear
- Pasterns and fetlocks: joints clean; slopes at about 40 degrees in front

Hooves: They are in proportion to size of the horse. Most have white hooves, while some are striped with black.

Barrel: The ribs are deep and well sprung.

Topline and loin: The topline is level, although some horses show a slight rise to the point of the

National Spotted Horses carry their heads naturally high.
Daniel Johnson

croup. Most have short backs with strong loin. The underline is deep throughout, and the flank is relatively deep, without too much tuck-up.

Hindquarters: The hindquarters are broad and well muscled viewed from either side or the rear. Other features are listed as follows:

- Hips: deep and well muscled
- Croup: moderate length, rounded, and slightly sloping
- Tailset: high
- Thigh and stifle: uniformly well muscled

Muscling: The horse is well muscled; it is not as developed as a Quarter Horse, but has more of a heavier build than the Tennessee Walking Horse. The muscles are smooth, not bulgy or knotty, and balanced with muscle development of forehand and rear equal. (This is true with most breeds that perform the smooth or easy gaits, as they push with the rear and pull with the front.)

Disposition: Typically gentle and easy to handle.

Way of going: The breed is shown at three gaits: the flat walk, show pleasure, and canter. All three gaits are performed as a four-year-old or older; only two gaits are required prior to that time.

For the **flat walk**, the horse should be striding behind, breaking in front (picking his feet up smartly), with good head carriage, style and conformation.

The **show pleasure** gait is like the flat walk, but with a noticeable increase in speed and flashiness.

Canter is not a fast gallop. The horse should be under control at all times, and should be on the correct lead. A stepping pace, rack, or any type saddle gait other than a trot is acceptable.

The horse should back straight in the line-up at all times and should not throw its head or open its mouth. Only keg shod horses back up. The Style Pleasure Class (similar to Show Pleasure Class, but more animated) is the only performance class that is not judged on backing up.

The National Spotted Saddle Horse is shown in a number of different classes: In-Hand, Pleasure, Breeding, Under Harness, Adult Riders, and Youth Riders. Classes are also divided by sex and/or age of either horse or rider and by the height of horses. Horses that are 14.2 hands and shorter may compete in both the smaller height horse classes and the regular horse classes.

Horses are shown with the type of bridle similar to those used for the Tennessee Walking Horse, except rhinestone or colored browbands are prohibited. They should be made of leather featuring either buck stitching or silver, or they can be plain. Saddles are western, as is the riding attire.

Credit: National Spotted Saddle Horse Association, Inc.

NATIONAL WALKING HORSE

The ideal Walking Horse has a smooth, great stride, with rhythm and natural motion. *Courtesy Gordon Lawler/National Walking Horse Association*

National Walking Horse Association

Kentucky Horse Park
4059 Iron Works Parkway, Suite 4
Lexington, Kentucky 40511
www.nwha.com

The naturally gaited National Walking Horse is one of the very few breeds of horses that originated in the United States. It is as much a part of the American heritage as the Quarter Horse. What the Quarter Horse is to cattle ranching and western life, the Walking Horse is to southern plantations, quail hunting, and field trial competitions throughout the eastern and southern states. It carried generals in the American Civil War, plowed fields for farmers, and pulled the family buggy to church on Sundays.

Generally called a Plantation Horse back then, it was one of the Tennessee farmer's most prized possessions. Owners enjoyed overseeing their huge plantations in comfort and style while astride their Plantation Horses. These wonderful horses glided along with a natural, ground-covering gait, providing an easy ride and at the same time looking quite beautiful. Their gaits were so smooth and straight that the owner could ride all day up and down the planted furrows, checking the crops while never disturbing the plants.

The Walking Horse has a distinct conformation with a high neck, deep girth, and medium chest. *Courtesy Gordon Lawler/ National Walking Horse Association*

The breed's popularity grew, and in the 1940s it was fast becoming the mount of choice on bridle paths and trail rides across the country because of its smooth gait and wonderful disposition. A Walking Horse was even used in the movies of that time as one of the mounts of the singing cowboy star, Roy Rogers. It was one of his famous and beloved Palominos, Trigger Jr., a Walking Horse that was a star in his own right. This was truly an era of unequaled popularity for the breed that has not been seen since.

In the Show Ring

As Walking Horses became more popular, competitions in the show ring increased. The more animated the gait of a horse, the higher it placed, thus increasing its value for breeding and showing. Therefore, different methods were employed to create a more exciting movement and enhance the gait.

Soring is one of those methods. Soring of Walking Horses for performance is believed to have begun in the 1950s. Deliberate and painful soring to the legs and pasterns of horses was done, causing them to exaggerate their stride for a better "look" in the show ring. Still done today, soring employs methods that includes, but is not limited to, caustic chemicals applied to the horse's front pasterns, foreign objects placed between the built up pads or shoes and the sole of the hoof, and intentional foundering.

Most horses carry 55 percent of their weight on their front legs, with the back legs carrying about 45 percent. If a horse's front legs are sored, the weight carrying percentages are reversed, causing the horse to stride longer with its hind legs and carry more weight on its rear. When viewed from the rear, the sored horse's back legs stand very wide apart, spreading its weight out as much as possible to keep its balance and attempt to stay off the painful front feet. Action devices (boots, chains, and others) were also introduced to get more action in the front legs. The more weight on a hoof or the more sore it is, the higher a horse will lift it.

From the 1950s, the accepted treatment for a bowed tendon on a horse was to blister it with a chemical agent, so the chemicals necessary to sore a Walker were readily available. It was not unusual to see a horse bleeding around the pastern areas on the front legs while in the show ring. Most of the show horses had terrible scars and calluses in that area.

The addition of elevating pads between the shoe and actual hoof was also introduced to get even more front end action. In the late 1950s and through the 1960s, pads grew 2 to 3 inches thick, and action devices could weigh as much as 40 ounces each. Today, action devices are limited to a 6-ounce chain per front foot.

The Walker's naturally beautiful four-beat gait was almost lost during the last half century because those involved in showing the Big Lick performance horse found that to get the look they wanted in the show ring, they had to breed horses with a tendency to pace. Trainers then artificially "squared up" pacing horses with a variety of methods to create the Big Lick gait, which was valued in the show ring and is still exhibited in many show rings today. Since these horses would go on to become world champions, many were popular for breeding, which produced more pacey horses and the process continued.

The American Horse Protection Association and other humane organizations became involved and brought public attention to the issue of soring in the Walking Horse industry. In 1970, the Horse Protection Act (HPA) was passed in Congress, making it a federal offence to show any horse, regardless of breed, that had been intentionally sored to alter its gait. It states, "Although the HPA covers all horse breeds, Tennessee Walking Horses and other high-stepping breeds are the most frequent victims of soring." Responsibility for its enforcement was given to the U.S. Department of Agriculture

(USDA). Though the HPA has been in existence since 1970, soring of Walking Horses has remained a problem.

For five decades, the controversial training and showing practices of the Walking Horse has attached a stigma to the breed, stunting its acceptance and growth. As the artificial gait changed the direction of the breed, the true gaits, which originally made the breed popular, were almost lost forever.

Registry

A concerned group of Walking Horse owners, breeders, and professionals were saddened by the pain show horses had to endure to produce the artificial gaits. They felt it was time for a new approach to the problems of soring and use of other caustic methods and wanted more stringent steps to be taken by the Walking Horse industry at large. Thus the National Walking Horse Association (NWHA) was founded in 1998 to ensure that horses would no longer be subjected to abusive methods for more pronounced gaits in its show ring.

Registration papers were, and still are, not required to participate, as the NWHA did not have any way to verify them. Initially, it allowed padded (commonly referred to as performance) horses to be exhibited in its affiliated shows, but these classes were not supported and were dropped. NWHA then became an all flat shod Walking Horse association.

The NWHA provides shows where no soring and no scars indicative of soring are allowed. Also no chains, pads, or built up shoes are allowed either in the show ring or on the show grounds of any NWHA affiliated show. Only horses in full compliance with the HPA can compete in its show ring. It also created a training and inspection program that strictly enforces zero tolerance for soring, scarring, and inhumane gaiting procedures at all its shows, which exceeds the USDA's policies now in practice.

Beginning in 1998, NWHA became a Horse Industry Organization (HIO), certified by the USDA. It trains its own judges from within the

The National Walking Horse has an attractive head with pointed ears and large eyes.
Henri Williams

association to recognize talented, naturally gaited horses whose gaits have been developed by humane practices. NWHA sets rules that are more stringent than other HIOs and strictly enforces them.

The first National Championship Walking Horse Show (the National) was held in 2001 with almost nine hundred entries. A more recent national show held in 2007 boasted over 1,750 entries hailing from 25 states. To date, this is the largest all flat shod Walking Horse show ever held in the nation. These numbers prove the increasing desire for shows that are fair and considerate competitions, with the wellbeing of the beloved Walking Horse in mind.

More gaited horse lovers are being drawn to the National Walking Horse as the word gets out that these horses perform, in and out of the show ring, without the need for special shoes. Even barefoot horses can be shown in the NWHA arena. NWHA member and former heavyweight boxing champion, George Foreman, has commented, "I instantly loved Walking Horses. They are beautiful. It's the horse of a heavyweight champion; you can have a good time, look good, and not fall off!" Foreman is an avid supporter of flat shod Walking Horses.

Progress

Simply having a place to exhibit a sound horse on a level playing field and having it judged by certified judges whose specialty is humanely trained, flat shod horses, were instrumental factors to a dramatic improvement in naturally gaited Walking Horses. More trainers became involved in training only naturally gaited, flat shod horses because they now had a venue for their product.

A versatility program was established, providing classes for jumping, driving, trail obstacles, obstacle driving, barrels, poles, western riding, reining, and dressage, among others. The National Walking Horse is extremely talented and can do anything any other horse can do, including trail riding, competitive trail events, field trials, and more.

The NWHA Tracking Registry (NWHATR) began in 2004 to track the performance of horses competing in the NWHA show circuit against other humanely trained Walking Horses. Breeders wanted to know which lineages crossed the best to produce well mannered, naturally gaited horses—ones that can perform a true flat walk and running walk, rather than a pace or stepping pace. Horses qualify for the NWHATR either through the Gait and Conformation Process, or by submission of its sire and dam's Walking Horse lineage of at least four generations. Any offspring of the initially registered horse must be DNA matched to its parents. Once in the NWHATR, the performance of the horse is tracked as it participates in competitive events or trail rides.

Standards

Horses are not required to be registered Tennessee Walking Horses to participate in NWHA events.

All horses, including Spotted Saddle Horses, Racking Horses, or Walking Ponies, are accepted into the registry if they have Walking Horse lineage or can do the walking gaits as certified by the Gait and Conformation requirement. The Gait and Conformation Appendix Registry was organized to recognize and register horses of Walking Horse breeding that are not currently, or have not been formally, registered, perhaps because of failure to maintain pedigrees or a rule change by a registry.

It is the goal of NWHA to bring recognition to horses of Walking Horse breeding by offering an opportunity for formal registration. Horses may enter the Appendix Registry on the basis of gait and conformation. To qualify, horses shall exhibit a true four-beat flat walk and running walk with no extreme abnormalities of conformation. The progeny of horses in the Appendix Registry will be eligible for registration in this registry without certification of gait and conformation if the other parent is a registered Walking Horse. All progeny must be parentage verified by DNA typing.

Size and color: There are no size or color restrictions. Horses and ponies under 14 hands are allowed.

Conformation: The composition and design of the Walking Horse should enable the horse to be a functional athlete that can perform the gaits specific to the breed. Its conformation has balance, structural correctness, adequate muscling, and breed and sex characteristics that are key components to athleticism, desired movement, and image for the breed. Added to those components is a distinct style of conformation that should include a neck that rises higher out of the shoulders than most breeds, as well as, more hip and hock angulation.

The ideal Walking Horse should possess these features: an attractive head; well-shaped and pointed ears; large, kind, clear, and alert eyes; a tapered muzzle; long and graceful neck with a refined throatlatch; long, sloping shoulders; deep heart girth; chest width that is neither too wide nor too narrow; short to medium length back with strong coupling at the loin; and sloping croup with lower-set tail. The hip is sloped and long from point of hip to hip joint, shorter from hip joint to stifle, and long from stifle to hock, with muscular development extending down toward the hocks. The rear cannon bones are short. The underline is longer than the topline.

Extremes in any conformation component are not desirable. Soundness of limbs should be of utmost importance.

Temperament: Experienced horsemen sometimes state that the Walking Horse is the most loving, accepting, and willing of all breeds. It enjoys being with people of all ages. It is always willing to learn something new and, once taught, rarely forgets. With its fantastic temperament and smooth, ground-covering gaits, the naturally gaited National Walking Horse is the perfect companion, pleasure and show horse for riders of all ages.

Qualifying Gaits

Trail walk: The trail walk is a true walk with a loose rein and no appearance of strain on the part of the horse or rider. The appearance should be that of a pleasure riding horse that is relaxed, content, and manageable.

Flat walk: The flat walk should be bold and four-cornered, with an evenly timed one–two–three–four beat. In the flat walk, the horse should break at the knees, reaching and pulling with the front legs in a movement that originates from the shoulder. The horse should have impulsion and exhibit stride and drive with the hind legs. There should be no wringing or twisting of the hocks, or any excessive hock action. The horse should demonstrate a loose way of going with plenty of motion. Overstride is important but should be in accord with the conformation and length of the back and legs. A horse with a good flat walk will naturally have a straight up–and–down head motion in time with the overall rhythm of the walk.

Within the flat walk lies the foundation for a good running walk, and it should be judged as equally important as the latter. The flat walk should be a distinctive *flat* walk, not a slow running walk, with each leg impacting the ground

National Walking Horses can also jump. *Julie Claire*

with distinction. The flat walk is more bold and purposeful in movement than the running walk. Form should never be sacrificed for speed.

Running walk: The running walk has the same beat, or evenly timed footfall (one–two–three–four), as the flat walk, but is much smoother, with greater stride, rhythm, and natural motion. The increased rear leg stride and increased reach in the shoulder create this smoother ride and propel the horse at a faster speed without changing the cadence of the leg motion. As with the flat walk, the horse will naturally have a straight up–and–down vertical

The Walking Horse has a pleasant face with a kind eye and compatible, willing attitude. *Julie Claire*

head motion in time with the overall rhythm of the running walk.

A correctly performed running walk is truly a gait of ease, producing a clearly and easily counted, four-beat tempo. It should be straight and loose, four-cornered, and exhibit overall balance without any trace or degree of a rack, trot, foxtrot, pace, or stepping pace. There should be no excessive winging, crossing, or ropewalking (putting one front foot directly in front of the track left by the other front foot). Horses exhibiting an exaggerated, hesitating way of going with a tendency to point with the front hooves are not in form.

The horse should reach and pull in the front with powerful shoulder movement and demonstrate obvious impulsion from behind: pushing, striding, and setting its feet firmly on the ground. When correctly engaged, the horse will naturally drop its hip. Overstride is important but should be in accord with the conformation and length of the back and legs of the horse. Speed at the running walk while maintaining correct form is a positive attribute, though form should never be sacrificed for speed.

Canter: The canter should be consistent, smooth, and straight on both leads. The horse should not be walking behind, but cantering on both ends with a rolling or rocking-chair motion, comfortably collected, neck slightly arched, head slightly tucked, and giving the appearance of ease and grace. The horse should be relaxed, performing in rhythm, with head motion in perfect harmony with leg movement. The canter is not too fast, with speed somewhat dependent upon the individual horse's conformation and size; this shall be considered in judging. While in the canter, the horse should cover some ground, but should not rock up and down unnecessarily without covering adequate ground. A horse that is on the wrong lead or is cross-cantering will be penalized.

General: The Walking Horse should move freely in each gait and proceed in a smooth fluid, rhythmic manner. Form is not to be sacrificed for speed. At all gaits, the horse should be flexed at the poll with muzzle slightly tucked. Any tendency to rack, pace, step-pace, trot, foxtrot, or otherwise deviate from the true walking gaits is not typical of the breed. It is important to remember that gait and overstride are what sets the Walking Horse apart from other gaited breeds.

Overstride is measured by how far the rear foot steps over the track of the front foot on the same side. Other gaited type horses can barely step up to their front track, let alone overstep it. It is overstride that makes the Walking gaits so ground covering and smooth.

Credit: National Walking Horse Association

PASO FINO

Paso Fino Horse Association, Inc.
101 North Collins
Plant City, Florida 33563
www.pfha.org

The Paso Fino is a graceful, agile, and supple athlete, with an incredibly smooth gait. It has captured the hearts of horse lovers everywhere with its proud carriage and elegance that reflects its Spanish heritage. It is the oldest true native breed of horse in the Western Hemisphere, having ties to a glorious past. Spanish conquistadors proudly rode this magnificent horse when they set out to conquer the New World.

Its gait is one of its most outstanding attributes. Paso Fino means "fine step." The Paso Fino's inherently smooth gait utilizes all four legs with precision and harmony. It is born with this gait that is unique to the breed and normally exhibits it from birth. After newborn Paso Fino foals struggle to their feet, they take their first faltering steps in gait.

The Paso's gait allows riders to enjoy long hours in the saddle without tiring, thus opening up a whole new world for horse lovers. When it comes to comfort, performance, and elegance, the Paso Fino horse is the natural choice. It does it all with a ride that provides unparalleled comfort. With its lively but controlled spirit, natural gait, presence, and responsive attitude, the Paso Fino is indeed a rare and treasured equine partner.

Some people have the mistaken notion that Paso Finos are like little wind-up toys that just go round and round a show arena. That myth, however, is being dispelled every day as more discriminating equestrians get on a Paso Fino and discover that it has something special to offer—its remarkably

A beautiful gray stallion depicts the perfect conformation for the Paso Fino. *Paso Fino Horse Association*

smooth ride and versatility. It is growing in popularity, and the ancient history of the Paso Fino is fast-becoming the future for show and pleasure horses in the United States and beyond.

History

Over five hundred years ago, on his second voyage from Spain, Christopher Columbus brought a select group of mares and stallions from the provinces of Andalusia and Cordela to Santa Domingo. These horses were a mixture of Spanish Barb from North Africa, Andalusian, and the smooth gaited Spanish Jennet (which is now extinct as a breed). Spanish conquistadors continued the importation of these breeds, which served as the foundation stock for remount stations for them.

With additional Spanish settlers bringing more horses to the New World, Spanish horses were called upon to perform a diverse role, first in the conquest, and then in the exploration and development of the Americas. Descendents of these horses are believed to have spread into North America after the Spanish soldiers forayed for a brief time into that territory. Modern-day mustangs still have traces of these Spanish forbears.

As Paso Finos drifted into the hands of the Native Americans, their gait became highly prized. An example of this is the Nez Perce Indian tribe, renowned for its expert horsemanship and sophisticated knowledge of breeding spotted horses. The tribe may have mixed some Spanish stock into its famous Appaloosas in their tribal land in the Pacific Northwest. Chief Joseph of the Nez Perce tribe had a favorite horse that was gaited and was envied by all his warriors.

For nearly five hundred years Paso Fino horses were selectively bred in the Western Hemisphere. With the more perfected breeding done by those who colonized the Caribbean area and Latin America, variations in types of Spanish horses were produced. Among them was a special horse that flourished initially in Puerto Rico and Colombia, and later in many other Latin American countries (primarily Cuba, the Dominican Republic, Aruba,

and Venezuela). Bred for its stamina, smooth gait, and beauty, it eventually came to be known as los Caballos de Paso Fino—the horse with the fine walk.

Coming primarily from Latin America, the Paso Fino as we know it today did not spread beyond those countries until after World War II. U.S. servicemen came into contact with stunning Paso Fino horses while stationed in Puerto Rico and began importing them from there in the mid 1940s. Two decades later, many Paso Fino horses began to be imported from Colombia as well.

For a while, there was some contention as to which country produced the "true" Paso Fino. Though there are still some self-professed purists who advocate for one country or another, the American Paso Fino is often a blend of the best of Puerto Rican and Colombian bloodlines.

Registry

The Paso Fino Horse Association was founded in 1972 and has continued to grow at an astonishing rate of 5 percent per year for the last five years. There are twenty-four regions within the association, twenty-one in the continental United States and one each in Europe, Canada, and Columbia. Currently, there are in excess of 52,500 registered Paso Finos.

There are more than two hundred thousand Paso Fino horses throughout Central and South America. La Confederación Internacional de Caballos de Paso (Confepaso), a confederation of ten countries (Germany, Switzerland, United States, Puerto Rico, Colombia, Venezuela, Dominican Republic, Panama, Aruba, and Ecuador), was established in 1990 for the purpose of international competition. There have been seven Mundial (World Cups) since 1993.

From the Florida Keys to the Pacific Northwest, from southern California to New England, and from eastern Canada to Puerto Rico and Colombia, the Paso Fino is now expanding in popularity as the horse for all seasons, climates, and purposes. Its remarkable versatility is not just for the show ring,

This Paso Fino Pinto stallion is colorful as well as graceful and agile. *Darlene Wohlart/equinephotography.com*

but also has been demonstrated in competitive trail and endurance rides, dressage, rodeo performances, and ranch work.

Standards

The Paso Fino has a noble appearance. Modern care and selective breeding have enhanced its beauty, refinement, and well-proportioned conformation conveying strength and power without extreme muscling. It is bred for good physical balance and is extremely quick, surefooted, and athletic. It is a willing and spirited horse, yet very gentle at hand and easily managed. It is people-oriented, enjoying its human companion and always striving to please.

One feature that is always noticed is its long, beautifully flowing, luxurious mane, tail, and fore-lock. No artificial additions are allowed. The tail is carried gracefully when the horse is in motion.

The head is refined and in good proportion to the body of the horse, neither extremely large nor small, with a preferred straight profile. The neck has a graceful arch, and the shoulders slop into the withers with great depth through the heart. While the chest is moderate in width, the midsection is moderate in length with a well-sprung ribcage. The Paso Fino horse's legs show well defined tendons and refined bones with longer forearms and shorter cannons. The hooves are durable and are seldom shod unless traveling on rocky surfaces.

Size will vary between 13.2 and 15.2 hands in height, with the average being slightly over 14 hands. The normal weight will range from 700 to 1,100 pounds. Full size may not be attained until the fifth year.

The breed can be found in every equine color, with or without white markings, including bay, black, buckskin, palomino, chestnut, gray, roan, and even pinto.

Gait

The breed's attitude seems to transmit to the observer that it knows its gait is a very special gift that must be executed with style and pride. Sometimes it is said the Paso Fino is a horse with brio, which is the inner spirit it has and is evident when observing its proud nobility. These horses walk freely, and many of them can perform a col-lected canter, or a relaxed lope, and can gallop like

A regal Paso Fino stallion and rider in traditional Colombian tack. *Darlene Wohlart/equinephotography.com*

other horses, but their preferred way of going is their own natural four-beat lateral gait.

The Paso Fino executes a gait that is smooth, rhythmic, purposeful, straight, and balanced in flexion and synchronization from front to rear, resulting in unequalled comfort and smoothness for the rider. The cadence of the one-two-three-four beat is rhythmic, with equal time intervals between hoof beats. There is very little up and down movement in either the croup or the shoulder of the horse. It is an evenly spaced, four-beat lateral gait, with each foot contacting the ground independently in a regular sequence at precise intervals, creating a rapid, unbroken rhythm. Executed perfectly, the four hoof beats are absolutely even in both cadence and impact, resulting in extreme smoothness and comfort for the rider.

The Paso Fino gait is performed at three forward speeds and with varying degrees of collection that decreases as speed increases. In all speeds of the gait, the rider should appear virtually motionless in the saddle, and there should be no perceptible up and down motion of the horse's croup.

The first of the three speeds is Classic Fino. During this step, the horse holds itself fully collected and balanced, with very slow forward speed. The footfall is extremely rapid, while the steps and extensions are exceedingly short. Leg motion is smooth and extravagant, with each hoof hitting the ground in rapid succession. This gait is used for show purposes only and is performed with the same forward impulsion as a slow walk, yet with a rapid footfall that is calculated, crisp, and precise.

The Paso Corto is comparable in speed to the trot, but is the average trail gait. Forward speed is moderate, unhurried, and executed with medium extension and stride. A well-conditioned horse may travel at the Paso Corto for hours without tiring, and due to the smooth gait, so can the rider.

The Paso Largo is the fastest speed of the three gaits and is executed with a longer extension and stride, with varying degrees of collection. Forward speed varies with the individual horse, since each one should attain its top speed in harmony with its own natural stride and cadence.

No matter if the horse is executing the highly collected Classic Fino or the fully extended Largo, the Paso Fino's performance is a pleasure for both the rider and performer. The breed is born with this completely natural gait, thus there are no external aids that help promote it, or are involved in the training for it. The only training that is used is to help with the collection of the gait and other requirements of the particular class in which the horse is to be shown.

The Paso Fino is capable of executing other gaits that are natural to horses, including the relaxed walk and lope or canter. It competes in western classes such as Trail and Versatility, as well as Costume and Pleasure Driving. Known for their diverse abilities, Paso Finos are also being seen in cow penning, trail riding, and endurance competitions and are winning ribbons in these events.

Credit: Paso Fino Horse Association, Inc.

PERUVIAN HORSE

The noble Peruvian Horse is a unique and stylish breed with a sloped croup and deep girth. *Lorraine Swanson/Shutterstock*

North American Peruvian Horse Association
3095 Burleson Retta Road, Suite B
Burleson, Texas 76028
www.napha.net

Webster's defines "luxury" as "the use and enjoyment of the best, most precious things that offer the most physical comfort and satisfaction." Thus, luxury may be the single best word in the English language to describe the Peruvian Horse.

This breed combines the world's smoothest gait with the most spectacularly stylish action known of all the equine breeds. It is the Cadillac of the horse world.

The Peruvian Horse is an enigmatic blend of extremes. It has the fire of the old Spanish war-horse, and yet is noted for tractability. It is an animal of refined beauty with the strength and endurance to cover many miles a day, year after year. No artificial devices or special training aids are necessary to enable the horse to perform its specialty—a natural four-beat footfall of medium speed that provides a ride of incomparable smoothness and harmony of movement. These are the qualities genetically locked in by centuries of selection.

It is a truly unique breed of horse, but only during the past thirty years has it been well known in the United States. In Peru, it has been cherished and selectively bred for centuries.

History

The judicious fusion of several Old World breeds constitute the Peruvian Horse's foundation. Most of its ancestors came from Spain with the Spanish conquistador, Francisco Pizarro, and were of Andalusian, African Barb, and Spanish Jennet blood. The Spanish Jennet passed on its even temperament and smooth ambling gait. The African Barb contributed great energy, strength, and stamina, while the Andalusian imparted its excellent conformation, action, proud carriage, and beauty to the new breed.

These Spanish horses were largely credited by historians for causing the fall of the centuries-old Inca Empire, as they gave the conquistadors a distinct advantage over the Incas. Explorers were aware of their horses' importance and reportedly valued them so much that many were shod with silver and young foals were carried by porters in hammocks during the long marches.

Subsequent settlers to the Peru area bred the Spanish horses selectively. At the time when Lima became the vice royalty of New Spain, the owners of Peru's large haciendas favored horses with fast, smooth gaits, thus succeeding generations of strict selection genetically fixed these traits.

The Peruvians did not breed exclusively for gait, as disposition was equally important. The horses were used for transportation, and riders did not want to deal with temperamental, stubborn, or nervous horses, which were culled out. In fact, the disposition of the Peruvian Horse has become its most appealing virtue, although the smooth gait is more renowned.

Once established, the Peruvian Horse was maintained in its native country as a closed population, isolated by geography and the dedication of its breeders from the influence of additional outside blood. Eventually, it became the national horse of Peru.

As a result of its strict culling, the Peruvian Horse remains elegant, intelligent, tractable, and eager to please. It is enjoyed by anyone looking for the thrill and luxury of a Cadillac ride. Additionally, it has retained the presence and arrogance of its warhorse ancestors. The modern day Peruvian Horse still travels like a conqueror.

Peruvian Horse and Paso Fino

Many people assume there is a close relationship between the Peruvian Horse and the Paso Fino. While the Peruvian horsemen were developing their native horses, other countries in Central and South America were also breeding horses from original Spanish stock. These later became known as Paso Finos.

Although these horses originated from the same Old World foundation bloods, they were bred for different purposes and characteristics. They came to the New World with different groups of settlers and were generated in entirely separate environments for different purposes.

The Paso Fino was developed in and around the Caribbean and Central and South America, while the Peruvian Horse was born within the borders of its namesake country. Over the ensuing four hundred years, the Paso Fino has become a distinct breed. Their favored gait does not require the length of stride essential for traveling long distances.

Both have a high head carriage and front leg lift, are smooth to ride, and exhibit basically the same four-beat footfall, although each executes it differently. The Peruvian, however, differs in that it is somewhat larger and deeper in the body and wider.

In the United States

In the United States, the Peruvian Horse's adopted homeland, there is an enthusiastic and dedicated

The Peruvian Horse is graceful and refined. Its walk is lateral. *Thomas Barrat/Shutterstock*

group of horse people who believe the breed rightly belongs in the United States and naturally fits in with the American way of life. They encourage others to find this best kept secret for themselves.

As one of the world's last remaining naturally gaited breeds, the Peruvian Paso has become a sensation among American horse enthusiasts for several very good reasons. It can guarantee 100 percent transmission of its gait to all purebred foals. There is something for everyone with the Peruvian Paso: riding comfort and stamina for the avid trail rider; calm tractable disposition so important in the family mount; and arrogant, flashy presence and action that set the exhibitor and parade team apart from others. For knowledgeable American horse people, the Peruvian Horse offers investment

potential solidly supported by its relative rarity and increasing popularity.

Owners have the privilege of preserving a unique breed that can never be duplicated. While the heritage of the Peruvian Horse cannot—and should not—be denied, its purely recreational role in the United States is shaping an animal that appeals particularly to the American sense of beauty and function. As a result, more and more American horse people are discovering the great joy, comfort, and excitement of owning the marvelous Peruvian Horse.

In 2005, two long-standing Peruvian Horse registries—the Peruvian Paso Horse Registry of North America (PPHRNA) and the American Association of Owners and Breeders of Peruvian

The Peruvian Horse's action combines *termino* with knee and fetlock flex. *Thomas Barrat/Shutterstock*

Paso Horses (AAOBPPH)—merged to become the North American Peruvian Horse Association. PPHRNA and AAOBPPH were founded in the early 1970s by serious breeders who had imported stock from Peru. In a few short years, the breed gained tremendous recognition and popularity in the United States. Since their importation to North America, many Peruvian Horses have proven their ability to adapt to all climates and continue their easy keeping capabilities. They are used for show, pleasure, trail, endurance, and parade riding. American breeders have already exported horses to Europe, Australia, East Asia, and Canada.

The registry has sustained moderate growth throughout its history, even during times when other breeds had seen some decline in numbers. The show ring, even at national levels, is full of amateur and junior riders who compete and win in every type of halter and performance class.

Standard

The Peruvian Horse should have the appearance of energy, grace, and refinement. Size ranges from 14.1 to 15.2 hands, with the average being about 14.2 hands.

Acceptable colors are bay, black, brown, buckskin, chestnut, dun, gray, grullo, palomino, and roan. Solid colors, grays, and dark skin are preferred.

The Peruvian Horse tends to boast long, luxurious manes and tails. The mane is abundant with fine, lustrous hair that may be wavy or straight, though tails are not as wavy due to their weight. Tails are set low, and when viewed from the rear, they are carried quietly and straight, and are held close to the buttocks.

The head is of medium size with a straight or slightly concave profile, small muzzle, oblong nostrils that extend easily, dark skin, dark expressive eyes set well apart, moderately marked jowls, and medium length ears with fine tips curved slightly inward.

The neck is of medium length with a graceful arch to the crest; it is slightly heavier in proportion to the body than that of most light saddle breeds.

The back is medium to short in length, strong, and rounded. Loins are broad and well muscled over the kidney area. The croup should be long, wide, nicely rounded, and fairly muscular with moderate slope.

The chest is wide with moderate muscling. The girth is deep, with the length of leg and depth of body approximately equal. Ribcage is well sprung and deep, as is the barrel. The underline is nearly level from the last rib to the brisket. Flanks are moderately short, full, and deep.

Quarters should be strong and of medium roundness and width. Shoulders are long, well inclined and well muscled, especially at the withers. Bones of the lower limbs should be well aligned and well articulated so that the long bones line up with each other correctly above and below the joints, with the skin tight against the bone and strong, prominent tendons. Pasterns are of medium length and springy without showing weakness. Any horse whose angle of the pastern is below horizontal, that is, the fetlock is level with or below the level of the coronet, will be heavily penalized. Cannon bones are short. There is slightly more angle to the hock than that of other light saddle breeds.

Gait Style and Training

In addition to an easy gait, early Peruvian Horse breeders desired their new breed to retain brilliant action combined with *termino*, typified by high lift as the knee and fetlock flex. This movement of the front legs is similar to the loose, outward rolling of a swimmer's arms in the crawl. The outward rolling happens during front limb extension while striding and is a characteristic trademark of the Peruvian Horse. This showy action gives the Peruvian Horse the appearance of always being "on parade" and is also completely natural due to selective breeding. It is not a wing or paddle stride, but instead originates in the shoulder, giving the horse the ability to swing the leg forward with minimum vertical force to the back.

The horse exhibits termino at the walk, Paso Llano, Sobreandando (the basic gaits of the breed), and canter. It is probably most evident in the slower gaits, simply because it is easier to see. The horses are very wise with their use of termino; if they are on a trail with a lot of shrubs or a narrow path, they will accommodate themselves to it and move with less or no termino.

Perhaps the most misunderstood of all traits that distinguishes the Peruvian Horse is brio, a quality of spirit that enables it to perform with arrogance and exuberance that can only be described as thrilling. Brio and stamina give the Peruvian its willingness and ability to perform tirelessly for many hours and many miles in the service of its rider.

A major philosophy among Peruvian breeders about training is that great Peruvian Horses are born—not trained. Training is designed to bring out the animal's inherent ability, but not modify it artificially. To help ensure retention of completely natural action and gait, no horse is allowed in the show ring with shoes or with hooves longer than 4 inches. All Peruvian breeders use basically the same training methods and equipment so that no advantage is gained through artificial devices or aids. If a horse will not collect properly or cannot be managed with a mild bit, it is not deemed suitable for breeding. If a horse lacks termino, well known exercises to increase this trait are not used, as this would only prolong the existence of the fault in future generations. The guiding philosophy is that it is easier to cull undesirable qualities immediately than to deal with them in future generations.

Gaits

The gait of the Peruvian Paso is a broken pace that gives the rider neither the vertical movement of the trot nor the lateral motion of the pace. It is undoubtedly the smoothest ride in the horse world.

The Paso Llano and Sobreandando, along with the walk, are the basic gaits of the breed.

The Paso Llano is a totally equal, four-beat gait. The timing and footfall is: one-two-three-four, which is left hind–left front–right hind–right front.

The Sobreandando is a slightly more lateral gait and usually faster. The footfall is the same: left hind–left front, right hind–right front, but the timing is more lateral. The left hind hits, then the left fore. There is a slight pause, the right hind hits, and then the right fore. So the timing and footfall are more like one-two . . . three-four; left hind–left front . . . right hind–right front.

The walk should be a relaxed, equal four-beat lateral movement. The horse should be on the bit, but the contact is light. The head should be steady.

A horse should be penalized if it does not walk or does not "cap." Cap means that at a slow speed, the rear lateral hoof will step, or preferably extend over (step farther forward than), the print of the front hoof. This is also called overreach. When the gait is extended, the rear hoof print will always reach over the front hoof print. This type of motion allows the horse to cover more ground with less effort. It also allows for a greater smoothness of gait and greater longevity of the limbs. The rear foot should reach to about the midsection of the horse and within 6 inches of a line extending down from the cinch area.

Horses that do not gait (Paso Llano or Sobreandando) at all should be dismissed from the class, and one that breaks gait should be heavily penalized.

The Enfrenadura is specifically a Peruvian Paso class and is the equivalent of a Peruvian reining class. The poncho is to be folded on the saddle. The show premium must specify exact patterns and sequences. The following patterns are those of the Traditional Peruvian Reining Class:

(a) Horse is to be stopped twice, once with the right hind leg farthest under the horse, and once with the left hind leg farthest under.

(b) Horse backs at least eight steps either straight back, or quartering to left and/or right, with the horse facing squarely forward. When the movement to the rear stops, the horse should pick both forelegs up and surge forward off the hind legs before gaiting forward.

(c) Horse should make a circle of 20 to 30 feet in diameter, which is completed at least three times with the horse following exactly the same circle. The hind legs should not *cuarteado* (inside hind leg stepping into or across the path of the outside hind leg in the turn).

(d) To perform the *caracol*, the horse first travels in a 30-foot circle and then gradually makes smaller and smaller concentric circles until it reaches the center. As the concentric circles become smaller, the horse will begin cuarteando and will begin turning its head in toward the center of the circle, with the amount of cuarteando becoming greater as the circle becomes smaller. When the horse reaches the center of the circle, it will have its head turned into the inside stirrup, and its hindquarters will make a complete circle around its forequarters. Then the process is reversed without stopping, and the concentric circles gradually become larger until the original starting point is reached. The carocal may be done to the left and/or right and may also be reversed in the center of the circle.

(e) The figure six is done in both directions; that is, with the loop of the "6" to the right once and to the left once. At the discretion of the judge, this maneuver may be done at a gallop.

(f) The figure eight should be composed of two perfect circles and not have an "X" in the center.

(g) Spurs are mandatory. No type of *gamarilla*, *bozalillo*, or *maquinaria* (pieces of headgear which tie the mouth shut or in any way lift the bit up from its normal position in the mouth) is permitted. Opening of the horse's mouth shall be penalized.

The class is judged 80 percent on performance, with emphasis on a soft mouth and a horse that is responsive to subtle aids; 10 percent on condition; and 10 percent on gait. Entries that do not follow the pattern should be heavily penalized or disqualified.

Credit: North American Peruvian Horse Association

RACKING HORSE

The Racking Horse has both style and grace with an easy gait, providing a luxurious ride. *Butch Housman*

Racking Horse Breeders' Association of America

67 Horse Center Road
Decatur, Alabama 35603
www.rackinghorse.com

Since the founding of the United States, the Racking Horse has been legendary for its beauty, stamina, and disposition. It could be ridden comfortably for hours because of its smooth, natural gait. This noble animal's popularity grew strong on the great southern plantations before the American Civil War. It was known for its easy ride, strength, longevity, surefootedness, and calmness when owners inspected their large estates.

As time went on, the Racking Horse was used for many other tasks and became more important and renowned for its unique attributes. It was especially appreciated for its ability to travel long distances, and for years it was the favorite mount of those who traveled by horse for many miles because of work or pleasure.

Having been around for so many years, it was declared by the U.S. Department of Agriculture (USDA) in May 1971 to be a breed of its own because of its special natural racking gait. In 1975, the Alabama legislature declared the Racking Horse as the official state horse of Alabama. This notoriety, as well as the comfortable ride and flashy stride, made the Racking Horse a favorite both in the show ring and on the trail.

Amateur riders find the Racking Horse to be the answer to their prayers, not only for the extremely comfortable ride, but also for its unusual friendliness to people. Beginners and veterans alike appreciate the opportunities generated by this intelligent, family-oriented breed that is so good natured. Long time breeders, and show judges can recall the time when Racking Horses were used for everything on southern farms, regardless of who was handling them.

Today more than ever, the Racking Horse is appreciated outside the show ring and is being used as a trail horse on every kind of terrain all over the United States. This is due to its surefootedness and gait that is easy on both rider and horse. It has very long strides that cover lots of ground at a good speed. When all these qualities are put together in a trail horse, riding to a destination is done quickly, calmly, and smoothly. Amateurs love this natural ability of the breed.

The Racking Horse has also been used on endurance rides, hunting trips, large farms, police patrols, and just for good fun and enjoyment. The Racking Horse is an exciting breed with unique gaiting attributes and versatility. It is a do-every-thing horse that does it all smoothly, with a rack.

Breed Gait

The ancestry of the Plantation Horse was due in large part to the infusion of Morgan blood. At the time when the Racking Horse was separated from other pleasure riding horses and declared the official horse of Alabama, it was the fastest growing breed. Breeders, however, incorporated Walking Horse blood before understanding Racking Horse ancestry. They discovered they did not like the way Walking Horses moved and they wanted to retain the natural four-beat, single-foot gait, which was not the pacing type gait Walking Horses began to

demonstrate. So breeders changed their programs back to Racking Horse ancestry and away from Walking Horses.

The Racking Horse has its own definite gait not usually associated with other pleasure type breeds, and there is a significant difference in their gait compared to others. It has a single-foot movement, meaning that only one foot is on the ground at a time when the horse is gaiting. This is easier to see in a photograph than by eye alone. It produces an extraordinary movement that is extremely easy to sit, versus the awkward side to side movement of a pace.

The Racking Horse cannot have hock action and is the only breed that does a "step pace" or show walk. It is unique since most gaited horses cannot be this versatile. The head bobs only at a walk, but then the head should stiffen as it goes into a faster gait (a one-two-three-four beat gait). At the rack, there is no overstriding the front feet, which is the key difference between the Racking Horse and the Walking Horse. There are no steps past the center of gravity to cause head motion. Most Racking Horses do not have as high of a leg lift or as deep of a stride as Walking Horses. Since they do not reach as far forward in the rear, there is no need for the head to bob.

This ability is bred into the Racking Horse and goes back to the original Plantation Horse. It is not an easy gait to produce, thus breeders have found it necessary to stay within the Racking Horse breed instead of using outside breeds, for the best results. Even so, sometimes only 50 percent of horses with Racking Horse breeding have a passing racking gait. Those that have a hint of pacing can be shod to train for a better racking gait, but the goal of all Racking Horse breeders is to produce horses that can naturally rack.

Breed Shows

To better promote natural racking gaits, shows hold futurity classes whereby foals, weanlings, and yearlings, as well as other young stock, are shown and judged on a lead to demonstrate their natural movement without any training aids.

This is a platform for breeders to show off what their horses can do and serves as an incentive to produce horses capable of proper Racking Horse gaits without any training devices.

Racking Horses start training for performance classes at about twenty-two to twenty-four months of age. As they mature and their value increases, they become ready to compete, which includes all aspects of the industry under saddle and also in harness. Most people hear and learn about the breed through shows, which range from small saddle club shows, to large area shows and state held shows.

Anyone can ride and show a Racking Horse, which is a midrange horse as far as its expense. The need for big training stables is not as apparent as for other gaited breeds and not as necessary for the show ring. Although show classes can have horses with headstalls and ribbons similar to Tennessee Walking Horses, some classes do not have them since exhibitors find they do not need fancy bridles or ribbons to compete.

Riders interested in showing need to be taught how to ride a rack, or how to help the horse perform it in the show ring. Especially "high lift" horses need to have riders who know a little bit about how to manage it. Posture should be erect in the saddle, and the horse should be kept under control, which can be a little tricky. Knowing the right kind of pressure to put on the horse's mouth needs to be learned, as well as when to apply it. The goal is for the horse to be controlled with minimum effort—a push-button reaction to a slight touch of the reins. Once this is learned, the horse easily maintains it.

The RHBBA has programs such as: Futurity Breeders' Association, Pleasure Association, Pro-fessional Trainers Association, Amateurs' Association, Juvenile Auxiliary, and Ladies Auxiliary. The purpose of these divisions is to help members experience the natural abilities of the Racking Horse in its native environment in and outside the show ring, thus keeping sharp the skill of both rider and horse under saddle and in harness.

One fun class offered at shows is the Water Glass Class. Riders enter the arena holding a glass filled with a certain amount of water. The horses are put through their gaits the same way as for any other gaited class, and the amount of water they have at the end is measured to see which one spilled the least, proving which entrant is the smoothest and the winner.

Shows for Racking Horses are different than other breed shows. Organ music and much excitement provide an electrifying atmosphere. The racking gait is a huge crowd pleaser with clapping, cheering, and calling out (in an orderly manner), providing a good time for all. Being quiet is not the norm, and the horses are not disturbed by the noise. There is also a speed class where horses rack at an astounding speed; one horse was even recorded racking at 41 miles per hour!

Registry

In early 1971, a group of Alabama horsemen formed the Racking Horse Breeders' Association of America (RHBAA). It requires that a horse be evaluated by a RHBAA commissioner for its ability to gait naturally before it can be accepted for registration. Foals can demonstrate their movement on a loose lead for this inspection. Horses from other gaited breeds can qualify as long as their gait is approved, but unless they have Racking Horse ancestry, it is rare that they will demonstrate the correct gait.

Registered Racking Horses are presently found throughout the United States and in several foreign countries, including Germany, Canada, and Australia. Over eighty-one thousand horses are registered with the RHBAA.

Standards

The Racking Horse is attractive and gracefully built, with a long sloping neck, full flanks, well boned, smooth legs, and finely textured hair. It is considered a light horse in comparison with other breeds, averaging 15.2 hands and weighing about 1,000 pounds.

Desirable points of conformation of the Racking Horse are as follows:

- General character: gentle, intelligent, and affectionate
- Color: sorrel, chestnut, black, roan, white, bay, brown, gray, yellow, dun, palomino, buckskin, champagne, cremello, and sometimes spotted or roan
- Markings: face—star, strip, blaze, snip, and bald; legs—coronet, fetlock, sock, and stocking; body—sometimes has white markings
- Head: intelligent and neat
- Eyes: bright
- Ears: well-shaped and pointed
- Nostrils: prominent and open
- Neck: long and graceful
- Shoulders: well-muscled and sloping
- Legs: slender and well boned
- Feet: sound and ample size to challenge lameness
- Tail: long and full, infrequently white, but often flaxen
- Size: average height is 15.2 hands; average weight is 1,000 pounds

Gaits

Racking horses shall be shown in each of the three natural gaits: the Show Walk, the Slow Rack, and the Fast Rack, as defined herein:

(a) The Show Walk is a smooth, collected, slow, and easy gait. It is a distinctive four-beat gait displaying both style and grace. The horse is alert and mounted well in the bridle.

(b) The Slow Rack is a relaxed four-beat gait with both style and action; it is neither a pace nor a trot. The neck is arched with the head and ears alert. The gait should be straight, smooth, and in form at all times.

(c) The Fast Rack is the same in form as the Slow Rack, displaying style, speed, and action. The Fast Rack is faster than either of the other gaits, but form may not be sacrificed for speed.

In each of the three gaits, the horse must be collected and presented well, and the rider must be relaxed and smooth in the saddle. At no time may the horse exemplify a gait with animated hock action. The Racking Horse must exhibit good conformation and be free of blemishes and unsoundness, other than healed permanent scars.

The rack is a bilateral four-beat gait that is neither a pace nor a trot. It is often called a single-foot because only one foot strikes the ground at a time. The breed comes by this gait as naturally as walking or trotting comes to others. The Racking Horse is not to be confused with other breeds whose rack is artificially achieved as a result of special training.

The Racking Horse must not exhibit an exaggerated head nod in the Slow Rack or the Fast Rack, nor exhibit an exaggerated hock action with the rear legs; its stride should be long and natural. The front leg action must exhibit a curved rolling motion rather than following a straight line, commonly termed as pitching or pointing. Abusive treatment and/or training techniques designed to produce an alteration of the gaits are not condoned.

Exceptions to the three gaits are for Trail Pleasure, Western Pleasure, Style Pleasure, Fine Harness, Juvenile Twelve Years and Under, Two-Year-Old, Two- and Three-Year-Old combined, and Style classes and shall be determined by the rules promulgated by the board of directors from time to time.

The gaits performed by the Racking Horse do not alter between the trail and the show ring. Though it may be shown under saddle, in-hand, or in harness, as well as flat shod or with pads, it still performs the smooth, collected gait that made the breed famous as a pleasure mount.

Although the Racking Horse can be shown in both Western and English classes, most of the classes are English. Classes are divided according to how the horses move and are shod. All horses are expected to compete without breaking their gait. The horse/rider team can be penalized for excessive speed.

Credit: Racking Horse Breeders' Association of America

ROCKY MOUNTAIN HORSE

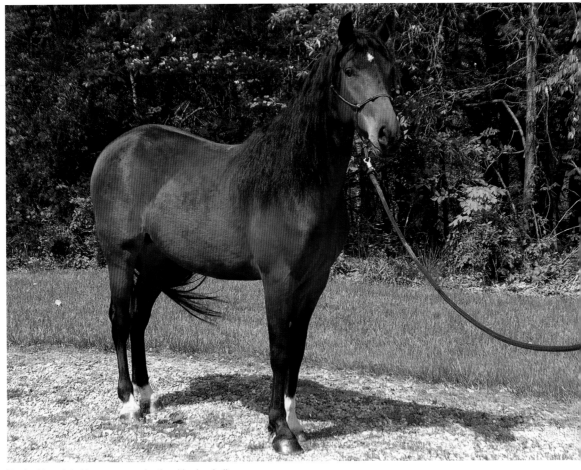

Rocky Mountain Horses are majestic with classic lines.

Rocky Mountain Horse Association
4037 Iron Works Parkway
Suite 160
Lexington, Kentucky 40511
www.rmhorse.com

To describe the majestic Rocky Mountain Horse defies the imagination. When speaking of it, words like regal, magnificent, beautiful, and marvelous, along with a full array of other superlatives are appropriate for this true American breed. Owners soon discover this horse is not just a beautiful animal, but also a part of their life, defining who they are, how they live, and their outlook on life. The Rocky Mountain Horse's ability to quickly bond with people captures the owners' hearts and minds, and even their souls. The history and versatility of the Rocky Mountain Horse leave those who have not owned and loved one with the feeling that the breed must have been something created within the imagination of a movie screenwriter—but they are far more than a writer's fantasy.

"One horse for all occasions" defines this unique breed of horse that, in just slightly more than two decades, has gone from becoming a near extinct breed to having more than seventeen thousand registered horses. From only twenty-six Rocky Mountain Horses located in an isolated area of the Appalachian Mountains in 1986, they have spread to forty-seven states and internationally to eleven countries. To understand what makes the breed so popular only requires the knowledge of their unique characteristics.

Characteristics

The Rocky Mountain Horse naturally demonstrates a smooth, ambling, four-beat gait that glides forward. It moves its feet with minimal ground clearance, as well as minimal knee and hock action. People are often astounded when a newborn foal steps right into this inherent gait when it is first turned out to pasture with the dam. Since this gait does not waste motion, it enables both the horse and the rider to travel long distances with minimal fatigue. While maintaining its natural gait, the horse can move at speeds from 7 to 20 miles per hour.

The beauty of the gait has made the Rocky Mountain Horse popular at horse shows across the country. The surefootedness of its gait has brought a whole new equine star to trail riding enthusiasts, from the casual trail rider, to competitive and endurance contenders. Often misunderstood by those not familiar with it, the Rocky can also perform the same basic gaits as non-gaited horses, such as walk, trot, canter, and gallop.

While the smooth gait is often the first skill that sparks the interest of many riders, it is the breed's beauty that catches the eye. There is nothing more beautiful than a group of Rockies moving around the pasture with long flowing manes and tails and a wonderful range of solid body colors. The chocolate body color with a mane and tail that can range from a dark flaxen to nearly white comes to mind when many think of the Rocky. There are also beautiful blacks, grays, bays, duns, buckskins, sorrels, roans, and palominos, to name a few. Beyond the beauty of the horses is their temperament and gait, which are the attributes that most owners rank right at the top.

Nothing shows the disposition of the Rocky Mountain horse like a stallion on a trail ride with other horses, including mares, or being ridden around a pasture by a preteen youngster. Their affinity for humans has become legendary. Owners smile when seeing articles on how to catch a horse to bring in from the pasture. Just calling them or walking out and waiting is sufficient for the Rockies; they soon come to see if something is wanted of them. Due to their natural curiosity and fondness of humans, they will often wander up to where someone may be working around the barn to see what they are doing, or maybe even "supervise."

Between the smooth gait and gentle disposition, the Rocky Mountain Horse is an ideal family horse, making it a natural for the beginning young rider. These same traits have also made the Rocky a natural choice for a growing population of senior citizens whose aging bones and muscles previously prevented them from riding. It is not unusual for seventy-year-old riders to find themselves being referred to as "the kids" by other riders in the group. Additionally, horse lovers who had given up on being able to continue riding because of injuries or inherent back or leg problems can now enjoy horseback activities on the back of a Rocky Mountain Horse. Many riding programs for the disabled have been adding Rockies to their stables because of what seems to be an instinctive intuition to their rider's special needs.

A good example of this is an elderly rider by the name of Jacklyn Hammitt of California. After her first ride on a Rocky, she acquired her own. Now at age seventy-six and with ten years of riding her Rocky, she is still riding along western trails two and three times a week. As she often says, "When my time on this earth is over, I hope it ends as I'm sitting squarely in my saddle and watching my last sunset." Gloria Northcote, also from California, introduced Hammitt to Rockies and has been through the same experiences due to her leg problems. As a

Chocolate colored with flaxen mane and tail is popular in Rocky Mountain horses. *Kim Levinson*

member of the Rocky Mountain Horse Association (RMHA) Trail Program, Northcote logged more than ten thousand miles of trail riding in just four years. Another example is Chris Balan, a member of the West Coast Rocky Mountain Horse Club, who on occasion will remove her prosthetic leg and strap it on her saddle with no problem. At a disabled camp program in the Southeast, a middle-aged blind man, after riding a Rocky around a pasture, expressed amazement: "I would have never believed a blind man could have ridden a horse." The sensitivity of the Rocky Mountain Horse to riders with special needs seems to have no limits. Testaments like these about the Rocky Mountain Horse are not unusual.

The versatility of the breed seems only to be limited by what a rider is willing to try. Rockies are used in competitive events, endurance rides, barrel racing, pole bending, working cattle, pulling buggies and carts, show classes, trail riding, jumping, and dressage. Dressage trainers have reported that the Rocky can be trained in far less time than other breeds. They are proving they truly are "one horse for all occasions."

Most Rocky Mountain Horses are considered easy keepers. It is not unusual for many Rocky owners to seldom find a need for feeding grain if good pastureland is available. During wintertime or in areas where good pasture is limited, most owners feed them local quality hay. Like all breeds, an individual horse may have slightly different needs, thus the owner should watch for weight problems and adjust feed accordingly.

Basic routine veterinary care and feeding will normally lead to a long healthy life. It is not unusual for Rockies to live into their thirties. Depending on the terrain and riding habits of the owner, some owners keep their Rockies barefoot.

As so many Rocky Mountain Horse owners like to say, "You can't own just one. You don't just own and ride the Rocky Mountain Horse, you experience them." The short history of the breed has shown that the introduction of a Rocky into an area for the first time seems to open the floodgates. As friends, neighbors, other trail riders, or show enthusiasts see and experience the breed, they soon become established in what some have called "Rocky Mountain Horse enclaves." From Florida to Minnesota and California to across the globe, the number of Rockies has increased as their popularity continues to grow.

History

The RMHA history of the breed began when a gaited colt was brought from the Rocky Mountain region of the United States, to the foothills of the Appalachian Mountains in eastern Kentucky around 1890. His name is unknown, but he was referred to as "the Rocky Mountain Horse" by the local Kentucky people after the region from which he had come. He is the horse credited for the start of the Rocky Mountain Horse breed. Little is known about this foundation stallion, but oral history indicated he was chocolate colored with flaxen mane and tail and possessed a superior gait. The stallion was bred to the local Appalachian saddle mares in a relatively small geographical area, and the basic characteristics of a strong genetic line continued. This prized line of horses increased in numbers as the years went by and became known as Rocky Mountain Horses.

Sam Tuttle, the most prominent breeder of Rocky Mountain Horses for the first three-quarters of the twentieth century, owned a stallion he named Tobe, sired by the original Rocky Mountain Horse. Tobe was the primary Rocky stallion used in Tuttle's breeding program and was always in demand for stud service. People brought their mares to Tobe from several different states, and he was as famous in Estill County as Man O'War was in Lexington, Kentucky.

In the early 1960s, Tuttle managed the trail riding concession at the Natural Bridge State Park in Powell County, Kentucky. He had as many as fifty horses including Tobe, who was often seen tied to the hitching post alongside all the mares. Besides breeding, Tobe was also used as a trail horse and became quite well known in the years he was ridden there. He carried Tuttle, and sometimes the trail guides, with surefooted ease over mountainous terrain for many years. Tuttle allowed other people to ride Tobe occasionally, and everyone who did enjoyed his gentle temperament and comfortable gait. It amazed people to know the well mannered horse they were riding was indeed a breeding stallion.

Tobe was used for breeding until he was thirty-four and passed on his gait, disposition, and other great qualities to his offspring, which were said to have followed in his "perfectly timed" footsteps. He left a legacy of many fine horses before his death at the ripe old age of thirty-seven.

Registry

The Rocky Mountain Horse Association (RMHA) was founded in 1986, but the work to save the breed began six years earlier through the efforts of Rea Swan. As a child, Swan rode one of Tuttle's horses, her first Rocky Mountain Horse. She acquired her first Rocky in 1980 and shortly after began a quest to save the breed that was in danger of becoming extinct because of its uncontrolled distribution and breeding. During the following five years, Swan traveled thousands of miles through surrounding counties and states to locate horses with Tobe's genes and characteristics.

By 1986, thirty-three people representing twenty-six progeny of Tobe gathered in Winchester, Kentucky, and the Rocky Mountain Horse Association (RMHA) became a reality. These founders made every effort for the Rocky Mountain Horse to become *breed specific* for the protection of the breed and to assure its future. RMHA maintains the original breed characteristics of the Rocky Mountain Horse, such as the natural gait, height requirements, conformation, color, markings and others.

The adherence to the original breed standard is maintained through a rigidly controlled two-step registration and certification process. For a foal to be registered, it is required to have DNA parental verification by the association through independent genetics laboratories. The test must verify that both the sire and dam are registered and the DNA matches the parentage listed on the registration application. After the horse is at least twenty-three months old, the horse must be inspected by three trained and official RMHA examiners. If they deem that the horse meets the conformation and gait standards of the RMHA, then a certification seal is placed on the registration papers. The RMHA is one of the few registries that require certification before breeding to produce offspring eligible for registration and certification.

This certification process is unique to most U.S. breed associations and is the reason RMHA was issued a certification mark by the U.S. Patent and Trademark Office. The certification mark specifically states: "The certification mark, as used by persons authorized by the certifier, certifies that the horses have been examined by the certifier and meet the certifier's standards regarding height, body, gait, temperament and color."

Rocky Mountain Horses are extremely gentle, making ideal family horses.
Phyllis Rocha

To the prospective buyer of a Rocky Mountain Horse, this certification mark indicates that the RMHA is committed to making every effort possible to keep the breed pure, from its early beginning into future generations, and to assure it is the finest of horse breeds,. The desire of the RMHA is that all owners can remain confident that their children and grandchildren in future years will have the advantage of owning and riding this same great breed.

Standards

The conformation of the Rocky Mountain Horse has remained constant throughout the breed's history.

Height: The height of the horse should be no less than 14.2 hands (58 inches) and no more than 16 hands (64 inches).

Head: It should have bold eyes, well-shaped ears, and a face that is neither dished nor protruding. The head should be medium sized and in proportion to the body with medium jaws.

Neck: The neck should be gracefully arched, medium in length, and set on an angle to allow a natural carriage, with a break at the poll.

Body size: The horse should have medium-sized bones with medium-sized feet in proportion to the body.

Legs: It should have a wide and deep chest with a span between the forelegs. The fore and hind legs should be free of noticeable deformity.

Body: The horse should have sloping shoulders, ideally with an angle of 45 degrees.

Color: The horse must have a solid body color. There shall be no white above the knee or hock except on the face, where modest amounts of white markings are acceptable. Excessive facial markings, such as a bald face, are not acceptable.

Gait: The Rocky Mountain Horse naturally demonstrates a smooth, ambling gait that glides forward. The horse moves out with a lateral gait in which one can count four distinct hoof beats producing a cadence of near equal rhythm. The speed may vary, but the four-beat rhythm remains constant. The gait may technically be described as the simultaneous but asynchronous motion of the legs of the same side of the body, followed by the movement of the legs on the opposite side. The gait is initiated by the hind leg. The length of stride for both hind and foreleg should be nearly equal. The Rocky Mountain Horse moves its feet with minimal ground clearance and minimal knee and hock action.

Credit: Rocky Mountain Horse Association

The history provided here includes excerpts from the book, *Rocky Mountain Horses*, by Bonnie Hodge (Viola, AR: Wildfire Enterprises, 2005), now in its second printing.

STANDARDBRED

Standardbred conformation can include hips higher than withers and a deep girth. *Daniel Johnson*

U.S. Trotting Association
750 Michigan Avenue
Columbus, Ohio 43215
www.ustrotting.com

**Standardbred Pleasure Horse
Organization of Maine**
SPHO-ME
45 Old Falls Road
Kennebunk, Maine 04043
www.sphomaine.net

While Thoroughbred racing became known as the sport of kings, the dependable, athletic Standardbred brought racing to the common person. Standardbred racing has long been known as the sport of the people, and both the sport and the breed are as much a part of American life as cowboys and apple pie.

With its origin dating back to early colonial times, the Standardbred is truly an American treasure. Its contribution to U.S. history is immeasurable. Immortalized by Currier and Ives, this was the horse that pulled doctors to their patients and served alongside soldiers in the American Civil

War. The Standardbred was everyone's horse.

It was only natural that the horse that was so vital to workday life was called upon to serve for recreation as well. During the days when a roadster stood in almost every stable, the thrill of holding the lines behind a fast trotter was not for the wealthy alone. Harness racing began with heartpounding duels along community dirt roads and gradually progressed into the sport it is today.

It began as friendly competitions between neighbors and grew into a celebrated sport of athleticism and skill at state-of-the-art racetracks. The first harness racing tracks opened in the mid 1800s, but harness racing could be found as early as 1825 at county fairs. By the late nineteenth century, harness racing was the most popular sport in the United States. Harnessed and ridden horses of all shapes, sizes, and bloodlines raced and eventually developed into a breed of their own, one known for its durability, intelligence, versatility, and speed—the Standardbred.

The name Standardbred originated from a certain standard time a horse was required to trot per mile to be registered in the original 1871 studbook. The time started off with traveling 1 mile in 3 minutes and was later revised to 1 mile in 2 minutes and 30 seconds for the trotters, and 1 mile in 2 minutes and 25 seconds for the pacers. The mile is still the standard distance covered in nearly every harness race today. The fastest pacers today attain speeds of up to 35 miles an hour, compared to a Thoroughbred, which travels just under 40 miles an hour.

With the genes for pacing, Standardbreds have contributed to the foundation for gaited breeds such as the Saddlebred and the Tennessee Walking Horse.

Standardbreds are known for their docile and willing temperaments. With their inherent desire to please and capacity to learn quickly, many former racers are reconditioned for use in regular riding. It is their athletic build and willing attitude that allows so many Standardbreds to make the transition from racetrack warrior to show horse, from fierce competitor to family companion.

History

The origin of the Standardbred traces back to Messenger, an English Thoroughbred foaled in 1780 and exported to the United States in 1788. He was used to improve running horses in America, but when a reform movement began putting pressure on the breeders of runners, trotting horse owners started to breed Messenger with their mares. Although Messenger was never raced, for unknown reasons his offspring became the fastest and best gaited trotters. His descendents spread to all parts of the United States and Canada.

Messenger was the great-grandsire of Hambletonian, a famous trotting sire that became the foundation of the Standardbred breed. Foaled in 1849 in New York Hambletonian's dam was called the Charles Kent Mare and he was sired by a horse named Abdalla. Owned by a hired hand, William Ryskyk, Hambletonian made his debut at the Orange County Fair in New York. He was well received, but not taken seriously as a trotting sire until he did a match race at the New York State Fair with his half-brother Abdallah Chief. Later, his offspring so dominated the trotting races that all of today's American Standardbreds trace back to Hambletonian. He was the first to have what is now called the "trotters pitch," being higher in his haunches than his withers.

Messenger and Hambletonian were bred to Canadian Pacers, Narragansett Pacers, and Morgan horses of New England to create the Standardbred breed. (The Narragansett Pacer probably became the Canadian Pacer, both of which disappeared from the United States.)

Racing Greats

As the sport evolved, harness racing gave the United States some of its first sport heroes, including the great Dan Patch and the big gray horse, Greyhound.

Dan Patch was a hugely influential horse to the breed, born in 1896. He was a well bred pacer, and during his career, it is claimed that he paced 75 miles at an average speed of 1:59.5. He set many records and never lost a race. In 1905, he set a record for pacers of 1:55.25 at Lexington, Kentucky, that stood for 33 years. He became a legend in his own time and was America's most famous athlete, human or equine, at the turn of the twentieth century. He traveled around the country making public appearances.

Greyhound was foaled in 1932 and was not impressive as a youngster, but the big gelding developed into a trotting machine with a 27-foot stride. Due to his terrific speed, he had very few challengers. In 1938, he set the world record for trotting the mile at 1:55.25, which stood for many years.

A more recently famous Standardbred was the pacer, Niatross, born in 1977. He won Horse of the Year in 1979 and was considered America's super horse. At three, he won the 1980 Pacing Triple Crown and another Horse of the Year title. The same year, he beat the existing world record for pacers by 3 full seconds to 1:49.1. He entered the stud in 1981 as the fastest and richest Standardbred, with earnings of $2,019,213. He sired two Little Brown Jug winners in his first two foal crops and was considered by some to be the greatest Standardbred in history.

The Standardbred breed continues to improve each year, with athletes setting records not even dreamed of when horses raced with high-wheeled sulkies and 1 mile in 2 minutes was the mark of a truly great horse. Now horses are timed at 1:50 or faster, meaning that if a standard bred horse from today raced a champion from 1900, the former would win by a football field.

Racing Types

Standardbred racing is contested on two gaits, the trot and the pace. Trotters race trotters and pacers race pacers. Any trotter or pacer that breaks into a canter or gallop during a race must be pulled back to its correct gait and either lose ground to its competitors, or be disqualified from the race.

Trotters move with a diagonal gait: the left front and right rear legs move in unison, as do the right front and left rear. It requires skill by the trainer to

get a trotter to move perfectly at high speeds without breaking the trot, even though the trotting gait is a natural one in the animal world.

Pacers, on the other hand, move the legs on one side of their body in tandem: left front and rear, and right front and rear move in unison. This action shows why pacers are often called "side-wheelers." Pacers account for about 80 percent of the performers in harness racing and are the faster of the two gaits. They are aided in maintaining their gait by plastic loops called "hobbles," which keep their legs moving in synchronization.

Trotters make up one in five existing Standardbred horses and take more time and patience to develop. Talented trotters, however, have less competition while having the opportunity to win as much, or more, than pacers.

Since pacers are generally seconds faster than trotters and it takes considerable time and effort to develop a good trotter, the majority of today's Standardbreds are raced as pacers. Pacers "get to the races faster," meaning there is a faster return on investment, yet it takes a very fast pacer to be truly successful. Although many horses are trained to pace when racing, the majority trot naturally when they are no longer at the racetrack.

Selective breeding has encouraged pacing bloodlines, but there are very few natural pacers. It is believed that the combination of genes and temperament—which allows so much outside influence such as hobbles holding them on gait—is what makes the breed to be the most successful pacers. Long legs and backs seem to be some of the conformation features that stand out in this breed, as they are seen in both the trotter and pacer bloodlines.

Like other racing breeds, Standardbreds are becoming more delicate, bred for "young" speed with less stamina. The original trotting races were won by horses that set their speed records when in their teens. Now most Standardbreds start racing as two- or three-year-olds and the best retire at the age of four. The original trotting races were done in multiple heats, with some horses racing almost twenty miles in an afternoon, compared to most races today that are one mile.

While the majority of Standardbred racing takes place with a driver and sulky, there is a new type of racing under saddle, which was popular early in the breed's development and has once again become popular in the United States.

Racetracks

Racing takes place at numerous tracks and fairs across North America, although harness racing is most popular in the Midwest and the East Coast.

Some of North America's top trotting races are the Peter Haughton Memorial for two-year-olds and the World Trotting Derby, Yonkers Trot, Hambletonian, and Kentucky Futurity for three-year-olds. The latter three races make up the Trotting Triple Crown.

For pacers, top races include the Woodrow Wilson Pace and Metro Pace for two-year-olds and the Little Brown Jug, Meadowlands Pace, North American Cup, and Adios Pace for three-year-olds. The Pacing Triple Crown is made up of the Little Brown Jug, the Messenger Stake, and the Cane Pace.

Other Talents

Although names such as Hambletonian, Dan Patch, Greyhound, and Niatross have made racing Standardbreds mainstream heroes, the breed itself remains one of the equine world's best kept secrets. They are the world's fastest horse in harness, but for all their stamina and speed, Standardbreds make willing and intelligent companions off the track. They excel in a variety of disciplines, from barrel racing to dressage, saddle seat to combined driving. They have been trained to compete in speed racking competitions, as well as smooth gaited trail horses.

Standardbreds face every task put before them with gentleness and patience, and it is their wonderful temperament that is so crucial to the retraining process. Trail horses, 4-H mounts, carriage horses, team penners, backyard pleasure horses, and eventers are just a few of these horses' new careers.

Riding a horse that paces can be a bit uncomfortable. The motion of the back is side to side with some suspension. Holding the horse a little "between gears" creates a variation of a stepping pace, or rack, and smoothes out the gait so it feels similar to other gaited breeds, such as the Tennessee Walker or Fox Trotter. Standardbreds can be very smooth and very fast.

Those who know Standardbreds love them for their temperament and work ethic. Due to their training on the track, it is usually an easy task to retrain them for pleasure or show. They have a heart that knows no limits and the versatility to go with it. Beginning hard work at a young age, they typically become overachievers. They are bred to accept the restrictions of hobbles, as well as lots of other confining equipment with no regular running allowed, thus saddles and riders do not seem to bother them much. They are extremely tolerant of what people do to them.

This tolerance carries over when retraining them for other disciplines, like riding. Standardbred horses are speedsters. Riding them is like driving a sports car instead of a sedan. They have an on-demand overdrive, but are gentle enough for the novice owner.

Registry and Breed Organizations

The U.S. Trotting Association in Columbus, Ohio, was created in 1939 and is the official breed registry for Standardbreds in the United States. It represents nearly twenty-four thousand Standardbred racing and breeding professionals and promotes harness racing across the country and around the world. Besides administering the studbook, it formulates the rules for racing and licenses drivers and trainers.

Since it promotes Standardbred horses on all fronts, it instituted the Standardbred Equestrian Program (SEP) in 1996. SEP is designed to work with adoption groups so non-racing Standardbreds can be used for pleasure or show, or find retirement homes. The program offers much to the Standardbred pleasure enthusiast, including the

Plastic hobbles keep the pacing Standardbred's legs moving in synchronization. *Daniel Johnson*

annual High Point awards program for competitors and the Medallion program for non-competitors. SEP also offers retraining tips, help with identification of horses (via lip tattoo or neck freeze brand), and other services.

Another helpful group is the Standardbred Pleasure Horse Organization (SPHO), founded in 1983 by Jane Warrington in New Jersey. As the wife of a successful race trainer, Warrington felt that there was a need to market non-racing horses. SPHO supports pleasure Standardbred horse owners and acts as a clearing house for racehorses to find new homes. It helps with the retraining process of racing horses both in the United States and abroad. SPHO organized the first all Standardbred horse show and first Standardbred drill team.

Standards

The U.S. Trotting Association is the regulatory, record-keeping, and registration association for all American Standardbreds. A registered Standardbred foal must have both parents registered. (Qualifying bloodlines are necessary for registration.) Racing Standardbreds must perform with a qualifying time in order to race. The time set to qualify racers changes according to racing criteria.

In many respects, the Standardbred resembles the Thoroughbred, but it is often more muscled and longer in body and it does not stand as tall. The breed has been changing in the last few years to be more refined, combining the well muscled type that is typical of the Morgan physique with the lean Thoroughbred type. The Standardbred is unique in that it is bred for one specific purpose (racing) and then asked to switch to another job (pleasure), which has different conformation requirements.

Standardbreds average between 15 and 16 hands, although the range can be from 14 to 17 hands. They weigh between 800 and 1,000 pounds.

Although bay is by far the most common color, they can be black, brown, chestnut, gray, and roan. White markings on the face and legs are sometimes seen.

The head is bigger and may even sport a Roman nose. The eyes are wideset, the jaw is wide, and the neck is straight and average length.

Shoulders are at a 45-degree angle. Withers are well defined to hold the harness, and there should be a deep heart girth.

Many have long backs and hind legs. For a gaited saddle horse, the longer hind legs can be helpful to gait properly. The rump sometimes is slightly higher than the withers. The tailset should be high with a heavily muscled croup.

For a balanced athlete, the bottomline should be longer than the topline. The chest is powerful, and the legs and feet are straight. They are known for having strong bone, tendons and hard feet.

Standardbreds have wonderful temperaments and try hard to please; they are steady and willing. They have been bred for years to accept a lot of manmade restrictions, such as harness and racing equipment and the training not to run at a gallop. Those that did not tolerate the training were culled out. This left a breed that has a submissive nature and a strong work ethic.

Credit: U.S. Trotting Association and Standardbred Pleasure Horse Organization of Maine

TENNESSEE WALKING HORSE

This beautiful horse epitomizes the ideal Tennessee Walking Horse. *Stuart Vesty/Tennessee Walking Horse Breeders' & Exhibitors' Association*

Tennessee Walking Horse Breeders' and Exhibitors' Association
P.O. Box 286
Lewisburg, Tennessee 37091
www.twhbea.com

The Tennessee Walking Horse has impressed the world with its gentle disposition and kindly manner, and it continues to prove itself as one of the most versatile horses in the land. Its docile temperament and smooth, easy gaits are why it has become much in demand across the United States and abroad. It is an exciting performance horse, but also a fun ride outside the show ring.

It is perfect for pleasure and trail riding, as well as a working horse. Whether it is English or western pleasure, it serves nobly as a mount for the young, the aged, and the timid, as well as the experienced rider, along pleasant paths and trails. Due to its easy gaits and even temperament, a rider can comfortably stay in the saddle many hours longer than on other breeds.

With the increased interest in trail and endurance rides across the United States, the riding value of the Tennessee Walker is steadily climbing. Highly used in the Ride-A-Thons of yesteryear (huge community trail rides back in the 1920s and 1930s), one cannot argue with its success. Consequently, the Tennessee Walking Horse's talent as both a pleasure and trail horse is being more widely recognized, and it is seen more frequently on trail rides throughout the country. With its durability, strength, and smoothness, both horse and rider come through less fatigued.

The Tennessee Walking Horse requires no special equipment. Its saddle and bridle are no different from other saddles and bridles used on any other breed. Most often, a type of western saddle is used to enjoy the trails, but some prefer the flat, cut back English type saddle for recreation and show.

A calm, docile temperament, combined with naturally smooth and easy gaits and immense versatility, has ensured the Tennessee Walking Horse's future in the equine world.

History

For those who think the Tennessee Walker is comparatively new on the equine scene, pages of history reflect the strong influence the animal has had in the building of America and in the daily lives of its forefathers. Mainly used as utility and riding stock and known as the Plantation-type Horse, it gained wide popularity for the ease of its gait and ability to stride faultlessly over hills and through the valleys of the rocky middle Tennessee terrain. Being used for all types of farm work, as well as family transportation and recreation, the Plantation-type horse was not trained for showing in those days. Its natural

gait was most often inherited from its breeding and came to be known as the running walk.

The foundation for this light pleasure breed is no mystery. In the beginning came the Narragansett and Canadian Pacer. The War Between the States occasioned the crossbreeding of the Confederate Pacers and Union Trotters, thus the Southern Plantation Walking Horse, or Tennessee Pacer, came into being. Next came the blood of the Thoroughbred, Standardbred, Morgan, and the American Saddlebred. All bloodlines were fused into one animal in the middle Tennessee Bluegrass region. The result over countless years of this selective breeding was the world's greatest pleasure, trail, and show horse—the Tennessee Walking Horse.

An historic stallion named Black Allen was instrumental in bringing the breed to the forefront. In 1886, a cross between a stallion called Allendorf, from the Hambletonian family of trotters, and Maggie Marshall, a Morgan mare, resulted in the colt, Black Allen. He developed into a small stallion with a gentle temperament and smooth walking gait that he passed on to his offspring. A cross between Black Allen and Tennessee Pacers helped produce today's Tennessee Walking Horse.

Registry

In 1935, admirers and breeders of this unique breed met to form the Tennessee Walking Horse Breeders' Association of America (now known as the Tennessee Walking Horse Breeders' and Exhibitors' Association). The organization selected 115 animals as foundation stock, which represented the tributaries that combined to produce the mainstream of the breed. Black Allen was chosen as the number one foundation sire and was given the title Allen F-1 to denote him as the first horse listed in the Tennessee Walking Horse studbook.

In the first year, 208 horses were registered; near the end of the century, the number increased to over 350,000. Now with association membership in excess of twenty thousand, the Tennessee Walking Horse has became one of the fastest growing breeds in the nation. It has firmly established

Tennessee Walkers should be moderate, but proportional, in their muscle design. *Daniel Johnson*

itself as one of the top ten recognized horse breeds in the United States.

The Tennessee Walking Horse studbook was closed in 1947, meaning that from 1948 onwards, to be registered as a Tennessee Walking Horse, a prospective horse's parents must also be so registered. The Tennessee Walking Horse was officially recognized as a distinct breed of light horse by the U.S. Department of Agriculture (USDA) in 1950.

Standards

Tennessee Walkers are a light breed, generally ranging from 14.3 to 17 hands and weighing 900 to 1,200 pounds.

Colors include all the solid colors, plus white and spotted patterns. Patterns include tobiano and overo, as well as sabino and a combination of sabino and tobiano. Sabino is white that extends up the legs in ragged patches and then onto the body from the belly area. A sabino/tobiano blend is common

in Tennessee Walkers. It combines characteristics of both patterns and usually has white that crosses over the topline. Its main identifying characteristic is excessive white on the face, under the chin, and under the jaw. Blue eyes or blue spots in the eyes indicate the presence of the sabino gene.

Dilution colors include dun with a prominent dorsal stripe, shoulder stripes, and horizontal leg stripes. Silver dilutes the gene that affects only the black pigment of the mane and tail, and dilutes body color only slightly. The mane and tail are lightened to a silver or blonde shade, and the eyes can range from hazel to dark brown. Bay silver horses appear to be chestnuts with flaxen or silver manes and tails. There can also be black silver, classic champagne silver, and other colors. There is an array of diverse choices to please any horse enthusiast, and different colors should not be discriminated against.

The modern Tennessee Walking Horse possesses a pretty head that is in proportion to the rest of the animal's body. The head and throatlatch should be refined and clean-cut, with the facial bone exhibiting a chiseled appearance. The eyes should be clear and bright, showing character and being of good size and well placed, with good width between the eyes. The face should be straight, rather than convex (Roman nosed) or concave (dish faced). The ears should be well set, medium to small in size, and they should be carried forward showing attentiveness. The muzzle should be small, with large, sensitive nostrils. The upper and lower teeth should meet when the mouth is closed. The jaw should show bone structure, but not excessive thickness.

The head should join the neck at approximately a 45-degree angle, with a distinct space between the jawbone and neck. The neck should be medium to long in length, and the head should be carried high. In the adult, the neck should be slightly arched. It should be lean and muscled and blend smoothly into the shoulders and withers. Excessive arching or a crested neck is undesirable.

The shoulder should be long and slope forward at a 45-degree angle from the withers to the point of the shoulder. The shoulder should be smooth, yet well muscled. The withers should be at least as high as the top of the rump.

The topline of the Tennessee Walking Horse should be level, or slightly sloping to the hindquarters. The back should be short to medium length, with a short, strong loin. Spring of rib and depth of heart girth is proportional. The croup should be long with good muscling and a well-set tail. It should also slope moderately from the point of the hip bone to the point of the buttock.

The underline is longer than the topline, allowing for a long stride. The hindquarters should be of moderate thickness and depth, and well muscled when viewed from the side and rear. The muscling should be evident inside and out on the rear legs.

The hock joint should be fairly wide and deep with the joint and be clean. The cannon area should be vertical from the hock to the pastern, with the latter showing a 45-degree angle with the ground. It is acceptable for a Tennessee Walker to stand under in the rear slightly, or be slightly cow-hocked or sickle-hocked.

Typically, Tennessee Walking Horses should be moderate, but proportional, in their muscle design. Masculinity in stallions is distinguished by more prominence of jaw and heavy muscling. The mares should be more refined and feminine, with adequate muscling and cleaner necks than stallions. Geldings should fit somewhere in between stallions and mares, but are generally not as massive in muscle as stallions. Refinement is also desired in geldings.

All horses should have a blending of structures and a balanced appearance, with all parts being proportionate to each other. In a model class (halter), the horse should be shown in a bridle, led into the ring, and parked (forelegs straight and hind legs extended back) for judging. Conformation and condition are paramount. Horses must stand quietly, and unruly entries are excused.

Gaits

In general, the Tennessee Walking Horse should travel in a straight, direct motion, never winging, crossing, or swinging. It performs three distinct gaits: the flat foot walk, running walk, and canter. These gaits are what the Tennessee Walker is famous for. They are natural, inherited gaits and can easily be recognized from the time a young foal starts to amble beside its mother, with rhythmic coordination of legs, head, and body movement. Many are also able to perform the rack, stepping pace, foxtrot, single-foot, and other variations of the famous running walk. While not desirable in the show ring, they are good alternatives as smooth, easy, trail riding gaits.

The **flat walk** is a brisk, long-reaching walk that can cover from 4 to 8 miles an hour. This is a four-cornered gait, with each of the horse's feet hitting the ground separately at regular intervals. The horse will glide over the track left by the front foot with its hind foot: right rear over right front, left rear over left front. The action of the back foot slipping over the front track is known as overstride, which is unique to the Walking Horse breed. The hock should show only forward motion; vertical hock action is highly undesirable. The flat walk should be loose, bold, and square with plenty of shoulder motion.

The **running walk** is the gait for which the Walking Horse is most noted. This extra-smooth, gliding gait is basically the same as the flat walk, except for a noticeable difference in the rate of speed. The horse can travel 10 to 20 miles per hour at this gait. As the speed is increased, the horse oversteps the front track with the back by a distance of 6 to 18 inches. The more "stride" the horse has, the better "walker" it is considered to be. It is this motion that gives the rider a feeling of gliding through the air as if propelled by a powerful smooth-running machine.

The running walk is as smooth and easy for the horses as it is for the riders. Since the gait is easy for them to perform, some Walkers relax certain muscles while executing it; they may flop their ears in rhythm and some may even snap their teeth.

They nod their heads while performing the running walk and will do it in rhythm with the cadence

Tennessee Walkers have an extrasmooth gliding gait that they easily perform. *Daniel Johnson*

of their feet. If the head motion of the horse is not nodding, then it is not walking. This nodding head motion along with overstride are two features that are unique to the breed and are considered when judging the running walk.

The running walk should also be executed with loose ease of movement—pulling the forefeet and pushing and driving with the hind. There should be a noticeable difference in the rate of speed between the flat walk and the running walk. However, they should not be judged by speed, but rather by the true form exhibited, as proper form should never be sacrificed for excessive speed.

The third gait is the **canter**, which is a collected gallop. The canter is performed in much the same way as other breeds, but the Tennessee Walking Horse seems to have a more relaxed way of executing this gait. The canter is a forward movement performed in a diagonal manner to the right or to the left. On the right lead, the horse should start the gait in this order: left hind, right hind and left fore together, then right fore. The footfall for the left lead is right hind, left hind and right fore, then left fore.

When performed in a ring, the animal should lead its canter with the foreleg to the inside of the ring. The canter has an abundance of ease, with lots

of spring and rhythm, and with proper rise and fall, providing a thrill to the rider. The canter lifts the front end, giving an easy rising and falling motion, much like that of a rocking chair, thus it is often referred to as the rocking-chair gait. It is a high rolling gallop, with distinct head motion performed with chin tucked, and is a smooth, collected movement.

Shoeing

Performance horses of the Tennessee Walking Horse breed are commonly shown with double- and triple-nailed pads to add dimension to the hoof, provide a sounder base, and change certain angles and paths in the motion of the hoof. Pads are an integral part of the training of the performance Tennessee Walking Horse, as they serve various functions. When utilized properly, they aid greatly toward accentuating the gaits of the show horse. Pads are essentially training devices, and their effectiveness and usefulness will vary with each individual horse.

On average, shoeing is at a slightly lower angle, with more natural toe than some of the western type horses. If a horse is shod when bought, the local farrier usually checks the angles of the horse's shoes before the horse loses a shoe or its foot grows beyond the desired length and angle. It is best to keep a record of these angles and lengths and have them handy for the farrier.

Otherwise, care of Tennessee Walking Horses is no different from other breeds of horses, and those that are used for pleasure riding require no special shoes.

Judging

The Tennessee Walking Horse is shown under both English and western tack and attire. There are divisions for both padded and flat shod horses in the show ring.

When the performance Tennessee Walking Horse is shown in English attire and tack, it is exhibited with hoof pads. It executes the basic gaits with more animation and accentuated brilliance.

The flat shod segment of the breed has grown due to the easy training of the breed and the inherited gaits. Many people are able to maintain their horse without the aid of a professional trainer.

The flat shod plantation pleasure horse should display brilliance and show presence while performing true walking gaits. Any tendency to pace, rack, or trot should be penalized. Form is more important than speed. The horse is to be well mannered and manageable on a light rein. Manners are paramount for a pleasure horse and should be given serious consideration in judging. The horse should be well balanced, both fore and rear. It must back readily on command and respond to the rider's signals to perform all gaits without necessity of bumping or pumping of the reins. English tack and attire are mandatory for this class.

Western pleasure entries are flat shod and shall reflect the suitability of a Tennessee Walking Horse as a western working horse, exhibiting an exceptionally smooth, comfortable ride without excessive animation. A good western pleasure horse should have a balanced, flowing motion with a free and easy gait. The horse should be ridden on a loose rein and should exhibit a true, four-beat walking gait with a cadenced head nod. The head set should be natural, neither excessively nosed out nor over-flexed at the poll. The head should not be high, but the horse should exhibit the type of head carriage natural for a Tennessee Walking Horse being used as a western working horse. If a western horse does not stand quietly, it must be penalized. If a western horse has a fast, uncontrollable canter or requires pumping or bumping by the rider, it must be penalized.

Other classes Tennessee Walkers excel at are barrel racing, reining, driving, jumping, and dressage.

Credit: Tennessee Walking Horse Breeders' and Exhibitors' Association

---

Opposite: The correct chiseled and clean-cut headpiece is on this chestnut Tennessee Walking stallion. *Darlene Wohlart/ equinephotography.com*

TIGER HORSE

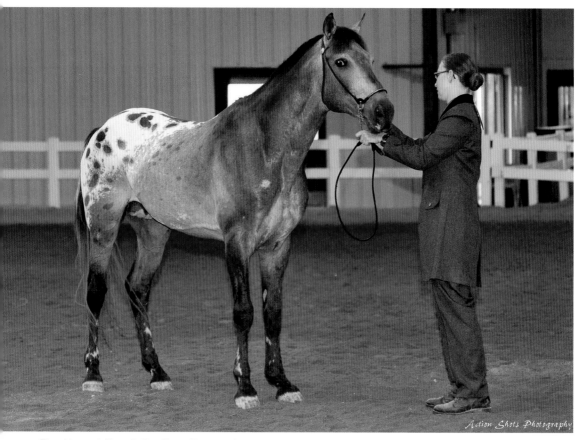

Tiger Horse stallion. *Action Shots Photography*

The Tiger Horse Association
1604 Fescue Circle
Huddleston, Virginia 24104
www.tigerhorses.org

Does it have stripes? Does it roar instead of neigh? Well no, but the Tiger Horse is certainly worth roaring about! It is a colorful saddle horse with distinct Spanish conformation and a comfortable riding gait. As an added bonus, it has the striking color patterns found on such modern breeds as Appaloosa horses. With its gait and Appaloosa type spotting, it is a rare and unique breed.

El Caballo Tigre has a long, proud history that stretches back into the mists of Spanish antiquity. Its smooth four-beat intermediate gaits and beautiful color patterns made it a favorite of the nobility and wealthy. It carried both conquerors and the conquered while forming new empires all across the world. It had a dramatic impact on Native American tribes, changing the course of their history. Both the Spanish and Native Americans knew and loved these superior, beautiful travel horses. Today this spotted, smooth riding breed can be found almost unchanged living in sheltered pockets across the American West.

European History

Thirty thousand years ago in the caves of Spain, unknown artists painted horses wearing rope halters. Some of the these horses were distinctively marked with leopard spotting or white hip blanket patterns, which are now known to be largely controlled by the incompletely dominant Leopard Complex (Lp) gene. These horses were members of the proto-warmblood herds that roamed Europe. Over the millennia, Iberian breeders infused the blood of horses from northern climates, East Asia, and North Africa into the proto warmbloods and gradually produced horses with smooth gait and great pride, upon which the Spanish Jennet breed was developed.

Centuries later, the Jennet horse experienced an upswing when Ferdinand II came to the Spanish throne in 1479 and passed the Gentleman's Law, which stated that "all gentlemen must ride stallions." Due to the fact that not all "fine gentlemen" were good horsemen, this law intensified the breeding of horses that had great presence, but were gentle and docile in nature. These influences ensured that the Jennet would remain a favorite riding mount of European horsemen from the fifteenth through eighteenth centuries. In 1593 Salomon de al Broue, horse master to Henry IV of France, wrote of the Spanish Jennet: "Comparing the better horses in order to appreciate their greater perfection, I must place the Spanish at the top and give it my vote for being the most noble, the best conformed, the bravest and the most worthy of being mounted by a Great King."

Jennet horses in wild color patterns became quite popular during the colonizing period of Europe. Many paintings of the time depict colorful Spanish horses in all patterns, from sabino, overo, and tobiano pintos, to the patterns variously called blooded, blood spotted, trouite (French for trout-like speckling) and leopard or tiger, which were various descriptions of the Lp patterned horses. Horses with these patterns were referred to by the Spanish as *Caballo Tigre*, or Tiger Horses. The Spanish still use the word "tiger" for all patterned cats, as there is no word for leopard in the Spanish language. This habit carried over into the description of other animals. Thus the name "tiger" was used to describe horses of the eye-catching and exotic spotted color patterns that are today associated with the Appaloosa, Knabstrupper, and Noriker horse breeds, all of which share the Tiger Horse of the Jennet breed as a common ancestor.

U.S. History

In the early 1500s, the Spanish began exporting horses to the American continents, and by the mid 1500s, they established important breeding centers in Central and South America. With the English colonization of the New World, however, Spanish horses began to lose favor in the face of the influence of the English Thoroughbred. Many Jennet horses, including those with the Tiger pattern, were exported as trade goods to Canadian colonies, where they rapidly spread across the North American Continent. Thus the Jennet became the ancestor of all North American gaited breeds.

By this time, Native American tribes began acquiring horses, and the southern and western tribes had the purest Spanish mounts, which came directly from Spain and the West Indies. Many of these horses exhibited four-beat or ambling gaits, and they came in all colors and patterns, reflecting their Jennet heritage. Native tribes dearly loved all the wildest color patterns, and this love helped to preserve Tiger Horses.

The Ni Mii Pu (Nez Perce) tribe of the Pacific Northwest was known for its spotted horses. Its first horses would have had very pure Spanish blood and were acquired from the Shoshone in the 1700 to 1730 time frame. Ni Mii Pu Indians became premier horse breeders and developed excellent herds; they even improved the technique of gelding. They especially prized Tiger patterns, which were not plentiful, and traded to acquire them whenever possible.

By the mid 1700s, a significant population of imported Dutch crossed leopard horses were brought to the southwestern parts of Canada and to the Pacific Northwest of the United States. They were from stock originating with Prince Phillip of Spain who bred spotted Iberian horses by crossing Dutch warmbloods with Jennets. This new style of Iberians was closer in type to the modern Lipizzaner and Lusitano and was enormously popular in Europe.

Particularly popular were leopard spotted horses, and in fact, leopard spotted Iberians from that bloodstock became the foundation for the modern Lipizzaner. Just around the turn of the 1700s, the spotted Iberian began to be less admired, which was the reason the horses were sent in large numbers to North America, especially Canada and the northern tier of the United States.

The Ni Mii Pu obtained these horses through trade and added them to their breeding pool, which was producing a distinctive and superior horse with strong Spanish/American characteristics. The new Iberian type of spotted Tigers figured strongly into their breeding programs, which were perhaps the finest of any of the Native American tribes.

Not only did the Ni Mii Pu acquire Tiger Horses from Canadian traders, but tribal oral history also tells of special stallions bought from Russian traders. These light horses, called Ghostwind Stallions, seem to have been of a color pattern that is now called few-spot or snowcap and would have been very light horses — homozygous for the Lp gene (leopard complex), making them nearly 100 percent producers of Tiger patterned horses. These horses were not Russian, but Spanish, and most likely were obtained from the Spanish in California where Russians established farms.

Thus the breeding programs of the Ni Mii Pu were heavily influenced by the blood of the horse "most worthy of being mounted by a Great King." The excellence of Ni Mii Pu horses is recorded in the journal of Meriwether Lewis, written during the Lewis and Clark expedition in 1804. Lewis wrote: "Some of those horses are pied with large spots of white irregularly scattered and intermixed with [a dark color] much like our best blooded horses in Virginia, which they resemble as well in

fleetness and bottom as in form and color."

The Ni Mii Pu bred their horses to be fast, tough, and easy keepers. Temperament was also important, as they had a relationship with their horses reminiscent of what the Bedouins had with their desert horses. Of critical importance was that the horses had to be surefooted and smooth moving to handle the rough terrain of the Ni Mii Pu homeland. This was one trait that was particularly retained from their Spanish heritage, and it was common for the Ni Mii Pu herds to have the ability to perform a four-beat intermediate gait or saddle gait. It came to be called the "Indian Shuffle" by white settlers and was a comfortable riding gait that was highly prized. Since it was much easier on horse, rider, and equipment, cowboys would pay as much as $50 or more for a "Shuffler" at a time when a good broke cowpony would go for around $30.

In 1877, war between the Ni Mii Pu and the U.S. Army lead the cavalry on an extensive chase after the Ni Mii Pu. The tribe's horses were able to outrun, outmaneuver, and outlast everything the U.S. Cavalry could send against them while living off the winter countryside. The only reason the Ni Mii Pu were caught was due to the advantage the army had with the telegraph, by which means it was able to lay an ambush.

The conquest and relocation of the tribe brought a near total dispersal of its huge horse herds. Many of the Tiger type horses, however, could still be found in the Pacific Northwest because they had been well distributed among the Native American tribes through trade. Also some ranchers either owned Tiger Horses or held portions of the Ni Mii Pu herds until the tribe's eventual return. Records also show that most of the military confiscated horses were shipped back east because they had proven their superiority to the cavalry's horses.

Registry

In 1938, Claude Thompson, an Oregon farmer, established a registry to preserve the spotted horses believed to have been developed by the Ni Mii Pu. Although the founding of the Appaloosa Horse

Tiger Horse gelding (left) and mare. *Action Shots Photography*

registration of horses that resembled the original Tiger Horse.

In order to understand exactly what should be looked for, a comprehensive breed standard was developed with the assistance of experts like Dr. D. Phillip Sponenberg, a specialist in color genetics and Spanish horses, and Dr. Deb Bennett, a horse historian and conformation expert, as well as many members of the Ni Mii Pu who contributed oral history to the research. Dr. Gus Cothran, an equine geneticist, now continues the DNA work for the association to ensure proper records of parentages and the genetic health of the Tiger Horse breed, as well as charting the advances made toward establishing a true breed.

Results from these efforts have produced some outstanding examples of what Tiger Horses are all about. A Tiger Horse named Snowline Romeo is the first stallion of any gaited breed to finish a 100-mile endurance race and has participated in several others, with 1,015 miles of endurance races now completed. This demonstrates the heartiness of the breed.

In 2007, the Tiger Horse Association joined with Friends of Sound Horses (FOSH), which enforces zero tolerance for soring of gaited horses for performance. (Soring is the deliberate application of products that produce better elevation of the horse's legs for the show ring, but cause the horse pain). It also became part of the Independent Judges Association and contributed to its rulebook. These partnerships mean that Tiger Horse Association members can show their Tiger Horses in any FOSH or affiliated show anywhere in North America. The first National Tiger Horse Association show was held as part of the North American Pleasure Gaited Horse Championship of FOSH.

Tiger Horses are well represented at shows. At their first national show and with limited horses, they placed in fourteen Open Gaited Breed Classes in addition to the five Tiger specific classes offered. The placements included a first and second in Gaited Dressage, first in In-Hand Trail Obstacle, and second and third in Pole Bending.

Club brought attention to these horses and prevented their total extinction, it also brought a crossbreeding program of Arabian, Thoroughbred, and Quarter Horse blood, which mostly eliminated original Tiger characteristics from the modern Appaloosa. There remained, however, pockets of the original type in Canada, remote areas of the Pacific Northwest, and those herds held in trust by ranch families. In addition, there were breeders who had always adhered to foundation breeding and had regularly produced horses of the ancient Tiger type and four-beat gaits.

In 1991, a small group started a research project to learn the origins of gait in Appaloosas. This turned out to be an endeavor that lasted more than three years and unearthed a significant amount of information differing markedly from the accepted Appaloosa history. It was then decided that a new organization was needed to find and preserve what was left of the ancient Tiger type horses. In 1994, the Tiger Horse Association was founded and began

Registration Requirements

The Tiger Horse Association accepts horses that display the Tiger Horse characteristics of leopard complex (Appaloosa) color patterns, an even four-beat intermediate gait, and some elements of Spanish conformation as its base foundation stock. These horses can come from the Appaloosas, Spanish Mustangs, Paso breeds, Native American or wild horse herds, or some of the less well known Spanish based breeds, such as the Florida Cracker Horse.

As a direct descendant of the Spanish Jennet, the Tiger Horse is a much older breed type than the Quarter Horse, Arabian, and Thoroughbred. In order to maintain the original Spanish conformation and four-beat gait, no horse that is primarily of these modern breeds' conformation is eligible for registration or should be used for breeding.

If a Tiger Horse does not clearly show an intermediate four-beat gait, then it is not accepted for registration. Since the ability to gait has been actively bred out of leopard complex horses, it is understood that outside gaited blood must be brought in to strengthen the gaiting ability of Tiger Horses, but all outcross breeding is allowed for one generation only.

While the four-beat gait is a trait of paramount importance in the breed, the Spanish conformation and color patterns are equally important. The leopard complex gene (Lp), which is responsible for the Tiger color patterns, is not always inherited, or sometimes when inherited, it does not show strong characteristics. Therefore, offspring of registered Tiger Horses that do not show the Lp characteristics are still eligible for full THA registration, though they cannot be awarded a Permanent Championship. While offspring of registered Tiger Horses that do not exhibit any of the Tiger characteristics can be fully registered for any performance or breeding purposes, they are to be disqualified from the Model Categories.

All Tiger horse breeding stock must be DNA tested. No horse with the graying gene or *pintado* markings is acceptable for registration.

Breed and Show Criteria

The Tiger Horse is an easy gaited riding horse with a specific color preference. It is a rare and unique breed that is not necessarily right for everyone and should not be altered to meet the whims of an individual or the marketplace

In the performances show ring, the horse should "cap," or show moderate overstride, with some horses showing more overstride as speed increases. The horse should have enough lift in front to cover uneven ground, and the stride should be medium in length.

All horses shown in Tiger Horse classes must be barefoot or trail shod with hoof and shoe lengths suitable for sustained long distance travel. Tail and mane extensions are not allowed in the show ring.

In the event that a judge has more than one individual exhibiting breed excellence, preference should be given to the one with the most striking coat pattern.

Standards

General impression: The Tiger Horse is a colorful, gaited, light horse breed that is well balanced and sturdy with no extreme muscling.

Head: Ears are of medium length, generally curved and notched, mobile, and alert. Eyes are large and prominent, with white sclera surrounding the iris, which can give a surprised expression. Viewed from the front, the head should look lean, with no cheekiness. A broad flat forehead between widely spaced eyes should taper to a fine muzzle with large sensitive nostrils. Profile can be straight to slightly convex. The ideal profile is an undulating Nató profile, in which the convex curve does not extend up between the eyes. Concave or dish profile is not typical or desirable, nor is an extreme Roman nose.

Neck: The neck should be set high, is moderate to long, well balanced, and blends smoothly into the wither. The neck of both sexes should be well arched with a clean throatlatch. Ewe neck, short straight neck, or a neck set carried too low to be properly raised and arched are serious faults. A jowly throatlatch is to be faulted.

Forehand: Withers should be well defined with a sloping shoulder. The ideal shoulder angle is 45 degrees. There should be a good depth of heart girth, and legs should be straight with a long, strong upper arm. The knees, set low, should be large, flat, and shield shaped. Cannons should be short and dense. Viewed from the front, the chest is of medium width, frequently with a well defined "V" between the forelegs. Muscling of the forehand should be long and flat. Heavy, bunchy muscling of the chest, shoulder, and upper arm is not acceptable. Extremely wide or narrow chest, A-frame front, upright shoulder, buck or calf knees, and toeing in or out are serious faults. Long cannons should be faulted.

Back: The back should be short coupled and strong, with a well muscled loin. Insufficient muscling to the loin, a long, weak back, or any crookedness are serious faults.

Hindquarters: The sloping croup should be level (in height) with, or lower than, the withers and the tail should be set low. Thighs are medium to long, with a well developed stifle and gaskin of equal length. Hocks should be well let down with short dense cannons. Hocks in some individuals will have slightly more angle, and some will have a slight tendency to toe out in the rear. Extreme sickle hocks or cow hocks are serious faults. Viewed from behind, the horse's thighs should be fairly flat, and the hips should tend toward the "rafter" build. The hindquarters should be strongly muscled, but it should be long, flat muscle. Heavy, bunchy muscling giving the appearance of the apple- or heart-shaped rear is not acceptable. Croups that are higher than the withers, poorly muscled rears, and weak stifles or hocks are serious faults. Long cannons should also be faulted.

Legs: They should be sturdy with dense substantial bone, as well as clean with strong dry tendons and moderate, strong, flexible pasterns. Hooves are dense, resilient, substantial, and usually striped. Front hooves should be round, while rear ones are usually slightly smaller and more oval. Neither toes nor heels should be long. Legs and hooves should not appear clumsy or drafty. Very fine or fragile legs and feet are not desirable. Extremely long and low pasterns, or extremely short and upright pasterns, are a serious fault.

Size: The Tiger Horse ranges from 14 to 16 hands, with the height between 14.2 and 15.2 hands being most typical and desirable. Weight can range from 700 to 1,300 pounds.

Mane and tail: Hair can range from being nearly nonexistent to extremely long and full, but it should always be completely natural. Any artificial or surgical methods used to alter the natural set, carriage, or movement of the tail is strictly forbidden, as is tail docking. While braiding, roaching, pulling, and trimming of mane and tail hair is tolerated for horses that are actively being exhibited in disciplines requiring such alterations, these practices are *not* encouraged and will not be called for in Tiger Horse showing, including Model Category.

Temperament: The Tiger Horse is affectionate, gentle, and sensible with excellent learning capacity and a great deal of heart. A controlled spirit and great sense of pride, often referred to as brio, is common.

Gait: The Tiger Horse is primarily a gaited, working saddle horse that, in addition to a walk and canter, must perform an even, natural intermediate four-beat gait. Evenness of gait and the ability to hold gait are of great importance, as are the athleticism, soundness, and smoothness of the gait. All gaits should have good fluid movement, with excellent reach and drive. *Termino*, while allowed, is not a sought-after and, when present, must be carefully evaluated for soundness. All gaits must be completely natural. The ability to perform a range of speed and collection in gait is highly desirable. A horse that can only perform a trot or two-beat pace is not eligible for registration.

Any attempt to alter the horse's natural way of going, such as varying the length and angles of the hooves, padding the hooves, weighting the feet in any manner, or inflicting deliberate pain on the horse, is strictly forbidden.

Color: The Tiger Horse is a gaited breed with

Tiger Horse mare and foal. White eye sclera, mottled skin, and spotting are evident. *Kellswater Farm*

a color preference. Any base coat color (black, bay, or similar others) is acceptable. In the ideal Tiger Horse, visible Tiger characteristics and coat pattern should be present. Characteristics include prominent white sclera around the iris of the eye, striped hooves, and parti-colored or mottled skin.

Common coat patterns include leopard, blanket (with or without spots), roan (with or without spots), and snowflake.

Credit: The Tiger Horse Association

VIRGINIA HIGHLANDER

Virginia Highlander Horse Association
1463 Teas Road
Sugar Grove, Virginia 24375
www.highlandfarm.iceryder.net

Located in the beautiful Blue Ridge Mountains of Virginia near Mount Rogers, a wonderful breed of small, naturally gaited horses known as Virginia Highlanders were developed. They are the culmination of the efforts of a breeder named William M. Pugh, who began a quest for a smaller, gentler horse that would be perfect for women and children. He also wanted an enduring horse with easy gaits that anyone could sit. He set these traits as high criteria on his horse farm.

The process began around 1960 when he brought home a small Arabian–Tennessee Walking Horse mare from Kentucky that foaled a lovely colt the following May. The colt appeared to have been sired by a Welsh Pony. He was exceptional in that he was small, flashy looking, extraordinarily gentle, and could both trot and single-foot like none other. The foal was named Pogo and he became the inspiration and prototype for the Virginia Highlander.

Today, half a century after the birth of Pogo, the beautiful green pastures of the Highland stud farm are dotted with the legacy of Pugh's dream—small horses with correct conformation, gentle character, and eye-catching color patterns.

Breed Foundation

Focusing on his dream, Pugh developed a breeding program that has continued since its inception in the 1960s. He bred Pogo to specially chosen mares and selected only the best offspring for further breeding. His efforts produced a unique

The small, naturally gaited Virginia Highlander is gentle and easy to train.
Susan Slider

breed founded upon the combination of several others: Welsh and Hackney Ponies for their hardiness, Arabians for their legendary endurance and "sparkle," and American Saddlebred and Tennessee Walking Horses for their gait. As the final key ingredient, he carefully added Morgan blood for their size, powerful compact correctness, and gentle, tractable temperament. A distinct breed began to appear out of this blend.

From a continuation of this mix, Pugh produced his foundation stock. As soon as he got a stallion that met his expectations, the previous stallion was sold. The yearlings and mares that did not fit into his vision for the breed were also sold.

Pugh's two foundation stallions were Pugh's Red Cloud and Shadow of the Ridge. By 1991, these two stallions and twenty mares formed the foundation of the new Virginia Highlander Horse Association.

Pugh's Red Cloud was a beautiful reddish chestnut with a flaxen mane and tail, flashy blaze, and stockings. Many of the breed's second generation broodmares are Red Cloud daughters. The foundation mares Pugh picked varied from black to white in color, with many having sabino and/or overo pinto characteristics.

Shadow of the Ridge is a blue roan sabino pinto with flaxen mane and tail. Shadow shows the type that Pugh felt was the perfect example of what he wanted to achieve in the breed. He was Pugh's personal mount and was known locally as "a Cadillac among riding horses," exactly what a Virginia Highlander should be. Pugh continued riding Shadow well into his seventies.

As a Breed

While its larger cousins in the horse world are easily found, well gaited small horses under 15 hands seemed to be quite difficult to locate. Pugh wanted horses like this that were also nice tempered and had large pony size, but retained the horse conformation. The Virginia Highlander fills this niche. Due to its size, it is easy for women, children, and older riders to mount, and even men, both young and old, have enjoyed its soft ride and responsive personality.

A trotting pony on a trail ride with big horses will be hard pressed to keep up without bouncing the rider all over the saddle. A gaited Virginia Highlander, however, can easily keep up and not leave the rider fatigued and sore. Additionally, it has a kind personality, keen intelligence, good health, and soundness.

Although the breed is quite rare, registered Virginia Highlanders can be found in nine states, including Virginia, West Virginia, Tennessee, Kentucky, North Carolina, South Carolina, Missouri, Kansas, and Pennsylvania. The number of registered non-foundation stock is now over two hundred, thus proving Pugh's dream has come to fruition. More importantly, many families have come to know and love this friendly type horse.

Pugh's daughter, Ellen Pugh Cooper, and her husband, Paul, continue the tradition of the original Highland Farm, tending the horses and fields. They are seeing renewed interest in the breed and expect the numbers to grow. After many decades of development, this small compatible mount offers now, more than ever, what buyers are currently looking for—a horse gentle enough for grandchildren and large enough to carry baby boomers comfortably.

Standards

Small, gaited grade mares with no Appaloosa blood and no more than one-quarter Quarter Horse can be bred to Virginia Highlander stallions to produce foals qualified for registration in the Virginia Highlander Horse Association.

Virginia Highlanders are constructed like horses, but of a smaller, more compact nature. The overall impression of the breed is of an intelligent and correct animal with the promise of power and balance under saddle. Both stallions and mares show the grace and compactness so favored by Pugh.

Their heads tend to be short, clean, and pleasant with straight or slightly concave profiles. Their eyes are wide set and large, reminiscent of their Arabian ancestors. They have good flare of jaw and short, well-set mouths with large nostrils. Their necks are well set with a long, clean throatlatch.

The breed as a whole is short backed and well coupled with correct angulation in the long, sloping shoulders; it has a good set of withers for correct rotation of the shoulder, allowing a ground-covering gait to be achieved with little effort. The hips are long and powerful, with evidence of the Morgan ancestry showing in the length of hip and the strong angulation in the stifle joint. Morgan influence is also evident in strong muscling throughout, but especially evident in the well developed gaskins. Without exception, the breed has short cannons, long, well angled pasterns, and round, flinty, hard hooves.

The tail is usually lower set. Nearly all members of the breed have heavy, long, flowing manes, tails, and forelocks. Some have almost marcel like curls appearing in their manes, while others have manes so abundant that it falls on both sides of their necks. Like feral horses, their tails are often thick and heavy to provide protection as they turn their tails to the cold mountain winter winds.

Temperament was of vital importance to Pugh, who selected only the best. The breed—from stallions to mares or youngsters—is trusting, calm, receptive, and easily trained once its confidence is gained.

Most Virginia Highlanders, if not all, are naturally gaited, although nearly all trot and some quite strongly. The majority are blessed with a natural single-foot gait that was Pugh's preference, and all show a long-strided, ground-covering flat walk.

Those that are strongly gaited show a typical gaited horse rocking-chair canter, while others have a more classic canter.

The average size of a mature Virginia Highlander is between 13 and 14 hands, with a few individuals above or below. The breed comes in all colors; black, white, chestnut, and bay with sabino/overo characteristics, commonly appearing both with and without roaning. Appaloosa color patterns and characteristics are not evident, nor are they allowed in the breed.

Pugh believed the limestone rich soil of his farm and the Blue Ridge Mountain climate made for an ideal location in which to breed and raise horses, but it could get cool and inclement. A former cattle farmer, he felt that horses were better left outside in all but the very worst icy rain type of weather. As a result, the Virginia Highlander is a hardy breed and an easy keeper.

Virginia Highlanders are versatile and can transition all the way from pleasure riding to competing in 4-H or Pony Club shows. They can jump easily and, above all, are equine athletes. They also compete in gymkhana, speed and agility events, and in trail and pleasure classes against all breeds, both gaited and non-gaited. After gaming all day, they can then turn around and willingly give the smoothest trail ride ever experienced.

As a trail horse, a show horse, or a devoted family pet, the Virginia Highlander wins hearts and admiring glances wherever it goes.

Credit: Catherine Stuart and the Virginia Highlander Horse Association

PART 4

THE DRAFT BREEDS

POWERHOUSE HORSES

From the brawn of spectacular heavy drafts to the muscle and ability of their smaller counterparts, a job is never too big. Herein are the mighty titans that established countries and kingdoms with their devotion and pounding strength. They clashed in tournaments, moved mountains, and shaped nations with a hardiness and steadiness that will never go out of style. Some still perform the same duties they did in their ancient past, while others are showcased as the best in parades or exhibitions. With a surge of power and might, they strike an awesome picture. Beholding them in action is an unforgettable and breathtaking experience.

Other hardworking breeds also extended their robust capabilities to get a job done. Quietly and humbly, they contributed their service and partnership. Their gentle perseverance carrying a precious load or hauling the master's wagon over difficult terrain required as much courage and deft ability as their bigger cousins.

These are the profound allies of man, without which the progression of civilization could not have happened.

AMERICAN CREAM DRAFT

With their calm, gentle demeanor, a team of American Cream Drafts can be driven by anyone.

American Cream Draft Horse Association
193 Crossover Road
Bennington, Vermont 05201
www.acdha.org

The American Cream Draft is a rare cream colored draft horse that most people know little or nothing about. This is amazing since it is the only draft horse native to America. It is built like the original drafts that worked on farms in the breadbasket of America before the age of mechanization. The American Cream is a unique breed, possessing all the beauty and movement of a top athlete, and projecting a graceful power that is easily directed. These gentle giants have come a long way toward being ideal drafts in the horse world of today and are appealing for work, riding, driving, or show.

Blood testing has proven that the American Cream is, in fact, a distinct group among the draft breeds. Though cream colored with white mane and tail, it is not a palomino, albino, or cremello, but has traits and blood type specific to itself. Its cream color is one of three main physical characteristics manifested by the "champagne" gene. The other two traits are obvious in American Creams, which are pink skin and amber eyes. These three defining traits result from the champagne gene and make the breed unique compared to other drafts. It is truly the "cream" of the draft horses.

History

The most frequently asked question by those who see American Creams for the first time refers to where they originated. Like some other breeds, there was one special horse that is credited for starting it all—Old Granny. She was an outstanding cream colored mare born in the early 1900s in central Iowa, but was of unknown draft type ancestry. She left her stamp on the horse world as the founder of a breed which distinctly and

Cream Drafts have long manes and tails, short coupling, and well-muscled hindquarters.

consistently resembled her in beautiful color and type. By mating her offspring to other well-known draft breeds, the American Cream type and quality were improved, while the color was maintained.

Many times it has been questioned if the Belgian drafts might have started the Cream breed. There is no evidence to support that theory, only the oral memory of Old Granny. She displayed the type of conformation and color now specified as required traits for American Creams. Belgians were used to further the breed, but so were other drafts.

From the first, American Creams were admired by all who saw them, yet it was not until approximately 1935 that any special effort was put forth to make a distinct breed of them. At that time, a few foresighted breeders began line-breeding and inbreeding with the hopes of establishing a new draft breed. In 1944, a group of breeders in Iowa formed the American Cream Draft Horse Association and was granted a charter for registrations and transfers

by the state. In 1950, the association was recognized as standard by the Iowa Department of Agriculture. This gave it all the privileges granted to older established breeds in the state.

Following the untimely death of the association's president in 1957, registrations and transfers steadily declined. Although bylaws in effect at that time stated that after five years, no animal would be registered unless both sire and dam were registered American Creams, applications for registrations failed to verify whether the ruling ever went into effect.

Then the advent of the internal combustion engine and the popularity of tractors during the 1950s ushered in the slaughter of millions of draft horses. With the demise of so many draft horses that were deemed to no longer have any purpose, the American Cream Draft breed, which was in its infancy, became all but extinct. The registration numbers that had grown to over two hundred were diminished to fewer than twenty-five. It was only due to the efforts of a few headstrong Iowa horsepeople who refused to trade their Creams for tractors that the breed survived at all.

In 1982, the association reorganized and re-opened the books, which had become inactive. As of 2008, the number of registered Creams was 402, an increase of 20 from the previous year. With these kinds of numbers, the American Livestock Breeds Conservancy and the Equus Survival Trust placed American Creams on the critically endangered breeds list.

Preservation

As word of American Creams being on the critical breeds list surfaced, owners and breeders accepted the challenge to come together as an association and replenish the numbers to stop the loss of this great draft. Members pledged to develop and improve the breed through careful study, yet maintain the breed as it had existed for the past century, rather than yield to the temptation to breed a more modern or "hitchy" type of animal. In an effort to obtain these goals, a herd book was updated semi-annually and provided free to members. Each American Cream horse owned by a member had first to be registered before being entered in the herd book, and if sold, registration papers had to be transferred to the new owner.

Blood-typing recommended by genetic specialist Dr. Gus Cothran began in 1982. It established that, compared with other draft breeds and based upon gene marker data, the American Cream was a distinct breed within the draft horses.

The association recognized artificial insemination and embryo transfer as a means of breeding registered stock, a service that is now offered by some members. Also, the association has been proactive in testing its registered animals for junctional epidermolysis bullosa (JEB) ever since the disease was discovered and test procedures were developed. (This disease is an inherited, soft tissue, terminal defect found in some drafts and other horses.)

Though it was found that the champagne gene is dominant, not every breeding resulted in a foal with pink skin, rich cream color, white mane and tail, and amber eyes. Dr. D. Phillip Sponenberg, another reputable geneticist, recommended an appendix registration for foals with Cream breeding that were too dark for full registration.

Today, though numbers of Cream horses are increasing, they are still dangerously low. Creams can be found all over the United States, with the highest concentration still in the Midwest.

Renewed Popularity

Guidelines for showing Creams have been developed, and several shows now hold classes in which they can compete. Youth of member families can attend clinics for training Creams that are not available to them locally. Through patience and quiet training, almost anyone can learn to drive American Creams. They are not so tall that a step-ladder is needed to put on a collar and harness, or a stool to mount for riding.

With their calm, willing demeanor, Creams are a good choice for those just starting in draft horse competitions, such as David and Nancy Lively from Vermont. They entered their two-year-old Cream filly team in the Billings Farm Plowing Contest and placed higher than fifth out of a field of forty-plus teams. Their team's calm behavior toward the crowd, the cows (oxen), and the many other teams and teamsters was flawless.

David commented, "They actually made me look good, for I had never plowed with a team of horses prior to this. They stood dead still when asked and showed no nervousness or uncertainty, listening to quiet commands and cues from [me sitting behind them]. . . . These young horses are built for power. When we measured them for a harness as two year olds, we found their girth was longer than their length! . . . [They have a] thick chest and sturdy legs . . . and they work unshod."

The American Cream's temperament is exemplary, as evidenced by the Livelys' American Cream stallion that follows them around the pen like a puppy.

Registry Requirements

American Creams can be fully registered if both parents are registered.

Cream foals with one registered Cream parent and another registered draft horse qualify for the appendix registry, if they meet certain requirements. From that point there is an upgrade system to ensure the offspring will be mated to fully registered Creams. The association believes this will strengthen, rather than dilute, the genes and enable the breed's numbers to increase more rapidly.

At some point, it is likely that the books will be closed to outside breeding and only offspring of Cream-to-Cream breeding will qualify for registry. Until that time, a Cream mare with dark skin and light mane and tail is still accepted for foundation stock, yet stallions must have pink skin and white manes and tails to be eligible for registration.

Standards

The American Cream is a draft animal that possesses the cream coat, pink skin, and amber colored eyes. It is strictly of draft breeding and must not be confused with palominos or other light breeds. The association's records tracing back to the beginning of the twentieth century do not indicate any other than draft breeding.

The American Cream is a medium-heavy draft. Mature (five years) height and weight of mares is 15 to 16 hands and 1,600 to 1,800 pounds, respectively. Mature stallions are 16 to 16.3 hands, and they weigh from 1,800 to 2,000 pounds.

American Creams have light, medium, or dark cream color on pink skin, white manes and tails, and amber or hazel eyes. Foals' eyes are almost white during the first year, but begin to darken and, by maturity, turn to amber. White markings on the face and legs are also desirable. The association does not allow roaching the manes or docking the tails. All Creams must have long manes and tails to be registered

Through the use of selective and line breeding, the breed has been refined to the standard it is at today. Creams exhibit a refined head that is well

American Cream Draft Horse gelding, 16.2 hands.
Suzanne Solieri and Pamela Jerrett

proportioned to the body, wide-set, large, intelligent eyes, small expressive ears, and a flat nose profile.

They are short coupled with well muscled hindquarters, a wide chest, good sloping shoulders, and a short, strong back. They are deep throughout the heart girth. Ribs are well sprung, with good strong legs that are in proportion to the body and set wide apart with strong, sure feet.

Their movement is smooth and easy, picking up their feet and setting them squarely on the ground.

A characteristic of the Creams that makes a lasting impression on those who have handled them, and is probably the most important feature, is their excellent disposition. They are best described as amiable, easygoing, willing, ready to please, and trustworthy.

Credit: American Cream Draft Horse Association

BELGIAN

The Belgian Draft Horse Corporation of America
125 Southwood Drive
P.O. Box 335
Wabash, Indiana 46992
www.belgiancorp.com

The Belgian is a spectacular animal and America's favorite draft horse, outnumbering all other draft breeds combined. It is a big, tall, powerful fellow with lots of action and one that carries its head high and proud. Its confident demeanor and high stepping movement are show stoppers, and yet the Belgian is easily handled. Compared to other major American draft breeds, the Belgian is the most outstanding. It is the best in any pulling field, outnumbering any other breed wherever there are pulling contests because it puts its heart into it and does not give up. For that reason, this horse is the most popular breed with the Amish and farmers who are serious about draft type work. They know the Belgian is the best. Whether the purpose is that of work, show, advertising, or just pleasure, the Belgian fits the need. The Belgian was no overnight success. Its popularity has been hard won over the last century on thousands of farms and ranches, in countless pulling contests and show rings, and on American streets where hitches once pulled freight wagons of food for numerous people. Its staying power proves its worth. This breed did not become America's favorite draft horse by being second best. It is the "American Draft Horse Supreme."

The Belgian is tall and powerful, carrying his head high and proud. *Belgian Draft Horse Corporation of America*

The Belgian foot is important; it should be deep, strong, and have adequate size. *Belgian Draft Horse Corporation of America*

History

Heavy type horses were known to exist in western Europe during the time of Julius Caesar. Most notable were the large black horses known as Flemish horses, which later carried armored knights into battle during the Middle Ages. With their great strength and size, they could handle the extra weight of armor and were referred to as the "Great Horse" by medieval writers. These horses provided the genetic material from which nearly all modern draft breeds are fashioned, yet the Belgian draft horses of today are the most direct lineal descendants of the Great Horse.

As the ancestral home of the Great Horse, Belgium lies in the heart of Flemish horse country. Although small, Belgium has fertile soil that is perfect for agriculture, and from early times its farmers used native stock to develop a heavy, powerful breed of horse necessary for the area's abundant farming and commerce.

Stallions from Belgium were exported to many other parts of Europe as the need for larger draft animals rose for industrial and farm use. There was no reason to import other horses into Belgium, which already had the best stock. It only needed to refine and stabilize the type of genetic material it already had at hand. This was accomplished with the Belgium government's energetic participation in establishing a system of district shows, culminating in the famous National Show in Brussels. At this international showcase for the breed, the prizes were generous, and there were inspection committees in place for stallions standing for public service.

The result was a rapid improvement into a fixed breed type, and the draft horses of Belgium were regarded as a national treasure, as well as part of its heritage. As an example, in 1891 Belgium exported stallions to the government stables of Russia, Italy, Germany, France, and the Austro-Hungary Empire. The movement of horses out of Belgium for breeding purposes was tremendous in scope and financially rewarding for its breeders for decades.

In the United States

The heavy draft stallions of Belgium were imported to the United States as its civilization moved west. Homesteaders needed heavier horses than the mustangs of the West to break the prairie ground for planting and pull large freight wagons. This created a need for a U.S. organization to keep imported animals and their descendants pure and protected. Thus the American Association of Importers and Breeders of Belgian Draft Horses was founded in 1887 in Indiana, with its name changing to the Belgian Draft Horse Corporation of America in 1937.

Progress of the Belgian horse was slow until after the turn of the century. In 1903, the government of Belgium sent an exhibit of horses to the St. Louis World's Fair and the International Livestock Exposition in Chicago. While this effort created plenty of controversy over which type of horse best suited Americans, it also generated a great deal of interest in the breed.

From that point forward, the breed's acceptance grew steadily. Nearly every major importer in the country included Belgians in their offering. In terms of importing seed stock and establishing new breeders, this was none too soon, for the onset of World War I in 1914 brought all importations to a halt. Suddenly, American Belgian breeders were on their own, but fortunately they had plenty of stock with which to develop their own style of Belgian horse.

It was during the draft horse decline in the 1920s when the Belgian moved into a very solid number-two position in the United States, just behind the Percheron. Thus it was not surprising that during that decade, there was a resumption of small-scale importations from Belgium. With the dramatic upturn in draft horse fortunes in the mid-1930s, horses imported from Belgium again assumed major proportions for a few years. The last importation was timely, landing in New York four months after World War II had begun and four months before the German invasion of Belgium.

Around that time, a number of events conspired to nearly end draft horse breeding of any kind. The labor shortage of World War II, the introduction of small, rubber-tired row-crop tractors, and the tremendous push for mechanization in the wake of World War II put all draft breeds under severe pressure. The decline of interest in draft horse breeding was precipitous, and the number of annual Belgian registrations dropped under the two hundred mark for a couple of years during the early 1950s.

Slowly, the return of the draft horse proceeded. As the price of horses recovered, so did the breeding. Registrations and transfers made slow but steady gains until, in 1980, they surpassed the all-time high set in 1937. An average for the next five years was over four thousand registrations and close to six thousand transfers—easily the greatest five-year period in the breed's history.

That is where the Belgian horse is today—way out in front.

Popularity

There are different reasons that fuel the resurgence in draft fortunes, explain its remarkable success, and support its current popularity, particularly of the Belgian. One is the growing ecological awareness that certain tools and methods of modern agriculture farming are destructive, causing many to seek

alternatives. The Belgian is also a very different and rewarding source of power for logging, plowing, or hauling.

Another reason more are turning to Belgians is an economic crunch that necessitates better farming methods, such as using homegrown power that can run on natural fuel and can, in turn, enrich the soil in the form of manure. The Belgian reproduces itself, provides surplus foals for sale, and appreciates in value for the first half of its life. Besides being used for the production of a cash crop, it can be bred for sorrel and blonde mules with the size and color so prized today.

Additionally, the Belgian's beauty is a consideration. Once discontinued at some fairs for being behind the times, it has now been welcomed back as a crowd pleaser. More increasingly big commercial firms are also looking to the Belgian hitch as an advertising vehicle.

Current popularity makes the purchase of Belgians easier than ever. The fact that Belgians are by far the most numerous of all draft breeds in the United States makes them more accessible for those contemplating the thrill of driving a powerful team or single draft horse, or just beginning a breeding program. Since they are mostly a one-color breed, it is easier to breed them, pair them up as a team, and enjoy a much bigger market when it comes time to sell.

Lastly, nostalgia plays a role, albeit a minor one. Increasing numbers of horse-minded people are finding their pleasure horses are in the form of a team of Belgians. Their good disposition and willingness to work make them a favorite for small, part-time "sundowner and weekender" type farms, which continue to increase in number.

Major Breed Changes

Many of the first Belgians imported into the United States were roundly criticized for being too thick, too low headed, straight shouldered, and round boned. There was even an expression for it: the Dutchman's type. Regardless of their faults, early Belgians made friends because they were easy

A six-up hitch. Belgians are high stepping, which is a show stopper, yet they are easily handled. *Belgian Draft Horse Corporation of America*

keepers and willing workers with amiable dispositions. American farmers decided that the breed's assets far outweighed its faults, and set out to retain what was right and remedy what was wrong.

This concerted effort has been one of the great success stories in animal breeding. American breeders of the Belgian horse achieved more in improvements than breeders of any other species of livestock. Today's modern Belgian is very different from that of the European type. It is a horse with far more style, particularly in the head and neck, with more slope to both shoulder and pastern, and possessing the good, clean, flat bone that goes hand-in-hand with such qualities. The American Belgian retains the drafty middle, shapely foot, good bone, heavy muscling, and amiable disposition of early Belgians. Its qualities as an easy keeper, a good shipper, and a willing worker are intact. The modern Belgian is still great in harness and has become a great wagon horse. The fact that Belgians are equally effective in pulling competitions as in hitch competitions says it all.

Standards

Color has also changed drastically from the early Belgian. Black, gray, red roan with black points, brown, and bay have given way to the predominant colors of today's Belgian, which are blonde, sorrel, and roan with light points and chestnut shading. In all of these colors there are different variations. Most all the colors do have light colored legs, though this does not necessarily mean that the horse has white socks. White socks are more desirable to some people than others. The white manes and tails are the most desirable, and the white face strip, which can vary in width, is also sought after.

The Belgian retains the thick middle, heavy muscling, close coupling, and easy-keeping qualities of its earlier ancestors.

It has a pleasing head. It is undesirable to have a large head that is not in proportion with the rest of the horse. The ears should be moderate, not too short or too long. The width between the eyes should coincide with the size of the horse. A Roman nose is frowned upon, but can happen occasionally.

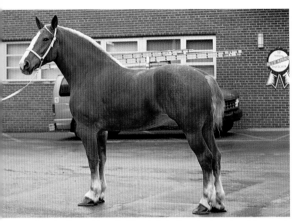

Neck of good length blends into the sloping shoulder, and the back is level of the ideal Belgian. *Belgian Draft Horse Corporation of America*

The Belgian horse should have large attractive eyes which are pleasant to look at. It is undesirable for a Belgian to have small, or "pig," eyes.

The Belgian horse should have a nice neck with good length that blends into the shoulder. It has sloping shoulders and pasterns and a strong, level back. There is a certain amount of slope to the hip (croup), with the tailset neither too high nor too low. Docked tails are desirable for the sake of safety, especially when working or driving.

Belgians have lots of bone. Hocks should be clean and straight, and hind legs placed properly. The foot should be deep, strong, and adequate for whatever size the horse may be. In judging the Belgian, this is one of the significant characteristics looked for and can be one reason why some horses do not place first in the show ring.

The horse should move well at both the walk and trot. Some important considerations for judging are: draft type, soundness, size, conformation, quality, and action at both the walk and trot.

The height of the Belgian can range from 16 to 19 hands, with a few individuals more than this.

As for the temperament of the Belgian, the horse is generally gentle, but this depends on the individual horse. There is no one set pattern for any breed when it comes to temperament.

The Belgian horse is quite diversified. It is used as a source of farm power and for showing in both Halter and Hitch classes, as well as pulling competitions and Pleasure class. Show classes include unicorn (three horses, one in the lead) and four-, six- and eight-horse hitches. Other classes that can be offered are for Tallest Horse and Draft Under Saddle, both western and English.

Junctional Epidermolysis Bullosa (JEB)

The Belgian Draft Horse Corporation of America has contracted with the Veterinary Genetics Lab at the University of California, Davis, to handle genetic testing for the junctional epidermolysis bullosa (JEB) condition. This is the new name for an old disease originally called epitheliogenesis imperfecto (EI), or hairless foal. JEB is a skin defect that is terminal in certain newborn Belgian foals. It affects the skin protein that holds the skin to the body. Affected foals are typically born alive and well, but soon develop patches of hair and skin loss over points of wear. These patches soon become larger and encompass large areas of the foal's body. Hoof attachment is also dependent on the protein; with its absence, this leads to the loss of the hoof wall. The foal's front teeth are in at birth, but many oral ulcers are also present. The foal dies, or is euthanized for severe infection and discomfort, at three to eight days of age.

Belgian breeders have been plagued with this annoying disease for centuries. There are scientific reports of the condition dating back to 1934 in Sweden, 1936 in the Netherlands, and there were twenty-eight cases reported in Germany from 1935 to 1944. JEB is a simple recessive genetic mutation that can be controlled through screened breeding. Breeding two horses that carry the genetic mutation can cause the birth of a JEB foal. The gene site of the mutation was isolated in 2002, so now testing for parentage verification of the disease can be performed.

Belgian owners can submit registration papers to the Belgian Draft Horse Corporation of America office requesting the JEB test. The corporate office

Hocks of the Belgian should be clean and straight and hind legs placed properly.

then sends back bar-coded paperwork and an envelope to collect mane or tail hairs for testing. When the samples are sent to the lab, it performs the genetic testing to determine the carrier or non-carrier status and parentage verification to confirm it was the animal specified. The results are returned to the corporate office and printed on the registration paper as "carrier of JEB," or "non-carrier of JEB." Public access of the horse's carrier status is allowed to help breeders identify those horses with JEB. Registration papers are then returned to the owner.

The test is only mandatory for new breeding stallions. If they have been blood-typed for the registration of their offspring, testing is totally voluntary. If they have not been blood-typed, however, it is mandatory for them to be JEB- and DNA-tested before their offspring can be registered. Blood typing is being replaced by DNA testing. Mares are done strictly on a voluntary basis. The purpose of this program is to inhibit two carrier horses from being bred together, so there would never be another JEB foal born.

Credit: The Belgian Draft Horse Corporation of America

BRABANT

American Brabant Association
2331A Oak Drive
Ijamsville, Maryland 21754
www.theamericanbrabantassociation.com

Those who see a Brabant for the first time often make remarks like "What is that? It's so beautiful!" or, "It looks like a wooly mammoth!" (in winter), or "What color is that?" One look and it is evident that the Brabant is a remarkably different draft horse with its massive bulk and impressive presence.

The Brabant (br*uh*´-b*uh* nt) is a true draft horse with lots of bone and an amiable personality. It is the heaviest draft, yet considered the most docile of all draft horses in the world. It is an excellent choice for the small farmer engaged in hobby farming or sustainable agriculture. Brabants are easy keepers with excellent feet. With the heart to pull, their stable disposition makes them steady, reliable work partners. They are excellent as starter horses for inexperienced people because, as a group, they are so quiet and willing.

The Brabant is the foundation for the American Belgian, and they were essentially the same horse until about 1940. Although they share a common origin, the Brabant has retained its working draft characteristics. After World War II, the Brabant was bred in Europe to be thicker bodied and more draft-like, with heavy feathering on the legs, while in the United States the Belgian was bred to be taller, lighter bodied, and clean legged. The Brabant remains the gentle giant of yesteryear, making it an ideal choice as a working farm horse.

History

Draft horses of today are thought to be descended from the Forest Horse of northern Europe that survived the last ice age. This horse developed on lands where abundant rainfall produced lush grasslands and heavy forests, thus resulting in a thick, slow-moving animal.

The earliest recognizable horse type or breed was the Ardennes, a strain of bulky pony that evolved in the area along what is now the French–Belgian border. The Ardennes is an ancient draft

This Brabant stallion has the ideal massive bone, short neck, and sloped croup.
Karen Gruner

breed mentioned in the writings of Julius Caesar, and even in those times it was highly valued. It possibly descended from the fifty-thousand-year-old horses whose remains were found in Solutre, France. The Ardennes was a short horse of about 13.2 hands, and was stout and hairy. In the year 732 CE, the Ardennes was crossed with the Barb, resulting in a slightly taller, lighter bodied horse better suited for mounted warfare. In the Middle Ages, the height of the horse was further increased for agricultural work.

In the early 1800s, the strain of Ardennes found along the Belgian border was crossed with Belgian horses to produce a horse called the Trait du Nord in France. The most successful of these crosses was created in the province of Brabant in Belgium, and the resulting strain took its name from there. These Brabant horses were the foundation Belgian draft horse, which was the undisputed number one draft breed at the time. Its official name was the Belgian Draught Horse.

By the late 1800s, Belgian drafts had three types that differed primarily in size rather than conformational type. Since all draft breeds developed from the black horses (the modern remnant are the Friesians) of the northern lowlands along the Dutch–Belgian border, these black horses produced the indigenous Belgian horse—the Gros de la Dendre. This was a tall, heavy, coarse horse that was predominantly bay in color. A stallion of this group, Gros le Wynhuyze, was an ancestor of Orange I, one of the foundation stallions of the Belgian horse of the early 1900s.

The second strain was known as the Greys of Hainault. These horses were smaller and less sluggish than the Gros de la Dendre type. As their name suggests, they tended to be gray, dappled gray, or roan in color. Baptiste de la Croyette, a stallion of the early 1800s, was the ancestor of Bayard, another foundation stallion for the Belgian horse of the early 1900s.

The Colosses de la Mehaigne, the tallest of the three types, was bred in the agricultural region of southern Belgium. These lighter bodied horses that

A bay roan Brabant mare is deep bodied with short coupling and thick neck. *Karen Gruner*

held their heads up were mostly red bay, black, and chestnut in color.

These three lines were interbred to form the Belgian horse of the early 1900s. It was massive and deep bodied with short, stout, clean legs, a moderately sloped croup, broad back, wide chest, and well sprung ribs. It retained all the colors of its ancestors including chestnut, red bay, dark bay, gray, black, and roan.

Belgian draft horses were imported to the United States starting in the late 1800s. Until World War I, some thirty-five thousand animals were sold each year in the United States, Canada, and Russia. Between 1850 and 1930, the price tag for a stallion could be up to a million francs. American Belgians were the same type as Belgian drafts in Europe until after World War II, when mechanization of farming meant the end of large-scale Belgian importations to the United States. The breeders in Europe continued to breed a massive, heavy bodied horse, which remained truer to the original type of the early 1900s, while the American breeders began to breed a lighter bodied horse. By 1950, the European Belgian and the American Belgian had significantly drifted apart in type.

Around 1930, Belgium breeders started producing heavier feathering on their Brabant horses, but a little-known disease affecting the horses' legs progressed to the detriment of the breed, with some horses dying as young as five or six. Around the turn of the twenty-first century, a group of breeders began to publicly address the issue, and a concerned group in Belgium started working to correct the problem. The Belgium people dearly love their big draft horses and continue to produce them, breeding toward more functionality. There are now about fifteen thousand Brabants in Belgium.

European countries that raise the Brabant have different names for it, depending on the country of origin. In southern Belgium, the Brabant is called the Cheval de Trait Belge, or Brabançon, while in northern Belgium, people call it the Belgisch Trekpaard. In France, it is the Cheval Trait du Nord, and in Holland it is the Nederlands Trekpaard. The Brabant is also raised in Denmark, Luxembourg, and Germany.

In the United States

There are four main bloodlines of Brabants in the United States: Babar de Wolvertem, Eros van Berrekenshof, Eminent van Berrekenshof, and Bloc van Velzeke. Two of these stallions are deceased, and the other two are twenty-two years old. At the turn of the twenty-first century, American Brabant Association members imported twenty new horses, thereby increasing the pool of unrelated horses to ensure genetic diversity for the future.

Interest in the breed is growing in the United States, but competition from local and cheaper draft horses hinders the marketability of Brabants. There is concern of losing the Brabant as a breed in the United States and as a type in Europe, yet it is difficult to predict its future. Most people interested in Brabants want them for work on a small farm, either hobby or low-income agriculture.

As the trend toward a lighter bodied draft horse continues, the importance of the Brabant retaining its heavy structure is becoming imperative. According to Deb Bennett, a conformation specialist, for each 1,000 pounds of body weight, the horse should have 8 inches of cannon bone for maximum skeletal integrity and soundness. Horses that have cannons of this width can be expected to remain sound over a long term. This is especially important for riding horses. Most light horses are a little short of this rule, but most draft breeds fall very short. Modern American Belgians have, on average, 5 inches of bone per 1,000 pounds of body weight. Brabants do a little better, as exampled by the mares owned by Brabant breeder Karen Gruner. Her mares weigh about 1,800 pounds and have 11 inches of bone (6.5 inches per 1,000 pounds). The rule of 8 inches of bone per 1,000 pounds is often difficult to achieve.

Registry

In the 1980s, a breeder named Anne Harper became interested in the European Belgian horse and began importing a few stallions and mares to cross with American Belgians. She was the major breeder of European Belgian horses in the United States up until the mid 1990s. About that time, Karen Gruner became interested in the breed when she saw a photo in *The Draft Horse Journal* of Babar de Wolvertem, a stallion Harper imported. Like others who view the Brabant for the first time, Gruner was impressed with the breed. One look at Babar, and she stopped looking at other drafts and started saving money toward the purchase of her first Brabant.

Shortly after Harper dispersed her herd, Gruner decided to form the American Brabant Association (ABA). The European Belgian, or more accurately, the Belgian Draught Horse, was called its old name "Brabant" to avoid confusing it with the American Belgian.

The goal of the ABA is to preserve the European type Belgian horse in North America and to provide communication between breeders of Brabants and Brabant crosses. The ABA encourages the conservation of the heavy, drafty, workhorse Brabant through careful breeding. With more Brabant crosses in the United States than pure Brabants, it stresses that outcrossing should be done carefully and provides information for

Brabants are quiet, willing, and phenomenal for any draft-type work.
Karen Gruner

maintaining good, genetically diverse lines of pure Brabants as a reservoir for the future.

In more recent years, Europe has noticeably been breeding a more modern type of Belgian Draft that is lighter bodied and leggier. If this trend continues, Gruner speculates that in another ten to twenty years, American Brabants will be truer to the old type (circa 1900) than the Brabants in Europe.

The ABA does not have a registry. Horses of pure Brabant breeding and American Belgian–Brabant crosses are registered with the Belgian Draft Horse Corporation of America. The ABA publishes a member-breeder list and otherwise promotes the breed.

Standards

With its massive bone and general draft characteristics, the Brabant really looks like a farm or logging horse, not a big carriage horse. It tends to appear more like the old-style Shetland Pony, only scaled up in size. It is very calm natured and a willing worker.

The modern Brabant stands 15.2 hands to 17 hands, with the most common size being 16.0 to 16.2 hands. It generally weighs between 1,800 and 2,200 pounds, with 2,000 pounds being average.

Unlike the American Belgian, the Brabant comes in many colors, the most common being red bay and bay roan. Also seen are dark bay (brown), blue roan, black (which is rare), sorrel, strawberry roan, and even gray (also rare).

The Brabant in the United States has a substantial, but neat, head and a short thick neck. Its body is deep and close-coupled. It has a broad chest, stout legs, moderately sloped croup, broad back, and well sprung ribs.

It has a thick, double mane and a long, full tail, which is often cut off evenly with the hocks when not docked because it is so heavy. The Brabant has moderate to heavy feathering on the lower legs, making its legs look even thicker than they actually are. There is plenty of bone in the legs. Big cannon bones are desirable.

The Brabant's greatest asset is its calm temperament. It is an easy keeper with a quiet, gentle, and willing disposition. And it is an ideal breed for the small farmer with a smaller farm who is interested in sustainable agriculture.

Credit: Karen Gruner; American Brabant Association

CANADIAN

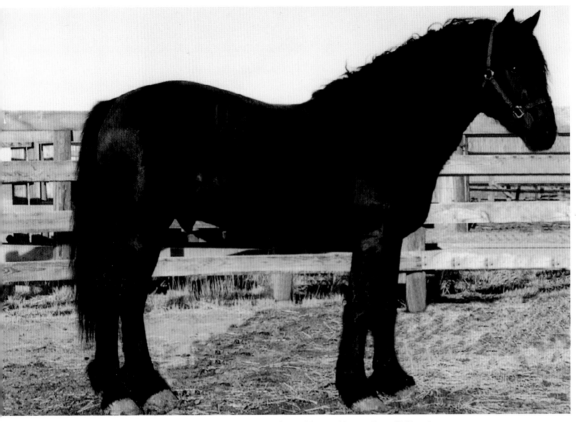

The Canadian has a well-proportioned body and sturdy legs with good bone. *Lazy D Ranch*

Canadian Horse Breeder's Association
59 rue Monfette Suite #108
Victoriaville, Quebec G6P 1JA, Canada
www.lechevalcanadien.ca

"Big, brave heart." "More athletic than a warmblood, calmer than a sport horse, faster learning than a hot blood, and more beautiful than any breed I have ever met!" "Very hard to find equals in other breeds." These are some of the comments recorded by judges about the incredible Canadian horse.

Despite such glowing reviews, the Canadian breed may be one of the best kept secrets of the century. It is an unsung hero in the development of the United States and a horse well known to North American colonists. Although a major contributor to Central American horse breeds, today even many Canadian residents are unaware of the breed. It is a 340-year-old Canadian secret.

The Canadian Horse can be called a general utility animal, with strength and endurance that is legendary. It is said that the Canadian is capable of generating more power per hundred pounds of body weight than any other breed. This low maintenance animal is intelligent, willing, incredibly athletic, and sound. It is a hardy breed and easily lives up to its nickname, "the Little Iron Horse."

History

The Canadian Horse, or Le Cheval Canadien, originated from horses sent to Quebec in 1665 by King Louis XIV, who instructed that only the best animals of the kingdom be sent. Thus the two stallions and twenty mares that went to New France (Canada) were from his Royal Stables of Normandy and Brittany, which at that time were the two most renowned horse breeding provinces of France. He also sent additional shipments in 1667 and in 1670, which together formed the basis of the new breed, called the French Canadian horse of the Old Regime. The Old English name for it was simply French Canadian horse.

The horses that were sent were of Breton, French Norman, Arabian, Andalusian, and Spanish Barb descent. The heavy Breton draft horse, although small, was noted for its soundness and vigor. The Norman horse closely resembled the Breton, but gave more evidence of infusion of oriental blood, possibly Arabian, Turkish, or Barb. Most likely the French Canadian descended from Andalusian sires brought into Normandy and La Perche (habitat of the Percheron breed) for breeding purposes.★

As a general purpose horse, the French Canadian was unsurpassed, useful both on the winter roads of Lower Canada and in light farm work. It was once remarked that the habitants would "never possess a better or more suitable breed of horse for this country than the real Canadian of good size."

After almost one hundred years in Canada, the breed's appearance was scarcely altered from its prototype, as it still closely resembled the Norman and Percheron. Until the British conquest of 1780, the French Canadian bred true to form without any mixture of foreign horses. After the conquest, other horses began to be imported from the British Isles and the United States in increasing numbers. These horses were crossed with the French Canadian and contributed to the development of new, distinctive varieties within Lower Canada, as well as diversification of the entire Canadian horse population.

New settlements that were established by the loyalists in 1784 in the future Upper Canada obtained most of their horses from the St. Lawrence Valley rather than from the United States. The result was that the French Canadian horse came to provide the foundation for the later development of the common horses of Upper Canada.

In the United States

About the time of the American Revolution, the Canadian was becoming very well known. Many (perhaps most) of the French Canadian horses were sold or traded to northern New England freighters or farmers. Articles written in New England in the 1700s and early 1800s praised the Canadian Horse. The historian Taillon described the Canadian as not only a sturdy and versatile steed, but also as being "small, but robust, hocks of steel, thick mane floating in the wind, bright and lively eyes . . . spirited, gentle. . . ."

The distribution of the horses broadened to include the western settlements in Detroit, Illinois, and the Great Plains, where they mixed with feral horses. Others spread to further destinations, such as those Benedict Arnold drove from Quebec over the ice of Lake Champlain to be shipped to the West Indies. Those that did reach the West Indies met with favor, for they could stand the climate better than either American or British horses. It is believed they contributed to the paso gaited breeds there.

Numerous French Canadian horses were also brought to the western part of Vermont. Within a few years (probably before the War of 1812 and certainly before 1820), they interbred to a considerable extent with the nondescript local horses.

The result was that by the 1820s and 1830s, New England's horses became so noted for their strength, endurance, and freedom from disease that the operators of the celebrated line of stages running between Boston and Portland preferred them above all others. Their popularity with the drivers was legendary.★

The trade southward for French Canadian horses continued actively up until the outbreak of the War of 1812, and then resumed and grew rapidly afterwards. The Canadian continued to be known as a driving horse in the northern states in the mid 1800s, and it was considered a prize to own one. Droves were collected by American dealers each year, mostly at Montreal, Quebec City, Trois-Rivieres (the Eastern Townships), and Lower Canada. In 1849, William Evans remarked, "There is a constant market at Montreal and other places for the sale of Canadian horses ... to ... the United States." By that time, the Canadian Horse numbered more than 150,000.

The purebred Canadian horse as it existed in 1850 was scarcely altered from its breed type of one hundred years before. Although there were considerable variations within the pure French Canadian breed, all of its members still had a clearly impressed general character stamped on each. Thus there was no disagreement among observers as to what the typical French Canadian horse of the mid nineteenth century was like. In spite of more than a century of separate breeding, it still very closely resembled the small horse of Normandy and the Percheron. When Edward Harris of Moorestown, New Jersey, the importer of the first Percherons brought to the United States, was looking for a way to describe the diligence of a Percheron, he stated, "Those who are acquainted with the thoroughbred Canadian Horse, will see in him a perfect model, on a small scale, of the Percheron horse." Edward A. Barnard, director of agriculture for the province of Quebec, writing in the early 1880s, was of the same opinion: "We know from experience in France, that they [the Percherons] are as good a breed as can be found of their size and they resemble the French-Canadian horse more closely than any other breed in the world."★

So great was the drain into the United States of the pure Canadian Horse, particularly during the American Civil War, that numbers in Canada were reduced alarmingly.★ The Canadian horse played a major role in the history of that war; it has even been said that the North won simply on the fact that its soldiers had the better horse—the Canadian. Its primary role was being an artillery mount due to its versatility as a riding/driving horse and its

endurance, strength, quiet disposition (important traits under battle conditions), and easy-keeping tendencies when given minimal forage. It was also used extensively as a cavalry mount. The Canadian was the true warhorse, but was never recognized as such. Some suggest that the Canadian's fatalities in the American Civil War contributed greatly to the breed's rapid decline in numbers throughout the late 1800s from its previously high population.

After hard use, sparse feed, and extreme weather conditions, the Canadian developed into the easy-keeping, strong, and hardy animal, fulfilling its reputation today as the Little Iron Horse.

Breed Influence

As the greatest contributor to the development of the common stock of Quebec, the French Canadian horse is worthy of the lasting respect of breeders and historians.★ Even comparatively inferior Canadian sires had the capacity of improving the common stock. With the use of average or superior stallions, the results were often surprising, as George Barnard pointed out: "Many of our best, and some of our largest horses in this district [the Eastern Townships,] are out of common mares of less than 15 hands and got by Canadians of 14 [hands]. The offspring of such often grow to 15½ and sometimes to 16 hands and are both heavy and agile. The loss of the coarser marks of the parents in these crosses is sometimes astonishing." Lower Canada was the only place where such stallions could be obtained, for the French Canadian horse was almost never bred in its purity in the United States.

Beneficial results of crossing the Canadian with the ordinary stock of the adjacent United States were universally admitted. In America, it was surpassed only by the Thoroughbred as a contributor to the development of the leading breeds at the end of the nineteenth century.

Breeders from Kentucky reported in 1853 that there had been "recently imported from Canada the Norman French horse and others from Vermont of the same breed, which have been crossed on our English race mare, and produced a most valuable stock."

In 1830, it was reported that most of the trotters in the northern United States were of French Canadian origin. Perhaps the most important debtors to the Canadian were the families of Standardbreds, whether trotters or pacers. "The American trotting horse is an American creation," states an article in the *National Live Stock Journal* in 1881, "[which] has been taken from various sources, but more lately from the short, quick-stepping French Canadians than from any other source. We run against the Canuck blood almost everywhere in our trotting pedigrees. . . . The Kentucky trotting pedigrees are full of it. . . . New York trotting pedigrees are full of it. . . . The New England pedigrees are full of it . . . and on Maine-bred horses, you encounter this Canuck blood on almost every page."

As well as the Standardbred, many purebred French Canadian horses were entered into the early studbook of the American Saddlebred. Foundation sires of these breeds were often pure Canadian or were mated to Canadian mares. The Tennessee Walking Horse and Missouri Fox Trotter can also claim Canadian ancestry.

Additionally, it was in the early studbook of the Morgan, which certainly had a considerable amount of French Canadian blood. This is indicated by specific characteristics, such as the excellent legs and feet, and above all by the heavy, crimpy mane and tail.★ Harris wrote in 1842 that French Canadian horses "are well known and highly prized in this section of the country [New Jersey], and still more to the north, where they have, undoubtedly, given . . . stamina and character to the horses of Vermont."★ (Vermont is homeland of the Morgan.)

In Michigan, the French Canadian horse preserved its identity for much longer than in Illinois. It seems to have remained entirely in the hands of the Old French settlers around Detroit, perhaps on account of a prejudice against it from others, who considered it a poor man's horse. As late as 1872, a Detroit historian, writing about the French settlers'

horses, affirmed that "they receive literally no care whatever and roam in bands, scouring along the roads with the speed of liberty."★

In the nineteenth century, throughout Upper Canada and the states of the Old Northwest, as well as in the Native American areas of the upper Mississippi Valley and the Canadian Northwest, there was a considerable intermixture of the blood of the French Canadian Horse with that of southwestern plains mustangs. Those found in Upper Canada in the 1820s and 1830s, especially among the Mohawks along the Grand River, represented one extreme. They were smaller than typical French Canadian horses, being under 13 hands, but in other respects they resembled Canadians so closely that it was difficult to identify any trace of mustang inheritance. At the end of the nineteenth century, the superiority of the northern Indian pony to the pure bronco in disposition, intelligence, and conformation was ascribed to the fact that the former was partly French Canadian in origin.★

Registry

Toward the end of the nineteenth century, however, the breed was in extreme danger of extinction. Due to the desire for large draft breeds and the advent of farm machinery, their numbers dwindled. A few concerned Canadian horse admirers tried to preserve what remained. They produced the first studbook in 1886 and founded the Canadian Horse Breed Registry, which has been administered by the Canadian Livestock Records Corporation since 1904.

In 1907, the Canadian federal government livestock commissioner started a new stud book with improved standards and formal inspections. Entries were permitted only to stallions and mares that could meet the newly defined standards. By late 1908, the studbook was officially closed to the addition of foundation stock. In the next year, a total of 2,528 horses had been presented for registration, but the commission saw fit to approve only 134 stallions and 835 mares, rejecting no less than 345 animals that had been in the previous studbook of 1886.★

Unfortunately, only horses primarily in Quebec were inspected, with some limited inspections possibly done in Ontario. There was neither adequate time nor funds to inspect horses elsewhere in Canada (particularly in the Prairies and Maritimes, where there was known to be quite a few Canadian Horses). Thus it occurred that Canadian Horses existed throughout North America, but were not recognized in the official stud book This, coupled with the advent of mechanization, eventually lead to the nearly complete disappearance of the Canadian Horse everywhere outside of Quebec and Ontario throughout the century.

In 1913, the Canadian Ministry of Agriculture set up a breeding program at Cap-Rouge, Quebec, where one of the foundation stallions was used for breeding. By the 1940s, eight bloodlines were established to supply uniformity of size, style, conformation, and vitality. When the federal government was occupied with the war, it closed down the operation in 1940 and sold off the breeding stock. The Quebec government reestablished the stud under the provincial department of agriculture at Deschambault, Quebec.

In the 1970s, the Canadian was once again threatened by extinction with less than four hundred registered horses in total and less than five registrations per year. Eleven years later, the Deschambault Research Station was closed and all stock sold at public auction. At this time, the peril of the breed was recognized and a concerted effort was made by diligent breeders to bring the Canadian back from the verge of extinction.

In 1991, when promotion of the Canadian Horses at Spruce Meadows and the Calgary Stampede began, there were only 1,500 Canadian Horses in existence. The breed status was classified as critical and endangered by the American Livestock Breeds Conservancy. Since that time, the breed has steadily grown in numbers. With the increased numbers, the Canadian was upgraded from critical to the rare category. Today, the Canadian Horse is growing in popularity across North America, but the demand far exceeds the availability of these still rare horses, which number about four thousand.

This horse became one of the very few breeds granted breed status in Canada. In 1999, the Canadian breed was made the official heritage horse of Quebec. During this time, Canadian horse owners and admirers across the country united in strong support, lobbying for the breed to be recognized as the national horse of Canada. Never before had Canadian Horse enthusiasts, owners, and politicians pulled together in such a dedicated expression of patriotism and unity for this much loved breed. In 2002, the bill received royal assent and was made law. The Canadian is now officially the national horse of Canada, a long overdue and well deserved honor. The 340-year-old Canadian secret has finally been uncovered.

Breed Qualities

The Canadian exhibits power, agility, finesse, strength, vigor, and natural balance. It is elegant and noble in carriage and movement. Bones are dense and clean; joints are lean and clean. Its joints bend freely and have lots of action. It is an enthusiastic, but gentle horse, being versatile, easy-keeping, resistant to disease, and strong, as well as known for its endurance and robustness. Mares are extraordinarily fertile and reproduce regularly until the age of twenty or older.

Canadian horses have fine heads and arched necks, along with long, thick, and often wavy tails and manes. They have sturdy legs with good bone and exceptionally hard, strong feet.

Good natured and truly versatile, the Canadian can be found doing almost any type of equine discipline. Perhaps best known for their driving ability, Canadian horses have won many prestigious driving awards throughout North America and in Europe. Generally easy to handle, their calmness, hardworking nature, and people oriented personality make the Canadian Horse ideal for use in the tourism industry. They pull carriages and are used as backcountry trail horses in the mountain parks. Some serve on the Montreal and Calgary City police forces and are used for mounted patrol.

This young Canadian mare displays the breed's agility, finesse, and vigor.
Jacqueline Kinsey

The Canadian's strength and docility make it ideal for dressage, hunter/jumper competitions, eventing, driving, endurance riding, packing, ranch work, and logging.

Standards

As a general purpose animal, the Canadian shows a well proportioned body, good setting of limbs, sturdy legs with good bone, and has exceptionally hard, strong feet. The forearm and gaskin are especially well muscled. The mane and tail are thick, long, and usually wavy.

Canadians are recognizable by their finely chiseled heads and arched necks. The head shows intelligence, spirit, and no excess of nervousness.

Generally, the Canadian Horse is black, but colors also range from bay or brown to light chestnut. Although there once were gray horses in the breed, it appears that the gene for gray coloration was lost when the breed numbers became severely depleted during the 1970s.

Stallions should weigh from 1,050 to 1,350 pounds, and mares from 1,000 to 1,250.

Canadians should exhibit:

- Head: square, or rather shorter than longer, with all over straight lines; lean, carried high and slanting from the bottom and from back to front; forehead and face are broad and flat
- Ears: set well apart, thin, mobile, and rather shorter than longer
- Eyes: wide apart, flush with head (neither sunken nor protruding); large, moderately convex, bright, kind, and active; eyelids are thin, distinct, clean, and mobile
- Nostrils: large, mobile, and wide apart
- Lips: thin, firm, mobile, and covered in delicate skin
- Mouth: rather small
- Jaw: slightly wide through the jaw and broad at the lower angle, with a wide, lean, well hollowed jaw cavity
- Cheeks: well developed, firm but lean
- Throat: medium width across; throatlatch slightly smaller
- Neck: fairly arched, broad at base and narrower at the top, medium length, sides slightly rounded and firmly muscled, elegantly attached to head and gracefully merging into shoulders
- Mane: proud mane with an abundance of long, fine, wavy hair
- Chest: broad and deep, girth well developed; large, protruding and firmly muscled breast
- Ribs: long, broad, well arched

- Withers: lean, large at the base, thin at the top; clean, long, slightly raised and extending toward the rear
- Back: strong, straight, well proportioned, broad, and short
- Loins: broad, well proportioned to back, well attached to croup, and strongly muscled
- Belly: well supported and melding with curve of ribs and with short, well-rounded flanks
- Shoulders: long, sloping, and well muscled
- Forearms and elbows: long, in right direction, with firm covering of muscles; elbows broad, parallel to axis of body, as well as being set apart
- Knees: lean, long, broad, substantial, clean, and bending neither inward nor outward
- Front cannons: short, flat, substantial, lean, clean, and perpendicular, with tendons well detached
- Fetlocks: broad, substantial, lean, and clean; hair acceptable
- Front pasterns: substantial, average length, moderately sloping
- Front feet: average size, standing squarely, frontline following angle of pastern, and heels open; equal size, landing vertically on the ground; hollow sole and thick wall; well-developed fork
- Hips: slightly protruding and symmetrical
- Croup: average; fairly broad, slightly sloped, and well muscled
- Tail: large at root, attached rather high, and carried well, with abundance of fine, long hair
- Buttocks: broad and substantial, with strong well developed loin muscles
- Stifles: clean, close to belly, and turned slightly outward
- Thighs: descending as close to hock as possible; firm, dense, and well muscled
- Legs: long, heavy but not plump, well-developed muscles, and slightly bowed to the outside, with heavy cord well-detached from bone

- Hocks: clean, lean, wide, substantial, flat-faced, parallel to incline of body, and flexible
- Back cannons: short, broad, flat, lean, clean, and perpendicular; tendons well separated from bones; large and firm
- Back pasterns: broad, substantial, lean, clean, long, and slightly sloping
- Back feet: same size and qualities as front feet, but less developed with more of an oval shape and with higher and more spread-apart heels
- Height: 14 to 16 hands, although during the survey taken in 2000, the majority of responding members considered the ideal size for the Canadian horse to be between 15 and 16 hands
- Weight: proportionate to horse
- Silhouette: showing power and health, as well as agility through perfect alignment of the horse's various components that are well balanced and of good quality
- Finesse: simultaneously showing quality and strength; coat soft and shining, mane thick and long, skin soft and elastic, bones dense and clean, joints lean and clean
- Gaits: free and vigorous movement; hocks, knees, fetlocks, pasterns all bending well in higher movements; harmonious
- Appearance: graceful gait and carriage, symmetrical shape, standing squarely
- Temperament: energetic and spirited without nervousness; calm and docile
- Colors: black, chestnut, bay, and dark brown

★ Jones, Robert Leslie. "The Old French Canadian Horse: Its History in Canada And The United States," *The Canadian Historical Review* 28(2): 125–155.

Credits: Canadian Horse Breeders Group, Rocky Mountain District; Canadian Horse Breeders Association; Lazy D Ranch; Gary and Elaine Ayre; Tammie and Dennis Dyck; Tammie Eastman; Dave Flato; and Yvonne Hillsden

CLYDESDALE

Clydesdales are massive with incredible strength and a distinctive look. *Greg Oakes*

Clydesdale Breeders of the USA
17346 Kelley Road
Pecatonica, Illinois 61063
www.clydesusa.com

The Clydesdale Horse merits the most serious consideration. It is utterly synonymous with the word "horsepower," with its massive build and extraordinary strength exemplifying what the ideal draft horse is all about. It has the most wonderful willing temperament and truly is a gentle giant.

A Clydesdale can pull many times more than its own weight, which is why it was so popular in the cities pulling large wagons of goods. There is nothing so impressive as the power of a team of Clydesdales strutting down a street with their white feathers punctuating each stride.

The Clydesdale is a rare breed, classified as "at risk" by the Rare Breeds Survival Trust. Having reached rock bottom in the 1960s, there are now more people breeding these wonderful animals, and numbers are steadily increasing.

History

The Clydesdale began to develop as a breed in the early part of the 1700s in Scotland. As the name implies, it originated from the valley of the River Clyde and in the area comprising the upper wards (districts) of the county of Lanarkshire, which was previously known as Clydesdale.

The Scottish farmers began using some of the large English and Flemish stallions on their smaller local mares. The horses from England were heavy because they were originally developed to carry armor-clad knights into battle.

The Flemish stallions were big and black. Legend has it that they were imported to Scotland from the Low Countries of Europe by one of the Dukes of Hamilton who wanted to "cut a dash" with some splendid coaching stallions. He generously allowed his tenant farmers to mate their Scottish mares with his imported blood. The resultant offspring were considered superior to both the sires and dams.

The farmers eventually produced a powerful horse with a long stride and a sizable hoof, perfect for working in the soft soils of the rough Scottish land. They realized that they had something rather special in the way of horse flesh and carefully developed the breed among themselves.

Before long, they had an animal that was widely sought after. It was bred to meet not only the agricultural needs of the local farmers, but also the demands of commerce for the coalfields of Lanarkshire and all types of heavy hauling both on the streets of Glasgow and over long distances. At one point, there were as many Clydesdales working in the towns and cities as there were in the countryside tilling the soil.

The Clydesdale breed spread rapidly from its base in southern Central Scotland northward through Scotland, southward to Northern England, and westward to Ireland. In the heyday of the breed, the sales at the market town of Lanark became renowned for its hundreds, if not thousands, of horses being sold in a matter of days.

The Clydesdale has a long neck, short back, and long, white feathered legs. *Shutterstock*

In the late nineteenth century, the popularity of the Clydesdale breed continued to flourish, leading to large numbers being exported to the British Commonwealth countries of Australia, New Zealand, and Canada, and some were also sent to the United States. Indeed, the Clydesdale is credited with aiding the advancement of Australia. Today, the Clydesdale is virtually the only draft breed in its native Scotland and is still a favorite in all of these Commonwealth nations and the United States.

The development of the railways, motorized transport, and farm tractors almost spelled the end of the Clydesdale as a working animal, although not perhaps as quickly as might be imagined since there was still use for them. When the railways were being constructed, Clydesdale Horses were used to transport the building materials and remove the waste soil and rocks that were dug out to fashion a level track bed. Over time, however, the horse work became redundant, and the breeding of these magnificent animals was left in the hands of a dwindling number of farming families. Due to sentiment, the farmers could not bear to see the breed, or the bloodlines that had been developed toward perfection over the decades, lost forever.

The distinct Clydesdale white faces on these foals are characteristic. *John Knelsen/ Shuterstock*

The Clydesdale saw a resurgence in popularity in the latter part of the twentieth century. Although replaced by the tractor on most farms, this beloved horse still works in agriculture and forestry where tractors are unable to be used or are unwanted.

Characteristics

The original Clydesdale Horse was a stocky, close-coupled animal around 16 hands, with good feathering on the legs, an active movement, and a good sloping shoulder. Today, Clydesdales are bigger than their original counterparts, as 17 hands and taller is not at all uncommon.

Originally, most Clydesdales were a solid dark bay brown or black color. Today, when people think of the Clydesdale, they immediately think of white blazes and white legs, but that was a fashion that was introduced later. Since genetics is not an exact science, as more white was introduced to the breed, the white hair occasionally strayed onto the Clydesdales' body, giving some a roan color. Purists frowned upon these animals, believing that only a good solid color was correct. Most people today, however, believe that a good horse cannot be a bad color, so roan horses and those with white

areas on the body are acceptable. Depending on their age and the amount of work they do, an adult Clydesdale may eat 25 to 50 pounds of hay and 2 to 10 pounds of grain or other supplements per day.

The majority of Clydesdales throughout the world today are kept for breeding and showing. They do not have to work for their living anymore. In the United Kingdom, a breeder is usually one with the family farm where the horses will very likely be the descendents of those kept by the preceding generation who ran that farm. They are not there to earn their keep like the dairy cows, beef cows, or sheep with which they may share a field. Instead, they are bred and shown at various agricultural shows held during the summer. They are a hobby (if not an expensive one!) for the farmer.

Increasingly, the public relations power of these lovely animals has been reconized. Companies are now using the horses to pull drays and carts as advertising vehicles for a variety of businesses. Breweries and whisky companies were the first to latch on to this idea, and now their names are emblazoned across the carts. City councils, such as the ones in Aberdeen, Dundee, and Glasgow in Scotland, keep Clydesdales for work within the cities and parks departments and for use as publicity

Clydesdales are increasingly being appreciated for riding.
Andrew Olscher/Shutterstock

tools. Clydesdale Horses also have joined the wedding industry, getting dressed up in their finery to pull the bride in a carriage to the church and make a memorable day even more so.

In the United States

In the United States, the versatility of the breed is evidenced by the increasing number of equine activities in which it participates. The Clydesdale is also popular with carriage services, for which it is well suited and always attracts public admiration. Street parades are not complete without the high stepping hooves of a Clydesdale hitch passing by.

The Clydesdale is playing a significant role in the "green" world, too. With the recognition that timber extraction and logging in environmentally sensitive areas can do untold damage to delicate ecosystems, utilizing draft teams for the work has been taken more seriously. The return to the horse as a substitute for machinery can minimize damage when carrying out necessary maintenance and extraction.

Today, Clydesdales are increasingly being ridden like any other breed of horse. They can be seen occasionally in dressage, as hunter jumpers, taking part in trail and endurance rides, used for therapeutic riding, or simply enjoyed as a gentle hack—possibly for the larger rider.

Crossbred Clydesdales can also be found at the top of all the equestrian fields as hunters, three- and one-day eventers, show jumpers, and so on. They seem to have an inbuilt spring and impetus that makes them good jumpers, and they possess the quality of movement that is so necessary for these sports.

Registry

The original breed registry is the Clydesdale Horse Society in Scotland. The Clydesdale Breeders of the USA was incorporated in 1879 and is the member organization for the Clydesdale horse. It sponsors national and regional horse shows, awarding special recognition to top quality U.S.-bred stallions, mares, and geldings, in addition to the usual Hitch and Halter classes. It registers six hundred new horses annually.

As with many other horse breeds, breeding and showing are a large part of the Clydesdale business. Breeders exhibit their horses in the Scottish tradition of line and harness events at county and state fairs and at national exhibitions.

The All American contest is an unusual Clydesdale competition. It is intended to give breeders and owners from all over the United States and Canada a chance to compete against each other, even though their horses may never be in the same show ring together. This is accomplished by mailing out a ballot with photos and qualified placings from the show season to all those who judged at the designated shows.

Standards

The modern Clydesdale is a horse of quality with a fine head, intelligent eye, excellent paces, and a fluidity of movement. It stands between 16 and 19 hands tall and weighs from 1,600 to 2,400 pounds—as much as a Volkswagen Beetle.

While this is larger than the original Scottish horse, one cardinal feature has been retained: the

The horsepower of a matching Clydesdale six-horse team is impressive. *Margo Harrison/Shutterstock*

breed's substantial underpinning. The old adage "no foot, no horse" has always held true. Thus an importance has been attached to maintaining sound hooves and legs within the breed. Clydesdales are known for the size of their feet. One of their horseshoes is about the size of a dinner plate. By comparison, a Thoroughbred race horse has a shoe about half of that size.

The Clydesdale has a very distinctive look when compared to other breeds. The combination of vivid body colors, bright white faces, and long, white, feathered legs with high stepping gait and a head held high leave no question that it is a Clydesdale. The feather is the long silky hair on the legs that flows to the ground and accentuates the high knee action and hock flexing.

A Clydesdale should have a nice open forehead, broad between the eyes, a flat (neither Roman-nosed nor dished) profile, a wide muzzle, large nostrils, bright clear intelligent eyes, and big ears. It should have a well arched, long neck springing out of an oblique shoulder with high withers. The back should be short, and the ribs well sprung from the backbone. The quarters should be long, and the thighs well packed with muscle and sinew. The hocks should be lean, flat bone, not rounded. The hind legs must be planted closely together, with

the points of the hocks turned inward rather than outward. The feather should be silky, not thick or hanging straight.

The most common body color is bay, followed by black, brown, and chestnut. The roan trait (solid body color with white hairs throughout the coat) is found in all the colors. Popular markings for today's big hitches are four white legs to the knees and hocks and a well-defined blaze or bald face. The show ring, however, does not discriminate on color, with light roans and dark legs being considered equally with solid colored horses and traditional markings.

Three words—strength, agility, and docility—depict, in brief, the main characteristics of the Clydesdale. The impression created by this thoroughly well built horse is that of strength and activity with a minimum of superfluous tissue. The idea is not grossness and bulk, but quality and weight. The horse must also exhibit action, lifting the foot high and taking a long stride to cover ground rapidly and easily.

Intelligence and willingness make the Clydesdale a welcome partner at work or play. It is stylish and active, yet tractable, intelligent, and serviceable for draft work, show, or simple pleasure.

Credit: Clydesdale Breeders of the USA

DOLE HORSE

North American Dole Horse Registry
9650 46th Street NE
Doyon, North Dakota 58327
www.dolehorseusa.com

Dole Horse. *Marte Holen Stensli*

The Dole Horse is the largest of the Norwegian native breeds. It is an all-around horse, adept as both a pulling horse and riding horse. It is also known as the Gudbrandsdal or East Country Horse, denoting the area in Norway where it was originally developed.

Writings about Dole Horses date back to the 1530s, when Archbishop Olaus Magnus mentioned them. As early as the 1870s, the breed type was established, with the heavier type being most preferred. The first stud book was published in 1902, but many of the pedigrees can be traced back to about 1865. In 1947, the breed name of Dølehest was officially recognized by the Royal Norwegian Ministry of Agriculture and Food, but Døle Horse (or Dole Horse) was, and still is, commonly used.

The Dole Horse is primarily used for farming or logging, but it also pulls light carts or carriages, which is what originally created the Norwegians' desire to have a horse that carried itself in a refined manner and a flashy trot. Its conformation and disposition are a result of this, and it continues to have staunch supporters who appreciate its versatility and distinctive character.

It is a curious horse that has a quiet disposition and is easy to train. Dole Horses that have been trained once for a particular exercise will always remember it, even if they do not repeat the exercise again until years later. The Dole Horse tries hard to please and does a good job at whatever task it is given. Expending its all when working or performing, the horse will not stop if asked to work longer and will keep going until it drops.

The Dole is a versatile breed and can be used for riding, driving, lower classes of dressage, or jumping as a sport. Driving allows more freedom of having family time together during a great outing. The Dole is especially good in harness and loves to trot. With its calm temperament, it is often found in riding schools and used in riding classes for people with disabilities. It is a naturally healthy breed and is frequently active or working into its twenties.

In Norway

Veikle Balder is considered to be the foundation stallion of the breed. He was the first state-owned stallion to run with mares in the mountain summer pastures of Heimdalen and Sikkilsdalen in Norway between 1862 and 1869. Interestingly, on his sire's side he is descended from the Thoroughbred, Odin, by Partisan and Rachel. Though Friesian traders were known to be in Norway from 400 to 800 AD, allowing the possibility of its influence on the Dole Horse, no one knows the ancestors of the breed for sure. It does, however, look similar to the Dale and Fell pony—breeds similar to the Friesian—only larger.

There are two types of Doles, but both are part of the same family and can be registered in the Norwegian registry. One is the heavier type, and the lighter of the two is the Norwegian Cold-Blooded Trotter, which was developed about 1880 or 1890. Both types have always been interbred, but each has its own registry with the Norwegian registry—one for the Dole and one for the Cold-Blooded Trotter. The Trotter is sometimes used for harness racing in Scandinavia, just like harness racing in America. Both types are good riding horses.

In Norway, Dole and Fjord horses are still used in forestry for thinning out and transporting logs over short distances. They cause less damage to the forest floor and can navigate narrower roads than tractors and logging rigs. In recent years, there has been a renewed interest in these traditional uses of horses.

The Dole Horse has also been used in the tourist industry for a very long time. As early as the end of the eighteenth century, farmers, especially in western Norway, earned additional income by driving tourists around. The horse-drawn transport for tourism is once again growing in many parts of the country. Sleigh rides and transportation for wedding celebrations are extremely popular.

Many horses in Norway are sold on the first Tuesday in November at the Stav market in Gudbrandsdalen Valley, which has over one hundred years of horse trading traditions.

Norway's Breeding

Norway has another unique tradition when it comes to its Dole Horses. For more than 130 years, around June 15 to September 1, mares are turned loose to run in the free-range mountain pastures with stallions. Studs are chosen by the breed association, and herds are separated into different areas. The mares are grouped according to the stud with which each owner wants his mares to breed. Yearling and two-year-old stallions are also released in summer pastures to teach them good social behavior. It also helps develop their agility and coordination. Grazing in the pastures prevents them from getting fat and enhances muscle development.

Since the mares are pasture bred in Norway, they foal later than in the United States. Often the mares will foal while in the mountains, where the weather sometimes becomes inclement and the foals are born in a snowstorm. Thus only the strongest foals survive, based on natural selection.

There is also the possibility of attack by bears (Norway has small brown bears), but horse owners are not worried about predators because of the studs' ability to defend their herd. The last known case was in 1998 when a stud named Haugvar protected his herd from an attacking bear. This stallion circled the mares and foals and chased the bear around the outside, fighting it off. He was found the next day with deep gashes on his rump and hind legs; he was also very weak and having difficulty breathing. After close examination, his wind pipe was found to be restricted by bear fur he had pulled during the fight.

Dole Horse. *Marte Holen Stensli*

Norway's Shows

The first official horse show was held by the Royal Norwegian Ministry of Agriculture and Food in Lillehammer in 1857. Shows are still held in the Lillehammer area by the Ministry of Agriculture, The stallion show, however, has been separated from the mare show and is a three-day event that is always held at the end of April.

On the first day of the show, all the stallions' legs are x-rayed. The x-rays are examined to ensure proper bone structure and bone mass. Stallions are also measured for height and are weighed. They are judged on their abilities to perform in driving and are shown at halter, although in Norway, bridles are used instead of halters. The horses' temperament is also judged. Only stallions that excel in all these areas are prized, and only stallions that are prized at an official horse show can be used for breeding. If the stallion is not prized, the offspring cannot be registered, unless homebred under certain rules of application.

While the show is going on, there are about thirty to forty three-year-olds and ten to fifteen four-year-old stallions around the outside of the arena, each waiting their turn. Stallions that were not prized as three-year-olds may try again as four-year-olds. Stallions enter the arena one at a time at one end and exit at the other arena end. Unlike in the United States where there is only one judge, in Norway there are four judges evaluating the same stallion at the same time, which takes about fifteen minutes per horse.

Four-year-old prized stallions are then sent to a testing facility for a month. There they are tested on their abilities in riding, driving, and log hauling. All of the testing is done by the same person, who is a qualified riding and driving instructor. A stallion that does not pass this round of testing loses its certification. Stallions are then re-tested at six and nine years of age. Again if they do not pass, they lose their certification. This gives a certain amount of control over pedigrees and ensures the quality of breeding stock. Many stallions typically change hands at these shows.

Mares are shown in spring and fall, but in a totally different kind of show, in which they only have to demonstrate obedience in harness. Unlike the stallions, their legs are not x-rayed, and they do not have an open arena liberty type class. Geldings are not shown. Foals are shown with the mares, but there are very few foal classes.

All of Norway's registered Dole Horses are blood typed and DNA tested, which was instituted in the 1980s. Also, all horses born in Norway after 1999 have a microchip.

The Dole Horse population as of 2000 was about four thousand. About 175 foals were registered that year. Norway does not register Dole horses in the United States.

In the United States

The first Dole Horse to be brought to the United State was Vollaug Silver, brought in 2001 by Marte Holen Stensli. Stensli grew up on a small dairy farm in Brumunddal, Norway. Silver was her constant companion during the last two years she lived in Norway, when Stensli oversaw two hundred cows on mountain pastures, keeping the cows and bulls in their respective areas. There were other herds three miles away, with the only barrier being a river whose banks Stensli and Silver patrolled to make sure each herd remained on its own side. They also returned straying cows and kept out a herd of reindeer that occasionally trespassed, chasing the herd back around difficult marshy land. This work entailed a heartiness for which Dole Horses are known.

Stensli's family always kept Dole Horses, even when tractors became popular in the early 1970s. During the oil shortage in the mid 1970s, Stensli's mother took a mare and drove her with a sleigh down the main highway in their hometown so residents could borrow it. Horse and sleigh were a great help to those in need at a time when most did not have working horses anymore.

After Stensli married and moved to North Dakota, she transported Silver over and began to bring him to local shows, which was the first time

Dole Horse team. *Marte Holen Stensli*

a Dole Horse was displayed in North America. She exhibited him in a string of state horse events, including many held by the North Dakota Draft Horse Association, which created much interest in the breed. In 2003, she imported three more Dole Horses—one stallion and two mares. One mare was a bay that foaled a black filly, and the other was a dun mare that foaled a palomino filly. The sire of both these foals was Stensli's black stud named Skogstad Svarten (*svarten* is Norwegian for "black") that later won Reserve Champion at the North Dakota State Fair. Stensli bred Svarten to her Bureau of Land Management (BLM) mustang mare, which foaled a sorrel colt. Thus began the first herd of Dole Horses in the Western Hemisphere. Stensli also began the first registry for both pure and part bred Dole Horses in North America named the North American Dole Horse Registry. Doles are still rare in North America, as there are only about twelve Doles in the United States.

Standards

The Dole Horse should be low, rectangular, strongly built, muscular, well coupled, and have good bone and limb position. The overall impression should be one of a quality, all-around horse. Foals applying for registration must be from registered parents.

Height should be between 14 and 16 hands. The head should be well formed, not too heavy, with a good, wide forehead. The head should be well set on a well formed neck.

The Dole has a rectangular build and is much longer in the back than other breeds. It stands squarely and is not close or cowhocked in the rear. It should be deep through the heart, have good width in the chest, and be well ribbed up. A Quarter Horse saddle fits adequately on its back.

The back and loins should be well muscled, and the quarters lengthy, broad, and strong. Stallions and mares should have a wide chest, though mares' chests are not as wide as stallions. Doles have a rounded croup and a medium tailset. Bone is medium, and the hooves are round shaped.

Doles usually have an abundant, full-length tail and thick mane, depending on the bloodline. Leg feathering is also profuse and similar to the Friesian—more than a Percheron, and not as much as a Gypsy Vanner. Feathering does not stay wet as long as that of other horses, but dries up faster because it is shorter and the quality of hair is different. It is stiffer, almost like a bristle brush, and would hurt if rubbed the wrong way with a hand. Cockleburs do not stick to Dole feathering.

Black, bay, chestnut, and sorrel are the predominate colors, but there are also duns, dapple grays, and palominos. White is considered an undesirable color for a Dole Horse, but markings such as a blaze, star, or socks are frequently seen. Spotted or paint coloration was last seen in the breed in the 1970s. No spotted stallion has ever been prized. This coloration used to be carried in the mares but was eventually bred out.

Movement should be active and free. Doles are great trotters and can turn quickly. They are good at an obstacle course under harness and can do tight corners easily. Their favorite gait is a trot, which is very smooth and easy to sit.

Dole Horses should have a calm but alert and inquisitive disposition. They try very hard to please.

Dole Horses are easy keepers. They do not need alfalfa, which is not grown in Norway. Any horse imported from there should not have any amount of alfalfa.

Dole Horses can live to an old age, up to twenty-five to thirty years, and can work most of that time.

Credit: Marte Holen Stensli

DONKEY

American Donkey and Mule Society, Inc.
P.O. Box 1210
Lewisville, Texas 75067
www.lovelongears.com

Standard donkeys are loveable characters. *Leah Patton*

The donkey, or *Equus asinus*, has been used since the beginning of recorded history as a beast of burden, packing animal, harness worker, and saddle mount. It is one of the three branches of the equine family, which is made up of horses, asses, and zebras. Domesticated donkeys are descended from wild asses, a few subspecies of which survive today. These are the Kulan, Kiang, Somali Wild Ass, and the Onager. No one is exactly sure when the first wild ass was captured and the domestication process begun, but animals resembling Onagers are depicted in Egyptian art alongside mules and horses.

In times past, the donkey was held in low esteem and earned the unfortunate reputation as the horse's poor relation, but in fact the donkey and its hybrid offspring, the mule, have played an enormous role in the shaping of the world. Donkeys are still used in many countries as the primary means of transport, but in the United States they are enjoying a new revival as a saddle mount, companion, and pet.

The answer to the frequently asked question directed to those who own donkeys, "Why own a long ear?" is "Why not?" Donkeys are hard working, hearty, and love to be "in your pocket." Throw away the view of the donkey as lowly and down-trodden, and the experience of their comic relief is a way to uplift spirits at the end of a hard day. They welcome with their hearty bray and a secret smile behind their inquisitive eyes. Those who love them belong to a special kind of club with a growing membership: Bitten by the long-ear bug!

Types

Donkeys now come in a variety of types and sizes, with few pure breeds left. Most old bloodline breeds have very limited gene pools, and only a few small populations of true recorded breeds exist in the United States. In fact, the type of large donkey known as Mammoth Jackstock was created specifically to blend all of the best known breeds together into a new type.

French Poitou: The best document of the recorded pure breeds is the Baudet du Poitou, or French Poitou ass. Less than five hundred specimens of this primitive donkey breed are left in the world, with approximately one hundred residing in the United States. This huge, dark brown (*bai/brun*) donkey stands 56 inches and taller and is covered in long, matted, shaggy hair. *Bai/brun* is the official French term for the color "bay/brown," which is the only accepted color in the French standard for the Poitou. The breed has remained unchanged for nearly one hundred years. Since 1977 when the world population was a mere forty-four animals, dedicated U.S. breeders contributed to the efforts to bring this breed back from extinction.

Miniature: The Miniature Mediterranean breed of donkey, quite popular in the United States and growing in demand elsewhere in the world, was originally developed from small animals imported from Sicily, Sardinia, and Ethiopia. If the Italian base stock of the Miniature was a bred-down animal, it happened many centuries ago, for there is now some evidence that it may have a distinct DNA marker setting it aside from other types of donkeys. Careful selection of these tiny individuals has produced a fairly stable gene pool of animals that mature less than 36 inches at the withers.

All donkey colors are found in the Miniature, with spotted, solid black, and dark red being the most sought after. The original color, still most frequent, is gray dun, similar to grullo, with a grayish body, black mane and tail, and a distinctive dark dorsal stripe and shoulder bar, known as the cross.

The Miniature Donkey Registry was founded in 1958 by Bea Langfeld and is still maintained today by the American Donkey and Mule Society (ADMS), founded in 1967. Miniatures have increased dramatically since their separate registry first began, and their numbers continue to grow. Today, there are over fifty-four thousand registered Miniature Donkeys in the United States with an estimated population of four times that number.

They have maintained their popularity over the years and still sustain one of the higher-price ranges of donkey sales. They can be ridden by small children, are stylish in harness, can be driven by adults, and make loving pets. These small donkeys with big personalities are favored by couples who are contemplating retirement, yet do not want to leave breeding and showing entirely.

Standard: Standard donkeys can be of three sizes: small standards are less than 40 inches, medium standards range up to 48 inches, and large standards are up to 54 inches (jennets) or 56 inches (jacks). (Donkeys are usually measured in inches as opposed to hands.)

Most records indicate that standard donkeys are blends either of ancestral breeds or of Spanish origin. One subgroup within the standard donkey group is the feral Wild Burro. These animals are descendants of the gold-miners' pack donkeys of the American West that were turned loose to run wild. Their population has remained strong, and now they are rounded up by the Bureau of Land Management (BLM) and adopted by the public as a measure of control.

Standard donkeys are popular as livestock guardians, given the donkey's natural dislike for members of the canine family. Some geldings and jennets (females) make excellent guard animals, but as with any type of guardian, not all perform as desired. Those not suited for guard duty can still be useful as children's mounts, as garden workers, in harness, ridden under saddle, or just as pets. Large standard donkeys make admirable saddle mounts, and large standard jacks (intact males) are often used as mule sires.

Mammoth Jackstock: The American Mammoth Jack, also known as Mammoth Jackstock, is a blend of many different breeds, and thus is found in many colors and body types. Solid black with white "points" or spotting are popular. Saddle jacks are often preferred to be lighter in limb and build. Draft-type jacks hearken back to the Andalusian type, and many are dappled red, gray roan, or dark red in coloration. These jacks are used to sire heavy working and draft mules.

Records for Jackstock production date back into the 1800s. The original Mammoth Jackstock registry still exists, but most common donkeys were never recorded or inscribed into any kind of studbook.

Today the ADMS operates five different registry books for donkeys and mules.

Since interbreeding between donkeys and horses produces a sterile mule, the only way a gene pool of donkeys can be improved is by adding those from other locals. As the U.S. population of donkeys is not in any danger, it is rare to bring in donkeys from other countries, but stock here is very important for export to other countries. Mammoths have been exported to many countries for use in breeding up for larger saddle donkeys, and Miniatures have been shipped worldwide as show or breeding stock.

Characteristics

Pound for pound, the donkey requires less feed than a horse, is more suited to harsh environments, and can carry a larger load with fewer long-term side effects. The phrase "in donkey's years" (meaning a very long time) stems from the fact that donkeys in general can live to be elderly more frequently than horses, outliving them by ten to fifteen years. The average lifespan of a Miniature Donkey is thirty years, with some jennets producing foals well into their late twenties. Ages of 45, 47, and 50 are not uncommon in donkeys.

Some terms used in reference to donkeys are unique to these long-eared equines. Intact males are called jacks rather than stallions in the United States, and a female is a jennet. Castrated males are called the same term as their horse counterparts—geldings. A mule jack is one that is bred solely to produce mules, while a jennet jack is one bred only to jennets in order to produce more donkeys.

As the donkey evolved for life in a desert environment, several factors of conformation, as well as genetics, set it aside and made it noticeably different from its equine cousin, the horse. The donkey neither nickers nor whinnies, but instead has a loud, honking call referred to as a bray. Its ears are large and open, more than twice the size of a horse's ear. The eyes are set into a D-shaped eye socket, and often the donkey has a look of aggrieved patience on its face. The face is straight or slightly convex, and the nostrils set low. Most donkeys have white points, such as white eye rings and belly, and a mealy muzzle. These features helped to deflect heat and cool the body.

The tail of the donkey is the other distinguishing feature. It is covered in long hair only at the switch end, while the rest has smooth, short hair as on the body. Usually, one can quickly tell the difference between a donkey and mule by first looking at the tail, as mules have a more horse-like, full-haired tail, and then by accessing the overall body shape. The majority of donkeys have stiff, upright manes with no true forelock, and very few have a laying mane over the neck.

The donkey is also narrower than the horse, with finer legs and smaller feet. Most donkeys have a very straight neck and less pronounced withers than a horse. The topline is more level, lacking the saddle dip from shoulder to hip. The shape of the pelvis also differs, as it is more angular. The haunch of the donkey lacks the full, double-muscle curve of the horse, but this does not diminish its power. Mules inherit the donkey's unique ability to high-jump from a standing start, due to the natural conformation of the donkey haunch.

Some of these features in the donkey's build make tack-fitting more of a challenge. Narrower saddle trees, breastplates, and cruppers are common parts of donkey gear. In fitting a bridle, a larger overall headstall may be needed, while the noseband and bit may need to be adjusted. The larger head and deeper jaw of the donkey often look deceivingly smaller when it is the size of a pony, but donkeys take full horse halters or bridles.

The white patterns are different in donkeys than in horses. Dapples are reversed in donkeys, which is called roan, and is not like a dapple-gray horse. There are no dark-headed roan donkeys. Roan donkeys are light-faced and light legged with dark-centered dapples, which is somewhat like a horse roan, but also like a horse gray. Since it really is not either, it is not called a gray.

Tobiano and appaloosa spotting are just not in the donkey genetics. There are some that look a little similar to a frame overo and hint of sabino, but the white often crosses the topline and stockings are involved. While it suggests tobiano type markings, those types do not breed like tobianos or have the tobiano pattern.

There are over fifteen years of research behind what is currently known about donkey color genetics, but more understanding is needed on some of the nuances. Lab testing to produce DNA color tests began in 2007 and continues on today.

Standards

Head: The head should be in proportion to body and not overly large. In Miniatures, face may be straight or slightly dished. Coarse heads and extreme Roman noses should be avoided. No more than one-fourth inch of bite deviation is allowed in breeding stock.

This is a donkey jack, an intact male donkey, used for breeding to other donkeys or to horses. *Courtesy American Donkey and Mule Society*

Neck: The neck should be straight and set well into shoulder. Extreme ewe or swan neck is penalized. Fat rolls are allowed, but are unsightly.

Forelegs: They should be set on well, with clear projection of chest in front. Shoulders are often straight and a gentle slope is preferred. Legs should be square and straight when viewed from the front and side.

Barrel: The barrel should be deep with plenty of heart girth and should not be long and weak. Smooth level topline and slight wither rise are preferred.

Hip: A shallow hip with no angle should be severely penalized. Gentle slope and deep pelvis are preferred.

Hind limbs: The donkey should stand square without being stretched. The hind legs should be set well under without being sickle-hocked. When viewed from behind, the hind legs should be straight with a small degree of cowhocks allowed. Severe cowhocks or crooked legs are to be penalized.

Hooves: Pasterns are more upright, but pastern and hoof angles should match. Club foot and long, broken angles are severely penalized.

Movement: The donkey moves with a short, flat-kneed action at the walk or trot. Exaggerated high-stepping action is not found, partially due to the upright angle of the shoulder. The hocks are the powertrain and should be well engaged. At the canter, many donkeys will move with the head lowered and neck slightly outstretched. A few donkeys will perform an interim gait similar to the single-foot or rack; these are prized as saddle animals and for use in breeding gaited mules. The true pace is rarely seen, but can occur.

Color: Any color is acceptable. The ancestral donkey color is gray dun (similar to grullo) with brown, black, red (sorrel), spotted, roan, frosted (aged gray/roan), brindle, and ivory (recessive blue-eyed white) also occurring. A newly documented color still under investigation, called "cameo," has been found in Australia. These dilute donkeys with light eyes are descended from a single jack. Horse colors of tobiano, appaloosa spotting, and cream dilutes (palomino) are not found in donkeys. Dark dorsal bar and cross are evident in most cases, even on very dark animals.

Regardless of size, the donkey should be balanced and not coarse. The head, while larger in proportion the body, should not be so heavy as to make it appear oversized. A very thin swan or ewe neck is a fault. Overshot or undershot jaws should be faulted. The hip should be gently sloped and full with dipped loins. Weak hindquarters are a severe fault. The hindquarters are lighter in general, but should not have a severe shallow croup or weak, high-set tail.

Credit: American Donkey and Mule Society, Inc.

DRUM HORSE

Drum Horses are uniquely eloquent and have abundant manes, tails, and feathering. *Stan Phaneuf*

Gypsy Cob and Drum Horse Association, Inc.
1812 E. 100 N.
Danville, Indiana 46122
www.gcdha.com

Nearly everyone who has met a Drum Horse has quickly said how wonderful it is. It captures the imagination with its stunning good looks and stately air. Often seen as a larger version of the Gypsy Cob, the Drum Horse stands at 16 hands and taller and utilizes the bloodlines of the Clydesdale, Shire, Friesian, and Gypsy Cob. It is a heavy, tall horse, yet also elegant and unique, with lovely feathering, varied coloring, and an exceptional disposition.

The Drum Horse is fashioned after the great war horses of England, with a beauty, stature, and dignity not found in any other existing breed. It originated with enthusiasts who were inspired by a particular working type of British cavalry horse and wanted to develop it as a breed in the United States.

Recently there has been more interest in the Drum Horse due to the popularity of the Gypsy

Cob. Many people love the Gypsy Cob, but prefer a larger horse. That need is met in the wonderful Drum Horse, which follows the pattern of a Gypsy Cob but only in a bigger frame. With its symbiotic relationship to the smaller and popular Gypsy Cob, the Drum Horse is a worthy and complementary counterpart.

There have been conflicting stories and opinions about the two horses, however, adding to the general confusion between them. The facts about the Drum Horse and its job, as well as its future development as a breed, are therefore important to clarify by its registry.

The Drum Horse as a Job Title

The term "drum horse" is used in Britain to describe the horse that carries a rider and two silver kettledrums during certain processions, exhibitions, and ceremonies of state. Throughout history, the preferred type of horse to do this job has varied with the era and the regiment with which it performed. The one common factor is that it has to be a large, strong horse with an even temperament. The size and strength is required because the combined weight of the drums and rider can easily exceed three hundred pounds. It has to have an easy disposition because of the parade type atmosphere where it often performs. Additionally, to make things just a little more difficult, the rider's hands have to be free to beat the drums, so the reins have to be attached to the rider's stirrups. The drums are large and ornamental, one on each side of the saddle, straddling the area just in front of the rider. The horse has to be able to walk calmly with the drums playing and not be affected either by that or the cheering crowds.

In 1888, Rudyard Kipling immortalized the Drum Horse and its job in the amusing story *The Rout of the White Hussars*. In this tale, he writes, "The soul of the Regiment lives in the Drum-Horse who carries the silver kettle-drums. He is nearly always a big piebald Waler. That is a point of honour; and a Regiment will spend anything you please on a piebald."

Drum Horses are a tall, heavy breed, yet stately.
Daniel Johnson

Once a horse graduates from training to become a full-fledged Drum Horse, it stays in service for many years. A good Drum Horse will typically serve from ten to fifteen years, after which it is placed in a retirement home. Many Drum Horses go at least partially deaf by the time they retire, due to the loud sounds of the drum.

In recent times, many of the Drum Horses have been high colored Clydesdales or crosses of Shires and the older, larger bloodlines of Gypsy Cobs, or with Dutch Warmbloods. This is the reason for the extensive feathering now seen in Drum Horses.

Drum Horses have had a long and colorful history in the British military. Some of the earliest regiments documenting Drum Horses were the Royal Scots Greys (1678), the Royal Dragoon Guards and the 3rd Hussars (both in 1685), the 5th Royal Irish Lancers (1689), the 10th Royal Hussars, and 9th Queen's Royal Lancers (both in 1715). These horses and their successors saw service wherever their regiments were sent, including India, Flanders, Crimea, and Palestine.

The regiments loved their Drum Horses and had their favorites, such as the first black horse used by the Royal Scots Greys, setting a tradition with that regiment of continuing to use black horses as often as possible. In 1832, the Queen's Royal Lancers were presented with two cream colored colts by the royal couple for use in the band. Thereafter it became customary, whenever possible, for the Queen's Royal Lancers to have a royal cream as the Drum Horse. By 1934, unable to obtain fresh blood from Germany during the war, the cream horses disappeared from the Royal Mews (stables).

The regiments did, however, use horses of other colors, including a piebald horse named Music Box, which was used at the Delhi Horse Show in 1931. The 9th Queen's Royal Lancers obtained a splendid skewbald gelding that was the subject of a painting by R. Miltais. Colored reproductions of this painting were used for the regimental Christmas card.

Ireland has always had a reputation for producing magnificent horses and it has been the birthplace of a number of highly respected Drum Horses as well. One of the best known was the much celebrated Plum Duff, which was the Drum Horse for the Royal Scots Greys for more than thirteen years. Another favorite was Mary, a beautiful gray mare belonging to the 3rd Hussars. She was sent from England to join the regiment in India in late 1927. A painting by Trickett was commissioned by the regiment to commemorate her sixteen years as a Drum Horse.

The Drum Horse as a Breed

The trend toward a larger Gypsy Cob horse in North America brought a quicker development of the Drum Horse, thus saving the future of the true Gypsy Cob. The Drum Horse provides a larger Gypsy type horse to fill that need and brings together the Gypsy heritage with the British tradition.

The ideal Drum Horse displays the calm disposition, heavy bone, and profuse feathering of those that serve in the Queen of England's cavalry. The purpose of the Drum Horse is to be a quintessential heavy riding horse, utilizing the bloodlines of the Gypsy Cob, Shire, Clydesdale, and Friesian. It has the agility, movement, and athleticism to excel in a variety of disciplines, including low-level dressage,

Drum Horses have a generous jaw, square muzzle, and well-set ears. *Daniel Johnson*

eventing, hunting, saddle seat, trail, and pleasure, and of course it makes an excellent driving horse.

The importation of Gypsy Cobs and the breeding of Drum Horses spurred a need for a registry in the United States; thus the Gypsy Cob and Drum Horse Association (GCDHA), Inc., was founded in 2002. Creating a DNA database was its first priority, and this was quickly instituted with the help of the University of Kentucky and Dr. Gus Cothran. Samples are taken from horses internationally, as well as locally, and are recorded in a single, global DNA bank.

The registry needed to verify what a Gypsy Cob or Drum Horse is in relation to all the other names that have been used to describe both these breeds. Names like colored cobs, traditional cobs, Irish Cobs, and Irish Tinkers are used throughout Ireland, the United Kingdom, western Europe, and the United States. The term Vanner was particularly confusing, as it has been used in North America to describe the Gypsy Cob. In Britain, however, a Vanner used to apply to any heavy workhorse of indiscriminate breeding that was used to pull milk floats and heavy drays. Currently the British description of a Vanner has changed to refer to a large pinto colored horse with feathers, which is called a Drum Horse in the United States. Neither is associated with the horses bred by Gypsies.

With such a confusing array of names, many North Americans did not know how to classify Drum Horses. Are they light horse breeds or draft horses? Most breeders wholeheartedly agree they are draft horses that often disguise themselves as a heavy, light horse. Yet the draft horse world has been very slow to accept them as draft breeds, while light horse breeds consider them to be light draft horses and thus do not readily accept them either.

The GCDHA addresses this problem by strongly promoting selective programs that solidify the Drum Horse as a breed and identify it with its proper name. GCDHA requires licensing of all breeding stallions through physical inspection that accurately certifies conformation, movement, quality of hair and bone, disposition and character.

Registration Requirements

All mares and stallions must be DNA tested. Geldings of known parentage are also required to submit DNA results, but geldings of unknown parentage do not have to do so.

Registered Drum Horses are a combination of Gypsy Cob, Clydesdale, Shire, and/or Friesian and must have no less than one-eighth Gypsy Cob breeding, but cannot be full Gypsy Cobs. Shires, Clydesdales, and Friesians being used to produce Drum Horse foals must apply for an Identification Certificate and submit DNA samples.

A non-feathered draft cannot be registered, as feathering is a mark of the Drum Horse breed in the United States. The horse must be a blend of one or more of the Clydesdale, Shire, Friesian, or Gypsy Cob *heavily feathered* draft breeds. Since feather is a recessive gene, the only way to preserve the heavy feathering of the Drum Horse is to breed two horses that both have the gene. Breeding a smooth legged horse to a feathered horse will result in a smooth legged or lightly feathered horse, which would not meet the Drum Horse registration requirements.

To be registered, horses must meet the physical criteria described in the breed standard, be certified as being a minimum of 16 hands on or before their fifth birthday, and have parents that both are no less than 15 hands. For regular registration status, the smaller of the two parents must be at least 15 hands.

Horses that do not reach 16 hands, have one parent under 15 hands, or fall below the minimum one-eighth Gypsy Cob breeding can be registered as Breeding Stock Drum Horses. The only exceptions are geldings that reach 16 hands but have one parent less than 15 hands. They are eligible for regular registration.

Standards

General appearance: The overall appearance of a Drum Horse should give the impression of intelligence, kindness, strength, and agility. The Drum Horse is considered a heavy riding horse and should display the athleticism for a pleasant day of hunting, hacking, or other ridden discipline. The ideal Drum Horse should also excel at driving. It should be a large well-muscled horse of either medium or heavy weight, with good quality bone, a sturdy body, kind expression, and abundant hair.

Size: It should be a minimum of 16 hands and upward.

Disposition: The Drum Horse should be, above all else, a kind and willing partner. It should display an intelligent character and docile temperament with a calm and sensible attitude.

Hair: Mane and tail should be long and thick. Abundant feather should start at the knees and hocks, preferably with some hair running down the front of the leg as well as the back. Feathers should be soft and silky, but may be straight or curling, and should cover the hoof. Docking of tails is not permissible. Trimming of any mane, tail, or feathering is frowned upon, unless required in a discipline in which the horse competes. A small bridle path is allowed, as is the trimming of facial and belly hair if so desired.

Color: The Drum Horse may be any color: solid, pinto, or appaloosa spotted.

Movement: When in motion, the ideal Drum

Horse should move with action, power, grace, and agility. Head carriage and collection should appear natural, not overly exaggerated or forced. Movement should be free, straight, and square with ample impulsion. Knee action should be somewhat snappy, but a long, free moving shoulder should allow the ability to reach forward in a classic extension. The horse should move up under itself with a smooth, powerful stride, be light on the forehand, and exhibit three good gaits. The Drum Horse's movement should be suitable for a variety of ridden and driven disciplines.

Head: The head should be in proportion to the body, neither too large nor too small, with broad forehead, generous jaw, square muzzle, and even bite. The ears should be cleanly shaped and well set on. The eyes should be large, set well apart, and have an intelligent, kind expression. Eyes can be any color, including blue, which shall not be penalized. Both convex and straight profiles are acceptable. Stallions and geldings should have a masculine appearance to the head, and mares a feminine appearance.

Neck: The neck should be substantial and well muscled with a defined arch. It should be clean through the throat, not too short, and tie in well at the shoulder and withers. Stallions may exhibit a masculine crest in proper relationship to the size and thickness of neck.

Chest: The chest should be broad with ample muscle. The muscle along the bottom of the chest should appear in an inverted "V" shape as it ties into the forearm.

Shoulders: The shoulders should be deep, powerful, and of a correct slope to allow for ample, free movement.

Withers: Withers should be average in height, not too high, with a generous layer of muscle.

Back: The back should be short, supple, and well muscled and should tie in strongly at the loin.

Barrel: The barrel should be deep with well sprung ribs and a solid covering of muscle. The flank should be as deep as the girth. The loin should be strong and tie into the croup with a smooth, well muscled appearance.

Hindquarters: The hindquarters should be smooth and rounded across a long croup with a medium to high tailset, long hip with wide pelvis, and well muscled thighs and buttocks.

Feet and legs: The legs should be set squarely and straight under the body, with clean joints, and should have plenty of dense, flat bone. Forearms and thighs should be well muscled. Hind legs should display clean and well defined hocks that are broad, deep, flat, and wide when viewed from the side. The Drum Horse may or may not exhibit the influence of the draft horse hock set. Pasterns should be long enough to allow a proper slope of about 45 degrees from the hoof head to the fetlock joint. Feet must be sound and substantial, with a generous, open heel.

Inspections

Only breeding stallions are required to be inspected and licensed for breeding. Inspections consist of two divisions: one for horses two years of age and older (Status Testing and Stallion Approval), and one for horses under two years of age (Premium Grading). Height measurements are taken on all mature horses.

Stallions seeking breeding licenses have to undergo a vet exam. The exam includes (as a minimum) an inspection to determine that both testicles are fully descended with no obvious abnormalities, as well as a soundness test (including heart, lungs, and flexion test) and inspection of the mouth/bite and eyes. This exam is to be done prior to the inspection.

Licensing approval for two-year-old stallions is only provisional, and those stallions must be re-inspected by the end of their fourth year before being issued permanent approval. Stallions that pass their inspection at three years of age or older are given permanent approval. Stallion licenses, permanent or provisional, are not issued to any horse less than two years of age. Licensed stallions that have been proven to consistently produce poor quality offspring, or offspring with genetic abnormalities, may have their licenses suspended and/or revoked.

Drum Horse herd. Black pinto spotting is a favorite color. *Daniel Johnson*

Stallions not scoring well can be brought back the following year for re-evaluation. Only one passed inspection is necessary for licensing.

Status levels and stallion licensing: All horses applying for licensing are shown in-hand and are judged on movement, as well as quiet demeanor while being examined. Inspectors touch the legs, check the bite, and perform other inspections.

Level I: Inspection criteria include breed characteristics, conformation, movement, soundness, and temperament. Level I is the minimum requirement for stallions seeking licensing approval. All horses passing the Level I testing are designated as an Approved horse. Horses passing the test with a high enough score are designated as Star status.

Level II: All Level II inspections require the horse to be presented working, either by driving or under saddle. Horses being presented in Level II should be working quietly and safely in the chosen discipline and stand quietly upon request. A simple pattern may be requested, but shall not include lead changes or hand gallops. Scoring includes marks from the Level I inspection, plus additional marks on brilliance of working movement, safety, soundness, willingness, and work ethic.

Horses passing both Level I and II testing are designated as Model. Those horses that were designated as Star from the Level I test and also pass Level II with a high enough score are designated as Preferred Model.

Level III: This highest level of inspection is geared toward breeding mares and stallions, and requires the horses to have first been presented in Levels I and II. Level III is based on the horse's previous Level I and II scores, plus on the scores of a minimum number of registered offspring (which include Drum Horses and Gypsy Cobs, but no part-breds).

Horses passing Levels I, II, and III are designated as Elite. Horses previously designated as Preferred Model that pass Level III testing with a high enough score are designated as Elite Gold.

Since geldings cannot be judged on offspring, to attain Elite status they must be judged in both ridden and driven disciplines.

Inspections for licensing of stallions are the same for both the Drum Horse and Gypsy Cob.

Credit: Gypsy Cob and Drum Horse Association, Inc.

GYPSY COB

Gypsy Waggons on their way to Appleby Fair. *R. Glover*

Gypsy Cob and Drum Horse Association, Inc.
1812 E. 100 N.
Danville, Indiana 46122
www.gcdha.com

Gypsy Cobs are easily recognized as sturdy little horses with an amazing amount of hair. Thick manes that fall below the shoulder and tails that drag on the ground are typical, with the crowning glory being an abundant silky leg feathering. The Gypsy Cob is also well known for its strength, tractability, and feed efficiency. Its designer looks are achieved through the perfect union of heavy, flat bone, a powerful body, intelligence, a docile nature, and the ever-flowing mane, tail, and feathering.

Gypsy horses were developed by the Romany people, or Gypsies, of Great Britain and Ireland. They were used to pull the colorful wagons known as the family vardo, or caravan. Gypsies have had horses for as long as their culture has been in existence, but the horse recognized today as the Gypsy Cob has only emerged within the past century. As it was originally a harness horse, it has always excelled at driving, but is now found in nearly all riding disciplines.

Foundation

Gypsy horses were used for nearly every aspect of Gypsies' traveling nomadic culture, from pulling the colorful wagons that were the Gypsies' homes, to pulling the smaller wagons used for work. Horses have always been the Gypsies' means of travel and employment, as well as their greatest source of pride. They are held near and dear to the Gypsies' heart and heritage. As one Gypsy remarked, "It is the horse born from the dream inside my head."

Coming from a culture that traditionally did not have written records, the best bloodlines were kept and recorded only by memory. Generations of breeding were handed down from father to son without the means of documentation. Horses with names like the Lob Eared Horse, the Kent Horse, and the Roadsweeper were considered greats of the breed.

The Romany people took great pride in the horses they bred and used. Since the horses traveled many roads and were often cared for by children, it was essential that they were both strong and kind with a willing disposition. They also had to be sound with a hardy nature and easy to keep, as there were no special provisions made for food or shelter. They lived on the vacant land and grass strips found alongside the road.

Although today many Romany people have settled into more modern housing, the horse-drawn vardo can still be found here and there on the roads. With less need for the larger, draft type horse, however, Gypsies now prefer a smaller cob or pony type with an active and speedy trot. As these horses are not used for working anymore, Gypsies love to "flash" them in front of onlookers.

The literal definition of a cob is a short, heavy or thickset horse. Nearly all cob breeders would probably describe it as a large pony or small horse that exhibits heavy bone, thick body, and some specific characteristics, such as head type, that could be found in either a pony or horse. Gypsies deliberately bred the cob type body because of its sturdy structure, small but heavy and powerful size, and dense bone. Although there is a broad spectrum in size, the average Gypsy Cob stands between 14 and 15 hands. Regardless of height, it displays the perfect cob type of a strong body, set legs on flat, dense bone, abundant hair, and a kind, intelligent expression.

There are other types of horses bred by Gypsies, and these larger cob and horse types are still used as wagon horses and as great all-around horses by non-Gypsy families. However, it is the Gypsy Cob that has received worldwide acclaim and recognition. It is considered *the* breed to have due to its striking looks and calm presence.

Gypsy Cobs come in nearly all colors, and most have pinto markings. Some Europeans are even breeding for the appaloosa spots and/or "pintaloosa" markings in their cobs. It is said that Gypsies started breeding for loud colored horses during World War I and World War II so the army would not confiscate them. While documentation that substantiates this is not readily available, it is believed to be true among the Gypsies

Registry

For many years, the Gypsy Cob suffered from a certain lack of appreciation within the mainstream equestrian society. Recently, however, Gypsy Cobs have developed an enthusiastic following throughout Europe and North America and can even be found in Australia. The beauty of these horses is surpassed only by their gentle and intelligent nature, making them now highly sought after outside the Romany culture. Beyond their natural role as a harness horse, many are used as safe and sane mounts for novice riders, and most riding schools and trekking centers also like to use these kind and willing partners.

With the widespread popularity of the breed crossing not only international borders, but also cultural boundaries, it became imperative that proper parentage verification be administered and documented. Of the utmost importance was the development of a genetic database. The U.S. importation of Gypsy Cobs and the breeding of Drum Horses also spurred a need for a registry. Thus the Gypsy Cob and Drum Horse Association (GCDHA), Inc., was founded in 2002 in the United States.

A DNA database was the first priority of the membership and was quickly instituted with the help of the University of Kentucky and Dr. Gus Cothran. DNA testing was established to form a modern database.

The association also established the definition of a Gypsy Cob in relation to many other names that have been used to describe it. There was confusion about whether it was a light horse breed or a draft horse, although most Gypsy Cob enthusiasts agreed it was a draft horse disguised as a heavy light breed. Yet the breeders of draft horses were slow in recognizing it as a draft, and light horse breeders considered it to be a draft. The GCDHA corrected the misconceptions by providing boundaries and breed distinctions drawing upon the already established Gypsy lines. Through these efforts, the breed's colorful history and bright future are preserved as the wonderful breed that it is.

Standards

For registration, all stallions and mares must be DNA tested. Geldings of known parentage are also required to submit DNA results, while those geldings claiming unknown parentage are exempted. Owners of Gypsy Cobs must provide a veterinarian height certification between the ages of three and five years, and Gypsy Cobs must meet the standard for registration.

General appearance: The overall appearance of a Gypsy Cob should give the impression of intelligence, kindness, strength, soundness, and agility. It should be of good bone, either medium or heavy weight, and be well muscled with a sturdy body, kind expression, and abundant hair.

Size: The Gypsy Cob can be any size and may be of the pony, cob, or horse variety.

Head: The head should be in proportion to the body, neither too large nor too small, with broad forehead, generous jaw, square muzzle, and even bite. The ears should be neat and well set on. The eyes should be large and set well apart with an intelligent, kind expression.

Neck: The neck should be slightly arched, well muscled, clean through the throat, not too short, and tie in well at the shoulder and withers.

Chest: The chest should be broad with ample muscle. The muscle along the bottom of the chest should appear in an inverted "V" shape as it ties into the forearm.

Shoulders: The shoulders should be deep, powerful, and well sloped.

Withers: Withers should be average in height, not too high, with a good cover of muscle.

Back: The back should be short and well muscled, and should tie in strongly at the loin.

Barrel: The barrel should be deep, with well sprung ribs and a solid covering of muscle. The flank should be as deep as the girth.

Legs: The legs should be set well under the body, straight, clean, and have plenty of dense, flat bone. Forearms and gaskins should be well muscled, and knees and hocks set close to the ground. Feet should be substantial with a generous, open heel.

Hindquarters: The hindquarters should be smooth and rounded across the croup, with a long hip, a wide pelvis, and well muscled buttocks and thighs.

Hair: Mane and tail should be long and thick. Abundant feathering starts at the knees and hocks, preferably with hair running down the front of the leg, as well as the back. Feathers may be straight or curling and should cover the hoof.

Color: The Gypsy Cob may be any color and can include either solid or spotted (pinto or appaloosa).

Disposition: The Gypsy Cob should be, above all else, a kind and willing partner. It should display an intelligent character and docile temperament.

Inspections

All breeding stallions must be inspected and licensed for breeding. Inspections for licensing of stallions are the same for both the Drum Horse and Gypsy Cob.

Inspections consist of two divisions: one for horses two years of age and older (Status Testing and Stallion Approval), and one for horses under two years of age (Premium Grading). Stallion licenses are not issued to any horse less than two

This Gypsy Cob has an abundant mane and square muzzle. *R. Glover*

years of age. Height measurements are taken on all mature horses.

Stallions seeking breeding licenses must undergo a vet exam. The exam includes (as a minimum) an inspection to determine that both testicles are fully descended with no obvious abnormalities, a soundness test (including heart, lungs, and flexion test), and inspection of the mouth/bite and eyes. This exam is to be done prior to the inspection.

Licensing approval for two-year-old stallions is only a provisional license, and those stallions must be re-inspected by the end of their fourth year before being issued permanent approval. Stallions passing their inspection at three years of age or older are given permanent approval. Licensed stallions that have been proven to consistently produce poor quality offspring, or offspring with genetic abnormalities, may have their licenses suspended and/or revoked. Stallions not scoring well can be brought back the following year for re-evaluation. Only one passed inspection is necessary for licensing.

Status levels and stallion licensing: All horses applying for licensing are shown in-hand and are judged on movement, as well as quiet demeanor, while being examined. Inspectors touch the legs, check the bite, and perform other inspections.

Level I: Inspection criteria include breed characteristics, conformation, movement, soundness, and temperament. Level I is the minimum requirement for stallions seeking licensing approval. All horses passing the Level I testing are designated as an Approved horse. Horses passing the test with a high enough score are designated as Star status.

Level II: All Level II inspections require the horse to be presented working, either by driving or under saddle, and should be quiet and safe. A simple pattern may be requested, but shall not include lead changes or hand gallops. Scoring includes marks from the Level I inspection, plus additional marks on brilliance of working movement, safety, soundness, willingness, and work ethic.

Horses passing both Level I and II testing are designated as Model horse. Those horses designated as Star from the Level I test that also pass Level II with a high enough score are designated as Preferred Model.

Level III: This highest level of inspection is geared toward breeding mares and stallions and requires them to first be presented in Levels I and II. Level III is based on the horses' previous Level I and II scores, plus on the scores of a minimum number of registered offspring, which includes Drum Horses and Gypsy Cobs, but no part-breds.

Horses passing Levels I, II, and III are designated as Elite. Horses previously designated as Preferred Model that pass Level III testing with a high enough score are designated as Elite Gold.

Since geldings cannot be judged on offspring, to attain Elite status they must be judged in both ridden and driven disciplines.

Credit: Gypsy Cob and Drum Horse Association, Inc.

GYPSY VANNER HORSE

The Gypsy's dream horse has a special look and charm that is rare to find. *Mark J. Barrett/WR Ranch*

The Gypsy Vanner Horse Society
P.O. Box 177
Marlboro, New York 12542
www.gypsyvannerhorsesociety.org

A vision was born over half a century ago to create a special horse to pull the colorful caravans that Gypsies call home. Until recently, that vision was shared by only a few, but the love affair between Gypsies and their horses is legendary. Mystery and magic have always been part of the Gypsies' charm, and this heritage is expressed in their beautiful and rare horses. Those encountering a Gypsy Vanner for the first time are awed by the presence of something beyond just a pretty animal. They experience the same passion Gypsies feel for a breathtaking animal, one filled with enchanting charisma and charm. The captivating Gypsy Vanner Horse inspires an amazing reaction wherever it goes.

"It's a proper Vanner," is a Gypsy expression meaning a horse that has the look most admired by the culture and is best suited to pull an owner's caravan. The word "vanner" is simply short for caravan, but it also refers to a large Gypsy horse that pulls the biggest caravans. The name then evolved into a term of endearment, identifying the look of a Gypsy's dream horse.

Proper Vanner horses are rare and can only be found in a certain small segment of the Gypsy horse population. Similar to small Shires, they have abundant leg feathering and a prettier head than most draft horses. They are bred with much love and pride by dedicated Gypsies, who rarely part with them and frequently keep them hidden from others. The deep feeling they have for their Proper Vanner horse is the same feeling all horse lovers know when they see the horse of their dreams.

Life of a Gypsy

To understand the Gypsy Vanner, it is important to understand Gypsies. The word "Gypsy" evolved from the word "Egypt," or "little Egypt." At one time, it was believed that Egypt was the original home of this society that had an inexplicable urge to roam. As Gypsies traveled throughout eastern and western Europe, they maintained a cultural likeness, even while developing other differences. Still, the love of music, horses, and the freedom to roam was a common thread bonding all people known as Gypsies.

They originally lived in what were called bender tents before they were replaced with caravans, which came into existence a little more than the past one hundred years. Today, Gypsy carts and caravans can still be found in many European countries, but it is only in Great Britain where the Gypsy caravan has become an art form, making the English Gypsy caravan the most highly decorated kind in the world. Gypsies want the perfect horse to pull their colorful castles of the open road and therefore only in Great Britain can quality Vanners be found.

The beginning of selectively bred horses for the English Gypsy caravan started about sixty or seventy years ago. The first horses that pulled Gypsy caravans and carts were not a defined type, nor were they spotted. The vast majority were bought and sold as a means of simple commerce and often were dramatically different from each other.

Like their horses, Gypsies evolved in unique and different ways. There are Gypsies of pure Romany heritage, there are half Romany Gypsies called Diddikoi, and there are non-Romany Gypsies who live the Gypsy lifestyle over many generations. The word "Travelers" is a common and accepted term to

A pretty head and abundant mane are outstanding features of the Gypsy Vanner. *Mark J. Barrett/WR Ranch*

describe a broad group of people that live a Gypsy lifestyle. There are also people in Great Britain, and more specifically Ireland and Scotland, called "Travellers" who live the same non-conventional, Gypsy-like lives outside the norm of mainstream society. Not all of these groups are the Gypsies who breed the true Gypsy Vanner Horse as the breed is known in the United States today.

Foundation

It was the Romany Gypsies who created the Vanner horse primarily by using native breeds, such as the Shire, Clydesdale, Dales Pony (the heaviest pony breed in Britain), and the Fell Pony (in the lighter type). The Friesian is included in the Vanner's background, because it was an important genetic element in the development of these other breeds, all of which have the wonderful personality of the cold-blooded draft. Originally, the Vanner was not recognized as a breed and had no name. Gypsy horses were primarily referred to as colored or piebald and skewbald horses, because most of them had spotted patterns.

Great Gypsy horse breeders, who fit every description of respected equine breeders, selectively bred toward the vision of the perfect caravan horse. After half a century, a few private Gypsy families succeeded in producing horses with this specific Vanner look. They proudly showed them off, but only to other Gypsies and kept them a secret from all others.

These horses were not easily sold, if ever, and never sold to outside cultures. Instead, they were passed down to succeeding generations as heirloom gifts and were not available for purchase. For such special horses to be sold by their Gypsy breeder was comparable to selling his heart and life's work. This attitude is hard to explain or be understood by other societies. Simply said, a Gypsy Vanner horse easily bought is not "a proper Vanner."

Characteristics

Due to their gentle natures and the natural culling process that takes place with a nomadic lifestyle, the Gypsy Vanner has one of the kindest dispositions of any horse. Gypsies had no tolerance for animals that might endanger lives, thus any horse displaying an ill temper was banished immediately. This led to the Gypsy Vanner Horse becoming one of the gentlest

and most docile horses in the world, which must be experienced to be believed. It was common for a Gypsy mother to tell her children to stop bothering the horses as they crawled over and under them. The horses have a unique love for people, comparable only to the Gypsies' love of their horses.

By the nature of its demanding existence, the Gypsy Vanner is extremely sound and easy to maintain, essential elements for a life of travel. Gypsies stake their horses on thirty-foot chains or ropes and move them daily. A Gypsy will tell you that a good Gypsy horse should live "under the hedge," which simply means that it should thrive on very little, and it typically does. The cold-blooded genetics in the Vanner contribute to its thriftiness. The horses stand with their rear ends to the cold wind and rain and either flourish or get sick. The sick ones do not last; the hardy ones that stay healthy, do.

An abundance of mane, tail, and feathering not only give the horses protection from the elements, but also give the animal a look true to its heritage. There are many Gypsy horses that developed from non-feathered or smooth legged breeds, but

Gypsy Vanner pulling caravan with its feathering emphasizing each stride. *WR Ranch*

a quality, magical feathered look is the signature of the Gypsy Vanner breed. Feathering is a cumulative or additive gene, thus horses with feathering must be bred to other horses with feathering to create and preserve this feature.

Gypsy Vanners are outstanding riding and driving horses, but to serious Gypsy breeders, they are primarily status symbols, a source of pride, and a means of cash flow. It is common for the best horses to reach very high levels of recognition and value. All serious Gypsy breeders know the great mares and stallions of heritage. These quality horses are a source of pride in the Gypsy community and are the centerpiece of the breed.

History

In 1994, horse breeders Dennis and Cindy Thompson of Florida traveled to England and, while there, noticed an unusual looking horse in a distant field. While pursuing more information about this special horse, they met a Gypsy named Fred Walker. He had a band of mares that looked just like the stallion and that he usually kept hidden due to their great value. The Thompsons spent the day in the Gypsy camp, listening to Walker as he expressed a deep sense of respect for the stallion they saw, called The Log, and explained Gypsy Vanner Horses to them.

Walker was a British Gypsy legend and pillar in the Gypsy community who lived in a horse-drawn caravan his entire life. He began his focus on breeding the perfect caravan horse in 1948 when he was only nineteen, and he maintained the genetics of his fifty-nine-year Vanner vision throughout his lifetime. He personally knew the stallions that inspired and began his Vanner breed. Over the decades of dedicated breeding, he produced or owned many of the most famous sires and dams.

Walker could trace The Log's heritage through three countries. His dam and sire were in one country, while his grandparents were in another. Dedicated Gypsy breeders who focused on producing horses with a specific look raised each of these generations. The breeder and owner of The

Log, Tom Price, treasured the day this stallion was born, recalling, "I held him in my arms and I knew he was special. He's the best colt I ever raised!" In 1992, The Log was valued as the highest priced Gypsy horse colt at Appleby Fair, one of the oldest Gypsy fairs in the world, and was recognized as one of the finest bred Gypsy horses in all of Great Britain.

The Thompsons began a relationship with Walker that entailed learning more about Gypsy culture and their horses over the following years and, in the process, earned Walker's trust. This was a feat in itself, because of the closed nature of the Gypsy society, particularly when it came to their Vanner Horses. Walker shared his passion for the Vanner horse, as well as the history and genetics of the breed with them. "It was like having Justin Morgan call you every two weeks to reminisce about his stallion," recalls Dennis Thompson.

The Thompsons were amazed that Walker's stunning horses were not recognized as a breed and had no name. After they spent four years learning about these treasured horses and the handful of Gypsies who created them, they began a search for their own herd. After two years, only three stallions were identified that had the look, heritage, and proven ability to consistently produce the quality of a "proper Vanner." They resided in the United Kingdom, which, until recently, was the only place beautiful Gypsy Vanner Horses of this type could be found. One was known as The King, which the Gypsies admired for his ability to reproduce his remarkable traits. There was also The Log and a third stallion, which was the pride of the Walker family. He was produced by two generations of magnificent Walker stallions and was never sold. In 1996, several fillies from this stallion were sold to the Thompsons and became the first Gypsy Vanner Horses imported to North America.

The Thompsons understood and respected the years of deep and careful thought that went into Gypsy Vanner breeding. It was their intent to select only the special type of horses that Walker approved of as foundation horses for their herd. They also established the Gypsy Vanner Horse Society as a registry in 1996, the first of its kind in North America.

Walker helped them pick the name Gypsy Vanner Horse for the new breed, which they registered as a trademark solely to establish the breed with a definable and focused look until an understanding of the new breed was achieved. Once the look was recognizable, it would be easier to identify the correct type and select specimens worthy of classification as Gypsy Vanner Horses.

By establishing trust over the years with established Gypsy Vanner breeders such as Walker, the Thompsons were able to buy and import The Log in 1997, renaming him Cushti Bok, which in the language of the Gypsies means "good luck." He became the first Gypsy Vanner stallion to be imported to North America, and was soon followed by The King, which was imported a year later. The King was the sire of Dolly, one of the first imported fillies. He is now known throughout the world as The Gypsy King.

The other imported mare named Bat was bred to The King, producing Kuchi in 1999. *ABC News with Peter Jennings* reported the birth of Kuchi, the first U.S.-born Gypsy Vanner Horse. The name Kuchi means "nomad" and is also the name of a Gypsy tribe famous for the dance the *huchi kuchi*. The name proved to be appropriate, as Kuchi dances when she walks. She is a stunning example of the power of genetics. Her colt, Destiny, has the blood of all three stallions: Kuchi's sire, The King; her grandfather, who was the pride of the Walker family; and Cushti Bok, Destiny's sire. This foundation bloodline is extremely valuable for the correct type and quality of the Gyspy Vanner Horse in North America.

In 1998, the Thompson's Gypsy Vanner Horses were introduced to the American public at Equitana USA in Louisville, Kentucky. It was love at first sight for everyone who saw them. The passion that the horses created with the crowds is the same that Gypsies know so well.

The Gypsy Vanner Horse became an instant hit in the United States. Its image was chosen for the cover photo of the Horse Feathers calendar by renowned equine photographer, Mark J. Barrett. Additionally, segments on Animal Planet and American Health Network showcased Gypsy Vanner Horses.

The Gypsy King's image has appeared in *Vogue* with the magazine's model of the year. His model became one of the top ten models for the Breyer Model Horses Company for 2001 and was chosen to be showcased and sold on QVC. Again the magic was felt as he made a special guest appearance at BreyerFest in Lexington, Kentucky.

This exposure brought recognition to Gypsies as one of the world's most colorful and least understood societies, as well as the horses they love so dearly.

Breed Overview

What the American public is experiencing and responding to when it sees Gypsy Vanner Horses are the same feelings a Gypsy feels. It stirs the heart and excites the soul to see such an amazingly beautiful and unique animal. However, not all Gypsy horses create this magic, and not all Gypsy horses should be recognized as examples of the breed. If the look is lost, so is the magic.

There are an estimated four thousand to five thousand Gypsy horses in the United Kingdom. The selectively bred Gypsy Vanner horses, however, are very rare. Their numbers are estimated to be only about 20 percent of the total Gypsy horse population. It was the discovery of one of those rare horses, along with the dedication to understanding the Gypsy dream, that created the opportunity to establish the breed in the United States. Only quality Gypsy horses that were approved by Walker and complemented the vision of a proper Vanner were imported by the Thompsons.

Opposite: In addition to the Vanner's amazing looks, it is friendly and engaging. *Mark J. Barrett/WR Ranch*

Gypsy Vanner Horses are colorful and compact, with the muscling to provide the power to pull the caravans so integral to the Gypsy society. Heavy bones, flat knees, and ample hooves give this magnificent horse the foundation to sustain a body that includes a broad chest and heavy hips. The withers are rounded, making the horse suitable for harness and the bareback riding style of Gypsy children. In addition to the Vanner's amazing looks, it possesses a temperament that is friendly and engaging.

Feathering is important to the Vanner look. According to Fred Walker, there is no question that only feathered horses were used to develop the breed. It is the intention of the Gypsy Vanner Horse Society to establish the breed with only feathered foundation animals. Genetics dictate that the degree of feathering on the offspring of those foundation animals can range from minimal to profuse. Breeding stallions should always have an abundance of feather.

The Gypsy Vanner is extremely easy to train, strong, intelligent, docile, athletic, distinctive, and willing, with excellent endurance. It is the perfect horse for any number of pursuits, such as English and western pleasure, freestyle riding, driving, carriage, dressage, hunt seat, saddle seat, hack classes, trail classes, jumping, or bareback riding. It is exceptional for trail rides due to its unflappable nature.

Gypsy Vanners can be shown both at Gypsy Vanner shows and any other show they qualify for. The Gypsy Vanner Horse Society is associated with the United States Equestrian Federation (USEF), United States Dressage Federation (USDF) All-Breeds Program, and the Ontario Equestrian Federation. There are just over 1,200 registered Gypsy Vanner Horses in North America as of 2008.

Vanners are becoming very popular for trail riding, due to their unflappable personality. They create a sensation wherever they go. One owner who trail rides her champion Vanner stallion is continually stopped by others who want to talk to her about her horse.

The first long distance Vanner was a gelding named Spenser, owned by Julie Anthony. Spenser did a 25 mile ride in 2008 with thirty-one other horses and finished 26th. This is remarkable, considering that most distance runners are Arabian or similar horses. Everyone was amazed that Spenser's pulse rate and overall hardiness handled the distance so well.

Vanners create a sensation wherever they go. At exhibitions, there are so many people who are enthralled with the Vanners, that the reaction is the same as to that of a rock star. The Vanners have to be continually moved around the crowds, who want to touch and mob the horses.

Breed Types

The Gypsy Vanner Horse is no different than other well known breeds that evolved over half a century, often producing different types through clear and carefully orchestrated plans of the breeders. Like other breed types named after a group or area of people who bred for a specific capacity and look, Gypsy horses experienced the same diversity of types within the original group. Just as there are different types of people referred to as Gypsies, there are different types of horses referred to as Gypsy horses.

There are three primary types of Gypsy horses: Gypsy Trotters, common types, and the classic types, or "proper Vanners."

Gypsy Trotters are typically a cross between a colored Gypsy horse stallion and usually a Standardbred mare. They are a lighter, leaner horse used for roadracing, and they can become quite valuable. Roadracing colored Gypsy trotters are very much a passion of Gypsies.

Common types of Gypsy horses evolved from many different breeds and are not easily definable. Smooth legged riding horses were often involved, which gives these horses a lighter, less distinct look. The majority of these horses can't be defined as a breed and are typically very inexpensive.

Classic types may be referred to as proper Vanners and have the look of a small Shire or light draft. They are the direct result of a focused breeding goal instituted sixty or seventy years ago.

Vanners are the perfect horse to pull the colorful Gypsy caravan. *Mark J. Barrett/WR Ranch*

Their history is documented and their look is easily defined. They were developed exclusively by Gypsies who were breeders of this type. Like all breeds, great stallions and great mares can be identified and are an important part of their history. The Classic type is recognized as the correct type horse of The Gypsy Vanner Horse Society (GVHS) in the United States.

This type has a short back, heavy flat bone (flat at the knee), broad chest and hips, and also has what a Gypsy would call a "sweet head." This simply means its head is more refined than that of most draft horses.

Feathering starts at the knee on the front legs and at, or near, the hock on the rear legs. The feathering is typically profuse and almost always covers the front hooves.

The height is between 13.2 and 15.2 hands tall. Their average weight is from 1,100 to 1,700 pounds.

There is a similar, lighter **Sport Gypsy horse**, which also has a set look that is worthy of recognition as a breed type, because its heritage and look are distinct. Its value rises with its quality, and like most things of value, quality is rare. The best stallions of this type can cost £20,000 ($30,000) or more. In recent years, there has been a trend by Gypsies to place great value on this smaller, lighter sport Gypsy horse rather than the larger Gypsy Classic type.

The word "lighter" is a relative word, as these quality horses have substantial bodies and lots of feathering. They simply have a lighter look than the heavier draft appearance of the Classic Gypsy Vanner Horse. Dedicated Gypsy breeders know this type of quality horse very well.

It is very likely that the Fells Pony contributed more to this lighter quality type, along with the other primary breeds that created the heavier Classic Gypsy Vanner Horse. The Fells Pony is a lighter quality pony with a feathered Friesian look similar to the Dales pony, only lighter in build. It is also important to note that the weight a horse carries can influence its look.

Registry Requirements

Horses with both parents registered in the GVHS are automatically eligible for registration. Eligible horses must be approved by the registration committee; they must have an acceptable score at a Gypsy Vanner evaluation performed by the registration committee, which is available in different parts of the United States. Since the stud book is still open, other horses can also apply for registration, but must pass the evaluation by the registration committee. The GVHS provides judging seminars to teach the judging and evaluation of the breed.

Standards

The Gypsy Vanner Horse Society respects the standards established by the oral history of Gypsies who spent their lifetime perfecting the caravan horse. The breed standards were reviewed and approved in detail by Fred Walker, who maintained the same genetics of his vision for the perfect Vanner horse for more than fifty-six years. The Gypsy Vanner is a "people sized" draft horse with heavy bone and broad body, but on a smaller scale than the large draft breeds.

Color: The Gypsy Vanner Horse is not a color breed, it is a body type. Therefore all colors, markings, and patterns are acceptable, with piebald and skewbald being the most common.

In honor of the British Gypsy heritage of the breed, the following names are used to describe Gypsy Vanner Horse colors:

- Piebald: black and white
- Skewbald: red and white, brown and white, tri-color
- Odd coloured: any other color
- Blagdon: solid color with white splashed up from underneath

Height: The Vanner is 13.2 to 15.2 hands, although there may be a few individuals outside of this range.

Body: The Vanner has the look of a small to average size horse with a draft horse type body. The back should be short coupled and in proportion to overall body. Withers are well rounded, not high, and fine. The chest should be deep and broad with well sprung ribs; and shoulders are sloping with well developed muscle. The hindquarters should have heavy, powerful hips with a well muscled and rounded croup; tail should be not set too low. Slab sided or severely sloping hindquarters are considered a fault. The neck should be strong and of ample length. Stallions must display a bold look with a rainbow (well arched) crest.

Legs: The legs should be clean, with heavy to medium-heavy bone set on a medium to large hoof. The front legs should be set square and muscular, with broad, flat, well developed knees. Rear legs should have hocks that are broad and clean. A Vanner will have the modified closer hock set of a pulling horse, but not as close as the modern draft horse. Set back or sickle hocks are a fault. Hooves are large, round, and open at the heels with well developed frogs. Small contracted hooves are considered a fault. Leg movement should be clean, straight, and true, with an energetic, distinctive, and effortless trot.

Hair: Ideal hair is straight and silky with some wave, curl, and body being acceptable. Kinky hair is a fault. Abundant feathering should begin at the back of the knees on the front legs and at, or near, the hocks on the rear, extending over the front of the hooves. Mane, forelock, and tail should be ample to profusely abundant; double manes are common, but not required.

Head: The Vanner should have a sweet head (more refined head than a typical Shire horse) set on a strong neck in harmony with the horse's overall look. The horse should have a clean throatlatch and jaw. The nose should be flat and tapered. A slightly Roman nose is acceptable if it goes with the horse's overall look, but a heavy Roman nose is not acceptable. Eyes can be any color and should be wide set, bright, alert, and kind. Ears should be in proportion to the head and not too large.

Nature: A Vanner should be alert and willing, with traits of intelligence, kindness and docility—a Golden Retriever with hooves.

Credit: The Gypsy Vanner Horse Society

MULE

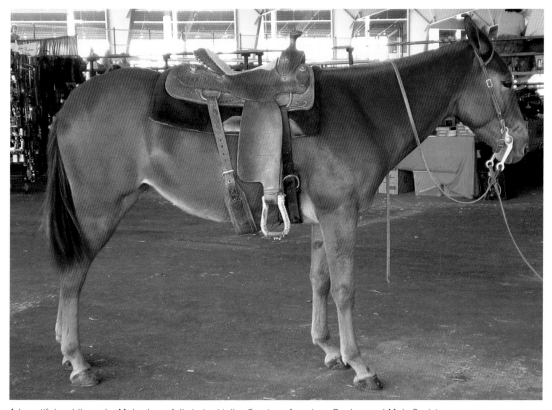

A beautiful saddle mule. Mules have fully haired tails. *Courtesy American Donkey and Mule Society*

American Donkey and Mule Society, Inc.
P.O. Box 1210
Lewisville, Texas 75067
www.lovelongears.com

The mule is not a species in the truest sense of the word, but instead it is a hybrid resulting from the cross of two related equine species, the horse and the donkey (ass). Like both parent breeds, mules have a past that dates far back into antiquity

They once were thought of only as work or draft animals and historically were utilized for their hardworking capabilities. With their steadfastness in harness, they proved repeatedly over the centuries that they were invaluable in shaping world history. In early America, thousands of mules were bred and sold for army use, and in some areas of the country where a horse could not withstand the working conditions, mules were used exclusively. They hauled huge wagon trains of coal, borax, and supplies across the harsh, dry expanses of Death Valley, where most horses would not survive.

No records of breeding or exact numbers were kept or any registry book started for mules back then. In recent years, however, they have been viewed as recreation animals, and today there are at least three registries for mules, as well as numerous clubs for their promotion and showing all over the United States.

The Mighty Mule

The mule will take much of its overall build and looks from the mare (or horse sire in hinnies), but also acquire the unique features and hybrid vigor contributed by the donkey parent. Due to this hybrid vigor, the mule is a heartier animal than the horse. It is more suited for heavy work with less damaging effects, although this does not condone overworking it. The mule is a more efficient converter of feed to energy. When a side-by-side comparison of horse and mule is done, the mule can carry a heavier load for a longer amount of time on less feed and with greater stamina. Additionally, it has an overall longer working life, and those aged forty years or older are not unheard of.

Mules will not endanger themselves in the way that some horses will (such as when Pony Express riders often rode horses to death), but instead will stop before injuring themselves. This self-preserving nature has led to the bad reputation of mules being stubborn, but it is actually a lack of communication and interpretation on the human's part.

Mules can be "customized" to any type or purpose, and therefore are probably the most versatile equine of all. With more stamina, a greater weight carrying capacity, and a willing but cautious nature, the mule can perform all of the tasks and disciplines of the horse and some that it cannot. Depending on the breed of mare, the mule can be bred for endurance (Arab breeding), riding (stock or warmblood), ranch work (mustang and stock breeds), miniature (pony and Miniature Horse), packing, harness, gaited, or draft. It can range in size and type from the smallest miniature (record is 25 inches) to the largest draft (recorded at 19.1 hands). Almost every breed of horse, at one time or another, has been used for mule breeding, either en masse or as an experiment by jack owners. Just as in the past,

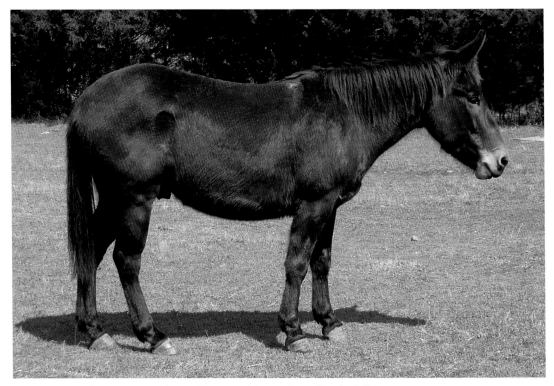

This saddle mule (Standard jack x Quarter Horse mare) is more horse-like. *Leah Patton*

good mules can still bring higher prices than saddle horses due to the increased demand.

At large shows across the nation, the same mule can compete and win in a variety of events, from western pleasure to hunter over fences, obstacle driving to children's lead-line, and from barrel racing to the mule's unique sport of coon jumping. The latter is a high-jump from a standing start, where mules have been known to jump more than a foot higher than their own ears in height. Mules are even used for racing. In 2003, history was made when the first equine ever to be cloned was born— a full brother to a top winning racing mule.

Genetics

In the strictest sense of the word, the mule is the result of breeding a jack (male) donkey to a mare (female) horse. The hybrid offspring can be either a male mule, called "horse mule," or female mare mule. The opposite pairing of a horse stallion to a donkey jennet results in a "hinny." Mules and hinnies are virtually identical for all practical purposes and are often cataloged together under the single generic term "mule." There is actually more variety in the physical appearance of mules and hinnies in general, than there is between the two.

Unless it is verified whether the sire was a stallion or a jack, all mule-appearing hybrids are listed as mules. There is no 100 percent reliable way, outside of DNA verification, to tell a hinny from a mule, and very few people, even experts on mules, can catalog mules and hinnies just by visual inspection. One supposedly foolproof way in sorting mules and hinnies of unverified parentage is to turn the animal into a mixed group of horses and donkeys. The mule reportedly chooses horses for company, while the hinny will go with the donkeys, both preferring to be with their mother types.

Breeding for mules is actually far more profitable and easier than breeding for hinnies. The overall fertility rate of horses is thought to be around 65 percent. This is not affected if the mare is bred to a jack; in fact, there are many old tales about previously barren mares being bred by jacks and raising healthy mule foals. When the gene tables are turned, however, and the chromosome count of the female (in this case the donkey jennet with sixty-two chromosomes) is lower than that of the male (sixty-four in the horse stallion), the conception and birth rate drops off sharply. Only about one in ten breedings in crossing for hinnies will result in a successful birth.

It is also far easier to keep one jack and a number of mares than to have a horse stallion to breed only to jennets. Jacks will usually willingly breed mares, especially if they are brought up with a mare, but a jack that is good on mares should not be put to the jennets as a rule. Horse stallions are more difficult to breed to jennets, as it is not as normal for them to be with donkeys.

Mules and hinnies both are sterile due to an imbalance of the sex chromosomes, but they are anatomically normal and behave as such. Female mules and hinnies will still come into heat, and males will show a strong sex drive. Since they often will go into a kind of rut to the exclusion of all other outside factors, male hybrids should always be castrated (preferably as soon as the testicles are descended). Uncastrated (stud) mules can be one of the most unpredictable and dangerous of all equines. Intact male mules were often let out with range mare bands at the turn of the twentieth century, as the mule would defend his mares to the death. This was done also as a way of population control, since no foals would result in the coverings.

Once in a great while, a report of a female mule or hinny giving birth surfaces. Until recent years, these were impossible to verify. With the advent of DNA testing, it can now be reported that about one in 1 million female mules may actually be fertile. It was once thought that the fertile mare mule contributed a complete set of maternal chromosomes, but at least two DNA verified hybrid offspring from fertile mare mules and hinnies have been shown to have mixed maternal gene sets (both horse and donkey). These events are highly publicized, hotly debated, and intensely studied when they do occur. No male mule has ever been known to have sired a foal, but the occurrence of female hybrid fertility has been documented in several other animal species as well.

Conformation Characteristics

Drawing on the unique features of the donkey parent, the mule is an unusual blend of horse and ass. The head is usually horse-like, but many mules have the deeper jaw, shorter face, and D-shaped eye socket of the donkey parent. Donkeys and many mules have an expression of perpetual surprise or patience due in part to the eye shape.

The mule's ears are noticeably larger than that of a horse, but not typically so large or open as donkey ears. The neck is rarely muscled or arched, a straight neck being more common. Depending on the exact cross of parents, the neck may be thin or drafty, but ewe necks, thin, weedy swan necks, or overly short necks are not preferred in the working mule.

The barrel is wider than that of a donkey, but many mules inherit the flat withers of the jack. This makes for a level topline that blends smoothly into a rounded rump. The shoulders are often straighter (more upright), but some mules, especially those of gaited breeding, may have deep sloping shoulders. The haunches of the mule are powerful, but still not overly muscled or heavily clad as the bunchy muscle of the stock bred horse.

The mule in general will have a smooth appearance resulting from the smooth body form of the donkey, rather than the clearly defined heavy muscle of some horse breeds. Even draft mules from the largest Belgian or Percheron mares will be less bulky in shape and form and will usually have abundant bone, but are clean limbed with very little or no leg feathering.

The mane of the mule is often unruly, many being sparse and tending to stand upright like the donkey's mane. There are numerous mane styles that can be worn on mules; preference is given to the style that best enhances the looks of the individual. It is common to see mules with very short, upright trimmed manes of only an inch or so in length, hogged (roached) flat to the neck, or trimmed in a standing curve. A few mules will have manes of both length and texture suited to laying flat on the neck; these may be thinned, braided, or banded for show. As the donkey has no falling forelock, many mules have thin or short forelocks that are usually taken off if the mane is clipped.

A more distinctive mule with white legs is the offspring of a jack with a tobiano spotted mare. *Courtesy American Donkey and Mule Society*

Tail styles also vary regionally and according to the preference of the owner. While a mule's tail is fully haired from the dock to the root (unlike the cow-like switch of the donkey), mules in the past had the top portions of the tail shaved down from 4 to 10 inches. This practice helped to accentuate the haunches. Alternately, army mules had "bells" of hair clipped into the tail, in order to signify the amount of training the mule had received.

Color

Colors in the mule run nearly every gamut of horse and donkey color, every combination imaginable, and can include a few variations that are unique to the hybrids. Bay, black, brown, chestnut, buckskin, and dun are common, and most of these colors have lighter "mealy" points (or blond,

pangare points) around the eyes, muzzle, and belly inherited from the donkey parent. Some have dorsal stripes and shoulder bars. Since there is no cream gene in the donkeys, mules cannot be cremello or perlino, but there are registered mules of silver dapple, champagne, and champagne/cream shades.

Random white markings such as a star, blaze, or white socks are actually uncommon in mules. The extent of random white in donkeys is usually limited to a forehead star (a blaze face, or blaze in combination with a white foot, indicates spotting in the donkey). This may be due to a masking of a sabino gene that is readily inherited by the mule.

Tobiano patterns from the horse are not transmitted in complete form to the mule or hinny offspring. Most often a mule from a tobiano mare will have only four white stockings and a white tail marking.

Very few mules appear to be true tobiano in pattern, but many exhibit what is known as "skewing" of the pattern. The patches of white appear irregularly, are displaced, or are an unusual size on the mule. Skewing can occur with the tobiano pattern (true overo and sabino being almost unheard of), the donkey spot pattern (with a solid colored horse parent and spotted donkey parent), and most dramatically in the Appaloosa bred mule. Combinations of Appaloosa horse and spotted donkey can result in wildly spectacular patterns of splash and spot, or even in all-white, pink skinned, blue eyed mules.

Breeding for color on mules is a true spin of the roulette wheel, and color is always figured into the equation as the icing on the cake, with temperament and conformation being the first goals in breeding.

Standards

The American Donkey and Mule Society, founded in 1967, operates five books for donkeys, mules, and zebra hybrids, including the registry for racing mules, which are popular in Nevada and California.

The mule should follow, in part, the breed of the horse parent with regard to head carriage, gait, and body shape. The main ideal for a mule is to be well balanced, straight, and clean legged, with no major conformation flaws outside the "equine normal" (severely ewed neck, cowhocks, or crooked legs for example).

Heads should be in proportion to the body and not overly large. Unlike other horse breeds with infusions of Arab blood, Arabian mules may have straight faces. Heavy Roman noses or coarse heads do not hamper a working mule, but are not preferred for showing.

Bite should be even, with less than one-fourth inch deviation preferred. Neck should be straight and set well into shoulder. Extreme ewe or swan necks are penalized, and very short, thick or Long, thin necks are not preferred in show stock, but do not affect most working mules.

Forelegs should be set on well with clear projection of chest in front. Shoulders are often straight, but a gentle slope is preferred. Legs should be square and straight when viewed from front and side.

Chests should be broad with defined, double-lobed breast musculature.

Barrels should be deep with plenty of heart girth and should not be long and weak.

Flatter withers than horses are not uncommon, but good withers and saddle dip are preferred in riding animals.

Underlines should be long and straight, tying into flank at a deeper set than horses.

Hips should be long and smooth; haunches large and well muscled; hindquarters should be in balance to shoulders. Very shallow hindquarters and weak hind ends are to be penalized.

The hind limbs of saddle or draft mules are shown standing square, while gaited mules may be stretched. The hind legs should be set under well without being sickle hocked. When viewed from behind, the hind legs should be straight with a small degree of cowhocks allowed. Severe cowhocks or crooked legs are to be penalized.

Pasterns are slightly more upright than what is normal in horses, but pastern and hoof angles should match. Club feet and long, broken hoof angles are severely penalized.

Mules perform all known gaits; those from Walking Horse mares may rack, amble, or single-foot. Exaggerated high-stepping action can be enhanced in the naturally gaited mule.

The hocks are the power "train" and should be well engaged. Headset should be that of the breed/usage of the mule.

Credit: American Donkey and Mule Society, Inc.

NORTH AMERICAN SPOTTED DRAFT

The North American Spotted Draft Horse Association
17594 U.S. Highway 20
Goshen, Indiana 46528
www.nasdha.net

The North American Spotted Draft is an impressive, full bodied horse, not only with massive draft features, but with outstanding color. As the name implies, it is a draft horse that is Paint or Pinto spotted. Those observing the Spotted Draft are caught up in the fascination of such a splendid animal. It moves with the directness and presence that only a draft can have and catches the eye with its beautiful color.

Spotted draft horses can be found throughout history. They were used as warhorses in medieval times, and there was a brown and white draft horse in Queen Elizabeth's Court, believed to be a Drum Horse (parade horse carrying large drums). Spotted draft horses also share a long history in the United States; one breeder in Iowa had over twenty spotted draft horses in the mid 1960s.

Breeding Basics

The simplest way of producing a North American Spotted Draft is to cross a full draft horse breed, such as a Belgian or Clydesdale, with a Paint Horse. The resulting foal will hopefully exhibit the tobiano or overo color pattern with a somewhat drafty build. (The possibility of creating a solid colored colt can also occur.) From here, the newly formed spotted half draft is bred back to a full draft, producing a three-quarter draft. Breeding a three-quarter draft horse to a full draft again produces a seven-eighths draft horse, now considered a full draft. The goal is to have the spotting pattern remain all the way to this last cross.

Spotted Draft Horses have pleasant heads with active ears. *Daniel Johnson*

Spotting Pattern Inheritance

Color genetics play a key role in producing Spotted Draft Horses. The desire is to produce a well marked, colored draft type horse. The most recognized Pinto spotting pattern is tobiano, whose major feature is having white appear somewhere along the spine and descend vertically. Other characteristics include spots similar to ink spots or paw prints, four white legs with irregular edged spotting, dark hooves, and patches of color around the chestnuts. Face markings are the same as on normal horses.

Horses that possess different alleles in any gene pair are referred to as heterozygous, and those that have the same alleles are called homozygous. Breeders try to select individuals that are known tobiano producers based on a high percentage of tobiano offspring (though they may be heterozygous for tobiano), or those that are homozygous. Since the homozygous horse has two copies of the tobiano gene, it will produce 100 percent tobiano progeny to a mate of any color. This is due to simple genetic rules; it only takes one copy of the tobiano gene to exhibit characteristics of the tobiano pattern. Since mating results in each parent contributing one half of the genetic make-up of the resulting foal, a homozygous individual will always pass one copy of the tobiano gene to that foal. The modifying genes, which control the extent of the white markings in the tobiano, are probably present in all horses, but they rely on the presence of the tobiano gene to express themselves.

No color pattern has been the subject of as much confusion over its identification and inheritance as the overo spotting pattern. In many respects, the overo is the opposite (or negative) of the tobiano. Overo displays as a dominant pattern of white patches that appears to spread horizontally along the ribs, neck, and body, leaving the topline and legs colored. Usually the face has a large, asymmetric white area, often referred to as a bald face. Oftentimes, an overo individual will have blue, or wall, eyes. An overo must have one overo parent, even if that individual is not completely marked.

A homozygous overo foal is born white and dies soon after birth from lethal defects, most commonly a defective bowel formation. This is known as lethal white syndrome. By never breeding an overo to an overo, and always overo to a solid colored horse, a good percentage of overo foals can occur without producing a lethal white individual.

The tovero spotting pattern looks like a combination of tobiano and overo, but does not exactly fit either one.

Opinions vary, but the overall preferred percentage of color on a Spotted Draft seems to be the tobiano pattern, with 60:40 black to white combination. Homozygous testing for tobiano can be performed through a simple genetic test using pulled mane hairs. The test utilizes the DNA located in the root bulb. Testing can be done at certain equine laboratories across the country.

Registry

The North American Spotted Draft Horse Association (NASDHA) was formed in 1995 to register and preserve these beautiful and rare horses. Since then, it has grown by leaps and bounds throughout the United States and Canada. To date, there are over 2,500 Spotted Drafts registered. It is the first and foremost registry for Spotted Drafts. This is not a color-only horse registry, but signifies a new draft breed.

Horses accepted into the association can be of any draft breed mixture, including Percheron, Belgian, Clydesdale, Shire, Suffolk Punch, and the American Cream. Percheron crosses seem to be the most popular because of the black and white color, though other crosses are also common.

The association holds no official position on tail docking, but as there is an escalation of more Spotted Draft horses being ridden, the general populous prefers a non-docked tail.

Registration

There are four registration divisions: Premium Draft, Regular Draft, Breeding Stock, and Indexing.
- Premium: seven-eighths to full draft
- Regular: one-half to three-quarters draft
- Breeding: solid colored breeding stock
- Indexing: allows registration of horses that are obviously at least one-half draft, yet whose parentage is unknown

Horses eligible for registration must be at least one-half draft of any breed. Horses must have obvious tobiano or overo pinto markings in order to be eligible for registration in the Premium and Regular divisions.

Standards

Spotted Drafts should have conformation that closely reflects the draft type they most resemble, such as Percheron or Belgian, Suffolk, Shire or Clydesdale, or other draft types.

Generally, the frame should be large and supported by clean, dense bone. It should have short, strong, muscled forearms and thighs. Legs should be placed well under the body. They have intelligent heads with active ears and powerful, arching necks, which are clean-cut at the throat. Shoulders tend to be upright, suitable for power rather than action. The back is short and strong, and ribs spring high from the backbone. The hindquarters are long and smooth to the root of the tail, which springs higher up than other breeds. The hip bones are wide apart and smoothly covered, and the croup is usually level. Depth and thickness from the withers to the legs are essential, as they should be as deep in the flank as over the heart.

Height: The average height of the Spotted Draft is 16 to 17 hands, but some are sometimes larger.

Color: Spotted Draft horses are most often tobianos, but overos and toveros do exist. Any base color is acceptable, though most popular colors are black, bay, and sorrel. Blue eyes are uncommon, but acceptable.

Disposition and use: The Spotted Draft has a splendid disposition and an easy temperament. It exhibits a ready willingness to work, great endurance, and a desired quality known as heart, which means they do not easily give up on a task. They are most often used for agricultural work, pleasure driving, parades, commercial carriages, showing, logging, western and English riding and games.

Interest in Spotted Draft horses has risen strongly in the past few years. As their popularity increases, they are seen more often at various expositions around the country, such as the Massachusetts Equine Affaire, Horse and Mule Progress Days, and the Texas Expo, to name a few. Due to their good

More riders are enjoying Spotted Drafts because of their calm attitudes. *Daniel Johnson*

nature, they are being used as trail horses for older folks who want a calm, relaxed trail buddy, or a "husband's" horse because of their stocky frame.

The versatility of the Spotted Draft continues to be apparent. Currently a member of the North American Spotted Draft Horse Association rides her Spotted Draft sidesaddle at demonstrations and events across the United States.

Credit: The North American Spotted Draft Horse Association

Norwegian Fjord Horse

Beautiful Fjord herd on a beautiful landscape. Fjords do well in various climates. *Crown Jewel Resort Ranch*

Norwegian Fjord Horse Registry
1203 Appian Drive
Webster, New York 14580
www.nfhr.com

The Norwegian Fjord Horse has become known as the little horse with a big heart, whether it is in the competition ring or patiently bearing the first-time horse owner. The sincerity of this breed, which gives unconditionally and trusts generously, has endeared it to people throughout the world.

The Norwegian Fjord possesses a charming, gentle disposition and a strong body structure that enables it to perform all types of riding, driving, and draft work. It is a unique, pure, and beautiful horse.

The Fjord has the reputation of being an agile and trusted workhorse with extraordinary power for its small size, as it is proportionally stronger than most horses. It is hardy, long lived, and willing. It learns fast and has an amazing ability to retain what it has learned, even after long periods of inactivity. Its versatility and compactness is enhanced by its extreme surefootedness. Its wonderful temperament and graceful, balanced gaits both under saddle and in harness make it the ideal all-purpose horse.

The Fjord's rugged and people-loving nature has made it a family favorite for centuries in Norway. It is often used as a schooling horse for the young or inexperienced rider, yet is large and powerful enough for adults to ride and enjoy. Its willingness to please, honest work ethic, and cleverness make it the perfect partner in the show world or in front of a farm implement. Remaining unchanged for centuries, it has become that rare breed of horse that is able to do it all in a world of specialization.

Breed Overview

The Norwegian Fjord Horse is one of the world's oldest and purest breeds. It is believed that the original Fjord horse migrated to Norway. After the last ice age, herds of wild Fjord horses existed there, which were domesticated over four thousand years ago. The mountainous district of Vestlandet (western Norway) is the breed's place of origin in Scandinavia. The breed still exhibits strong survival instincts and remains healthy, fertile, and useful well into its long life. Fjords are efficient foragers and thrive equally well in the pasture or stable, adapting easily to the weather conditions of their environment, be it hot and dry, or cold and wet.

One unique characteristic of the Norwegian Fjord Horse is its mane. The center hair of the mane is dark (usually black), while the outer hair is white. The mane is trimmed short, so it will stand erect in a characteristic crescent shape to emphasize the graceful curve of the neck. The white outer hair is trimmed slightly shorter than the dark inner hair to display the dramatic dark stripe. The mane is one of the breed's trademarks and complements the horse's frame and structure well.

Without a doubt, the nature of the Norwegian Fjord Horse is one of its greatest qualities. Possessing a mild mannered, sensible, and predictable disposition has earned the Fjord a home with many families. It loves attention, is people-orientated,

and is happiest when working. Its eagerness to please makes it very trainable.

With its calm and noble character, the Fjord is often the breed winning in competition. It can be seen in dressage, jumping, reining, cutting, packing, both light and heavy harness work, combined driving events, weight pulling, logging, and farm work. It is now distinctly making its name as a top competitor in sanctioned equine events, such as in U.S. Equestrian Federation (USEF) level dressage, advanced level American Driving Society (ADS) combined driving events, elite carriage driving, and USA Equestrian approved hunter shows.

Norwegian people hold the Fjord in such high esteem that it is regarded as a national treasure and is one of the national symbols. The Norwegian Registry is called Norges Fjordhestlag.

The first Fjord, a colt, brought to the United States was in 1888 by publisher J. B. Lippincott. Warren Delano, uncle of President Franklin Delano Roosevelt, imported the first stallion and six mares in 1906. It was not until the 1950s and early 1960s when most of America's original foundation stock was imported, many bloodlines of which may be found in the pedigrees of current registrations.

In the 1980s, an evaluation committee began to pen the process for evaluations of Fjord horses in the United States through the training of qualified judges (evaluators). The first qualified evaluators went to the Fjord show in Norway in 1990. The first evaluation using the new U.S. rules was held in Libby, Montana, in 1994. Since then, the Fjord has progressed to the popular breed it is today in North America. The future looks bright for this beautiful, gentle horse.

Colors

In some countries, there is confusion as to which Fjord colors are genuine and accepted and what the correct terms should be. Norway has established fixed names of the different colors, which have been official since 1922.

Approximately 90 percent of all Fjord horses are brown dun in color. The other 10 percent can be red dun, gray (blue dun), white dun, or yellow (gold) dun. The brown dun, red dun (chestnut), and gray are also called "wild colors" because they are the same kind found on Przewalski's Horse, the wild horse of Central Asia—and the Tarpan, the European wild horse. In addition, yellow dun and white dun are genuine colors of the breed, although yellow dun is a very rare color. It is seldom seen even in Norway.

The white dun was the dominant color among the earliest registered Fjord horses in the Norwegian stud book. It is a diluted color and a variety of the brown dun color caused by a factor that reduces the production of pigment. The color of the body is an off-white or yellowish-white. It came into disrepute because early in the breed's history, no one knew how the different colors were inherited. Thus white duns were bred to white duns, which sometimes resulted in white and walleyed foals, called *kvit*.

In 1980, the Norges Fjordhestlag (Norwegian registry) acknowledged these five colors—brown dun, red dun, gray, yellow dun, and white dun—as the genuine and typical colors of the Fjord horse. This decision was supported by scientific fact.

There have been changing opinions on what color is the most fashionable, and for this reason, different kinds of dun colors have fluctuated in number at different times. The brown dun color in particular has increased in popularity recently, especially the lighter shades, and is now the dominating color. At present, there is interest in preserving all five dun colors.

Markings

Fjords also retain primitive markings, which include horizontal zebra stripes on the legs and a dorsal stripe that runs from the forelock, down the neck and back, and into the tail. Dark stripes may also be seen over the withers. Red duns have reddish-brown stripes and body markings. Gray duns have black or very dark gray stripes and markings. Pale or white dun is a very light body color with a black or gray stripe and markings. Yellow dun has a

darker yellow stripe and markings, and it may have a completely white forelock, mane, and tail.

The last marking is very seldom seen; some individuals can have small, brown spots on their body, for instance on their thigh or cheek. This marking is called *Njals-merke* (mark of Njal), after the foundation stallion of the modern Norwegian Fjord Horse, Njal 166, which had such spots on his cheeks.

The color of these markings differs according to the main body color. On a red or yellow dun horse with a monochrome forelock, mane, and tail, the dorsal stripe can be indistinct and zebra stripes may not be present at all. On very light shades of brown dun, zebra stripes can be very weak or lacking.

Zebra stripes have the same color, though often a lighter shade, as the mane and the other markings, and are more noticeable in the horse's summer coat. The stripes are most prominent and in greatest numbers on the forelegs. Foals lack zebra stripes, but they will appear by the first shedding of their foal-coat. In some cases, the zebra stripes are lacking on the grays and white duns. On these, the legs can be of the same color as the body, or dark up to the knees and hocks. A white star is acceptable only on mares, but not preferred.

Registry

According to the European Convention on domestic animals, the breed's motherland, Norway, has the responsibility to preserve and develop the Fjord horses' breed type. Around 1850, breeding and certification of the Fjord was instituted by the Norwegian government. The Norwegian Fjord Horse Registry maintains a stud book in the United States and works in conjunction with Europeans and the Fjord Horse International Association.

In the early 1980s, there were two U.S.-based Norwegian Fjord registries. They merged in 2003 to become the Norwegian Fjord Horse Registry, Inc., the official registry for Fjords based in the United States. It requires that Norwegian foals must have registered parents to be registered and have to be DNA tested to confirm parentage.

The ideal Fjord Horse is short coupled with good body depth and muscling. *Sandy North*

The Norwegian Fjord Horse Registry has an independent evaluation program in which horses are evaluated in-hand for conformation. Performance evaluations are also offered at Introductory and Advanced levels in three disciplines: Riding (English or western), Driving, and Draft. Although optional, evaluations are strongly encouraged, especially for breeding stock. Evaluation results are published in the Evaluation Record Book.

Standards

The breed standard is difficult to express in precise terminology. Norwegians describe their impression as "got mote," which means a horse should have a nice and pleasant appearance. Historically, Fjords have had different shapes, models, or body types, according to the particular needs of the time.

Body structure within the breed ranges the entire spectrum, from flatter, lighter muscling to a more round, heavier muscling. This wide genetic pool has produced the versatile Fjord of today, which is not a specialized breed, but has varying types for a wide variety of activities. All horses that meet the set conditions and demands of quality are equally acceptable.

Temperament: Norwegian Fjord Horses have a calm presence and a curious, active character with an obvious display of either masculine or feminine traits.

Size: Fjords generally range in size at maturity from 13.2 to 14.2 hands (54 to 58 inches) and weigh about 900 to 1,200 pounds, with a few individuals ranging outside these measurements.

General conformation: The head and neck

Fjord Horses are naturally adept for harness work in all kinds of conditions.
Else Bigton

Else Bigton 2006

should present an appearance of elegance without coarseness. The body is short coupled with good depth, large heart girth, and well developed muscles.

Conformation should be harmoniously balanced and must always be complemented by substance of body and ample bone. A combination of correct conformation, movement, and breed type is more important than extremes of beauty, elegance, and extravagant movement. What is most important is the ability of the horse to use and develop its inborn qualities.

Head: Medium-sized, with a broad, flat forehead, a straight or slightly dished profile, and good definition. Ears are small and truncated, wideset, and alert. Eyes are large, round, expressive, dark in color, well set on head. Jowls are well rounded and muscular. Jaws are quite large, with a definitive ridge and a good distance between them.

Muzzle: A wide and fleshy muzzle should be present, with large, softly elastic, outlined nostrils. On a mature Fjord Horse, incisors must be properly occluded. A malocclusion of less than or equal to one-quarter of a tooth width should be considered a minor fault, while more than one-quarter tooth width should be considered a major fault, regardless of sex.

Throatlatch: Slightly deeper than most other breeds, but must be sufficiently refined to allow proper flexing at the poll, while still providing for normal respiration. The poll should have sufficient length to allow for proper flexion. The neck bones approach the skull from behind the ears rather than inserted from below.

Neck: Is well muscled and crested. It should be supple, forming a natural arch, and appear rather heavy, but well raised and in proportion to the entire horse. The topline should be longer than the bottom line. Placement of the neck on the shoulder should run smoothly into the withers and chest, creating an upward- and outward-flexing image, giving the balance and carriage necessary to maintain the look of the Fjord horse.

Shoulder: Well muscled with good length and angulation. The shoulder and neck should be viewed as a balanced, functional unit.

Withers: Moderately defined and long, extending into the back.

Chest: Wide, demonstrating muscling proportional to gender and body size. Girth is deep, with an ample spring of rib to provide circulatory and respiratory capacity.

Back: Well muscled and broad; short to

The Fjord has a reputation for its agility as well as its power in a compact size. *Sandy North*

moderately long. (The back is considered moderately long when it has the same length as the shoulder.)

Loins: Well muscled with an even transition to the croup.

Croup: The shape of the hindquarter may vary, and it is important that the back, loins, croup, and quarters are in harmony. The tail should be set moderately high and carried naturally while at rest and in action.

Hips: Long, deep and well-developed; substantial and in proportion to the shoulder.

Thigh and gaskin: Strong and well muscled, carrying plenty of flesh; appear well muscled when viewed from behind.

Stifle: The stifle is located deep in the hindquarter with strength and full range of motion.

Hocks: Well developed, large in proportion to the horse, and positioned with a well-marked point.

Legs: Powerful with substantial bone. Should be correct and sound with a slightly longer forearm than cannon, well-defined joints, clean cannons, flat bone, and an appearance of overall substance and strength. When the legs are viewed from the side, front, and rear, they should be parallel and nearly vertical to the ground, except for the angulation of the pasterns. There is some feathering on the legs, but not profuse.

A lovely Fjord colt with a promising future. *Sandy North*

Pasterns: Should have moderately proportional length and angulation to provide reasonable flexion and support.

Hooves: Dense, round, large, and black or dark in color. Their attachment at the coronary band should be a continued angle of the pastern with proportional heel length. Fjords have excellent feet.

Movement: The Fjord horse's athletic action is straight, even, and true with good forward movement. The gaits are well balanced with a regular cadence and a length of stride in which the hind hoof print oversteps the front hoof print at the walk and trot. The Fjord has a ground-covering walk, powerful trot, and free moving canter.

- Walk: The Fjord horse is eager and efficient, moving in a four-beat cadence.

- Trot: It has a true two-beat diagonal gait. Being a powerful gait, the trot demonstrates the characteristic traits of speed, comfort, and athletic ability. The trot comes naturally and is the most favored gait of the horse.

- Canter: It should be balanced and free with good forward movement.

Markings and colors: The most common and/or desirable markings found on Fjords are: Primitive markings, such as small brown marks over the eyes and on the cheeks and thighs. Dark horizontal stripes on the legs, especially the forelegs. One or more dark stripes over the withers (very seldom seen).

Other markings that may occur are dark ear outlines and tips, a darker mid-section in the forelock,

Fjords have extraordinary power for their small size, being proportionally stronger than most horses. *Crown Jewel Resort Ranch*

mane and tail, and a full-length, darker dorsal stripe. Dark hoof color may be present and may range to amber in red and yellow dun horses. Some striping may occur.

Markings that are not typical for the breed should be avoided. A small star is acceptable only on mares, but is not preferred. Other white or flesh-colored markings are not accepted.

It is important to preserve all of the accepted Fjord horse colors and their variations. Coat colors and marking combinations are described as follows:

- Brown dun: coat color is pale yellow-brown and can vary from creamy yellow to nearly brown, with the dorsal stripe (forelock through tail) being black or dark brown
- Gray (blue dun): coat color ranges from light

Fjords are powerful enough for adults to ride, and many do. *Sandy North*

silver gray to dark slate gray; stripe in mane, dorsal stripe, and tail stripe are dark gray to black; muzzle is generally a darker shade of gray than body color

- Red dun: coat color is pale red-yellow in lighter or darker shades; the dorsal stripe is red or red-brown and always darker than the coat color, but never black. On the lighter shades of red duns, the forelock, mane, and tail can be completely white
- White dun: coat color is white or yellow-white; dorsal stripe is black or gray
- Yellow dun: coat color is yellow-white; dorsal stripe is a darker shade of yellow, but may be indistinct; forelock, mane, and tail may be completely white

Undesirable Aspects of Conformation

- Head: long or narrow-shaped head; high-set, or small (pig) eyes; white sclera around the eye; eye discoloration (walleye); extreme convex profile; small, underdeveloped jaws; long ears; narrow placement or poor angulation of ears (lop ears); small, pinched nostrils; improper occlusion (bite); lack of appropriate gender characteristics
- Neck: depression in front of withers (ewe neck); tied in too low on shoulder; thick throatlatch; heavy underside of the neck; insufficient muscling; lack of gender-related crest; length longer or shorter than body proportions; insufficient length of poll
- Legs and hooves: short, straight pasterns; broken-axis pastern; long, weak pasterns; over at the knees (buck knees); back at the knees (calf knees); offset knees; tied in at the knees; base wide or narrow; narrow, flat, or low heels; platter hooves; ringbone; laminitis (founder); spavin; curbs; stringhalt; straight or sickle hocks; cow hocks
- Withers: excessively round (mutton withers)
- Shoulder and forequarters: too straight (lack of angulation); upright shoulder; short arm

Fjords possess a charming, gentle disposition, making them a family favorite. *Paula Chmura*

or forearm; too wide, muscled, or narrow (lacking capacity and muscling)
- Body and hindquarters: long or low back; roach back; long, weak coupling; high hip/croup; too narrow (lacking capacity and muscling); steep croup; rafter hips; wry or low-set tail
- Movement: irregular stride and/or cadence; extravagant action; short stride behind; overreaching; forging; winging; paddling
- Gender: retained testicles (one or both); malformed vulva

Credit: Norwegian Fjord Horse Registry

PERCHERON

Percheron horse, showing its strong musculature. *Daniel Johnson*

Percheron Horse Association of America
P.O. Box 141, 10330 Quaker Road
Fredericktown, Ohio 43019
www.percheronhorse.org

The Percheron is an intelligent, hardworking, classic draft that can easily get a job done. It is a versatile athlete that readily adapts to varying climates and conditions. It has the strength to pull heavy loads and the graceful style to pull a fine carriage. The Percheron can be ridden, and some have been known to make fine jumpers. Long before the invention of the motorized truck or tractor, Percherons provided the power

to build and feed many nations. Now this noble horse provides the power, substance, beauty, and style as America's work and recreation horse for the twenty-first century.

History

As with any ancient breed, the origins of the Percheron are shrouded in myth, as the foundations of the breed precede any documentation by several centuries.

The breed derives its name from the area that served as its cradle. Le Perche is an old province about 55 by 66 miles in size and located some 50 miles southwest of Paris. It borders Normandy to

A six-horse team of Percherons displays their power. *Shutterstock*

the northeast and Beauce to the east. It is a gently rolling, well-watered, and fertile place with a benign climate, pre-eminently suited to the raising of livestock. It was thus ideally suited to capitalize on trade opportunities as they arose following the Middle Ages and well into the modern era.

From the earliest known times, the people of Le Perche were producers of horses, but not often buyers; they were always free sellers to the adjacent areas and, ultimately, the world. In the matter of breeding horses, they were a world unto themselves. They prized their horses and entire families cared for them, causing the horses to develop docility and affection toward people. This is similar to the Arabian heritage, a breed that also played a role in the development of the Percheron.

By the time of the Crusades, the Percheron was widely recognized as an outstanding horse for its substance and soundness, as well as for its characteristic beauty and style. Traditionally, it has been a breed with a preponderance of grays, confirmed by old paintings and crude drawings from the Middle Ages. French knights were almost always portrayed on gray or white chargers that had considerable substance for that time, yet without coarseness.

By the seventeenth century, horses produced in Le Perche had attained widespread fame and were in demand for many different uses. When the day of the warhorse was over, their color, substance, and style were made to order for heavy stagecoaches in France. There were three turnpikes from Paris to the coastal ports of Normandy that ran through Le Perche, so the French did not have to look far. They needed a horse that could trot from seven to ten miles per hour and had the endurance to do it all day and night. The Percheron of this time showed less scale, usually 15 to 16 hands high, and easily adapted to pulling at a trot, the heavy mail and passenger coaches for the kings of France. The light colored grays and whites were preferred because of their visibility at night. Percherons were called a diligence horse, as the stagecoaches were called diligences.

When rail replaced the diligences, omnibus horses were needed in Paris and other French cities. The job called for a little heavier horse, thus the breeders of the Le Perche altered their local breed enough to do the job. At the same time, faster and stronger horses were replacing oxen in agriculture. An example was the nearby Beauce, known as the granary of France, which needed a bigger horse for farming. Also, as trade and commerce grew, so did the need for horses of heavy draft to move large loads from docks and railheads. These businesses needed an even larger horse than the farmers, so again, the breeders of Le Perche complied. Another change to the Percheon type occurred in the early nineteenth century, when the French government established its own Percheron stud at Le Pin for the development of army mounts.

About 1823, a famous foundation horse named Jean le Blanc was foaled in Le Perche, and all of today's Percheron bloodlines trace directly to him. He was a white stallion that greatly improved the breed more than any other and was descended from the famous Arabian stallion, Gallipoly. A great number of horses raised in Le Perche over the next fifty years had Jean le Blanc as an ancestor. This influence of the Arabian horse, along with selective breeding, led to the superiority of the Percheron, which surpassed all other draft breeds in excellence.

From warhorse (heavy saddler) to diligence horse (heavy coacher or light draft) to the true heavy draft, the breeders of Le Perche sculpted away on their beloved indigenous breed for hundreds of years, altering the animal to meet the demands of the times and to entice the buyer.

In the United States
The decades of the 1870s and 1880s were years of massive importations from Europe to the United

States. Literally thousands of draft-type horses, especially stallions, were imported primarily from France and Great Britain. As the trade grew and importers ventured farther inland into France in search of the best horses, the little province of Le Perche and its superior draft horses were discovered.

The United States was experiencing the same changes as Europe: from stagecoach to rail, from agrarian to industrial, and from sail to steam. Horse stock had been heavily depleted because of the American Civil War in the 1860s. The West was being settled, its cities were growing, and there came the same cry for bigger, stronger horses than before, just as in continental Europe. The only source of draft stock at the time was from western Europe.

Percherons were first imported to the United States in 1839 by Edward Harris of Moorestown, New Jersey. Then the Percheron stallions Normandy and Louis Napoleon were imported to Ohio in 1851. Louis Napoleon was later sold to someone in Illinois and wound up in the hands of the Dillon family, which was instrumental in forming the Percheron Association.

The age of purebred livestock had dawned, with stud books and herd books rapidly spawning on both sides of the Atlantic. In the winter of 1875–1876 in Chicago, Illinois, the National Association of Importers and Breeders of Norman Horses was launched, becoming the first purebred livestock association formed in the United States. By the time the second volume of the stud book was published, the name was altered to the Percheron-Norman Society, and in a matter of just a few years, the hyphenated version disappeared to become simply Percheron.

Percherons quickly became America's favorite horse. In the decade of the 1880s, almost 5,000 stallions and over 2,500 mares were imported to the United States from France, mostly from Le Perche, which exceeded importations from Great Britain and the rest of continental Europe. This lasted until the financial panic of 1893. There were virtually no importations from 1894 to 1898, and breeding in United States came to a standstill. Much of the seed stock from the earlier period was lost or squandered, as people were either too broke or too cautious to spend the money they had.

Importations resumed in 1898, averaging about seven hundred head annually from that time to 1905. In 1906 they reached the enormous number of thirteen thousand stallions and two hundred mares. In 1905, Percheron breeders again met in Chicago and formed the Percheron Society of America. Annual registrations reached ten thousand per year by the next decade. The Percheron quickly regained its status as the favorite of both the American farmer, and the teamster who moved freight on the nation's city streets.

With World War I in 1914, the days of large horse importations were forever gone. With the role of tractors and trucks in the cities, the United States equine population crested in 1920. The draft horse was subjected to a losing battle, particularly in the cities. It held its own on the farms in the 1920s, but even there, interest was waning. However, in the 1930s, corn was cheap, and farmers were broke, so drafts were once again in demand. Registrations more than doubled in a few short years.

In 1934, the Percheron Society of America discontinued when the Percheron Horse Association of America was founded. Registrations in 1937 reached 4,611, a figure not seen in over a decade. Percherons were so popular that by 1930, the government census showed that there were three times as many Percherons as the other four draft breeds combined (Belgian, Shire, Clydesdale, and Suffolk).

The tides turned again during the 1940s, with the invention of the modern farm tractor, and the use of drafters declined, leading to the near extinction of the Percheron. After World War II, the greatest liquidation of draft horse stock in history began and kept right on going through the 1950s, until drafts were no longer considered worth counting in the official U.S. agriculture census of the United States. As the country modernized

and mechanized, the Percheron was all but forgotten. The low point in Percheron registrations came in 1954, when just eighty-five head were recorded. The term "endangered species" would have been appropriate, though it was not yet in common use.

It was a relatively small handful of farmers dedicated to the breed and unwilling to relinquish its equine heritage who kept the Percheron alive. They were aided by the thousands of Amish farmers throughout the country who stuck with the draft horse as their source of motive power. They kept the breed alive through the next twenty years of the draft horse depression, which lasted through the 1950s and 1960s.

By the late 1960s, a renaissance in the draft horse business began, as Americans rediscovered draft horse usefulness. They enjoyed the pleasure of working with Percherons on non-farm tasks, and the horses proved to be very handy in saving young trees in the smaller woodlot operation while extracting other trees. They did not need a wide road to get to a dense wood site and could work where even the most modern tractors failed. Their independent "four-wheel-drive" conquered mud and snow to the shame of all manmade machines. Additionally, equine shows welcomed them back, and a growing recreation business discovered their attractiveness at ski lodges and similar places. Thus their comeback involved a combination of niche markets.

The Breed Today

At its height, the Percheron Horse Association of America registered in excess of ten thousand head per year and was the largest draft horse association in the world. It set many of the registration standards that are still in widespread use in other livestock breed registries.

Percherons are now back on small farms and working in the forests. Thousands of Percherons are used for recreation, such as hayrides, sleigh rides, and parades. They are shown in competitive hitching, halter, and riding classes at many state and county fairs across the country. They are used in advertising and promotions and are a common sight on streets, as the carriage business has flourished in many of the larger cities.

The resurgence in numbers and values has been nothing short of amazing. Registrations totaled 1,088 in 1988, and in 2006, there were 2,032 registrations from forty-three states and Canada. The Percheron Horse Association of America, whose membership includes all fifty states, has a National Show and sponsors a World Percheron Congress every four years, which had its thirteenth show in 2008.

This is not, as was sometimes true in the old days, a case of a few people importing and recording hundreds of horses. The ownership of the breed is in many hands for many uses.

In the 1930s, the conventional wisdom was that the draft horse's battle with the truck and tractor was lost completely. So a deliberate effort to downsize the breed was undertaken. The appeal of the big hitches has reversed that trend, and the demand for draft horses now reaches in several directions at the same time. The times call for a versatile horse. At that, the Percheron has had a lot of practice.

Standards

Percherons need to have registered parents to be eligible for registration. Those from foreign countries need to be registered in their country before they can be registered in the Percheron Horse Association of America.

Temperament: The Percheron has a very pleasing disposition. It is proud, alert, intelligent, and a willing worker. It is also expected to be of marked tractability and an easy keeper.

Color: Percherons are usually black or gray, but there are also sorrels, bays, roans, and other various colors. Many Percherons have white markings on the head and feet, but excessive white is undesirable.

Size: Percherons can range in height from 15 to 19 hands, but most are between 16.2 and 17.3 hands. They can weigh up to 2,600 pounds, with

Percherons have a more classic styled head than most drafts. *Lincoln Rogers/Shutterstock*

the average being around 1,900.

Head: The Percheron head and neck are the most attractive of its draft horse characteristics. Good Percherons have large and full prominent eyes, a broad and full forehead, and a straight face. Their strong jaw and refined ears, attractively set and carried with animation, suggests an Arabian ancestry. Stallions should have a ruggedness about the head, and mares should have a feminine look.

Body: The ideal horse should have a fairly long, level croup with a big, round hip. It should be close coupled and wide and deep through the chest, with plenty of back rib. The muscles of the arms, forearms, croup, and gaskins are especially emphasized in a good drafter. The Percherhon is noted for heavy muscling on the lower thighs and for an aspect of unusual ruggedness and power. Also characteristic of the Percheron is the high quality of the feet and legs.

Movement: Ease and balance of gait is essential. A characteristic of the Percheron is its clean action.

Credit: Percheron Horse Association of America

PINTO DRAFT HORSE

Pinto Draft Registry, Inc.
P.O. Box 738
Estancia, New Mexico 87016
www.pinto-draft-registry.com

The Pinto Draft Horse is a beautiful horse of Pinto color. In breeding, is half to full draft horse. The combination of Pinto coloring and draft substance was for emphasis on color and strength in a magnificent, flashy draft horse. It is ideal for those who appreciate the power and full body of a draft, together with eye-catching spots.

Mention of Pinto Draft Horses can be found throughout European history and date back to medieval times, when they were used as warhorses. Knights rode them into battle and used them for jousts.

Queen Elizabeth II of the United Kingdom has had Pinto Draft Horses at her court and in her breeding program. They were used to carry two big drums in parades and special events. During these parades, the horses were ridden with a big drum on each side, which were played by the rider. The most famous of these horses is the 17 hand Gypsy Drum Horse, Galway Warrior, which stood at stud in the Queen's royal stable for several years before he was imported to the United States in 2002 when he was nineteen years old. He now resides in Colorado, where he stands at stud along with a Gypsy Vanner stallion.

In the United States, the horses are known as Gypsy Drum Horses and stand 16 hands and taller. They are eligible for registration as both a Drum Horse and Pinto Draft Horse.

Pinto colored draft horses in the United States can be traced back to the 1920s, and were called "Spots" by the old-timers. In the 1920s and 1930s, these horses were used for farming. Originally, there was no registry for these beautiful colored draft horses. Like the other draft breeds, they became fewer in number as the tractor took over farming.

Recent History

Horse breeders Lowell and Gayle Clark had been breeding drafts for Pinto color since the mid 1970s. In 1977, they bought their first team of

The Pinto Draft is known for its willingness to work, endurance, and great heart. *Gayle Clark/ Pinto Draft Registry*

Combining color and great strength, Pinto Drafts are magnificent flashy horses. *Ginny Gable/ Pinto Draft Registry*

black, tobiano draft horses, Dick and Jane, and used the team in pulling contests in Colorado and New Mexico. The horses were an impressive team, standing at 16.3 hands, and their flashy coloring turned many heads. Dick and Jane were Colorado State Pulling Horses from 1978 to 1980, when the Clarks moved to New Mexico. The horses drew much interest in colored drafts, resulting in many questions about the origins of their coloring. Dick and Jane were traced back to their previous owner, Lynn Roller of Iowa, who at one time had twenty teams of Pinto spotted drafts. Dick and Jane were half brother and sister, and their common sire was a black Percheron stallion that was one of the finest Percheron horses in the United States.

In 1980, the Clarks bought a seven-month-old stallion named Pecos Chief at a horse auction in Kansas. His dam was a big, black tobiano draft mare, and his sire was a black Percheron. In 1981, the Clarks showed Pecos Chief at the tender age of one at the National Western Stock Show in Denver, where he won third place in the Open Draft Halter Class, competing among twelve other draft horses.

That is when the queries really started coming: "Wow! What a beautiful horse!" "What kind is it?" "There should be a registry for these magnificent horses." Wherever the Clarks went, they heard these were familiar comments, which showed there was an obvious interest in the horses like this throughout the United States.

Dick, Jane, and Pecos Chief were used in pulling contests and shown at many fairs in Colorado. The biggest show was the National Western Stock Show in Denver, where the Clarks' horses drew great interest. The Clarks drove a Pinto draft, four-up team (four-horse hitch), in the Great Circus Parade in Milwaukee, Wisconsin, from 1993 through 1997. They also drove their team in many other parades, such as the Scottsdale, Arizona, parade, the largest of all horse parades west of the Mississippi River. As always, their horses drew much attention, and the main question was, "When will there be a registry for these beautiful horses?"

The question was finally answered when the Clarks founded the registry for Pinto Spotted Draft Horses in 1995, with some help from Leonard and Kittie Tostenson of Minnesota. The Clarks promoted the breed with their stallion, Pecos Chief. It was also promoted through the Horse Progress Days in Indiana and Ohio and at the first-ever Equitana USA, held in 1996 in Louisville, Kentucky.

Their efforts were successful, as the horses' presence at these events really sparked interest in the Pinto Spotted Draft. At the end of the registry's third year, there were 234 horses registered, and by 2000, there were 1,331 registered. A top-selling stallion brought $14,500 at the Kalona Draft Horse Sale in Iowa, and the top-selling mare sold for $95,000.

In 2000, the registry split, and the Pinto Draft Registry (PDR), Inc., was founded in 2002 by Gayle Clark, which accepted full and half draft horses of Pinto color. PDR is a color registry and was established to promote beautiful draft horses of Pinto color.

Outstanding Pinto Drafts

Pecos Chief held the title of Supreme Champion Stallion at the New Mexico State Fair for many years. This was an award for the top winner of points in all classes, from Halter to show and Fun classes. His get also won many show awards. After turning twenty-eight years old in 2008, Pecos Chief produced a lifetime of show wins and outstanding progeny, several of which were homozygous offspring. (This means they carry the dominant genes that will produce coat pattern no matter what color horse they are bred to, whether solid or pinto marked.)

The Clarks now have six generations of Pinto Drafts of Percheron breeding in their horses. Pecos Chief and his offspring—many of which are all over the United States—have proven themselves in the show ring and in breeding. In 1998, Peter Stone made a model horse of Pecos Chief, and the following year he made the model of Pecos Banner's Papoose, a granddaughter of Pecos Chief. They are now collector models.

Today in the show ring, the Half-Draft/Sport colored horses are making a name for themselves.

At this time they can only be shown in Open and Fun classes, like Farm Team Race, Obstacle Course, and Farm classes. Open classes can be any of the show classes identified as that. In 2002, there was a show in Texas just for the Pinto/Spotted Draft, and a year later, the Florida State Fair added show classes for the Pinto/Spotted Draft for the first time. Little by little, they are being added into the show world.

Demand for Pinto Drafts is becoming more evident. One of the Clarks' horses, a bay tobiano named Toby, was trained as a hunter and vaulting horse and sold for $20,000. He was a three-quarter draft gelding whose bay dam was half Quarter Horse and half Percheron. Breyer made a model of him, also.

One of Pecos Chief sons, Kashari, sold for $20,000 in 1995 after he won the Training Level at an Arizona show. He was trained as a three-day event horse and was out of a half Appaloosa, half draft mare. This stunning black tobiano was sold before the registry began.

The breed is certain to grow in popularity in the years to come. There is much interest in the Pinto Draft and the Half-Draft/Sport Horse today. Many like the color of the Pinto on a 17-plus hand horse weighing 1,800-plus pounds. It is an awesome sight.

Standards

Horses accepted in the registry must be half of any of the six draft breeds, which are Percheron, Belgian, Clydesdale, Shire, Suffolk Punch, and American Cream. The half division must be that of one-half of one of these draft breeds. The light horse breeds accepted for cross-breeding are Thoroughbred, American Quarter Horse, Pinto, Paint, Morgan, Arabian, any sport horse, Friesian and three gaited Saddlebred, and Gypsy Drum Horse. No Appaloosa, Walking Horse, Racking Horse, American Saddlebred, Standardbred, pony, or donkey bloodlines are allowed. Stallions must have a DNA test done and have a breeding report on file with PDR before their get can be registered.

Increasingly, Pinto Drafts are enjoyed for riding. This is a foundation stallion. *Ginny Gable/Pinto Draft Registry*

There are three divisions:

- **Division A:** Pinto Draft—has seven-eighths or more of draft breeding and has a Pinto spotting pattern. It must mature to 15 hands or taller. With one generation of pedigree, the papers will read: A-Pinto Draft. If the pedigree is unknown, the papers will read A-Pinto Draft Grade.
- **Division B:** Pinto Half-Draft/Sport Horse—has at least one-half, and up to seven-eighths, draft breeding and has a Pinto spotting pattern. Must be 15 hands or taller when mature.
- **Division C:** Breeding Stock are horses that qualify for Divisions A and B, but are horses of solid color. They can be full Pinto Draft or Pinto Half-Draft/Sport Horse. The papers will be marked as stated previously.

Geldings will be accepted under Divisions A and B, but no solid colored geldings will be accepted under Division C.

The Pinto Draft should have conformation that closely reflects the draft type they most resemble—Percheron, Belgian, Suffolk, Shire, or Clydesdale type.

Generally, the frame should be large, supported by clean dense bone and strong muscled forearms and thighs. Legs are placed well under the horse. They have intelligent heads with active ears and powerful, arching necks, which are clean cut at the throat. Shoulders tend to be upright, suitable for power rather than action, and the back is short and strong. Ribs spring high from the backbone. The hindquarters are long and smooth to the root of the tail, which springs up higher than other breeds. The hip bones are wide apart and smoothly covered; the croup is usually level. Depth and thickness from the withers to the legs are essential, and should be deep in the flank and over the heart.

Most of the horses in the draft divisions have their tails docked, but it is up to the individual owner's discretion. The half-draft horses' tails are left long.

The average height of the Pinto Draft is 15 to 17 hands. They weigh from 1,600 to 1,900 pounds.

The Pinto Draft Horse is impressive with its flashy color and draft substance. *Ginny Gable/Pinto Draft Registry*

Color Requirements

Pinto Drafts are most often tobiano or overo spotted in pattern and can also be a combination of the two patterns, called tovero. Any base color is acceptable, though the most popular is black, bay, or sorrel. The PDR is a color registry, thus the horses must display Paint or Pinto color markings.

The three recognized color patterns are:

Tobiano: A horse with tobiano (toe-bee-ah´-no) spotting appears to be white with large spots of color often overlapping on the horse, with a greater percentage of color than white. Spots of color typically originate from the head, chest, flank, and buttock and often include the tail. Legs are generally white, giving the appearance of a white horse with large, flowing spots of color.

Overo: An overo spotted horse appears to be a colored horse with white markings. These spots of white appear to be jagged and originate on the horse's side or belly, spreading toward the neck, tail, legs, and back. Color appears to frame the white spots, thus an overo often has a dark tail, mane, legs, and back line. Bald or white faces often accompany this pattern. Some overos show white legs along with splashy white markings, seemingly made up of many round lacy spots. The location of the white is generally not the same on overo horses as tobiano, although white legs appear to be more common. White almost never crosses the back on an overo.

Tovero: A horse that shows characteristics of both the tobiano and overo.

The Pinto Colored Draft has a splendid disposition. It exhibits a ready willingness to work, great endurance, and a quality known as heart, for which it is well known. It is used for agricultural work, pleasure driving, parades, commercial carriage pulling, showing, logging, and riding, as well as a vaulting horse (broad-backed circus type horses used with gymnastic maneuvers).

In general, the Pinto Draft is an easy keeper, like that of many draft horses. It exhibits the mild, laidback temperament of the draft horse that makes them so desirable. Their best quality is the conformation and easygoing attitude of the draft horse.

Credit: Pinto Draft Registry, Inc.

SHIRE

A beautiful Shire colt with well-set eyes and ears of good length. *Des Surles*

American Shire Horse Association
1211 Hill Harrell Road
Effingham, South Carolina 29541
www.shirehorse.org

The Shire is a strikingly beautiful horse with its arched, massive neck, and classic movement. It is one of the largest horses in the world and yet probably the gentlest. Reaching as tall as 19 hands, the Shire is a full-bodied horse with amazing strength. It easily stands out from other drafts with its stunning colors, usually accentuated with profuse white leg feathering and a fine head. Many Shires are a true black, but vibrant bays and an occasional gray can also be seen.

People are often attracted to the Shire because it is big and impressive and has those wonderful feathered feet. But they fall in love with the Shire because of its heart and kindness.

The Shire holds its value due to the fact that it is a rare breed, but those who really know the Shire mostly appreciate the reserved pride and self assurance it possesses without any trace of arrogance. It is a calm, majestic, and noble animal.

History

The Shire is one of the oldest of the defined draft breeds. It originated in the shires of England and traces back to the time of Roman occupation of the island. Records from the Romans praised the native island horses for their conformation and constitution.

Records in the early medieval period show there were importations of several Flemish stallions from what is now the Netherlands. These were described by horsemen of the time as being black in color, with white on their faces and heavy feathering on their legs. When crossed with the native island stock, a tall, rangy, muscular horse with broad, flat limbs was the result.

These crosses became English warhorses from medieval times to the beginning of the Renaissance period. This was verified by paintings dating back to the fifteenth century depicting Shires of perfect form. Several English monarchs issued laws mandating strict regulations for their breeding, which required that the noble class keep and breed quality stock while culling out inferior horses. In an effort to increase the size of the animals, Henry VIII ordered the destruction of all horses under 15.2 hands. The resulting breed was big and strong enough to carry over four hundred pounds of knight and armor into battle. This powerful warhorse was considered the best in Europe, and anyone exporting one to the Continent committed treason, punishable by death.

With the introduction of more modern warfare techniques, the need for warhorses went into decline, but the horses did not disappear. With the beginning of the Industrial Revolution in the early 1800s, the horses now known as Shires became nothing less than national treasures to the businessmen of England.

Every type of raw material came to England's ports for manufacturing, and they needed to be hauled from the ports to the manufacturing cities and back again. Roads at that time went through muddy fens and over rolling hills and were often nothing more than dirt tracks. The loads were heavy, necessitating a horse of enormous bulk, prodigious strength, and quiet demeanor. The pride of the businessman required a horse of style to pull his wagons with alacrity at delivering the goods to their destination on time. And so the modern Shire was created.

The first organization for Shires, the English Cart Horse Society, was established in London in 1877 and printed its first stud book in 1880. A few years later, the name was changed to its current one,

the Shire Horse Society (SHS). The first predominant stallion recognized by the SHS was a horse named Honest Tom, whose likeness is used as the symbol of the American Shire Horse Association (ASHA), which was established in 1885.

The Shire was imported rather heavily into the United States at that time, both to establish the breed and to be crossbred with the existing stock to improve its quality. An acknowledged equine expert of the time wrote, "I have had opportunity for extended personal observations and inquiry as to the result of crossing them [Shires] on native American mares, as well as on the grades and crosses of other breeds, and the evidence is of unqualified satisfaction. They have been found competent to transmit and impress their own characteristics with a remarkable certainty, and the name 'Shire Horse' has become a synonym for strength, constitution, energy, and endurance."

At that time in the United States, the Shire played a role in helping to establish the major draft breeds seen today by adding size and temperament to the settler's existing stock. These breeds would return the favor after the drop in Shire numbers with the advent of the tractor and semi, but especially after World War II.

In the aftermath of World War II, the Shire population in England was decimated by the export of horses to feed the people of the Continent. If not for a few breweries in England that continued to make their London deliveries by Shire (and still do so today), a few dedicated enthusiasts, and the royal family, the English would have lost the breed entirely. Numbers of Shires worldwide became frightfully small.

In the United States, the ASHA went dormant, but in the mid 1960s a group of ranchers in Idaho pooled its resources and bought the last remaining Shire herd of any size left in the United States. With the help of a Clydesdale breeder, the old stud books were brought up to date. In 1968, the first Shire to be imported from the United Kingdom since before World War II was sent to Idaho, and the breed began to make steady gains in popularity.

Correct rear quarters on a Shire: long legs with heavy bone, set wide and full of muscle. *Solveig Nesse*

Since the gene pool was so small, a grading up registry was implemented. Draft mares of other breeds were bred to fully registered Shire stallions. The resulting fillies were registered as half Shires and bred back to a Shire stallion and so on. When the concentration of Shire blood reached fifteen-sixteenths, the next generation's foals were fully registered. The ASHA closed this book in the late 1980s. Thus, the draft breeds that benefited from an infusion of Shire blood before World War II returned the favor by reestablishing the breed in the United States and abroad.

Shires Today

Although it is still in the rare breeds registry, the Shire is flourishing today. While making its comeback from very few numbers, the Shire remains one of the most genetically sound breeds to be found. It is used for work, pleasure, and once again, to help establish other breeds. Shires are adept in harness for the farm and ranch. No matter how cold it gets, they can handle it. In their shaggy winter coats (and sometimes even in summer), they frequently sport the unique trait of an upper lip moustache, a comical and endearing feature.

The Shire is an outstanding worker in agriculture as a heavy draft horse and is immensely strong. The average adult Shire weighs about one hundred pounds per hand and is capable of hauling a five ton load. They have excellent "cordy" limbs (having tendons that are well separated and defined beneath the knees and hocks).

Shires haul everything from garbage wagons in small towns, to tourists in the ski areas or the United States' honored dead at Arlington National Cemetery. Under saddle, they led the inaugural parade of the first President Bush and also work as patrol horses in the streets of some towns. Their kind gentility makes them ideal therapy horses. They can hunt foxes or take a favorite aunt for a stroll on the trail.

When crossbred to light horses, the result can be a spectacular athlete with a calm, clever mind that enjoys work and usually gives more than is asked,

which actually can lead to problems. Shires and Shire sport horses are slow to fully mature, taking six years to do so. Since they usually are so willing and athletic, it is very tempting to push them too fast in their training or use, thus causing injuries.

Registry

The ASHA provides a National Show and Regional shows. Shires can now be seen in draft competitions and at American Driving Society events. Beside the regular registry, the ASHA has established the Shire Sporthorse Registry that accepts the offspring of a registered Shire and a light horse. These horses have also been accepted into various warmblood societies and are very competitive.

Due to many factors, the modern ASHA has always been on the cutting edge of equine technology. It was the first association in the world to require parent verification of all foals registered in its book, first by blood factors and also by DNA, when it became available. Artificial insemination has long been accepted and practiced by North American Shire breeders. One of the first successful equine embryo transfers resulted in a Shire colt in 1985.

Standards

The Shire stallion should possess a masculine head and good neck crest, with sloping, not upright, shoulders, running well into the back. The back should be short and well coupled with the loins. The tail should be set well up, but the horse should not be goose-rumped. Both head and tail should be carried erect. The ribs should be well sprung, not flat sided, with good middle that generally denotes good constitution.

The most essential parts of a stallion are his feet and joints; the feet should have open heels, big around the coronets, with plenty of length in the pasterns. When in motion, he should go with force, using both knees and hocks, which should be kept close together. He should go straight and true, before and behind.

Mares should conform to the stallion standards,

A magnificent Shire stallion boldly travels with force, using both knees and hocks. *Des Surles*

except that they may be slightly smaller with a feminine and matronly appearance. A mare should have plenty of room to carry a foal. Geldings should conform to stallion standards, with the exception of the thick, masculine neck.

- Color: black, brown, bay, gray, or chestnut are the preferred colors. Excessive white markings and roaning are undesirable.
- Height: Minimum 16.2 hands and upwards, with the average being 17.1 hands
- Head: Long and lean, neither too large nor too small, with long neck in proportion to the body; large jaw bone should be avoided
- Eyes: Large, well set and alert; wall eyes should be avoided
- Nose: Nostrils thin and wide, lips together, and nose slightly convex
- Ears: Long, lean, sharp, and sensitive
- Throat: Clean cut and lean
- Shoulder: Deep, oblique, and wide enough to support a collar
- Neck: Long, slightly arched, and well set on to give the horse a commanding appearance
- Girth: Deep, with adequate width in proportion with the rest of the body
- Back: Short, strong, and muscular; should not be dipped or roached
- Loins: Standing well up, denoting a strong constitution
- Fore end: Wide across the chest, with legs

well under the body and well developed in muscle; otherwise, action is impeded

- Hindquarters: Long and sweeping, wide and full of muscle, and well let down toward the thighs
- Ribs: Round, deep, well sprung, and not flat
- Forelegs: Should be as straight as possible down to the pasterns
- Pasterns: Fairly long and sloped at about a 45-degree angle
- Hind legs: Hocks should be clean, broad, deep, flat, and wide when viewed from the side; set at a correct angle for leverage, in line with the hindquarters, and of heavy bone; puffy and sickle hocks are to be avoided; the leg sinews should be clean cut, hard, and clear of the cannon bone
- Feet: Moderately deep and wide at the heels; coronets open
- Feather: Fine, straight, and silky

Class Requirements

All stallions and foals must be registered. Mares registered as three-quarter Shire or seven-eighth Shire may be shown with fully registered mares. Geldings registered as three-quarters, seven-eighths, or fifteen-sixteenths Shire may be shown with fully registered geldings. Geldings not registered must be of Shire type to be shown in a grade gelding class. All horses shown in group classes must be registered (get, produce, mare and foal, herd). Shire- cross sport horses are not eligible to show in draft performances, unless permitted by the host show.

Performance classes can include cart, hitch, and unicorn classes where Clydesdales can be included to complete the hitch. Shire Under Saddle is another performance class.

For In-Hand classes, the handler can carry a show stick, often used to guide the horse. A trailer is a designated person who follows about ten feet behind the horse.

The horse's front legs should be set up even and square to the shoulder; hind legs should be close together and one hind leg can be slightly in front of the other. It is suggested that legs be wrapped from mid-cannon to pasterns prior to the class, and then removed just before the class to allow "spats" to lie down and emphasize the bone and angles of the lower legs. (This is unlike some draft breeds, where feathering from the hock on down are groomed to be full.)

Tails should be braided or put up in some manner so there is no untied hair, giving the judge an unobstructed view of the hindquarters. Scotch knots are traditional for docked tails, and French braids or scotch knots for long tails. Manes should be rolled or plaited on stallions and geldings over one year of age for Halter classes. A bridle path can be clipped in. Pulling of the mane to approximately one-third of the width of the neck is also a standard practice. Braiding manes on mares or foals is optional. Braiding of forelocks is also optional, but they are not shaved for the show ring.

Shires are traditionally shown in russet or black show bridles, but white or other colors may be used. Stallion girths (rollers) are encouraged on stallions over two years of age, as they make stallions easier to manage and enhance their appearance.

Over-shoeing is discouraged, but older horses should be shod. Hooves should not be blackened or whitened. Dye or other substances should not be used to alter the coat color or markings.

Credit: Des Surles and the American Shire Horse Association

SUFFOLK

The Suffolk is a chestnut-colored, full-bodied horse, with massive bone and great muscling. *American Suffolk Horse Association*

The American Suffolk Horse Association
4240 Goehring Road
Ledbetter, Texas 78946
www.suffolkpunch.com

Today's best known breeds of draft horses are said to have descended from the great war-horses of medieval times. While these titans clashed in mortal combat, however, the quiet farmers of eastern England went about developing their own breed of heavy horse, the Suffolk, sometimes called the Suffolk Punch. Today, the Suffolk is the least known of the major drafts in the United States, and yet it has perhaps the most appealing qualities to a breeder than any of the better known draft horses. It is outstanding as a utility animal and has beautiful conformation. This versatile horse is being both shown and used to perform the agricultural tasks for which it was bred.

History

The homeland of the Suffolk Horse is Norfolk and Suffolk Counties of England. These counties are bordered by the North Sea to the north, east, and south, and by the Fens, an area of low marshy land, to the west. Isolated from their neighbors, the farmers of Suffolk independently developed breeds of livestock to fit their particular way of life. To plow the heavy clay soil, they needed an agricultural horse that not only was powerful, but also had stamina, good health, life longevity, and docility. Accordingly, these fine husbandmen produced the Suffolk horse and bred into it these attributes.

Suffolk farmers used their horses to till and harvest their own lands, so seldom did they have horses to sell. This not only kept the Suffolk relatively unknown, but also pure, remaining unchanged and true to its original purpose—to be a strong and faithful worker for its master.

Of all the draft breeds, the Suffolk is one of the oldest in existence, with records dating back to 1880. Crisp's Horse of Ufford, the foundation stallion of the entire breed, was foaled in 1768.

The first Suffolks were imported to North America in the 1880s and the American Suffolk Horse Association was founded shortly thereafter.

The Suffolk in North America was hard hit by the headlong mechanization of the post–World War II period. When tractors were favored over horses, numbers dwindled. Although the breed had made great strides in popularity during the 1930s, the Suffolk still did not have the numerical base necessary to withstand the onslaught of the 1950s. For a few years, the American Suffolk Horse Association ceased to function. Then in the early 1960s, as the draft horse market began to recover, a few widely scattered breeders who had kept faith with their Suffolks reorganized.

The early 1970s saw some outstanding importations from England. While interest in the draft horse in general was expanding, the demand for Suffolks also began to increase. The early 1980s saw an encouraging increase in the number of Suffolks registered, along with more excellent importations from England. With continuing importations and a substantial increase in the number of registered Suffolks, the 1990s showed tremendous progress for the breed.

Today, there are between 1,500 and 2,000 Suffolks in North America. This is an approximate number because some are never registered for a variety of reasons. On average, the association registers one hundred horses a year, but it has only been in the last five years that it has hit the triple digits. With less than three hundred Suffolks in England and less than twenty-five hundred in global population, it is listed in the critical category with the Equus Survival Trust.

Characteristics

There is a consistency like none other in the Suffolk horse. Every Suffolk is a chestnut color and there is great uniformity in the breed type. The Suffolk appears to be shorter legged, but this is only due to the great muscling of the upper legs. Its back is short and strong, and the horse has massive bone and impressive strength. The Suffolk body type is in perfect harmony with all its parts, producing a very balanced horse. Its rounded, full bodied structure and brawn is utilized efficiently to get a job done. It is not an unusually tall or rangy horse, but carries the immense bulk of a true draft breed.

Suffolks are excellent workhorses, parade horses, or show horses. They have never been bred for high knee action. Their short cannon bone combined with a long forearm creates a wonderful, ground covering stride.

Suffolks are determined, yet gentle horses. They do not give up easily on any task, but accomplish it with a quiet focus that is greatly appreciated. They are patient with any handler, and most amateurs can safely handle a well-trained Suffolk team. Suffolks have wonderful temperaments and are a joy to work with, since they try hard to understand

and do whatever needs to be done. Suffolk stallions are also great and willing workers that are much happier when they are working.

With the new trend toward a more ecological agricultural system, generally utilized on smaller farm lots, the horse has proven to have far less negative impact (on soil compaction and pollution, as examples) than a tractor. Suffolks in particular are efficient at maneuvering around wood sites without destroying young plants.

Suffolks are known as easy keepers. Good pasture and hay are sometimes supplemented with grain, but how much depends on many factors, including age, workload, where they live, and more. Suffolks need more grain when they are working, lactating, or breeding.

Standards

Suffolks applying for registration in the American Suffolk Horse Association must have a registered sire and dam. There are no part-bred registrations.

Suffolks are large, symmetrical, and uniform in color and type. Characteristically the whole appearance of Suffolk Horses is that of a pleasant, roundly modeled whole that pertains—like the singleness of color—to no other breed.

Suffolks possess intelligent heads with active ears. They have powerful, arching necks that are clean cut at the throat.

The shoulders are inclined to be upright, suitable for power rather than action. The back is short and strong, with the ribs springing high from the backbone. The quarters are long and smooth to the root of the tail, which springs higher up than in other breeds. The hipbones are wide apart, but smoothly covered, and the croup is usually level.

Depth and thickness from the withers to the legs are essential, and Suffolks should be as deep in the flank as over the heart.

Their frames are supported by clean, dense bone. Due to their extreme draftiness, the legs appear short and are strongly muscled in forearms and thighs. The legs are placed well under the horse and are free of long hair, helping to easily shed the soil. Their excellent feet are round, of fair size, and wear extremely well, shod or unshod.

The height of Suffolks is between 15.2 and 16.2 hands, with the average being 16.1, but many stallions stand up to 17 hands and more. They can weigh anywhere between 1,400 to 2,100 pounds at maturity.

Their coat is a beautiful chestnut color, though there are many shades ranging from light golden, to red, to dark liver. The mane and tail can also vary in shade. White markings can occur, but in general are not as prominent as in other breeds, most of them being confined to a star or snip and white ankles or fetlocks. No other color is admissible to register the horse in the studbook.

Suffolks are horses of splendid disposition and easy temperament. They exhibit a ready willingness to work, and have great endurance and a quality known as heart, the inner determination to push on. A Suffolk farmer referred to this quality when he said that he valued the Suffolk as "a puller of dead weight and indeed a good drawer."

Credit: The American Suffolk Horse Association

Part 5

Ponies and Small Horses

Small Size, Big Heart

Ponies and small horses are wonderfully diverse and remarkable in their own right and heritage. They have been everywhere throughout the world and have been present throughout history, often doing jobs bigger horses could not do. They influenced societies and undergirded many cultures. As endearing children's companions, their impact has been huge, with their maxi-sized affection and devotion. Their hardworking faithfulness has been relevant to countless lives. They inspire with their tender sensitivity, hardy capabilities, mischievousness, and gutsy spirit when tackling a job. They compete alongside horses and provide solid foundations to future equine interests. Bringing laughter and joy with their miniature antics and movements, they create a festive atmosphere at any event.

Here are those special and lovable characters that warm the heart with their selfless giving and sacrificing. Without them, the equine world would not be complete.

AMERICAN MINIATURE HORSE

Miniatures come in all colors and have great strength for their size. *Jodie French/American Miniature Horse Registry*

American Miniature Horse Association
5601 South Interstate 35W
Alvarado, Texas 76009
www.amha.org

American Miniature Horse Registry
81 B Queenwood Road
Morton, Illinois 61550
www.shetlandminiature.com

"The smallest horse that makes for the biggest smile," is the best statement describing the American Miniature Horse. One cannot help but smile when first introduced to this amazing little animal. Radiant with color, it brings a sense of adventure and playfulness. Its miniature movements and endearing personality are enjoyable just to be around. It is big fun in a little package.

Over the centuries, the Miniature Horse has served in a broad spectrum of equine roles; from royal gift, devoted pet, novelty item, or public exhibit, to mine worker and research animal. Yet it has remained an endearing and special little horse. It comes in a variety of colors, markings, and types. No bigger than a large dog, it possesses the conformation characteristics found in most equine horses, ranging from the draft to the Arabian. Even in its diminutive height, it continues to maintain

This trophy is bigger than the gray colt who won it. Miniatures are fun to show. *Lot-Sa-Fun Miniature Horses*

the big horse look. Its stunning beauty is magnificent, displaying an elegant, scaled-down version of a regular-sized horse.

Miniatures can provide all the fun and excitement of any equine breed but in a much handier package. They make it possible to own a horse without a big pasture and large barn. One acre can support as many as three Miniature Horses. They take a proportionately smaller amount of feed and stabling; the cost of maintaining a Miniature is about one-tenth that of a large horse. The feeding program is basically the same, but the care and clean-up detail is significantly less and can be performed safely by persons of any age, including children. Miniatures tend to thrive on pasture, sunshine, and room to run and play.

Their Lilliputian size is just the first of many attributes that make them special to people of all ages, from young children to senior citizens. Eager to please, they make a gentle and affectionate companion well suited for everyone, from novice horse

person to the consummate show professional. Their roles vary from backyard pet or companion of the elderly, to gorgeous show horse or therapy horse for the handicapped. Large numbers of fans of all ages are attracted to Miniature Horse shows hosted around the United States. There are a variety of classes to choose from, including obstacle driving and speedy roadster driving.

As an investment, show partner, or companion, Miniatures are appreciated and valued. Along with horse shows, Miniatures can be seen at parades, parties, nursing homes, schools, and backyards, where the fun is shared with others.

History

The Miniature Horse's history is as diverse as its color patterns. The first small horses existed in prehistoric times and were most likely the products of survival in harsh natural climates and limited feed. After standard sized horses developed, smaller horses became more unique to breed. Over the years, progressively smaller equines of various types were developed. Finally, a diminutive horse was produced for a broad range of uses, from European court pets to hauling ore carts in mines.

Historians tend to support the idea that the Miniature Horse is a derivative of many different breed sources. Popular belief is that its bloodlines trace back to English and Dutch mine horses. As documented in the pedigrees of Miniatures today, they also drew upon the blood of the Shetland Pony.

The first mention of small horses being imported from Great Britain to the United States was in 1888. Some were purchased to work in the Appalachian coal mines as late as 1950 where a small hauling horse was necessary. Research shows there was little public awareness of true Miniatures until 1960.

Those who recognized the value of the little horses started breeding for quality as well as a diminutive size. The goal was to produce a small equine with the looks of a standard sized breed type. Further breeding specifically for a small size was aided by an increased knowledge of genetics. As a result of nearly four hundred years of selective breeding, the Miniature Horse today has become a miniature version of a well-balanced, standard sized horse. It comes in a rainbow of colors and patterns and several body types.

The Mighty Miniature

Miniatures are in fact horses with the same reactions and motivations of other, larger horses, and their small size does not make them fragile. Many who observe them marvel at their strength and agility as well as their size. They are extremely versatile and excel in many disciplines including driving, halter, hunter/jumper, costume, obstacle, and others. The obstacle class is performed in-hand with horses led through a trail-like course. They can also be driven through an obstacle course. Both classes are extremely popular with the youth.

While Miniatures tend to be affectionate and easy to handle, as with all equines, temperaments and abilities vary with each individual. Miniatures are prone to overeating, so it is important to monitor their nutritional needs and avoid excessive food intake. With average adult Miniatures weighing only 150 to 250 pounds, they should never be ridden by anyone but the smallest children (under 70 pounds).

Children develop an immediate affinity for Miniatures. Small children, perhaps afraid of the standard-sized horse, will often jump at the chance to embrace a Miniature Horse or its foal. Miniature foals are particularly lovable due to their petite size, ranging from 16 to 21 inches in height at birth. Guiding a young child through the proper care of the Miniature Horse encourages discipline, responsibility, and respect, while working with one builds confidence and self-esteem—important qualities that carry over into adult life.

Adults also have realized the great rewards of sharing their lives with Miniature Horses. Transcending generations, it is not uncommon to see entire families, from grandparents to grandchildren, working together to care for, or work with, their horses. Miniature Horse ownership provides a wonderful learning experience and a great sense of accomplishment.

Individuals with special needs have found the Miniature Horse is an excellent substitute for full-sized horses that might compromise their condition or ability. Miniature Horses have long been utilized for therapeutic and special needs programs with positive results. Additionally, older people who are no longer as mobile as they used to be and cannot continue to manage a standard sized horse, can enjoy all the benefits of Miniature Horse ownership, whether for competition, recreation, or investment.

Classically elegant, gentle by nature, and appealing to people of all ages and abilities, the Miniature Horse is truly the horse for everyone. It unites youth, adults, those with special needs, and older individuals together in the love and admiration of this amazingly unique breed.

American Miniature Horse Association

The American Miniature Horse Association (AMHA), Inc., was founded in 1978 in Texas. It is

This beautiful Miniature mare is classically elegant and a good example of the breed. *Lot-Sa-Fun Miniature Horses*

the world's leading Miniature Horse registry, with nearly 160,000 horses and more than 12,000 members in thirty-seven countries and provinces. Its standard for Miniatures sets the breed apart from ponies and other small equines, and it has taken great strides since its inception to ensure the accuracy of pedigrees. One such step was closing the registry on December 31, 1987, allowing only horses with AMHA registered parents to be registered. Horses born after 1995 must be blood-typed and/or DNA tested before their offspring can be registered.

Horses registered with AMHA must meet its Standard of Perfection and cannot exceed 34 inches in height at the withers. Temporary papers are issued to eligible Miniature Horses whose parents are both registered with AMHA. If a horse is 34 inches or less after five years of age, it can become permanently registered.

AMHA Standard of Perfection

General impression: This is a small, sound, well-balanced horse possessing the correct conformation characteristics required of most breeds. Refinement and femininity should be present in the mare, and boldness and masculinity in the stallion. The general impression should be one of symmetry, strength, agility, and alertness. Since the breed objective is for the smallest possible horse, the preference in judging shall be given the smaller horse, with other characteristics being approximately equal.

Size: Must measure not more than 34 inches at the withers at the last hairs of the mane.

Head: In proportion to length of neck and body. Broad forehead with large prominent eyes set wide apart. Comparatively short distance between eyes and muzzle. Profile straight or slightly concave below the eyes. Large nostrils. Clean, refined muzzle, and an even bite.

Ears: Medium in size, pointed, and carried alertly, with tips curving slightly inward.

Throatlatch: Clean and well defined, allowing ample flexion at the poll.

Neck: Flexible, lengthy, in proportion to body and type, and blending smoothly into the withers.

Shoulder: Long, sloping, and well angulated, allowing a free-swinging stride and alert head/neck carriage. Well-muscled forearms.

Body: Well muscled with ample bone and substance. Balanced and well proportioned. Short back and loins in relation to length of underline. Smooth and generally level topline. Deep girth and flank. Trim barrel.

Hindquarters: Long, well-muscled hip, thigh, and gaskin. Highest point of croup to be the same height as withers. Tailset is neither excessively high nor low, but smoothly rounding off rump.

Legs: Set straight and parallel when viewed from front or back. Straight, true, and squarely set when viewed from the side, with hooves pointing directly ahead. Pasterns slope about 45 degrees and blend smoothly, with no change of angle from the hooves to the ground. Hooves are round, compact, and trimmed as short as practical for an unshod horse. Smooth, fluid gait in motion.

Color: Any color or marking pattern and any eye color is equally acceptable. The hair should be lustrous and silky.

Disqualification: Height in excess of 34 inches. Cryptorchism in senior stallions. Any unsoundness or inheritable deformity. If in doubt, the show judge may request the opinion of the show veterinarian. Non-disfiguring blemishes not associated with unsoundness or injuries, and that are temporary, should not be penalized unless they impair the general appearance and/or action of the horse.

American Miniature Horse Registry

The American Miniature Horse Registry (AMHR) is another large organization for Miniature Horses. It was founded in 1972 and has recognized clubs throughout the United States and Canada. Its parent registry is the American Shetland Pony Club, which was founded in 1888 as a registry for Shetlands being imported from Europe at that time. This registry expanded into two breeds registries: The American Shetland Pony Club and the American Miniature Horse Registry. The AMHR is the oldest and most versatile of its kind for small equines in the United States today. It hosts the annual National Championships, which has become one of the largest Miniature Horse shows, with an average of five thousand entries annually.

The size of AMHR registered Miniatures ranges from 34 inches and under for Division A, and 34 to 38 inches for Division B. No horse over 38 inches is eligible for registration with AMHR. The two divisions of horses never compete against each other.

AMHR Standards

General impression: AMHR Miniatures are not skittish. Otherwise, the AMHR has the same objective as the AMHA, except for the inclusion that the disposition should be eager and friendly.

Size: The same as the AMHA, except the American Miniature Horse must measure not more than 34 inches at the base of the last hair on the mane for Division A, and not more than 38

inches for Division B. Since the breed objective is the smallest possible conformation-perfect horse, preference in judging shall be given to the smallest, with all other factors being equal. In no case shall a smaller horse be placed over a larger horse with better conformation. Priority in judging shall be in this order:

1. Soundness
2. Balance and conformity to the standard of perfection
3. Size

Head: In proportion to the body, neither excessively long nor short. The eyes should be large, alert, and prominent with no discrimination in color. The ears are open toward the front and carried erect. The teeth should show no signs of parrot mouth or undershot jaw.

Neck: Strong, muscular, and proportionate to body and the type of horse being represented.

Body: Well muscled with good bone and substance, well sprung ribs, and level topline, with the height in withers and rump being as near to equal as possible. Fore and hindquarters should be well angulated, so that the horse in movement shows a smooth gait.

Legs: Straight, clean, and sound.

Hooves: Round, compact, trimmed as short as practical for an unshod horse, and in condition.

Color: Any color, eye color, and/or marking pattern is equally acceptable.

Throatlatch, shoulders, and hindquarters: These are the same as the AMHA standards.

Disqualifications: Height in excess of 34 inches for Division A and 38 inches for Division B Miniatures. Dwarfism, blindness, unsoundness, and cryptorchidism in aged stallions. Horses are shown with full mane and tail (no full roach). Mane and tail length shall be left to the decision and discretion of the exhibitor. Thinning, pulling, or shortening of mane and tail is permissible.

Credit: American Miniature Horse Association and American Miniature Horse Registry

CASPIAN HORSE

Caspian Horse Society of the Americas
www.caspianhorse.com

Despite of the fact that the Caspian is diminutive, many mistake it for a sizable horse. Nothing could be further from the truth. This is a breed standing under 12 hands, but appears deceivingly like a larger, well proportioned horse. A photo of a Caspian without a person standing beside it for perspective gives the illusion of the much larger Thoroughbred or Arabian.

In fact it looks like a miniature Arabian, yet it is a distinct and unique breed. It has the floating Arabian action with the head and tail held high. The delicate head of the Arabian with classic dished face, protruding eyes, wide flaring nostrils, silky mane, and flowing tail are attributes of the Caspian, except it is even more exquisitely refined and elegant than an Arabian, but in a pony size. It is a horse, however, not a pony, because of its perfect proportions and gaits, although it stands at only 11 to 12 hands on average.

The Caspian Horse is the ultimate athlete. It is small and tractable enough to be easily handled by the youngest child or the most inexperienced adult. Its remarkable endurance, fluid movement, natural jumping abilities, and kind, willing temperament make it an all-around superb horse, excelling both under saddle and under harness.

The Caspian Horse has great intelligence and courage. It learns quickly, is extremely curious, and loves to be active. It is people friendly, affectionate toward its owner, and very entertaining for spectators. The Caspian Horse is notorious for stealing hearts away.

History

This little horse has been traced back to 3000 BC, almost 5,000 years ago, making it possibly one of the oldest breeds of horses in the world. Its history is as colorful as the horse itself.

Though under 12 hands, the Caspian is an elegant little horse. *Kristull Ranch*

As a small, wild horse, it roamed west central Iran seemingly forever. Since its territory was bounded by the sea on one side and mountains on the other, its purity was maintained over the centuries.

It was a highly prized breed. In ancient history, the Caspian Horse was used in royal ceremonies and was offered to Persian kings as treasured gifts. Pictures of Caspians decorated the walls of ancient palaces.

An image of a Caspian Horse graced the seal of King Darius the Great; on his trilingual emblem of 600 BC, small horses are depicted pulling the chariot of the king as he shoots arrows at a fierce lion. It was important for King Darius to have a horse that was agile, quick, and reflected well upon his own athletic prowess and courage.

King Shapur is also depicted on a bas-relief being carried in triumph by a Caspian with the king's feet nearly touching the ground. Another relief shows the investiture of King Ardashir with small Caspian Horses. In the Oxus treasure, small horses are portrayed in gold pulling a royal golden chariot.

In more recent history, the shah of Iran hosted a celebration in 1971 at the ancient palace of

Proportionate head with a long neck add to the Caspian's horse appearance. *Victoria Tollman*

Persepolis. During the celebration, Prince Philip and Princess Anne visited the royal stables, which housed Caspian Horses. They watched eight-year-old children race with Caspian stallions, which was quite impressive to the British royal guests.

During this visit, Prince Philip expressed his concern about the rare breed, so small in numbers and vulnerable because they were only located in one region. Little did he know how prophetic his concerns were, because several years later the Iranian Revolution broke out, making future exports of the Caspian Horse almost impossible. Before the revolution took place, the Shah of Iran presented Prince Philip with a pair of Caspians, which was exported to Great Britain.

Prince Philip was also instrumental in helping export several other small shipments to Great Britain before the Iranian Revolution. Most of the Caspians living and being bred outside of Iran in the last thirty years came from these crucial shipments. In England, the Caspians participated in various royal events, and Queen Elizabeth presented ribbons at several Caspian breed shows.

Conservation of Historical Importance

Louise Firouz, a U.S.-born Cornell graduate, and her new husband, an aristocrat linked to the former shah of Iran, moved to Iran in 1957, which was Mr. Firouz's native country. The couple established the Norouzabad Equestrian Center for children of families living in the country's capital of Tehran. One of the difficulties Firouz faced was providing appropriate mounts for some of the smaller riders. This proved to be a catalyst for her pursuit of what were rumored to be very small horses in the remote villages around the Caspian Sea. Her search eventually led to the rediscovery and preservation of this ancient lost breed of the royals—the Caspian Horse.

Firouz and her husband lived close to the ancient Persian capital, Persepolis. On the walls of this ancient palace, there were rock relief carvings of the Lydian Horse, which had a small, prominent skull formation similar to that found in many other artifacts resembling the small Caspian. These ancient carvings depicted a small horse of the royals that had the same appearance as the Caspians. Firouz's knowledge of these artifacts, combined with her first sighting of a Caspian Horse, resulted in the historical rediscovery of the ancient lost horse. She first saw the small breed in the mid 1960s on a horseback expedition in the remote mountainous regions of Iran, just south of the Caspian Sea.

In 1965, a study was initiated to determine the range, nature, and historical precedent for a horse of this size in Iran. Archeologists, zoologists, equine historians, and genetic researchers contributed a wealth of information to the investigation. From this research, among many other extensive findings, it was determined that the horse depicted on the walls of the ancient palace of Persepolis did actually exist and the depictions were not mere renderings of an imaginary small horse. The study's results supported Firouz's theory that the little horse residing by the Caspian Sea was indeed the five-thousand-year-old lost royal horse of Persia and probably the most ancient domestic breed in existence.

In 1965, when Firouz first saw the horses, they appeared somewhat rough from lack of nourishment and were covered with ticks and parasites. Upon close inspection, however, these horses showed distinctive characteristics similar to the

This yearling colt has the Caspian's characteristically slim build with a deep girth. *CaspianHorse.org*

ancient artifacts with which she was familiar. They had the same large, protruding eyes, a prominent jaw, large nostrils, a dished head, and a high tailset. During her first trip, Firouz rescued three horses, which were dubbed Caspians. The former owners of these misused, overworked horses had no idea of the ancient breed's near extinction.

Between 1965 and 1968, Firouz conducted a careful survey and estimated that there were only fifty Caspians along the entire southern coast of the Caspian Sea. She painstakingly built and nurtured several Caspian foundation herds beginning in 1965. One herd consisted of seven mares and six stallions that she had purchased to form the foundation stock for a Caspian breeding center in Iran. After her breeding successes, the Royal Horse Society (RHS) of Iran confiscated her herd in 1974.

She started a second private herd in 1975, consisting of twenty mares and three stallions. In 1977, this second Caspian breeding center was forced to close its doors, and the RHS declared a ban on all Caspian exports and collected all remaining Caspians. Sadly, due to the political climate, most of the RHS horses were lost. Fortunately, Firouz was able to export nine stallions and seventeen mares, representing nineteen different Caspian horse bloodlines, from Iran to Europe during the early 1970s. These twenty-six horses made up the European foundation herd.

Due to her efforts to save Caspian Horses from starvation and slaughter by exporting them during the early years of the Islamic Revolution, in 1979 she and her husband were repeatedly arrested and detained. At one point, Firouz went on a hunger strike to gain her release and left the prison emaciated and weak. She experienced the decimation of her beloved Caspians when they were run across land mines, used for food, and attacked by wolves during their escape to foreign countries in hopes of survival. She worked side by side with leading researchers and presented information about

Caspians to worldwide audiences of scientists and archaeologists. She was the guest speaker for the first International Caspian Conference held in Houston, Texas, in 1999.

With Iran's many political upheavals during the 1980s—the overthrow of the Shah, the Islamic Revolution, bombing during the protracted Iran–Iraq War, threats of famine—and the Caspian's close association with royalty, its survival remained precarious. The Caspian breed fluctuated between political honoraria as a national treasure and the threat of political seizure as wartime food.

At the end of the Iran–Iraq War, the 1992 International Caspian Studbook listed just thirty-eight registered Caspian horses still surviving in Iran. Firouz captured additional feral horses or purchased them when she could during travels throughout the country. Working with modern genetic methods, she established the fact that none of these horses were lineal relations of the European horses. DNA studies proved they were all part of the same unique gene pool and were all purebred Caspian Horses.

The number of Caspians in Iran is still quite small, and exportations out of Iran are still extremely difficult. The last exports occurred in the early 1990s with a small shipment arriving in Great Britain after a tortuous journey through a war zone where bandits attacked and robbed the convoy. In December 2003, there was a small herd of Caspians housed just outside Bam, Iran, that was reduced to one stallion due to an earthquake, a tragedy for such small numbers of remaining Iranian Caspians. Conserving the Caspian also became more of an issue with the death of Firouz in early 2008.

The Caspian Horse is listed by the Equus Survival Trust as a critically endangered breed. It is indeed a rare breed, as there are only nine hundred Caspians in existence. The breeding of the remaining horses is carefully managed, and their numbers are slowly growing worldwide. Due to their unusual history, there is little chance the breed will become too interbred to remain viable.

Scientific Research

Elwyn Hartley Edwards, an equine historian and author of *The Encyclopedia of the Horse*, relates that the Caspian to the fourth horse type from which all modern-day breeds derive. Dr. Gus Cothran, who has conducted extensive DNA research, concurs that the Caspian Horse is in an ancestral position to most breeds.

Among the other fascinating findings of extensive research are the four basic skeletal differences found between the Caspian and all other breeds:

1. The Caspian skull shows a pronounced elevation of the interparietal bones, and the Caspian possesses no parietal crest.

2. The scapula is wider than in other breeds.

3. The metacarpal and metatarsal bones are much longer and slimmer in comparison to the height of the horse. The spinous processes of the first six thoracic vertebrae show a pronounced elongation.

4. The Caspian has maintained its small, elegant stature of approximately 10 to 12 hands for almost 5,000 years. Research has demonstrated that the Caspian has kept its small size under all types of demographic and environmental conditions, further evidence of its purity, distinction, and unique lineage over many centuries.

Introduction to the United States

In 1966, the first Caspian stallion was imported into the United States, but never sired any purebred Caspians. In 1973, another Caspian stallion was imported and also did not sire any purebreds. In 1994, the first herd of seven Caspians was imported to Texas for the purpose of breeding pure Caspians. They were brought to the Monastery of St. Clare Miniature Horse Farm in Brenham, Texas. From there, they spread to all corners of the United States. With additional imports and local breeding, this band has grown to a dynamic mini-herd of nearly five hundred as of 2003. Three of its stallions made the largest Caspian public appearance at Equitana USA in 1996 and stunned the crowds with their beauty and gentle temperament.

Diminutive gray Caspian stallion with the perfect conformation of a refined horse. *Kristull Ranch*

The Caspian Horse Society of the Americas (CHSA) was incorporated in 1994 to maintain a purebred and part-bred permanent registry devoted to the interests of the Caspian Horse in the Western Hemisphere. It is a member of the International Caspian Society.

Standards

General appearance: The Caspian is a horse, not a pony, and therefore should be viewed in the same manner as when judging a Thoroughbred—that is, the limbs, body, and head should all be in proportion to each other. Foreshortened limbs or a head out of proportion to neck or body are faults. The overall impression should be of a well-bred, elegant horse in miniature form.

Eyes: Almond shaped, large, dark, set low, and often prominent.

Nostrils: Large, low set, finely chiseled, and capable of considerable dilation during action.

Ears: Short, wide apart, alert, finely drawn, and often noticeably in-pricked at the tips.

Head: Wide, vaulted forehead (in most cases the parietal bones do not form a crest, but remain open to the occipital crest). Frontal bone should blend into nasal bone in a pleasing slope. It has very deep, prominent cheekbones with great width between them where they join at the throat. Head tapers to a fine, firm muzzle.

Neck: Long, supple neck with a finely modeled throatlatch.

Shoulders and withers: Long, sloping, well modeled, with good wither.

Body: Characteristically slim with deep girth. Chest width is in proportion to width of body; it is a fault to have "both legs out of the same hole." It is close-coupled, with well-defined hindquarters and good saddle space.

Hindquarters: Long and sloping from hip to point of buttocks, with great length from stifle to hock.

Hocks: Owing to their mountain origin, Caspians may have a more angled hock than lowland breeds.

Limbs: Characteristically slender with dense, flat bone, and flat knees. Good slope to pasterns, neither upright nor over-sloping.

Hooves: Both front and back hooves are oval and neat, with immensely strong wall and sole and very little frog. The horse only requires shoeing on the roughest ground.

Coat, skin and hair: Skin is thin, fine, supple, and dark except under white markings. Coat is silky and flat, often with an iridescent sheen in summer. In the winter, the coat can become dense, making the Caspian adaptable to various climates. Mane and tail are abundant, but fine and silky. Mane usually lies flat (as in Thoroughbreds), but can grow to great lengths. Tail is carried gaily in action. Limbs are generally clean with little or no feathering at the fetlock. Some Caspians carry a dorsal stripe. The bone structure is very dense, defying the Caspian's refined appearance.

Colors: All colors, except piebald or skewbald (pinto). Grays will go through many shades of roan, often dappling and fading to near white at maturity. The main colors are chestnut, bay, and gray. Occasionally, a black or dun color may appear.

Height: Varies with feeding, care, and climate. Recorded specimens have ranged from 10 hands to more than 12 hands. Growth rate in the young is extremely rapid, with the young Caspian reaching most of its height in the first eighteen months, then filling out with maturity.

Action and performance: Natural floating action at all gaits. Long, low swinging trot with spectacular use of the shoulder, as well as a smooth, rocking canter and rapid, flat gallop. Since the Caspian has origins in the mountainous regions of Iran, they have deer-like movements of agility and are superb jumpers.

Temperament: Highly intelligent and alert, but very kind and willing.

When turned out in a field of other breeds of horses, they will most often prefer to graze with their own kind. Caspian stallions most often prefer Caspian mares, and this may be the reason for their intact survival.

Credits: Francie Stull, Kristull Ranch

CHINCOTEAGUE PONY

National Chincoteague Pony Association
2595 Jensen Road
Bellingham, Washington 98226
www.pony-chincoteague.com

There is a race of hardy ponies that live on the islands of Chincoteague and Assateague off the coast of Virginia and Maryland. They are small, compact and good natured. Legend has it that their ancestors swam ashore from a Spanish vessel, a galleon named the *Santo Cristo*, which had capsized off the coast around the year 1600. The ship had been headed for Panama, but never made land. Its cargo of horses was to go to the viceroy of Peru to help in the gold mines. The horses lost at sea are believed to have swum to the nearby islands, and their descendants have been living there ever since.

Life on the islands was tough, and the growth of the horses in succeeding generations became stunted due to the harsh environment. To keep from starving they ate coarse saltmarsh cordgrass, American beach grass, thorny greenbrier stems, bayberry twigs, seaweed, and even poison ivy. When their freshwater sources froze during cold winters or dried up during the hot summers, they learned to survive on small amounts of seawater which, at times, gave them the appearance of being fat or bloated. Thus the horses bred down in size and became the unique breed known today as the Chincoteague Pony.

Today, there are two groups of wild ponies descended from the original horses that survived the famous shipwreck. These two groups are the Maryland Herd and the Virginia Herd. The Maryland Herd consists of approximately 140 head and is owned by the Maryland Park Service. The Virginia Herd consists of approximately 150 head and is overseen by the Chincoteague Volunteer Fire Company. Both wild herds are now on one island, Assateague Island, Virginia–Maryland, which has no human populations. The ponies graze in the

The pleasant Chincoteague head belies its wild background. *Daniel Johnson*

Chincoteague National Wildlife Refuge, located on the Virginia portion of Assateague Island. There is a secure wire fence dividing the island and the herds. The Maryland Herd has anti-fertilization shots to keep them from reproducing.

The famous annual Pony Round-Up and Pony Swim are held each year during the month of July. This roundup began in 1927 after the town on Chincoteague burned down due to not having a fire department, thus the pony auction was instituted to help finance one. The proceeds helped to build a large firehouse on Chincoteague Island, and the auction continues to provide money for the upkeep of the ponies and local charities.

On pony penning day, the Chincoteague volunteer firemen drive the Virginia Herd ponies off the wildlife refuge on Assateague Island, through the seawater channel at slack tide, and to Chincoteague Island in Virginia. This is when the water is at its calmest and the tide is neither coming in nor going out, making it the easiest time for the ponies to swim across the channel. Traditionally, this roundup happens during the last Wednesday of every July. Then the ponies are gathered for the auction, which takes place the next day. Here the foals are auctioned off to the highest bidder.

People from all over the world come to the annual Pony Swim and penning, and it is a favorite event particularly with local children. Chincoteague Island, unlike Assateague, is well populated with people and has seafood restaurants and hotels accommodating the crowds that come to see the ponies year round. The crowds are especially heavy during the last Wednesday and Thursday of July, when the famous pony auction takes place. In 2001, the highest bid ever for a pony was $10,305, setting a new record. The foal was a black and white pinto filly.

After the foals are sold, the stallion and mares are taken back to Assateague Island, again swimming the channel at slack tide. About three to four stallions are returned with all the mares, and sometimes the foals too young to leave their mothers are also returned.

There are three bands of the Virginia Herd running on the wildlife refuge on the island. Each band consists of one herd of ponies with one stallion. All are mixed up at the pony penning, and when they are returned to their home on Assateauge island, the bands are formed once again . The whole process of the Pony Round-Up, auction, and return swim takes three days. There is also an auction in the autumn for the very last foals to be sold for the year.

The movie *Misty*, a Twentieth Century Fox Production released in 1961, depicted the Pony Swim and auction, and one young boy's quest for

ownership of a beloved Chincoteague Pony. This movie was based on a series of children's books about the Chincoteague Pony by Marguerite Henry. The first of the series and her most popular book, *Misty of Chincoteague*, is a children's classic based on a true story and was first published in 1947. Famous for her many horse novels, she subsequently wrote many more tales about these ponies including *Stormy, Misty's Foal*, and *Sea Star: Orphan of Chincoteague*, which introduced many young readers to the Chincoteague Pony. Henry's books and the movie brought sudden popularity to this little breed, and it has enjoyed recognition ever since. There are now approximately 3,980 privately owned Chincoteague Ponies scattered across the United States and Canada.

Registry

In 1983, after obtaining three Chincoteague Ponies in 1975, a breeder named Gale Park Frederick founded a non-profit organization for the breed, named the National Chincoteague Pony Association, which is now the oldest Chincoteague Pony registry. Subsequently, the ponies were recognized as a pure and rare breed.

Park is the only known breeder of the ponies. After purchasing her original three Chincoteague Ponies, she transferred them to her farm in Bellingham, Washington, and has been successfully breeding Chincotagues ever since. For over thirty-four years, she has been keeping the bloodlines pure through selective breeding. Every twelfth foal born is a Misty or Stormy look-alike. A herd size of thirteen ponies ensures that five lucky people can purchase a new pony each year from her place.

In recent years, the Chincoteague Volunteer Fire Company introduced a few mustang horses and purebred Arabians into the Assateague herd to strengthen and diversify the bloodline. Due to this, purebred Chincoteague Ponies are even harder to find and more valuable.

Opposite: The petite Chincoteague Pony retains characteristics of its horse ancestors. *Daniel Johnson*

Standards

Color: Most Chincoteague Ponies have pinto/ paint spotting: overo (solid color with white splashes), or tobiano (white base with irregular patches of solid or roan color). Spotting colors include palomino to dark bay on white, dark red on white (tobiano) with black points, and strawberry roan on white (tobiano). Other color variations include solid black, solid sorrel with flaxen mane and tail, and solid chestnut with flaxen mane and tail. Currently, on the Assateague Island the ponies come in all colors.

Conformation: The Chincoteague Pony is a well-proportioned horse with a strong and muscular, compact body. They typically stand 14.2 hands or less and weigh between 800 and 900 pounds.

The body tends to have a unique style and balanced conformation that includes a well-rounded rump. The tail sits low on the rump. Manes and tails are extra long, and the tail may touch the ground and flag when the pony runs.

With its strong hooves, the pony makes for an excellent long distance runner and can gallop very fast for its size.

Coat: The hair of a Chincoteague Pony is strong and thick. An extra thick mane and tail can grow to a great length, if allowed, and may also grow long on the forehead. The forehead has one or two cowlicks. Fetlocks have light feathering, adding to the unique appearance of the pony. During the winter months, the pony grows a heavy coat of hair, causing it to become shaggy in appearance. This helps the Chincoteague Pony stay warm on the island and makes it a good choice for those who live in cold climate areas.

Disposition: The Chincoteague Pony is well known to be good natured, kind, sweet, and gentle. It has a love of people and is highly intelligent, versatile, and well suited for children. The personality of a Chincoteague Pony has been described to be like a puppy. It is very brave, honorable, and loves to play and learn new things.

Traits: The Chincoteague Pony requires little food compared to an adult horse. It has a reputation as an easy keeper and will do nicely in a weed patch, plus hay, a salt block, grain, and fresh water. There is a saying about the ponies: A Chincoteague Pony can get fat on a cement slab.

A Chincoteague Pony will only use one corner of its stall, paddock, or pasture to deposit fecal matter, making for easy cleanup. This is a trait learned from island living to protect their limited grazing land.

English or western saddles can be used on Chincoteague Ponies. They are natural in dressage and perform well in hunt seat, jumping, driving, and trail riding. They respond well to gentle training techniques because of their easy attachment to their owners as well as other horses. Their colorfully marked coats are a particular favorite in pony halter classes.

In Park's experience raising Chincoteague Ponies, she has gathered many delightful observations about them. She had a mare that liked to have help in birthing her foal while she was lying down, eating grass! There was an incident when a Chincoteague dam confronted a large stallion to protect another pony in the field from being harassed too much. Another time, a stallion diverted its position in a herd and protected Park by shielding her from the herd rushing up toward her.

Chincoteague Ponies thrive on the attention and love that people give them. When cars drive up, the ponies come running in from the pasture and stand by the fence, waiting for someone to come see them. They love the smiles and petting that delighted visitors are so generous in giving.

"If we stand and clap and laugh, the Chincoteague Ponies run, jump, gallop, and frolic in the green pastures," says Park. "They love the attention and provide hours of amusement. Each pony has its own personality."

Credit: Gale Park Frederick and the National Chincoteague Pony Association

CONNEMARA

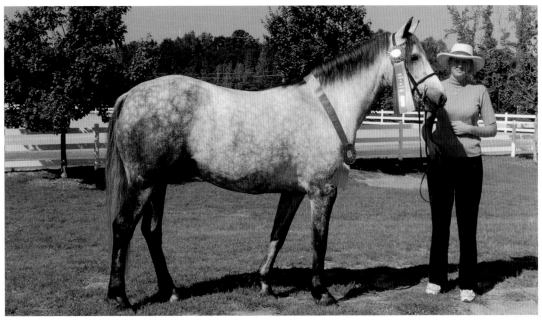

The Connemara has horse genes, and some outgrow their pony status. *American Connemara Pony Society*

The American Connemara Pony Society
P.O. Box 100
Middlebrook, Virginia 24459
www.acps.org

Humans can take little credit for the development of the Connemara. Over many centuries, it evolved as naturally as other wild species have grown and changed. If it had any foresight, this little horse might have picked a friendlier native land than Connemara, the western-most spear of Ireland that juts out into the Atlantic. But then it would not have been a Connemara, for the breed is the product of its environment.

Distinct and sturdy physical qualities of the Connemara evolved over generations on this extremely rugged and·rocky Irish seacoast. Living there was hard for ponies left out in such inclement weather. Their "stall" during the fiercest winter storm was perhaps the lee of a rock or a sheltered valley. Moisture is harder for equines to bear than low temperatures, and in Ireland there is constant moisture. If it is not actively raining or snowing, sea-spray dashes up and around, or an Irish mist comes down.

Forage is not any easier to find in this land of rocks and bogs. Connemaras learned to eat whatever was offered from spring's first thin grass to gorse, heather or seaweed, all cover so sparse that a day's rations might require an animal to travel miles over rocky terrain or chancy mountain trails. This made for a varied diet that all the conditions in the world could not equal.

Since humans had little to do with the breed's origins, there are no ancient records of matings, desirable nicks, or prepotent stallions. Without the help of humans, the Connemara became a sturdy, self-reliant animal that could fend for itself in the most difficult environment. Nature selected the best and rejected the unfit.

Living wild in the mountains and rocks of Connemara gradually eliminated all individuals with bad feet or legs, until the breed possessed magnificent bone and hooves as hard as the native marble. It was the nimble and surefooted that survived while traversing the dangerous ledges and precipices. One wrong step could mean certain death. Clearing the endless rock walls to claim a tender bit of grass bred into the breed a disdain for any barrier. This talent was so instilled through the generations that the Connemara became a natural jumper.

The ponies were originally used in Ireland to work the land. They also transported seaweed for fertilizer, peat for fuel, produce to market, and the family to church. The driving career of a much loved pony often began once a child had outgrown it. Its size made Connemaras easy to harness and their strength enabled them to pull a carriage with several adults. Due to the lack of highways and post roads suitable for carriage travel in Ireland, the Connemaras continued to flourish as saddle and work animals long after comparable breeds had become extinct in other countries.

As in many agricultural cultures, the Connemara's forebears were often handled by women who tilled the soil and hauled the turf while the men were away at war, fishing, or otherwise trying to earn a living. Consequently, any horse with a mean or tricky streak was soon weeded out. So too were the stupid and lazy until each succeeding generation of the Connemara stabilized as a willing, intelligent, sweet-tempered animal, making it an eager partner in any equine enterprise.

Foundation

The strong dun strain in the Connemara suggests some link with the older Norwegian Dun and possibly, before that, the Mongol horse during the millennia when the British Isles were still part of the European continent. Less conjecture than educated guess, it is presumed that Spanish and Barb stallions from the wrecked Spanish Armada swam ashore to Ireland, where they lived and crossed on native mares, for there is a distinct Arabian–Spanish influence in the breed.

Spanish horses then were of two distinct types: the lighter-boned Jennet and the Andalusian (a forerunner of Lipizzaners, which may explain its resemblance to the Connemara). It seems probable that both lines blended with each other and the local Irish stock, resulting in a soft-gaited riding animal much desired by riders of all stations. The English termed these Irish ponies "Hobbies." The first Connemara Hobby of any historical note was a fine dark dun shipped from Galway to London to be presented to King James I in 1606. This was perhaps the first Connemara exportation on record and signifies the quality of the breed even at that time.

In 1900, Dr. J. C. Ewart of Edinburgh University, an expert on equine genetics and a breeder of ponies, was commissioned by the English government as part of a remount program to study the actual condition and possibilities of the Connemara pony. In his report, he described the old dun type of Connemara as being "capable of living where all but wild ponies would starve" and "strong and hardy as mules." He states that the Connemara breed was extremely valuable, "fertile and free from hereditary disease [and] their extinction would be a national loss."

Not until 1923 were the Irish to benefit by his advice, when the Connemara Pony Breeders Society was founded, incorporating into its program Ewart's recommendations from a quarter century before. Nine carefully selected stallions were entered into the first studbook as foundation sires and ninety-three mares were admitted after inspection. Some forty years later, during which time the most painstaking work of inspecting and approving ponies for inclusion was carried out, the studbook was closed, having listed three thousand mares and two hundred stallions.

The Connemara Pony Breeders Society has staged an annual Connemara Pony Show each August in Clifden, Galway, which is unlike any other show in the world. Gaelic-speaking exhibitors bring their distinct culture to the show and compete to win the red rosette (in Ireland red is first place, blue is second), qualifying their ponies as a valuable cash crop.

In a letter referring to the show, Sir Alfred Pease, an English horse breeding expert in the early 1900s, said, "I have judged all classes of light horses, hunters, ponies, etc., in England, and have bred all classes—and being struck with the substance and quality and beauty of this Connemara breed, wonder how it has ever been evolved. I have never seen such a collection anywhere which combined so much substance and quality. I feel that you have in this breed a national asset of great value." Pease reported that he saw "some of the cleanest, flattest, and hardest legs that are possible to find."

Human nature, however, was not satisfied with how excellent the Connemara might have already been. Accordingly, a few stallions of other breeds were introduced into the breed. Two Thoroughbreds of the 1940s, Winter and Little Heaven, had a considerable influence on the modern Connemara, and also a part-bred Arab of the 1950s and 1960s, named Clonkeehan Auratum. Traits of others, such as Mayboy, an Irish draft, survive in a few of today's ponies.

Performance Connemaras

The naturally selective process of living on the Atlantic seacoast developed the conformation and ability of the Connemara to respond to an extremely wide range of work requirements under a variety of conditions. It has, above all else, proven and demonstrated its ability to work with, not against, its human partner. It is so people-oriented, eager to please, and athletic that its versatility is almost legendary.

There is perhaps no better suited horse or pony than a Connemara for eventing. The Connemara is naturally agile, careful, and typically an eager jumper, proving that what it lacks in height can easily be made up for with its style and athletic ability. More trainers, riders, and eventing enthusiasts are realizing that big horses are not necessarily superior to their smaller competitors, and many are actually

Connemaras make great hunter/jumpers with their sure-footedness, grace, and balance. *Greg Oakes*

looking for more compact, able mounts to manage tricky distances and varied terrain.

It is no surprise then that the Connemara, though still relatively small in numbers in the United States, has excelled in upper level eventing for a number of years. Known for its relatively big stride and even bigger heart, the Connemara is a natural choice for Pony Club and similar disciplines besides eventing. The Connemara stallion, Hideaway's Erin Go-Bragh, is a celebrity to young and old, being a Breyer horse model and honored guest of the U.S. Combined Training Association (USCTA, now the U.S. Eventing Association) at Equitana 1999. Go Bragh ranks as the winningest stallion in USCTA history. He and other Connemaras, including his half-bred daughter, Black Points Tilly Go-Bragh, have proven to the eventing world that a big heart and innate athleticism overcome a small stature.

The willing nature and ground-covering stride of the Connemara make it an ideal prospect for the sport of dressage. It is not unusual to see a Connemara doing well at this event, even when competing against warmbloods. Perhaps the best known Connemaras in the dressage arena are the half-breds, Seldom Scene and Last Scene, both of which competed to the Grand Prix level ridden by Lendon Grey. She credits her rise to the top of U.S. dressage to the big heart in the little package of Seldom Scene. This 14.2-hand gray half-bred carried her to championship titles both in the United States and in Europe.

Other heroes also include the purebreds Blue Ridge Tiger in endurance and three-time U.S. Equestrian Federation (USEF) Hunter Pony Award winner, Kerrymor Autumn Hope. The USEF awards the Clifden Trophy annually to the high point Connemara in hunter classes. The McKenna Trophy is awarded by USEF to the overall best Connemara in combined training and the United States Eventing Association awards other yearly trophies.

Connemaras possess the stamina, ground-covering stride, and balanced way of going, which makes them ideal performers in the discipline of combined driving. With excellent feet and legs, they manage the speed, quick turns, rolling terrain, and changes in road surfaces often associated with cross-country driving.

Due to their good length of rein, straight true action, free moving shoulders, strong backs, and powerful hindquarters, Connemaras used in driven dressage are elegant and graceful. The stallion, Hideaway's Erin Smithereen, was well known for his expertise in combined driving.

The greatest compliment for the breed, though, is the hundreds of Connemaras that carry their riders, junior and senior alike, wherever the riders' fancy leads. Their unique temperament and kindly responsiveness to people make them highly valued as companion animals. Their sensitive nature

has made them wonderful therapeutic ride and drive ponies.

In the United States

The first notice of Connemaras by the United States was mentioned by a New York admirer, Henry William Herbert. In 1859, Herbert (also known as Frank Forester) wrote in his book, *Hints to Horse-Keepers*: "In Spain there existed from an early date in the middle ages a peculiar breed of very small, high-bred horses, scarcely to be called ponies, known as the Andalusian jennet, the descendants of which are said still to exist in the Connemara horse, peculiar to Galway in Ireland. . . . In that district they were long famous for their endurance, speed, docility and easiness of gait as well as for the high and courageous spirit."

Connemaras were first imported to the United States in 1951, when a dun stallion, a black stallion, and four mares were brought to Virginia. By 1957, there were enough owners to join forces, and the American Connemara Pony Society was formed "in recognition of the need for a pony of great stamina and versatility, capable of carrying an adult in the hunt field, yet gentle and tractable enough for a young child, fearless as a show jumper, yet suitable and steady as a driving pony."

The society published its first studbook that same year, with a total of 155 purebred Connemaras registered. Since that date, the number of registered ponies has doubled and redoubled, so that now the Society has recorded over 4,000 purebreds and some 2,500 half-breds.

Standards

The American Connemara Pony Society breed standards are applied in the show ring. It is of utmost importance that the Connnemara be judged to maintain the unique characteristics and qualities that make the breed what it is. Breed characteristics and qualities should be considered foremost, and judging should maintain the breed standards. Judging should not be influenced by the features of any other breed.

The Connemara is foremost a using breed, meaning one that has not been restricted to only one activity or purpose.

It has horse genes, so in the "land of milk and honey" (the United States), some outgrow pony status, or 14.2 hands. Throughout the rest of the world, the Connemara is registered only as a pony (14.2 or under), and only after meeting the breed registry standards and inspection. North America is the one exception, where the Connemara is allowed to be registered as a small horse as well as a pony. The judge should recognize the influence of the Connemara's pony heritage, while giving balanced consideration to the effects of larger size on overall conformation.

With this general description, the following are standards for judging the American Connemara pony and horse:

Size: A purebred pony ranges in size from 13 to 15.2 hands.

Temperament: Mannerly, manageable, kind, responsive, and possessing good sense and basic intelligence. Good temperament is one of the most important breed prerequisites.

Type: Rugged and sturdy, with its body compact and deep through the heart, as well as with well-sprung ribcage and broad chest.

Action: Straight and true both front and rear, with free movement in the shoulders. Connemaras should move underneath themselves and should be surefooted, athletic, and clever, covering a lot of ground.

Head and neck: Kind eye and a well shaped and balanced head in proportion to the rest of the body. The neck should be of good length and definition, meeting the shoulder smoothly.

Shoulders: Long and well laid back with good slope.

Back: Strong and muscular; some length of back is normal in Connemaras, especially in mares.

Hindquarters: Well rounded and deep, with good length from the point of the hip through the haunch, and should balance the shoulders.

Bone: Clean, hard, flat, and proportionately substantial. Forearms and gaskins should be long and muscular, while cannons should be short and very dense.

Feet and joints: The feet are hard and strong, and the joints are large and well defined.

Colors: Gray, dun, bay, brown, black, roan, and a few are chestnuts. No piebalds or skewbalds are accepted.

The ideal Connemara always has the sloped shoulder of a riding horse, well balanced head and neck, and clean, hard, flat bone measuring approximately 8 inches below the knee. Predominant characteristics are hardiness of constitution, stamina, docility, intelligence, and soundness.

Credit: American Connemara Pony Society

DALES PONY

Dales Pony Society of America
32 Welsh Road
Lebanon, New Jersey 08833
www.dalesponies.com

Dales Pony Association of North America
P.O. Box 733
Walkerton, Ontario
Canada, N0G 2 V0
www.dalesponyassoc.com

The Dales is one of nine British Native Pony breeds referred to as Mountain and Moorland ponies, which developed in the rugged mountains and moors of Britain and Ireland. Native to northeastern England near the Scottish border, the Dales Pony possesses unusual strength, high courage, and great beauty. Fashioned by harsh and unforgiving conditions, Dales Ponies are tough, surefooted, and thrifty, while maintaining an inherent level-headedness often lacking in horses and other pony breeds. With its keen intelligence, superb temperament, and tremendous athletic ability, the Dales Pony is that rare commodity among equine breeds: a large pony that can take the amateur or professional equestrian far in a variety of athletic pursuits, while remaining a safe and enjoyable mount for family riding.

Dales Ponies were bred for a specific job in an inhospitable and tough environment, however, when their job requirements changed, they rapidly adapted to other uses. Today, the ponies demonstrate all the traits and talents that brought their ancestors such distinction. The combination of strength, talent, agility, and high courage with a kind and intelligent nature makes the Dales Pony a top-notch riding, driving, and draft pony.

Even among the remarkable Mountain and Moorland breeds, the Dales Pony represents something unique—an extremely powerful, well-

Dales stallion, exhibited in traditional stallion tack, in a Mixed Mountain and Moorland Pony class. *Courtesy Davidson Dales Pony Farm*

A herd of Dales mares and foals in Wisconsin. *Courtesy Raspotnik Farm*

muscled equine more than capable of forestry and draft work. At the same time, it demonstrates the extraordinary charisma and ground-covering trot with just the right amount of sparkle that makes even the most casual observer take notice. As these exceptional ponies establish their reputation throughout North America, it is hoped that dedicated breeders and committed enthusiasts ensure their traditional characteristics—those traits that make a Dales a Dales—are never lost.

History

Separated by the Pennines in Northern England, the Dales and Fell Pony breeds share a common genetic heritage and similar, though distinct, histories. Once believed to be two types of the same breed, today the Dales and Fell are divided into separate studbooks and societies. Dales Ponies were bred as pack ponies in the eighteenth and nineteenth centuries in England for the Pennines lead mining industry and won fame for their ability to quickly traverse rough country under daunting loads. The ponies easily carried up to 240 pounds of lead from the mines, across the Pennines, and to the lead washing stations. The trek could cover fifty miles a day over perilously narrow trails, demanding a very surefooted and fast gait to make good time. As railways emerged and road systems improved, the Dales were less sought after as pack animals, but quickly found a niche on the small farms in and around the Yorkshire Dales. With their unusual strength, sensible nature, and remarkable agility, they offered great advantages over larger draft breeds to the small farmer.

The modern Dales Pony can trace its ancestry to the Pennine Pony (native to Yorkshire, Lancashire, Cumbria, and County Durham) and the Scotch Galloway, both now extinct. During the late

Dales stallion enjoying some quiet time with a young friend. *Courtesy Davidson Dales Pony Farm*

eighteenth century, when road improvement was on an upswing in England, demand surged for fast-trotting horses for mail carriages and transportation coaches. These fast trotters were called "roadsters," and the most sought after of these was the Norfolk Cob. The foundation Norfolk Cob sire was Shales the Original, foaled in 1755 and a direct descendent of the Thoroughbred, Flying Childers, by the Darley Arabian. (The Darley Arabian was one of three stallions considered to be the founders of the modern Thoroughbred.) Shales the Original was the foundation sire of many of the best trotting breeds, and most Dales Ponies today can trace their pedigree back to this remarkable stallion.

The Norfolk Cob was used to create the splendid Yorkshire Roadsters of the mid-nineteenth century, and fashionable trotters became the rage. Farmers in and around the Yorkshire Dales (known as Dalesmen) set great store in the famous trotting races of the time, but most found it impractical to keep a pony solely for racing. The Dalesmen

bred the best of the Norfolk Cob and the Pennine Pony–Scottish Galloway blood to create spectacular trotting action without spoiling the pony's ability to work the land and transport cargo and people. These fast trotting, hardworking, and increasingly stylish ponies became the modern-day Dales Pony. It was comfortable to ride, strong enough for draft work, and thrifty enough to flourish on the bleak grazing provided on the dales—the precise qualities prized by the Dalesmen. Family farmers also recognized in the hardworking Dales an innate jumping talent, thus many became the preferred mount for a good day's fox hunt, easily carrying an adult of 250 pounds or more. In short, the Dales Pony literally did it all for the farmer and his family, thoroughly earning the breed's reputation as the "Great All-Rounder."

Early in the twentieth century, there was a tremendous demand for active "vanners" (a smaller, lighter version of a full-sized draft carriage horse) for town work, and "gunners" (horses that transported artillery and munitions) for the army. At this time, many fine Clydesdale stallions were traveling the districts and were bred to Dales mares to produce vanners, which gave the farmer a good return financially, but proved a significant threat to the purity of the breed. The addition of Clydesdale blood was viewed by many proponents of the Dales breed as both a mistake and a failure.

Partially in response to this situation, the Dales Pony Improvement Society was formed in 1916, and the Dales Pony Studbook opened, helping to ensure the preservation of the purebred Dales Pony. In testament to the value of the breed, the United Kingdom's Board of Agriculture offered to Dales stallion owners a Stallion Premium—a monetary award given to the stallion owner to help cover the costs of standing and traveling a stallion—after an inspection of a number of ponies by Capt. A. Campbell of the British Army. Campbell stated in his report regarding the Dales Ponies, "Your breed has one superb asset, possessed of every specimen I saw, i.e., the most perfect foot in the British Isles."

Sadly, because of their compact size, relaxed

Dales stallion going nicely over fences. *Courtesy Davidson Dales Pony Farm*

temperament, bravery, and legendary strength, Dales Ponies were used extensively by the British Army in both World War I and World War II. Their small size enabled them to be more efficiently transported to the continent than the larger draft horses, while their strength made them a favorite choice for the movement of munitions and other supplies. The need was great and numerous Dales Ponies were conscripted. Some died during battle, while others were sold for meat when the British troops necessarily left the ponies behind when they returned home.

Their numbers also suffered when the advent of mechanized farm machinery caused Dales Ponies to no longer be essential to the farmer's way of

life, and thus far fewer ponies were bred. By the mid 1950s, only a very small number of registered Dales Ponies remained. Fortunately, through the support of dedicated breeders and the work of conservation organizations, their numbers have gradually increased, and the overall quality of the breed remains high.

In North America

Denise and Colin Dunkley brought the first Dales Ponies to North America when they moved to Canada from their native England in 1991 and set up Canadale Dales Pony Stud. A few years later, Dales Ponies arrived in the United States when

Dales mare and her young rider in a Novice Ridden Pony class. *Courtesy Davidson Dales Pony Farm*

Stephen and Marian Barker established Blooming Dales Pony Farm in Oregon in 1994, after importing a stallion and three Section A mares. All foals bred by Blooming Dales carry the Redprairie prefix in their names—the first Dales prefix established in the United States.

Since then, Dales Ponies have increased in popularity, and small breeding operations have sprung up across the nation, with the greatest density being on the East Coast. Many of these breeding farms still import ponies from the United Kingdom to ensure the quality of their homebred stock.

Dales Ponies have made a name for themselves in many equestrian disciplines, as the reputation of Mountain and Moorland ponies continues to grow in the United States. Across the country, Dales compete successfully in dressage, three-day eventing, and all forms of carriage driving competitions, most notably Combined Driving. They are highly sought after in the United Kingdom as mounts for disabled riders and drivers, and it is expected that as their numbers increase in the United States, they will find similar jobs. Dales even find work hauling timber or maple sap with harness and sleigh over silent, snowbound landscapes. Dales Ponies have much to offer children and adults, as well as backyard pony owners and serious competitors alike. As the Great All-rounder, the breed is becoming firmly established in North America.

With approximately 2,000 Dales Ponies worldwide and fewer than 250 in North America, the breed is classified as endangered by the Rare Breeds Survival Trust in the United Kingdom and as critical by the Equus Survival Trust in the United States. Although today they are more commonly sought after for equestrian pursuits, many Dales Ponies still actively work the land both in the United Kingdom and in North America.

The Rare Breeds Survival Trust has recognized the importance of the breed's affinity for utility work as it relates to its future survival, as shown in this statement: "Although competitive sporting events are likely to continue to be a significant factor in the future use of most [endangered] breeds, the Trust is concerned about re-establishing utility values of native breeds outside the leisure industry and is exploring their use in activities such as forestry and farming. Dales Ponies, Suffolk Punch and Clydesdale heavy horses have all demonstrated their worth in forestry work, and a proven efficient function is the best safeguard for the future security of rare breeds."

Registry

In 1964, the Dales Pony Society (DPS) of the United Kingdom was reorganized, and "Improvement" was dropped from the name. Unregistered but high quality ponies were sought for inclusion into the registry. A grading-up register was initiated whereby unregistered mares or mares with half a pedigree were registered as Section D if they were true to type, color, and height. Foals from Section D mares that were bred to a fully registered stallion were then graded-up in the registry to Section C. Similarly, offspring of Section C mares were registered as Section B and offspring of Section B mares were registered as Section A. This grading-up register was closed in 1969, along with Section D of the registry. Thankfully, the grading-up scheme significantly increased the number of registered Dales while ensuring the quality of the breed today. The DPS is now the mother society for all approved registries throughout the world.

The Dales Pony Society of America (DPSA) is a daughter registry for both purebred and part-bred ponies in the United States, Canada, and Mexico. Fredericka and George Wagner founded the DPSA in 1999 when they imported ten Dales Ponies from the United Kingdom. The society became a non-profit corporation and member-owned in 2005, and a fully sanctioned daughter registry of the DPS in 2008.

Breed Description

Ideally, the Dales stand between 14 and 14.2 hands. The vast majority are black or dark brown, but bay and gray are found, with a few roan mixed in for good measure. White markings are closely monitored, and only a star above the eyes, a snip, and white up to the fetlocks on the hind legs are allowed for a pony to be registered as a Section A in the main studbook. Ponies with more white than this are registered as a Section B. Colts born to Section B dams are ineligible for stallion status even if correctly marked.

The Dales head profile should be straight or slightly convex; any dishing is viewed as a fault. The neck is strong and muscular, and a good pony possesses a deep, short-coupled trunk with well-sprung ribs. The cannons must display 8 to 9 inches of flat bone, and pasterns should be of good length and covered with silky feather to match the ample, flowing mane and tail. The famous eye-catching Dales trot is a rounded, ground-covering gait with no wasted action, full of propulsion, and a joy to watch.

Standards

General impression: Strong, active pony, full of quality and spirit, yet gentle and kind.

Head: Neat and pony-like, and broad between the eyes, which should be bright and alert. Pony ears are slightly incurving, and it should have a long forelock of hair down the face.

Neck: Strong and of ample length. Stallions should display a bold outlook with a well arched crest. Throat and jaw line should be well defined, and the pony should have a long, flowing mane.

Shoulders: Well-laid, long, sloping shoulders with well-developed muscles. Withers should not be too fine.

Dales mare competing in a Pleasure Driving class.
Courtesy Davidson Dales Pony Farm

Forearms: Set square, short, and very muscular with broad, well developed knees.

Body: Short coupled and deep through the chest with well sprung ribs.

Hindquarters: Deep, lengthy, and powerful, with the second thighs well developed and very muscular. Tail well set on, but not too high, with plenty of long luxurious hair reaching the ground.

Hocks: Broad, flat, clean, and well let down, with plenty of dense, flat bone.

Feet, legs, and joints: The very best of feet and legs should be present with flexible joints, showing quality with no coarseness. The cannons should display 8 to 9 inches of flat, flinty bone and well defined tendons. Pasterns should be nicely sloping and have good length. There should be ample silky feathers and the feet should be large, round, and open at the heels with well-developed frogs.

Preferred height: 14 to 14.2 hands is desirable.

Colors: Black, brown, some gray and bay colors, and a few are roan. White markings should only appear as a star, snip, and to fetlocks of hind legs only.

Movement: Clean, straight and true, with it going forward on "all fours" with tremendous energy. The knee is lifted, and the hind legs flexed well under the body for powerful drive.

Character: True pony character and alert, courageous, intelligent, and kind.

Registration requirements: Ponies will be accepted by the DPSA from any country including Canada and Mexico, provided they have proper documentation and DNA records, up until two full years of age. Imported ponies already registered with the DPS in the United Kingdom or with another registry recognized by the DPS will be accepted regardless of age. All purebred Dales Ponies registered with the DPSA are DNA qualified (sire, dam, and foal) and must be micro-chipped prior to registration.

Colt registrations: Colts eligible for stallion status must be sired by a licensed stallion out of a Section A mare and must display correct markings. All stallions must be licensed from three years of age and all are re-entered in the Stud Book when licensed. Colts out of Section B mares or mismatched colts from Section A mares are not eligible for stallion status. These colts will be issued a registration with a gelding number and must be castrated at a suitable age.

Mare, filly and gelding registrations: The registration is divided by two sections:

- Section A: by a licensed stallion, out of either a Section A or Section B mare, and displaying correct markings
- Section B: by a licensed stallion and out of a Section A or Section B mare, but displaying incorrect markings

Part-bred pony registrations: The DPSA maintains a Part-bred Registry to encourage the production of horses and ponies of good quality with substance, courage, and agility from Dales stallions. Crossbreeding of Dales mares is discouraged, as the breed is still recovering from near extinction. The Part-bred Registry will register crossbred foals that are the offspring of a licensed Dales stallion as one-half, three-quarters, or seven-eighths Dales, but it is not possible to achieve a purebred Dales by means of up-grading. DNA testing is not required for the part-bred foals or for the dams.

Credits: Kelly Davidson Chou, with assistance from the Dales Pony Society, United Kingdom, and Dales Pony Society of America

DARTMOOR PONY

As a hearty moorland breed, the Dartmoor is stalwart and athletic. *American Dartmoor Pony Association*

American Dartmoor Pony Association
203 Kendall Oaks Drive
Boerne, Texas 78006

Dartmoor Pony Registry of America
295 Upper Ridgeview Road
Columbus, North Carolina 28722
www.dartmoorpony.com

The Dartmoor is an attractive and ancient pony originating from the moors of Devon in southwest England. Through the centuries, the rough, rocky terrain and sparse grazing produced a sure-footed, strong, and hardy pony quite capable of excelling in any number of pursuits.

The Dartmoor of today has a wonderfully calm temperament and friendly nature, making it an excellent choice for adults and children alike. The pony provides riders of all ages with wonderful experiences due to its versatility and adaptability. Its well laid-back shoulder and long, low stride provide a smooth and comfortable ride that adults like to sit. With its gentle, calm nature, the Dartmoor is very much in demand as a child's first riding mount. It is not unusual for the same pony to patiently carry a toddler on lead-line, compete with an older child in 4-H or Pony Club, and then happily take parents for a Sunday drive.

Typically, once a Dartmoor Pony belongs to a family, it is rarely sold. Fondness for Dartmoors is such that when children outgrow one as a riding mount, it continues on with the family as a harness pony or is passed on to relatives to introduce their young ones to the love of riding and caring for a pony.

The Dartmoor is perfect for showing, hunting or trail riding. Its good looks, pleasant manner, and brave nature make it an excellent candidate for both pleasure and competitive driving.

The Dartmoor is the best possible foundation stock for breeding larger children's ponies. It contributes its substance of bone for a small warmblood type of pony with versatility and strength and, most importantly, that Dartmoor good nature.

History

Ponies on Dartmoor are believed to have been in existence for centuries, surviving unbelievable hardships from both nature and humans. Hoof prints assumed to be from domestic animals—possibly Dartmoor Ponies—were discovered on England's Shaugh Moor within the boundaries of a Bronze Age settlement dating back to approximately 2000 BC.

The Dartmoor Pony originated on High Willhays, one of the tallest peaks and highest points of southern England located on the southwest coast in the county of Devon. The pony received its name from a wild area of moorland called Dartmoor, which stands over one thousand feet above sea level. Dartmoor is about 365 square miles of almost solid granite highlands, which are very rocky with sparse vegetation. A thin layer of soil covers protruding rocks throughout with little fields, grassy slopes, and wooded valleys along the edges. Dartmoor's weather can be quite intense, receiving full force gales from the Atlantic Ocean. Being able to survive such bleak conditions, the

Dartmoor Pony became known as a race of pony that was surefooted, hardy, and full of stamina, enabling it to survive in almost any terrain or climate in the world.

One of the earliest recorded references to Dartmoor Ponies is in the will of Awifwold of Credition, a Saxon bishop who died in 1012. Another example was during the reign of Henry I (1100–1135), when a stallion was taken from Dartmoor (then a royal forest) to be bred with his royal mares.

Much later, however, there was less need for ponies, as it was necessary to breed a horse of considerable frame to carry soldiers and their heavy armor. The plight of English ponies became even more pronounced in 1535 when Dartmoor Ponies, along with all other ponies of the British Isles, almost became extinct after Henry VIII passed a law to eliminate "nags of small stature." Fines were imposed on anyone using a stallion under 14 hands. Six years later, another law was passed by Henry VIII prohibiting the use of any "horse under 15 hands" and all "unprofitable beasts." Smaller ponies were caught and destroyed, but some slipped through the cracks because they were too far away to police. Queen Elizabeth I later annulled these laws.

In the 1820s, Dartmoor Ponies became very popular in the nearby towns for their ability to cross the rough and mountainous roads. King Edward VII valued Dartmoors for his polo teams, and there followed a huge comeback in the breed until World Wars I and II. During the wars, Dartmoors and other ponies once again declined in numbers, as they were more usable for meat instead of work. Since that time, however, the Dartmoor has made steady progress in numbers due to strict breeding practices and demands.

Registration in England

It was not until 1898 when the Polo and Riding Pony Society—later known as the National Pony Society—set up local committees to provide descriptions of native breeds of ponies, giving each a section of the Stud Book for registration. More

Dartmoor herd racing. Dartmoors show consistency in type, size, and color. *Bob Langrish*

Dartmoors were initially registered than any other native British breed. With exception of the height, the original description of the Dartmoor is almost identical to today's standard. The height limit for a stallion at that time was 14 hands and 14.2 hands for mares, but very few ponies came close to that.

The 1920s were an important time for the Darties. From 1924 to 1927, the Dartmoor Pony Society came into existence and set the height limit at 12.2 hands. It knew there were many other outlets beyond polo in which the Dartmoor could perform for both profit and enjoyment.

Some of the most influential bloodlines still utilized today were first noticed in the 1920s. Ponies of this era include Judy V, a champion mare bred by E. P. Northey, who produced the first breed standard and got the first Dartmoor Stud Book off the ground. The Leat, another champion, was bred by the Prince of Wales at his Ducy Stud at Tor Royal near Princetown. These two champions bred together and produced Juliet IV, yet another

champion that in turn produced the outstanding show and stud success, Jude, in 1941.

In the 1940s, very few Dartmoors were registered, partially due to World War II. Registration by inspection was introduced, and prizewinners at selected shows became eligible for registration. By the end of the 1950s, the breed was in much better shape. Registration by inspection finished in 1957. All future registrations in the National Pony Society's Stud Book were of ponies whose parents were already registered. The Dartmoor Pony Society continued with membership, breeding, inspections, and showing, but did not take over the registration process until 1977.

Preservation of Ponies on Dartmoor

Throughout history, the Dartmoor Pony has been used for a variety of services, including pulling carts to and from market and packing wool, granite, and tin as well as other materials from the mines. At the start of the twentieth century until the 1960s,

Beautiful Dartmoor stallion with naturally full mane and tail. *Pam Norton*

Dartmoor Prison officials raised unregistered ponies for the warders to ride while escorting inmates to and from their duties outside the prison.

When not in service, the ponies were left to roam free on the moor. Over the years, the quality and number of pure Dartmoor Ponies on the moorland declined. Since the moor is common land, there are no restrictions as to what can be turned out. Some farms on Dartmoor have been given grazing rights on the commons for a specific number of cattle, sheep, and ponies. Breeds such as the Shetland, Arabian, and Thoroughbred have been turned out on the moor at various times. Consequently, a pony coming from Dartmoor does not necessarily mean it is a Dartmoor Pony.

The Dartmoor area also reflected what was popular for the current times. In the 1940s, there was a demand for small pit ponies. In the 1950s, pinto ponies were popular and pony classes were on the rise, requiring a warmblood type pony. Ponies on Dartmoor began to decline by the crossbreeding with these less hardy breeds. While the breed was being kept pure by stud farms, it was evident with each trend, a toll was taken on the quality of the pure Dartmoor. A plan had to be formed to preserve the breed.

In 1951, Dartmoor was designated a national park and the pony was chosen to be on its logo. In 1987, the Duchy of Cornwall (of which Prince Charles is the Duke) joined the Dartmoor Pony Society, along with the Dartmoor National Park Authority and the Ministry of Agriculture, to improve the quality of the moor ponies. They developed the Dartmoor Pony Support Scheme, which allowed inspected and approved typey mares to run with a pedigreed stallion on one of several newtakes (an enclosed, controlled part of the moor that is separated from the commons and used for breeding purposes). Newtakes are owned by Prince Charles and maintained for the purpose of producing the type of pure Dartmoor that is as hardy as its ancestors. It was hoped that this scheme would encourage local farmers to breed the true-to-type Dartmoor that is able to survive the highland's harsh environment.

The Dartmoor Pony Society opened a supplemental register to include the inspected mares as foundation stock, and there was a noticeable improvement of the foals over the years. It was hoped that the majority of the fillies that were upgraded after inspection would return to the scheme and eventually replace the original mares. This would give breeders a new genetic pool, which was important to future breeding. It also provided park visitors a chance to see the Dartmoor Pony in its natural habitat.

One such example of the scheme's success with mares from the newtakes is Lizwell Gambling Queen, a four-time National Combined Driving Champion that competed successfully in three World Championships in Europe representing the United States. This smart-moving mare finished in the top ten twice and won the silver medal for dressage in Denmark—an amazing feat!

Beneficial Crossbreds

Every breed of equine has a special purpose and is not meant to be good at every discipline. Due to this and to meet the current trend, breed registries have often added outside blood to make their breed come closer to what the market demands. Dartmoors are no different, and as early as the twelfth century, blood from other breeds had been introduced, sometimes to create the perfect replacement pony for children who had outgrown their Dartie. In turn, the pure Dartmoor has remained invaluable for its own unique qualities that have been transmitted to create other breeds worldwide.

The Dartmoor Pony contributes both its kind disposition (a very important quality for a child's mount) and substance of bone to produce a pony with versatility, strength, and intelligence. Thus the present-day Dartmoor Pony has been beneficially crossbred to create the Dartmoor Sport Pony, an elegant, talented, kind-hearted, riding and driving pony that is also an exceptional jumper.

Initially, there was concern that the Dartmoor would lose its valuable foundation bloodlines and original quality so necessary for preservation, such as other pure breeds have experienced when crossbred. To prevent this from happening, the American Dartmoor Sport Pony registry was created by the American Dartmoor Pony Association. With this addition to the registry, breeders could obtain the special qualities of the Dartmoor in an equine suited to their needs and discipline without depleting the number of pure Dartmoor Ponies.

The Dartmoor Sport Pony has at least 50 percent Dartmoor Pony blood and is created by crossing Dartmoor stallions with mares of other breeds. Sport Ponies come in various builds and sizes suitable for all types of disciplines and can be bred to another American Dartmoor Sport Pony or Dartmoor Pony.

The Dartmoor Sport Ponies have helped purebred Dartmoors as well. Since purebreds are rare and can only come from the limited number of mares available to breed with stallions, the process of increasing numbers is slow. With low worldwide numbers, it is hard to get the publicity needed to increase interest, breeding, and marketing. Since the number of mares of other breeds is endless, the Dartmoor Sport Ponies are being bred at a higher rate. As they enter shows where their talents are being displayed, they increase awareness of the Dartmoor Pony and its contribution to the equine world. With this added exposure, the purebred Dartmoor is on the rise. This pattern of improvement by crossing other breeds to pure Dartmoor stallions has caused the Dartie to become one of the most successful of all British Isle pony breeds.

The Dartmoor Market

Virtually all registered English Dartmoors now reside on private property, and stud farms throughout Great Britain have been breeding and showing their registered Dartmoors. They are constantly striving to keep the breed true to its origins to provide others a chance to own a first class pony. Dartmoors are now being raised throughout Europe, the United States, Australia, and smaller countries. Breeding societies worldwide are working hard at retaining quality and increasing Dartmoor numbers to fill the demand for reliable and sensible ponies.

The increase in Dartmoor demand is due to several reasons: Darties average around 12 hands, making it easy for a child to groom, saddle, and mount them. They move with a low, smooth stride, making their riders feel like they are on a much larger mount. They are not readily excitable like some of their cousins. They are quiet, dependable, easy to train, and possess a gentle and kind heart, not unlike the family Labrador dog. In the show ring, they have competed at Federation Equestre Internationale (FEI) levels and have had outstanding success against other breeds in jumping, cross-country, and dressage, proving that they are a breed to be reckoned with in competition. When used as harness ponies, they can hold their own against much larger equines, displaying toughness and courage allied with their calmness.

By careful selection, breeding through the stud farms, and the preservation efforts of the farmers' ponies on the moor, Dartmoor numbers have a chance of rising to that of other popular pony breeds. Globally, however, there are very few Dartmoor Ponies compared to their cousins. The breed is listed with the Equus Survival Trust as vulnerable, with five thousand to seven thousand active adult purebred breeding mares.

In the United States

The Dartmoor Pony was first introduced to North America in the 1930s. Although still considered a rare breed, its population has been growing steadily in the United States. Recently, there has been a number of quality imports from England as more people have become interested in breeding and owning Dartmoors. Today, there are about 350 purebreds in the United States.

There are two U.S. registries: American Dartmoor Pony Association (ADPA) and Dartmoor Pony Registry of America (DPRA).

Founded in 1993, ADPA was started by breeders who felt it important to have a registry that preserved and promoted the Dartmoor Pony by the standards of the Dartmoor Pony Society in the United Kingdom. This was first accomplished through blood-typing and parentage verification, and later upgraded to DNA-typing with parentage verification. Ponies that can trace back 100 percent to pure United Kingdom stock are registered as purebreds, while Dartmoor crosses of 50 percent or more are registered as American Dartmoor Sport Ponies.

Founded in 1956, the DPRA was started by Joan Dunning of Virginia who imported her first Dartmoors in 1936. Dunning, as well as her daughter, Hetty Abeles, are still among the leading breeders and supporters of Dartmoor Ponies today.

The DPRA is the organization that maintains the official studbook for Dartmoor Ponies in the United States. It has been registering Dartmoors since 1956 and also maintains a database on DPRA-registered Dartmoors. The DPRA uses its database records and DNA to maintain an accurate account of the breed in the United States.

Standards

Overall impression: The Dartmoor is a very good-looking riding pony, sturdily built yet possessing quality. The mane and tail should be full and natural. As a hearty moorland breed, the Dartmoor is stalwart in conformation, more similar to a warmblood type than the elegant Welsh. Its distinctiveness and consistency of appearance make the Dartmoor easy to pick out in a crowd, as well as easy to match to other ponies for a driving team.

Height: Ranging in height from 11 to 12.2 hands, but is not to exceed 12.2 hands (127 centimeters or 50 inches).

Color: Bay, black, brown, chestnut, gray, and roan. Bay and brown are the most dominant colors, followed by black and gray. White markings on the head and legs should be minimal. Excessive white markings are discouraged, and piebald and skewbald are not allowed.

Head and neck: The head should be small with large kindly eyes and small alert ears. It should be well set on a good neck of medium length. The throat and jaws should be fine and show no signs of coarseness or throatiness. Stallions have a moderate crest.

Shoulders: Good shoulders are most important. They should be well laid back and sloping, but not too fine at the withers.

Body: Of medium length, strong, and well-ribbed up with a good depth of girth giving plenty of heart room.

Loin and hindquarters: Strong and well covered with muscle. The hindquarters should be of medium length and neither level nor steeply sloping. The tail should be well set up.

Limbs: The hocks should be well let down, with plenty of length from hip to hock, and clean-cut with plenty of bone below the hock. There should be a strong second thigh. Legs should not be sickle-hocked or cow-hocked, and the forelegs should not be tied in at the elbows. The forearm should be muscular and relatively long, with the knee fairly large and flat on the front. The cannons should be short with ample good, flat, flinty bone. The pasterns should be sloping, but not too long, and the feet should be hard and well shaped.

Temperament: The Dartmoor makes an excellent choice for a child's first pony. Its calm, consistent, quiet disposition encourages novice riders both in and out of the show ring. It has an exceptional mental attitude.

Movement: Low and straight coming from the shoulder with good hock action, but without exaggeration.

Abilities: Dartmoors are perfect as children's riding and show ponies.

Being very brave and possessing powerful rear quarters, they are solid and safe jumpers, thus making them ideal for small children learning to jump. Combining a quiet disposition, inherent hardiness, and a great work ethic, the ponies excel in competition or pleasure driving for both older children and adults. For those not willing to give up the wonderful Dartmoor qualities when they grow too tall for purebreds, the larger Dartmoor Sport Pony is a good choice.

Credit: American Dartmoor Pony Association

EXMOOR PONY

This Exmoor stallion is an excellent example of the breed type. *Kathryn A. Lasky*

Exmoor Pony Association International
P.O. Box 1517
Litchfield, Connecticut 06759
www.exmoorpony.com

Exmoor Pony Enthusiasts
P.O. Box 155
Ripley, Ontario N0G 2R0
Canada
http://exmoorenthusiasts.fortunecity.com

Canadian Livestock Records Corporation
2417 Holly Lane
Ottawa, Ontario K1V 0M7
Canada
www.clrc.ca

The Exmoor Pony certainly is special. Here is no inanimate relic dug up from the past; here is a living, breathing animal of great antiquity that came to Britain long before humans did. It has seen humans evolve from the Stone Age to the beginning of agriculture, through the Industrial Revolution to the Age of Technology. It is considered the purest of England's Mountain and Moorland pony breeds and is an enormously important part of British heritage. It still resembles wild ponies that roamed England ten thousand years ago. To this day, it continues to live on one of the most remote moors of England, Exmoor, for which it is named.

The Exmoor is talented and strong, and is a very rare and treasured breed. It is a hardy pony, shaped by nature for survival over many centuries, and as

Identical characteristics are obvious in this Exmoor Pony herd. *Ona Kiser*

such is an easy keeper. While it is genetically invaluable for its unique history and hardiness, there is the added bonus of its versatility. Its intelligence, robust nature, and natural agility results in a pony ideally suited for riding and driving, whether for pleasure or competition. It is stocky and strong enough to carry an adult fox hunting. Its action is long, low, and more comfortable than many other ponies its size. The mountain and moorland habitat of the Exmoor has bred into the breed balance, agility, and surefootedness.

The Exmoor is wonderful to live with, easy to care for, easy to fall in love with, and sensible enough to learn all things equine—and more! It is the Original Off-Roader.

History

The first wild ponies came to Britain between ten thousand and twenty thousand years ago, walking across a swampy plain that was later to become the English Channel. They became widespread throughout Britain, living alongside mammoths and preyed upon by saber-toothed tigers, wolves, and bears. Their presence in Britain ebbed and flowed until drastic climate changes in the Mesolithic period brought a covering of trees in the lowland areas. Open grazing habitats became available only on the mountains and hills of Britain, and consequently the pony populations became restricted to those areas.

When the English Channel formed five thousand to eight thousand years ago, equine populations became isolated on the British Isles with no possible further interference. Some scientists theorize that the British hill pony was hunted to extinction, and then re-introduced by Celts. Other scientists believe they remained in reduced numbers on the isolated uplands.

The Exmoor Pony is a wonderful riding and family pony.
Exmoor Ponies of North America

When farmers settled the lowland areas and divided the land into fields and agricultural holdings, British hill ponies became isolated from each other and their destinies followed different paths. This resulted in the nine recognized native breeds of Mountain and Moorland ponies in Britain today. In each area, human interference led to the mixing of different genetic ingredients to produce distinctive breeds. As an example, when Roman mercenaries brought their horses to Northern England, these breeds blended with British hill ponies to produce the Fell Pony.

On Exmoor, a very different story unfolded. In every other part of Britain, outside equine blood was introduced to a degree that drastically altered the appearance of the British hill pony; on Exmoor, this did not happen. Most of the changes to ponies elsewhere in Britain took place in the last few hundred years. These changes can be linked to the influences of major trade routes and ports introducing new ideas and new animals, or to the influences of landowners doing the same.

Exmoor, however, until very recently, was a forgotten place with no such routes across it or large ports nearby, and few landowners feature in its history. It is situated in the southwest of Britain, spanning the borders of Devon and Somerset, its northern boundary being the high cliffs of the Bristol Channel. It is an area of high moorland divided by steep wooded valleys and fragmented by farmland. The moorland provides a varied diet of grasses, rushes, heather, and gorse and is where wild red deer survived as well as the hill ponies and farm stock. The area is subject to very wet winters, cold temperatures, and driving winds. It is, in effect, a social island within the British Isles, and because of this the original type of pony survived.

A few people on Exmoor followed the trend for crossing and "improving" the local pony, but it is significant that these herds died out and left no legacy. Exmoor Ponies of today are descended from stock that was managed on the principle that nature had the best design and introducing outside blood would lead to dilution of hardiness. Thus the Exmoor of today remains the closest surviving breed to the British hill pony.

Until 1818, most of the open expanse of Exmoor was designated a Royal Forest, with "forest" in this sense meaning a hunting ground. A warden worked for the crown and managed Exmoor as an upland grazing expanse where farmers from its fringes could graze their stock (ponies, sheep, and cattle) upon payment of fees. The warden alone ran the stallions that, as it is recorded, were of the original native type.

In 1818, the Royal Forest was sold to John Knight, an industrialist who believed he could tame the Exmoor land and make it a more productive agricultural system. He considered that whatever nature had created, he could improve upon, including the ponies. Knight and a few others experimented, but they produced ponies that could not thrive living out in Exmoor's harsh winters.

The outgoing warden, Sir Thomas Acland, took thirty of the pure Exmoor Ponies that had lived in the forest to his own estate. Other local farmers who had worked with him bought up small numbers of ponies at the 1818 dispersal sale and began their own breeding herds. Sir Thomas and his colleagues were perhaps some of the first conservationists, breeding the Exmoor ponies true to type.

Most of the significant traits from these outside infusions in the last of the crossed herds, which had lived separately from the true Exmoors, died out early in the twentieth century. The Acland ponies continued and their descendants now form the famous Anchor herd that runs on Winsford Hill. In most cases, those farming families that had saved ponies back in 1818 are still involved today, inbreeding Exmoors.

Having survived the dispersal in 1818 and the fashion for "improvement," which could have changed them beyond recognition, Exmoor Ponies were nearly exterminated during World War II. They were used for training troops, some of which practiced on live targets, including ponies. Gates were left open and grazing areas were no longer safe for stock. Many ponies were stolen and transported away to cities to feed hungry people. By the end of the war, it is estimated that no more than fifty Exmoor ponies survived.

A breeder on Exmoor named Mary Etherington rallied farmers and landowners to revive Exmoor pony breeding and build up numbers. She even exhibited two Exmoors at the London Zoo to draw attention to their plight. Cattle grids were installed, and stock was returned to the commons and moors. Steadily, the Exmoor Pony population began to recover and grow.

Although numbers increased gradually, even by the mid 1970s just around thirty Exmoor foals a year were being registered. In the late 1970s,

attention was once again focused on their zoological importance and rarity. Enthusiasm for breeding Exmoors returned as demand for foals increased, and many new owners bought Exmoors as a commitment to their conservation. While numbers rose away from Exmoor, the population of free-roaming ponies that lived on the moor and were subjected to the laws of nature remained under two hundred.

Today, the majority of Exmoors are bred off the moors. The few remaining herds on the moors have experienced significant inbreeding and are managed by their owners only during yearly roundups, weanling sales, and stallion selections. Otherwise, they fend for themselves on the cold, windy, and wet moor.

Uses

A boost to this free living population came in the 1980s with the recognition that Exmoor Ponies can be a useful conservation tool themselves. The National Trust, English Nature (now part of Natural England), and several county wildlife trusts set up small, free-living herds on sensitive nature reserves to manage the vegetation. This is proving most successful and is benefiting the conservation of the Exmoor Pony alongside the conservation of whole habitats.

Prior to the use of mechanization, which came comparatively late to Exmoor, the local pony was used for a wide variety of tasks on the hill farms. A pony could be used for driving, shepherding, plowing, harrowing, hunting, and carrying the farmer to market, as well as being children's show ponies. Some were even used for the post (mail) rounds, while others were mounts for the British Home Guard during World War II. Exmoors were also used in crossbreeding programs to improve the soundness of other breeds and tap into their jumping ability. Those that were one-quarter to one-eighth Exmoor crosses (usually crossed with Thoroughbreds) were used as steeplechasers in the United Kingdom.

As well as being able to serve many family members, the Exmoor found favor because it was economical to keep. In fact, one of the most important aspects of caring for an Exmoor is to ensure that it does not get too much food, even if it is pastured.

Today, Exmoor Ponies are seldom used for farm work, but throughout Britain they participate in every sphere of equestrian activity, be it showing, riding, driving, jumping, long-distance riding, or riding and driving for the disabled. Their considerable strength makes them highly suited to driving, but it also means that they require a competent child rider rather than a rank beginner.

Registries

Back in 1921, the owners of herds in the United Kingdom, who believed that the purebred Exmoor should continue to exist and not be lost through crossbreeding, gathered together and formed the Exmoor Pony Society to promote and encourage the breeding of purebred Exmoor Ponies. The Society set in place a system whereby foals from registered Exmoor parents have to be inspected and passed as free from disqualifying faults before they can be registered. A foal with any concentrations of white hairs on the body, or in the mane or tail, or white patches on its feet, fails to qualify for registration.

Each autumn the herds are gathered off the moor to their home farms for inspection and branding. There are many more Exmoors bred in Britain's domesticated situations, thus the society inspectors travel throughout Britain assessing these foals, as well as the moorland ones. If a foal passes, it is hot branded with the Exmoor Pony Society's four-pointed star above its left shoulder. Beneath this—except for the Anchor herd—is the mare owner's herd number, and the left flank is branded with the foal's individual number. The Anchor herd has no herd number, but instead has an anchor symbol brand over the individual number. Each registered Exmoor therefore carries its individual identity for life, and by checking this in the studbook, its breeding is also known.

In the United States, the Exmoor Pony Association International was founded in 2001 and does registrations based on DNA testing. The goal is to include all Exmoors and be able to assess their genetic status and numbers. It has three levels of registration. Section A is for those that are DNA tested and have a veterinary exam, plus they are presented to a panel of three judges to assess breed type and pass. Section B is for those that are DNA tested plus they have an exam for physical defects. Section C is for those ponies that are DNA tested. The registry also includes Exmoor crosses of 50 percent or more.

Another registry is the Canadian Livestock Records Corporation, which registers Exmoor Ponies under its General Stud and Herd Book and is open to all purebred ponies born in Canada or the United States.

Due to Exmoors being very rare, there is much concern about their low numbers. The Exmoor population on the moor in England is limited to about 150 ponies; there are less than 100 Exmoors in North America and only some 2,000 in the world. The breed is listed in the critical category by the Equus Survival Trust, and the Rare Breeds Survival Trust (United Kingdom) lists it as endangered as of 2007.

Breed Characteristics

All Exmoor Ponies are essentially identical, conforming to a natural blueprint. Variation in color and markings, which are typical in breeds humans have created, is noticeably absent. This suggests that the Exmoor remains more a wild race than a selected breed. Characteristics of Exmoor Ponies are all survival adaptations for avoiding predators as well as coping with hostile elements.

The ponies' moorland living has given them an efficient digestive system. They have a large girth and stomach capacity and unusual prehensile lips. Whereas they thrive on gorse bushes, they will get fat on too much hay or pasture. They are easy keepers personified; however, as with other breeds, they need to be fed adequately if they are working hard.

Their hooves are unusually tough. Typically, they do not need shoes unless they are driven on pave-

Exmoors are stocky and robust ponies resembling their ancient ancestors. *Ona Kiser*

ment, and hoof trimming is needed far less than with most other breeds. They have an almost cat-like jumping ability with remarkable agility and can often make a significant jump even from a standstill.

Their temperament is intelligent, sensible, and independent, but it usually takes some experience as a rider to get the best work out of them.

Overall appearance: Exmoor Ponies are hardy, vigorous, alert, and symmetrical in appearance. They are stocky and strong with deep chests and large girths. The large capacity of their digestive system is important in winter, as they consume large quantities of coarse plant material that provides them with internal warmth. They have an alert expression and general poise indicating balance and symmetry of movement with fine, clean bone.

Color: At first glance, all Exmoor Ponies look alike. They come in bay, brown, and mouse dun (a dilute of the basic bay gene) and usually have darker legs, although browns may have brown legs. They all have striking mealy (oatmeal) colored markings on the muzzle, around the eyes, and sometimes under the belly, but no white markings anywhere else. The mane and tail are usually a darker brown than the body, sometimes almost black, but occasionally they are lighter and more mousy in color. The shade of brown of the coat ranges from a light rich brown, termed "bay," through every shade of brown, to just a few individuals that are almost black.

This pattern of coloring/marking, which is uniform throughout the population, is a primitive design and found elsewhere in the horse family (Przewalski's Horse) and is displayed by many herbivorous prey animals in other animal families, such as cattle, sheep, and antelopes. Exmoors blend in very well against the background of mixed heather, grass, and bracken in their moorland habitat, camouflaging them from predators. Additionally, the mealy muzzle and mealy eye ring perhaps serve to break up the outline of the head, making its movements less obvious to a predator. Exmoor foals are born with the mealy markings set against a much lighter coat color. This changes as they grow their first winter coat, and it may take up to two years for them to match the adults in color.

Size: There is relatively little variation in size between adult Exmoors. They naturally range from 11.1 to 13.1 hands (46 to 53 inches), with the majority being around 12.2 hands (50 inches). Heights of above 12.2 hands occur more frequently in domestication. The preferred height range in stallions and geldings is 11.3 to 12.3 hands at maturity, while mares should be 11.2 to 12.2 hands at maturity.

Exmoors are immensely strong ponies for their size. They have plentiful bone, with 6.5 to 7 inches minimum circumference for cannon bones (6.5 inches minimum for mares and 7 inches minimum for stallions and geldings). They also have three-quarters of an inch more in circumference on their hind cannon bones than their front ones. (It is professionally recommended that all equines have 7 inches per 1,000 pounds of body weight, and Exmoors are well over that.) They have broad loins allowing them to carry relatively more weight for their size, making them an ideal family pony as they can carry adults as well as children.

Temperament: Exmoors are loyal and kind if well treated. They are also intelligent, sensible, and independent.

Bite: The Exmoor Pony presents an example of high efficiency in the business of finding, gathering, chewing, and digesting food. The teeth are well adapted to a coarse diet. The incisors (biting teeth) are curved so that they meet vertically, like a pair of pliers, and therefore cut cleanly and effectively. The efficiency of the bite does not appear to decline so rapidly with age as is seen in many other horses. The molars (chewing teeth) are very large and set into the jaw, so that the maximum chewing pressure can be exerted on tough plants.

Contrary to many publications, Exmoor Ponies do not have an extra seventh molar tooth. This misconception arose from the mistranslation of some German research, which in fact was referring to an extra branch off the blood supply to the lower jaw (this might have been the beginnings of the evolution of an extra tooth). This feature does not seem to be confined to Exmoors and is perhaps simply present in animals with large lower jaws.

Head: The face is clean-cut with a wide forehead. Ears of the Exmoor are short, thick, and pointed. The eyes are large and wide apart, giving them an extra-wide field of vision and a distinctive, appealing expression. The eyes are prominent "toad," or hooded, eyes, which are often erroneously thought to relate to the mealy colored ring. It refers, however, to the raised fleshy rim above and below the eye that the coloring accentuates. This rim serves to protect the eye from rainwater by diverting it down the length of the head to run off the lower jaw.

Body: The Exmoor has a clean throatlatch and good length of neck. The shoulders are clean, fine at the top, and well laid back. The chest is deep and wide between and behind forelegs. Ribs are long, well-sprung, and wide apart. The back is level, broad and also level across the loins. The tail is neatly set in.

Legs: The legs are clean and short with a strong cannon bone. Forelegs are straight, well apart, and squarely set. Hind legs are well apart and nearly perpendicular from hock to fetlock, with point of hock in line with pelvis bone. There is a wide curve from flank to hock joint, and legs are free in motion with no tendency to sweep or turn. The feet are outstandingly hard and neat, and are slate blue/black in color.

Movement: When moving, the Exmoor is straight and smooth without exaggerated action. The limbs are designed for movement over hilly terrain.

Coat: One of the major forces of natural selection is climate. The Exmoor Pony's external anatomy is designed to withstand extremes of cold and, most importantly, rain. These are the descendants of a mountain pony prototype that evolved

A thrilling scene: an Exmoor herd cavorting in a country setting. *Ona Kiser*

to live in wet upland environments.

The coat grows in two phases, providing summer and winter coats. The winter hair grows in two layers that, in effect, provides a sort of thermal underwear and a raincoat. The hairs next to the skin forming the undercoat (like thermal underwear) are fine and springy in texture and form an insulating layer. The outer hairs act as a raincoat, being coarse and water-repellent, which water beads off of like a well waxed car or polished furniture. The efficiency of this double layered coat is evident from the phenomenon of snow-thatching—the coat insulates them so well that in cold weather, snow does not melt on them. It collects on the ponies' backs as insufficient body heat escapes to melt it. Thus the body is not chilled by melting snow, and the collected snow is shaken off periodically.

Body hair is good at channeling rain off so that it never touches the skin. It grows in a surface drainage pattern: it lies in an arrangement of whorls (cowlicks) and vortices, which maximize water dispersal away from the vulnerable parts of the body and body openings.

The tail, mane, forelock, and, in winter, the beard all show water-shedding specialization. The fan of short hairs near the root of the tail is called a snowchute, but its function is to channel rainwater out over the buttocks so that it does not run under the tail. The long, fully haired mane and tail, which contrast with the upright mane and partially haired tail of a Przewalski, are adaptations to this prime need of dispersing water from the body.

The Exmoor Pony sheds its winter coat by late spring, and for a short time, until about late August, sports its summer coat. This retains the drainage properties but consists of just a single, short layer, since insulation is unnecessary. It is a hard, flat, shiny coat. Most Exmoors with good nutrition show extensive dappling. Seasonal dappling is a result of the sooty (smutty like) gene.

Certain bloodlines have a tendency for "sweet itch," an allergic dermatitis to insect bites, especially gnats.

Credits: Exmoor Pony Association International and Exmoor Pony Enthusiasts

FALABELLA MINIATURE HORSE

Falabella Miniature Horse Association
33222 N. Fairfield Road
Round Lake, Illinois 60073
www.falabellafmha.com

The Falabella is a rare Argentine breed of Miniature Horse that has been kept pure by breeding only pure Falabellas to each other for countless generations. It is known as the original Miniature Horse breed, yet the miniature size is secondary to the pure heritage, which is more than 150 years old. It is a true purebred with a unique and historic ancestry, which is one of its greatest attributes. The other is the fact that the Falabella name is recognized all over the world. Breed ancestry has been kept pure by the Falabella Farm and by small groups of dedicated breeders who want to preserve the little horse's precious heritage. Falabellas were produced through both natural and selective breeding over many generations.

The Falabella is an exquisitely small horse that has always been rare due to the limited number within its ancestry gene pool. Estimates indicate that only a few thousand of them exist in the entire world. The most desirable feature of the Falabella and its primary value is that of its rarity and pure ancestry. It is very prestigious to own and is highly prized by those who have one.

Beside its intrinsic value, the Falabella can provide family enjoyment as a beloved pet or companion for anyone, from tots to teens and adults. Most Falabellas can be ridden by small children. Although some may be too small for riding, the breed is strong for its size, thus driving them is very popular, especially in shows and parades.

History

Many historic facts and fables have been told of the famous Falabella in books, magazines, and equine news articles. It was said that the original little horses were descendants of Andalusian and Spanish Barb horses brought to Argentina by the Spaniards when they first arrived in the fifteenth century. The Spanish intended to conquer Argentina, but were defeated, and the horses were left behind, free to roam. Over the next few centuries, inbreeding and the harsh environment caused a reduction in size, which culminated in naturally small horses.

By the 1840s, these small equines were seen mixed within herds near the southern Buenos Aires area by a breeder named Patrick Newell, who decided to build a herd with the smallest horses he could find. It was from this point when selective breeding began to develop a true small horse. Newell learned how to improve the horses and passed his breeding knowledge to his son-in-law, Juan Falabella, who in turn shared his knowledge with his son Emilio, who then passed it on to his son, Julio.

As Julio worked to develop the breed with his father throughout his younger years, he gained all the knowledge his father had received from previous generations. Over many years, they used a variety of equines, including the native Argentine Criollo horse and others with Pinto and Appaloosa markings, to breed down in size, continually keeping the smallest and best quality in each generation.

By the 1950s, Julio took over the Falabella Farm and created horses in every color. The greatest development and perfection of the Falabella breed was achieved by Julio when he created his little horses in varied colors, including pintos and some very rare and colorful Appaloosas, which were his favorites. Through dedication and knowledge, he was able to produce perfect little horses that were some of the smallest in the world.

Once the tiny sizes in all colors were attained, a century of natural heritage and breed development

A Falabella pinto-spotted youngster is inquisitive. *Iofoto/Shutterstock*

was completed, and Julio set out to show his Falabella Miniature Horses to the world. By the early 1960s, he was exporting his Falabellas to the United States and other countries. Several articles about the Falabella Miniature Horse were written in *National Geographic* magazine, *Western Horseman*, and horse magazines. When reporters traveled to Argentina to interview him, Julio was the first ever

to call diminutive equines "Miniature Horses," as well as the first to market them by that name. News spread like wildfire about this Miniature Horse breed that was centuries in the making. Julio and his Falabella Miniature Horses became famous as he continued to export them to all parts of the world. Some of the richest and most famous people—kings, princes, presidents, and movie stars—bought them, usually paying astronomical prices for some of Julio's smallest and best horses.

Through the 1970s Falabella Miniature Horses were being imported in small groups. By this time, Julio had a large number of Falabellas on his ranch in sizes as small as 28 inches with perfect conformation in all colors. Some of Julio's best and most colorful stallions and mares were sent to the United States and other countries around the world. It was during these years that the Falabella Miniature Horse became a registered breed through the Falabella Miniature Horse Association (FMHA). When Julio passed away in 1980, the Falabella Farm and his life's work were continued in Argentina by his wife and her sons. Julio's daughter, Maria Angelica Falabella, also continued the breed when she moved to the United States in 1995. She brought her very best Falabellas with her, including her smallest and most colorful Pintos and Appaloosas. Both Falabella farms continued to be primary producers and exporters of the breed all over the world until Maria Angelica Falabella's retirement in 2006. The Falabella Farm in Argentina still has the little horses, and there are also other breeding farms located in the United States, Canada, Europe, the United Kingdom, and in a number of other countries.

The most famous Falabella to be imported to the United States was Chianti, a beautiful black leopard Appaloosa stallion foaled in 1964 that was imported with Falabella mares to the Regina Winery in California in the 1960s. Chianti became an immediate sensation and has since been featured in many equine news articles. Chianti and his mares produced some of the first Falabella foals born in the United States and some of the very first Appaloosas within the Miniature breed, making Chianti a founding sire.

One of the best known and finest stallions in the United States was Toyland Zodiac, a 31-inch, top-quality, black leopard Appaloosa foaled in 1976. Toyland Zodiac was the leading sire and grandsire of more show-quality and top-winning offspring than any other Falabella stallion in the United

States. Some of the most beautiful and finest quality Falabellas have bloodlines that trace back to Toyland Zodiac, firmly establishing him as a prominent founding sire in the breed.

Breeding Incentives

Specializing in Falabellas is a popular choice for those who are looking for something different. A growing number of Miniature Horse breeders and owners are adding Falabellas to their farms, as they see the many advantages in breeding these rare little horses. Being highly popular, but limited in number, they offer an exclusive marketing advantage. This is especially attractive since there are few Falabella breeders, but a large number of Miniature Horse owners who are potential buyers.

They are strong color producers and are available in all colors and sizes, offering a wide variety of choices to please everyone. They can be shown in all Miniature Horse shows and registered in all Miniature Horse registries in the world. Most importantly, they have their own FMHA registration certificate to authenticate their historic ancestry.

With many top farm names coming and going over the years, the Falabella name has withstood the test of time by retaining its status. Falabellas are known and shown worldwide and the name creates its own market, which is a unique advertising and promotional advantage available to breeders. This offers an exclusive opportunity to use the Falabella name to market them, which draws enquiries from Miniature Horse owners as well as Falabella fanciers. Only FMHA registered horses have the inherited right to claim the Falabella name.

As with other horse breeds, Falabellas come in all price ranges. Some can be expensive and carry premium prices, yet, most can be acquired at affordable prices. Foals are especially desirable, being adorable and affectionate, and cost less than adults. They are ideal for those who want a few horses, a sire for future breeding stock, or want show prospects. They retain their value and are adorable and fun to raise. They add herd value if kept, or generate

Falabellas come in all colors and can have any color of eyes. *Iofoto/ Shutterstock*

income each year if sold. A one-time purchase of breeding stock can give financial returns through foal sales for twenty years or more.

There are distinct differences between Falabellas and American Miniature Horses. As of 2008, there are less than 1,500 Falabellas registered in the FMHA since its incorporation in 1973, compared to the hundreds of thousands of registered Miniature Horses. Only small herds of Falabellas are known to exist in the United States and most other countries, and their number is estimated to be only several thousand in the entire world. This creates a strong demand and limited supply due to the small number in existence. Although both Falabellas and American Miniature Horses have made great strides toward meeting the standard of perfection in the past twenty years, the purebred ancestry documentation of every Falabella and its rarity are what primarily set it apart from all other breeds.

Because they are so special, however, the primary reason to have Falabellas is to protect and preserve the breed through dedicated breeding by keeping the bloodlines pure.

Showing

Beyond generating an income, many enjoy the thrill of showing and winning ribbons, trophies, and special awards, which can bring show titles, recognition, and added value to Falabellas. Since they meet the requirements and breed standards of other Miniature Horse registries, they can be registered

A good example of breed type, this Appaloosa Falabella is a foundation stallion. *Falabella Miniature Horse Association*

and shown in Miniature Horse shows around the world. With there so few Falabellas in existence, there would hardly be enough to put on a big show like the larger Miniature Horse registries do.

Both adults and children can show in a variety of Miniature Horse classes. The horses are easy to train for driving and very rewarding to show. Being a versatile breed, Falabellas can do all the things that any Miniature Horse can do. Show-quality Falabellas compete side by side with today's American Miniatures and have taken ribbons and national titles. Some have taken top awards on an international basis.

For those who cannot get to the shows, Falabellas do not have to be shown to maintain their high value and good marketability. Their true value is in what they are—rare Falabella Miniature Horses.

Argentina Falabella Registry

All Falabellas have their origins from the Falabella Farm in Argentina, which still continues to breed and export its little horses around the world. The Falabella Farm has developed its own Asociación de Criadores de Caballos Falabella (ACCF) registry, which records the original ancestry of their sires,

dams, and offspring born on the Falabella Farm. The breed name is protected by the Falabella Farm in Argentina through ACCF. When a Falabella is exported from Argentina, its ancestry continues to be protected by registration internationally with an ACCF registration document that authenticates its Falabella Farm heritage.

Falabella Miniature Horse Association

With continued importations of Falabellas in the 1970s and additional offspring being born, there was a need for a registry in the United States. By this time, Falabellas were already becoming popular, and a number of breeders were importing them to other parts of the world as well as across the country. In 1973 the Falabella Miniature Horse Association (FMHA) was incorporated in the United States as the first Falabella Miniature Horse registry in the world. The Argentina ancestral pedigrees were recorded, and FMHA registration certificates were issued to all purebreds and their offspring. Today, FMHA continues as an international registry for Falabellas all over the world.

Only purebred Falabellas are accepted for registration. They must have an FMHA registered sire and dam, or documented proof of every ancestor tracing their original ancestry to the Falabella Farm in Argentina. Those that originate from the Falabella Farm and have a Falabella prefix on their pedigree are honored for registration. FMHA also honors all pure descendants of imported Fallabellas having ACCF registration certificates from the Argentina Falabella Farm and from other Falabella registries in other countries.

Other U.S. Registries

An additional and important advantage of the breed is that most Falabellas in the United States can also be registered in the American Miniature Horse Association (AMHA) and/or the American Miniature Horse Registry (AMHR). This triple registration option gives owners the opportunity to register, breed, and show their Falabellas in the registries of their choice and still maintain a pure Falabella breeding program.

The American Miniature Horse is extremely popular and has become one of the top choice breeds. Proof of their popularity is shown as the count of AMHA and AMHR registrations are over two hundred thousand since their inception. In comparison, there are less than 1,500 Falbellas registered in FMHA since its inception in 1973, attesting to their rarity. Pure Falabellas make up only a tiny part of the growing number of other registered Miniature Horses; however they are a big attraction for Miniature Horse breeders and Falabella fanciers, who enjoy the option of showing and breeding Falabellas with other Miniatures.

FMHA Breed Standard

The first and most important breed standard for any Falabella Miniature Horse is to possess documentation of pure Falabella ancestry, meaning that every ancestor has been verified to be a purebred Falabella, which is authenticated by a FMHA registration certificate.

Disposition: Falabellas are sweet natured, easy to handle, and enjoy being with anyone, from children, to adults and seniors.

Quality: The quality of a Falabella is most important, having an overall appearance of a well balanced horse with a pleasing look, good legs, a good bite, and good conformation—the same as required to show. Falabellas with the finest show quality are highly desirable.

Breed type: All breed types are acceptable. As development of the Falabella evolved, selective breeding created a variety of types. Some of the most popular breed types seen in Falabellas are Arabian, Thoroughbred, Quarter Horse, Pinto, and Appaloosa, but the most important factor is always their pure Falabella ancestry. Emphasis has been toward breeding for refinement, with well balanced conformation and the look of a true horse in the breed type they resemble.

Size: Birth heights can be as small as 12 inches or up to 22 inches or more, and mature heights are usually attained at three years of age. Since they are naturally a small equine breed, mature heights can be 25 to 34 inches and more, but most Falabellas mature in the 30 to 34-inch height range. They were continually bred for the smallest sizes, and records show they breed true for their inherited traits. They have long been known for producing some of the smallest equines in the world and for passing on their small sizes to their offspring. All sizes are accepted for registration in FMHA. In essence, size does not take away from their pure ancestry or value. Their pure heritage has always been the first and foremost reason to acquire them, and they are still a rare and special breed regardless of their height. Once pure Falabellas are accepted for registration, they remain registered in FMHA for life.

Colors: Falabellas come in all solid colors and a wide variety of colorful pinto and appaloosa patterns. An unusual "pintaloosa" pattern can also occur, showing both pinto and appaloosa markings. Some of the most colorful are in strong demand, but limited in number.

Credit: Falabella Miniature Horse Association

FALABELLA BLEND MINIATURE HORSE

Falabella Blend Registry
33222 N. Fairfield Road
Round Lake, Illinois 60073
www.falabellafmha.com

A Falabella Blend Miniature Horse is a blend of pure Falabella ancestry combined with the bloodlines of an American Miniature Horse or another Miniature. It was created through breeding pure Falabellas with American Miniature Horses starting in the 1960s, when the first Falabellas were imported from Argentina to the United States. As more continued to be imported over succeeding years, the breeding of Falabellas to American Miniatures continued and the Falabella Blends gained in popularity.

In the 1980s, a longtime Falabella breeder from Illinois named Laurie Stevens, bred her Falabella stallions to American Miniature mares and advertised the offspring as Falabella Blends. Over the years, Falabella Blends became popular as the name caught on, and by the 1990s the Falabella Blends were well known. Breeders liked the idea that the petite little horses carried the historic Falabella bloodline. Today, Falabella Blends are in many parts of the world.

They come in a variety of sizes and colors and are versatile in many ways. Falabella Blends can be easily trained for children to ride or to pull a cart or small wagon. They are quick to learn tricks and can be shown by both children and adults to win ribbons and awards at the shows. Foals are adorable and can add herd value if kept, or can generate income from foal sales. Falabella Blends are an excellent choice to breed for fun and for profit.

Registry

Since there was no specific registry for the Falabella Blends in earlier years, they were registered and shown by the American Miniature Horse

Falabella Blend bay appaloosa mare. *Falabella Miniature Horse Association*

Association (AMHA), American Miniature Horse Registry (AMHR), or other Miniature registries. This still continues today, since the Falabella Blends will always be an integral part of both the Falabella and the American Miniature Horse breed.

As the Falabella Blend became more popular, there was a need for a registry to authenticate its ancestry, and in 2001 the Falabella Blend Registry (FBR) was founded by Laurie Stevens as a separate associate registry to the Falabella Miniature Horse Association (FMHA), which was established in 1973. Since that time, the Falabella Blend has become a popular specialty breed, and the FBR became an international registry for all Falabella Blends in the world.

Any Miniature Horse that is out of an FMHA sire or dam, or has one or more ancestors that have Falabella Blend or pure Falabella ancestry can be registered. This is verified through a pedigree search in FMHA and FBR studbook records. Any Miniature Horse from any other association or registry that is verified to have an ancestral combination of pure Falabella and Miniature Horse ancestry is accepted for registration. A true Falabella Blend Miniature has the prestige and honor of carrying the unique Falabella bloodlines. There are many AMHA and AMHR Falabella Blends that are not yet registered in FBR. If the ancestry is from the Falabella Farms in Argentina, that is acceptable as well.

To stay within FBR breeding guidelines, it is recommended breeding toward the ideal blend of 25 to 75 percent Falabella ancestry whenever possible. If a Falabella Blend is less than 25 percent Falabella, it is recommended to increase the Falabella ancestry. Using a pure Falabella stallion or breeding two Falabella Blends together produces the best and most valued foals. Most breeders start with a pure Falabella colt or stallion to maintain the best lineage in their Falabella Blend breeding program. It takes only one pure Falabella stallion to produce Falabella Blends.

The difference between the Falabella Blend and other Miniature Horses is the former is a separate breed that combines pure Falabella ancestry with Miniature Horse ancestry within their pedigree. The breed is strictly an ancestral breed, and everyone must maintain a combined *blend* of the pure Argentine Falabella and American bloodlines in order to be accepted for registration. The American Miniature is strictly a size breed that must maintain a specific height, but may have a variety of all Miniature bloodlines from any Miniature Horse in the United States or from other parts of the world. These differences separate the Falabella Blend from the American Miniature.

An increasing number of Miniature Horse farms in the United States and all over the world are creating some lovely show quality Falabella Blends and finding it much to their liking. The Falabella name is well known worldwide, giving added appeal to foals with Falabella Blend registration certificates.

Specializing in Blends

The American Miniature Horse is extremely popular and can be found throughout the United States and the rest of the world. In comparison, there are less than one thousand Falabella Blends registered in the FBR that can only be found through certain breeders who have them. This puts Falabella Blends in their own unique and separate category and allows breeders to promote and specialize with them. They are popular, beautiful, and are perfect for the breeder who wants something different.

Since they are a true Miniature breed in size, AMHA and/or AMHR certificates add value and desirability for American breeders. FMHA or FBR registration certificates bring additional value.

Pure Falabellas and Falabella Blends are but a small part of AMHA and AMHR registered American Miniatures. Their uniqueness makes them popular with breeders looking for a distinct kind of miniature.

Since they can be registered in all Miniature Horse registries, they can also be bred to American or other Miniatures to produce foals that are also Falabella Blends. They can compete for regional and national wins like other Miniatures registered in any other Miniature association, registry, or society. A number of Falabellas and Falabella Blends have taken winner's ribbons and special regional and national wins in the United States and internationally.

As a specialty breed, the Falabella and Falabella Blend breed names are known worldwide, giving added appeal and value to foals with Falabella Blend registration. Using the Falabella Blend name attracts other Miniature breeders, as the breed has been popular among breeders since the first pure Falabellas were imported in the 1960s. A number of them started with Falabella Blends by acquiring a pure Falabella colt or stallion to breed with their Miniature mares, while others have Falabella Blends because they like the combined American and Falabella lines. Having both American Miniatures and Falabella Blends in one breeding program is to offer something for everyone.

Although most Falabella Blends are acquired for breeding, they can also be enjoyed by families in a variety of ways. It is fun having Blend foals, as

Falabella Blend foals are especially adorable. *Falabella Miniature Horse Association*

they are especially petite and adorable and make great family pets. They can be shown by adults and children in a variety of Miniature Horse classes or in parades. They can be ridden by small children under seventy pounds, and most can be driven in a small cart. Like the Falabellas, they are strong for their size and driving them is popular. Falabella Blends come in all sizes, colors, and personalities, providing a variety of uses to please everyone.

Standard of Perfection

The first and most important breed standard for any Falabella Blend Miniature Horse is to have its heritage verified with a registration certificate from the FBR.

Breed type: All equine breed types are acceptable, but the Arabian, Quarter Horse, Thoroughbred, Pinto, and Appaloosa are some of the most popular. The most important factors are always the Falabella part of the horse's ancestry and good conformation with a pleasing look. Over the last twenty years, emphasis has

gradually been on breeding for more refinement in all Miniature breed types. This trend is gaining in popularity worldwide among breeders and at the shows.

Color: The Falabella Blend comes in every known color of every breed of equine. They come in all solid colors and a wide array of beautiful pinto and appaloosa patterns. Unusual "pintaloosa" patterns can also occur, showing both pinto and appaloosa markings. There is no limit to their endless variety of colors.

Size: A variety of sizes are accepted for FBR registration. The most popular Falabella Blend size ranges from 30 to 34 inches. They reproduce well and can throw toy-sized foals that mature at 30 inches and under if they carry toy-size ancestry. Emphasis is put on breeding for a small size while maintaining a true horse look. The smallest and most perfect in conformation are the most desirable.

Birth heights can be as petite as 12 inches or up to 22 inches or more. Toy-sized Falabella Blends can mature under 27 inches or up to 29.75 inches. They are highly prized for their tiny size, but are limited in number and can be hard to find. The smallest and most perfect can have very high value.

Some Falabella Blends mature over 34 inches, but since they naturally inherit their size as well as their pure Falabella and Miniature Horse ancestry, they are accepted for registration in FBR. No matter what size they are, it does not take away their ancestry or their value as Falabella Blends. They are still a unique and special breed. Once a Falabella Blend is accepted for registration in FBR, they remain registered for life.

Disposition: The Falabella Blend has a naturally good disposition inherited from both the Falabella and the Miniature Horse breeds. They can be a wonderful farm friend for anyone. They are generally sweet natured, easy to handle, and enjoy being with people of all ages.

Credit: Falabella Blend Registry

FELL PONY

Fell Pony Society and Conservancy
of the Americas
775 Flippin Road
Lowgap, North Carolina 27024
www.fellpony.org

Fell Pony Society
Ion House, Great Asby
Appleby, Cumbria CA16 6HD
United Kingdom
www.fellponysociety.org

Although Fells have become popular show and pleasure riding ponies in England, it has always been their *work ethic* that the hill breeders of Cumbria have admired and taken pains to preserve. As the world shrinks and the ponies' territory enlarges, true stewards of the breed are looking for innovative ways to maintain the heart and soul of this blue-collar pony.

The Fell Pony is one of the nine recognized Mountain and Moorland pony breeds of Britain. It is a hardy and versatile working breed of exceedingly good temperament and intelligence. With sturdy legs, hard hooves, and plenty of dense, flat bone below the knee, it is a wonderfully strong pony. Tireless, surefooted, and thrifty, the Fell Pony is renowned for its ground-covering trot, straight, silky feathering, and profuse mane and tail. The lay of its shoulder makes the pony a comfortable long-distance riding mount, and the depth of its girth and soundness of limbs make it a trouble-free competitor for driving, jumping, or dressage.

History

This rare pony hails from Northern England and the Scottish border, where they derive their name, Fell, from the Norse word for "hill." The breed's origins go back to the four centuries of Roman occupation on this border, when auxiliary

Fell Pony mare at a trot. *Sue Millard*

Fells grazing. Fells come in different colors, but black is the prevailing color. *Sue Millard*

troops were brought in to help at Hadrian's Wall, which separated the two countries of England and Scotland. The troops also maintained law and order throughout the area, as they did in most of the British Isles. French, Dutch, German, Polish, Spanish, and Eastern European cavalrymen were posted there, as were their horses. Also foreign horses of several types, from slender Arab types to coarse workhorses, are known to have been there from archaeology in northern Britain.

A cross between those foreign horses and the Celtic pony might have produced an animal closer to horse size, but anything over 13.2 hands high was not suited to the northern fells. Big animals could not survive without extra feeding, so by natural selection, the breed stabilized as a pony.

By the second century, the Galloway pony in southern Scotland was established as a breed, as was the Fell across the northern counties of England. The two were geographically close and are said to have been very similar, probably bred from the same stock and containing types ranging from the taller Dales and Highland Ponies, to the smaller end of the Fells. Old farmers still sometimes refer to

a Fell as a Galloway. Most of the ponies were probably of subdued colors such as brown, dun, black, or dark bay with limited white markings.

Gray was the common horse color for those in the north of England in the early 1500s. It is believed that gray in the Fell breed partly traces back to those owned by the Cistercian Order or Grey Friars, who resided in the Lake District in Northwest England.

From the time of the Roman withdrawal in the fourth century until the eighteenth century, well maintained road surfaces were few and far between, and pack ponies were the only reliable means of transporting goods. The Fell was particularly useful for this purpose, being a fast and steady walker.

Through the eighteenth and nineteenth centuries, when canals, roadways, and train lines were developed, the ponies were gradually superseded for distance transport and became once more mainly local assets. In the nineteenth century, Fell Ponies were utilized for trotting races and sports events, as well as light arable farm work, shepherding, and transport such as carrying mail or goods to market by trap.

In the twentieth century, Fell Ponies were used only occasionally as pit ponies (in mines) due to their taller pony height. In some areas, they were used for deer stalking, an endeavor that required a steady, surefooted pack pony that could carry the dead stag down hill inclines for the hunter.

The Fell Pony Society (FPS) was formed in 1916. It now has Queen Elizabeth II as its patron, who is a knowledgeable owner and breeder. Her husband, Prince Philip, often competes in driving events with a four-in-hand Fell team.

Today's Fell Pony

Although most Fell Ponies today are bred in Cumbria, Southwest Scotland, and the North of England, there are also Fells all over the United Kingdom, with studs established in Holland, Germany, France, Switzerland, the Czech Republic, Belgium, Denmark, Australia, Canada, and the United States.

Fells still have the reputation of being easy to maintain and able to work all day on a small ration, thriving where a more highly bred animal would find it difficult just to survive. They average from 13.1 to 13.2 hands high and are allowed a maximum height of 14 hands. Fells come in four different colors, with black becoming the predominant color over the last few decades, followed by brown, bay, and gray. A star and/or a little white on or below the hind fetlock are acceptable. Although an excess of white markings is discouraged, such ponies are still eligible for registration.

Fell Ponies, like some horses, mature late—sometimes not until seven years of age. Most Fells in their native country are left to run free until the age of two or three and are not overfed. At that time, they are lightly trained and then often turned back out until four to five years, when they begin light and straight riding without much bending of their spines. In general, they do not start any weight bearing training until three years of age. These precautions are generally adhered to, except for the Fells bred on the hills, which may well be sold at weaning (usually in October) unless they are retained as future breeding stock. It is suggested that mares should not be bred until they are at least three years of age, or otherwise irreparable damage may be done to their internal and reproductive organs and it may restrict their own growth and maturity.

Making this breed come off of their native fells to be raised and introduced to new environments and trends can be a detriment to the retention of traditional breed type. One such dangerous trend is the notion that Fells are a small version of the Friesian Horse. This perception is partially due to the fact that black is now the most common color for Fells, as well as the growing popular awareness of the Friesian breed.

The FPS strongly disapproves of the comparison with other breeds to describe the Fell, which is not a mini version of any other breed. If the focus and presentation of a breed is compromised by such a perception, it may lead to a change in the direction of breeding standards, as has happened with many other breeds in the past. A careful study of the Fell Pony breed standard reveals that the body type, structure, and movement of the Fell Pony clearly differ from those of the Friesian horse. DNA studies also bear this out. By observing the Fell in its natural environment with its various body types and range of colors, its true unique nature and scope becomes apparent.

The unseen traits are as important as the outer traits, as Sue Millard, a British author, pony judge, FPS Council member, and driving enthusiast points out in her remarks that the Fells have "sensible temperaments, hardiness, vigor, self reliance and brains. These are vital to the breed but are not visible. They're the inner pony, the bits that you only get to know by doing the job and living the life. These invisible characteristics can't be retained without giving the pony a job of work to do and, if possible, allowing it to live and reproduce as its ancestors did and still do."

The traditional hill breeders of Britain have carefully conserved this rare breed's ancestral type, as well as the hardiness and savvy of the Celtic mountain ponies—and so the purebred Fell should remain. It is currently used in activities such as pleasure riding, endurance riding, competitive driving, showing, and farming. For work or play, it has often been said, "You cannot put a Fell to the wrong job."

A Fell Pony is capable of carrying a grown man all day with ease; many are gentle enough for capable children and, with correct training, are perfect for the disabled. Their temperament is like that of other British native pony breeds, whose instinct for survival has been essential to them for centuries. This instinct, combined with the intelligence, curiosity, stamina, and mischievousness of a Fell, can pose unique challenges to the inexperienced or over confident person. Sensible horse training is always paramount, but when working with a Fell, there needs to be a cooperative partnership mentality. Fells, just like all equines, are individuals, and each can vary in temperament. They could be compared to working dog breeds, in that they are meant for activity that engages their mind and curiosity.

Registry

All Fell Ponies in North America are currently registered via the mother registry in England, the FPS. The FPS does recognize support groups in foreign countries as overseas branches. The Fell Pony Society and Conservancy of the Americas is the oldest Fell pony organization in North America and is an approved overseas branch of the FPS. Originally known as the Fell Pony Conservancy of North America, it was founded in 1999 and included all the known North American breeders at that time. It was officially restructured and incorporated as an educational organization in 2004 with the sanctioning of the mother society, and it hosted the first Fell Pony Nationals of North America in 2008.

Globally there are fewer than five hundred registered breeding mares; however, the integrity and usefulness of the breed has recently come to light and exportations are on the rise. Numbers of ponies in North America, while still relatively low, continue to rise steadily. Currently, there are about

350 Fell Ponies in North America and an estimated figure of 6,000 worldwide.

Fells are registered in the Fell Pony Society Studbook in Britain, the recognized authority on the breed.

Breed Description

Fell Ponies are presented at shows well groomed, yet untrimmed to emphasize their natural state. They should always be presented as an example of their own breed and not a version of another.

- **Height:** Not exceeding 14 hands (142.2 centimeters)
- **Color:** Black, brown, bay, and gray; chestnuts, piebalds, and skewbalds are debarred; a star and/or a little white on or below the hind fetlock is acceptable; excess of white markings is discouraged, but such ponies are still eligible for registration
- **Head:** Small, well chiseled in outline, well set on, forehead broad, tapering to nose
- **Nostrils:** Large and expanding
- **Eyes:** Prominent, bright, mild, and intelligent
- **Ears:** Neatly set, well formed, and small
- **Throat and jaw:** Fine, showing no signs of throatiness or coarseness
- **Neck:** Of proportionate length, giving good length of rein; strong and not too heavy; moderate crest in case of a stallion
- **Shoulders:** Most important feature; well laid back and sloping; not too fine at withers or loaded at the points; a good, long shoulder blade; muscles well developed
- **Carcass (underlying structure or frame):** Good strong back of good outline; muscular loins; deep carcass; thick through the heart; round ribbed from shoulders to flank; short and well coupled; hindquarters square and strong with tail well set on
- **Feet, legs, and joints:** Feet of good size, round and well formed, open at heels with the characteristic blue horn (keratin that makes up the hoof); fair sloping pasterns but

Fell Ponies serving as pack ponies. *Sue Millard*

not too long; forelegs straight, well placed, not tied at elbows; big well-formed knees, short cannon bone, plenty of good flat bone below knees (8 inches at least); great muscularity of arm
- **Hind legs:** Good thighs and second thighs, very muscular; hocks well let down and clean-cut; plenty of bone below the joint; no sickle-hocks or cow-hocks
- **Mane, tail, and feather:** Plenty of fine hair at heels; coarse hair objectionable; all fine hair except that at point of heel may be cast (shed) in summer; mane and tail left to grow long
- **Action:** Walk, smart and true; trot, well-balanced all round, with good knee and hock action going well from the shoulder and flexing the hocks; not going too wide or near behind; should show great pace

and endurance, bringing the hind legs well under the body when going
- **General character:** Constitutionally as hard as iron and should show good pony characteristics with unmistakable appearance of hardiness peculiar to mountain ponies; lively and alert appearance and great bone

Scale of points

Height and color 5
Head, nostrils, eyes, ears, throat/jaw, and neck 10
Shoulders 15
Carcass 20
Feet, legs, joints, and hind legs 25
Action 25
General characteristics 25

Credit: Fell Pony Society and Conservancy of the Americas

GOTLAND PONY

Gotlands are lightly built with deep chests and sloping croups. *Frances Aprille*

Gotland Russ Association of North America
811 Carpenter Hill Road
Medford, Oregon 97501
www.gotlandponies.org

On the island of Gotland, Sweden, in the Baltic Sea lives a herd of a semi-wild pony—the Gotland Pony, or Russ as it is called locally. A herd of these handy little ponies lives on a protected area here. The European Union has classified the breed as uniquely Swedish, and it is considered part of the Swedish cultural heritage.

The Gotland Pony is an ancient breed relatively free from outside blood. Although it has been refined over the years, the Gotland has remained true to its ancestry. This sturdy pony has withstood outside pressure of breeding it to be larger, thus avoiding such common fads in the horse world that have often produced structure and temperament problems.

Gotlands are great companions for young and old alike. Due to their longevity of life, versatility, and friendly disposition, the Gotland is a family favorite. Many of them live into their thirties, so the

Gotland Pony mare and foal. *Joyce Moreno*

same Gotland Pony can be around to see as many as three generations in one family. With their gentle temperament and small size (11.3 to 13.1 hands), they are ideal for children of all ages and make perfect first mounts. Keeping Gotland Ponies does not have to be expensive or complicated. They are easy to train, safe for children and smaller adults, and great for both riding and driving. They are level-headed and not easily spooked.

Everyone who meets a Gotland in the performance arena or on the trail comments on its engaging appearance and terrific temperament.

History

Probable ancestors to the breed lived in isolation and kept their moderate size and attractive, relatively primitive look since the Stone Age. Theories about their introduction to the island include traveling on a land bridge that existed thousands of years ago, or people bringing them by boat. Traces of horses on Gotland date back to about 3000 BC and show that early humans kept horses in a semi-domestic fashion on the island, using them to perform various tasks as well as a source of food. It is not known for certain, however, if these remnants are related to the breed seen today, just as it is uncertain how the ponies came to Gotland. The truth is that they seem to be related to Przewalski's Horse, a very primitive wild horse.

Other stories, such as their being used for warfare, carrying Vikings, or sacking Rome with the Goths on their backs are false. (The Goths did not live on Gotland or even mainland Sweden, but came from southwestern Europe.) Some Gotland ponies were domesticated and used for farm work, and new ponies were brought in from the moors when they were needed. During cold winters, the wild ponies foraged for themselves and often would eat from the farmers' haystacks.

At the beginning of the nineteenth century, the ponies could be found throughout Gotland. When farmers claimed the formerly public land and

established property boundaries, the land became sectioned off and was fenced, interfering with the free forested land the wild ponies grazed on. Many wild ponies were rounded up and exported to Belgium, England, and Germany, where they read-justed to new lives often as cart ponies or as work ponies on farms or in coal mines.

They were a popular export at this time because they were easy keepers, versatile, and strong in rela-tion to their size. In fact, they were so popular that they almost became extinct in Sweden. Around 1880, there were about 11,500 ponies roaming the moors of Gotland, but this number dropped consid-erably once the exportations to England, Germany, and Belgium began. Additionally, the meat ration-ing and food shortages of World War I led to a further demise of the breed, and those left in the forest on Gotland were near extinction. By 1930, there were only thirty active broodmares left.

Planned breeding and cooperation between breeders on Gotland and the mainland of Sweden helped re-establish the breed. When inbreed-ing threatened the Gotland's existence, carefully selected new blood helped to revitalize the breed. This included the introduction of a Syrian stallion in 1886 and two Welsh stallions in the early 1950s.

Today, local farmers, breeders, and the Gotland Agricultural Society own and maintain a herd of about 150 Gotland Ponies on the moors of Lojsta in the southern part of Gotland. Though the ponies live in relative freedom, the society keeps records on them and they are overseen with a watchful eye; a caretaker visits the herd almost daily and, in winter, supplements their forage with feed every other day.

A few times each year, the ponies are rounded up for hoof trims and checked for overall health and wellbeing. Each season is marked by the annual Gotland activities of releasing a stallion into the herd each June, judging in July, and weaning the foals from the mares in November.

There is a Swedish registry named Svenska Russavelsföreningen—the Swedish Russ Breeders' Association—as well as Finish, Norwegian, and Danish registries for the breed. Each one adheres to the same breed standards set by the Swedish organization.

Globally, there are about nine thousand Russ in Sweden, Gotland, Denmark, Finland, Norway, Canada, and the United States. About one hun-dred new foals are registered in Sweden each year. In the United States, registrations are currently down, with no foals being registered in 2008 and none expected for 2009. During the peak of breeding Gotlands in the United States and Canada, up to thirty foals were registered per year. Now there are only about 170 registered ponies living in North America, indicating they are a very rare breed there.

In the United States

Gotlands were first imported to the United States in 1957 by banker Max Miller, for his ranch in Wyoming. Miller had come in contact with Gotland Ponies while on a family vacation to the island and thought they would be ideal for his grandchildren, who spent the summers on his Wyoming ranch. He was so impressed by his ponies that in 1959 he, along with Donald Howe and Jess Thurmond, formed the Gotland Horse Farms based in Nebraska. The company imported three colts and eighteen fillies in 1959. From this, the American Gotland Horse Association (AGHA) was founded in 1960 for "the registration, development and marketing of the Gotland Horse in America."

In 1960, U.S. Naval Admiral Robert C. Lee (Retired) and his wife imported two buckskin colored foals from Gotland and established their Leeward Farm in Missouri. From humble beginnings with only two Russ, they became the largest and most influential breeders in the United States. They built their stock carefully with an emphasis on functionality. Leeward Farm was a cattle ranch, and Lee's three sons, all skilled riders, used the ponies for all types of farm work, as well as competed with them in every riding discipline.

Mrs. Lee used the ponies in a riding program for disabled children, for which she discovered the ponies were well suited. She became the secretary for the AGHA's registry, and after her death in 1984, a friend from the cattle business, Jack Jungroth, salvaged the registry from her estate. Jungroth became registrar and spent hours imputing data from all the registrations into an early computer program so the records would not be lost.

In 1990, the American Livestock Breeds Conservancy (ALBC) contacted a breeder, Leslie Bebensee, about taking on a herd of Gotland mares and a stallion to start a breeding program to preserve the Gotland Pony. Bebensee agreed and in the next couple of years other breeders and owners made contact with ALBC for the same purpose. In 1994, Jungroth turned the records of the AGHA over to ALBC.

That same year, breeders in Gotland, mainland Sweden, and Denmark donated three yearling colts to the breeders in North America, as there were only two stallions residing there at the time. These colts were received by Pat Phelan of Russ Haven Farm in Manitoba, Canada. Consequently, there are now ten breeding stallions available to North American breeders.

In 1997, the ALBC turned the registry over to the newly formed Gotland Russ Association of North America (GRANA), which remains as the current registry for Gotlands in North America. Through the efforts of the registry's first president, Gunilla Combs, GRANA became a daughter organization of the Svenska Russavelsföreningen; it currently holds the same standards as Gotlands in Sweden.

Since 1996, GRANA has required DNA testing for all breeding stock and for foal registrations. It has also attempted to get inspections for breeding stock

Gotlands are well-proportioned, light, and elegant ponies.
Pat Phelan

Gotland Ponies resting with riders at Pony Club Camp. *Renee Riley Adams*

performed in North America. Several stallions and mares have already been approved for breeding by licensed inspectors from Sweden, either in person or via DVD.

The breed and its association have struggled for a place in the general U.S. equine market. While the Gotland is a very versatile breed, its following remains small.

Characteristics

The best qualities of the breed are its people-oriented attitude and intelligence. As the saying goes in Sweden, the only people who do not like Gotlands are those who have been outsmarted by one. Besides their lively intelligence, they are easy keepers and are very healthy in general, thriving in an outdoor environment all year round. They are strong, energetic, long lived, and friendly.

They are wonderful companion ponies with gentle dispositions. They also are athletic, excelling as trotters and jumpers. Though strong enough for an adult to ride, they are primarily used for driving and as children's mounts.

They have a well proportioned appearance and are light, elegant ponies, yet also hardy and sturdy. They are a gentle but strong breed, with superb gaits, movement, and temperament. Their frame is narrow and lightly built, but they have great endurance.

Their height is 11.3 to 13.1 hands (115 to 130 centimeters), with 12.2 to 12.3 hands being ideal. The mostly brown coloring of the Russ camouflages them well. Dun and bay predominate in the breed, but all colors are allowed except albinos, roans, and piebalds.

They have broad foreheads and shapely muzzles, with short and flexible necks and full manes. Their chests are deep, and their shoulders, though long and strong, are relatively upright. They have good withers, a long back, and a sloping croup. Their legs are strong and their hooves are very hard. They have a good, free-flowing movement. No other horse of comparable size can out-trot a Gotland Russ.

In Sweden, these versatile ponies reap great success in the show ring, as well as in three-day eventing, show-jumping, dressage, driving, and harness racing. A Swedish Gotland mare, Snaeckan, holds the world record for harness racing for ponies, Section B (up to 130 centimeters).

In North America, the Gotland has proven itself by performing well in western riding, endurance, dressage, show jumping, eventing, and trail riding disciplines, as well as pleasure and combined driving.

Credits: Joyce Moreno, president and registrar, and the Gotland Russ Association of North America, with references to articles by Pernilla Jobs and Gunilla Combs

HAFLINGER

American Haflinger Registry
1686 East Waterloo Road
Akron, Ohio 44306
www.haflingerhorse.com

The specialness of the Haflinger lies, of course, in its unique golden chestnut coloring with the long, flowing, white mane and tail, the coloring all Haflingers have. More unique than its coloring is its people-loving, willing, and forgiving temperament that was established over centuries of living alongside and working with mountain peasants. The Haflinger served in every capacity possible for all family members and very simply became part of the family.

This beautiful and versatile horse is now one of North America's fastest growing horse breeds.

It is being discovered by the horse-loving public who want an equine companion that is safe, loveable, and dependable. Intelligence, character, grace, stamina, athleticism, and long life are qualities of the Haflinger. It continues to capture hearts and enrich lives, as it has for centuries. Its beauty and charm steals hearts forever.

History

The history of the Haflinger Horse can be traced to medieval times, when writings told of an Oriental race of horse found in the Southern Tyrolean Mountains of present-day Austria and northern Italy. Many of the villages and farms in the Tyrol were accessible only by narrow paths requiring agile and surefooted horses for transporting and packing. Artwork in the early 1800s from the

This Haflinger stallion shows harmony of conformation and elegance. *American Haflinger Registry*

A noble Haflinger stallion. *American Haflinger Registry*

emphasis on a small, yet solid constitution. A horse versatile enough for both riding and driving was developed with substantial bone and an uncomplicated personality.

Haflinger Horses were first introduced into the United States in 1958. The first importation was acquired by Tempel Smith of Chicago, Illinois, who sent his farm manager to Europe to find a unique breed of horse that could be brought to the United States. In 1958, thirteen Haflingers—one two-year-old stallion, nine broodmares, and three foals—left Hamburg, Germany, tucked away in stalls built on the deck of a steel-hauling ship, which arrived in New York nine days later. Haflingers have proceeded to become more popular in North America ever since.

The modern Haflinger is now found all over the world, active in such varied uses as draft work, packing, light harness and combined driving, western and trail riding, endurance riding, dressage, jumping, vaulting, and therapeutic riding programs. Haflingers hold their own in competition with other breeds, often showing surprising athleticism and strength for their size.

In the United States

The American Haflinger Registry was formed in 1998 from the combined memberships of the Haflinger Association of America and the Haflinger Registry of North America. It represents approximately nine thousand North American Haflinger owners with over thirty thousand Haflingers now recorded in the studbook.

The World Haflinger Federation sets the standards, and the American Haflinger Registry follows that standard today. A Haflinger must have a purebred, registered sire and dam to be registered. The American Haflinger Registry conducts a voluntary Inspection and Classification Program open to both mares and stallions. Breeding animals are presented before a panel of judges who evaluate the horse against the accepted breed standard using a ten-point system with written scorecard. The following is examined:

region depicted a small, noble, chestnut horse with packs and riders traversing steep mountain trails.

The first official documentation of the present-day Haflinger (named for the Tyrolean village of Hafling) was in 1874, when the foundation stallion, 249 Folie, was born by the Half Arabian stallion, 133 El' Bedavi XXII, that was crossed with a refined native Tyrolean mare. All modern purebred Haflingers trace their ancestry directly to Folie through seven different stallion lines: A, B, N, S, ST, and W. With documentation of pure lines, this makes the Haflinger breed much older than one century.

During the years of World War II, there was a significant shift in breeding practices, as pack horses were needed by the military, thus a shorter, draftier Haflinger was produced. Postwar, the breeding practices were modified again in order to restore the height and refinement of the breed, still with an

- Character and temperament as observed by the judges during the inspection and measurement process
- Conformation, shown standing in-hand
- Basic gaits (walk and trot) shown on the triangle
- Free schooling, including canter or gallop

The classification of Breeding Horses aged six and over are final decisions; the judgments are not revised up or down afterwards. An owner is entitled to one appeal, however, and may be given the opportunity to re-present the horse one time only at a later inspection under different judges. The decision and score at the second inspection is final and overrides the original score.

Standards

The standards apply to both inspections and judging at halter.

Color: Color may range from light chestnut to dark liver chestnut with white or flaxen mane and tail. Color impurities in the base color, such as roaning, black spots, or others, are undesirable; excessive deviations will be judged as negative, and using such animals for breeding purposes is strongly discouraged. Color impurities in the mane and tail are undesirable; excessive deviation from white or flaxen will also be judged as negative, and using such animals for breeding purposes is strongly discouraged.

Markings: Head markings are desirable, but not a prerequisite. Too many markings are undesirable and can go as far as being strongly discouraged. Leg markings are not desirable: One white leg (which is a white sock that extends above the fetlock joint) will not be penalized; two white legs will result in a one-point deduction; three white legs will result in a two-point deduction; and horses with four white legs or white above the knees or hocks will be strongly discouraged from breeding. White markings are signified by a change in skin pigment.

Size: The desired size is from 54 to 60 inches. Horses not reaching the minimum size should result in them being strongly discouraged from breeding.

Horses outside this parameter may still be used for breeding in the case of an excellent or outstanding evaluation of all other characteristics.

Type: A desirable appearance of the horse is one of elegance and harmony. To this belong a lean and expressive head with large eyes, well formed neck, and supple mid-section. The croup should be neither too divided nor too short, and the horse should have a distinct musculature as well as correct, defined limbs with good joints.

Stallions and mares for breeding should have clearly defined masculine or feminine features.

Haflinger clearing a jump. Haflingers are graceful and athletic. *American Haflinger Registry*

The Halflinger is an elegant chestnut horse with a long, white mane and tail. *American Haflinger Registry*

Body structure: The body structure should be harmonious and suitable for an all-around pleasure horse.

The **head** should be noble and lean, and the size in harmony with the horse, with large forward-pointing eyes and wide nostrils. It should have enough poll freedom to allow for correct flexion, a clean connection of the head to neck through the jowl area, and correct positioning of the ears.

The **neck** should be medium long and slimmer toward the head, with no bulky lower line. It should not be too wide and should demonstrate good freedom of the lower jaw muscles.

A pronounced **withers** reaching well into the back, large diagonally lying shoulders, and sufficient depth of chest are the most striking features of the forehand. The **back** should be medium long and muscular, as well as display swinging, load-bearing capacity and balance in its movement. The **hindquarters** should be long and slightly sloping, but not too steep, with a not too obviously divided, yet well-muscled croup. The tail should not be set too low. All in all, a harmonious distribution of the forehand, mid-section, and hindquarters is the goal.

Front and hind limbs are extremely important. They should have correct conformation and clearly pronounced joints, with a broad and flat knee joint and a broad strong hock. A full range of bone measurements proportionate to height shall be considered, with special attention to the quality of the cannon bone, as indicated by an oval shape, clean connection to both the fetlock and pastern joints, and clear definition of the tendons and ligaments. Seen from the front and behind, limbs should show straight conformation; seen from the side, a straight standing foreleg and hind leg angled at approximately 150 degrees at the hock are desirable, as is a hoof angle of approximately 45 to 5 degrees to the ground. The pasterns should be moderately long and well developed. The hooves should be round, distinct, and hard.

Movements for basic gaits: The stride should be correct, supple, and of a pure rhythm without serious faults. The horse should have a good, long-reaching, swinging stride at its disposal, with an elastic and not too flat gait, showing good impulsion from behind.

Desirable are hardworking rhythmic and swinging basic gaits: walk, four-time; trot, two-time; and canter, three-time. The movements at a walk should be relaxed, energetic, and elevated. The movements at the trot and gallop should be supple, swinging, and light on the feet, with a noticeable swinging phase and a natural suspension. The clear thrust of the foot from an active working hindquarter should be transferred over a loosely swinging back to the anticipating forehand that is moving freely from the shoulder. Some knee action is desirable. In particular, the canter should demonstrate a clear forward- and upward-springing sequence.

Internal characteristics and health: Desirable is a horse with an even temperament and a strong, excellent character without vices. It should be an all around horse, good natured, strong, eager, and able to perform, easy feeder, resistant to disease, and easy to adapt to be useful for all purposes. In particular, this is valid for riding, driving, and vaulting in the pleasure and sport sector, but also as a working horse for pulling and carrying.

Credit: American Haflinger Registry

HIGHLAND

Highland Pony Enthusiasts Club of America
1651 Barren Road
Oxford, Pennsylvania 19363
www.hpeca.org

Scottish Highland Pony Society of North America
P.O. Box 425
Boonville, California 95415
www.highland-pony.org

The Highland Pony is an ancient and versatile breed native to Scotland and has been found in its Highlands since the eighth century BC. Many ponies had also existed in the Hebrides, which are Scottish islands off the northwest coast of the mainland. Wild, hardy ponies lived for centuries on the highlands in the northern mountains of Scotland, which consists mostly of rough, windswept moors or heaths with high peaks, steep hills, and deep valleys. Conditions are cold and harsh, but the native ponies adapted to the severity of conditions by developing into rugged, robust animals.

The Highland Pony came from these tough, survivors and inherited their endurance, making it a good choice for any work in adverse conditions. It is a compact, kind, and strong breed.

History

Highland Ponies are the descendants of crofters' (Scottish farmers) ponies, so they were subjected to little controlled breeding. For hundreds of years they were used for transportation and as an all-purpose draft animal on the small Highland farms, or crofts. They became a dependable asset for agricultural needs in the highlands and islands of Scotland. The ease of their upkeep, as well as their sturdiness and courage, was much preferred over horses. They were an integral part of the crofter's family, without which life would have been more extreme and difficult. Their strength and abilities were much appreciated and well known throughout the country by rural folk and royalty alike.

Besides being used as agricultural animals, they were utilized as mounts during wartime. In 1314, Robert the Bruce allegedly rode a Highland Pony

Curious Highland foals. Highlands are a muscular and substantial breed. *Courtesy the Highland Pony Society*

to fight Sir Henry de Bohun, who was riding a larger warhorse and was in full armor. Robert won on his much smaller Highland Pony, a great tribute to its tenacity. Highlands were also reportedly used in the Boer Wars in the late nineteenth century. Agriculture surveys and travel accounts from the eighteenth century describe a pony smaller in stature than present-day Highland Ponies. Most likely at that time, they were still primarily an unimproved product of their harsh environment. The original Highland Ponies were athletic as well as smaller, perhaps more similar to the now extinct Scottish Galloway that was used by Scottish cattle drovers. The larger Highlands of today would not have maintained their height and size on the terrain they traditionally lived on, so the breed has been "improved" since the 1700s. Consequently, the pony that Robert the Bruce rode would not have been instantly recognizable as a Highland Pony to people today.

Lingcropper, a famous stallion dating back to 1745, was one of these older, smaller types, probably of Scottish origin and most likely a Scottish Galloway. He was a sire of great importance to the Highland breed, also having a substantial influence on the Fell Pony breed, though he predated the first registered Fells by 150 years. He was undoubtedly a pony of some distinction, as his name is mentioned regularly in ballads and stories popular at the time.

Following the Scottish uprising of 1745, there was a change in the land tenure system, and with that came oppression. In the late 1770 to the 1800s, Scottish landlords drove thousands of crofters from the Highlands. Highland pony numbers declined throughout this period, as land previously available to cattle and ponies was turned into large-scale sheep farms. In 1886, the Crofters' Act gave the crofters more rights to what little land remained, but the depopulation of the Highland Ponies continued even into the twentieth century, as voluntary emigration replaced forced emigration.

Highland Ponies experienced an upswing in propagation when Queen Victoria patronized them and bred many of them after 1850 at Balmoral Castle and Estate. Today, Queen Elizabeth II is their patron and continues the breeding of Highland Ponies, maintaining a herd on the Balmoral Estate.

Although the Highland Pony has traceable bloodlines dating back to the 1830s, the studbook was not established until the 1880s. Recording pedigrees began in 1896, and the Highland Pony Society was founded in 1923.

Like many other British native ponies, Highlands saw a steep decline in numbers after World War II and with the coming of mechanization. Then in the 1950s, trekking (trail riding) through rough Scottish terrain became popular; thus the pony's quiet nature, surefootedness, and weight-carrying capabilities were once again in demand. Highlands were patient with every kind of rider and could carry the heaviest to the lightest, from the expert rider to the amateur. Tourism flourished with trekking, and many ponies were bought by their riders. Since then, Highlands have experienced a resurgence in numbers.

Highland Uses

Overall, Highland Ponies are hardy, docile, healthy, and fun to have. They live long and are generally introduced to ride by tack at age three, but used only sparingly. By five or six, they are mature enough to begin many productive years of life. Even today, they can handle all severe weather conditions, subsisting easily where horses would find it too difficult. They are easy keepers, thriving on coarse grazing and usually foaling without difficulty.

For centuries, Highland Ponies were, and still are, used on the Scottish crofts for farm work, pulling carts and logging (called snigging). Besides working the land, they were also relied on as pack animals. Often they hauled peat used for fuel, packing it home from the marshy bogs. Highlands have continued to be used for plowing, pulling carts on small crofts, and transporting materials and people. They are also used for forestry work, being much easier to navigate in thick forests and more economical than a tractor. Additionally, they do not

Highland Ponies have short, pretty heads. Gray is a common color. *Linda Macpherson/Shutterstock*

destroy the underbrush like a tractor would and can drag and haul in places too marshy or steep for a tractor.

For the past two centuries, Highland Ponies, using special pack saddles, have been the primary means of transporting deer and other game off the hills. Hunting is a necessary sport in the Highlands, and the ponies are efficient and helpful partners. They are still used for carrying grouse panniers on many Scottish estates to this day, as well as bringing the "bag" (stags) down from the hills. They are not used much for hunting with hounds (which was banned in Scotland and throughout Britain in 2005), but they are utilized for shooting, trekking, and packing where their great strength for carrying heavy loads over rough cover is valued. Their intelligence, ability for hauling bulky loads, and calm personalities are appreciated by hunters.

They are ideal for families with members of all ages and sizes due to their strength, surefootedness,

dependability, and quiet nature. They have been used safely for the disabled for whom their unflappable temperament is paramount. They can stand patiently for hours, and their size is ideal for easy mounting, while their strength and broad backs can handle varying weights.

Some Highlands pull specially built carts that can hold both the disabled person in his or her wheelchair and a companion. This allows the disabled to experience the independence of driving the pony by himself or herself, providing a much appreciated and thrilling time. The Highland's burly strength is perfect for this, and such activities have increased its popularity.

As an occasional hack, Highlands are exceptional. If they are needed for more extensive work, they can easily make a quick transition. They adapt effortlessly to equestrian disciplines as diverse as Pony Club events, trail riding, dressage, driving, western riding, and long distance endurance or cross-country riding. They are also respectable jumpers. Their talents are appreciated especially in harness, as their consistency in color makes a matched pair easy to find. They are also used in tandems and four-in-hand teams.

Their substance, bone, and temperament also mean they cross well with other breeds, both horse and pony sized. In Britain, Highlands and Thoroughbreds are a popular cross, producing warmblood type performance horses for eventing, show jumping, and dressage.

In the United States

The first Highlands brought to the United States came with the colonial settlers. More evidence of recent importations goes back to the early 1960s, when various individuals imported Highlands, a few of which went to the Maryland area. Some of these ponies competed in driving classes at the Devon, Pennsylvania, show.

Most early Highlands were imported as safe driving ponies or for interbreeding to others. In the last decade or so, however, foundation breeding lines have experienced more stability in North

America, though numbers are still low. Presently, there are an estimated seventy Highlands in North America as of 2008, making them a very rare breed for the continent. They are listed as vulnerable on the Equus Survival Trust list, with most Highlands still residing in Scotland.

The Highland Pony Enthusiasts Club of America (HPEC) was founded in 2004 and is affiliated with the Highland Pony Society of Scotland (HPS). As with all other Highland Pony Society affiliated Enthusiast Clubs worldwide, the HPEC is a social club designed to promote the principles of HPS. It encourages registrations with it and has sponsored Mountain and Moorland classes in the United States. (Mountain and Moorland breeds are the native ponies of the British Isles.)

The Scottish Highland Pony Society of North America (SHPSNA) was established in 2001. It has registration services, documentation of bloodlines, and census-taking for Highlands in North America. It has separate studbooks for purebred Highland ponies and part-bred Highlands. DNA testing is done under contract with the Veterinary Genetics Laboratory at the University of California, Davis, for identification and parentage verification purposes.

Presently, SHPSNA is not affiliated with the United Kingdom's registry, the Highland Pony Society, but it does encourage members to support the Highland breed internationally by joining the Highland Pony Society, which is considered the world Highland Pony authority. SHPSNA has also sponsored Mountain and Moorland classes in the United States.

The National Pony Society in the United Kingdom has approved sanctioned shows throughout the United States and offers award programs for all Mountain and Moorland breeds, including Highland ponies and other British riding ponies.

Breed Description

The Highland Pony developed as a landrace—a breed that has evolved primarily as a product of its environment, and to a smaller degree by its agricultural usage or shaping by humans. As such, it has developed several survival type characteristics.

Overall, it is muscular with plenty of substantial bone and exhibits powerful strength with the commonly accepted standards of good conformation. It has plenty of substance, along with the classic beauty of a native pony. The Highland Pony should have compact conformation that is shorter legged than the length of its body, making it longer in body than its height. Yet the Highland presents a balanced, pleasant appearance.

Coat: The Highland Pony has a winter coat of stiff coarse hair covering a soft thick undercoat. This enables the pony to thrive in all kinds of cold and wet conditions that other breeds cannot tolerate, with both coats giving ample protection. The outer coat sheds out in spring to a smooth summer coat.

Leg feathering is only a tuft of straight hair in the summer, but winter feathering can go all the way up to the knees. Manes and tails are thick, long and full.

Colors: Gray and various shades of dun are the most common coat colors. These can range from various shades of mouse, yellow, and cream dun to black. Sometimes a bay or a liver chestnut with a silver mane and tail can be found. Some have dorsal stripes, some have shoulders stripes, and some even have zebra markings on their legs.

Broken colors are not allowed. A small star is acceptable, but other white markings, such as white legs or hooves, are not allowed in the show ring. Stallions with white markings other than a small star are not licensed for breeding.

Foals typically experience color changes, as do some adults as they grow older. Some can go through color changes with the seasons. Gray is by far the most common color in the breed, and those with the gray gene can be born any color and fade to gray over time. The silver dilution is often found in ponies with island bloodlines. The Isle of Rum ponies are especially known for this.

Size: The breed standard encourages the size of ponies to be between 13 hands and 14.2 hands, but many registered ponies are outside this range.

A beautiful Highland herd. Highlands are rugged and robust. *Paula Gent/Shutterstock*

Head: The head is well carried and alert. It is small and short with width between the eyes and is fairly long from ear to eye. It has a square, broad muzzle, large nostrils, and large, kind eyes. Ears are set wide and erect and are not too large. The jowls are deep.

Neck: The neck is of medium length and is well set in the withers; it is powerful and naturally arched, but clearly tapering at the throatlatch. The head is carried high and forward.

Body: The body should have a deep chest and barrel, a short, strong back, and ribs that are well sprung. The shoulders are long and slope well with very defined withers. The quarters are broad and long with the tail set not too low.

Legs: The forearms are well placed, long, and strong. The hind legs also are strong with powerful thighs, strong second thighs, and flat hocks. The legs have flat, hard bone, broad knees, and short cannon bones. Knees and hocks are large and low set, with lots of clean, flat bone below them. Pasterns are medium long and oblique. The hooves are large,

well shaped and open, as well as dark colored and comparatively hard.

Movement: The Highland's movement is straight and powerful without high knee action. The walk is naturally fast, a trait that historically suited the work once required of the pony. Here is where the Highland excels like no other. It can travel a steady 4 miles per hour at a quick, rhythmic walk, hauling loads through the roughest of terrains.

The other gaits should be correct and straight. Dishing, straddling, and wide hock movements are obvious faults. Knees, pasterns, and hocks should be freely and powerfully flexed. The action is free moving without any undue knee action.

Disposition: The Highland's hardiness and stable, even temperament has established it as the mount of choice.

It is a sensible, brave companion, willing and steady, yet full of personality.

Credit: Victoria Tollman, Equus Survival Trust

NEW FOREST PONY

The New Forest Pony is an elegant, high-quality children's riding pony. *Okjen Farm*

The New Forest Pony Association, Inc., and Registry of North America
P.O. Box 206
Pascoag, Rhode Island 02859
www.newforestpony.net

The New Forest Pony is known as a medium to large pony with three good gaits (not the short, fast pony gait) and a calm, quiet temperament that is well suited for children. It is a low maintenance pony that is elegant, without sacrificing hardiness, and loves to work. It is also a good performance pony with excellent temperament and can perform at the professional level. The breeding goals are to produce the highest quality riding pony for children, as well as other specific ideals such as elegance and durability, but always keeping in mind that it is solely for children to ride.

The breed stands out from other ponies due to its more horse-like gait and looks. The New Forest Ponies are flat ribbed, making it easy for children to get their legs around, unlike many of the round ribbed, barrel like ponies. They also resemble and perform like warmbloods, but in a smaller package. They are noted for their intelligence, strength, versatility, and quiet, willing-to-please temperament. As easy keepers with giving personalities, they are a wonderful choice for families and especially for children.

One owner, after discovering the breed for herself, remarked, "I had grown up with horses and, over the years, had ridden or owned horses of many breeds. However, I found that once I got over forty, I didn't bounce like I used to. Knowing it's a fact of life that if you ride, you may take a tumble every now and then, I thought that falling from 14.2 instead of 17.2 hands held a lot of appeal. Plus, I found that I didn't have the same confidence that I did as a young rider."

The New Forest is an all-encompassing pony: loving temperament, beautiful looks, warmblood movement, excellent athletic ability, and tons of versatility for dressage, driving, and jumping. It has comfortable gaits and is as smooth as any horse. It rides big, unlike most of the other pony breeds, and is very intelligent. It picks up quickly on training and learning new exercises, trying greatly not to disappoint.

The New Forest loves to be around people and makes an effort, even from a distance, to come for a pat or visit. It has excellent hooves, which are very strong; trimming and shoeing are not a constant necessity as with other breeds. It is a very economical pony to feed and own. Owners find that feeding and stall cleaning finishes a lot quicker because the ponies are not usually messy in their stalls.

History

The New Forest Pony is one of the recognized breeds of Mountain and Moorland ponies of the British Isles. They originated in, and were named after, the New Forest area located in Hampshire on the South Coast of England, which spreads out over ninety thousand acres. New Forest has remained a protected region over the years, and semi-feral New Forest Ponies still inhabit the area.

Although Canute's Forest Law of 1016 records the presence of horses among the other wild animals of the forest, there are few written references about them. Just how and when all the New Forest Ponies passed into private ownership is not certain, but in general they seemed to have been valued locally for their docility, hardiness, strength, and sureness of foot. Thoroughbred and Arabian blood was introduced from time to time to improve their looks and increase height, but it was not until the end of the nineteenth century that systematic efforts to improve the breed were made.

In 1891, the Society for the Improvement of New Forest Ponies was founded to offer premiums to suitable stallions to run on the forest. In 1906, the Burley and District New Forest Pony Breeding and Cattle Society started to register mares and young stock and published its first Stud Book in 1910. There was a current theory that the best way of improving the breed was to introduce stallions from other native breeds, and as the earliest Stud Book shows, there were acceptable sires from a curious assortment.

From 1914 to 1959, registrations were recorded in the National Pony Society's Stud Book. In 1938, the two local societies amalgamated, and no outside blood has been permitted since the mid 1930s. In 1960, the New Forest Pony Breeding and Cattle Society published its own Stud Book and has done so ever since. A notable significance of New Forest Pony breeding in recent years has been the increase in both the numbers of ponies bred in private studs (breeding farms) outside the New Forest and in the numbers of ponies exported. There are now flourishing studs of registered New Forest Ponies not only in the United Kingdom, but all over Europe as well as in North America and Australia.

Performance Pony

In recent years, higher standards have been achieved by the breed due to the increased performance level required by the sports of dressage, jumping, and driving. To meet the demands for a modern sport type pony, the registries have selectively bred for better movement in all three gaits and toward a versatile, luxury sport pony.

The demand for good sport ponies has continuously grown worldwide, with an increased interest particularly in the United States in recent years. With the promotion of dressage as a junior/young rider's sport by the U.S. Dressage Federation (USDF), the demand for dressage ponies has increased significantly. The New Forest Pony is a proven athlete and is capable of performing at the highest levels.

Many of the top European riders started their careers riding well-bred New Forest Ponies. At the 1991 European Pony Championships, the New Forest Pony was represented by five highly bred individuals, and their abilities would have been considered world class had they been horses. In 1977, New Foresters competed at the World Four-In-Hand Driving Championship. In 1993, a pony named Calypso won the USDF Bronze Medal in third-level dressage ridden by a nine-year-old girl.

New Forest Ponies are shown in Devon for under saddle and in-hand classes. They are seen at the International Sporthorse Registry (ISR)/Oldenburg inspections and at the American Warmblood Society (AWS), where they are approved and registered in the Sport Pony division. (ISR/Oldenburg is a warmblood sport horse and sport pony registry in which the horses and/or ponies are judged during an inspection on type, conformation correctness, and movement.)

In the United States

The herd in the United States began with twenty-two purebred champion ponies imported from England in 1950. Most of the original imports were brought to North America by Mr. and Mrs. Piel from Maine, Mary Wilson from Massachusetts, and Dr. and Mrs. Holbrook from Ontario, Canada. These individuals shared stories and ponies among themselves.

The New Forest Pony Association (NFPA) and Registry of North America was founded in 1989 by Lucille Guibault and Jody Waltz, both Rhode Island residents. It uses the same standards and forms as the New Forest Pony Breeding and Cattle Society in England. After Guibault reviewed all the studbooks from England to locate ponies in North America, she and Waltz eventually tracked down some pure New Foresters that had been bred, but never registered. The society sanctioned the Welsh Pony Show to include a New Forest Pony Division from 1990 to 1995 with a qualified pony judge from England and Wales. Enthusiasts from Canada also included a New Forest Pony Division at the Ancaster Fair from 1995 to 1999.

In the mid 1990s, Linda Kindle, now the president of the registry, became involved. Kindle was born and raised in the Netherlands, and her parents owned and operated a riding academy that had mostly New Forest Ponies. "The main reason we purchased New Forest Ponies for our riding school was their steady temperament and their ability to perform well," says Kindle. "Over the twenty years that we ran the riding academy, there was never an incident where anyone was injured on these ponies. In general, they are very tolerant and willing to please."

Other breeders started to recognize the potential of these sport ponies and began to import new blood into North America. Canada imported from England, and the East Coast of the United States also imported an approved stallion along with some New Forest Pony mares from Holland.

In 1992, the NFPA expanded its responsibilities and commitment to the breed by becoming a fully operational registry for the United States and Canada, and produced its first studbook in the same year. The NFPA is the only licensed and recognized registry for the breed in North America, and it follows the same guidelines and standards as in England. Since the association's expansion, the NFPA has been responsible for more than three hundred registrations of New Forest foals and ponies brought from England and Holland.

Registration

A pony is eligible for registration in the NFPA Stud Book if its sire and dam are registered in a recognized New Forest Pony Stud Book, provided that it meets the recognized breed standards. Its sire must be registered and licensed before the mare was covered.

Most European countries have inspections and a performance test that stallions must complete to become a breeding stallion. Inspection is where the pony is shown in-hand on both hard and soft footing, performs free-jumping, and completes a veterinarian exam. In the performance test, the pony is judged under saddle in dressage, free-jumping, stadium jumping with a rider, and cross-country jumping with a rider, and then has another veterinarian examination.

Due to the fairly small amount of registrations and large distances between breeders, it is difficult for the NFPA to have the same inspections as in Europe. The Registry is, however, working toward organizing an inspection tour with European judges to inspect all New Forest Ponies in North America.

Currently, there is a veterinary exam required for the stallion at the age of two and one-half years. If it passes the exam, it receives a temporary license to breed New Forest mares. During this time, the stallion must enter in an Open Halter Class or inspection in a pony division and registry, such as ISR/Oldenburg, USDF, or the American Warmblood Society, all of which are accepted.

After the age of three years, the pony stallion must have performed a first-level dressage test with a minimum score of 58 percent, or have performed in a Hunter Jumper class and placed in the top three. For the final stallion approval, another veterinary exam is performed when the stallion is five years old. Before the age of six, performance testing must have been completed.

Section A main Stud Book is for purebred New Forest Ponies with three generations of registered New Forest Ponies on the sire and dam sides. Section F main Stud Book is for Canadian-born ponies that are purebred New Forests with three generations of registered New Forests on the sire and dam sides. There must also be DNA test results on file for both the sire and dam.

Entry in the First Cross Section is open to the progeny of registered New Forest Ponies mated to a registered purebred horse or pony of a different breed, but not any color breeds. Part-bred ponies are not accepted for regular registration.

Standards

New Forest Ponies range in size from 12 to 14.2 hands. The colors allowed for registration are bay, brown, gray, chestnut, roan, and black. Limited white markings are allowed on the head and legs, otherwise they are not allowed unless they were acquired from scars. Blue-eyed creams, palominos, piebalds, and skewbalds are not permitted.

Well-bred New Foresters display free, well balanced, straight movement, plenty of bone, strong quarters, and good depth of body; they must be a riding type with substance.

New Forest Ponies are suited to a kaleidoscope of activities, from dressage, driving, jumping, Pony Club, polo, and gymkhana, and are successfully trained to carry disabled riders.

One of their most endearing qualities is their natural, gentle manner. Their calm dispositions naturally make them excellent choices for children.

"As with a lot of the people who own these ponies, I have had a great companionship with the ponies I owned," says Kindle. "One of the ponies I had, named Sasha, was one of the special ones that became a one-person horse. She became my favorite and we did everything together. . . . When I had grown out of her, we had to find a new home for Sasha. It took three tries to find her a good home because she didn't want to accept any of the people wanting to buy her. A mother was looking for a companion for her daughter who was born deaf and had a speech impairment. When the little girl approached Sasha, she immediately connected with her and the two became inseparable. This was the first horse the little girl ever owned and she soon learned to ride on her. It became an incredible bond, and they spent hours on end together."

The future of the breed looks very promising. Not only kids, but smaller adults looking for a top-

The New Forest is a noble, yet gentle pony. *Okjen Farm*

level performance prospect are turning to New Forest Ponies because of their versatile capabilities. They are also shaking up the world in top-level competitive driving with frequent wins.

Breeding Goals

The first prerequisite is for a functional pony. The second is to produce a type that matches the market demands. There should be selective breeding toward a performance pony that today's rider wants, one that can perform more. The original type should not be lost, but there can be a little more elegance and the capability to compete against hunter/jumper ponies in the United States, Canada, and Europe beyond the typical riding pony.

Specializing in breeding could produce a dressage type, which should have correct gaits with a good overstepping walk, an extended trot pushing from behind, and a round, well balanced canter, as well as exhibiting talent besides good conformation and pedigree. A hunter/jumper should have jumping talent with scope, good canter, good jumping blood in the pedigree, and exterior soundness. An English and western pleasure pony should be calm with a pleasant, flat-moving trot and canter, and a good exterior and pedigree. The conformation of a dressage pony can be good for jumping also, yet a good hunter/jumper is not always a good dressage pony. Likewise, an English and western pleasure mount is not always a good jumper and, gait-wise, will not always make a good dressage pony.

The best selection would be for the all-around pony. Jumping can make heavy demands on any animal, especially on one already more susceptible to injury. With the added burden of the rider, the pony is most at risk when landing after a jump. The legs of dressage ponies are also subject to injuries and infections more frequently than is most often assumed. Classical dressage often consists of very strongly collected gaits, which place a greater burden on joints and tendons.

Credit: The New Forest Pony Association, Inc. and Registry of North America

NEWFOUNDLAND PONY

Newfoundland Pony Society
P.O. Box 8132
St. John's, Newfoundland and Labrador
A1B 3M9
Canada
www.newfoundlandpony.com

The Newfoundland Pony is a special and historic pony, used for riding, driving, and light draft work. It makes an excellent mount for children and adults, and excels under saddle and in harness. It is a multi-talented, enduring, hardy, dedicated worker and easy keeper.

This is a rare breed, unique in its history and capabilities. For four hundred years, the Newfoundland survived in the harshest of conditions that only the hardiest creatures could endure. At the same time, it never lost its affinity for working side by side with people. It is a strong, adaptable, and congenial pony, but most of all, it is a survivor.

The Newfoundland Pony of today has all of the assets of its ancestors, and probably a few more. It is a sturdy mount that is hardworking, eager to please, and learns quickly. Since these features are combined with good feet, robust good health, and a pleasing temperament, it is a pony that is hard to match. It is an all-purpose pony with many desirable characteristics: strength, stamina, courage, intelligence, obedience, willingness, and common sense.

The Newfoundland Pony is excellent for riding. *Greg Oakes*

History

The arrival of Moorland breeds in New Founde Land, as it was called when first discovered, began in the 1600s when Lord Falkland attempted a settlement there. Those were tough times for both human and beast, with conditions on the island being extremely harsh, indicating a need for horses of the hardy type. Falkland sent an order to Bristol, England, requesting livestock that "can live in hard ground and in the wood without fodder in the winter." These were the expectations of imported ponies and conditions that they would need to have for survival.

When early English fishermen became involved in the rich fishing grounds of Newfoundland and settled there in the seventeenth and eighteenth centuries, the robust native ponies they brought from the British Isles possessed the type of resilient attributes Falkland described. These breeds became ancestors to the Newfoundland Pony and were primarily Exmoor, Dartmoor, and New Forest Ponies from England, and to a lesser extent, Welsh Mountain Ponies from Wales, Galloway (now extinct) and Highland Ponies from Scotland, and Connemara Ponies from Ireland. These were sturdy creatures, already well adapted to the harsh climate of the islands of the North Atlantic and were used for work side by side with the moorland and highland crofters. They were perfect helpmates to "live in the hard ground and wood" in Newfoundland's harsh climate and rocky terrain. They were fully accustomed to the plough, harrow, back pack, cart, and heavy work.

In time, the resident pony population of Newfoundland increased to the point where local supply could satisfy demand and further British imports were no longer necessary. Isolated on the island, these various British native breeds interbred, and over three centuries and with little outside influence, the hardiest of them eventually evolved into one common pony type perfectly suited to the rough Newfoundland environment. That pony is now recognized as the Newfoundland Pony.

The Newfoundland Pony was primarily a work pony used in the field and on the fishing wharf. It hauled firewood, timber, kelp, the fish catch, and rocks and pulled the plow. It transported its owners by back, cart, and wagon in times before the car. This remarkable little pony was an integral part of Newfoundland life right up to the late 1940s and 1950s, and in some remote villages up to the late 1960s and early 1970s.

By 1935 the population of ponies on the island was recorded as 9,025, while the horse population was recorded at 5,658. The pony had greater and wider use and therefore outnumbered the larger equines. Healthy numbers of Newfoundland Ponies existed into the 1970s and 1980s.

After that, the population dropped rapidly due to a number of factors. While once a necessity for rural and city life, increased modernization made the pony's traditional role obsolete. This occurred with the replacement of horse power by mechanical power, so working ponies were no longer needed. The Newfoundland Pony had been used to plow gardens, haul fishing nets or kelp and wood, gather hay, and provide families with transportation around the island. When these functions were replaced and the pony population plummeted, there was the possibility of its extinction. Also anti-roaming legislation was passed in many communities, thus limiting the pony's food supply and curtailing the traditional method of breeding during the summer pasture months. Owners were being encouraged to geld their stallions. Due to the decreased need for the pony, thousands were exported for meat to processing plants in Quebec, which then sold the meat to Belgium and France for human consumption.

This exceptional animal that for over four hundred years had helped Newfoundlanders secure a place in the New World almost disappeared completely. Had it not been for a number of dedicated individual breeders and pony protection groups, the Newfoundland Pony would have become extinct.

From an estimated population of twelve thousand in the 1970s, pony numbers dropped to fewer than one hundred in the 1980s. By the early 1990s, the population was thought to still be under two hundred, with many of these not being used for breeding purposes.

Preservation Measures

The Newfoundland Pony Society was founded in 1979 and incorporated in 1981. It proceeded to lobby the government of Newfoundland and Labrador to have the Newfoundland Pony recognized as a living part of the province's cultural history and have it protected from extinction.

In 1997, the provincial government of Newfoundland passed the Heritage Animals Act, which gave both the Newfoundland Pony and the Newfoundland Pony Society official designation. It provided legal protection for Newfoundland Ponies, with the assistance of the Newfoundland Pony Society, by making it illegal to transport the ponies off the island without export permits. This ensured

The Newfoundland is a hardy breed that often has fine legs. *Diana Wright*

that ponies leaving the island were headed only to breeders and pony lovers—not meatpacking plants. The act also designated the Newfoundland Pony Society as the public group responsible for registering, promoting, and protecting the Newfoundland Pony. The society identifies and maintains a listing of Newfoundland Ponies, as well as doing inspections where necessary and promoting the Newfoundland Pony in Newfoundland.

Additionally, an ongoing effort on the part of concerned individuals stabilized the Newfoundland Pony population, but the Newfoundland Pony has continued to be classified as critically endangered by Rare Breeds Canada. The current Newfoundland Pony population totals less than four hundred animals, but many of them are geldings and aged mares. The number of ponies able to carry on the breed is relatively small—approximately 250. The Newfoundland population is spread across

Canada, with the majority of the ponies located in Newfoundland, Nova Scotia, and Ontario.

The Future

There are many dedicated Newfoundland Pony owners and breeders located across Canada, as well as a few in the United States, producing Newfoundland Ponies that are listed and recognized by the Newfoundland Pony Society. The Newfoundland Pony is not an officially recognized "breed," however. Although it has been purebred for centuries, it is considered a pony "type" by the government. Pedigrees were not formally recorded for the pony until the 1980s.

Breeders and owners of Newfoundland Ponies are seeking to have the Newfoundland Pony recognized as a national breed in Canada under the Animal Pedigree Act (APA). The act makes no consideration for any historical significance of the pony, so it is within this context that the Newfoundland Pony must make a place for itself in today's equine world. The Newfoundland Pony Society is cooperating with breeders and owners in this effort.

Rare Breeds Canada is supporting a blood-typing project for two ponies, the Newfoundland Pony and the Lac La Croix Indian Pony. The Newfoundland Pony has a diverse ancestry in its background, but the isolation of the various lines in the Newfoundland community is unique. In recent years, the breeding pool has been significantly reduced. The presence of radical changers, the incidence of cryptorchism, and the variation in size are all subject to speculation. Knowledge of the genetic diversity will be key to understanding the level of risk to the pony.

Foundation breeds of the Newfoundland Pony are:

Connemara
Dartmoor
Exmoor
Fell
Galloway
Highland
New Forest
Section A: Welsh Mountain Pony
Section B: Welsh Pony
Section C: Welsh Pony of Cob Type
Section D: Welsh Cob

With continued support from concerned individuals, groups, and corporations in Newfoundland, across Canada, and beyond, the prospect for the survival of the Newfoundland Pony, while not yet assured, is improving annually. With the dedication of countless volunteers, it is hoped the Newfoundland Pony known and loved across North America will eventually be recognized as one of the most historically significant pony breeds in the world.

Standards

For listing with the Newfoundland Pony Society as a Heritage Newfoundland Pony, DNA parental verification is required. The standards may vary in the event that a more detailed survey of the breed carried out at a later date shows evidence of any discrepancy. The applicant pony must conform to the following standards in order to be registered as a Newfoundland Pony in the Newfoundland Pony Society:

- Demonstrates and/or documents ancestry to the Newfoundland Pony acceptable to the society
- Has a good temperament and is docile and easy to work with
- Is a good winter animal, being all-around hardy
- Is surefooted
- Has a structure that can vary from fine boned types to larger stocky types
- Has a height that can vary from 11 to 14.2 hands
- Has a coat color of bay, black, brown, chestnut, dun, gray, roan, and white (with pink skin), but no piebalds and skewbalds (pintos) are acceptable
- Has a heavy coat, which sometimes changes color and character seasonally
- Has a thick mane and tail
- Has a low-set tail
- Has feathered fetlocks with hair extending below fetlock points
- Has flint hard hooves
- Has, typically, dark limb points, though white or light color on limbs is acceptable
- Is free of defects that might endanger the ability to live a normal, healthy life

Credit: Newfoundland Pony Society

PONY OF THE AMERICAS

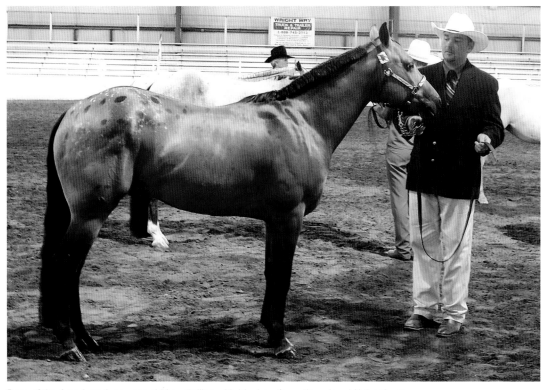

Pony of the Americas three-year-old bay stallion with ideal conformation. *Jared Katzenberger*

Pony of the Americas Club, Inc.
3828 South Emerson Avenue
Indianapolis, Indiana 46203
www.poac.org

The Pony of the Americas is the largest pony breed in the United States created exclusively for children. It was produced to be the mount for youth in their growth years. Initially, it was a special gift to the children of the United States, but it has become so popular that the breed is now all over the world. Its origins are derived from one of the oldest known American horse breeds, the Appaloosa. Today, many Pony of the Americas, or POAs as they are more conveniently called, look like little Appaloosa horses.

The purpose of the POA is to be a tractable and beautiful breed suitable for youth that bridges the gap between a small pony and a horse. A pony of this size provides an avenue for family participation that is wholesome and friendly. Due to its longevity of life, a POA can serve more than one generation, and many outstanding POAs are participating and winning in the show ring well into their twenties. They are useful in disabled riding schools long after their showing days are over. The reason for this fact, besides their pony heritage, may be the treatment they receive in the hands of their owners. With their connection to children, POAs are regarded as a member of the family.

In the show ring, emphasis is on versatility, as one POA can be asked to perform in a variety of extremely diverse classes, all in one show. This can range all the way from western pleasure, trail, reining, and western riding, to the English disciplines of pleasure, hunter under saddle and over fences, open jumping, pleasure driving, and gymkhana timed events. In addition to the show ring, the stamina and versatility of the POA has been found to be valuable on the farm and even for track racing. As a durable mount, it is perfect for trail and endurance riding, ranch work, and hunting. Its gentle, willing nature makes the POA easy to be trained, handled, and loved by children.

The goal was for a child-sized equine that could give boys or girls confidence and a sense of responsibility, qualities that would serve them well in later life. The POA motto is "Try hard, win humbly, lose gracefully, and, if you must, protest with dignity." This, perhaps more than anything else, sets POA exhibitors apart from others in the world of horse show competition. Boys and girls cheer for one another, even though they are competing against each other. Deep friendships are made that last entire lifetimes for both parents and children from coast to coast.

History

In 1954, attorney and Shetland breeder, Les Boomhower from Iowa, acquired a black and white Appaloosa spotted mare that appeared to have some Arabian in her. At her side was her day-old foal, supposedly sired by a black Shetland stallion. The foal had the same basic white body color as the mother, with the same black spots that looked like paint smears. On his left flank, the spots appeared to form a black handprint, so he was named Black Hand. At the time Boomhower bought the mare, she was not registered with the Appaloosa Horse Club, although she fit the requirements. He named and registered her as Manitoba No. 454.

There was no more information about Black Hand's sire until much later. In 1990, a POA owner named Julius Peterson stopped at a farm in Iowa, where he noticed and admired some spotted horses grazing in a pasture. Peterson talked with the owner, Bud Drape, and learned that he had been the breeder of the foal that was Black Hand. When Manitoba was a two-year-old, Drape bred her to a dappled chestnut Shetland stallion with a light mane and tail that he had purchased at a local sale. He knew nothing of the stallion's lineage, but thought he appeared to have some Welsh in him. Before the mare foaled in 1954, she had changed hands about three times by the time she was sold to Boomhower, which accounts for the misinformation about the color of the Shetland.

When Boomhower was watching his children with Black Hand, he had an idea about a good kid's pony—a breed for children who had outgrown the Shetland but were too small for a full-sized horse. He called a meeting of his Shetland breeder friends to discuss it, and in 1954, the Pony of the Americas Club was formed. Boomhower was elected the first president, and he registered the organization with the state of Iowa the same year. Prior to this, no western pony breed had been developed in the United States for a particular purpose.

Using Black Hand, now a coming yearling, as the type-standard, the group set the requirements for registration of equines with his characteristics: small ears, small, slightly dished Arabian type head, and body muscled like the Quarter Horse with Appaloosa characteristics visible at forty feet. Height requirements were set between 44 and 52 inches, which Boomhower was very adamant about enforcing because he felt there should be a distinct difference between POAs and Appaloosas. The age of a child showing the new breed was set at sixteen years old and under, for this was to be a breed for children to ride and show. Adults could only show a POA at halter or with a cart. So POAs must also be gentle and easy to train.

Founding Lines

Black Hand became POA No. 1. The second pony to apply for registration was a beautiful red, black, and white leopard colt from Arizona that was the product of an Arabian leopard stallion and a Welsh mare. His name was Siri Chief and he was 50 inches

Pony of the Americas blue roan gelding with blanket and spots, 51 inches tall. *Jared Katzenberger*

tall. After Les saw his picture, Siri Chief became POA No. 2.

Applications for registration in the new breed came from all over the country. Among the firsts were Na-na Su-Kin (Little Chief) No. 14, whose ancestors came from the Nez Perce Indian ponies of Montana, and Corette's Scottish Chieftain No. 18, found on a boatload of Highland cattle shipped to Canada from Scotland. In 1957, two Texas brothers obtained a wild mustang stallion named Dragon from Mexico, along with his band of mares. He became POA No. 103. From England came Stewart's Danny Boy No. 282, imported by breeders in Pennsylvania.

Black Hand, Siri Chief, Na-na Su-Kin, Corette's Scottish Chieftain, Dragon, and Stewart's Danny Boy all became founding sires of the POA breed. As other applications came pouring in, each was carefully considered based on strict guidelines before registration was granted.

As the breed grew, a second generation of bloodlines joined the founding sires in prominence. Lady of Paint was a mare of only 50 inches at maturity and was a descendant of Kawliga (one of the founding sires of the Appaloosa breed) on her sire's side, and she had an American Quarter Horse on her dam's side. She became a halter and performance champion in her own right, but her greatest

Pony of the Americas chestnut snowcap colt.
Jared Katzenberger

accomplishment was producing the Warrior line of performance POAs through her first foal, a colt named Lady's Warrior. He became one of the first premier sires of the breed.

The first Supreme Champion Stallion, Chief Little Britches, produced the famous Britches line of performance POAs, noted for their trainability and intelligence. Joining them was another Appaloosa sired colt named East Acres Double Tough. His balance and symmetry, as well as his substance and style, earned him consistent national halter championships in the 1980s. These qualities were passed on as Double Tough foals names were added to the list of International Champions.

A registered Appaloosa stallion named Gold Prince became a POA when the height limit was raised to 56 inches. He was bred to POA mares to produce halter and performance National Champions.

The Warrior, Britches, Double Tough, and Gold Prince lines joined the founding sires to lead the breed in producing outstanding POAs. The unknowns disappeared from pedigrees as POA lines became more established.

Progress

As the years progressed, the POA Club began to evolve and grow, and state and regional shows began to emerge. In 1959 the first International Show for the Pony of the Americas was held in Mason City, Iowa, and became an annual event. It also included a POA track racing with a 100-yard race. From that first competition, racing grew to 220 yards and gradually increased to 440 yards, with a grading and qualifications standard. The POAs raced in two divisions divided by size, and the jockeys were the children. The practice was discontinued at the International Show after 1967 for safety reasons, but the POA rulebook carried the rules and standards for track racing until 1997.

Other events were added to the International Show after racing was dropped. Freestyle reining (reining program to music) was held from 1990 to 2000. A versatility class began at the 1985 International Show, with contestants showing in four classes: western pleasure, English pleasure, reining, and barrel racing. (Each rider was allowed two grooms and had to change clothes and tack between classes without ever leaving the show ring and within a time limit.) A World Championship Show was added to the show schedule in 1976, but the International has remained the premier showcase for POAs every year.

In 1963, it was voted to raise the height limit of a POA from 44 to 46 inches at the lower limit, and from 52 to 54 inches at the upper limit. It was about this time when the Shetland began to disappear from the POA breeding program. Larger ponies, such as the Welsh, and small horses, like the wild mustang and the Arabian, were combined with Indian ponies, Quarter Horses, and Appaloosas by the breeders to achieve that little horse look.

In 1973, the age of a child showing was raised to eighteen and under, and in 1985 the upper limit of the POA was raised to 56 inches. Adults could only show POAs at halter or pleasure driving, otherwise only children could compete with their POAs. Only for training purposes were the nineteen-and-over riding futurity classes instituted for young stock in 1987, as these classes were lobbied for by boys and girls who had aged out of POA showing. While a two-, three-, or four-year-old POA was being shown in these futurity classes, they could not be shown in eighteen-and-under competition, thus keeping the separation of child and adult.

Throughout all of these events, the POA has always been associated with family values, fun, and competition.

International Interest

Since the founding of the breed in 1954, the registry went from one pony, Black Hand, to over forty-five thousand POAs in 2003.

The breed also expanded into other countries. In 1997, Germany imported its first POA, named Bounce Back Val. As more POAs were imported to Germany, the first German Pony of the Americas Breeders Club was founded in Unteralpen, Germany, in 1999. POAs located in Canada now have affiliation with those in the United States. To address this situation, Canada and Mexico, along with other countries within the continents of Central and South America and Europe, are now included in the area elections.

The size and substance of the POAs was used in the formation of a new breed in Australia. Australia's Palouse breed was developed in 1974 using Appaloosa studs and pony mares. Shortly thereafter, POAs and English ponies were imported to improve the stock. In 1978, the unbeatable POA, MP's Jim's Silverpiece, was sold to an Australian breeder. Silverpiece received the highest rating on the inspection score ever given an animal imported into Australia. The formation of the first U. S. POA Equestrian Team was finalized in 1993 through an exchange program with the Australian Palouse organization.

In England, an animal portrait artist and a director in the Spotted Horse and Pony Society, Adrienne Walsh, chose a leopard POA, Super Intimidator, for her painting depicting the perfect spotted equine to commemorate the tenth anniversary of the founding of that society in 2002.

Breed Overview

POAs are not small Appaloosas since they have a finer look. However, when someone asks, "What is a POA?" and a quick answer is needed, the easiest reply is, "A small Appaloosa."

For show purposes there are definite height limits for weanlings, yearlings, and two-, three-, and four-year-olds. Permanent registration is only given at six years of age. Temporary registration is given if the pony fits the color, height, and conformation standards. There is also a hardship clause for ponies with unknown registry, or for Appaloosas that remain small enough to meet the height requirements if they fit the color and conformation standards.

POAs still must have color that is recognizable from forty feet, mottled skin, and white sclera to be registered. Sclera is the white of the eye and usually is readily visible, resembling the human eye. Mottled skin is a blotchy pattern of pigmented and non-pigmented skin (usually with black spots) found on the muzzle, around the eyes, and genital areas. Bold, vertical, clearly defined, light or dark stripes on the hooves are another POA characteristic, but are not required for registration.

Pinto coloration and bald faces are disqualifications for the POA registry as are white stockings that rise above the middle of the knee.

Standards

General appearance: Pony of the Americas should show beauty and symmetry. It should also be a balanced individual, regardless of size, and correct in all aspects of conformation, exhibiting approved color patterns and characteristics.

Quality of a POA: Quality refers to substance, style, and refinement. The ponies should be well proportioned and in good health and flesh (not too fat or too thin), with soft, pliable skin, and the overall appearance of refinement, style, beauty, and substance.

Size: The POA is between 46 and 56 inches in height at maturity.

Head: The head should be proportionate in size to the body, with clean-cut features. The symmetrical and smooth head is clean-cut and slightly dished, showing mottled skin around the nostrils and lips. The forehead is wide and sclera of eyes is white, adding distinctiveness to head's appearance. The eyes should be medium size, pointedly alert, and well carried.

Neck: Showing style, quality and character, the neck should be slightly arched and clean-cut, with distinctly defined throatlatch and large windpipe.

Body: The body should be round, full ribbed, and heavily muscled with well-sprung ribs. The back is straight and both the back and loin are short, wide, and well muscled. The underline is long with flank well let down.

Forehand: The arm and forearm should show muscle; shoulders should be deep and well laid in, sloping 45 degrees. The withers should be prominent and well-defined with good saddle base.

Chest: The chest should be fairly wide, deep, and full, and blend into well-muscled, sloping shoulders.

Hindquarters: The croup should be long, level, and muscular, and the quarters and gaskins, deep and muscular. The hocks should be clean-cut and supporting. Hips are smoothly covered, being long, sloping, and muscular. Thighs are long, muscular, and deep, blending into well-rounded quarters. Gaskins are long, wide, and muscular, extending to clean, clearly defined, wide straight hocks.

Legs: The legs should be set squarely under the body, straight and true at each corner so that the animal is well balanced and travels easily. They should be in correct position from front, side, and rear view. Forearm is well muscled, long, wide, and tapers down to a broad knee. Knees taper gradually into the cannon. Cannons should be lean, short, wide, and flat, with wide, smooth, and strongly supported fetlocks. The ankles should be firm, and the fetlocks are clean of excess hair. Pasterns are medium long and slope a medium 45-degree angle.

Feet: Hooves are striped, rounded, deep, open, and wide at heels. The feet should be proportionate to the size of the pony, of good shape, wide, and deep at the heels.

Gaits: This refers to a way of going. The walk should be straight with a long, easy stride, true and flat footed.

The western jog trot is soft, relaxed, and quiet with a definite two-beat gait. At no time should it resemble a running walk, nor should it be rough or stilted. The speed and stride should be compatible with the pony size.

The English trot should be a free-moving, ground-covering stride, executed in a long, low frame. Excessive knee or hock action is at no time desirable. Quick, short strides should be penalized.

Lope or canter should be rolling and comfortable with strong emphasis on a natural three-beat, soft lope. A four-beat lope is at no time desirable and should be penalized.

Manners: Good manners are demonstrated by the pony's obedience to all commands and includes the ability to stand quietly, back readily, walk, jog, lope, or stop as requested and, in general, guided by a light mouth. Pulling on the bit, head tossing, breaking stride, traveling in a sideways motion, and wringing the tail are objectionable.

Presence: Presence refers to animation, self-assurance, alertness, and personality that stem from good breeding, good grooming, good care, good training, and good handling. Evidence of being a "professional" is also present, in that the pony senses what is required and readily expends the effort necessary to obey the demands of its rider, driver, or handler.

Colors: The seven basic coat patterns recognized for the POA breed are:

- Snowflake pattern—basic dark body color with "snowflake" type white spots over all or part of the body
- Frost pattern—basic dark body color with "frost" type white sprinkled over all or part of the body
- Blanket pattern—basic dark body color with white "blanket" over croup, hindquarters, loins, and back (or over parts of these); blanket may have dark spots

The tractable nature of the POA is demonstrated in this red roan mare with blanket and spots. *Jared Katzenberger*

- Leopard pattern—basic white body color with dark spots over entire body and neck
- White with black spots on hindquarters—basic body color white with dark spots over hindquarters, loins, croup, and back (or over parts of these)
- Marbleized roan pattern—basic roan body color (including neck), being a mixture of light and dark hairs with light color predominant and with "varnish" marks
- Few-spotted leopard pattern—basic body color is white with no or few spots on body. Areas of solid color or dark roan may be found on the ears, behind the elbows, the flank, and usually the underside of the neck. Strong sclera (the area of the eye which encircles the iris) and mottled skin are required.

Coat patterns vary widely, and over time, some ponies develop additional color. One of the most popular colorations is the blanketed pattern, which is characterized by white over the loin and hips with dark, round, egg-shaped spots. These spots may vary in size, from tiny specks to spots 4 or more inches in diameter. Others will show white over the hips without the dark spots. This variation on the blanket pattern is known as "snowcapped."

Spotting over the entire body is commonly referred to as a leopard pattern. In both blanket and leopard patterns, the spots may be darker in the middle, with a lighter ring surrounding the spot. This unique look is called a halo.

When white hairs are mixed in the base coat color, the pattern is called roan. Often associated with this coat pattern variation are the descriptive terms of red, blue, and marbleized. Gray or roan ponies must have mottled skin and white sclera to qualify for registration.

Credit: Pony of the Americas Club, Inc.

SHETLAND PONY

The American Shetland Pony Club
81 B East Queenwood Road
Morton, Illinois 61550
www.shetlandminature.com

Shetland Ponies have been known for more than a century as "the most remarkable of ponies." They are the perfect-sized riding pony for children and are hardy and reliable, ready to share in any adventure. They make great, trustworthy companions, suitable for most any youngster to ride and handle. The love and devotion these ponies offer is giant sized, and a bond with them is never outgrown. Shetlands are relaxing and fun to own with an appeal lasting beyond childhood.

With their maximum height of 48 inches, they are an easy fit for lighter adults as well. For those desiring a larger Shetland, the National Show Pony (half Shetland) is now available. Since they have retained an innate driving ability, well trained Shetlands excel in driving classes and can be shown by both adults and older children. Pony hitches have livened up many a parade and are used regularly in a working environment.

Shetlands are fine family pets requiring minimal maintenance. They can undertake most any pursuit a standard horse can, only in a smaller, less expensive package. They require the same healthcare as horses, only their feed and stabling is in proportionately smaller amounts. Owning a Shetland does not require expensive equipment. It can range from the barest essentials such as a halter, bridle, saddle, and simple grooming tools, to all the equipment necessary for a hitch of performance ponies pulling an elegant, antique carriage.

A well trained Shetland not only excels at driving, but it also has a multitude of other uses. Lead-line classes for small children are always fun. Shetlands have also been used successfully in therapeutic programs for the physically and mentally challenged. There is an activity suited for anyone with the Shetland.

Classic Shetland stallion showing ideal breed type. *Courtesy Dorie Tennessen/TNT Farm*

History

The Shetland Islands on the storm-lashed northern most part of the British Isles is the home of the Shetland Pony. On those islands, its ancestry roamed the hills and moors, developing into hardy little animals well adapted to their environment. It is uncertain from where the ponies came from before then, but they have been on the islands as far back as any knowledge of Britain. Nowadays, the Shetland Pony is raised and kept only on a few of the islands, i.e., the Mainland, Bressay, Fair Isle, Fetlar, Yell, and Unst.

It is said that sometime in the sixteenth century, Spanish Armada ships went ashore there (possibly aground), having had onboard some fine horses belonging to the admiral's stud (horse farm). Supposedly the cross of these horses imparted much of the beauty and fleetness now evident in the pony.

The islands' rough terrain obviously had much to do with establishing the characteristics of the ponies. They are renowned for their sound feet and legs, strong symmetrical body, good eyes, wonderful endurance, and good temperament. The ponies generally ran at large on the hills and lived on the heather and the scant grass they found. They were seldom fed a handful of grain or hay during the long, cold winter and were driven to the extremity of eating seaweed. It has been said that they also would, under pressure of great hunger, eat the dead fish that were washed in with the seaweed, but this is questionable. Hence, "survival of the fittest" accounts for their symmetry of form and great constitution.

In the mid 1800s, Shetlands were used for pulling ore carts in coal mines and carried peat from the hills for the family. The peat, which was used for fuel, was packed in "cassies," each one containing not less than 60 or 70 pounds. Two of these cassies were slung across a pony's back on a kind of pack saddle in the shape of a sawhorse and were fastened in position by a breast collar, a girth or two, and breeching. The whole load weighed as much as a good-sized man and was often carried for several miles up and down hills, across marshes, through storms, and in washed out paths and gullies without halting. So the Shetland's feet had to be good, its back strong, and its eyes clear to pick its way. The pony was never used in its native home in harness, but only to ride and pack. Any good Shetland pony could pack half of its own weight and go many miles without halting.

Not all ponies from the Shetland Islands were small. Eli Elliott, an early Shetland Pony historian from Iowa, remarked, "Some years ago they brought larger ponies from the highlands of Scotland and crossed them with little mares. These are not 'right Shetlands' as they grew to be 46 to 48 inches. 'Rights' are 40 to 43 inches, with some 36 to 38 inches." As to size, the smaller the better, which the Shetlander was not slow in finding out. When Elliott imported 126 Shetlands in the year of 1888, he had to pay 50 percent more for 8 little mares that were 36 inches and under fully grown. He remarked, "As long as you can get them straight in the legs and round in the body, you can not get them too small. We often hear of marvelously small ponies and I have made it a point to look for them: but the smallest grown pony I have ever seen was 34 inches high and weighed under 200 pounds."

Elliott imported all the Shetlands he could buy for two years straight and said, "I am fully convinced that we have more and better Shetland Ponies today in America than they have on the whole group of the Shetland Isles.... As a rule the [sucklings] and yearlings are straight in their legs. The mares seldom breed oftener than every other year, but keep at it to a great age. I saw one mare thirty years old and about to drop another colt."

It is a well known fact that on a part of the island of Fetlar, a titled lady of Scotland, Lady Nicholson, had for years crossed small Arabian stallions to Shetland mares. This produced remarkable ponies 46 to 48 inches tall, some of which were extremely fine, and they became known as Fetlar or Lady Nicholson ponies. Iceland's ponies were also released on the island of Bressay, with which Shetland stallions were then crossed. Consequently, a pony coming from the Shetland Islands does not prove it is a pure Shetland.

Shetland mare with the refinement of the Modern type.
Courtesy Dorie Tennessen/TNT Farm

Elliott proclaimed, "I have seen work horses there that would weigh from 1,200 to 1,500 pounds and I saw one colt, the produce of such a mare and a Shetland stallion. Hence [there is] wisdom of having a competent committee to examine each and every applicant for entry in our Stud Book!"

Registry

In 1888, the American Shetland Pony Club (ASPC) was founded, and the first Shetlands were registered in the United States. Over a hundred years later, the American Shetland Pony is still popular and thriving. Now after more than a century of selective breeding, the Shetland has developed refinement, resulting in a sturdy but elegant pony.

Shetlands are divided into four registries: the American Show Pony, the Modern American Shetland Pony, the Classic American Shetland Pony, and the National Show Pony. Each type of American Shetland Pony has its own division for competition and its own criteria.

The newest registry recognized by the American Shetland Pony Club is the National Show Pony, which is required to have only one purebred Shetland or Miniature Horse parent and can measure up to a full 14.2 hands at the withers. National

Show Ponies have a division for hunters, western riding, and driving.

Shetlands must be registered with the ASPC, which is also the parent registry of the American Miniature Horse Registry. The ASPC has remained closed since 1955 to imported Shetlands. The exceptions to this rule are ponies that are registered in Canada with American parentage.

American Show Pony

American Show Ponies are similar to the Modern American Shetland Pony with its animated gait and brilliance. These larger, flashy ponies are especially suited to driving and draw a lot of attention in the show ring.

Any pony that is registered with the American Shetland Pony Club, the American Hackney Horse Society, or any offspring of a registered Shetland bred to a registered Hackney pony is eligible to be recorded in the American Show Pony Stud Book. It also must meet the dual height requirements: there must be a maximum overall exhibition height of 48 inches or less as measured from the highest point of the withers to the measuring surface; also the height from the highest point of the withers to the hairline of the coronary band at the heel shall not exceed 46 inches (that is, 47 inches over-all height with a 1-inch heel, or 48 inches overall height that would include up to a 2-inch heel).

This breed, like the Modern, is an elegant and stylish show pony. Although it can be slightly larger, its rules and shows are similar to the Modern American Shetland Pony.

Modern American Shetland Pony

This pony is elegance in motion. It combines the historic hardiness of the Classic Shetland Pony with an outcross of an animated and more supe-rior, refined breed. This cross produces a long, shapely necked and fine-boned pony with extreme action and a spirited, but sophisticated, personality that lends itself well to the show ring. Moderns can come in any color, but are not to exceed 46 inches.

The Modern American Shetland Pony is shown in two height divisions: less than 43 inches, and 43 to 46 inches. Besides halter classes, they can be shown in performance classes, which include road-ster, harness, and pleasure driving.

A well trained Modern American Shetland makes an agile, intelligent mount for a child and can be used for everything from gymkhana ponies to hunter/jumpers. A good headset, superb car-riage, and high action most often define a great Modern Shetland performance pony. This is an ele-gant animal with all the pomp and sophistication of a carriage horse, yet possessing the sturdiness of a pony.

Modern Shetlands are thrilling to watch, with the fiery energy and style they bring to the show ring, as well as the fun and quick thinking they achieve in event competition. They can also add elegance to a casual carriage ride down the lane. They have high-stepping action and the excitement of the larger breeds, with the handiness of a pony.

Standards for American Show Pony and Modern American Shetland Pony

Conformation should be that of a strong, attrac-tive pony, blending the original Shetland type with refinement and quality resulting from American care and selective breeding. The head should be symmetrical and proportionate to the body with width between prominent eyes. It should have a fine jaw, short, sharp, erect ears, a small muzzle with flaring nostrils, and a refined throatlatch. The head should be carried high on a well arched neck. The barrel should be well rounded, and the back short and level with a flat croup. The pony's structure should be strong with refinement: high withers, sloping shoulders, flat boned, muscular legs (not cow- or sickle-hocked), strong springy pasterns and good, strong, serviceable feet. The mane and tail should be full.

Ears: Ears should be small, fine, alert, expressive, and set well on head.

Foretop: This should be long and full, but not bushy and wavy.

Eye: Eyes should be large and luminous, placed well on head, wide apart, and prominent on side of head.

Forehead: A wide and smooth forehead is desirable.

Face: The pony should have straight or very slightly concave profile.

Nose: The nose should be broad and flat, carry-ing width of muzzle.

Muzzle: The muzzle should be small and refined, with large nostrils and firm lips.

Chin: The chin should continue line from upper lip and should not be meaty or flappy.

Mandible: This should have a smooth bottom line and be wide between the branches.

Jaw: The jaw is not as pronounced and massive as on some breeds, but should show some bulge, particularly on stallions to denote masculinity.

Throat: The throat should be fine and pro-nounced. The previously mentioned parts of the head, when blended together, should be small and fine, and express personality.

Neck: The intersection of the neck into the head should be horizontal to give a fine rounded throatlatch and an arched neck with the head car-ried high.

Point of shoulder: This is pronounced, setting well forward at approximately a 45-degree angle from the withers.

Breast: The chest should be broad and deep, but not too wide and flat between the front legs.

Arm: This should be muscular, but not too bulgy or massive, and set forward on shoulder. The forearm should be long, smooth, but with pronounced muscles.

Cannon bone: The cannon bone should be short, wide, flat, and dense, with the tendons standing out.

Knee: The knees are smooth, well blended, and in straight line with forearm and cannon bone.

Fetlock joint: Clean and hard. There should be no puffiness, or cocked-over appearance. Fetlocks are light.

Pastern: The pasterns should be long and springy, but not at the expense of strength.

Hooves: The hard, dense hooves should be wider at the base than at the coronary band. The heels are open, and the angle is that of the pastern.

Foot: It should toe straight, not turned in or out.

Tendons: Broad and clearly defined. When felt between the fingers, the tendons should be hard and taut. They should not be overly cut-in below the knee and the hock.

Pisiform: This should be clear cut and clean (one of the signs of quality joints).

Elbow: The elbow should be close to barrel.

Chestnut: They should be heavy and course, as chestnuts seem to go with ponies.

Ribs: To have feed capacity, endurance, and good looks a pony must be well ribbed. There must be a combination of breed character, or quality, and the good spring of rib that the Shetland has been noted to possess for centuries. The ribs should be extended back as close as possible to the point of the hip. In other words, the pony should have a rounded barrel.

Girth: When viewed from the side, the pony should be deep in the heart girth.

Coupling: The back and the loin areas should be short, and the hip or croup long and level. If the pony has these features, then it is said to be short-coupled, which is desirable. From the side, the belly line is longer than the back line. This indicates several things: the heart-girth is deep, the ribs are well sprung, the coupling is short, and the foreleg is set well forward, which it must be to have the angle of shoulder necessary for good shoulder action.

Flank: The flank should not be "cut-up."

Stifle: The stifle should be round, full, and strong.

Hock joint: When a pony stands with the hind legs squarely under it, a plumb bob should fall from the point of the buttock, straight down the back of the hind leg from the hock to the ankle. From a posterior view, the point of the hock should be the same distance apart as the fetlocks. The joint itself should be large, but neat and clean, with the bones defined, or else the hock will look meaty.

Gaskin: The gaskin should be well rounded, wide, and muscular.

Thigh: The distance from the stifle to the buttock should be deep and full.

Point of buttock: The buttock should be gracefully and symmetrically rounded. When viewed from the rear, it should be wide.

Tail: The tail should spring from the line of the back, not hung down below as though an afterthought. The tail should be long and full.

Dock: This is the portion of the tail arising from the back and should come out boldly.

Croup: There should be a pleasing, gentle curve, but comparatively speaking, it is a horizontal croup. When viewed from behind, the croup should be oval, not broad and flat, and it should not come to a point.

Point of hip: This should be laid in smoothly to give a pleasing appearance. The angle of the line from the points of the buttocks should be low, and the distance should be great.

Loins: The loins should be full, broad, and strong, as well as blend smoothly.

Back: The back should be short and wide, not flat, and in proportion to the neck of the pony.

Withers: These should be clearly defined and

Shetlands are expressive with refined heads and large eyes. *Courtesy Johnny Robb*

is extended in a horizontal position. The elbow and the hocks should be flexed, with the feet well under the body and well off the ground. The body at all times should be in perfect balance, with the head carried high.

Manners: Good manners are demonstrated by the pony's obedience to all commands requested, and in general, the pony should be guided by a light mouth. Pulling on a bit, head tossing, and breaking stride are objectionable. Ladies, amateur, and children's ponies in harness should stand quietly and back readily.

Presence: Presence refers to the animation, self-assurance, alertness, and personality that stems from good breeding, good grooming, good care, good training, and good handling.

Soundness: As a minimum requirement, all Shetlands must be serviceably sound for show purposes. Any pony showing evidence of lameness, deformity in feet, broken wind, or complete loss of sight in either eye shall be refused an award.

Color: Shetlands may be any color, and either solid or mixed, but not appaloosa. No particular color is preferred. Additionally, no discrimination should be made because of the color of eyes, such as glass, watch, hazel, or blue.

Classic American Shetland Pony

This is a pony that possesses style and substance, being more refined than the original imported Shetland. It is a fun choice for the show ring, driving, trail, or open events. It exhibits a well balanced, strong, sturdy body in a compact package, while also having the willing, easygoing, and gentle disposition to be a suitable companion for all ages. It is a versatile animal, adept at pulling a cart, working in the field, or carrying a child.

To be eligible for registration, the Classic Shetland's height must not exceed 46 inches at the withers. For the Classic Shetland that is under three years of age, there are two major show ring height divisions and each has additional graduated divisions to accommodate different heights for varying ages.

narrow, but not pronounced, and should give a pleasing blend to the back and neck.

Poll: The poll is horizontal just behind ears.

Quality: The quality of the American Show Pony and the Modern Shetland has a general overall appearance of style, refinement, and beauty, as evidenced by fine-boned legs, well proportioned body, and skin that is soft and pliable, with the pony in good health and flesh (but not too fat).

Performance: Good performance shall consist of the walk (in breeding classes), in which the feet should be lifted well off of the ground and placed down flat. The stride is medium in length, brisk, elastic, and straight. The trot should be a straightforward, diagonal movement, with the forelegs being raised at least to a point where the forearm

The American Show Pony is flashy with its animated gaits and overall brilliance. *Courtesy Dorie Tennessen/TNT Farm*

The **Over Division** is for:
- Three-year-olds that are over 42 inches, but not exceeding 46 inches.
- Two-year-olds that are over 41 inches, but not exceeding 44.5 inches.
- One-year-olds that are over 40 inches, but not exceeding 43 inches.

The **Under Division** is for:
- Three-year-olds and older that are 42 inches and under.
- Two-year-olds that are 41 inches and under.
- One-year-olds that are 40 inches and under.
- Foals of current year that are 40 inches and under.

There is also a **Foundation Class** for those on which the breed has been founded. They are required to have a pedigree imprinted with a Foundation Shetland seal. They should be more conservative in type than an entry in Open Classes and should exhibit slightly more bone and substance. The maximum heel (barefoot or shod) for a Foundation pony, including the plate, does not exceed 1½ inches. It is for those Shetlands not exceeding 42 inches and is for exhibition purposes only:

Senior Class is for three-year-olds and older whose height does not exceed 42 inches.

Junior Class is for two-year-olds and under that are 41 inches or less.

Foals of Current Year who are 40 inches or less.

There is a broad diversity of types within the Classic Shetland Pony breed that can vary to a degree from one geographic region to another. The correct Classic American Shetland type should be based on the motto of "form follows function." The more correct type will be dictated by the discipline in which it is engaged or exhibited, such as halter class, light harness, heavy harness, hunter/jumper, competitive driving, or as a child's mount or pet.

Standards of Classic American Shetland Pony

The Classic American Shetland has a well-proportioned body that maintains the strong Shetland constitution with substance in the chest, body, and hindquarters. The short head is clean-cut, with a fine muzzle, large nostrils, brilliant eyes, wide forehead, and sharp, small, well-set ears. It possesses fineness of throatlatch, length of neck in proportion to the body, and a sloping shoulder. The legs are set properly under the body on the four corners, and the forearm is well muscled. The knee and cannon bones are broad and well defined and have an ideally shaped pastern with proper size and angle of pastern and foot. Its topline is straight, the back is short, and the loin is short and well muscled. The tail is set high on the croup. The body has plenty of depth, with well-rounded buttocks and well-muscled gaskins. The ribs should be well sprung and have a round barrel. The knees and hocks are well supported from below by strong, short cannons, joints, and hooves. The mane, foretop, and tail are full, and the coast is fine and silky. It has a natural, straight, and springy way of going. Extremes in length of neck, body, legs, and action are undesirable.

General character: Hardy, spirited, and pony-like.

Head: Small, short, and clean-cut; well set on the neck and tapering from wide set eyes to the muzzle.

Ears: Small, alert, and expressive, set well up on head and delicately curving to tip.

Foretop: Long and full.

Eyes: Expressive, large, bold, and luminous, placed well down from base of head, wide apart, and prominent on side of head. Placement of eyes should give the head a diamond shape from the front view.

Forehead: Wide, smooth, and full.

Face: Slightly concave, and dished is preferred, but a straight profile is permissible. Any indication of a convex (Roman) profile shall be severely faulted.

Nose: Narrow but flat nose is desirable, blending into the muzzle with a gentle curve. A Roman nose shall be severely faulted.

Nostrils: Prominent and open on a small and refined muzzle.

Muzzle: Small and refined, with large nostrils and firm lips.

Neck: Must be proportionate to the body, with extreme length of neck to be avoided. It should be well carried and be moderately lean without crestiness, in the case of mares. In the case of mature stallions, it is inclined to be slightly crested. A broken crest shall be faulted.

Angle of neck: The angle of the neck coming out of the shoulder should be from 45 to 60 degrees. The ideal angle of neck on the halter pony should not exceed 60 degrees.

Hock joint: This is the same as the other two registries, except that cow hocks or sickle hocks shall be faulted.

Action: Free, true, and forcibly straightforward. The walk should be a relaxed, flat footed walk and a four-beat straight movement. The trot should be easygoing and square with elasticity, and should have freedom of movement that is open, reaching, and capable of covering ground when asked to do so. Stiff legged extension (pea shooting) or lack of freedom of movement shall be faulted. Up and down motion (piston-like) without extension shall also be faulted.

Color: This is the same as the other two registries. Recognized Shetland colors are albino, bay, black, brown, buckskin, chestnut, cremello, dun, gray, grullo, palomino, perlino, pinto (tobiano, overo, tovero, and sabino) roan (bay, red, and blue), silver dapple, sorrel, and white.

All other parts of the standards are the same as the American Show Pony and Modern American Shetland Pony's criteria.

Credit: The American Shetland Pony Club

UNITED KINGDOM SHETLAND PONY

Personal Ponies Ltd
The Shetland Register
23 Sergio Way
Hot Springs Village, Arkansas 71909
www.personalponies.org

The United Kingdom (UK) Shetland Pony is a very special breed. It is the true Shetland Pony, the one that worked the coal and tin mines in Scotland, England, and Wales, and the peat fields in the Shetland Islands. These ponies are docile, kind, intelligent, sensitive, and capable of doing hard work. They have an amazing temperament, and are steady of mind and great of heart. However, they are definitely not world-class beauties! They are not sleek, slim-legged, high spirited show ponies. Quite the contrary, they mostly look like sturdy little trolls—short and stocky with shaggy coats and thick manes and tails. This is because they have more important work to do than jumping fences and prancing in show rings.

It was discovered that the UK Shetlands are extra sensitive to small children, especially those with special needs. Their job in the United States is to be loved, hugged, petted, and kissed, as they stand quietly and patiently while a child in braces, on crutches, or in a wheelchair brushes and combs, feeds, or caresses them. It is very important work.

Breed Origins

No one knows for sure how the UK Shetland Pony became an integral part of the history of the Shetland Islands, but about two thousand years ago there were ponies like today's UK Shetland living there. The Shetland Islands have severe weather due to their location, approximately one hundred miles south of the Arctic Circle and just north of Great Britain. Grass is scanty, the ground is hard, rocky, and wet, and there is a constant cold wind. Under

UK Shetlands are not elegant. The most beautiful part of them is their heart. *Personal Ponies Ltd.*

these conditions, animals that can get by with little to eat are more likely to survive, thus the process of natural selection resulted in smaller ponies. It is important to note that the smallness of UK Shetland Ponies is not the result of stunting due to the lack of food while they are growing; it is solely due to the ruthless action of natural selection in weeding out the genetically larger ponies.

These ponies have a long history of domestication and were best suited to work as draft animals; they were often described as "wide, round, and low to the ground." They were originally bred to haul peat and do farm work. Later they were used for draft work, when roads were built and carts

UK Shetlands are built low to the ground. They are like sturdy little trolls. *Personal Ponies Ltd.*

could be pulled along the roadways. They were not the same type as today's American Shetland or the American Miniature Horse, for they were far more stocky and rugged.

In the late nineteenth century, Shetland Ponies were used extensively in the coal mines of Scotland and Wales. Many were exported to the United States to be used in the mines of Pennsylvania, West Virginia, Kentucky, and Tennessee. Their patient, quiet, kind ways were ideal for the demanding work of pulling coal carts in the mines. It was at this time that their history took a dramatic turn, regarding the work in the coal mines.

Troubling History

Previous to the use of the UK Shetlands, from 1809 to 1842, hundreds of women and children were employed as "beasts of burden," working in the many iron or coal mines across England, Scotland, and Wales. Boys as young as four and girls as young as seven would draw coal out of the narrowest mine shafts by way of girdle and chain. From a belt around their waist, a chain was attached that went between their legs and was attached to a large tub without wheels. On hands and feet they would crawl, pulling the tub filled with ore or coal to the main shaft for fourteen hours a day.

In 1842, the Mines Act was passed, which prohibited women and children under the age of ten from working underground. When the labor law was enacted, UK Shetland Ponies were exported from their homeland by the thousands to replace the women and children who were no longer allowed to do the work. UK Shetlands were small in stature, heavy boned, and surefooted. These qualities, along with their strength and temperament, made them ideal for the grueling labor in the narrow mine shafts.

By the 1850s, only male ponies (stallions) were used. They were lowered down into the mines at age four, where they remained underground the rest of their lives—sometimes as long as thirty years. Tens of thousands of stallions worked together underground, which was certainly a testament to their kind nature and willingness to please their human companions. The ponies traveled more than three thousand miles per year and hauled as many tons of ore and coal.

This was a sad and heart-wrenching time. The ponies received inhumane treatment, as attested by a grandson of a collier in the United States to the founder of the Shetland Register. Not only were the ponies sent into the mines for life, but their eyes were also sometimes hammered out and sewn shut to eliminate coal dust infections! This cruel treatment was done in the coal mines in the United States as well.

The best and stoutest ponies were exported to the colliery (coal mine) owners, as large profits could be made selling them for mine work. This was attractive to farmers on the Shetland Islands, who lived at poverty level and could not afford to keep their best ponies. Only the more slender animals were kept or sold elsewhere, because the strongest were in demand for the heavy work in the mines, thus they were much more valuable. The smallest and strongest ponies had no counterparts for this demanding work.

In 1870, a stud (breeding farm) was established by the Fifth Marquis of Londonderry, a colliery owner. The sole purpose of the stud, located on the islands of Bressay and Noss, was to breed pit ponies. No expense was spared in purchasing UK Shetland stallions and mares from the islands, and the best became the foundation breeding stock for the Londonderry Stud. The formula for success in the development of the Londonderry pony was to produce those with "as much weight as possible and as near to the ground as can be got" without defects of conformation. Temperament was not compromised, as a tractable pony was essential for the work required in the mines.

The Shetland Pony Stud Book Society began in 1890 in England to preserve the breed from the drain of the best stallions being exported to the coal mines. It accepted only ponies less than 42 inches high, which encouraged breeders not to produce bigger Welsh-like ponies.

As the mines became progressively more mechanized, fewer ponies were needed. Ponies bred at the Londonderry Stud were sold to breeders in the United Kingdom as well as to breeders and mine owners in the United States. The Londonderry Stud was finally dispersed in 1899, yet up until the latter part of the 1970s, ponies still worked in isolated underground mines throughout Britain. Today, UK Shetlands are still used on the islands to haul peat as well as do other tasks, and a few still work in tin mines in Wales, but for the most part, pit ponies are no longer used in the mines.

After World War I, the British started breeding UK Shetlands as riding ponies for children, and the demand for riding and driving them became popular. Queen Elizabeth II and her siblings rode UK Shetlands, and the Queen Mother was the patroness of the breed until her death.

In 1956, the Shetland Islands Premium Stallion scheme was put into effect in Britain. The Department of Agriculture provided quality registered stallions to seven of the Shetland Islands to live on the common grazing grounds (scattolds), where UK Shetlands were allowed to roam. It also prohibited the use of inferior studs, ensuring foals of greater value.

In the United States

In 1984, Marianne Alexander of upstate New York bought two registered American Miniature Horses. She was captivated by their exceptionally kind and gentle dispositions, and amazed at the way they responded to her grandchildren and other children who visited her farm. They seemed to have a special sensitivity toward the children, who adored them.

Curious about their lineage, she began to trace their bloodlines and discovered that, although they were registered as American Miniature Horses, they were descendants of UK Shetlands imported to the United States in 1884 from the Londonderry Stud. This discovery piqued her curiosity, so she and her husband made a trip to England, Ireland, and Scotland to see the UK Shetland breed in its homeland hills, meet with Shetland breeders, and study the original studbooks in depth. It was their good fortune that they found some longtime

United Kingdom Shetland mare pulling a carriage. *Personal Ponies Ltd.*

UK Shetland breeders that had adhered to the Londonderry Shetland breed type. They offered the Alexanders firsthand knowledge about the UK Shetland that is barely known in the United States. This is when the Alexanders learned of the ponies' inhumane treatment in many of the mines. They also found that Shetlands in the United Kingdom are the true breed type—gentle, full-bodied, and good with children.

By the end of the trip, Marianne Alexander knew what she had to do; she wanted to give something back. "My personal intent was to make reparation for the inhumane treatment that thousands of Shetland Ponies received when sent into the mines for some thirty years—a life sentence." The ponies' incredible sensitivity to children convinced her that they were ideal companions for children with special needs. She wanted to spend her retirement breeding the ponies and offering them to children

who needed something to brighten their lives, to love, and to be a loyal friend.

Registry

Alexander began to assemble a breeding herd of UK type Shetlands in the United States and established The Shetland Register (TSR) in 1986. The philosophy of the register was based on the knowledge and interest of individuals who later participated in the development of Alexander's organization, Personal Ponies Ltd. (PPL), incorporated in New York in 1993. The primary purpose of this organization was to provide Shetland Pony companionship to children who are differently able, to make a difference in their lives, and to bring love and joy to them.

To assure that the true UK Shetland type and temperament would be acquired, the register began securing and importing ponies from

United Kingdom Shetlands have lots of depth. They are robust and sturdy. *Personal Ponies Ltd.*

the Shetland Islands, Scotland, and England. The majority of American Shetlands could not be used; although some could possibly trace their lineage to the UK Shetland, they did not resemble the breed. Only a few UK type Shetlands in the United States were used for breeding if their pedigrees traced back to the UK Shetlands imported in 1881, but these were infrequently found. TSR's goal was to develop and preserve this type of pony from the United Kingdom.

PPL's purpose was to bring a pony to a child with special needs—*their* pony—to love and care for, completely without charge. In a distinctly unique program, the ponies were placed with sponsors who brought them to the children, which made PPL the only organization of its kind in the world. There are riding centers and organizations dedicated to assisting children to learn to ride or drive a horse or pony in harness. Nothing, however, has been done for the very small child with special

needs that requires a smaller mount or an equine companion of small stature.

The ponies were placed strategically with their sponsors to help promote PPL and serve the wider community, such as visits to convalescent homes, daycare centers, therapeutic riding centers, and treatment centers. Ponies were brought anywhere children could benefit from seeing and interacting with them. Volunteers sponsored ponies by maintaining them so that they were available for visiting families unable to keep a pony at their home. These children could visit several times a week to see "their" pony and to care for it in any way they could, whether it be brushing, feeding, walking, or just being with their pony.

Dynamics

Since its humble beginning with only two individuals, PPL has expanded into an international organization. It has placed ponies with hundreds of children with special needs. There are programs in almost every state involving hundreds of volunteers throughout the country. The organization now has fifty-five breeding farms, sixty-five stallions standing at stud, about two hundred breeding mares, and more than one thousand registered ponies. Yet even with all this growth, there are still many children waiting for ponies.

Although small Shetland Ponies are far less expensive to maintain than big horses, building a quality herd of UK Shetlands is hard work and very expensive. The Personal Ponies organization is ever on the lookout for true-to-type Shetlands in the United States, but they are rarely found anymore. Thus importing quality UK Shetland stallions and mares for the breeding program is a priority. Without quality breeding stock, it is impossible to keep up with the requests of families with children who are differently able.

Finding and importing a mature (two-year-old) stallion or broodmare is both an expensive and complex undertaking. Today's market in the United Kingdom is focused on a riding type Shetland, making it difficult to find the draft Londonderry type pony of yesteryear. Once an individual that is suitable for the organization is located, there is the cost of the pony, the added cost of airfare, trucking, and veterinary approvals, as well as extensive quarantines and testing carried out by both the U.K. and U.S. governments. All of this means that the cost to import a mature individual of breeding quality is about $18,000 to $20,000.

TSR is open to utilizing modern biotechnology, such as artificial insemination, embryo transfer, and the possibility of cloning, as these technologies become available. It is hoped that the use of these and other modern scientific methods will dramatically enhance the number of quality UK Shetlands.

The organization consists of volunteers who raise, train, sponsor, and promote the ponies, and they assume the cost of maintaining the ponies they

A pregnant United Kingdom Shetland mare. *Personal Ponies Ltd.*

A little girl with her United Kingdom Shetland. *Personal Ponies Ltd.*

naturally kind nature, and singular enjoyment of human company, UK Shetlands are uniquely suited in temperament and size for small children.

The ponies are often very small, as small as 30 inches, and seldom taller than 39 inches. Most ponies are too small to be ridden (except minimally by a child of thirty pounds or less), although often they make fine driving ponies. The only requirement in the program, however, is that the ponies are offered as "best friends." In their average thirty-year lifetime, the ponies may serve many children. PPL's mission is always to bring joy and smiles into children's lives, and the UK Shetlands are remarkably suited in temperament and size to excel at this mission.

All the ponies must allow themselves to be bumped or leaned on by children on crutches, braces, or in wheelchairs. They must not be bothered by excited screams, clapping, or laughter as children hug, snuggle, pat, or kiss them. They must tolerate quick, erratic movements, or slow, clumsy fumbling, and stand patiently while a child brushes, combs, feeds, or walks them. They are the ideal pony to be a personal companion of "differently abled" children. "I like to think that being hugged on by little arms and feeling tiny fingers in his mane with a carrot treat or apple core snugged in a small fist is a far better job for a 'winged' (angel) pony than hauling coal," says Alexander.

There have been continuing examples of the lives of children with special needs being immeasurably enriched by having a small equine companion to love and care for. One example is the story of Krista, a little seven–year-old girl diagnosed with a terminal brain tumor, who wanted a white pony because "angels are white in heaven where I am going." A little white UK Shetland Pony named

are assigned. Families who receive ponies from the program are also responsible for the cost of maintaining and the care of the ponies they receive.

Attributes

UK Shetlands are perfectly suited for their intended new job in the United States of being a friend to a child with special needs. The requirement of a sweet disposition for easy handling is innate in the UK Shetland, giving them the tenderness needed to be lovable little equines. With their robust structure,

Sandman was sent to her, but the day before he arrived, Krista was hospitalized. Sandman was taken to the hospital the next day, and Krista was wheeled to the window so she could see *her* pony for the first time. She was given a photo of her pony to keep with her until she was well enough to come home and be with him. She treasured that photo. Later Krista's mom wrote that Krista went to heaven while lying in her mom's lap holding a picture of her "angel horse." From Krista's mom come these words, "The last few days of Krista's young life were greatly enriched by the generosity of your program. The smiles on her face every time her pony was mentioned were worth more than any amount of money in the world."

Soon after Krista's death, Sandman was sent to a little boy with the same condition who had heard about Sandman and asked if he was available. The stories go on about the love these little ponies bring to children with special needs.

Besides providing love and companionship to children who are differently able, the ponies are also "roving ambassadors" and are taken wherever people can benefit from interacting with them. They brighten the day of seniors in convalescent homes, lighten up an entire camp of cancer patients, and participate in programs for children who are emotionally disturbed. They go to parades, fairs, daycare centers, therapeutic riding centers; any place where smiles are needed, the ponies are there.

Standard of Excellence

General appearance: An important feature of the UK Shetland Pony is its general air of presence, stamina, and robustness.

Temperament: First and foremost in the standard of excellence for the breeding stock is a kind attitude and the innate ability to relate to children and be a loving companion. The pony must have an attitude and temperament in keeping with the true UK Shetland Pony; this number one requirement is being suitable for use by a child, especially a child who is differently able.

Height: The ideal ponies stay in the mini to midi range of 28 to 38 inches, with the goal of breeding toward the midi-size range of 32 to 38 inches. They must not exceed 42 inches at maturity. Regardless of size, all ponies must maintain the bone, substance, and temperament of the UK Shetland.

Color: Any color known in equines is acceptable, except appaloosa spotting.

Head: The head should be small, carried well, and in proportion. Ears should be small, erect, and wide set, but pointing well forward. The forehead should be broad with bold, dark, intelligent eyes. Blue or wall eyes are not acceptable. The muzzle must be broad with nostrils wide and open. Teeth must be correct with an even bite.

Body: The neck should be properly set onto the shoulders, which should be sloping, not upright. The body should be strong with plenty of heart room and well-sprung ribs; the loin is strong and muscular. The quarters should be broad and long with the tail set well up on it.

Forelegs: Front legs should be well-placed with sufficient good, flat bone, showing a strong forearm. They should have a short, balanced cannon bone and springy pasterns.

Hind legs: Thighs should be strong and muscular with well-shaped strong hocks, nicely let down. The hocks are neither hooky nor too straight. The hind legs should not be set too wide apart, nor should the hocks be turned in when viewing the pony from behind.

Feet: Feet should be tough, round, and well-shaped.

Action: The ponies should have straight, free action, tracking up well and using every joint.

Coat: The ponies carry a double coat in winter, with long guard hairs for shedding rain to keep the pony's skin protected and dry. Their short summer coat has a silky sheen. The mane, foretop, and tail hair should be long, straight, and profuse in both winter and summer coats. Feathering of the fetlocks must be straight and silky at all times.

Credit: Personal Ponies Ltd.

WELARA PONY

Arabian eloquence and Welsh sturdiness are apparent in this Welara. *Daniel Johnson*

American Welara Pony Registry
P.O. Box 3309
Landers, California 92285
www.welararegistry.com

The Welara is recognized as one of the most beautiful pony breeds in the world. Its homeland is England, but the breed additionally brings in the hardy Celtic ancestry of the Welsh Pony from the mountains of Wales. Additionally, the Arabian horse contributes its own shrouded mystique from the desert land of Bedouins and nomadic herdsmen.

The Welara utilizes the best of both breeds, which have been intentionally crossed for nearly a century. It possesses the dry, cut-sculptured beauty found in the Arabian, and the hardiness and versatility of the Welsh Pony. The pony has an arched neck, dished face, and small muzzle, along with a short back similar to the old-world Arabian and natural high tail carriage. Its gait is slightly animated without the use of training aids. The pony's greatest qualities are its beauty, refinement, hardiness, longevity, and an unusual bonding with humans.

The Welara has a distinct personality that exhibits more charisma than most other equine breeds, making it more enjoyable to work with in all disciplines. Its intelligence and playfulness make it stand out from other breeds.

Many breeders are so impressed with the Welara that they permanently included breeding it in their original Arabian or Welsh program. It is well known that as far back as the early part of the twentieth century, Lady Wentworth bred fine Welsh Ponies at her famed stud, Crabbet Park, to her foremost Arabian stallion and was interested in producing, what she termed, "the most beautiful pony on the face of the earth."

Welaras in England

In 1873, Wilfrid Scawen Blunt and his wife, Lady Anne, of the Crabbet Stud in England, began to acquire Arabians. Wilfrid became convinced that to infuse the blood of the Arabian into the native English racehorses was to revolutionize the world of racing, but Thoroughbred owners did not accept his beliefs.

In 1875, Wilfrid and Lady Anne traveled from Egypt to Damascus via Palestine, where they became well known among the tribes of those lands for their consuming interest in their horses. Bedouin tastes in horses with classic heads and shorter backs pleased the Blunts more than the long backs of English horses. Bedouin tribes brought horses for them to inspect and buy, and they conceived the idea of bringing some of the finest Arabians they could acquire to Crabbet for breeding.

Wilfrid bought and imported a horse by the name of Kars and several mares. In his promotion of the Arabian, Wilfrid entered Kars in a two-mile race in England. While the stallion did not win it, he gave such a good showing of himself that it must have come as a great shock to the English, who believed only a Thoroughbred could run. Some years later in 1882, Blunt entered a stallion by the name of Pharaoh in a match race and he won impressively, but Blunt never was able to alter the thinking of the racing community during his lifetime.

He and Lady Anne continued to purchase notable Arabians directly from their native lands. In 1878, the Blunts made the acquaintance of Ali Pasha Sherif and his Abbas Pasha Stud, which contained the finest Arabians. Years later when Ali Pasha Sherif was forced to sell his horses, the Blunts were able to have their pick. This greatly built up the quality of Crabbet horses.

The Blunts held promotional horse sales at Crabbet, but due to the English attitude toward the Arabian, most of the horses were sold to other countries. Some went to the United States, some to Australia, and a few went to Spain.

Wilfrid suffered through tuberculosis and subsequent moods of depression, probably due to morphine as a painkiller. In 1904, convinced he had not long to live, he turned Crabbet over to his daughter, Judith, who was known as Lady Wentworth and was married with children at the time. By 1906, Crabbet was divided by agreement and Wilfrid and Lady Anne lived apart. Lady Anne lived on their stud farm in Egypt, and when she died, she left her horses and her part of Crabbet to her granddaughters, under the control of Lady Wentworth.

Wilfrid sold some of his finest mares and stallions to interested parties in the United States, a tragic loss for England but a treasure for America. Also, the American cereal king, W. K. Kellogg, purchased some of Judith's finest horses, adding further quality to horses in the States.

Lady Wentworth was astute and capable of handling Crabbet, and in April of 1920, she purchased one of the most important Arabian stallions of all time. Bred at the Antoniny Stud in Poland and foaled in 1908, he was the beautiful gray named Skowronek, and he became a famous Arabian stallion at Crabbet. From the early 1920s, Lady Wentworth had also imported a number of Welsh Ponies. She had an interest in creating particularly refined ponies and bred a number of her Welsh Ponies to Skowronek.

Apparently she was pleased with the results. This is when she stated: "Welsh–Arabian as a cross produced the most beautiful pony on the face of the earth!" At the time of her death, she was crossing many Arabians with Welsh Ponies. Skowronek was one of the original studs used to create the Welara breed as it is known today. Another famous foundation stud was the Welsh stallion Dyoll Starlight, foaled in 1894 at Glanrannell Park Stud in Carmarthenshire, Wales. The importance of these two stallions cannot be overestimated, for they changed the equine world forever, establishing a legacy in the Welara.

It did not take many years for breeders to recognize the tremendous potential this breed possessed, especially in the show ring. Unfortunately, for many years the Welara was at a severe disadvantage due to the fact that there was no breed registry to promote or encourage the breeding and improvement of it.

U.S. Registry

In 1979 an American horse breeder named John Collins purchased an unusually beautiful thirteen-month-old Half Arabian, half Welsh colt. It excelled in horse show competitions, attracted admiration wherever it went, and started considerable controversy concerning the lack of an official breed registry or breed name for the Welsh–Arabian.

In 1980, Collins and a group of horse people joined together to form a breed registry and start a studbook. Most in the group were well-established West Coast Arabian and Welsh breeders and firm admirers of the Welara. They saw the breed as a living work of art and worth perpetuating.

The American Welara Pony Registry (AWPR) was founded on January 15, 1981. Collins named his beautiful colt Desert Shadow, and he became the first registered Welara stallion in the registry. In the summer of 1981, he won his first championship against twenty-three finalists. Since then, he has won countless shows and produced blue-ribbon-winning offspring throughout the West Coast.

The AWPR became the official international registry for the Welsh–Arabian (Welara) breed. The word "American" in the name only designated the registry's location, as the registry did not place any

limit or restrictions to registering animals in other counties. In fact, the AWPR today registers both Welara and foundation stock globally and has many international members, breeders, and stock.

The popularity of the Welara breed has grown phenomenally over the past two decades. Annual registrations have more than doubled in the last few years, and sale values have soared. Stallion fees have now reached competitive prices with the Arabian industry and have well surpassed most pony breeds. In 2003 alone, eighteen new Welara breeding farms were recorded in the United States.

The Welara has become a highly valued equine breed worldwide. Since the registry began, there have been Welara sale value increases of more than 500 percent, and in 2003, sale values surpassed the $23,000 mark. To date, the highest verified sale price of a registered Welara was $40,000, with the average sale value of a registered Welara being from $5,000 to $10,000.

There are Welara breeders throughout the United States, Canada, Australia, and the United Kingdom, though some foreign countries refer to the Welara breed as either a Sport Pony or a Riding Pony. The European names usually refer to the Welara as the Welsh–Arabian, but in some cases the name can also represent additional combinations of breeds, including the Thoroughbred, which is not acceptable for registration with the AWPR.

The registry only accepts pure Welsh–Arabian breeding and prefers that the sire and dam of a Welara are registered with their respective breeds' registry. This is to verify breed purity in an ongoing effort to maintain quality.

Registering the Pure Welara

The benefits of registering a Welara with the AWPR when the animal has already been previously registered with an Arabian registry as a Half Arabian or with a Welsh registry as a half Welsh, are many, as the following examples show:

1. Very few breeders are looking for, or are particularly interested in, prospective herd stallions or broodmares that are part-breds, since there is limited

market demand and value for such offspring. Many breeders have reported that the registered Welara is much easier to market.

2. The registered Welara is considered, in an ever-widening geographical area including the United States and many foreign countries, as a purebred equine breed unto itself. As with nearly every horse and pony breed, the Welara was originally a cross of two or more different breeds and was considered by most to be a part-bred in its early formative years. With the passing of time, however, along with the enthusiasm of breeders increasing production of such "new breeds," the general populace and knowledgeable horse people alike gradually accepted the Welara as a breed in itself, in other words, a purebred. This process of acceptance happened a long time ago with such breeds as the Welsh, Appaloosa, Morgan, Thoroughbred, and countless others, and is certainly happening now with the Welara.

3. Many owners and breeders have indicated they are not satisfied with the usual indifference of registries for their registration certificates, studbooks, and pedigree databases involving the other "outside breed" that is not directly related to the breed that particular registry represents. This can clearly be seen on registration certificates for those that are half Welsh or Half Arabian. The information included for the "outside breed" is frequently as cryptic as stating only "grade Welsh," or a similar referral. Not only is this disappointing and frustrating to the owner, but it also neglects one of the primary purposes of livestock registration: to permanently preserve the history, ancestry, and all known information for each and every animal registered. The AWPR, however, includes and preserves all information and the known pedigree of both breeds involved, the Arabian and the Welsh, as well as treating them as equally important and without discrimination.

4. Registered Welaras also have the additional benefit of being eligible for Year-End High Point awards, with purses available through the AWPR. All registered Welara and Foundation Stock, both

The Welara has a clean-cut head with gentle eyes and a refined muzzle. *Daniel Johnson*

domestic and international, can take advantage of this program.

Registry Requirements

The Welara is a cross between the Welsh Pony or Cob and the Arabian, with no other breeds or bloodlines involved. It can range in size from 46 inches (11.2 hands) to 60 inches (15 hands) at the withers. On rare occasions, a Welara at maturity may not meet size requirements of 46 to 60 inches, but this does not affect its eligibility for regular registration as a Welara, or its usefulness as a sire or dam to propagate the Welara breed. It could, however, affect its success in the show ring, since size requirements are accounted for at approved shows and events. On occasion, a particular show or event may offer special classes or activities where such individuals can still compete or perform.

Any color is eligible for registration, excluding Appaloosa characteristics. The cross must be part Arabian and part Welsh, and neither part may be less than one-eighth or more than seven-eighths.

On the Welsh side, Sections A, B, C, and D of the registry are accepted, but Sections B, C, and D usually are preferred due to size only (these are the larger sizes). Welara stallions at maturity should measure between 14 and 15 hands. A mature Welara mare should measure between 13.1 and 14.3 hands at the withers.

Breeding for a Welara is accomplished by crossing either an Arabian stallion with a Welsh mare or a Welsh stallion to an Arabian mare; the resulting offspring will be equally refined either way. Additionally, a cross of a Welara stallion to a Welara mare can produce beautifully refined animals of great potential. Each of these animals brings its particular qualities to create a uniquely intelligent and versatile pony of extreme beauty.

Welara Foundation Stock

The AWPR also maintains the Welara Foundation Stock, a registry of the Arabian and Welsh animals used to produce Welaras. This registry records an important part of the heritage of the Welara breed.

It is for Arabians or Welsh Ponies or Cobs from Section A, B, C, or D that produced Welaras. Welara Ponies that are too small (below 46 inches) to meet standard size requirements for regular registration are also recorded. Welara foundation animals are eligible to compete in AWPR sponsored or sanctioned shows and events. Both Welara and Foundation Stock also frequently compete in open shows, all-breed shows, shows that offer half Welsh or Half Arabian classes, and events sponsored or sanctioned by the Arabian Horse Association or the Welsh Pony and Cob Society of America.

Foundation animals must be pure Arabian, pure Welsh, or Welara Ponies that are too small (under 11.2 hands) to meet size requirements (which is rare). It is not mandatory for foundation animals to be registered with their respective breed registry, but it is preferred.

Foundation animals may be of any age or color, excluding appaloosa characteristics, to be eligible for registration. Only stallions and mares are eligible, as geldings and spayed mares may not be registered in this section.

Sport Pony

The Welara Sport Pony is part Welara and part of an outside breed. There are no restrictions as to which breed may be crossed with the Welara to produce a Sport Pony. The Thoroughbred combination is popular with hunter and jumper enthusiasts, but there are a multitude of possible combinations to fulfill the needs of many equine disciplines.

For eligibility as a Sport Pony, the animal must have 50 percent or more Welara breeding and the other 50 percent or less can be from an outside breed. The Welara (Welsh–Arabian) breeding must be verifiable by registration numbers or certificates that were issued from recognized registry sources for the Welara side, such as the AWPR, Arabian Horse Association, Canadian Arabian Horse Registry, Welsh Pony and Cob Society of America, Welsh Pony and Cob Society (United Kingdom), and other similar official registries. The Welara breeding may come solely from the sire or the dam. Any combination is permitted, as long as it can be verified and is 50 percent or greater Welara breeding.

Since the purebred Welara can have different percentages of Welsh and Arabian bloodlines—not necessarily 50/50—and neither part is less than one-eighth or more than seven-eighths, the 50 percent or more Welara bloodline required for the Sport Pony may also differ in the percentage of Welsh and Arabian blood and does not need to be equal for registration eligibility.

Because the Welara Sport Pony is partly an outside breed, there are no size or color restrictions. Stallions, mares, and geldings are eligible.

The arched neck and elevated tail are features of the Welara. *Daniel Johnson*

Standards

The Welara Pony should resemble a miniature coach horse, except more refined with a high tail carriage, slightly animated gait, and naturally arched neck.

There are several breed variations available to suit various needs and tastes. These variations include:

- Crossing an Arabian horse with a standard Section A Welsh Mountain Pony, which will produce a refined, smaller (under 13 hands) Welara suitable for younger children and light driving purposes
- Crossing an Arabian horse with a standard Section B Welsh Pony, which will produce a slightly larger (13 to 13.2 hand), refined Welara suitable for older children, light adults, and driving
- Crossing an Arabian horse with a Section C Welsh Pony of Cob Type, which will produce a larger (13.2 to 14.2 hand), heavier boned, yet refined Welara, frequently exhibiting feathered feet and excellent for average-sized adults, driving, showing, trail riding, and most other equine-related activities

- Crossing an Arabian horse with a Section D Welsh Cob, which will produce a large (13.3 to 15 hand), refined Welara suitable for average to slightly heavier adults for any type of driving, trail riding, showing, and most other equine-related activities

Characteristics

- General character: hardy, spirited, versatile, refined, and larger than most pony breeds, with a maximum height of 60 inches (15 hands), and a minimum size requirement of 46 inches (11.2 hands)
- Color: any color, excluding appaloosa characteristics
- Head: small, clean cut, well set on, and tapering to the muzzle, with the profile slightly concave below the eyes
- Eyes: bold and intelligent, but gentle
- Ears: well, placed, small, and pointed
- Nostrils: large and open
- Jaws and throat: clean and finely cut
- Neck: lengthy, arched, set on high, and running well back into the withers; fully matured stallions inclined to have a mild crest
- Shoulders: long and well laid back
- Forelegs: set square and true, with large flat knees
- Pasterns: moderately long and well sloped
- Hooves: round and heels open
- Back: short and muscular
- Croup: long and comparatively horizontal
- Tail: naturally high carriage
- Flanks: deep and muscular
- Hocks: large, strong and clean, with points prominent, to turn neither inward nor outward

Credit: American Welara Pony Registry and Heidi Tschida, Ponies Galore! Welsh Ponies

WELSH PONY AND COB

A Welsh Cob (Section D) mare turning heads in a Pleasure Driving class. *Courtesy of Davidson Dales Farm*

Welsh Pony and Cob Society of America
720 Green Street
Stephens City, Virginia 22655
www.welshpony.org

Undoubtedly the most popular of the nine Mountain and Moorland Pony breeds native to the British Isles is the strikingly attractive Welsh. It is the epitome of elegance and athleticism, and many experts consider it "the most beautiful pony in the world." Writing in *The Horse* in 1859, Youatt stated, "The Welsh Pony is one of the most beautiful little animals that can be imagined. He has a small head, high withers, deep, yet round barrel, short joints, flat legs and good round feet. He will live on any fare and never tire."

The Welsh Mountain Pony is renowned in the horse world for its gorgeous head and breathtaking movement, making it perhaps the most charismatic and eye-catching of all British native pony breeds. Like the other Mountain and Moorland breeds, the native Welsh Mountain Pony owes its sound constitution, iron-hard limbs, and great intelligence to a harsh and unforgiving environment that demanded much of the individuals who survived there. It was once written that they were "little animals who can survive where sheep and cattle die."

Today the breed is divided into four sections or types, all developed from the Welsh Mountain Pony. The four sections include:
• Section A: Welsh Mountain Pony
• Section B: Welsh Pony or Welsh Riding Pony

• Section C: Welsh Pony of Cob Type

• Section D: Welsh Cob

Many light horse breeders have utilized the characteristics of the Welsh Pony or Cob and the Half-Welsh can now also be registered.

In the United States and Canada, the four sections of Welsh Pony and Cob can be found successfully competing in a wide variety of disciplines including: hunter/jumpers, eventing, English and western pleasure, competitive trail and endurance, dressage, and combined driving events, among many others. Due to its popularity and great versatility, the breed is a fantastic introduction to the Mountain and Moorland breeds for families and other pony lovers. Its distinctive characteristics generate tremendous enthusiasm among breeders and pony lovers all over the world. Many of its most devoted admirers believe the companionship of a Welsh Pony or Cob is a delight and privilege that must be experienced to be truly understood.

History

The original Welsh Mountain Pony is thought to have evolved from the prehistoric Celtic pony and developed in Wales prior to the arrival of the Romans. Though its inhospitable habitat was daunting and harsh, the ponies managed not only to survive but ultimately flourish. The necessity of the "survival of the fittest" insured perpetuation of the breed through only the hardiest of stock.

The traits of hardiness, beauty, and intelligence, combined with the legendary Welsh temperament, reportedly caught the attention of Julius Caesar during his British campaign in 55 BC. It is believed that the Roman leader was so taken with the beautiful ponies that he kept a stud of native ponies on the shores of Lake Bala in Wales.

During the Roman occupation of Britain, Roman horses bred with the native ponies, producing hardy offspring with both substance and beauty. The characteristics of the Welsh breed as it is known today were likely established by the late fifteenth century, when the Crusaders returned to England with Arabian stallions obtained from the Middle East.

Even when Henry VIII (1509–1547) decreed that "nags of small stature" be destroyed (all stallions under 15 hands and all mares under 13 hands), enough of the small Welsh ponies resided in remote and desolate areas to avoid the onslaught. Like other surviving English pony breeds, such as the Dartmoor and Exmoor, the Welsh Mountain Pony's isolation from human scrutiny ensured a less than diligent execution of the monarch's edict, preserving it for future generations.

In past centuries the ponies were commonly bay, brown, dun, or black. One brilliant pony changed this: a gray stallion named Dyoll Starlight foaled in 1894 and considered by many to be the foundation stallion for the modern Welsh Mountain Pony. Starlight's lineage goes back to an Arabian horse, known as the Crawshay Baily Arab, who was turned out with a herd of Welsh Mountain Ponies in 1850. The Crawshay Baily Arab is believed to have also produced Starlight's dam, Dyoll Moonlight. Many Welsh experts believe that Dyoll Moonlight's Arabian blood is responsible for introducing the gray gene into the Welsh breed.

Though clearly developed from the smaller Welsh Mountain Pony, the history of the Welsh Cob is shrouded in mystery. In the twelfth century in the area of Powys in Wales, it was noted that Spanish stallions were bred with native pony mares producing the "Powis Horse" or what we now call the Welsh Cob. The Powis horse, also known as a Rouncy, was the most sought after of all mounts in Western Britain. An archbishop of Brecon recorded that the brave Welsh princes rode "swift and generous steeds" into battle. Descriptions of these preferred mounts of the time relate characteristics of the Welsh Cob that are still the ideal for the type today. In the nineteenth century a writer stated that the Welsh Cob was "strong enough for the farm, swift enough to fetch the doctor in an emergency, handy enough to put to the cannon, and good enough for the cavalry to ride." It's a very apt description of today's Welsh Cob.

Registries

The Welsh Pony and Cob Society, founded in Wales in 1901, published the first Welsh Stud Book in 1902. The original classification for Welsh Ponies was Section A: The Welsh Mountain Pony. Due to the demand for children's riding ponies, Section B: The Welsh Pony, was added in 1931.

In the United States, Welsh Ponies were imported by breeders as early as the 1880s. George E. Brown of Illinois appears to have been one of the first real Welsh enthusiasts in America, importing a large number of ponies between 1884 and 1910. He called the Welsh "the grandest little horse yet produced!"

Principally through the efforts of Brown and John Alexander, the Welsh Pony and Cob Society of America (WPCSA) was formed and certification for the establishment of a breed registry was issued by the U.S. Department of Agriculture in 1907. It was the concern of early importers and breeders that breed purity be maintained and this subject was regularly discussed with breeders in the United Kingdom. Brown summarized this in a report to the members of the WPCSA: "With a correct standard fixed and uniformly adhered to, nothing can block the advancement of Welsh to front rank in their classes." Interest in the Welsh Pony took a drop during the Depression years, but through the combined efforts of breeders, particularly those in the East, participation in shows and fairs continued.

The 1950s brought increased interest in the breed and WPCSA membership rose significantly. By 1957, a total of 2,881 Welsh had been registered in the United States and interest demanded annual publication of the Stud Book, demonstrating that the Welsh was becoming the fastest growing pony breed in the States.

With 2007 now marking the 100th anniversary of the Society, more than 48,000 Welsh Ponies have been registered since the WPCSA's inception. All Welsh Ponies and Cobs are descended directly and entirely from stock registered with the Welsh Pony and Cob Society in the United Kingdom.

Welsh Mountain Pony (Section A)

The diminutive Welsh Mountain Pony still roams in semi-feral herds in its native land. An animal of great beauty and refinement, it has the substance, stamina and soundness of his ancestors. With its friendly personality and even temperament, it is extremely intelligent and easily trained.

Well built and kind in nature, the Welsh Mountain Pony makes the ideal children's pony and can be used for small children for first riding lessons. In the show ring these ponies are extremely competitive in lead-line and first ridden classes. With older children they are very successful in breed competitions and in mixed Mountain and Moorland classes where available. The Welsh Mountain Pony is a willing and safe jumper for Pony Club and junior one-day events.

With its Mountain and Moorland heritage, these ponies are hardy and strong and live well on meager rations. It often puts weight on easily and can become fat if overfed and under-worked, so care in its management is advised.

Its general description includes a small head with neat, pony-like ears with a wide forehead. The eyes are big, bold and expressive. A clean-cut jaw tapers to a small muzzle which should be dished in profile and never straight or convex. The neck is of good length, well carried and set strongly into sloping shoulders and a well-defined withers. Limbs are set square with strong forearms, short cannon bones and good round hooves. The tail is set high and well carried. The action is spectacular, demonstrating power from the hind quarters and good free use of the shoulders. The movement must be straight in front and behind, quick and rhythmical. Well known for its friendly personality and even temperament, the Mountain Pony is extremely intelligent and easily trained.

The Welsh Mountain Pony (Section A) may not exceed 12.2 hands in the United Sates (12 hands in the United Kingdom). The Welsh Mountain Pony faces ever increasing threats to survival on its native land and needs support if it is to continue to survive in its semi-wild state. Widely acknowledged as the

Welsh Cob (Section D) gelding exhibits the tapered head and small ears. *Courtesy of Davidson Dales Farm*

world's most beautiful pony, it is essential that the traditional hill breeding of these Mountain Ponies continue.

Welsh (Riding) Pony (Section B)

The Welsh Pony has all the physical and personality characteristics of the Section A Mountain Pony, but was originally added to meet the demand for a larger riding type pony. The same general description of the Welsh Mountain Pony can be applied to the Welsh Pony, with greater emphasis being placed on riding pony qualities while still retaining the true Welsh quality with substance. For generations these ponies were the hill farmers' main means of transport, herding sheep and wild ponies over rough and mountainous country. They had to be hardy, balanced, and fast in order to survive, which ensured that only the best were bred from. These qualities, combined with a natural jumping ability and the temperament of their Welsh Mountain Pony forebears, make the Welsh Pony second to none in whatever field its rider may choose.

Today they hold their own among first class riding ponies, both in performance competitions and in the show ring. With the Welsh Mountain Pony as its foundation, the breed standard for Section B is the same as for Section A, but "more particularly the Section B pony shall be described as a riding pony, with quality, riding action, adequate bone and substance, hardiness and constitution and with pony character." The Welsh Pony is well known for its beautiful trotting action and athletic ability but still retains the substance and hardiness of its Welsh Mountain Pony lineage.

Section B ponies do not exceed 14.2 hands in the United States (13.2 hands in the United Kingdom), but have no lower height limit.

Welsh Pony of Cob Type (Section C)

The Welsh Pony of Cob Type first resulted by crossing the Welsh mountain pony (Section A) and the Welsh Cob (Section D). Today, some Section C ponies are still produced from this cross. Other breeds also influenced the Section C, including the Norfolk Trotter, the Hackney, and Yorkshire Coach Horse.

Welsh Ponies of Cob Type are strong, hardy and active with pony character and as much substance as possible. They have bold eyes, strong laid back shoulders, dense hooves, a moderate quantity of silky feather, lengthy hindquarters and powerful hocks.

Cob Type Ponies differ from the Section A and B ponies in that they demonstrate a heavier or "cob-like" build, tend to have less dishing of the face in profile, and have clean limbs with silky feathering at the heels. Their movement is high stepping, but with good reach in the shoulder and impulsion from the hindquarters. They have a round barrel and compact back with good muscling.

The Welsh Ponies of Cob Type is considered to have a more independent character than the Section A or B, yet they are known for their gentle nature. They are easy keepers and have excellent endurance.

Today, this type is used mainly in harness for competitive driving, yet many are beautiful jumpers and can make wonderful children's ponies. Their true worth has been more fully realized in the United States in recent years and their numbers have increased accordingly. Active, surefooted, hardy, and attractive, they are ideal for many purposes both for adults and children.

The Welsh Pony of Cob Type must not exceed 13.2 hands.

Welsh Cob (Section D)

Used as mounts for the British knights during the fifteenth century, the Welsh Cob was used to lead the mighty fighting horses, known as destriers. As the destrier's natural gait was the trot, Welsh Cobs had to cover great distances matching the much taller warhorses stride for stride at the trot. To this day, their forceful, ground-covering trot is legendary.

On the upland farms of Wales, Welsh Cobs would often have to do everything from plowing a field to carrying a farmer to market or driving a family to church on Sunday. Up until the mid twentieth century, its substance made it a popular mount in the British Army and for pulling heavy guns and equipment through rugged terrain. Prior to the automobile, the Welsh Cob was the quickest and most reliable transport for doctors and businessmen.

Aptly described as "the best ride and drive animal in the world," the Welsh Cob is well respected for its flashy trot, athletic prowess, and great endurance. Though they are the tallest and stockiest of the Welsh sections, the head remains full of pony character, with large eyes, and neat pony-like ears. Mature stallions have well formed necks with substantial crests giving the appearance of a strong and charismatic animal.

The legs should be relatively short, as it is still considered a pony type. Welsh Cob action must be straight, free, and forceful. The knees should be bent with the whole foreleg extended from the shoulders as far as possible with the hocks well flexed, producing powerful leverage.

Gray coloring is less common in both the Section C and D, but bold white markings are common.

The Welsh Cob is earning a sound reputation in both the hunter/jumper and dressage spheres, and many have had great success in the international driving scene. A strong and powerful animal, both Section C and D ponies have gentle natures and are extremely hardy. From backyard pony to internationally known sport horse, the Cob suits all needs. In the field of competition, the Welsh Cob is a tremendously competent athlete and is difficult to beat.

It should stand above 13.2 hands, and unlike any other Mountain and Moorland pony, there is no upper height limit.

Essential Points of Conformation For All Sections

- General character: Hardy, spirited and pony like
- Color: Any color except piebald and skewbald (pinto type spotting)
- Head: Small, clean-cut, well set on, and tapering to the muzzle
- Eyes: Bold, intelligent and expressive
- Nostrils: Prominent and open
- Jaw and throat: Clean and finely cut, with ample room at the angle of the jaw
- Neck: Lengthy, well carried, and moderately lean in the case of mares, but inclined to be "cresty" in the case of mature stallions
- Shoulders: Long and sloping well back. Withers moderately fine but not "knifey." The humerus is upright so that the foreleg is not set in under the body.
- Forelegs: Set square and true and not tied in at the elbows. Long strong forearm, well developed knee, short flat bone below the knee, pasterns of proportionate slope and length, feet well shaped and round, and hooves dense.

- Back and loins: Muscular, strong and well coupled
- Girth: Deep and well formed
- Ribs: Well sprung
- Hind quarters: Lengthy and fine. Not cobby, ragged or goose-rumped. Tail well set on and carried gaily.
- Hind legs: Hocks to be large, flat and clean with points prominent to turn neither inwards nor outwards. The hind leg not to be too bent. The hock not to be set behind a line from the point of the quarter to the fetlock joint. Pasterns of proportionate slope and length. Feet well shaped, hooves dense.
- Action: Quick, free and straight from the shoulder, well away in front. Hocks well flexed with straight and powerful leverage and well under the body.
- Height: Section A not exceeding 12.2 hands; 12 hands in the UK

Section B not exceeding 14.2 hands; 13.2 hands in the UK

Section C not exceeding 13.2 hands

Section D exceeding 13.2 hands with no upper height restriction

Mares and foals must be DNA typed and stallions must have a standard Stallion Service Report.

Half-Welsh

The breeders of both fine light horses and smaller ponies have successfully crossed with Welsh Ponies and Cobs. With an unusually high capacity for transmitting their best qualities through carefully selected crosses, Welsh have been found to improve many performance lines. Registered Half-Welsh horses/ponies must have either a purebred Welsh sire or dam registered with the Welsh Pony and Cob Society of America.

Credit: Kelly Davidson Chow and Welsh Pony and Cob Society of America, Inc.

PART 6

THE CLASSICS

WARMBLOODS AND PERFORMANCE HORSES

Hailing from the antiquity of Europe, these superb athletes have flourished down through the ages with their mettle still proven today. Many of them began as warhorses and have evolved with agilities for war maneuvers. They now excel at equestrian competitions and sports, such as racing, eventing, dressage, or driving. With their capacity to move quickly in any direction, they can bend, pivot, and "dance." Their inherent power and courage lifts them off the ground in effortless jumping. They display great muscling, yet are light on their feet and sensitive to the rider's subtle requests. Like beautiful music, they float when they move. They are the elites of the performance arena.

ANDALUSIAN

Andalusians in motion are awesome and breathtaking. *Richard Beard*

International Andalusian and Lusitano Horse Association
101 Carnoustie North, Box 200
Birmingham, Alabama 35242
www.ialha.org

The original, ancient type of hot-blooded Iberian horse that was once carved and painted on cave walls in France and Spain lives on in the modern Andalusian. Its hardiness and quality have stood the test of time, and it remains the aristocrat of the ages.

It is a breed of stout courage, stamina, and strength of body and character. Its willing intelligence and generosity of heart are the supreme traits for which the Andalusian has been celebrated in art, literature, and the arena for thousands of years. Centuries of riders were devoted to this remarkable horse, and the world-renowned skill of Iberian horse people have directly contributed to the development of classical dressage, in which the performance of horse and rider is considered as living, breathing art. Both the western stock seat and the classical seat used in dressage were born on the back of the Andalusian horse.

When contemporary Andalusian enthusiasts try to express their deep delight in this marvelous breed, they sometimes quote famous horsemen, like William Cavendish (1592–1676), the Duke of Newcastle. As one of the first authorities who approached teaching horses as an art, not an act of brutality and domination, he wrote of his favored mount, the Andalusian, "I vouch that it will be the noblest in the world and that from the tip of its ears to the tip of its hoofs there is none to match its cut. It has great vigor and energy but is very docile; it walks proudly and has a style of trot that is the most beautiful in the world. It is arrogant when galloping, is faster than any other race horse, and is much more noble and friendlier than them too; in short, on a day of triumph it is the best type of horse for a great monarch to display his glory to his people, or on a day of battle to lead his army."

Another famous horseman, the eighteenth century equine painter and noble practitioner of mounted arts, Baron d'Eisenberg, said, "Experience has clearly demonstrated that Spanish horses are undoubtedly the best in the world for dressage purposes . . . because of their figure, which is willing, vigorous and so docile that they are capable of understanding and executing to perfection anything that with skill and patience they are taught."

History

No one knows how long the ancestors of the Andalusian existed on the Iberian Peninsula (modern-day Spain and Portugal) or in what is now southern France. They are pictured on Cro-Magnon cave walls dating thirty thousand years ago. Using these horses, the fearsome Carthaginian cavalry defeated Roman troops, although they later were conquered by the Romans. Spanish horses then became the most sought after cattle and battle mounts throughout recorded history. In 711 AD, the Moorish conquerors of Spain admired and acquired these horses that were so unlike the Arabians they had at home.

Literally for centuries, families of horse breeders and cattle ranchers in the Iberian Peninsula consistently focused on selecting their stock for character, type, substance, conduct, and ability as working cow horses. From this desired ideal, families then concentrated on breeding for talents to suit their own farms and regions' needs, terrains, and interests. They always chose, however, with utmost care, horses whose nature, conformation, and beauty enhanced their reputation as superlative, keenly

desired dressage and cavalry horses for the discriminating rider.

For nearly a thousand years, Andalusians were exported to all the courts of Europe and revered by everyone, from princes to Shakespeare and Miguel de Cervantes—avid fans of splendid horses bred for hunting and war. Hernando Cortés brought Queen Isabella's donated Iberian horses from Spain to Mexico. Andalusian horses carried Hannibal's troops, the soldiers of Rome, and the Crusaders of France; they made possible the conquest of the New World, as well as the invention and exploration of the highest, most spiritually attuned aspirations of quality riding—classical dressage. In the cradle of dressage, the clever and impressive Andalusian was—and is—king.

From this illustrious, ancient history, dozens of Andalusian horse traditions still exist. One charming Spanish custom involves naming horses by a humorous connotation, such as calling an especially agile horse Slowpoke (in Spanish, *Lentado*), or using the name Sleepy (*Soñoliento*) for one that is extremely smart and watchful; this is a droll, ancient Gypsy joke many Iberian horse people still enjoy. There are many braids in this strand of Iberian life; the Andalusian people rejoice in a vibrant, complex culture with roots that run deeper than that of Rome—to Phoenician, Carthaginian, and prehistoric times.

The Name "Andalusian"

Perhaps because this breed has had such an enormous influence on civilization, marching through thousands of years of history with humankind, it is not surprising that the Andalusian horse is called by different names in different countries.

In Spain, this breed is now referred to as the Pure Spanish Horse (Pura Raza Española, or PRE). In Portugal and Brazil, it is called Puro Sangue Lusitano (PSL). In the United States and Canada, the breed is known as the Andalusian, although it is not uncommon for North American owners who register their horses in Spain to adopt the term PRE for their stock, and likewise those who register in Portugal or Brazil might refer to them as Lusitanos. Throughout North America and many other nations, Iberian horses are most often referred to as "Andalusian" in honor of their region of origin, the former Roman province of old Andalucia.

Regardless of passionate debates about what to call this ancient breed, the quality of Andalucia's horses has never been disputed. Worldwide fans admire the breed for its beauty, athleticism, brains, and disposition—splendid gifts handed down through the ages.

The Art of the *Vaquero*

One of the many Spanish disciplines at which the Andalusian and Andalusian crosses excel is Doma Vaquera, also called "dressage for the *vaquero*" and "the art of the *vaquero*." The *vaqueros*, who are the working stockmen, must daily move the fierce Iberian bulls and herds of cattle that are native to Spain and Portugal. In Doma Vaquera, working the cattle is taken to an artistic level, requiring a highly trained equine as well as a superb rider with balance, timing, and courage.

The horse must be athletic, intelligent, and instantly responsive to the rider's slightest command. The rider must exemplify the skills and instincts of a true horseman, with the horse virtually functioning as an extension of his own body. This is because, unlike most cattle in the United States, Iberian bulls as well as cows (even without calves), are bred to be exceptionally fearless. They will often savagely turn on the people who work them, thus the "simple" task of moving cattle from one pasture to another can be deadly. A rider who can cue the horse in response and anticipation to unpredictable, explosive Spanish cattle, even with just a thought, is essential to the partnership for this kind of work. A horse that can instantly perform a side-pass, pirouette, or roll-back, or can leap to a gallop and abruptly stop or change direction, is also necessary.

Doma Vaquera–inspired patterns and movements are also performed in North America. This discipline, in which a horse and rider perform the movements of the *vaquero* (without using cattle), is one of the classes offered in all International Andalusian and Lusitano Horse Association (IALHA) horse shows. It is a competitive discipline that transports the ideals of the working stockman to the arena and allows the skills and movements used by working *vaqueros* to be enjoyed by men, women, and children. Women can even perform Doma Vaquera side-saddle if they wish—a true exhibition of grace, skill, and horsemanship. This discipline is receiving more interest all across the country in natural horsemanship circles.

Doma Vaquera consists of three levels: Basico (Beginner), Intermedio (Intermediate), and Alta (Advanced). Like reining or dressage, Doma Vaquera competitions are based upon standardized written test patterns appropriate for the horse and rider's skill levels. The arena is the same size as a large dressage arena.

In Doma Vaquera, the rider holds the reins in the left hand with the right hand placed on the rider's right thigh at the walk. The thumb is pointed forward and held across the chest, and the hand is in a gentle fist at the canter or gallop. The horse performs at the walk, canter, and gallop: in Intermedio and Alta tests, there is no trot, while the Basico test does contain one very brief trot element. The Basic test includes movements like turn on the haunches, turn on the forehand, rein back, and a fast stop from canter (not to be confused with a reiner's sliding stop).

The Advanced test includes the half-pass, full-pass, canter pirouettes, flying lead changes, and a fast stop from the gallop. Whatever the test level, the horse and rider are judged on their precision, successful performance of each movement, and the élan (or flair) with which they flow together. The rider must epitomize pride of bearing, and the horse must display utmost willingness, grace, and instantaneous reflexes guided by the rider's aids, which should not be noticeable.

For riders wishing to take Doma Vaquera further, there are exciting disciplines of La Garrocha

This regal stallion fits the Andalusian title "the best horse for a great monarch." *Richard Beard*

(Spanish stock lance) and Doma Trabajo (working equitation.) A *garrocha* is the traditional Spanish cattle lance, which is a 13.1-foot resilient wooden pole *vaqueros* use to test Iberian bulls. The *garrocha* is used to keep bulls at a safe distance from the horses. It is too dangerous to put a rope on an Iberian bull, especially if rider and horse are attached at the rope's end! (Fighting cattle do not run away; they attack without warning.) *Garrochas* also test the young bulls in the field; two *garrochistas* (*vaqueros* using *garrocha* poles) ride on either side of a galloping bull in open country, and with careful timing, one rider will set his *garrocha* to push and unbalance the bull. If it immediately leaps to its feet, enraged, it is considered worthy of a stockman's herd. If the bull gets up slowly and goes calmly about its business, it is deemed too tame, and therefore unworthy, and is removed from the herd.

In the arena, the *garrocha* is used as the fixed central point to dance a mesmerizing display of skillful horsemanship. The horse and rider present intricate moves with multiple, spinning canter pirouettes below the *garrocha*, as the rider holds the lance just high enough for the pair to pass under while keeping the lance's end motionlessly planted in the arena's sand.

Doma Trabajo is similar to trail classes except it is timed and performed at the canter and gallop. It also includes actual arched bridges to cross, a *garrocha* with which the rider taps the silhouette of a galloping bull in passing, and a jump that the mounted pair must comfortably and cleanly take. At higher levels of the discipline, there is even an element made up of two poles lying parallel on the ground that the horse and rider must cross by going straight sideways across both poles at the canter in full-pass.

Exhilarating to work or watch, the Doma Trabajo showcases the skills honed through Doma Vaquera and La Garrocha, all dazzling tests of the horse and rider's artistry and competitive skills in riding, training, and communion of soul.

Breed Characteristics

Producing good temperament has always been of utmost importance to Iberian horse people. In the Iberian Peninsula, stallions are educated throughout their entire lives to conduct themselves as gentlemen in any company. Thus Andalusians hold a marked, extraordinary affinity for people. Good temperament requires an Andalusian horse to be extremely assertive against a dangerous bull one moment, yet pleasantly carry family members safely through traffic the next. A stallion could be required to cover mares early in the day and then work politely in harness together with mares pulling a carriage in the afternoon. Sometimes a stallion would be used by a *garrochista* to test Iberian fighting cattle in the morning and then would carry his master and his master's lady to a *feria*, or festival, in the afternoon.

Stallions also had to exhibit patience and great care with their riders, regardless of their rider's experience or skill. This kind temperament is clearly seen in the Andalusian's homeland, where young children commonly ride some of the country's finest stallions in competition, parades, and exhibitions. Daily across Portugal and Spain, Andalusian breeding stallions are seen politely awaiting their riders' instructions, tied right next to other stallions they have never met or seen before. This extraordinary combination of spirit, brio, and willingness is why so few Andalusian stallions are gelded.

Good Andalusian Horses are willing and glad to oblige an amateur lady, a novice adult, or an inexperienced child with pleasure for hours, simply out of courtesy and kindly good sense. They are sweet-natured, generous, and deeply intuitive to a rider's desires. Quality Andalusians are noble, carry their riders sensibly, and consider it their job to do their best by each person who guides them, according to that person's abilities, with courtesy of heart. Often they are devoted to just one particularly favorite rider, though a well-trained horse will work nicely with anyone.

After tactful, quiet training and handling, the mares are often the most loving and trustworthy steeds of all. However, while Andalusian mares are exceptionally generous and gentle, some may thrive best with a rider of great talent, sensitivity, and intuition. It is usual in Spain to teach mares to drive so they can work while carrying their highly valued foals. They are ridden less frequently, partly due to the long line of royal decrees allowing only *caballeros* to ride stallions—a sure way for the noblemen of past centuries to absorb the lessons of obedience, allegiance, and supreme horsemanship. However, this tradition is changing very slowly. In North America, of course, Andalusian mares are frequently ridden.

The mares are extremely perceptive and brave; they choose their friends and, once trust is established, dedicate themselves to giving their riders cheerful help. They bond faithfully to their humans, becoming dear friends with the people they elect as privileged riders and handlers. Andalusians have an avid desire to please and tend to be more forgiving than almost any other generous hearted horses. Andalusians flourish on fair, thoughtful, courteous treatment; they strive hard to do right and ardently want to please. In return, they only ask their handlers to guide them clearly and kindly, use them as well as they deserve to be ridden, and love them back.

Over the centuries, only horses with both a generous, gracious nature and the quick wittedness to preserve both riders and themselves in battle and the bullring were chosen for breeding. This careful breeding has paid off, as today Andalusians are proving to be splendid open jumpers, three-day eventers, carriage horses, and hunt field horses in North America and Europe. In the United States, Andalusians excel in disciplines as varied and challenging as marathon or dressage driving, reining, team penning, upper and lower-level dressage, and open jumping. With their capabilities for surefootedness, riders enjoy delving deep into rugged trail country. Andalusians bask in the spotlight at exhibitions, equestrian theater, jousts, or medieval games. They have been featured in films like *Braveheart*, *The Lord of the Rings*, *Gladiator*, and many more.

The Andalusian has a noble presence and classical movement. *Jacquelin D. Suechting*

Registry

The IALHA was formed in 1995 by the union of two previously existing associations. The stud book itself goes back about fifty years in the United States. The IALHA maintains one studbook for purebreds and another for Half-Andalusians.

The Purebred Registry is for purebreds of the Andalusian breed, which includes those of Spanish origin known as Caballo Pura Raza Española, and of Portuguese origin known as Cavalo Puro Sangue Lusitano. All horses born of two registered purebred Andalusian parents are eligible for inclusion in the Purebred Registry. For the Half-Andalusian Registry, a horse must have one parent registered in the IALHA Purebred Registry. Horses' parentage is verified through DNA testing.

Standards

The individual, physical elements that create an Andalusian's overall beauty are wonderfully appealing.

Size: Andalusians usually stand 15.2 to 16.2 hands at the withers.

Color: Color patterns of all types once existed in the Andalusian, as attested by many famous artists including Leonardo da Vinci, Diego Velasquez, Sir Anthony van Dyck, Rembrandt, and Peter Paul Rubens. Many of these coat patterns persist in the Andalusians' descendants, such as their North American relatives—Appaloosas and Paints/Pintos. About 80 percent of Andalusians today are gray, 15 percent are bay, and 5 percent are black, chestnut, palomino, or buckskin.

Head: The Andalusian's head can show either a straight profile or a somewhat sub-convex outline. It is never dished at all, and occasionally an Andalusian may have a more pronounced convexity between and just below the eyes. This is not a Roman nose because it is located somewhat below the eyes and too far up the horse's skull for that feature. A truly low-located Roman-style nose—any bulging very low on the face of an Andalusian—is considered a flaw. Horses with the sub-convex profile are thought to offer a truly battle-brave, strong-willed character, perhaps best suited for the fast, dangerous job of commanding and outmaneuvering the combative *toros bravos*, or fighting bulls.

Andalusian eyes are exceptionally attractive, with an unmistakable almond, almost triangular, cast. Any white sclera showing, or any hard, glaring expression toward their handler (not at a bull they are being asked to move or fight) is considered a serious flaw. Ears are neither too large nor too small. The jowls should not be too large, and throatlatch should be clean; nostrils should display a typical comma shape.

Neck: Andalusians possess a broad neck, particularly in stallions, whose well developed crests exalt their beauty. They often have a luxurious mane and tail, amazing to stroke, soft and gently curling like new lamb's wool.

Body: The Andalusian has a short coupled body, well sprung ribcage, rounded croup, and a low set tail carried flat against the rump. The shoulders are well sloped, and withers well defined. The chest and hindquarters are broad.

Legs: The Andalusian has short cannons, substantial hocks, and superb feet and bone.

Movement: The Andalusian's way of going is energetic and easily collected, with a marked and notable aptitude for lateral work, great agility, and capable (when properly taught) of excellent correct extensions. The Andalusian has tremendous presence, or brio. It gives a solid sense of power, is sturdy yet refined, without ever looking anything like a draft horse. These horses have splendid natural balance and aptitude for collection to boost their athletic prowess.

Credit: International Andalusian and Lusitano Horse Association

BELGIAN WARMBLOOD

Mare and foal. Belgian Warmbloods pass their quality on to their offspring. *Reg Corkum*

Belgian Warmblood Breeding Association
North American District
1979 CR 103
Georgetown, Texas 78626
www.belgianwarmblood.com

Being on a Belgian Warmblood is like sitting on a piece of history. For a breed that is only fifty years old, the accomplishments, the thrill, and the satisfaction it gives are immeasurable. Names like Darco, Jus de Pomme, and Big Ben are important characters in the story of the Belgian Warmblood.

The photograph of Jus de Pomme winning double gold in the Olympics held in Atlanta, Georgia, is one of the most exciting images for the registry. One of the most poignant pictures is one of four young children in Belgium sitting on the back of the famous Lugano van la Roche, demonstrating one of the other important qualities of the Belgian Warmblood—its wonderful temperament. This photograph hangs in the living room of one Belgium family of breeders that has been with the Belgium Warmblood Breeding Association (or Belgisch Warmbloedpaard, BWP) for decades, starting with Lugano van la Roche, and still active today with the exciting young stallion Adorado. Belgian Warmbloods continue to make history today, and it is a journey in which all breeders and riders of these special horses participate. The Belgian Warmblood has been carefully developed over several decades through the selective breeding of Belgium's finest cavalry and light agricultural horses crossed with Thoroughbreds, Anglo-Arabs, and other proven European warmbloods (Hanoverian, Holsteiner, Selle Francais, and Dutch). The resulting modern Belgian Warmblood is an ideal riding and competition sport horse of international quality, with its bloodlines being the world's finest. Talented and successful riders have been buying and competing with Belgian Warmbloods for many years, which consistently place at the top in world rankings for jumping and dressage. Their achievements have been phenomenal and have made a statement as to the athleticism and profound ability of the breed.

History

From the end of the nineteenth century to 1954, the breeding of agricultural riding horses that could be worked during the week and ridden on the weekend was outlawed in Belgium. The purpose of the ban was to protect the Belgian Draft horse breed, yet the ban was so extensive that Flemish riding horses completely disappeared. Once agriculture became mechanized in the 1950s, the ban was lifted.

As the need for heavy draft horses lessened and horses were only used for light agricultural work, the way was clear for the development of the recreational horse. The label "agricultural riding horse" was replaced with the name "warmblood." Belgian breeders first looked to Gelderland, the Netherlands, for foundation stock for the Belgian Warmblood and then quickly moved to France to the Selle Francais, Hanover, and finally Holstein. The offspring of the horse Ibrahim from France, the stallions Flugel and Lugano from Hanover, and the young stallion Codex from Holstein—all of which were bred to Dutch and French broodmares—comprised the origin of the Belgian Warmblood.

The Belgian Warmblood Breeding Association was founded in 1955 when the rural riding organization, Landelijke Ruiterij, imported stock from various countries for sporting purposes. Since the registry began from scratch, there was no need to build upon a gene pool that might have been unsuitable; rather the best horses and bloodlines for sport were incorporated as the foundation of the registry.

The BWP stands as a model for a Europe without borders and has a very open policy on the introduction of jumping genes from the surrounding breeding areas. Thus, the BWP has become a sort of melting pot of the most important European bloodlines with just a couple of thousand mares in its stock. The Belgian Warmblood breed continues to progressively change through utilization of the finest bloodlines of those warmblood breeds that are highly competitive in the sport horse and other performance arenas.

Famous Athletes

Belgian Warmblood horses have represented countries around the world in Olympic and World Cup competitions. At the 2000 World Cup, three of the top ten horses were Belgian Warmbloods. During the same year, Belgian Warmbloods won the Olympic individual bronze medal for show jumping, and fifth, sixth, and tenth place (one alternate) in the Olympian World Cup. They won a 1992 Olympic gold medal for team jumping, and two 1996 Olympic gold medals—one for individual and team jumping, and one for team show jumping.

Further successes include an individual bronze medal for show jumping for Saudi Arabia with Khashm al Aan at the 2000 Olympics in Sydney, while Parco and Clinton tied for fifth for Belgium at the 2004 Olympics in Athens in the show jumping competition. The 2004 and 2008 Summer Games saw U.S. team gold medals for Sapphire in show jumping. In fact, Belgian Warmbloods comprised half of the Olympic show jumping team and alternates for the 2008 games.

Although Belgian Warmbloods have been recognized primarily for their strengths in show jumping and eventing, they are becoming regulars

Belgian Warmlood in dressage, displaying its elastic stride.
Violetta Jackowski

in dressage competition as well. They competed in both the 1992 and 1996 Olympics in dressage. Each year, increasing numbers of BWP horses are competing and winning in United States Dressage Federation (USDF) sanctioned dressage competitions. Belgian Warmbloods are no longer Europe's best kept secret, as now they are being sought out by riders all over the world.

The Belgian Warmblood is also making an impact on the American sport horse industry. Many world-class American riders have been winning numerous championships, international events, and classes at prestigious breed shows across the country with Belgian Warmbloods. Examples are Soubrette, a domestically bred Belgian Warmblood that was the five-year-old Eastern League Young Jumper Champion in 2001, and Gray Slipper, honored with *The Chronicle of the Horse* Horse of the Year Award in 2007.

Since implementing performance requirements for its stallions in 1996, the BWP North American District (BWP-NAD) has had two champions at the one-hundred-day stallion testing in North America. In 1996, the approved stallion, Mannhattan, had the top jumping index at the testing in Rancho Santa Fe, California. In 1998, Puerto D'Azur was the overall champion at the one-hundred-day test in Batavia, Ohio. These stallions were competing against the finest warmblood stallions in the country that were from every recognized warmblood breed.

With such glowing achievements, there is no comparison to the amazing qualities of the Belgian Warmblood.

North American Registry

The Belgian Warmblood first entered the North American show scene in the 1970s, and the BWP-NAD was established in 1987. It was founded by a group of breeders, owners, and friends dedicated to the importation and preservation of the Belgian Warmblood in North America. It is a fully

Belgian Warmblood stallion evaluated on his free jumping.
Nancy McCallum Photography

recognized district of Belgium and serves as the sole administrating office for breeding practices on the North American continent.

In 1988, the North American District hosted the first official keuring tour for the inspection of breeding stock in the United States by Belgian judges. By monitoring through keurings, or approvals, the BWP-NAD ensures the selective breeding of the ideal sport horse. Since its inception, annual keuring events have grown to encompass more than twenty inspection sites throughout the continental United States (north to south and coast to coast), as well as Canada. These keurings serve to guarantee the continued success of horses by the BWP-NAD.

The BWP-NAD continues Belgium's fine breeding tradition by affording owners in North America the opportunity to breed mares and stallions approved by the Belgian jury. Its goal is to encourage the excellence of Belgian Warmbloods in all disciplines, ensure their position in the international marketplace, and bring joy to their owners. Each year, the BWP-NAD sponsors individual breed classes at major breed shows in the country, including dressage, futurities, combined eventing, and hunter/jumper competitions.

Lifetime achievement awards are based on a horse's performance in dressage, hunters/jumper competitions, or eventing. The BWP-NAD is developing a database to track both Belgian Warmbloods' performances in North America and horses that are for sale, as well as record offspring foaled in North America. The association is a charter member of the Federation of North American Sport Horse Organizations, participates in the all-breeds category of the USDF, and works with the United States Equestrian Federation (USEF) to ensure that every BWP foal born is assigned a lifetime number for performance tracking.

Registry Requirements

Only quality horses are admitted to the registry through the visual inspection and evaluation (keuring) of stallions, mares, and foals. They are selected for their athletic ability, conformation, and movement. They can be any color, and the average size is between 16 and 17 hands.

The Belgian jury looks for horses that have correct, modern conformation, athletic potential for the Olympic disciplines, proven bloodlines, good character, reliable temperament, and, above all, the potential to pass these traits on to their offspring. As a result, this selectivity ensures that buyers, riders, and breeders of Belgian Warmbloods are getting the highest quality horse possible.

Standards (Keurings)
Stallions

Stallions registered in certain European warmblood foal books are eligible for inspection by the BWP. They must be at least three years old, sired by approved stallions (not just registered or licensed) from a recognized European warmblood association, and out of main stud book dams. The stallion's sire and dam do not have to be of the breed, but they must be from proven competition bloodlines.

Judges first inspect the stallion's pedigree. If the judges feel that the stallion is of sufficient pedigree, then he is shown in hand at a walk and trot. If the quality of the gaits and conformation are sufficient, the stallion is then asked to free jump (jump without a rider) and is evaluated on jumping style. If a stallion is over the age of three, the judges require that he be seen under saddle. The ideal size for a stallion is 16.1 to 17.1 hands.

Prior to acquiring provisional approval, stallions must undergo a veterinary examination, which includes a semen analysis and radiographs of the forefeet (regular and navicular series), fore fetlocks, carpal joints, rear fetlocks, hocks, and stifles. This examination must show the stallion to be free of heritable diseases. He must also be tested for the presence of equine viral arteritis (EVA). Finally, all stallions must undergo an endoscopic laryngeal exam.

BWP has sixty-seven approved stallions as of 2008 in the United States.

Mares

Mares approved for breeding are entered into one of two stud books. The main stud book is for select registered mares of a recognized sport horse breed, including most other European warmbloods, Thoroughbreds, and Arabians. The auxiliary stud book is for select mares of unrecognized breeds or those of unverifiable pedigree. All mares must be over 15.1 hands to be eligible for inspection and inclusion into either book.

Mares are evaluated on their movement, elasticity, conformation, and general impression. Any mare producing consistently unacceptable foals may have her breeding status rescinded.

There are several stages that the mare must complete to obtain Elite status. The mare must be inspected twice between the ages of three and six (as opposed to three and four years of age) and must be recommended by the jury to receive a conformation label. She also must receive a veterinary label and a performance label, as well as have

produced at least one offspring. After completing all four steps, she is awarded Elite status.

For the conformation label, the mare must be presented at three years old, and again at four, to the Belgian jury. The mare must be recommended by the keuring jury for the label both years. If the mare is not presented at the age of three and four, she must have completed the rest of the elite mare requirements before she may be presented for this label.

For the veterinary label, the mare must submit to a thorough veterinary exam and x-rays. The radiographs needed are of the forefeet, hocks, and stifles. For the performance label, the mare must complete two years' worth of performance requirements at the same age and level as the stallions.

If all three labels are attained, elite status will be granted after the mare produces a BWP registered foal.

The Select Mare Program provides E-Label (conformation label) mares with the opportunity to take a performance test instead of completing performance requirements. The mare must still have an approved foal, but x-rays and veterinary exams are not required.

Foals

In order for a foal to be registered, it must be sired by a BWP-approved stallion and out of a dam that has been entered into either the main or the auxiliary stud book of BWP. With the advent of the European Union, it recently became possible to register foals that are sired by outside approved stallions and out of dams that have been entered into either the main or auxiliary stud book of BWP. These stallions must be approved for breeding by the European stud books of the Hanoverian, Oldenburg, Dutch, Selle Francais, or certain other recognized stud books. The stallions must be over six years old and have already completed their performance requirements at the time of breeding. All foals are DNA typed.

Credit: Belgian Warmblood Breeding Association, North American District

CLEVELAND BAY

Mares with the wide chests and leg muscling common to Cleveland Bays. *David Field*

Cleveland Bay Horse Society of North America
P.O. Box 483
Goshen, New Hampshire 03752
www.clevelandbay.org

The Cleveland Bay is a centuries-old breed that has always been intriguing. Appreciation for this superb horse is not solely because of its critically rare status—which, in and of itself, is unique—but also because of its intelligence, beauty, and temperament. It is truly an all-around horse. Cleveland Bays today do everything from trail riding, cross-country, and dressage, to jumping, driving, and even herding and working cattle. It is an honest horse that really wants to work hard for its owner.

The Cleveland Bay cross is also known for being an outstanding athlete, but without a doubt, the purebred Cleveland Bay can do anything the partbred can do. Unfortunately, this fact is under-estimated, contributing to its critically rare status; without purebreds, there would be no partbreds. The Cleveland Bay is a unique, rare horse that deserves to be preserved.

History

The Cleveland Bay originated in the Cleveland area of northern Yorkshire, England. Yorkshire is known as the source of two breeds, the Thoroughbred and the Cleveland Bay, but the latter is the oldest indigenous English horse breed. It can be traced back to approximately 1250 AD.[*] During that period, an abbot recorded that the native bay horses possessed exceptional strength and endurance. They were strong enough to carry a 600-pound pack 60 miles a day, four days a week, over rugged terrain. They could carry a knight and his provisions and still be agile enough to make lightning attacks and speedy retreats as needed. Cattle rustlers from the north also found them invaluable.★

Due to their exceptional ability, they were kept as a separate breed and excelled as all-around using horses. They were admired by journeymen merchants, locally called "chapmen," who exclusively used the horses, thus they became known first as chapmen horses.★ Bay colored mares from these native horses were crossed with oriental stallions during the seventeenth century for specific type, which is thought to have evolved eventually into the modern Cleveland Bay.

Shaped by a harsh environment, horses of durability, longevity, and quiet disposition resulted. These characteristics, combined with size, substance, and uniformity of the bay color, produced a versatile breed that was used as a hunt horse, coach or pack horse, and agricultural worker.★

These notable horses were so valued that the government gave contracts to Yorkshire men to mount crack cavalry units. Also, the East India Company supplied its studs (horse farms) with the stallions to upgrade the local Asian breeds (F. F. Rives, *The Southern Planter*, March 1855).

Over the centuries, only minimal additions of outside blood were allowed. It is known that during the reign of King Charles I from 1625 to 1649, the Spanish, or Andalusian, horse was introduced to England, and some of its blood was added to the Cleveland Bay.

During the eighteenth century, some thirty-two of the first offspring of the Arabian foundation sires of the Thoroughbred breed were bred to Cleveland mares. This practice ceased in the 1780s, and since then no outside crosses have been permitted. It is frequently stated that the reason the Thoroughbred and Arabian cross so successfully with the Cleveland Bay is because of the common ancestry the

Cleveland Bay has with the Thoroughbred.★ Due to the known prepotency of the Cleveland Bay, it was used as foundation stock or improvement sires for the Oldenburg, Anglo Norman (Selle Francais), Holsteiner, Clydesdale (Clydesdale stud book of 1887, volume 1), and other breeds.★

The breed's popularity peaked in the late 1880s. In 1884, the Cleveland Bay Horse Society of Great Britain published the first volume of its studbook, which contained stallions and mares selected for their purity and pedigrees tracing back over a century. Since then, the Cleveland Bay has remained relatively free from the influence of other breeds, thus it is extraordinarily dominant for producing uniformity of size, conformation, soundness, stamina, temperament, and color. As a breed, the Cleveland Bay has been kept purer than any other breed of British stock, except for the Thoroughbred. This makes it remarkable in its purity and ensures its value for crossing purposes. It was the sire of choice during the peak of the carriage era.★

During the nineteenth century, some Cleveland Bays were bred to Thoroughbreds, which produced the Yorkshire Coach Horse, a carriage horse with unmatched ability for speed, style, and power. With the advent of the mechanical age, however, numbers of Cleveland Bays and Yorkshire Coach Horses declined. By the early 1920s, very few pure Cleveland Bays were left in existence. The few remaining stallions and mares from the Yorkshire Coach Horse stud book were accepted into the Cleveland Bay stud book when the former's society ceased. A few other unregistered Cleveland mares in Yorkshire with an abundance of Cleveland bloodlines were accepted into the Grading registry. Progeny from these two mare lines have added some diversity to the gene pool.

The breed was in dire straights again when the horse were further decimated by being used as artillery horses during World War I. The breed survived in the region of its birthplace during these difficult times, but in the 1960s, only five or six mature stallions were known. A few dedicated breeders kept the breed going and were helped in the 1950s, when

Her Majesty Queen Elizabeth II purchased a Cleveland stallion and reinstated the King George V Challenge Cup for the highest breed award to encourage more breeding. Due to the foresight and determination of the Yorkshire admirers, the breed survived and numbers grew. The Queen of England became the patron of the breed and her Royal Mews (stable) continues the tradition of using Cleveland Bays and crossbreds in ceremonial duties.

In the United States

The first Cleveland Bay stallions imported into the United States were sent to Maryland, Virginia, and Massachusetts in the early 1800s. Later in 1884, the Upperville Colt and Horse Show in Virginia was created to showcase Colonel Dulany's imported Cleveland stallion, Scrivington, and his offspring.

Hundreds of Cleveland Bays were shipped to the United States to fulfill its demand for horses. They were commonly referred to as "coachers" or "English coach horses," as well as by breed name. This use of differing names for the same breed tended to obscure actual numbers and the influence the Cleveland Bay had in the States.★

When William F. "Buffalo Bill" Cody took his Wild West show to England to perform at the request of Queen Victoria, he was so impressed by what he saw of the Cleveland Bay horses that he purchased and imported a number of them to the United States. They were used in the Wild West show, and Buffalo Bill would culminate performances by driving six purebred stallions in a stagecoach hitch. Twelve stallions and fourteen mares were registered in the American Cleveland Bay stud book by William F. Cody.

The American West utilized the stallions in the breeding of range horses, appreciating their staying quality (endurance), easy maintenance, and ability to handle the biggest of steers. William Powell, whose father owned a large ranch in the West and several hundred head of horses, recalled, "Among the stallions was a Cleveland Bay, and of course he was bred to all kinds of range mares, but he turned out some of the best saddle horses in the country."

He continued by saying that they were capable of carrying a two-hundred-pound cowboy, plus all his equipment, through a full day of roundup and stock work. "They had a lot of staying quality, were easy keepers and it took a Thoroughbred to outrun one in a race. It took a big steer on the end of a rope to even worry one of the partbred Cleveland saddle horses." (*The Longhorn*, June 15, 1940)

To quote from a sales catalog prepared in 1889 by Jesse Harris, importer of horses at Fort Collins, Colorado: "We think we are safe in asserting that in no breed of horse known do the sires more faithfully mark their progeny than the Cleveland Bay .. . we can show mares of different grades and colours from Percheron to Cayuse and Broncho, all suckling bay colts by Cleveland Bay sires. [The breed] is a good disposition, easy to break and of superior intelligence."★

The Cleveland Bay Horse Society of North America (CBHSNA) was founded in 1885, with two thousand stallions and mares registered by 1907. It is one of the oldest warmblood registries and continues to this day. Originally imported as a superb coach horse, Cleveland Bay interest waned during mechanization, but was briefly revived in the 1930s when Alexander Mackey-Smith imported founding stock for hunters.

The Cleveland Bay has successfully been crossbred to Thoroughbred types to produce outstanding performance horses in dressage, driving, and jumping. Many other Cleveland Bay partbreds compete in all disciplines of horsemanship. It is through these quality animals that breed recognition is becoming known.

Presently there are only about 157 purebred Cleveland Bays in the United States and Canada. With the increase in numbers, some purebreds are competing along with their breeding duties, however the breed is still on the critical list of the Equus Survival Trust, with one hundred to three hundred active breeding mares. Cleveland Bay lovers from the United Kingdom, the United States, Canada, Japan, New Zealand, and Australia are dedicated to the conservation of this unique horse.

The Cleveland Bay is a calm, yet powerful horse with good body depth and substance. *Emerald Hill Farm Cleveland Bay Horses*

Registry Requirements

The CBHSNA requires that both pure and partbred Cleveland Bays are registered with the Cleveland Bay Horse Society of Great Britain. For purebreds it requires the following:

- The horse must be a purebred and sired by a licensed Cleveland Bay stallion and out of a registered Cleveland Bay mare in the CBHS stud book.
- The horse's sire should have been awarded the Basic License for purebred Cleveland Bays. This process involves CBHSNA with the Cleveland Bay Horse Society reviewing and approving the application. Application for the Basic License can begin when the horse is three.
- Only a breeder can enter a horse for registration.
- The horse must be bay with black points and no white markings other than a small white star. Roaning in the coat is not acceptable.
- An identification chart must be completed by a veterinarian to show at least five whorls and any scars or markings, or if the horse has a microchipped number.

Partbred Cleveland Bays have been referred to as Cleveland Bay Sport Horses; however, the

Cleveland Bay Horse Society's registry for them is called the Part Bred Registry. Stallions can apply for a license if they are a registered partbred.

For registering a partbred, the same criteria for registering purebreds apply except the horse must have at least one great grandparent in the full Cleveland Bay Horse Society stud book. If the horse is by a pure or partbred Cleveland Bay stallion, but the stallion is not licensed by the Cleveland Bay Horse Society, the entry will be accepted by virtue of its grandparents and proof of the covering. As well, there should be written evidence of the claimed breeding. Licensing is subject to an initial veterinary inspection and also a second one, three years later. The Society reserves the right to inspect any colt/stallion at any stage. Partbreds can also be registered with any other registry they qualify for.

The CBHSNA is the first contact for a horse applying for a Basic Stallion Breeding License in North America. The process involves CBHSNA Breeding Committee forwarding the completed application forms to the Cleveland Bay Horse Society, which reviews and makes a decision about the application.

Standards

The following standard of points are for the guidance of persons interested in the breed, as well as judges. These standards have been established by the Cleveland Bay Horse Society in Great Britain and are the standards that the CBHSNA follows.

Height: 16 to 16.2 hands, but height outside of these parameters should not disqualify an otherwise good sort.

Weight: Between 1,225 and 1,500 pounds.

Color: The horse must be bay with black points—that is, black legs, mane, and tail. Possessing gray hairs in mane and tail does not disqualify the horse, as it has long been recognized as a feature in certain strains of pure Cleveland blood. White is not admissible beyond a small, white star. Legs that are bay or red below the knees and hocks do not disqualify the horse, but are considered a fault as to color.

Body: The body should be wide and deep. The back should not be too long and should be strong with muscular loins. The shoulders should be sloping, deep, and muscular. Quarters should be level, powerful, long, and oval, with the tail springing well from the quarters.

Head and neck: The head should be bold and not too small. It should be well carried on a long, lean neck.

Eyes: The eyes should be large, well set, and kindly in expression.

Ears: The ears tend to be large and fine.

Limbs: Arms, thighs, and second thighs should be muscular. The knees and hocks should be large and well closed. There should be 9 inches or more of good flat bone below the knee when measured at the narrowest point on a tight tape. The pasterns should be strong, sloping, and not too long. The legs should be clean of superfluous hair and as clean and hard as possible.

Feet: One of the most important features of the breed is its feet. They must be of the best and should be blue in color. Feet that are shallow or narrow are undesirable. As the saying goes: No foot, no horse.

Action: The Cleveland's way of going must be true, straight, and free. High action is not characteristic of the breed. A Cleveland that moves well and is full of courage will move freely from the shoulder and will flex its knees and hocks sufficiently. The action required is free all around, gets over the ground, and fits the wear and tear qualities of the breed.

General: Cleveland Bay horses have the characteristics of being long-lived and prepotent, transmitting uniformity in type and substance. They are known for their calm temperament, intelligence, and soundness, which are ideal for hunting, dressage, and driving.

★Extracts from the article, "The Original Coach Horse—The Cleveland Bay," by Joanna Dorman (*Driving Digest Magazine*, May/June 1983)

Credit: Cleveland Bay Horse Society of North America

DUTCH WARMBLOOD

The Dutch Warmblood Studbook in North America
P.O. Box 0
Sutherlin, Oregon 97479
www.kwpn-na.org

The Dutch Warmblood is a modern sport horse derived from the selective breeding of German, French, and English horses crossed with native Dutch stock. Over the last two hundred years there have been frequent infusions of "foreign" blood—from France, Hanover, East Prussia, and England—as well as Arabian and Thoroughbred blood. The main Dutch breeds in the last century were the Gelderlander of Central Holland and the Groninger of Northern Holland. The Groninger was the same horse as the early German Oldenburg and similar to the present Danish Oldenburg.

Warmblood breeding in the Netherlands is over a century old, during which time the breeding objective has constantly adapted, with Dutch breeders producing what the market demands. In earlier days, there was a high demand for agricultural horses, but many farmers wanted to own a Sunday horse as well. This was a more noble type of horse that would move proudly and impressively and one that farmers could show off on their way to the market, church, or family visits. This competitive inclination was carefully preserved in Dutch breeding.

Annually about 12,000 foals are born in Holland, compared to about 60,000 in Germany, 5,000 in Sweden, and 14,000 in France, all of which are the major sport horse breeding countries. These horses supply the domestic market as well as being an important export product.

In a relatively short time, countless numbers of successful modernized Dutch sport horses have rocketed to international competitive importance. Dutch Warmblood horses, famous for their character, soundness, and athletic ability, are exported to

The Dutch Warmblood is a well-proportioned, balanced horse with suppleness. *Vey Martini*

all corners of the globe and are winners under the flags of many different nations in Olympic Games and other international competitions.

They consistently rank among the very top sport horse stud books in the world in jumper, dressage, and hunter classes. Some of the greatest, most successful Dutch Warmblood horses in North America are Roemer, Contango, Idocus, Ravel, Authentic, Judgement, and Hickstead.

Registry

The Royal Warmblood Studbook of the Netherlands (Koninklijk Warmbloed Paardenstamboek Nederland, or KWPN) is the registry and studbook for the Dutch Warmblood Sport Horse. It has a history dating back to early in the nineteenth century and deals with all matters pertaining to Dutch horses. With the help of one of the greatest horsemen in the world, the late Gert van der Veen, the North American Department was established in 1983 and remains closely related to KWPN. Gert van der Veen, the former head inspector and director of the KWPN, provided a great deal of the focus and guidance for the North America Department.

Evaluations

One of the interesting things about the KWPN is that it has the strictest selection requirements of any of the warmblood studbooks. A rigorous selection system and continuous evaluation of breeding stock, along with high-tech research and use of a statistical records department, bring the latest developments in science and technology to bear on the improvement of Dutch horses. In addition, the long horse breeding history and agricultural heritage of the Dutch bring generations of nearly ingrained expertise to the production of top quality horses.

One of the most predictable and positive traits of the KWPN is that it will shift its breeding focus quickly and drastically if the evidence becomes clear that it is necessary. This gives guidance to breeders and allows them to trust in the breeding goals of the stud book.

The main tools in the ongoing evolution and improvement of the Dutch horse are the keurings, or inspections, which are held in the Netherlands and in North America every year. At these keurings, horses are evaluated and rewarded according to their quality and fulfillment of the breeding goal. This system includes rigorous selection and testing for breeding stallions—one of the most selective and thorough in the world.

"Predicates" are an integral part of the Dutch grading system. They represent an individual horse's success in sport or in the keuring, which is the selection backbone of the success of the KWPN. Predicates include: *ster, keur, preferent*, IBOP (Instelling Bruikbaarheids Onderzoek Parrden, or loosely translated from Dutch as the Institution Usability Investigation Horses, i.e. testing performance talent of horses), elite, *prestatie*, sport, and crown. Each has its own meaning and merit.

Stud Book Requirements

There are two categories of stud book requirements, one for mares and one for stallions, and four distinct breeding categories.

Stallions: In the Dutch system, all stallions, regardless of discipline, are required to compete against other stallions at their level of training, especially in the first few years of their competition history. The finals of these competitions are held during the annual three-day Hengstenkeuring in Den Bosch, the Netherlands, during the first week of February. These competitions are judged by the same jury that originally approved the stallions, so that it can support the stallions continuing in the stud book. Additionally, the jury also must inspect the first foal crop, which includes three-year-olds at their stud book inspection, seven-year-olds in sport, and eleven-year-olds in sport. If a stallion is seen to contribute poorly to the breeding population—that is not producing successful sport horses at the appropriate ages—and/or does not compete well enough himself, he might lose his approval and be removed from the breeding population.

The system consists of three rounds of evaluations and a performance test. It begins with seven hundred to eight hundred stallion candidates that are evaluated on their pedigree, conformation, and free movement and/or free jumping. Out of those, about sixty to seventy coming three-year-olds are allowed to go on to the stallion performance test. At the end of this testing, perhaps only twenty to twenty-eight are eventually approved each year.

All of the stallions that pass the first round of testing must pass radiographic, endoscopic, and semen evaluations before they are allowed to go on to the second round. So when breeding to an approved stallion, not only he, but also all of the stallions in his pedigree have had clean x-rays, clean endoscopies, and good quality semen.

Mares: Mares in the Netherlands and the United States are also evaluated according to their quality and performance. Predicates show their status within the system.

Unlike some warmblood registries, KWPN

horses are not branded as foals based on the fact that they are registered. KWPN horses may be branded upon acceptance into the stud book at age three or older. To be accepted into the stud book, they are evaluated on conformation and free movement or free jumping. At this time, a linear score sheet comprising between twenty-eight and thirty-six conformation and movement characteristics is filled out for each horse.

Breed categories: The changes to the breed over the generations have reflected the needs of the times, from carriage horse and warhorse, to farm horse, transportation, and recreation. KWPN horses are split into four distinct breeding types: Dressage, Jumper, Harness (Tuigpaard), and Gelders.

By separating the stud book into types, the fastest and most efficient progress can be made toward the breeding goal. The concept is that, with a specialized selection process, there will be faster positive results in the population.

Riding Types

The riding horses, comprising Dressage and Jumper types, are by far the largest group. Riding horses are bred to excel in the disciplines of dressage and jumping, although they are frequently seen in other disciplines, such as combined driving. In North America, there is also a third type of riding horse: the Hunter. A breeding goal has been formulated for each breeding direction.

The more natural ability produced in the riding types, the greater the eventual results may be in sporting competitions. This is important because the lift inherent in the hind legs of KWPN riding horses is greatly appreciated and is genetically produced in breeding programs.

Breeding goal for Dressage horses: The breeding goal is to produce a Dressage horse that can perform at Grand Prix level and also possesses a healthy constitution, functional conformation, correct movement mechanism, a correct base, and a preferably attractive exterior.

To reach this goal, the Dressage horse should be long lined and have a correct model with balanced proportions. The horse should move correctly and be light footed, balanced, and supple with carrying power, impulsion, and good self-carriage. The Dressage horse should be easy to handle and ride, be intelligent, and have a willing and hard working character.

Breeding goal for Jumper horses: This is the same as for the Dressage horse, except that the Jumper horse has courage, jumps with quick reflexes, is careful, has good technique, and has a great deal of scope. A good Jumper snaps its hind leg under its body and lifts its withers, while naturally and automatically transferring the weight to its hind end and lifting the rider.

Breeding goal for Hunter horses: The breeding goal aims for a Hunter that is the same as the Dressage and Jumper horses, except that it can perform at the highest levels of hunter competition and has charm. The Hunter has a long, flowing stride that smoothly covers ground in a steady rhythm with little knee or hock action. It jumps with a beautiful rounded bascule and has a calm/brave character.

Harness Horse

The KWPN Harness horse, or Tuigpaard, is currently experiencing great popularity. It is uniquely bred to perform in driving competitions and harness classes. The Harness horse is almost a separate breed; its breeding stock is sometimes mixed with the Gelders horse, but generally not with any of the riding types. Some Hackney blood had been added at some point in its history to enhance hardiness and nobility.

In combination with its proud, high carriage, the Harness horse displays flashy, powerful movement with a long moment of suspension in the trot, broad foreleg movement with high knee action, and powerful carrying ability. It is generally harnessed in front of a light show carriage in order to demonstrate its spectacular trot. Ideally, it should bring the hindquarters under, which causes the front to rise and makes the horse appear progressively taller. It should carry most of its weight behind, generating

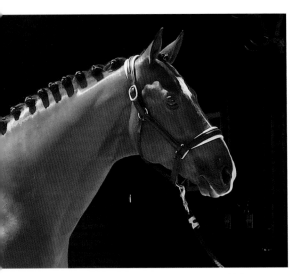

Belgian Warmbloods have attractive heads with long, muscular, high-set necks. *Vey Martini*

forward and upward power from its hindquarters in order to display its remarkable front action. The horse lifts the foreleg high from the shoulder and then places it well forward. The ideal action combines a long moment of suspension, good balance, rhythm, and fine coordination between fore and hindquarters with the lifted front—an unforgettable sight!

Breeding goal for Harness horses: This is the same as the Dressage horse, except it can perform in the highest levels of harness sport. The Harness horse should have good suspension in the trot with a foreleg that moves out well with high knee action, and a hind leg that steps under powerfully. The horse should also have proud self carriage with a long vertical neck.

Gelders Type

The Gelders horse is an elegant horse originating in the province Gelderland. Gelders bloodlines remain pure, as no foreign blood is allowed, and is therefore the smallest division within the KWPN horse. The Gelders horse has a rich front, plenty of bone and body, and impressive, proud movements displaying great power and action from behind. It

is a versatile performer, both in harness and under saddle, and is characterized by its enthusiastic show performance and willing temperament.

Breeding goal for Gelders horses: The breeding goal is to produce a Gelders horse that can be used for multiple purposes. The Gelders horse distinguishes itself both in harness and under saddle with its happy appearance and reliable, willing character. It should be suitable for use under saddle and in harness. It has an elegant build with substance, self carriage, and sufficiently developed legs providing big gaits. It has light knee action in the foreleg, and power and carrying ability from behind.

General Breeding Goal

The general KWPN Breeding Goal is to produce a performance horse that:
- can perform at Grand Prix level
- has a constitution that enables lasting usefulness
- has a character and will to perform, as well as being agreeable and good natured toward people
- has functional conformation and a correct movement mechanism that will enable good performance
- has an attractive exterior that is related to refinement, nobility, and quality

Registry Criteria

The selection of stallions is not only based on pedigree, but also on jumping and dressage talent for riding horses, harness talent for Harness horses, and any of these abilities for Gelders horses. The stallions must also have a good character, good semen quality, and good health and durability.

Stud book, foal book, and Register A mares, geldings, and stallions are eligible for stud book inspection at age three or older. Register A mares and geldings are usually by a sire that is approved with an outside stud book on a par with the KWPN with regard to breeding goals and worldwide performance. They must also complete those requirements not met by the sire (radiographs, endoscopy, and/or performance). Upon successful presentation, mares and stallions are accepted into the stud book, but geldings remain in or move to the foal book, since they are not used for breeding.

After a successful stud book inspection, mares and geldings receive new updated registration papers and may be branded on the left haunch with the traditional Dutch lion brand. Stallions may be branded if they are of star quality or better. Although horses have not been branded in the Netherlands since 2000 due to European regulations, those entering the stud book in North America may still be branded.

Horses that are 100 percent Thoroughbred, Anglo-Arab, Hackney, or American Saddlebred have no KWPN registration possibilities.

Stallion and mare DNA must be available for parentage verification. Names have to coincide with the year of birth. For instance in 2008, all registered names began with the letter "D," and in 2009 they start with the letter "E."

Standards

- Conformation: stands in rectangular model; is long lined with a proportional build; has an uphill build; has long legs; has a light head/neck connection; has a long neck that is raised and arched, with muscling in the topline; has a strongly built and strongly muscled back/loin formation; has a correct and hard foundation; and is attractive
- Movement: walk—a pure four-time gait that is active and has suppleness and impulsion; trot—a pure two-time gait that is active and has suppleness and impulsion, balance and self-carriage; canter—a pure three-time gait that is active, light with suppleness, impulsion, balance, and self-carriage; horse can lengthen and shorten easily in the canter movement, without losing rhythm, tact, balance, or self carriage; rises in the front (Dressage); has good posture; is light footed; shows flexion in the joints, engagement of the hindquarters, and freedom from the shoulder with a slight lift of the knee; should be obedient, alert, responsive, and move freely; pace should remain the same throughout the course
- Jumping: canter—light and balanced without making much front; remains more horizontal in the body; collects strongly during the last canter stride before the jump and places the hind leg far forward under the body in order to get a powerful takeoff; leaves the ground quickly with power; jumps with an upward wither with the highest point over the middle of the jump; brings the underarm above the horizontal and folds the cannon under the underarm
- Bascule: brings the neck down during the jump, with the rump following the direction of the neck, and opens the hindquarter
- Athletic ability: is supple and can develop forward motion over the jump, lands lightly, and canters off easily; is careful, efficient, and has much scope
- Hunter jumping: jumps with front legs folded high and evenly; head and neck should stretch out and down to insure a well-balanced jump; body and legs stay straight so the horse stays in the middle of the jump; leaves the ground smoothly; should clear each jump confidently, easily, and in good style; lands lightly and canters off smoothly; has a calm steady rhythm
- Character: willing, hardworking, and honest character; has the will to perform; is easy to handle; reacts quickly to the aids; has courage (Jumping); is intelligent; looks at and evaluates the jump (Jumping); has a calm, brave temperament (Hunter)

Credit: Scot Tolman and the Dutch Warmblood Studbook in North America

FRIESIAN

The bend at the poll, feathering, and elevated leg action mark this stallion unmistakably as a Friesian. *Cindy Bellamy/Friesian Heritage Horse & Sporthorse International*

The Friesian Horse Society, Inc.
17670 Pioneer Trail
Plattsmouth, Nebraska 68048
www.friesianhorsesociety.com

Despite all the adversities and changes the Friesian has faced over the centuries, it will always be viewed as one of the most mystical and magical horses. The Friesian is a magnificent and noble animal with an ancient heritage dating back to knights who proudly rode it long ago. With its dramatic and stunning looks, it strikes the beholder as a breed apart. Its extravagant beauty is breathtaking and the impression it makes is profound to those observing it. With its lofty stance, striking black coat, and draping mane and tail, the Friesian exudes a persona that sets it apart from all others. Though quiet and reserved, its presence incites awe.

The Friesian's trademarks are its overall distinctive exterior, especially the high-set neck with outstanding crest, broad chest, lightly accentuated croup, and relatively small head and ears. Most noticeable is the impressive stature, luxuriant mane, and the extra long tail. During performances, these features combine with the leg feathering and low tailset to emphasize the breed's powerful and elastic gait. Athletic ability, strength, loyalty, and elegance are its other outstanding gifts.

Beyond its fantastic exterior, the Friesian's versatility brings lasting appreciation, being equally skilled at multi-level dressage, trotting, and driving, singly or combined. Its high step and superb natural movement are the result of favor by breeders throughout northern Europe.

The Friesian beauty and attributes are more than skin deep. Its character is marked by friendliness, intelligence, adaptability, and an enormous willingness to work. It is this character especially that has drawn people to it throughout history and caused them to go through extreme trials for it. The Frisian is a gentleman: kind, honest, willing to please, well mannered, and a pleasant companion for riders of all ages and every level. Whether competing in upper level dressage tests, performing on the carriage driving circuit, or just going for a trail ride, the Friesian quickly becomes a member of the family.

The Dutch consider the Friesian to be "the Black Pearl of the Netherlands" and truly a treasure to cherish.

History

The Friesian is the only horse breed native to the Netherlands, where it has been known since as far back as the thirteenth century. At the start of the Christian era, the Friesian was used in battle[1] and Friesian troops were documented in Britannia. In the fourth century, English writer Anthony Dent[1] wrote about the presence of Friesian troops and their horses in Carlisle. Both cases probably involve Friesian mercenaries mounted on Friesian stallions. Anthony Dent and other writers' works indicate that the Friesian horse is the ancestor of both the Shire breed and the Fell pony.

In the eleventh century, William the Conqueror (Willem de Veroveraar)[1] used horses that had a remarkable resemblance to the Friesian breed. From this period, there are many illustrations of knights riding Friesian-looking horses. During the crusades and later, through the course of the Eighty Years' War, it is very probable that the Friesian breed was crossed with Arabian and Andalusian horses.

The first written evidence of use of the name "Friesian horse" was an announcement in 1544 that German Elector Johann Friedrich von Sachsen came to the Reichstag in Spiers riding a Friesian stallion.[2] Three years later, he rode the stallion in the Battle of Muhlberg and was recognized from afar by Emperor Charles V. Also an etching dating from 1568 of the stallion Phryso[1], belonging to Don Juan of Austria, in Naples is very well known. During the seventeenth century, the Friesian horse was well represented at the various riding schools where the haute école of equitation was practiced.

Use of the Friesian Horse, however, became increasingly limited to the current Dutch province of Friesland during the eighteenth and nineteenth centuries. Toward the end of the nineteenth century, the presence of the Friesian Horse in the countryside of Friesland became an expression of the owner's wealth, with the breed used mostly to bring upper-class farmers to church. The horse was additionally used for entertainment in the form of ridden short-track trotting races.[3] In these races, the horse was traditionally ridden with just a small orange blanket on its back. During this period, the Friesian Horse was very likely used in the breeding of the Orlov Trotter, as well as American trotting horses.

On May 1, 1879, in Roordahuizum, the Friesch Paarden-Stamboek (FPS), which is the stud book of the Friesian Horse, was established, and it has registered Friesian Horses ever since. Registration of the limited number of Friesian Horses remaining proved somewhat of a stimulus for the breed, but the popularity of the heavier breeds, the so-called Bovenlanders, continued to undermine the Friesian. Supporters of the Bovenlanders were often unnecessarily harsh in their judgments of the Friesian horse, criticizing that it would "dance" too much in front of the plow and therefore waste useful energy. There was some truth in what they said, but they failed to appreciate the history of the Friesian Horse and the profound affection between master and horse that is so often seen with the Friesian breed.[2]

At the end of the nineteenth and the start of the twentieth century, a very difficult period ensued during which the Friesian had to struggle to compete with the heavy breeds. The dancing show horses of the landed farmers were in fact less suited for heavy work. Farmers finally switched over to the heavier breeds or crossed the Friesian Horse with them, which proved almost fatal for the breed. By the start of the twentieth century, Friesian numbers had dwindled rapidly. In 1913, there were only three older stud book stallions available for breeding.[4]

Fortunately there were people in Friesland who wanted to save the native Friesian Horse breed from extinction. They bought the remaining quality purebred colts and saved the Friesian from disaster.[4] Among others, the royal stables in Borculo and the De Oorsprong breeding farm, which had been established by the family Van Eysinga at Huis ter Heide in 1885, played a role in its preservation.[3]

After 1913 and the Friesian's competition with heavier horses, some of its luxuriance was compromised for more horsepower. The Friesian therefore became a little smaller and heavier. As a result, a type of Friesian Horse emerged that was different from the type that is more desirable today, which has the original long lines of its forefathers.[4]

By the 1960s, the crisis resulting from farm mechanization made the agricultural horse redundant. Most farmers lacked the money to keep a horse for pleasure only, which meant that the horse disappeared from the farm yards. In 1965, only some five hundred mares were registered in the stud book.[2] Fortunately, there were now also great lovers of the breed who brought the horse to the attention of others. In 1967, the national

riding association, De Oorsprong, began a crusade through the Dutch province of Friesland to promote the Friesian horse. From March 28 to April 1, a parade of lovers of the breed traveled with their Friesian horses from Huis ter Heide to Workum (towns within the Netherlands).[3] The impact of the promotion campaign was evident in the rapid expansion of the breed in the two ensuing decades.

Many people have discovered the fabulous characteristics of the Friesian breed, and purebreds are now seen and enjoyed around the world. The Friesian has recently become one of Europe's most respected performance horse. Due to continued steady growth in numbers, as well as its tremendous surge in popularity, the Friesian's survival is now virtually guaranteed.

Breed Characteristics

A consistent breeding policy has produced the Friesian Horse exhibiting the unique characteristics of the breed and continuing to bear close resemblance to its ancestors. There are three modern bloodlines: Tetman 205, Age 168, and Ritske 202. Each of these sires traces its blood to Paulus 121, a Friesian stallion born in 1913 and entered into the stud book in 1916. He, in turn, can be traced back three generations to the original nineteenth century stud book foundation sire, Nemo 51, born in 1885. Today, all purebred Friesians trace back to these bloodlines.

The Friesian Horse has increasingly developed into a sports horse over the past decades, thus returning to its origins before the agricultural interlude. It is fast becoming the luxuriant aristocratic carriage horse it once was. Typical of these Black Pearls are the front, majestic mane, feathering of the lower legs, jet black color, and spacious, powerful, elevated gaits. The harmonious build and noble head set on a lightly arched neck complete the aristocratic and fiery appearance. Its amicable character is the key to a great utility breed.[5] Today, thanks to its typical functional characteristics, the Friesian horse now competes

Stunning Friesian stallion with the thick mane and tail, refined head, and feathering. *The Friesians of Freedom Farm L.L.C.*

with other breeds at the highest levels of equestrian sports.[5]

Nonetheless, the heavier and short-legged type is still much in evidence, partly due to it being used midway through the last century mainly as a harness horse in farming operations. Since there is a close relation between an animal's intended use and its exterior, Friesian Horses that were bred for agricultural use were more short-legged and compact than their ancestors, with forelegs a bit behind the vertical and a broad chest. With this broad chest, the horse was better able to throw itself "into the harness" and, in so doing, develop more pulling power. These exterior characteristics are less functional

these days in the riding arena, or in harness and driving horses. Because this type was bred for so many years, multiple generations are needed before it disappears from the breed.

These days, Friesians are kept for purposes of recreation, breeding, and sports, and often for some combination of these objectives. They are often seen in the dressage ring and in driving sports, while some of the more common uses are for ridden work under saddle, or as a harness or driving horse.

For work under saddle and driving sports, a functional build is key. The horse's body must have an uphill slope, where the distribution of weight is brought more onto the hindquarters in motion, enabling the horse to carry more with its hindquarters. For an uphill build, a relatively long foreleg is important, as is the stance of the foreleg. The stance of the foreleg is linked to the shoulder, whereby an angled and long shoulder provides the horse with space to extend its foreleg far out to the front. The harness horse often has a bit more vertical neckline than the riding and driving horse.

For an all-purpose horse, the Friesian must move fluidly through its entire body, with powerful hindquarters that transmit movements forward, enabling the horse to "grow" in front. This is a desired trait for both riding under the saddle and for driving in front of the wagon. For harness horses, a lot of knee action is desirable (but not this alone, as it must be combined with spaciousness of gaits and "carrying" hindquarters), while for riding horses and also driving horses, extravagant knee action is not always appreciated. For all purposes, a correct leg stance is a must.

U.S. Registry

Today the majority of Friesians are in the Netherlands. Most Dutch members are associated with breeding societies, which organize a large number of annual activities. As of 2007, more than forty thousand horses were registered by the Koninklijke Vereniging "Het Friesch Paarden-Stamboek" (KFPS) and some seven thousand breedings are now documented every year.[6] The result has been the establishment of daughter societies of KFPS outside the Netherlands.

Established in 1993 as a North American affiliate, the Friesian Horse Society (FHS) now serves as an American Friesian registry. It utilizes the strict registration standards that originated in the Netherlands and accepts all horses from the Friesian Horse Association of North America (FHANA) and German registered Friesenpferde Zuchtverband e.V. (FPZV) stallions for breeding. Only purebred horses with no unqualified stallions in their pedigrees receive registration papers. Purebreds with unqualified stallions receive only a birth certificate, and the documents are visibly different.

In the show ring, the FHS puts value on the exterior of a horse, but also considers the Friesian's performance in a variety of tests as equally important in rating it. The judge uses a checklist of all the possible characteristics of the typical Friesian, from appearance to temperament. The two main marks are "exterior" and "quality of gaits." The judge crosses out what is not apparent in the horse, leaving on the list the horse's remaining traits. This provides the owner with a grade that is easy to understand.

Registry Requirements

The annual judging of Friesian Horses take place at sites throughout North America. It is a subjective attempt to evaluate a horse against the standards for the ideal Friesian. Movement is 60 percent of the judging evaluation, and conformation is 40 percent. Horses must be sound for judging evaluations.

Foals

All foals whose lineage qualifies them for stud book registration may be entered in the foal book. There are no restrictions based on physical appearance or soundness. Foals resulting from embryo transfers are allowed, but cloning is not. Unless distance or other constraints make it impossible, all foals must be judged in the year of their birth at the side of their dams. Each calendar year, foal names must begin with specific letters designated by the KFPS. Names should be relatively simple, ideally consisting of a single word. Genetic samples for parentage verification are taken from all foals and their dams (if not already on file). All FHS registered horses must have DNA on file with the FHS.

Adults in the foal book: Some horses registered in the foal book will not be eligible as adults for registration in the stud books for mares, geldings, or stallions. Common reasons for permanent foal book status are unacceptable white markings, serious faults, or unsoundness. In addition, some gelding owners never present their horses for registration in the stud book for geldings. All stallions that do not qualify as Studbook Stallions remain in the foal book permanently.

Mares and Geldings

Mares and geldings entering the adult stud books are evaluated on a number of points that include various aspects of conformation, breed characteristics, and movement. They are scored on each point based on their positive or negative deviation from the average for the Friesian Horse population. They must be older than three years, and the evaluation is conducted annually.

Eligibility for the stud book for mares or the stud book for geldings requires that they be:

1. Registered in the foal book
2. At least 1.5 meters (14.3 hands) at the withers
3. Black and have no white, except for a small star or a few white hairs on the forehead or muzzle; white is not permitted on the body, legs, or hooves
4. Sound, as unsound horses cannot enter the stud book
5. Free of hereditary defects (mares with hereditary defects should not be used for breeding)

Criteria for acceptance in the stud books require a demonstration of conformation and movement that adequately meets the desired typical Friesian characteristics. Mares and geldings can also be judged for inclusion in the Star Mare and Gelding Register, and mares can be judged for the Model (Provisional), Preferential Mare, or Performance Mother (Prestatie) Registers.

Stallions

Stallions that successfully pass the Stallion Performance Test (SPT) will be entered in the stud book for stallions. The SPT can be conducted annually. Stallions that are three and older that are eligible for entering the stud book must be registered in the foal book.

To be eligible for consideration as a candidate for the SPT, stallions must:

1. Be at least 1.58 meters (15.2 ¼ hands) at age 3 and at least 1.60 meters (15.3 hands) at age 4
2. Be entirely black with no white markings, except for a small star or a few white hairs on the forehead or muzzle; white is not permitted on the body, legs, or hooves
3. Have an examination by a veterinarian; x-rays taken of knee joints that reveal the bones as sound; semen analysis conducted that shows the sample meets minimum motility standards; and blood typing performed on the stallion and his dam
4. Demonstrate to the inspection judges that its movement and conformation is of sufficiently exceptional quality to warrant consideration as a Studbook Stallion

Eligibility is also based on the pedigree and the dam. There are strict requirements for the pedigrees and dams of prospective Studbook Stallions. Evaluation of stallions is made by judges during the final days of the SPT. Stallions are rated in each of the following areas:

- Walk
- Trot
- Canter
- Performance under saddle
- Performance as a driving horse to demonstrate obedience
- Performance pulling a sledge
- Performance as a carriage show horse to demonstrate action
- Character and temperament
- Stable manners
- Training manners

Those stallions that enter the stud book for stallions will receive provisional approved breeding privileges until their offspring have been judged for the first time. When a stallion's oldest offspring become three years old, a percentage of the offspring from each year's foal crop is evaluated for quality, which determines if the stallion demonstrates a positive impact upon the breed. This qualifies the stallion for the continuation of approved breeding privileges.

Participation in sports by approved stallions: After the year of their registration in the stud book, and up to and including the year in which their descendants are presented, approved stallions must participate in at least one discipline of an official equestrian competition on four different competition days per season.

Stallion genetic testing: All stallions used for breeding must have appropriate genetic test results on file with the FHS before they can be granted approved breeding privileges or have their off-spring registered.

Offspring Judging I: When the stallion's oldest offspring become three years old, a percentage of the offspring from each year's foal crop will be evaluated for quality. Through the quality of his offspring, the stallion must demonstrate a positive impact upon the breed or he will no longer be granted approved breeding privileges. All Studbook Stallions with approved breeding privileges ideally should be judged annually.

Subsidiary Registers (B-Books): Purebred Friesian Horses of traceable lineage not eligible for the stud books (for example, its sire was not a Studbook Stallion with approved breeding privileges, or its dam was not registered in the stud book or foal book) may be registered in a Subsidiary Register (B-Book).

Breed Overview

The preferred build today of the Friesian is the lighter sport horse rather than the heavier draft type. The modern Friesian is strong but slightly taller and lighter on its feet than its coach-bred forebears. For this reason, the Friesian has re-emerged throughout Europe as both a champion dressage and driving performance horse.

The Friesian's aristocratic appearance is accentuated by big expressive eyes and a fine head carried high on an elegant and nicely curved neck. Compared to the body, the head seems rather small and either straight or slightly concave; the small ears are also typical. It has tough legs with good bone structure, resulting in an enduring and sure-footed horse. It is a powerful horse with high stepping action.

Today, the Friesian is bred to be exclusively black. Darker colors have always dominated, but up to the turn of the century, about 20 percent were chestnut or bay. The black color was advanced by strict selection. The only white spot allowed on the body is a star.

Typical Characteristics

The FHS advocates a modern Friesian Horse while maintaining typical characteristics of the breed.

The noble head has clear, intelligent eyes and small alert ears with tips pointing slightly toward each other. The neck is of adequate length and is lightly arched. A strong back joins a croup of good length, which does not slope too steeply. The shoulder is strong, long, and sloping, and the body is of good depth with well sprung ribs. The feet and legs are strong with a well developed forearm and proper stance. A height of 1.6 meters (15.3 hands) is considered ideal. The horse has fluid, elegant, and suspended gaits, which are emphasized by feathering on the lower legs, a fine mane, and beautiful, long tail. Jet black is the preferred color. This is a horse of luxurious and proud appearance, full of personality, honesty, and eagerness to work.

Ideal Conformation

The head is relatively short with a width that is proportional to the length. The ears are small and alert with the tips pointing slightly toward each other. The eyes are large and shining. The nasal bone is slightly hollow or straight; nostrils are wide. The lips are closed and the teeth meet properly. The jawbones are not heavy and are spread wide apart to allow the horse to breathe easily while at work. The head is set gracefully on the neck with adequate space for the throat. Overall, the head is dry and expressive, and it blends smoothly into the neck.

The neck is lightly arched at the crest, is long enough for the horse to bend properly, and is adequately muscled. The neck is set on high, and the lower neckline does not bulge between the throat and chest.

The withers are well developed and prominent; they particularly blend gradually into the back. The back is not too long and is well muscled. A slightly low back is allowed.

A beautiful head on a Friesian stallion in harness. Note the small, tipped ears, and refined muzzle. *Cheval Photography*

The loin is wide, strong, well muscled and makes a smooth transition into the croup. The croup is of good length, slopes slightly downward, and is wide and muscular. It neither forms a point nor is overly rounded. The tail is not set on too low. The gluteal muscle is long and well developed.

The shoulders are long, sloping, and set apart widely enough to form a good chest, which is neither too wide nor too narrow.

The ribs are long and curved, supplying ample space for the heart and lungs, without being rotund. The belly maintains sufficient depth toward the rear.

The forelegs are properly positioned and, when viewed from the front, are set parallel with a hoof width of space at the ground. Viewed from the side, they are perpendicular down through the fetlock joint. The cannon bone is not too long, while the forearm has good length. The pastern is resilient, of good length, and is at a 45-degree angle to the ground. The hoofs are wide and sound.

The hind legs, when viewed from the rear, are straight. When viewed from the side, the legs are set directly under the hindquarters and are strong with good, sound hooves. The hind cannon is a little longer than the front cannon; the gaskin is long, with well-developed muscle. The angle at the hock is approximately 150 degrees, and the rear pasterns are at a 55-degree angle to the ground.

The joints in the legs are dry, well developed, and provide a good foundation for the tendons and ligaments.

The overall appearance of the horse's body is more nearly a rectangle than a square. When the shoulder is long and sloping, the back is not too long, and the croup is of adequate length. The ratio of fore-, middle- and hindquarters can be an ideal one-to-one-to-one. The horse is neither too massive nor too light.

The walk is straight, vigorous, and springy. There is good length of stride, and the hindquarters swing forward with power.

The trot is a reaching and forward movement with power from the hindquarters. It is elevated and light-footed with a moment of suspension. The hock flexes as the horse moves forward, and the inside angle of the hind leg closes during each stride.

The canter is well supported and lively, with sufficient power from the hindquarters and flexion in the hock.

Breeding for Performance

The Friesian Horse is used in various equestrian sports: show driving, combined driving, dressage under saddle, and recreation. As driving horses, Friesians perform well, but to become more competitive in all sports, attention should be given to the following points:

- Strong, powerful hindquarters
- Luxurious build that is not too heavy, but has ample power
- Long, sloping shoulder
- Hard, dry legs
- Light-footed movements with a moment of suspension
- Neither too small nor too large in size, with the ideal range of height being 1.59 to 1.63 meters (15.2½ to 16 hands)
- Sufficiently long and well muscled forearm and gaskin
- Strong, smooth transition from loin to croup; long and well developed gluteal muscle
- Good, wide hooves with proper heels
- Good head/neck connection
- Honest character and eager to work
- Stamina

Sources

[1] Het Friese paard, ir. G. J. A. Bouma, E. Dijkstra and dr.ir. A. Osinga

[2] Article R. J. Zethoven, former board member of the KFPS

[3] Friese stamhengsten deel I, E. Dijkstra (citation from Dr. Geurts)

[4] Judging of the Friesian Horse, by P. de Boer, S. Minkema, and A. M. Teekens

[5] Taken from "Information about the KFPS" by Koninklijke Vereniging "Het Friesch Paarden-Stamboek"

[6] Taken from "The Friesian Horse History" by Koninklijke Vereniging "Het Friesch Paarden-Stamboek"

Credit: The Friesian Horse Society, Inc.

FRIESIAN HERITAGE HORSE

Magnificent Friesian/Saddlebred mare with an elastic stride and high-set neck. *Cindy Bellamy/Friesian Heritage Horse & Sporthorse International*

Friesian Heritage Horse and Sporthorse International
133 E. De La Guerra, #159
Santa Barbara, California 93101
www.friesianheritage.com

Commanding attention wherever they appear, horses of Friesian heritage have impacted the American equine world in a manner that will not soon be forgotten. Friesian Heritage Horses are the product of Friesians interbred with various other horses. This crossbreeding frequently results in intelligent individuals deserving of their stellar reputation. Proving their capabilities in all types of events, they are distinctive horses, commonly displaying athletic ability, proper balance, and an elegant appearance. They can offer the best of both worlds since some of the Friesian's distinct characteristics, agreeable disposition, and presence are often retained and can blend well with traits from other breeds.

Known for their versatility, Friesian crossbred horses can be suitable for anything from the show ring to the family camping trip. They have achieved popularity and success in many performance disciplines, especially dressage, eventing, driving, and combined driving. They are also commonly found in exhibitions, costumed events, parades, jousting, renaissance fairs, and are becoming increasingly more popular as western riding mounts, both for leisure and showing.

History

For centuries, the primary purpose of the Friesian was as a carriage horse and sometimes as a light agricultural animal. It was often a popular candidate for cross breeding and the original stud books provided for crossbred Friesians. In 1880, the first stud books in the Netherlands were created; Book A was a registration book for Friesian Horses and Book B was for registration of Friesian crossbreds. In 1907, books A and B were combined into one book to register all of the horses.

Eventually, modernization led to a dramatic decline in the Friesian population and the breed nearly became extinct. To preserve it, a small group formed the Friesian Horse Society, or *Het Friesche Paard*, in 1913. This society worked toward improving the Friesian horse by buying quality Friesian foals and awarding horses of good type. In 1915, the Society again opened two registration books: Book A for Friesian horses and Book B for crossbreds or "Upland horses." In 1943, Book B left the Stud Book, leaving the Friesian Stud Book to register only purebred Friesians.

In the United States, the popularity of the Friesian breed was ignited by the 1985 film *Ladyhawke*, which created interest in the Friesian. However, when Friesians were initially imported to America, the breed was rare and quite expensive. This resulted in the development of the Friesian crossbred horse.

Initially, the goal for many breeders who crossbred Friesians was to produce a Friesian "look-alike," primarily because ownership of a purebred was cost prohibitive for the average horse owner. However, as these crossbred horses matured and started entering the competition world, some were recognized for their sheer talent and athleticism. Also many breeders noticed that when crossing Friesians with another breed, better individuals with increased health and stamina often resulted. Not only were these crossbreds talented, but they also tended to maintain the agreeable temperament and trainability that the Friesian breed is known for. This allowed them to become popular with, and

well suited to, amateur horse owners and exhibitors as well as professionals.

Characteristics

The Friesian crossbred has been known by many different names: Friesian Heritage Horse, Friesian Cross, Friesian Sport Horse, Friesian Blood Horse, and Friesian Derivative—all meaning a horse that is partly Friesian and partly another breed or breed combination.

The secondary breed(s) selected depended on the goal of the individual breeder. Currently, due to the relative rarity of the Friesian breed as well as the fact that it is more cost effective, Friesian crossbreds are primarily the result of breeding Friesian stallions to mares of other breeds. Purebred mares are seldom used for crossbreeding.

The type and suitability of Friesian crossbreds vary widely, depending on what the Friesian is crossed with. In many breeding programs, crossing with Friesians is used to improve temperament, increase bone, improve joint articulation, achieve a higher neck set, or attain a curved body shape. Often the emphasis is placed on retaining the easy-going disposition and the regal presence of the Friesian.

The purebred Friesian has historically been bred as a high-stepping carriage horse. Therefore, some breeders cross it with more athletic, more forward moving breeds to develop a horse that can seriously compete in the sport horse disciplines.

Since the purebred Friesian is almost always solid black, for some cross breeders, the goal is to have a horse that strongly resembles the purebred Friesian, but with different coat colors and/or spotted patterns. Although Friesian crossbreds can be black, a great number of them are also bay. The chestnut (red) gene rarely occurs in the purebred Friesian and therefore is also rare in the crossbred. Any color is acceptable for crossbred registration.

Friesians crossed with Arabians, Morgans, Thoroughbreds and Saddlebreds are popular and typically result in a horse that has Friesian-like traits, yet has more refinement, agility, and stamina than a purebred Friesian. When baroque type breeds,

There are various Friesian-crossed horses. This is a superb young Friesian/Appaloosa stallion. *Cindy Bellamy/Friesian Heritage Horse & Sporthorse International*

such as the Andalusian, Lusitano, and the Lippizan have been used, typically the goal is to keep the "baroque look," but increase the stamina and collection of the horse. Friesians bred to American stock horse breeds, such as the Quarter Horse, Paint, and Appaloosa, are often used to produce pinto and appaloosa patterned horses or those with variant colors, such as buckskin, dun, or roan. These crossbreds rarely retain the typical stock horse look, build, or movement. Generally, they are built more uphill, have longer, higher gaits than the stock horse, tend to have a stronger hindquarter, and again, have more stamina than the purebred Friesian.

Tennessee Walkers and other gaited horses have been used with the goal of producing offspring with Friesian traits that are gaited—although they do not always inherit the intended gait. Draft horses crossed with Friesians are immensely popular as pleasure companions. In this situation the Friesian horse is commonly used to *refine* the draft horse characteristics and add the Friesian presence and showiness while preserving the easygoing temperament of both breeds.

Like Friesians, Friesian crossbreds tend to have quirky, very sociable, and clever personalities. They like to play in water and love attention. They are extremely curious, often investigating everything. They typically get along well with other horses and truly seem to enjoy the company of people. Even the stallions tend to be more tolerant of one

Wonderful Friesian/draft stallion. This is a nice blend, producing a colorful, eloquent horse. *Cindy Bellamy/ Friesian Heritage Horse & Sporthorse International*

another and are often seen working together without the typical stallion-to-stallion aggression. Their friendliness is often described as "puppy-dog" like.

Registry

There are many different Friesian based registries in existence, but they have different requirements and restrictions and sometimes vary greatly in their philosophies of what constitutes a register-able Friesian crossbred.

The Friesian Heritage Horse and Sporthorse International is an inclusive registry for Friesian crossbred and purebred Friesian horses that provides support and respect for both. The registry is casually referred to as "the Friesian Heritage Horse," "the Heritage Horse," or simply "the HH." For the purposes of the registry, "Friesian Heritage Horses" refers to all HH registered horses of 25 to 99.9 percent documented Friesian heritage (blood). Purebred Friesians registered with HH are simply referred to as "purebreds" or "Friesians." For crossbred registration, the secondary breed may be any breed or breed combination of horse or pony. Mules are not eligible for registration, even if they are part Friesian.

The HH maintains five separate books for horses (and/or ponies) of Friesian heritage. For entry into four of the five books, eligibility is based simply on the percentage of documented Friesian blood, except for the pony book, which also requires a mature height of under 15 hands. The fifth book, which is the Heritage Warmblood book, is the only book that requires inspection prior to entry. However, the HH encourages all breeders to utilize optional tools and inspections to help identify performance type and suitability for horses within any of the HH books.

For horses that earn the designations through inspection scores or accomplishments in Open showing, the HH provides performance designations, such as Sporthorse (SD), Park Performance (PD), and Utility (UD). These earned designations are recorded on the registration certificate. Participation in the suitability designation program is optional. The three suitability type designations of SD, PD, and UD may be earned by horses within any of the HH books, except for the Heritage Warmblood book, which is strictly for horses of sport horse type.

The five separate HH registration books for horses of Friesian heritage are:

Crossbred Friesian Book: 25 to 75 percent Friesian heritage

Crossbred Friesian Pony Book: 25 to 75 percent Friesian heritage with a mature height under 15 hands

Faux Friesian Book: 75.1 to 99.9 percent Friesian heritage

Purebred Friesian Book: 100 percent Friesian heritage

Heritage Warmblood: These horses cannot have a purebred parent, but must have 25 to 75 percent Friesian blood with Friesian lineage on both sides of the pedigree. They must have full DNA verification and meet strict inspection requirements on a sport horse (SD) standard prior to being accepted into the Heritage Warmblood book. It is hoped that the Heritage Warmblood will eventually evolve into a breed of its own.

Second generation and successive generations of Friesian Heritage Horses, which are not deemed to be sport horse in type or that score lower than the sport horse requirements of the Heritage Warmblood book, are still eligible for registration in the other three crossbred books and may still earn designation as PD, UD, or SD in their respective books.

Registry Requirements and Standards

To maintain integrity, the HH follows current horse industry standards by utilizing DNA testing and keeping updated and proactive on genetic issues. Horses registered with HH must submit a DNA hair sample before their subsequent offspring can be registered with HH.

Horses with Quarter Horse ancestry related to the stallion, Impressive, or horses with unknown lineage, must be tested for HYPP (hyperkalemic periodic paralysis), or the notation "Not HYPP Tested" will be clearly marked on their registration certificate. (HYPP is an inherited muscular disease.)

In order to fortify breeding programs and increase quality, the HH registry strongly encourages inspections be utilized in order to evaluate the conformation, suitability and movement of the Friesian and the Friesian Heritage Horse, particularly those used for breeding. Equally important is the inspection of horses of non-Friesian heritage that are utilized for breeding to Friesians.

The HH offers optional inspections through the services of Federated Equine Inspection Tours, LLC (FEIT). FEIT is an American based inspection circuit that is open to all breeds of horses. FEIT inspections are judged by licensed, highly experienced, USEF (United States Equestrian Federation) judges. In most cases at inspection locations where HH horses are attending, the judge is also accredited by USEF to judge the Friesian breed. Horses are presented individually, in-hand, and at liberty and the quality of the horse's conformation, walk, trot, and canter are evaluated, discussed, and scored by the judge.

Horses are scored 40 percent on conformation and 60 percent on movement. For horses that qualify, first (blue), second (red), and third (yellow) premiums are given and ribbons and certificates are awarded. All horses scoring 7.7 and over have their quality further acknowledged by also receiving an award of "High Merit." Horses with an overall score below 6.0 are not eligible for a premium and generally should not be considered as breeding prospects.

For the Friesian Heritage Horse, good, sound conformation is key, regardless of the type or suitability of a horse. Good conformation is basically the same for all types of horses. However, a few minor variations in structure, such as shoulder angle, may influence what a horse moves like and therefore becomes the determining factor in what discipline the horse may be suitable for.

FEIT currently offers a choice of four different standards that horses may be judged against:

- Sporthorse Standard (traditional Olympic disciplines)
- Park Standard (for riding or driving horses with high knee action)
- Utility Standard (for horses that do not move like a sport horse or a park horse. The movement may be flatter, making them more suitable for something like hunter work, jousting, or western disciplines)
- Purebred Friesian Standard (equivalent to the FPS standard in Holland)

Breed Quality

The goal of the HH is to promote horses of Friesian heritage in a manner that will secure and further improve the value of these wonderful horses, both now and into the future. It believes that in order to enhance the quality and credibility of the Friesian Heritage Horse in the equine community at large, the following Friesian myths should not be propagated.

Myth: Purebred Friesians are all dressage horses.

Truth: Friesians are, by and large, carriage horses and only a small percentage are truly suitable for the higher levels of dressage and other sport horse disciplines.

Myth: All Friesian crossbred horses are sport horses.

Truth: Any horse, regardless of breed, *could* be sport horse in type, but not all are. The term sport horse, by horse industry standards, does not simply mean a crossbred horse, but actually refers to a certain type of horse whose build and movement are suitable for the sport horse disciplines of dressage, jumping, and combined driving. Friesian crosses are capable of excelling in a variety of disciplines, but only some of the population has the type and movement necessary to excel as sport horses.

Myth: All purebred Friesians are high quality animals.

Truth: Friesians have faults and weaknesses just like any other breed of horse and not all of them are appropriate for breeding; this is why inspection of horses used for breeding is important.

Myth: All horses that have titles such as Qualified, Approved, or Ster are automatically better breeding candidates or better quality animals than those who do not have titles.

Truth: There are many things to be considered before accepting a title as the mark of a superior horse. Sometimes, depending on their accomplishments and offspring, there are horses that do not have registry titles at all, yet are equal in quality to horses that do have titles. Titles such as Qualified, Ster, Approved, Model, and Preferent, can be important, and depending on the registry and other factors, can be an indicator of superior quality. But when pertaining to the quality of a horse for purchase or for breeding potential, such titles alone don't qualify a horse, nor do they always address the specific suitability of a particular animal. Many additional factors other than titles need to be evaluated and considered. Questions such as, "Qualified for what?" and "What standard was the horse evaluated against?" are critical to ask as well as understanding the judging criteria on which the title was earned. (It is common for titled Friesians to be heavily invested in and later they are

discovered not to be suitable for the discipline they were chosen for.)

Until very recently, Friesians were historically not given titles based on their dressage or sport horse potential, but are traditionally awarded for how high and flashy they can lift during the trot—which is not ideal movement for a sport horse. Many "titled" Friesians who fit the breed standard for high action, and therefore score high, have poor quality canters and are generally more suited for harness than for riding. This is acceptable when the intended use for the horse is harness or saddleseat, but is disastrous when the intended use is for sport horse activities, and uncomfortable at best, when the intended use is leisure riding.

Sometimes titles are awarded based on competition scores alone with no formal conformation judging or inspection. This practice can indicate a good horse, but conformation is almost never judged during performance competition and many in-hand classes that do judge conformation don't evaluate the canter in any way. Since different registries have different requirements, the meaning of the same title can be completely different from one registry to another.

Furthermore, simple marketing ploys can sometimes take advantage of awarded titles by assigning titles simply based on the fact that the horse's owner paid to register the horse and nothing more—the horse was never actually evaluated by anyone, yet could still have titles, like Approved or Qualified.

Myth: Only purebred Friesians and Friesian crossbreds of *certain* registries can produce quality horses, and foreign-bred horses and foreign-based registries are better than their American counterparts.

Truth: Good horses exist in many different registries and can be either American-bred and born or imported. Evaluation of the individual horse first, before consideration of the registry or birthplace, is important. Frequently, Friesians are imported when they are mere babies—long before an age-appropriate appraisal of their breeding quality can be assessed. Furthermore, foals are often shipped

Friesian/Thoroughbred gelding performing at Prix St. George–level dressage. *David McWhirter Photography*

in groups, because it is more cost effective. These groups usually contain one, or maybe two, breeding quality individuals and those remaining are filler for the load—something to resell to pay for shipping costs. The fact that a horse was imported should never be considered as an automatic breeding qualification.

Myth: More hair (mane, tail, and feathering) indicates a better quality Friesian.

Truth: Mane, tail, and feathering are simply icing on the cake. Sometimes an overabundance of hair can be regarded as more grooming work and some owners opt to shave it off. Excess hair can lead to increased incidence of bacterial skin conditions and can cause other problems as well.

When evaluating an extremely hairy Friesian, it is advisable for the hair to be braided up and out of the way in order to clearly see the conformation and traits underneath all the hair, which can hide a multitude of faults. Unfortunately, in Friesian and Friesian crossbreds, abundance of hair is often the sole consideration in choosing a breeding horse. In terms of importance, hair should be the last thing considered, after it has been determined that everything else is suitable and/or superior.

Myth: Bigger is better and Friesians are always enormous.

Truth: The mature height of both Friesian and Friesian crossbred horses can vary significantly—anywhere from 14 to 17-plus hands. However, the vast majority of horses of Friesian heritage, on average, fall somewhere in the range of 15 to 16 hands tall. Although, due to their extremely high neck set and their substantial build, they often appear taller and their heights are frequently exaggerated—sometimes by quite a bit. Mature horses are typically measured during inspection and it is advisable to look for a verified record of height.

Factors taken into account when considering a very large size horse include the fact that excessively big horses can be harder to handle. They can potentially be more complicated and expensive to fit for saddles, tack, and trailers, particularly when they are big-bodied along with being tall. For the average size rider, they can be more arduous to ride, especially if the intended purpose is dressage. Sometimes size and athleticism can be a trade off—very large horses can be heavier in their movement and sometimes lack agility.

Furthermore, the stamina of big horses is not always the best. Since they often have a lot of extra body weight to carry, they can tire more easily and this can effect how competitive they may be. Additionally, more size can sometimes cause extra strain on the joints and consequently could lead to increased soundness issues.

Credit: Friesian Heritage Horse and Sporthorse International

GEORGIAN GRANDE

Carrying itself with graceful elegance, the Georgian Grande is dependable, quiet, and calm—perfect for trail riding.
International Georgian Grande Horse Registry

International Georgian Grande Horse Registry, Inc.
P.O. Box 845
Piketon, Ohio 45661
www.georgiangrande.com

The Georgian Grande horse has the graceful elegance and noble bearing of the Saddlebred perfectly blended with the size, good bone, and calm disposition of the Friesian or draft horse. The purpose of creating the Georgian Grande was to produce a breed that is a perfect blend of these great horses, having the best of both worlds and being better than either parent.

It has a natural self carriage that eludes description. Some call it presence, class, or style, but a superior air distinguishes every movement of the Georgian Grande. It is a proud, powerful, and vigorous horse, but it is always quiet and reserved.

Georgian Grandes grow large and stay sound. They are sturdy horses that are intelligent and alert, retaining the common sense of a working horse.

They possess strength, beauty, and a good mind. Overall, they are extremely versatile and are good at multiple disciplines. In fact their movement is that of upper level dressage, and they are adept at jumping. On trails they are dependable, quiet, and calm; they also excel at driving. They are easy to train and very willing to work. Such are the abilities and qualities of the incredible Georgian Grande.

History

During the 1970s, a breeder named George Wagner Jr. started crossing drafts to Saddlebreds to recreate and bring back the original, heavier boned, bigger Saddlebreds of the historic past, which were more robust and sensible. One example of the original type Saddlebred was General Robert E. Lee's horse, Traveler, which was Lee's favorite horse throughout his many battle campaigns. Other examples would be the noble Saddlebreds ridden by officers of the U.S. Calvary during the American Civil War. Those were the old fashioned, bigger Saddlebreds of yesteryear, yet the American Saddlebred of today has had a lot of its original appearance bred out of it. Occasionally, an old-fashioned, or baroque, style Saddlebred can still be found, but most have disappeared from the equine scene.

With Wagner's dedicated efforts, the original Saddlebred can again be seen, even nobler, calmer, and more beautiful than before, in the magnificent Georgian Grande. Its name means "George's Great Horse," and indeed George Wagner succeeded in producing a great horse after selectively breeding Georgian Grandes for thirty years. In 1994, the International Georgian Grande Horse Registry (IGGHR) was founded, and since then it has grown by leaps and bounds. IGGHR is now a member of the U.S. Dressage Federation (USDF) All-Breeds Council, as well as the American Horse Council. As a USDF participating breed, Georgian Grandes are eligible to compete for the U.S. Equestrian Federation (USEF)/USDF/IGGHR All-Breeds Award.

The breed is becoming quite popular, as its many abilities are being noticed and appreciated. There

Just a few days old, this colt shows off his striking spots with the typical Georgian Grande presence. *Flying W Farms*

are IGGHR horses winning in dressage, eventing, and show jumping, and they can be shown in English Pleasure, Hunt Seat, Hunter Hack, English Show Hack, Driving and Western Pleasure. They excel in Renaissance exhibitions and make wonderful and dependable trail horses for the entire family.

Registry Requirements

The acceptable blend to produce a Georgian Grande is that of the American Saddlebred with the Clydesdale, Shire, Percheron, Belgian, Friesian, or Irish Draught. Horses with a registered Georgian Grande sire or dam can be registered. Registered Drum Horses or Gypsy Vanner Horses can also be used for foundation breeding. Registered Spotted Draft Horses with a background of Clydesdale, Shire, Percheron or Belgian can be used for producing Georgian Grandes. Geldings can be a combination of Saddlebred and any draft breed.

No other light breed other than a Saddlebred can be crossed with a draft to produce a Georgian Grande. The percentage of Saddlebred blood may be up to 75 percent, but never less than 25 percent. In every case, the purpose of crossing the Saddlebred with the draft or Friesian is to produce offspring that are a perfect combination of both parents, but better than either parent individually.

Standards

Overall impression: The breed has grandeur and great power, yet very gentle and submissive to rider or handler. The Georgian Grande is a large, very impressive horse that commands attention wherever it is seen.

Conformation: The ideal Georgian Grande should definitely appear to be built uphill, carrying itself with deep hocks well up under the middle of the horse in movement. It should be in good flesh, with good muscle tone, and a smooth, glossy coat. Stallions should exhibit a masculine look, while femininity in mares is desired.

Size: Heights can range from 15.2 hands to 17 hands and taller. They weigh from 1,000 to 1,400 pounds or heavier.

Color: Any color is acceptable.

Head: The Georgia Grande has a well shaped head with broad flat forehead. Eyes should be large, luminous, expressive, and set wide apart. They can be any color; blue eyes shall not be penalized. Profile should be straight or slightly concave. Muzzle is relatively fine, but must have large nostrils and clean, smooth, strong jaw line. The ears should be expressive, well shaped, attractively set, and carried alertly. The bite is even.

Neck: The neck is one of the most important points of conformation in the Georgian Grande horse. It should be long and well muscled, denoting strength, suppleness, and power. It should be well arched and well flexed at the poll, with a good clean throatlatch. The throatlatch should be clean and fine enough to allow for flexion and "setting the head,"

yet also large enough to allow for plenty of airflow during competition. The ultra-fine throatlatch of the pure Saddlebred show horse of today is not desirable in the Georgian Grande. Rather it should be a sensible blend of the ultra-fine Saddlebred's throatlatch and the more practical, larger one of the Friesian or draft—in other words, a happy, commonsense medium.

Withers: These are well defined.

Shoulder: The shoulders should be deep, sloping, and well laid back, allowing for great freedom of movement.

Back: The back is strong and relatively short and supple in movement with well sprung ribs.

Croup: The croup is long, not table-top level, but slightly sloping; the tailset is high or moderately high. The hips are big, round, and powerful. The hindquarters should be strong and well muscled. The chest is proportionate to the size of the horse. The muscles of the forearms, croup, and gaskins are especially emphasized.

Legs: Front legs are set well forward under the shoulder. Rear legs are clean and correct, not cow-hocked or sicklehocked. Proper angulation of the rear legs allows for good jumping. Feathering on legs is acceptable, but not required, and horses may be shown with feathering or with legs clipped.

Knees: The knees are large, flat, and clean.

Hocks: The hocks are large, clean, flat in front and at the sides, and wide from front to back. Rear hocks should be positioned so that a line dropped from the horse's buttocks falls straight down the back of the hock and cannon. Legs should be straight with plenty of good, clean, flat bone. At maturity, there should be at least 9 inches (or more) of good, hard, flinty bone just below the knee (in circumference), and the more, the better. It should be noted that Georgian Grande horses are not fully mature until five to six years of age.

Cannons: Well made. When viewed from the side, should be flat and broad; tendons are well defined and tendons behind the cannon are firm and smooth. Pasterns are sloping.

Feet: Hooves should be of proper size to carry

This solid 17-hand stallion has the noble bearing of the Georgian Grande. *International Georgian Grande Horse Registry*

the weight of this big, beautiful animal. They are well built, round, open at the heel, and sound. May be shown shod or unshod.

Mane and tail: Both should be naturally full and flowing. For show purposes a Georgian Grande may be exhibited with the mane braided. The mane may also be pulled for Hunter/Jumper classes (optional). Tail is always natural, never docked (like the draft) or cut (like the Saddlebred).

Movement: The walk should be supple and very energetic with good "overtrack" (overreach from behind), marching forward with good swing to the hips showing suppleness through the back.

At the trot, the ideal Georgian Grande horse should move with floating suspension (lift) and power from behind (impulsion). There is great flexibility in the loins and freedom in the shoulder. Above all, the horse must be able to get its hocks well up under itself from behind, (deep hocks). The horse must be able to bend the hock and stifle deeply, as well as set the hind foot well under

its center of gravity. By bending the hind limb in this way, the horse lowers the entire hindquarters and thus appears to lift up the front end. The trot should be very light on the forehand, carrying most of the weight on the rear quarters, and exhibit good impulsion, suspension, and extension. The hind foot should actually contact the ground slightly before the front foot on the opposite side, (called diagonal advanced positioning or DAP). The front feet should not wing nor paddle, but move straight ahead.

The canter is balanced and round, with hocks well up under the horse. It should be a true three-beat canter, quiet through the back and unhurried.

Dressage and Sport Horse In-Hand Class

The ideal Georgian Grande is well proportioned and presents a beautiful overall picture. It carries itself with neck high and well arched, head up and ears forward, and every movement saying, "Look at me!" Large, wide-set expressive eyes and gracefully shaped ears set close together are positioned on a well-shaped head. The neck must be long and elegant with clean throatlatch. The neck is arched and well-flexed at the poll. A short heavy neck is to be penalized.

The horse has well-defined withers, while the shoulders are deep and sloping. The back is strong, and the hindquarters well muscled with a strong rounded croup. The legs are straight with broad flat bones and sloping pasterns. Georgian Grandes are built uphill (higher in front than in the back) and move that way. They have clean fluid action, which is straight and true.

The hocks are deep, and carried well up under the horse in movement, giving great impulsion from behind and lifting the front with beautiful suspension and extension at the trot.

Masculinity in stallions and femininity in mares are important qualities to be expressed. The Georgian Grande, with its conformation type, calm temperament, and stamina, is well suited for any discipline.

Horses should stand with front legs perpendicular to the ground. Front legs should be square; back legs should be positioned either squarely or with one slightly behind the other to give a clear view of the hocks. Horses should stand with ears forward, head up, and neck extended and arched. They are alert and attentive to the handler.

Horses are judged 50 percent on conformation and manners, and 50 percent on movement.

Serious conformation defects, such as an overbite, underbite, only one testicle descended (stallions) or any unsoundness, lameness, or similar conditions, are grounds for disqualifications. Manmade scars and blemishes shall not count against a horse. Excessively unruly behavior will result in disqualification in the show ring.

Performance Requirements

Age considerations: Horses are not considered mature until the age of six. Georgian Grandes cannot be shown under saddle until they are three years old. A Junior horse is five years and under.

A Senior horse is six years and older. Georgian Grandes cannot be shown in any driving class until they are two years old.

Show aids: The application of any foreign or caustic substance, such as ginger, mustard, pepper, or abrasives, that could alter or influence a horse's natural carriage, movement, or behavior is prohibited. The injecting of any foreign substance into a horse's tail or ears, the cutting of tail ligaments, soring, or maiming of feet, or any such practice that would alter or influence a horse's natural carriage, movement, or behavior, is prohibited. Uses of any devices or aides that alter the natural movement of the horse, such as chains, shackles, or rubber bands, are strictly prohibited in any competition. The use of color changing products on Georgian Grandes is prohibited, except for hoof polish. Gag and twisted bits of any type are prohibited.

The addition of supplemental hair in manes, tails, or feathers is prohibited. Georgian Grandes are to be shown in their natural splendor, with full natural flowing mane and tail for Open In-Hand classes. The exception is for In-Hand Dressage or Hunter class, for which manes may be braided or pulled.

Shoeing: Artificial lengthening of the hoof wall and use of any kind of material other than hoof packing or repair material is prohibited. The shoe is not to extend more than one-fourth inch beyond the hoof in front and beyond one-fourth inch of the bulb of the heel. Weighted shoes (toe, side, or heel weighted) are prohibited. The weight of shoes should be proportionate to the horse's height and weight. Excessive weight or that which causes unnatural action/movement is prohibited. Bar shoes, caulks, pads, wedges, and bandages of any kind are prohibited.

Weanlings and yearlings must be shown barefoot. Horses over the age of two may be shown without shoes, or flat shod in pleasure or dressage type shoes.

Credit: International Georgian Grande Horse Registry, Inc.

Hackney Horse and Pony

Classy little Hackney Pony pulling a cart. *Greg Oakes*

American Hackney Horse Society
4059 Iron Works Parkway, A-3
Lexington, Kentucky 40511
www.hackneysociety.com

The Hackney is a dynamic high stepper that comes in two versions, the horse and the pony, both of which are bred for their durability and brilliance in harness. The Hackney is loved for its animation, vigor, endurance, personality, and strong natural way of going. It is the high stepping aristocrat of the show ring and is not only captivating, but also breathtaking. The crisp trot with knees raised high at each step and powerfully propelled hindquarters amazes those who view the Hackney for the first time. Its bright spirit, gentle eye, and intelligence are all parts of the winning package that draws both young and old to the Hackney breed.

The Hackney loves to be driven and "do its owner proud," both in the show ring and on a quiet country road. Under saddle, it is equally affable. However it is presented, the image of the Hackney Horse and Pony is one of beauty and animation.

Today hundreds of Hackney Ponies and Horses are used as both stylish show horses and amiable family companions. The caring and sharing between children and Hackneys is one of life's greatest joys. They can teach a child lessons for life and are easy to keep, especially the ponies. They do not take up much space and are relatively inexpensive to buy and maintain. Their longevity and soundness are legendary—and they are so much fun!

Above all, Hackneys love to please, whether under the lights of a show ring or the canopy of green leaves on a country road.

History

The Hackney originated in Norfolk, England, where horses called Norfolk Trotters had been selectively bred for elegant style and speed. Seeking to improve on both accounts, breeders crossed their Norfolk mares to grandsons of the foundation sires of the Thoroughbred. The first Hackney Horse as we know the breed today is said to have been The Shale's Horse, foaled in 1760. He was renowned for his elegant style and speed and became a foundation in the breed. During the next fifty years, the Hackney continued to be selectively bred as a distinct breed.

The development of the Hackney matched stride-for-stride with the improvement in both the quality of English life and the use of public roadways in Britain. Vast advancements of roads in the mid-1800s contributed to the development of swift trotting horses. Originally these roads required heavy dray animals that could tug carts from deep ruts. Now, a driver could command, "Trot on," and really go!

Prosperous farmers, not nobility, were responsible for developing high-tech carriage and riding horses. As noblemen were busying themselves with fox hunters and Thoroughbred racehorses, wealthy farmers took to the roads to show off their prosperity with harness horses. A pair of perfectly matched bays with elegant head carriage, trotting along smartly, their knees rising almost to their noses—that was the proof of abundant crops, calves, and lambs.

This was the golden age of driving, when automobiles were not even a dream. The Hackney was the ultimate driving machine of the 1880s both in the United States and the United Kingdom. The breeding of Hackneys in Britain was formalized with the founding of the Hackney Stud Book Society in 1883.

The seas were being crossed regularly during the 1800s by ships bearing both Hackney Horses and the smaller ponies, which certain breeders were selectively encouraging. The first Hackney Pony imported to the United States was Stella 239, brought to Philadelphia by A. J. Cassatt in 1878. From 1890 until the Great Depression, wealthy Americans brought over boatload after boatload of horses and ponies of the most noted strains.

Owners of Hackney Horses throughout the western states wanted to form a society by first obtaining assurance of affiliation with the council of the English Hackney Society. After this was accomplished, in 1891 Cassatt and other Hackney enthusiasts founded the American Hackney Horse Society (AHHS), an organization and registry that continues today.

Breed Quality

The Hackney Horse and Pony inspire the same loyalty and affection from their owners as the Hackney of yesteryear. The remarkable high-stepping gait is exciting to watch as the Hackney transmits its exuberance, enthusiasm, and excitement to both owner and spectator. It is known as the "aristocrat of the show ring," carrying itself with an attitude that is seemingly explosive with great expression, while also remaining tractable.

Its diversity and temperament allow the Hackney to adapt to the challenge, be it show, pleasure, carriage, riding, or as a child's friend. When it is observed traveling smartly down a road, all other horses and ponies by comparison seem merely ordinary.

The action of the Hackney, which is its hallmark, is spectacular and highly distinctive. Its remarkable high stepping gait is exciting to watch. Shoulder action is fluid and free with a very high, ground covering knee action, and action of the hind legs is similar, but to a lesser degree. The hocks are brought under the body and raised high. All joints exhibit extreme flexion, and the action is straight and true. The whole effect is arresting and startling, showing extreme brilliance. The Hackney is truly elegance on the road!

Hackney Horse

Shown in a variety of ways, the Hackney Horse must stand over 14.2 hands. It can be shown in

The elegant Hackney pony has a long neck, prominent withers, and high-set tail. *American Hackney Horse Society*

Single, Pair, Four-In-Hand, and Obstacle classes and In-Hand. Some are shown under saddle, competing in Hunter/Jumper, Dressage, Eventing, English Pleasure, and competitive trail riding/driving.

Show carriage driving has classes for elegance and style appropriate for the horses. Among them are fun classes, such as obstacle courses involving flapping clotheslines, barking dogs, and farm animals. Hackney Horses have recently sparked an interest with junior exhibitors due to their intelligent and trainable temperament.

Pleasure driving clubs exist all over the country just for the fun of driving. No competition is involved here, just a learning experience and a delightful drive with camaraderie in the countryside.

Hackney Pony

The Pony was developed by crossing the Hackney Horse with ponies of good conformation and motion. Hackney Ponies are almost exclusively shown in harness, but they can also be shown in-hand (judged on conformation only). Due to their personalities, they make good pleasure carriage animals.

Hackney Ponies are shown in four divisions; the Hackney Pony (Cob Tail), Harness Pony (Long Tail), Roadster Pony, and Pleasure Pony.

The **Hackney Pony (or Cob Tail)** division is for ponies measuring over 12.2, but under 14.2 hands at the withers. These ponies must be shown with a shortened tail and a braided mane and forelock. They are shown with a four-wheel vehicle called a viceroy and are also shown in pairs.

The **Hackney Harness Pony (or Long Tail)** must measure 12.2 hands or under at the withers. It is shown with a long mane and undocked tail. Like the Cob Tail, it is also shown with the four-wheeled viceroy vehicle and can be shown in pairs.

Another class for either the Long Tail or Cob Tail is the Pleasure Driving Division. Ponies are shown with unbraided manes and tails with an appropriate pleasure vehicle, but only by amateurs, at a pleasure trot, road trot, and flat walk. They must stand quietly in the lineup and back when asked. They are to be quiet, easy to handle, and a pure joy to drive.

Hackney Roadster Ponies are the speedsters of the Hackney breed and are very popular. They measure below 13 hands and are shown at three separate trotting speeds: the jog trot, road gait, and at speed. They are shown with a two-wheeled bike with the driver wearing racing silks. They can also be shown under saddle by junior exhibitors wearing racing silks. A new division, Roadster Pony to Wagon, has the pony hitched to a miniature doctor's buggy.

Showing in the newest of the four Hackney pony divisions, the **Pleasure Pony** is 14.2 hands or under, well mannered, and a pleasure to drive. It can be either a Long Tail or Cob Tail and is shown with unbraided mane and tail and an appropriate vehicle in the Pleasure Driving Division, driven only by an amateur. They are required to stand quietly, back up, and be easy to handle.

Conformation Proportions for all Hackneys

Head: The head should be well shaped and in proportion to the size of the animal. The eyes

should be large and set wide apart, while the ears should be well shaped, set somewhat close together on top of the head, and carried alertly. The face should be straight with a fine muzzle, large nostrils, and a clean, smooth jaw line, with the mandible set wide apart for good air passage.

Neck: The neck should be set on top of the shoulder with a definite demarcation where it rises from the chest and attaches to the withers. The topline on the neck should be considerably longer than the underline, with a fine throatlatch and long poll to facilitate an attractive head carriage.

Body: The shoulder should be long and well angulated with prominent, well defined withers. The back should be somewhat level, with a shorter topline than underline. The hip should also be long, with a fairly flat croup and high set tail carriage.

Legs: The front legs should be attached well forward beneath the point of the shoulder and should be straight with a long forearm and short cannon bone. The pasterns should have sufficient length and angulation to provide a light, springy step. The hind legs should also be set on the corners of the body, with a long gaskin and a short

cannon bone. A slight sickle hocked appearance is not undesirable, and the hock and knee should be approximately the same distance from the ground.

Hooves: These should be in proportion to the size of the animal. They are open at the heel with a concave sole. A slight toeing out is not objectionable.

View from the front: Chest should be of moderate width and front legs should be perpendicular to the ground. A straight line through the forearm to the center of the knee and to the center of the coronet band is preferable.

View from the side: The topline represents a curve from the ears and poll to the back, giving the impression of the neck sitting on top of the withers rather than in front of them, and continuing to a straight back with relatively level croup rounding to a well muscled buttock. Tail should be attached high; at maturity the croup should not be higher than the withers. The underline should be longer than the topline, and the body should be deep through the heart, girth, and flank. The front legs should be straight, perpendicular to the ground, and attached well forward beneath the point of the shoulder. From the side view, the animal can be divided into distinct thirds: one third from the tip of the nose to withers, one third from withers to mid-loin, and one third from mid-loin to the tip of buttocks.

View from the rear: Croup should be well rounded, with well muscled thighs and gaskins. The gaskins should be relatively long in relation to the cannons.

Standards

All Hackney Horses and Ponies must have both parents registered with the American Hackney Horse Society and must have genetic DNA testing performed.

The modern Hackney is colored black, brown, and bay, with chestnut being the minority. They come with or without a face strip and white stockings. They should possess a small head, muzzle, and ears, giving the general impression of alertness. The neck should be long and blend into a broad chest and powerful shoulders. A compact body with a level back and round rib, a short strong loin and level croup with either a long or docked tail carried high are desired. The legs should be of medium length, the joints are large and of strong quality. The thighs and quarters are well muscled. Pasterns are of good length and slope. The Hackney has a good foot, and both the horse and pony have a good reputation for soundness.

- Head: carried relatively high; size and dimensions in proportion, with clear-cut features and well-chiseled, straight face line
- Muzzle: fine; nostrils large; lips thin, trim, and even
- Eyes: prominent orbit; large, full, bright, and clear, with a thin lid
- Ears: small, fine, alert, coming out of top of head, pointed, and set close
- Neck: supple and well-crested; throatlatch clean; head well set on
- Shoulders: very long and sloping, yet muscular
- Withers: high, muscular, and well-finished at top, extending well into the back
- Chest: medium-wide and deep
- Ribs: well-sprung, long, and close
- Back: Short, straight, strong, and broad
- Flank: deep, long, and full flank, not tucked; low underline
- Hips: broad, round and smooth
- Croup: long, level, and smooth; no goose rump
- Tail: comes out high from back; well-carried
- Thighs: full and muscular.
- Gaskins: broad and muscular
- Legs: sinewy; viewed from the rear, vertical line dropped from the point of the buttock should divide the leg and foot into lateral halves; when viewed from front, a vertical line from the point of the shoulder should divide the leg and foot into two lateral halves; viewed from the side, the same line should pass through the center of the elbow joint and the center of the foot
- Hocks: straight, wide, and point prominent; deep, clean cut, smooth, and well-supported.
- Forearm: long, broad, and muscular
- Knees: straight, wide, deep, and strongly supported
- Cannons: short, broad, flat, tendons sharply defined, and set well back
- Pasterns: long, sloping, smooth and strong, with a 45-degree angle from vertical
- Feet: round, uniform and straight; frog large and elastic; heels wide. Rear feet less round than in front, sole concave, heels wide and full
- Type: symmetry; overall ease of identification as a Hackney
- Quality: bone clean, dense, fine, yet indicating substance; tendons and joints sharply defined; hide and hair fine; general refinement
- Temperament: gentle, good disposition, active, and intelligent.

Credit: American Hackney Horse Society

HANOVERIAN

Hanoverian chestnut stallion. *Abramova Kseniya/Shutterstock*

The American Hanoverian Society
4067 Iron Works Parkway, Suite 1
Lexington, Kentucky 40511
www.hanoverian.org

For generations the Hanoverian Horse has been recognized as one of the most prominent and successful breeds of riding horse in the world. It retains the substantial bone, sturdiness, and stamina of its heritage.

Breeding stock is very carefully inspected and selected for correct conformation, athletic ability, and inner qualities, such as disposition and trainability. The Hanoverian has natural impulsion and light, elastic gaits characterized by a ground-covering walk, a floating trot, and a soft, round, rhythmic canter. Selective breeding for jumping ability enables the Hanoverian to excel in both the hunter and jumper rings, as well as eventing. It also has a long history of excellence in the dressage arena under professionals and amateurs alike.

The breeding aim is to produce a noble, correctly built warmblood horse capable of superior performance in dressage, eventing, hunting, jumping, and driving. It must have natural impulsion and space-gaining, elastic movements. It is a horse suited as an all-around riding horse because of its temperament, character, and willingness.

History

The Hanoverian originated in northern Germany in the state of Lower Saxony, the former kingdom of Hanover, where a flourishing horse breeding industry existed for four hundred years. Nearly three hundred years ago the Hanoverian was bred to serve as a sturdy carriage and military horse. The State Stud was established at Celle in 1735, and the Hanoverian stud book officially began in 1888.

Since the end of World War II, the breeding goal has been to produce exclusively a more versatile performance horse. After discovering the breed's athletic talent and rideability, American competitors began importing Hanoverians, creating a need to continue the German standard of selectivity for the breed in the United States. In 1978 the American Hanoverian Society (AHS) was incorporated for that purpose.

Over the years, the society has worked closely with the Hannoveraner Verband (or HV, the German Hanoverian breeding association, also known as Verband hannoverscher Warmblutzüchter), inspecting breeding stock, registering horses, and licensing and performance testing stallions. In 1995 the AHS assumed full responsibility for breeding Hanoverians in the United States and is now an internationally recognized organization. To maintain continuity, the AHS invites representatives of the HV to judge breeding stock. It adheres to the highly selective breeding standards as practiced since 1735 in Hanover, Germany, with its goal being to develop a horse on the North American continent with the same or better characteristics.

Registry Requirements

Quality performance horses are the result of the Hanoverian selection process. Each year, the AHS organizes a national inspection tour to register foals, inspect and performance test mares, and license stallions.

Foals: Only foals from AHS inspected and approved parents may be registered with the society. The parentage of foals must be verified by blood or DNA typing. The DNA types of the dam, sire, and foal must be on file before registration can be completed.

Foals have their movement and conformation evaluated by both American and German inspectors during the Annual Inspection Tour. This enables the inspection commission to evaluate the offspring of AHS stallions. Foals are registered at the inspection site, and traditionally they are branded as Hanoverian breeding stock, but this is optional. Foal names must begin with the first letter of their sire's registered name.

Mares: Mare inspections take place at the age of three or older. German and American inspectors evaluate mares for type, conformation, and gaits. The Mare Performance Test (MPT) scores a mare's rideability, gaits, and jumping talent. Eligible high-scoring Main Studbook mares that pass this performance test and produce an AHS registered foal are awarded the prestigious title of Elite Mare.

A Hanoverian mare's papers, her overall score, and her dam's stud book placement determine the stud book level in which she is entered. Registered mares three years of age or older must be inspected and entered into a section of the stud book before their foals can be registered.

Non-Hanoverian mares eligible for inspection are Jockey Club–registered Thoroughbreds, registered Arabians, registered Anglo-Arabians, and German-foaled warmblood mares.

Stallions: All stallion candidates must be presented for physical inspection. If scores on conformation, movement, and jumping ability are sufficient, a temporary breeding license is granted. Stallions must then either complete the Stallion Performance Test (SPT), which evaluates their gaits, trainability, and athletic ability in dressage, show jumping, and cross-country, or they must meet specified performance requirements.

Breeding eligibility is verified annually. Within two years of licensing, the stallion must successfully complete an AHS SPT. On the final weekend of the performance test, special guest riders also evaluate the stallions. Until the SPT is completed, the temporary breeding approval is limited to two

Lovely Hanoverian bay mare. *Abramova Kseniya/Shutterstock*

years, during which the stallion is restricted to the registration of a maximum of twenty AHS foals per year.

Non-Hanoverian: Certain non-Hanoverian mares and stallions are eligible for inspection and entry into the stud book if they meet strict breed and pedigree requirements and attain sufficient scores upon presentation. Non-Hanoverian mares and stallions may also be approved for breeding if they receive a sufficient score at inspection to be admitted to the Hanoverian breeding program.

Crossbreds: A horse with only one AHS approved parent can receive a Certificate of Pedigree (CP), which is equivalent to a birth certificate for a horse considered to be a crossbred. A horse can be issued a CP at any age, provided it has not been issued papers by any other breed society or registry.

CP horses are allowed participation in the performance divisions of the AHS Awards Program, but cannot participate in the breeding program. They are ineligible to participate in AHS-sponsored breed show High Placing Awards, Hanoverian Individual Breed Classes, or year-end awards in Sport Horse breed show divisions. For U.S. Dressage Federation (USDF) and other awards (eventing, hunters, and jumpers), the AHS requires that the CP horse be properly transferred into the ownership of a current-year AHS member. CP horses can be advertised in AHS publications, however, they may not be inspected and entered into the AHS breeding program or branded.

Breed Criteria

The principal criteria for evaluating breeding stock include the following:

1. Masculinity/femininity and typiness
2. Conformation
3. Correctness of gaits
4. Impulsion and elasticity of gaits

5. Walk

6. Overall impression and development as related to age

Stallions must have a distinctly masculine bearing and mares a distinctly feminine expression. A horse's type must correspond to the society's breeding goal.

Conformation

Head: The horse should have a noble head with expressive eyes sitting on a well proportioned and well put on neck.

Withers: The withers should be pronounced and extend far back.

Body: The main part of the body from the chest to the buttocks should fit into a rectangular (not square) frame, with all parts harmoniously integrated.

Shoulders: Shoulders should be sloping, with the angle between scapula and humerus being large and open.

Back: Preferably the back is strong, but not tight, and is well padded in the area of the kidney with a long, well sprung hind rib, and a broad, slightly sloping croup.

Hindquarters: Careful attention is paid to the hindquarters, particularly to their angulation, proportion, and joint formation.

Legs: Long, broad forearms are on correspondingly short cannon bones and straight legs. The hocks must be broad, clear, and well defined. The pasterns of all four legs must be of proper slope and length. The hooves should be well shaped, strong, and sound.

Gaits: Movement as seen from the front and the rear must be straight with no paddling, winging, or crossing over.

Impulsion and elasticity: Impulsion must clearly emanate from the hindquarters, traveling through a relaxed back swinging in rhythm with the gait. Movements should be big, yet light and springy.

Typy Hanoverian mare with long, flowing strides.
Pat Mitchell/Courtesy Wendy Webster

Walk: The walk must be ground covering, relaxed, and regular. Strides must be even, and footfalls must be correct in their sequence—not lateral or pacing. Freedom of shoulders and haunches and a supple back must be evident.

Overall impression and development: As to size, sound judgment should prevail. Horses should be neither excessively large nor too small. In all cases, height should be in proportion to the overall build. Harmony is more important than size. A horse's development must commensurate with its age. Horses are scored on a scale of one 1 to 10, with 1 being very bad, and 10 being excellent.

Famous Performers

Hanoverian Horses excel in a variety of disciplines. The AHS rewards performance success with year-end awards in dressage, show jumping, show hunters, eventing, and sport horse breeding.

The Hanoverian gelding of Canada, A Criminal Mind, successfully completed the prestigious 2001 Rolex Kentucky Three-Day Event, in Lexington, Kentucky. Other than the Olympics, Rolex Kentucky is the only Concours Complet International (CCI) four-star event—a rating for eventing given by the international governing body, Federation Equestre Internationale (FEI)—held in the United States. It is also one of only four such regularly scheduled events anywhere in the world. Competing at this level of eventing is indeed testimony to the versatility of the Hanoverian horse.

The Hanoverian's sought-after movement and trainability result in success at all levels of dressage. With stellar performances in both the 2003 Dressage World Cup and the 2002 World Equestrian Games, the chestnut mare named Brentina—honored as the AHS/USDF Grand Prix Horse of the Year—captured the attention of the international dressage community. In 2006, she won the team bronze at the World Equestrian Games and,

This Hanoverian mare has a noble head with expressive eyes and gentle demeanor. *Janne Bugtrup/Courtesy Wendy Webster*

in 2005, won third at the FEI World Cup in Las Vegas, Nevada, and the U.S. Equestrian Federation (USEF) Horse of the Year. Another very successful mare, Delicata, was the winner of five USDF dressage awards in one year.

Hanoverians also possess the versatility to serve as pleasure mounts when not showing. An example of this is the gelding, Ferguson, which won the High Point Hanoverian award at the Central States Dressage and Combined Training fall festival. Ferguson and his owner also enjoy quite a bit of trail riding. His owner remarked, "He is delightful; level headed at shows, trails, and around home."

Credit: The American Hanoverian Society

HOLSTEINER

The American Holsteiner Horse Association, Inc.
222 East Main Street, Suite 1
Georgetown, Kentucky 40324
www.holsteiner.com

A Holsteiner with beautiful form in dressage. This is an 18.3-hand gelding. *Vey Martini*

The Holsteiner Horse originated in the Schleswig-Holstein region of northern Germany and is the product of a systematic breeding program that originated over seven hundred years ago. Its breeders always included visionaries who recognized the outstanding traits of the breed, yet were not afraid to bring in new bloodlines to adapt their horses to the changing needs of the market.

The Holsteiner initially evolved from native North German stock, with monasteries of the region conducting its early breeding. This included special emphasis on producing a carriage horse that could also work the fields in the harsh climate of the area. Following the Reformation, breeding initiatives fell to the state and individual farmers. Great pride was taken in selecting the best quality mares and stallions and in keeping accurate breeding records. Numbers, called *stamms* or *stems*, were assigned to each new mare line and were passed down through the generations from mother to daughter. This practice is still in existence today.

The Holsteiner was in high demand by the military and royalty throughout Europe. As demand grew for a lighter horse, however, the elegant driving horses of the 1800s were produced through infusions of the Yorkshire Coach Horse and Cleveland Bay bloodlines with the importation of stallions of those breeds.

In response to the shift toward the breeding of horses especially suited to the Olympic disciplines of dressage, eventing, and show jumping, the Holsteiner Verband (the Elmshorn, Germany, registry) brought in English Thoroughbred, Anglo-Arab, and Selle Francais (Anglo-Norman) stallions to modernize the Holsteiner type. This began the shaping of the breed to a world-class performance horse.

With the progression toward superb quality, Holsteiner blood was also greatly valued in other warmblood breeds and can be found conspicuously in the Dutch Warmblood and Oldenburg horses of today.

Registry

In North America, the American Holsteiner Horse Association (AHHA), established in 1978, is dedicated to carrying out the breeding practices of the

German Holsteiner Verband. The AHHA functions as an independent organization while maintaining an informal working relationship with the Verband. It is committed to adhering as close as possible to the selective breeding standards practiced since the thirteenth century by the Holsteiner Horse breeders of the province of Schleswig-Holstein. It recognizes the Holsteiner Verband as the ultimate authority on the Holsteiner bloodlines.

In order to achieve its breeding goal, the AHHA conducts annual stallion and mare inspections. Only those horses that are of sufficient quality are eligible to produce registered offspring. It maintains a public registry of Holsteiner Horses and brands qualified stallions, mares, and foals with the AHHA brand. Mares are judged by an official inspection team and are presented standing, at the walk, and at the trot. Gaits, including canter, are observed with the mare at liberty as well. Mares may be presented for evaluation more than once without penalty.

To be eligible for listing in the stallion book, stallions must be registered by either the AHHA or the German Verband. They must have Holsteiner dams that have at least two generations of registered Holsteiner in their dam line. Stallions are judged by an official inspection team and must present a record of performance in sport, if applicable. The stallion also must be at least two years old at time of presentation for AHHA stallion inspection and stand at least 16 hands tall.

Stallions that are two years old and those that have not yet reached their sixth birthday may be presented for preliminary approval at an official AHHA inspection site. They are presented on hard ground and judged at liberty and free jumping. They must receive a type score of not less than 7 and not less than 6 in any other subgroup. Those that pass the preliminary approval are granted a temporary breeding permit and must complete performance sport requirements before their sixth year.

Mature and other qualifying stallions must pass the inspection with qualifying scores, as well as a veterinary inspection and drug screening. They must complete a performance test in order to demonstrate the stallion's versatility, athletic ability, and stamina as a saddle horse, as well as its soundness of mind and body to withstand the demands of the modern sport horse disciplines. The performance requirements are for dressage, show jumping, hunter, or combined training. Stallions may be presented more than once.

Standards

Traditional Holsteiner Verband standards and AHHA breeding goals serve as the standard for grading. The goal is to produce a well-balanced, sturdy horse possessing Holsteiner blood and an even, willing temperament that is physically and mentally able to perform at a level of excellence in the modern sport horse disciplines. Stallions and mares are graded on a scale from 1 to 10 for each of the following:

- Type
- Topline
- Front legs
- Hind legs
- Walk
- Trot
- Canter

Characteristics

The modern Holsteiner is of medium frame and stands 16 to 17 hands. A small lovely head with large, intelligent, kind eyes is carried on a beautifully arched neck. This arched neck rises upward out of the withers and from a well angled shoulder, producing elegance and lightness. It has a strong back and loin with a powerful hind leg, making it an exceptionally talented jumper.

The Holsteiner's conformation adapts easily to self carriage, that expressive, elegant quality so essential in modern equestrian sports. When the Holsteiner begins to move, its reputation as one of the world's finest sport horses is understood. The horse is well balanced with round, generous strides and a natural, elastic movement.

Its temperament is relaxed and willing, but sensitive, with good character and an eagerness for work.

Traditionally, the Holsteiner has been bay in color, with a preference for few or no white markings.

Performance Achievements

The Holsteiner stud book is one of the smallest studbooks in Germany, listing only approximately 6 percent of the total horse population, yet it has consistently produced some of the world's most successful international horses in all disciplines. At the 1976 Olympics in Montreal, Holsteiners dominated the proceedings by winning gold and silver medals in dressage and silver medals in three-day eventing and show jumping. The same year, the World Championship in combined driving was won with a team of four Holsteiners.

In 1996, Calvaro 5, an 18-hand gray gelding, won the individual silver medal in show jumping at the Atlanta Olympics and was voted Best Horse at the World Equestrian Games in 1998. Despite her Hanoverian brand, Olympic gold medalist Ratina Z is by the Holsteiner stallion Ramiro, and her second dam, or grandmother, is a Holsteiner mare that won the prestigious Grand Prix of Aachen, Germany. Landlady, an American bred mare, was short listed for the United States Equestrian Team (USET) three-day event team for the 1999 Pan American Games.

In North America, most of the top show jumping riders have had at least one Holsteiner in the barn. Holsteiner stallions continue to produce some of the United States' top dressage horses, including Lifetime, U.S. Dressage Federation (USDF) Horse of the Year at Second Level. In the Adult Amateur divisions, where good temperament is of the utmost importance, both Contango, USDF Horse of the Year at Grand Prix, and Jagger, USDF Fourth Level Horse of the Year, are by Holsteiner stallions.

That high performance quality has carried on into the present era. The 2008 Olympic Holsteiner winners included Marius, a fourteen-year-old gelding that won the individual gold and Eventing team gold for Germany in three-day eventing. In the Team Show Jumping, gold medals went to Carlsson Vom Dach, an eleven-year-old gelding, and Cedric, a ten-year-old gelding for the United States. In Team Show Jumping, a silver medal went to In Style, a thirteen-year-old gelding for Canada. Also Team Show Jumping's bronze medal team from Norway was entirely mounted on Holsteiners: Le Beau and Cattani were both thirteen-year-old geldings, Camiro was an eleven-year-old gelding, and Casino was a stallion bred in Holland.

Credit: The American Holsteiner Horse Association, Inc.

IRISH DRAUGHT

A strong, solid, yet elegant horse, the Irish Draught is an excellent jumper. *Irish Draught Horse Society North America*

Irish Draught Horse Society of North America
4037 Iron Works Parkway, No. 160
Lexington, Kentucky 40511
www.irishdraught.com

Though the name might imply it, the Irish Draught is not a draft horse in the usual sense of that category. While having the strength and even temperament of the working horse, the Irish Draught is neither as massive nor as heavily feathered as draft horses, and has movement that is smooth, free, and ground-covering without being heavy or ponderous. (An alternative spelling of "draught" is "draft" and it is pronounced the same way).

The Irish Draught is heralded as the world's best field hunter and can perform with style in harness. It is also impressive in dressage, and excels in eventing and show jumping.

The development of this breed began long before it had a name. Over a century of selection has produced a warmblooded breed that is sound with good bone, substance, and quality. Standing over a lot of ground, the Irish Draught has an exceptionally strong and sound constitution, great stamina, and an uncanny jumping ability. In addition, it has a fabulous, willing, intelligent, docile, and common-sense temperament.

The Irish Draught can take care of its rider in all types of situations and makes a perfect mount for children, amateurs, and adult riders. It possesses the ability and versatility to be an ideal family horse. Such exceptional qualities also make the Irish Draught an invaluable and irreplaceable element in the production of the highly successful Irish Draught Sport Horse.

Versatility, heart, athleticism, kind temperament, and easy-keeping attributes have been hallmarks of the Irish Draught and Irish Draught Sport Horse, instilled centuries ago, into what has become the athletes they are today.

History

The Irish Draught is a native Irish breed and has been in existence for centuries, though it has been nearly lost on several occasions. Ireland's soil, climate, and culture make it the most horse-friendly place on earth. The Irish Draught has benefited from this environment for longer than any other type of horse and, over time, has evolved into Ireland's unique contribution to the equine world.

It traces its roots back to Celtic times on its island home when horses were raced in ancient festivals or pulled chariots in epic battles. Influences of Spanish and Norman blood were added to that of the native ponies and Hobbies, which gradually evolved into animals with versatility beyond what the name "Irish Draught" implies.

This versatility in native horses of the late nineteenth and early twentieth century was needed by Irish farmers, who required more than what the popular heavy draft could provide. They needed an animal that could work the land throughout the week, go fox-hunting Saturday and jump anything it faced, and then be ready to bring the family to church on Sunday. It had to be docile, strong, and economical to keep. Its traditional winter feed was young gorse bushes chopped up, boiled turnips, and bran or meal that could be spared from the cows. It was from this need that the Irish Draught was born.

During periods of poverty and famine in Ireland's history, many breeders gave up breeding their horses, and large numbers of the heavy horses were sold as meat. Many were also exported for use in the military, where they served as remounts and artillery horses in various European conflicts. This practice continues to this day, although the horses are now used mostly as police mounts and for military ceremonial work.

The Irish Draught's major role, however, was that of the farmer's equine partner. In the countryside, it lived and worked closely with its farming family. Tilling fields during the week, hunting on weekends, and carting the family around, it served as an athletic, versatile, hardy, and durable companion.

In 1917, Ireland's Department of Agriculture recognized the Irish Draught as a distinct breed and established a stud book for horses of "Irish Draught type."

Irish (Draught) Sport Horse

A complete package in its purest form, the Irish Draught must also be acknowledged for its potent and unparalleled contribution in the creation of that magical cross, the Irish (Draught) Sport Horse, which has been so successful at international levels in eventing and show jumping.

Ever since show jumping had its birth in Ireland and went on to become an international sport at the end of the nineteenth century, the Irish Draught has played a major role in this event and in the sport horse world at large. During the turn of the twentieth century, farmers were also breeding their purebred mares to Thoroughbred stallions, producing a wonderful cross known as the Irish Draught Sport Horse. The even temperament, durability, and power of the Irish Draught mixed with the speed and athleticism of the Thoroughbred created a potent blend.

World famous for jumping and cross-country ability, the Irish Draught/Thoroughbred cross is not only a top caliber international athlete, but can serve as a perfect novice mount, adeptly boosting the confidence of a lower level rider. Although there have been crosses with other breeds, such as top quality warmbloods, Arabians, and Quarter Horses that are showing great promise, it is still the Registered Irish Draughts crossed with Thoroughbred, that has achieved and maintained worldwide fame.

This magical cross is referred to simply as the Irish Sport Horse (ISH) in Europe. Since this name is applied today to all Horse Sport Ireland registered animals of any breeding, however, the name has been modified in North America to Irish Draught Sport Horse. While this may seem confusing, there is a reason for the different names. The Sport Horse is recognized by the Irish Draught Horse Society of North America (IDHSNA) and Irish Draught Horse Society of Canada as a crossbred animal with a portion of Registered Irish Draught (RID) blood. The Irish Sport Horse, as recognized by Horse Sport Ireland, is an animal *bred* in Ireland of *any* breeding, which may or may not have Irish Draught blood in its pedigree. For example: an Arabian crossed with a Thoroughbred, a Thoroughbred crossed with a Connemara, or a pure Thoroughbred or an RID crossed with a Thoroughbred may all be classified as an Irish Sport Horse by Horse Sport Ireland. In North America, however, only a cross with RID blood is classified as an Irish Draught Sport Horse.

The Irish Draught Sport Horse is not a special breed, or a product of a U.S. breeding program; it is simply a moniker aimed at educating the public about the Irish Draught blood that is so prevalent in many of the top performance animals. Whether the cross is known as an Irish Draught Sport Horse, an Irish Sport Horse, or even an Irish Hunter, if there is Irish Draught blood running in those veins, it is one great horse!

Examples of this are horses like Cruising, Cagney, Ado Annie, Flexible, Carling King, and Hopes Are High, some of the shining stars of the Grand Prix circuit. Others like McKinlaigh, Custom Made, Supreme Rock, Giltedge, and Sailing have thrilled the eventing world. In fact, McKinlaigh earned an individual silver medal for eventing at the Beijing Olympics in 2008.

Preservation of the Purebred

Although the success of this cross fueled an economical upswing for the Irish, the sport horse breeding boon left many high-quality purebred mares reproducing crossbreds, severely reducing the number of purebred daughters. Falling numbers of breeding purebreds has posed a serious threat to the continuance of the breed. It was this eventual decline in numbers that saw the pure Irish Draught, while busy creating international super horses, be listed as At Risk with the Equus Survival Trust by 2008.

Fortunately, with a total world herd of less than 2,500 horses, the purebred has developed a new following of enthusiastic and dedicated breeders who want to preserve and perpetuate the much sought-after qualities of the purebred. The breed is currently experiencing a resurgence of both the outcross and rare lines

Registry and Inspections

The IDHSNA was established in 1993 and fosters appreciation for both the Irish Draught and the Irish Draught Sport Horse. It maintains a registry and stud books for qualified Irish Draught and part Irish Draught horses in North America. It is recognized by the Irish Draught Horse Society (IDHS) in Ireland and the Irish Horse Board, as is the IDHS of Canada, another recognized daughter society of the IDHS in Ireland.

Both societies in North America organize an annual inspection tour conducted by qualified Irish inspectors, provided by the IDHS in Ireland, to approve horses in the stud books of the daughter societies. This supports high standards of breeding and quality so North American Irish Draughts remain true to type. Every breeding purebred Irish Draught is required to be presented at an official inspection in order to be added to the official stud book.

Any purebred horse brought forward for inspection must be from approved parents; sport horses applying for breeding approval must have one approved parent. Mares and geldings may be presented at any time after two years of age, and stallions any time after three years of age. The inspections are carried out by a team of qualified Irish Draught inspectors, selected from the ranks of approved judges from within the IDHS in Ireland.

Mares and stallions in North America are required to pass the physical inspection for breed type. Conformation, movement, temperament, and athletic ability via loose line jumping are part of the inspection criteria. A medical exam is also performed by an attending veterinarian. Upon successful inspection, mares and stallions are registered into the stud book and carry "RID" after their names, or "RIDSH" for approved sport horses. Horses that fail the inspection are given an opportunity to be brought forward at a later date, as some take time to mature fully.

Standards

Type and character: The Irish Draught is an active, short shinned, powerful horse with substance and quality, proud of bearing, deep of girth and strong of back and quarters. Standing over a lot of ground, it has an exceptionally strong and sound constitution. It is graceful and surefooted, courageous and athletic, and possesses an inherent jumping ability. In addition to all these qualities, the Irish Draught has an intelligent, willing, people-oriented nature and is noted for its even temperament and common sense.

Height: Stallions are generally between 15.3 and 16.3 hands, while mares are generally between 15.1 and 16.1 hands. (Taller individuals may be accepted, as long as they meet the majority of Irish Draught standards.)

Bone: The Irish Draught has good, strong, clean bone.

Head: The horse has large, bold eyes, set well apart, as well as a wide forehead and long, well set ears. Head should be generous and pleasant, not coarse or hatchet headed, though a slight Roman nose is permissible. The jawbones should have enough room to take the gullet and allow ease of breathing.

Shoulders, neck, and front: Shoulders should be clean cut and not loaded, and withers are well defined, not coarse. The neck set in high and carried proudly, showing good length of rein. The chest should not be too broad and beefy. The forearms should be long and muscular, not caught in at the elbows, with the knee being large, generous, and set near the ground. The cannon bone should be straight and short with plenty of flat, clean bone, never back at the knee (calf-kneed)—that is, not sloping forward from knee to fetlock. The bone must not be round or coarse. The legs should be clean and hard with a little hair permissible at the back of the fetlock as a necessary protection. The pastern is strong and in proportion, not short and upright, or long and weak. The hoof should be generous and sound, not boxy or contracted, and there should be plenty of room at the heel.

Back and hindquarters: The back should be powerful, the girth deep. The loin must not be weak, but mares must have enough room to carry a foal. The croup to buttocks should be long and sloping, not short and rounded or flat topped, and hips are not wide and plain. From the back view, thighs are strong and powerful and at least as wide as the hips, with the second thighs long and developed. The hocks are near the ground and generous. Points of the hocks are not too close together or wide apart, but straight. They should not be out behind the horse, but should be in line from the back and the quarters to the heel to the ground. They should not be over bent or weak. The cannon bone for the foreleg should be short and strong.

Action: Movement should be smooth and free, without exaggeration and not heavy or ponderous. Walk and trot should be straight and true with good flexion in the hocks and freedom of the shoulders.

Color: The Irish Draught can come in any strong, whole color, including gray. White legs above the knees or hocks are not desirable, and paint/pinto patterns are not permissible.

Credit: Irish Draught Horse Society of North America

LIPIZZAN

Lipizzan Association of North America
P.O. Box 1133
Anderson, Indiana 46015
www.lipizzan.org

The ideal Lipizzan is the baroque, classical type. *Lipizzan Association of North America*

The Lipizzan is a revered and ancient horse tracing back to Iberian and Berber horses imported by Archduke Charles who founded a stud in Lipizza (in modern-day Slovenia) in 1580. As a ceremonial horse, the breed has nobility, brilliance, and style. It is a type of baroque mount that exhibits balanced agility, temperament, and good character as some of its distinguishing attributes. It is known for its docility and intelligence and has become world famous because of its connection with the Spanish Riding School in Vienna. The Lipizzan has been bred selectively to easily perform the high school movements of dressage and to be an elegant carriage horse.

Developed exclusively by the Hapsburg monarchy, the Lipizzan is the true horse of royalty. Four hundred years of selective breeding have made it one of Europe's oldest breeds, with its historical and cultural development enhancing its mystique. Physically capable of withstanding the demands of the skill called the "airs above the ground," the Lipizzan was bred to perform haute école dressage at the famous Spanish Riding School. Owners and breeders are dedicated to the Lipizzan because they appreciate its rarity, cultural importance, romantic history, intelligence, classic beauty, and harmonious, athletic way of moving.

By the late twentieth and presently in the twenty-first century, the Lipizzan has proved itself to be a successful competitor at all levels of dressage and driving, while continuing to be the ultimate mount for classical horsemanship. It has also been appreciated in other equestrian disciplines, including pleasure riding. Comments often heard from those seeing an American Lipizzan for the first time are, "I thought they were only in Europe," "I thought they were too rare for regular people to own," "Can they really be bought here?" and "They must really be expensive!" Surprisingly, Lipizzans can be purchased in the United States and have been successful endurance horses and trail competitors, as well as eventing and dressage horses.

History

The Hapsburg family controlled both Spain and Austria when the art of classical riding was revived in Europe during the Renaissance. There was a need for light, fast horses for use in the military and in the riding school. The Spanish horse, produced during Moorish rule by crossing Berber and Arab stallions with Iberian mares, was considered the most suitable mount because of its exceptional sturdiness, beauty, and intelligence.

In 1562, Maximilian II brought the Spanish horse to Austria and founded the court stud at Kladrub. His brother, Archduke Charles, established a similar private imperial stud farm with Spanish stock in 1580 at Lippiza (now named Lipizza Italian, or Lipica in Slovenian) near the Adriatic Sea. There on the karst plateau near Trieste, Italy, the type of horse bred was called the "Lippizaner." (Today in Europe the breed is still called Lipizzaner, while in the United States, it is Lipizzan.)

The Kladrub and Lipizza stock were bred to the native karst horses, and succeeding generations were crossed with the old Neapolitan breed and horses of Spanish descent obtained from Spain, Germany, and Denmark. The Kladrub stud produced heavy carriage horses and riding horses, while light carriage horses came from the Lipizza stud, although breeding stock was interchanged between the studs.

Of the sires used during the eighteenth and nineteenth centuries, only six had established sire lines: Conversano, a black Neapolitan, born in 1767; Favory, a dun born in 1779 and transferred from Kladrub; Maestoso, a gray crossbred born in 1819, transferred from Kladrub, having a Neapolitan sire and a Spanish dam; Neapolitano, a bay or brown from another Neapolitan sire, born in 1790; Pluto, a gray of Spanish origin and from the Danish stud, born in 1765; and Siglavy, a gray Arabian, born in 1810.

By the 1800s, there were no longer any original Spanish horses available, so Arabians were used to strengthen the lines. Of the seven Arabian stallions used, only Siglavy founded a separate dynasty. The two other stallion lines that did not find favor at the Lipizza stud were perpetuated at other studs within the boundaries of the Austrian empire. The Tulipan (Croatia) and Incitato (Transylvanian-Hungarian) lines are still found in Yugoslavia, Hungary, and other Eastern European countries, as well as North America. In addition to the sire lines, thirty-five mares established dominant families that are recognized today. Each country established traditions in naming, branding, and otherwise identifying their Lipizzans.

Spanish Riding School

An important establishment linked to the Lipizzan is the Spanish Riding School in Vienna. It was named after the early Spanish horses imported in the sixteenth century and is the oldest surviving institution of its kind in the world. Its primary purpose has remained the same throughout its history: to perpetuate the art of classical horsemanship in its purest form and transmit it from generation to generation. To this end, the school has used the Lipizzan exclusively as a horse capable of performing all the steps and movements of dressage, including the airs above the ground—the levade, the courbette, and the capriole.

A spectacular Lipizzan with crested neck, powerful shoulders, and short legs. *Lipizzan Association of North America and Tempel Lipizzans*

Breed Expansion

Until 1916, the Lipizzan stud farm remained a private possession of the Hapsburg monarchy, and the expansion of the breed was only affected by military conflicts over the centuries. Whenever warfare threatened the Lipizza stud, the horses were moved away. During these moves, individual horses were occasionally given or sold to other studs. From these horses came other small Lipizzan farms, usually within the boundaries of the Austrian empire.

During World War I, the breeding stock was relocated to Laxenburg near Vienna. The foals were placed in Kladrub, the other imperial stud farm. After World War I, central Europe was reorganized and the large Austrian-Hungarian Empire was divided into several new republics. Every new state inherited the possessions of the former monarchy, thus the breeding stock of the imperial stud farm of Lippiza (1580–1916) was divided over three different countries. The main portion went to Italy, and the village of Lipizza and its surroundings were also awarded stock. The 1913–1915 foals remained at Kladrub, which was then owned by the Czechoslovakian state. In 1919, the republic of Austria became the owner of the rest of the breeding stock and the stallions of the Spanish Riding School. In addition to Italy, Czechoslovakia, and Austria, other new states that continued the breeding of the Lipizzan horse were Hungary, Rumania, and Yugoslavia.

During World War II, the Lipizzan breed was again threatened with extinction when the mares and foals from Austria, Italy, and Yugoslavia were transferred to Hostau in Czechoslovakia by the German High Command. Through the heroic efforts of the Spanish Riding School's director, Alois Podhajsky, the school and its horses were saved, owing their survival also to the intervention of Gen. George S. Patton of the U.S. Army. The perpetuation of the breed was guaranteed by Patton, who retrieved the mares and returned them to Austrian soil. Today Lipizzans are found beyond the borders of what was once the Austrian-Hungarian Empire.

In the United States

The first Lipizzans brought to the United States were given to opera singer Countess Maria Jeritza, who received several as gifts from the Austrian government in 1937. In 1945, the U.S. Remount Service imported nine Lipizzans, but it was not until the late 1950s that Lipizzans were imported in any great number. Between 1958 and 1969, Tempel and Ester Smith of Illinois imported one stallion and thirteen mares from Austria, seven Lipizzaners from Hungary, and six from Yugoslavia. In 1959, Evelyn Dreitzler from Washington State began negotiations with the Austrian government and, between 1959 and 1973, imported three stallions and ten mares to the United States. Other importations have occurred during the past thirty years, each adding another dimension to the U.S. Lipizzan genetic base.

Today, with only about 1,500 Lipizzans in North America and an additional 2,000 in the rest of the world, the breed is considered rare and the number of foals born each year is correspondingly small. Extreme care has been taken by those involved in the production of Lipizzans to ensure that the purity of the breed is preserved.

Registration

In 1992, members of the oldest U.S. Lipizzan registry, the Lipizzan Association of America, joined with the Lipizzan Society of North America to form the Lipizzan Association of North America (LANA). LANA is a North American representative of the Lipizzan International Federation (LIF), a worldwide association of Lipizzan owners and breeders. LANA follows the LIF criteria defining a purebred and registers Lipizzans. Horses eligible for registration must trace without interruption to the recognized male lines and female families of official European stud farms and their approved breeding stock.

Lipizzans born and bred within the North American continent, as well as those that are imported, including those in utero, can be registered. If they have a sire or dam not registered with LANA, a five-generation pedigree of the unregistered sire and dam must be submitted. It is recommended that there be no duplication of ancestors in a pedigree closer than four generations. No Lipizzan can be transferred without first being registered.

DNA technology using microsatellites are used to identify equine parentage and provide information for future genetic traits and disease diagnosis. All LANA registered breeding stock within the continental United States must be DNA typed.

Lineage Requirements

Stallion lines: LANA recognizes as eligible for registration those Lipizzan stallions that are descended from the six stallion lines: Conversano, Favory, Maestoso, Neapolitano, Pluto, and Siglavy. The Incitato and Tulipan lines are also recognized as eligible for registration provided the pedigrees follow the LIF standards; both the sire's and dam's lineage must trace to approved breeding stock.

Mare lines: Lipizzan mares eligible for registration are descended from the classic mare lines or those mare families approved by the LIF that have been introduced through traditional breeding procedures, according to the plan of the individual studs.

Recognized European breeding experiments: Horses of Arab, Andalusian, and Kladrub breeding are occasionally accepted in the pedigree of Lipizzans by the LIF, and therefore LANA, provided these horses were incorporated in an historically and traditionally recognized and approved breeding program.

Naming

A horse eligible for registration in LANA must use the traditional procedure of naming the Lipizzan. Those imported from stud farms outside the North American continent keep their original registered name. Foals born on the North American continent are registered using LANA's naming procedure. To

A lovely dappled Lipizzan with convex head and correct, rectangular body. *Lipizzan Association of North America and Tempel Lipizzans*

In the *courbette*, the Lipizzan horse raises his forehand off the ground, tucks up his forelegs evenly, and then jumps forward on his hind legs. *Spanish Riding School*

standardize the procedure of naming a horse, every stallion has a double name, the first being the lineage name of sire and the second being that of the dam. For mares, LANA follows the Austrian Piber stud farm naming criteria and requires that all mare names should be complementary to the traditional Lipizzan line names and must end in the vowel "a."

The age of the horse shall be its true age as to the day, month, and year. However, for show purposes all horses born during one calendar year of January 1 to December 31 will be considered the same age.

Partbred Requirements

LANA provides a separate division that registers Lipizzan partbreds. They must have a minimum of half Lipizzan breeding with one purebred Lipizzan parent eligible for registration as a purebred. The Lipizzan portion of the pedigree must trace to the recognized male lines and female families of official European stud farms and their approved breeding stock. Partbreds do not have to be DNA tested, but the purebred parent must have blood type or DNA on record in order for the partbred to be registered.

Type and Conformation

By implementing strict standards, LANA encourages the development of the Lipizzan riding horse that is the epitome of beauty and harmony, possessing intelligence and docile temperament. The Lipizzan is noted for its sturdy body, brilliant action, and proud carriage.

Lipizzans are born dark colored and gradually turn white. *Drazen Vukelic/Shutterstock*

The head is usually straight or slightly convex. It is remarkable for its large, prominent, and appealing eyes, which are set wide apart. Its small ears are set rather wide apart and carried alertly; a small muzzle balances a prominent jaw.

The body is rectangular and compact, set off by a powerful, crested neck and muscular shoulders. It presents a picture of strength with broad back and loins, well-rounded, muscular hindquarters, and short, strong legs with well defined tendons and joints.

Not an exceedingly tall horse, the Lipizzan averages between 14.2 and 15.2 hands.

Lipizzans are genetically a type of gray. Born dark, black-brown, brown, or mouse-gray, Lipizzans gradually lighten until the white coat for which they are noted is pronounced somewhere between the ages of six and ten. The white hair coat has become dominant in the bred; only now and then is a black or brown adult produced. As late as two hundred years ago, blacks, browns, chestnuts, duns, piebalds, and skewbalds were found in the adult herd. Today non-white Lipizzans are a rarity, with only a black or bay found occasionally.

This Lipizzan shows brilliant form at the *piaffe* (trotting in place). *Sara Stafford*

Evaluations

Lipizzan breed evaluations have been held in the United States since 1986, and LANA continues to organize and host evaluations around the country. The first evaluation for foals and geldings is for educational purposes and to certify the breeding abilities of their sires and dams.

In the *levade*, the horse coils its loins and positions itself close to the ground, holding the pose at 30 to 35 degrees. *Spanish Riding School*

On European stud farms, horses under the age of three and one-half are evaluated at several points in their development. Likewise in the United States, all evaluations on foals and young horses are marked preliminary. Foals and youngsters two and under should be re-evaluated after age three to obtain their final approval; however, the evaluation process is continuous, even after approval for breeding. It is a constant education and review process, and nearly every horse passes. The purpose of evaluations is to eliminate probable genetic faults, such as really crooked legs.

In-hand evaluations are done when the horse is at liberty to properly judge the trot and canter. This is due to the fact that there are very few professional handlers in the United States, and in most cases, short people do not display a horse any better than a taller handler. (For in-hand classes of other breeds, handlers have been characteristically tall). For the fairest judging, the assistance of several arena helpers is used, and the horses are set free to "strut their stuff" and then be reclaimed by their handlers.

Horses scoring between 60 and 70 may be bred and their foals evaluated. If those horses produce well, they should continue the breeding process. If not, the animals should be used as riding or driving horses.

Horses are judged on:
- Conformation of head, neck, shoulders, withers, front and hind legs, back, loins, frame, and topline
- Breed type (excludes foals and geldings). Breed and type, and masculinity/femininity
- Correctness of gaits walk in-hand, trot in-hand and free, and canter free
- Impulsion and elasticity
- Temperament and obedience
- Overall impression

Evaluations for the Not-So-Classical Lipizzan

First and foremost, the primary purpose of LANA is to register Lipizzan horses, regardless of their body type. Some members prefer the baroque, classical type, while others prefer the more modern, competition type. The view of the judging criteria is that the classical, baroque Lipizzan is the epitome of the breed. Therefore, the further a horse deviates from the classical type, the lower the score will be in the Breed and Type section of the evaluation. Unless a horse is so unlike a Lipizzan that it receives a very low score in the Breed and Type section, it will be approved provided everything else is of good quality.

Credit: Lipizzan Association of North America

OLDENBURG

Oldenburg mare and foal. Inherited excellence is promoted through inspections. *Daniel Johnson*

Oldenburg Horse Breeders' Society

150 Hammocks Drive
West Palm Beach, Florida 33413
www.oldenburghorse.com

The Oldenburg horse belongs to one of Europe's oldest warmblood breeds. It is bred in the far northern part of Germany in the relatively small breeding area of the former kingdom of Oldenburg. An important aspect for Oldenburg's success is its horse breeding philosophy—take the best stallions and mares that can be found and include them into the breed.

Oldenburg never had a state stud or stallions owned by the association. Everything was always based on private stallion owners and the competition among them is probably one secret of the great success of the Oldenburg breed. Unlike other registries in Germany where the breeding programs were completely under government direction, Oldenburg breeding has been in the hands of private breeders and stallions owners since the 1600s. The success of the Oldenburg horse can be attributed to this fact of open competition between stock produced by private studs.

The result is that the Oldenburg sport horse is now one of the most modern and popular riding horses of the world. It is adept in jumping as well as in dressage and seen everywhere in sport horse arenas.

History

The Oldenburg breed began with Graf Johann XVI von Oldenburg (1573–1603) who founded many small breeding farms within the Oldenburg region for the purpose of producing war horses. These horses were given to important rulers and those who had distinguished themselves in battle. Graf Johann used Turkish, Neopolitan, Andalusian, and Danish stallions to improve his Friesian horses, described as being large and strong.

Further development of the Oldenburg breed was attributed to the work of Graf Johann's successor, Herzog Anton Gunther von Oldenburg, in the sixteenth century. He traveled even more extensively, bringing back stallions from Naples, Spain, Poland, England, Tartary, and Barbary (North Africa). He was also well known for his traditional dressage riding, most notably on his Oldenburg stallion, Kranich, which is portrayed with him in a well-known painting. He permitted his tenants and other commoners to use his stallions and soon the seventeenth-century Oldenburgs were in great demand throughout Europe, serving as elegant riding and carriage horses.

From the sixteenth through the eighteenth centuries, Oldenburg horses were mainly bred on private sovereign stud farms and owned by Europe's nobility. One such instance was when Leopold I, King of the Holy Roman Empire, rode through Vienna on his wedding day astride a black Oldenburg stallion. He was followed by his wife who sat in a splendid carriage pulled by eight dark bay Oldenburgs.

The period following was shaped by several important events: an Oldenburg State-appointed licensing committee was conceived and the first stallion approval was decreed by the state in 1820. This committee decided whether or not the stallions presented each year would be allowed to breed for the new society (this was after the Napoleonic wars and restructuring of the land). There was also the introduction of a register of origins in 1861, and the establishment of a foundation for two horse breeding societies by the Horse Breeding Act of April 9, 1897. These two societies merged in 1923 to form today's Verband der Züchter des Oldenburger Pferdes. Further progress in the breed occurred when the first measures towards refinement were introduced in 1935 with the addition of the Thoroughbred horse, Adonis.

Due to the introduction of modern transportation in the twentieth century, the demand for carriage horses dropped. In the early 1960s, the German Oldenburg breeding associations made the decision to produce a modern riding horse and embarked on an extensive cross-breeding program. The purpose of the program and the new breeding goal was to produce an outstanding sport horse.

More Thoroughbred stallions were approved and the turnaround in breeding towards the modern sport horse was underway. Oldenburg mares bred to top European Thoroughbred stallions produced more refinement. The resulting mares were bred to Europe's finest riding horse bloodlines, such as Trakehner, Anglo-Normans, and Anglo-Arabs. But also Hanoverians, Holsteiner, Westphalian, and Dutch stallions were used.

In 2002, it was decided that a separate breeding society dedicated to the pursuit of breeding top jumper horses would be created. It is called the Springpferdezuchtverband Oldenburg International e.V., or OS for short. It is still related to the main Oldenburg breeding society, but it has a separate breeding commission that concentrates on the jumping bloodlines and abilities of the stallions and mares.

Each November, approximately eighty young stallions are presented to the German Oldenburger Verband for three days. They are preselected from more than five hundred and are presented to the commission for stallion licensing. This process has produced the superbly athletic Oldenburg horse that is a successful sport horse in the dressage and jumping arenas around the world.

Today, the German Oldenburger Verband registration commissio) has nearly eight thousand registered mares and is one of the largest breeding associations in Germany (Hanover has approximately fifteen thousand mares, Westphalia has approximately ten thousand). Half of the Oldenburg registered mares live in the Oldenburg area in the northwest of Lower Saxony.

Distinctive Oldenburgs

Towards the end of the 1960s the French stallion, Condor, was proving to be very successful, so Oldenburg stallion owners turned to France to improve their lines. Practically no other breeding area was able to achieve the success Oldenburg reached with stallions of French origin.

Furioso II was the first Anglo-Norman of modern breeding times. Horse breeders the world over still have the highest regard for this sire. French Anglo-Arabians such as Inschallah AA were also used in Oldenburg in small doses with great success. By combining the various bloodlines on the base of Oldenburg mares, breeders were able to produce a horse in a relatively short period of time that now is in the top group of modern sport horse breeds.

In 1986, a privately owned Oldenburg stallion, Donnerhall, became the Deutsche Landwirts-chafts-Gesellschaft (German Agricultural Society) Champion for the first time. Donnerhall, born in 1981, was one of the most successful sires of his generation in Germany. As no other, he combined success in breeding and sport—in 1994 in The Hague, the Netherlands, he was a member of the German gold medal winning dressage team at the World Championships and won the individual bronze medal. He was also a member of the German European Championship team and won the individual bronze medal there as well.

The next legend in the making in the world of sport horse breeding is the Oldenburg bred, licensed, and approved stallion, Sandro Hit. He not only won the World Championships for the six-year-old dressage horses in 1999, but his offspring have dominated the young horse championships and are emerging with great success at Grand Prix in international competition. His daughter, Poetin, won both the German National Championships and the World Championships for five-year-old dressage horses in

2003 before selling for the record price of 2.5 million euros at the PSI auction the same year.

The success of Sandro Hit's daughters continues through the two time German Champion, Silberaster, and Samira, who also broke records winning the German National Championships in 2007 for the six-year-old dressage horses. Judge Christoph Hess commented about Samira, "We've never seen anything like this in this arena!" before awarding her two perfect scores of 10 resulting in an overall score of 9.7.

Sandro Hit's licensed and approved sons are also becoming dominant in the sport horse world. Sir Donnerhall, who combines the lines of Sandro Hit and Donnerhall, was the Reserve Champion of the five-year-old dressage horses at the 2006 World Championships and was the 2006 German National Champion for the same division. He has also proved himself as a sire, having produced the Reserve Champion of the 2007 Oldenburg stallion licensing, Sir Rubin, and the Champion of the 2008 Southern German stallion licensing, Sir Nymphenburg.

Oldenburgs are also well known in the jumper arenas around the world. In the past there have been jumper stars such as the mare, Weihaiwej, who incredibly accomplished the nearly impossible feat of winning double gold at the World Championships in 1994, and Sandro Boy who won the 2006 World Cup by putting in an amazing four clear rounds. More recently Air Jordan Z and Leena successfully competed in the 2007 World Cup in Las Vegas, and after winning individual gold at the Pan American Games, the incredible gelding, Special Ed, brought home the 2008 Olympic Team silver for Canada.

An outstanding stallion, Le Champ Ask, was the champion of the 2008 stallion licensing, and his talent was so clear, his character so assured, that he broke the German breeding society auction record, selling to Denmark for the sum of 1.1 million euros.

Around the globe today, Oldenburg jumpers and dressage horses, such as Salieri, Don Schufro,

The noble Oldenburg, a historic horse with modern athletic talent. *Daniel Johnson*

Silberaster, Deveroux, Don Angelo, Dolomit, and Ringo Starr, put fear into the hearts of competitors. Outstanding athletes such as these and Bonfire, who was ridden to unprecedented wins of five World Cup titles and an individual dressage gold medal in the Olympic Games in Sydney, Australia, are excellent examples of the high standards of breeding from the Oldenburg Verband that will surely continue into the future.

American Registry

In the United States, the Oldenburg breeding philosophy of using the best possible mares and stallions has also become successful. In 1982, the Verband der Zuecnter des Oldenburger Pferdes e.V. (direct English translation is "Oldenburg Horse Breeders Society") registered its first horses in North America. The Oldenburg Horse Breeders' Society (OHBS), using the successful breeding philosophy and breeding goals of the Oldenburger Verband in Germany, have been a strong force in producing top riding horses for the North American market.

The Oldenburg breed is an important part of the sport horse breeding in the United States. Since the Oldenburg breeding philosophy has limited restrictions against good mares or stallions from other Oldenburg accepted breeds, the registry is in the comfortable position of picking the best from what's available.

With the breeding of modern sport horses in North America and with the cross breeding with American Thoroughbreds, it became increasingly important to establish a uniform standard of evaluation and measurement to ensure the highest standards of breeding and consequently, of offspring. Based on this need, the OHBS provides uniform methods and means to evaluate, test, register and measure performance of sport horses participating in jumping, dressage, and eventing using the strict German standards as dictated by the Department of Agriculture. The approach, methods of evaluation, and overall objectives are developed from the many years of successful experiences in Europe.

The OHBS is supported 100 percent by the German Verband breeding director, Dr Wolfgang Schulze-Schleppinghof, as well as experienced breeders in North America. Its standards of measurement and registration are also regulated by the registry systems of the European horse-producing countries.

Only horses that are the sport horse type are eligible for entry into the OHBS. The principal goal of the registry is to assist in the development of top performance horses in North America using the established and effective criteria used in Europe. Horses are presented at specific sites and dates for inspection tests prior to approval of their registration.

Breeding of selected horses is aimed at producing a noble, large-framed and correct horse with dynamic, spacious, and elastic movements. It is well suited for dressage, hunter classes, show jumping, or eventing because of its temperament, character, and rideability.

Criteria for Scoring Mares

Mares need at least a four-generation pedigree of approved bloodlines. They must be three years old or older and may be eligible for one of four mare books: the Main Mare Book is for registered mares with a full pedigree and very good type; the Mare Book is for registered mares with perhaps one score that is lower or an incomplete pedigree; the Pre Mare Book I and Pre Mare Book II are for mares that are not eligible due to reasons of pedigree alone, but their quality must be of very good type. Mares are scored on: head, neck, saddle position, frame, forelegs, hindlegs, breed (sex type), walk in-hand, swing/elasticity, correctness of gaits, and overall impression and development.

Since 2008, the Registry offers mare performance tests for mares at a limited number of locations. All three-year-old or older mares that are registered with OHBS can participate in the Mare Performance Test, which is a one-day event. Basic gaits and free jumping are scored by three judges and rideability is evaluated by a test rider. Eligible mares are presented loose as well as under saddle.

Usually the test starts with the free jumping. Three judges evaluate the jumping ability, style, and technique. This is followed by the under saddle presentation of basic gaits. Mares should be able to lengthen strides in each gait and perform simple dressage movements, such as a three loop serpentine and free walk on a loose rein. The under saddle test is not a dressage test. However the mare should be able to walk, trot, and canter from 10 to 15 minutes. The mare should be presented well balanced and ridden forward in the three basic gaits. During the third and final part of the test, the mare is ridden by the registry's test rider for approximately 5 to 10 minutes.

Criteria for Scoring Foals

Foals are judged on conformation, type, and correctness, as well as swing, elasticity, and athletic ability of movement. Overall impression and development is evaluated as related to age.

Eligibility and Selection of Breeding Stallions

Stallions are eligible for presentation at one of the OHBS stallion inspections if they have a regular registration of a registry that is approved by

Oldenburg five-year-old stallion. *Jane Sommers*

the German Oldenburg Verband with at least a four-generation pedigree. The selection of breeding stallions is undertaken through a series of steps based upon the age, performance, and breeding results of the horse.

The initial inspection (Koerung) of two-and-a-half- and three-year-old stallions is done in-hand, with free jumping and lunging, which began in 2008. The Koerung for older stallions also includes an inspection under saddle. The next step on the way to a lifetime breeding license is passing a thirty-day test for three- and four-year-olds, followed by qualification for the National Championship with a specific high score, or passing a seventy-days test, or alternatively competing at the highest level of sport, finishing within the first three placings. In Dressage, it is also required that the scores must be of a specific high level. These are the three alternative possibilities at the final selection step for breeding stallions, the most sure being the seventy-days test, at this time.

It must be pointed out that although the criteria is tough, this is the only way to ensure that the sport has an influx of high quality horses being produced.

Credit: Oldenburg Horse Breeders' Society

PURA RAZA ESPAÑOLA

The Foundation for the Pure Spanish Horse
4001 Juan Tabo NE, Suite D
Albuquerque, New Mexico 87111
www.prehorse.org

The Pure Spanish Horse is a strong, athletic, and beautiful horse in both appearance and character. It is also called the Pura Raza Española (PRE) in Spain, the United States, and Canada. Perhaps its best quality is its willingness to work with the less than perfect human companions, exhibiting the nobility and grace it joyfully offers while performing anything requested of it, even after days unexercised. This is horse that is easily trained and easily ridden. When riding a PRE, the rider immediately feels a sensation so special that it is like a dream. With any indiscreet cue, the horse responds instantly, compensating its movement to best fit the rider. Immediately, the rider feels as one with the horse.

The Pura Raza Española is a graceful breed, best known for accommodating the rider. *Paco Rey*

The PRE is impressive, with its gallant presence and long flowing mane and tail. It comes in all colors, but mostly gray or white, and has been bred for centuries to bond with, understand, and relate to humans with timeless generosity. It was the majestic horse reserved for kings, queens, and elite government officials to make them look impressive and important. The PRE remains a magnificent animal, deserving of honor for all times.

History

The PRE is descended from one of the most ancient of equine breeds living on the Iberian Peninsula since prehistory, dating back thousands of years. In northeastern Spain, the prototype Spanish horse was painted on the cave walls being led by early man. The Pure Spanish Horse dates its ancestry back to these ancient horses that were esteemed for their quality and appearance since Roman times.

The Pure Spanish Horse's historical use in Spain was first as a farm horse to work with the brave bulls destined for the bull rings. The breed is still used in Spain to fight in the bull ring and still used to work stock on the farms. Back then, it was also used to carry lords into battle, and later in parades, it proudly carried the victors in their moments of triumph. In the Middle Ages, it carried knights and later became the treasured mount of European nobles.

The Pure Spanish Horse was unified as a breed between 1567 and 1593 by the Spanish king, Felipe II. He decided to bring to life the universally idealized historic horse whose image had endured for so long in both bronze sculptures and paintings. He looked at the basic horse bred in Spain, selected the best of those examples that came closest to the ideal, and directed the production of this type horse. He formally established the standards for the breed, which are recognized today in the Pure Spanish Horse.

Concurrent with his breeding program, the humanistic approach was spreading through Spain, and the teachings of the ancient Greek, Xenophon, were put into practice for the treatment and training of these carefully bred horses. This resulted in the Pure Spanish Horse being known and respected for its submission to the aids and the assistance it contributed to its rider.

Horsemen soon realized that the same qualities that made the Pure Spanish Horse a versatile warhorse in its early history could also be valuable in times of peace. It soon became the favorite of the grand riding academies, where dressage and high school riding began and flourished. It was used in dressage competitions and competitive driving in a single- or four-horse hitch. It was also utilized in the distinctly Spanish discipline called the Doma Vaquera—the formalized show ring version of farm work, most closely related to a reining pattern with combined dressage elements.

Today, the Pure Spanish Horse is considered one of the national treasures of Spain, an inheritance handed down from father to son through generations.

In the United States

The first time the Pure Spanish Horse was brought to the United States was in the cargo holds of the voyages of the conquistadors, beginning with the second voyage of Christopher Columbus. Despite its popularity, it did not make its second official appearance in the United States until the late 1960s. In fact, the PRE is one of the rarest breeds in the United States. As a result, many Americans have only seen one in Hollywood films, such as *The Lord of the Rings*, or television programs like *Wizard's First Rule*, with perhaps only a very few having seen a PRE in person.

The PRE, however, is experiencing a rapid growth in popularity in response to an active promotion. Many new owners are discovering the wonderful attributes of the breed at competitions that present an opportunity to show off in dressage and other performance classes.

In the United States there are no bullfights, but PRE horses are found to be adept at all the disciplines one could expect: dressage, hunt seat, saddle seat, driving, parades, trail, and western and English pleasure. Some even excel as open jumpers. The 2008 Summer Olympics brought two PRE horses into the spotlight. The stallion Rociero XV was the first PRE to qualify for the U.S. Olympic Selection Trials, and the stallion Fuego XII represented Spain in dressage at Beijing.

History of the PRE Name

The name "Andalusian" was used interchangeably in the past with "Spanish Horse" when describing the breed. The name "Andalusian" fell out of favor when two major events occurred: one national, one international. The national event in Spain was the growth of the breed in numbers, which meant that it expanded from its ancestral birthplace in the province of Andalusia—specifically the royal stables of Córdoba—to the entire nation of Spain. So as not to show partiality to the breeders in Andalusia, the horse became known as *el caballo de pura raza española*, or the PRE.

When the official Spanish studbook for the breed was first organized in 1911 and published in 1913, the name given to the registry was Caballos de Pura Raza Española (Horses of the Pure Spanish Breed). This is, to this day, the only correct name for the breed. The name has remained the same throughout the twenty-two published volumes of the stud book. It is the official, government-accepted, owner-recognized, national breed association–endorsed name of this breed of horse that is historically and currently produced throughout Spain and now in other countries around the world that adhere to Spanish breed standards and protocols. Even so, some owners continued to refer to the breed as Andalusian.

With the international event of the restoration of democracy in Portugal, there coincided strong national fervor, which ensured that Portugal's horse was named by the ancient Roman name for Portugal, Lusitania. The Portuguese horse from the mid 1970s was from then on formally known as the Lusitano, making a distinct and permanent international separation of horses in the two countries.

A Pura Raza Española stallion shows his stylish capabilities. *Jorge Monaltvo*

The Portuguese stud book, (volume I, published in 1989), was entitled the *Livro Genealógico Português de Equinos: Stud Book da Raca Lusitana.*

From this point forward, the breeders in Spain formally endorsed the idea of no longer using the regional name of Andalusian, but to uniformly use the national name Pura Raza Española (PRE), thereby encompassing breeders in all provinces of Spain. It was owners outside of Spain, who, perhaps because Pura Raza Española was more difficult to pronounce, chose to continue using the easier Andalusian name when referring to the breed. All over the world, however, the breed is called the Pura Raza Española, or PRE. This name has international recognition and translates to English as the Pure Spanish Horse.

Breeds Associated with the PRE

Lusitano, or Puro Sangue Lusitano (PSL): The Lusitano is a purebred horse of Portugal that is closely related to the PRE, as many Spanish horses served as foundation horses for the Lusitano; Portugal, however, considers its breed pure and separate from the PRE, and similarly, Spain recognizes the Puro Sangue Lusitano (PSL) as a pure breed separate from the PRE.

Pure Spanish Portuguese (PSP): The Pure Spanish Portuguese (PSP) is a cross between the PRE and the PSL, although the ratio need not be fifty-fifty. It is recognized in the International Andalusian and Lusitano Horse Association (IALHA) as a purebred Andalusian. This horse is not eligible for the revision or valoration process conducted by the Spanish government for the PRE, or for the similar process held by the Portuguese for the Lusitano.

The Spanish Horse Brand

There was a great confluence of events in 1998. In the United States, the Foundation for the Pure Spanish Horse was formed, and in Spain, D. Juan Carlos Altamirano published his monumental treatise, *Historia Y Origen del Caballo Español: Las caballerizas reales de Cordoba (The History and Origin of the Spanish Horse: The Royal Stables of Cordoba).*

In this seminal and definitive work, Altamirano describes the codification of the Spanish Horse under the reign of King Felipe II. Beginning with his royal decree of November 28, 1567, the breed was formalized, the standards were set, and a royal stable was established in the city of Cordoba. The brand for this stable was an "R" for *Real* (Royal) inside a "C" for Cordoba. A *corona* (crown) was added to the top of the "C" as an additional royal stamp. This brand was placed on horses that were produced in the royal stables, and was the first brand used on the first horses of the now organized breed.

Centuries later, when the royal stable of Cordoba was no longer a breeding station, the brand fell into disuse, then oblivion. It was Altamirano, who, in his studies, found the brand and re-registered it in his name. On hearing of the works and efforts of the Foundation for the Pure Spanish Horse in the

United States, he generously donated this brand to the organization for its sole and exclusive use.

Four years later in 2002, the royal stables in Cordoba were reopened and now serve as a home to the breed again. Altamirano has made a second and final gift of this logo to the royal stables for its use.

So the circle is complete: the brand associated with the birth of the breed has been revived and helped with the education of owners around the world through the works of the Foundation for the Pure Spanish Horse. It is now again at home in the place of its birth: the royal stables of Cordoba, Spain. Its use is authorized for only these two entities.

Registry Requirements

PRE horses registered with the Spanish stud book in Spain should have a Spanish passport for equines, which includes the *carta*, or registration certificate, within it. In 2007, the management of the Spanish PRE stud book was transferred and assigned to a Spanish breeder's group as the managing entity. Horses of the Spanish PRE stud book are qualified for inclusion by virtue of birth to registered parents and have the opportunity to be included on their own merits as reproducers by compliance with the requirements of *valoración* at their maturity.

In the United States in 2008, a new and independent worldwide PRE registry, the PRE Mundial, was created and is administered by the Foundation for the Pure Spanish Horse. Horses registered in the PRE Mundial Registry receive a *carta mundial*.

PRE horses have to pass a physical inspection and genetic testing as foals to receive their Spanish passport or *carta mundial*, which are recognized internationally as a guarantee ensuring a horse's lineage and authenticity. This process is called Inscription and is most often done when the foal is still nursing from its dam. When the horse reaches adulthood (usually three or four years old), it is examined again for minimum size, quality, transmissible faults, and breed fidelity. When it passes this approval, it is said to be *apto*, or qualified.

Standards

The PRE horse's physical appearance and flashy action make it one of the world's most desirable riding horses. Its conformation hints at the breed's capabilities. It is strongly built, yet elegant.

Size: Minimum height at the withers for males is 1.52 meters (59.84 inches, or almost 15 hands) and for females is 1.50 meters (59.05 inches, or 14.3 hands). The typical PRE stands 15.2 to 16.2 hands.

Color: About 70 percent of PRE horses are gray or white, 20 percent are bay, 5 percent are black, and 5 percent are chestnut, palomino, or dun. Grays and whites are born dark and lighten as they age, often going through various lightening stages. Some do not stop changing when they turn white, but continue on to develop freckles.

Head: The classically beautiful head is unique and an instant identifier. It is of medium length, rectangular, and lean. In profile, the face is straight or softly convex, moderately narrow, and without excess flesh. It has a broad forehead and well placed ears. The eyes are large, alive, and triangular, placed within an orbital arch. The comma-shaped nostrils can expand downward to bring in quantities of air, providing strength for extended efforts. The unique breed characteristics are obvious in the shape and dexterity of the upper lip, the sensitivity of the mouth, and the point of the chin.

Neck: The neck is reasonably long and broad, yet elegant and well crested in stallions. The mane is thick and abundant.

Body: Well defined withers precede a short back, and the quarters are broad and strong. It has strong boned legs, good slope to the shoulder, deep heart-girth, and round, powerful haunches. The croup is rounded and of medium length. The tail is abundant, set low, and lies tightly against the body.

Disqualifications: Having a fallen crest (accumulation of excess fat in the crest), inverted or U-neck, monorchidism, or cryptorchidism will be grounds for disqualification of a horse.

Credit: The Foundation for the Pure Spanish Horse and Gareth A. Selwood

SPANISH-NORMAN

Spanish-Norman Horse Registry, Inc.
P.O. Box 985
Woodbury, Connecticut 06798
www.spanish-norman.com

Thundering across the pages of history comes the epic warhorse of the ages, the medieval knight's noble steed—the Spanish-Norman Horse. Valiant horse chosen by battling knights, powerful warhorse of the crusaders, proud mount of the conquistadors—all describe the gallant horse that carried Spanish blood in its veins long ago. This courageous horse was immortalized in paintings, statues, and sculptures of the Middle Ages, leaving an indelible mark of the chivalry and pageantry from that era. It was a horse of extraordinary majesty, incredible power, and awesome presence. As magnificent as it was, the knight's horse of the Middle Ages did not survive the ensuing years after it last pounded over the battlefields of ancient Europe when it was so prominent.

Today, however, this magical horse has been re-created by blending the genes of the Andalusian of Spain and the Percheron of France. Research has proven that both the indigenous Spanish horse of the Iberian Peninsula (now called the Andalusian) and the French Le Perche horse carry a similar genetic strain of Barb blood left from the Moorish invasions. The Andalusian brings its perfect combination of artistry, elegance, and style to the breed, reflecting the principles of lightness and collection, which are important attributes of classical art

and dressage. The Percheron contributes its profound size, strength, and bone density. Its gentle, people-loving temperament adds stability.

With the union of these remarkable foundation lines, the historic warhorse of long ago has been brought to life once again in the Spanish-Norman. This unique sport horse is the genetic phenotype of the extinct Norman warhorse. It is an exclusive, rare breed that is a living symbol of the famous medieval horse now recreated and again making an impact in the equestrian world.

History

When the Moors invaded Spain in 711 AD, their Barb mounts were small, agile, and fiery, possessing great stamina. As Islamic forces advanced into Spain and France from North Africa, Europeans were faced with the Barb horse that was unsurpassed in combat. Hardy, courageous, and powerful, it was quick to respond to the rider's commands,

The Spanish-Norman is a gallant, strong, and spectacular breed.
Linda Osterman Hamid

and had an uncanny ability to engage its hindquarters and strike out in any direction. Confronted with this remarkable Moorish warhorse, Europeans realized the importance of breeding horses for battle. When the Moors lost their first conflict in 718, the victors were awarded the invaluable prize of Barb breeding stock and began combining them with their own horses. It was by this means of conquests and defeats through the centuries that the Barb horse became a great legacy in Europe of the Moorish invasions.

In this way, ancient Spanish horses were infused with Barb blood. It was not until the year 1492 when the Reconquista, or reclaiming of Al-Andalus (the Arabic name for the Iberian Peninsula), was complete, leaving in its wake the magnificent Iberian Horse that now possessed Barb blood, which would later be known as the Andalusian and Lusitano. Research shows these early Spanish horses influenced the development of the Norman horses of medieval France.

Barb blood was also used on native French horses, which contributed to the equine type that would come to be known as Percheron, after the Le Perche district of France. The mighty Percheron was renowned for its excellence on the battlefield. It was instrumental to the Norman invasion of England in 1066, which was carried out by fierce warriors called "destriers" mounted on warhorses. By the 1840s, these heavy horses were imported to the United States and were initially called Normans, but shortly reverted back to the name Percheron. In 1990, blood-typing studies on Percherons by Dr. Gus Cothran at the University of Kentucky confirmed that indeed the Percheron carried a Barb genetic link.

Therefore both horses of Andalusia and Normandy possessed an infusion of Barb blood from the Moorish invasions. With their common oriental ancestry, breeding Andalusians to Percherons produces amazing offspring approximating a type of the old Norman horse. Thus the Spanish-Norman breed recreates the phenotype of the medieval knight's charger.

Breed Ambassadors

Spanish-Normans are "the warhorse of the ages as the sport horse of today." They are attracting attention and admiration of equine aficionados worldwide. They can be found presenting the colors in breed exhibitions at the Kentucky Horse Park, mounted police competitions, performances at Equine Affaire's Fantasia, and in mounted medieval games or reining competitions in full reproduction armor or tournament garb.

They also perform in reining, dressage, western riding, open jumping, eventing, trail, field hunting, pleasure riding, parades, costumed exhibitions, and sidesaddle demonstrations.

Spain's premier, all-breed horse publication, *Ecuestre*, featured an extensive article with color photos entitled, "Spanish-Norman, El Retorno del Caballo Medieval," in its November 1998 issue. Other major equine publications in the United States, Canada, the United Kingdom, Germany, and Poland have spotlighted the Spanish-Norman.

The most famous Spanish-Norman to date is Romántico H. H. F., owned by breed cofounders Linda and Allan Hamid of Connecticut. The magnificent 16.1-hand gray stallion is an excellent example of the Spanish-Norman breed. He is the sole U.S.-bred horse of Spanish descent to win a U.S. Equestrian Team (USET) ribbon. This was won in Freestyle Reining at the June 2000 Festival of Champions at the USET Olympic Training Center in Gladstone, New Jersey. Donning medieval armor, he also competed at the 1999 All American Quarter Horse Congress in Columbus, Ohio, and won a fourth place ribbon in Open Freestyle Reining. Popular with audiences of all ages, Romántico has presented exhibitions at the Greenwich Polo Club in Connecticut, the Equine Affaire and the Fleet Jumper Classic, both in Massachusetts, and the BreyerFest in Kentucky. At numerous charity events, he has patiently posed for photos with children, exemplifying the outstanding temperament of the breed. As the Breed Ambassador, he also was selected for the collector's limited-edition Breyer horse model in 2005, honoring the

Spanish-Norman breed; he was immortalized in fine porcelain wearing his signature armor depicting the heritage of the Spanish-Norman breed.

Another example of the breed is Agincourt H. H. F., an American gelding that was exported to France where he now competes in three-day eventing. This exportation of a Spanish-Norman to Europe is an impressive tribute to the breed and an example of the competitive capabilities of the Spanish-Norman.

Sir Norman of Tiverton is a Spanish-Norman Horse that competes in Open Jumping classes at the 3 feet 6 inch and 3 feet 9 inch levels. His rider admires the Spanish-Norman for its natural ability, tractability, and good mind. He comments that Sir Norman "always gives 100 percent and is a brave, fun horse with a wonderful personality who craves attention and affection from his fans."

Another ambassador of the Spanish-Norman breed is Victoria of Fox Run from Kentucky. For several years, this lovely mare has represented the Spanish-Norman breed at the Kentucky Horse Park in Lexington, Kentucky, greeting visitors daily from around the world and participating in the Parade of Breeds.

After reading an article on the breed in a German horse publication, Katharina and Horst Fehring of Germany went to France and purchased the lovely Percheron mare, Helva de Fauveliere, to be bred to their Andalusian stallion, Orgulloso XL, imported from Spain. The Fehrings established their Spanish-Norman breeding farm in Germany with the goal of becoming the first breeders of Spanish-Normans in Europe. Their first Spanish-Norman was foaled in 2003.

Characteristics

The Spanish-Norman retains the attributes of the Andalusian, which possesses class, grace, and harmony. Renowned for its reliability and stamina, the Percheron adds its great size and stability. With the panache of the Andalusian and the easygoing work ethic of the Percheron, the Spanish-Norman projects the image of a large, exquisite horse. It has the

natural collection, athleticism, beauty, and elegance to compete in almost every discipline. Quite often the individual Spanish-Norman excels at more than one discipline or is simply a good all-around pleasure mount and companion.

The majority of Spanish-Norman fans are from the baby boomer generation who find the breed fits their needs. The Spanish-Norman is steady and willing, providing true companionship for those who may be rediscovering their passion for horses after taking time off for their career or to raise a family. One owner states of her second-level dressage horse, "I purchased my Spanish-Norman mare for myself as a new rider at fifty years old because of her temperament and I just fell in love with her. As a woman who never rode in her life until fifty, my Spanish-Norman has become my friend and partner. To me, she is a horse of a lifetime and she always draws attention wherever we go."

Men seem particularly attracted to the Spanish-Norman, possibly due to its historic persona of once being the knight's battle charger, but also because of the horse's powerful presence. It is the perfect mount for larger men who feel "under-horsed" with lighter breeds, but also want a competitive edge with the style and athleticism that the breed provides.

More important than all its other accomplishments and attributes is the special relationship between horse and human that the Spanish-Norman provides. It is very rare to find a trained adult horse available on the market, since most owners have a deep relationship with their Spanish-Norman.

Registry

Registry co-founder, Linda Hamid of Connecticut, was first attracted to the Andalusian horse while studying at the University of Madrid in 1965, and years later she introduced her husband, Allan Hamid, to the breed. An avid horseman, historian, and educator, Allan did research on the medieval warhorse. In the late 1980s, the Hamids began breeding Percheron mares to their Spanish imported Andalusian stallion, Embajador IX, of

Hamid Hill Farm, Ltd. This stallion was later to become the first foundation sire of the Spanish-Norman breed.

After the Hamids learned of the research at the University of Kentucky Gluck Equine Center that proved the Percheron of France, the Andalusian of Spain, and the Lusitano of Portugal shared common blood markers, they established the Spanish-Norman Horse Registry, Inc., in 1991. Its main goal is to produce an outstanding modern sport horse that retains the presence, physical prowess, and mental abilities of the classic medieval Norman warhorse.

The breed has since grown, with currently 135 Andalusian stallions registered as foundation sires of the Spanish-Norman Horse Registry. Additionally, there are Spanish-Norman horses located across the United States and Canada, with a few in Germany, England, Spain and France.

Registry Requirements

A Spanish-Norman must be a minimum of 50 percent Andalusian. A Spanish-Norman can be dual-registered as a Half-Andalusian with the International Andalusian and Lusitano Horse Association (IALHA) and compete in that organization's shows. Besides IALHA events, it can also compete in dressage, jumping, and/or any discipline at all-breed open shows. To establish and revitalize the former prestige and ability of the breed, an annual trophy honors the competing Spanish-Norman with the highest points.

Percheron mares must be registered with the Percheron Horse Association of America (PHAA) or the Canadian Percheron Association. Spanish-Norman mares can also be bred to an Andalusian stallion. A rare second-generation Spanish-Norman can be produced by breeding a Spanish-Norman to a Spanish-Norman.

Breed Characteristics

The Spanish-Norman embodies the proud heritage of its noble ancestors. It combines the beauty, boldness, and natural collection of the Andalusian with the Percheron's great willingness to work, as well as its size and excellent, stable disposition. Endowed with the unique combination of presence with docility, the Spanish-Norman possesses outstanding character and temperament, qualities essential to a successful performance horse. It is an athletic breed, yet a horse of substance and gentleness.

Height: The majestic Spanish-Norman stands between 15.3 and 17 hands.

Color: It is predominantly gray with some bays and blacks.

Head: The head shows a slightly convex to straight profile. It has large, expressive eyes and fine, thin ears that are of medium length.

Neck: It has a medium length neck. The mane is thick, luxuriant, and often wavy. A distinguished regal crest is characteristic of the breed.

Body: The body is muscular and short coupled with strong hindquarters, sloping shoulder, ample heart girth, and broad chest. The tail is usually abundant, long, and low set.

Legs: Sturdy feet and legs are present, and strong, wide hooves are the norm.

Movement: The Spanish-Norman is bred to move freely from the shoulder with elastic, fluid movement and impulsion. It displays agility, engagement, cadence, and elevation with extension, and projects an image of harmony, balance, and symmetry.

Disposition: It has a keen aptitude for learning, a strong work ethic, tractability, exceptional stamina, and enthusiasm for performing. It displays loyalty, affection, and an understanding of its human partner that is unique and seems to appear in a large majority of horses in the breed.

As a versatile sport horse, the Spanish-Norman has the potential to excel in a variety of equine disciplines including jumping, eventing, dressage, reining, and driving. An impressive exhibition and parade horse, the Spanish-Norman also performs in historic re-enactments, jousting, and medieval games.

Credit: Linda Osterman Hamid and Spanish-Norman Horse Registry, Inc.

SWEDISH WARMBLOOD

The Swedish Warmblood is a stellar jumper and athlete. *Courtesy Carol Reid*

Swedish Warmblood Association of North America
P.O. Box 788
Socorro, New Mexico 87801
www.swanaoffice.org

Breeders of the Swedish Warmblood Horse have good reasons to be proud: they and their predecessors have developed a sound, intelligent horse proven to be internationally competitive in all disciplines of equestrian sport and representing a well established type. The brilliance of the Swedish Horse is derived from a highly selective breeding program established more than a century ago. Only the very best stallions are approved for breeding after passing scrupulous tests and evaluations.

Originally the breeding was focused on producing durable cavalry horses, but at an early stage, more focus on top level sport horses began. Today Sweden has a long tradition in the latter field, along with a tradition of patience among breeders and trainers. Young Swedish Warmbloods are allowed to mature without stress and thus are able to work at their full potential for many years. Olympic statistics provide significant evidence of this fact.

Sweden's elaborate performance and progeny testing of stallions is based on both scientific analysis and practical experience. It stands as a guarantee for the further development of the breed. Credit is not only given to the breeding work done by Sweden's forefathers, but also points to performance based selections followed by sophisticated progeny testing. The result is the ability of the Swedish Warmblood to provide stellar performances in dressage, show-jumping, or three-day eventing, due to its rare combination of soundness, character, and heart—qualities appreciated by any rider.

History

The Swedish Warmblood is one of the oldest warmblood breeds in the world. Archeological evidence has been found showing the existence of horses in what is now Sweden dating to 4000 BC. Its history closely follows that of Scandinavian settlers. It was a simple working animal, meeting the basic needs of the people trying to survive the difficult conditions of the era and environment. The Scandinavian horse was small; as late as the sixteenth century it was 12 to 14 hands tall. It was a high-spirited and hardy breed, primarily used on farms.

In the sixteenth century, a program began to improve the quality of the native horses. The major centers of Swedish Warmblood breeding at that time were at the royal stud farms of Kungsör and Strömsholm. By royal decree, stallions were prohibited in large areas around the stud farms. Friesians were then imported from the Netherlands to increase the size of the native stock, and during the seventeenth century, Spanish horses were introduced for size and elegance.

In 1658 following the peace treaty with the Danes in Roskilde, Denmark, the Swedish king, Carl X Gustaf, ordered a royal stud to be established at Flyinge, now part of Sweden. Horses had previously been bred at Flyinge when it was Danish since the twelfth century when the Danish archbishops held a fortified stronghold with mounted troops there.

Sweden was plagued by unusually severe weather in the 1600s, even for this cold country, making it difficulty to produce quality horses. During this time, there was also heavy warfare, and the military campaign required about seven thousand horses. The demand for cavalry horses quickly exceeded the breeding capability of the little nation. Although Swedish horses had earned the reputation as resilient and dependable animals, Swedes were producing horses considerably smaller than those in the rest of Europe, and warfare necessitated large, robust horses.

The growth and shaping of the horse occurred more precisely with its use in the cavalry, which is when the history of the Swedish Warmblood truly began. By carefully selecting Thoroughbred and other warmblood horses for fresh blood, the Swedish military bred stallions which produced comfortable riding horses for the army. Farmers owned the mares and the army bought offspring suitable for its activities. The larger draft breeds were excluded. Due to increasing differences in needs between the two largest users of horses in Sweden—the army and farmers—the Swedish breeding program was divided. For centuries, the breed continued and was specifically developed for riding, while most other warmblood breeds at times were bred to be draft horses for farm work.

In the early 1800s, the Swedish government ordered the implementation of an organized breeding program for the nation. By this time, Sweden had adopted a policy of neutrality while most of Europe was occupied with the Napoleonic Wars. This translated to very little foreign stock available for breeding, with only Russia agreeing to sell two hundred horses to Sweden. This resulted in thirty-two stallions being sent to Flyinge and Strömsholm during this time.

A former cavalry officer and veterinarian, Clas Adam Ehrengranat, served as head of Flyinge from 1817 to 1837 and influenced the evolution of Swedish horses well beyond the Russian imports. Under his leadership, stallions were provided to cavalry units for their own military breeding stock as well as to farmers to increase horses in the country. Ehrengranat introduced horse biomechanics to Sweden, and his articles on horse movement helped mold Sweden's warhorse into the sport horse of modern times. They also helped preserve the French art of riding, a foundation to dressage, after it was nearly lost during the French Revolution.

As technology of war changed, so did the military role of the Swedish horse. The influence of outside breeds began with Thoroughbred imports, which increased significantly during the 1830s and were embraced for their rideability. This contributed to the final departure from the work horse Sweden had bred for so long. The military also began importing Anglo-Norman (now known as Selle Francais), Hanoverian, and Trakehner stallions to improve their stock. In order to direct the breeding efforts and consolidate the different breeds, the Swedish government began an examination system in 1874. This resulted in several excellent saddle breeds, including the Swedish Warmblood.

A complete register of broodmares and their foals was instituted in 1894 and the first official stud book for the Swedish Warmblood in which inspected and approved stallions and mares were entered was also published in the late 1800s.

At the turn of the century, the role of the cavalry diminished, and the Swedish horse had to adapt to new demands from the armed forces. Officers now wanted a lighter, more elegant horse for the new style of riding that became popular in the early 1900s, eventually known as dressage. The army also reduced their warmblood force by more than 60 percent, forcing farmers to consider producing work horses to stay in business. Since the Swedish army was the primary market for warmbloods, it established rider associations to educate Swedish breeders on training and breeding sport horses. This was an incentive to market trained horses, increasing the production of warmbloods in large numbers instead of work horses. A new sport horse type was developed with the goal of competition in jumping, dressage, and eventing circles.

The Swedish Warmblood association, Avelsföreningen för Svenska Varmblodiga Hästen (ASVH), was formed in 1928 by breeders, with encouragement from the army, to promote the development of uniform mares of high standard.

In the period between the world wars, the ASVH continued to focus on the production of excellent riding horses at a time when other warmbloods were bred primarily as agricultural draft horses. The Swedish cavalry remained the dominant force in international competitions throughout the first half of the twentieth century, until the army stopped using horses in 1972. Since then, the breeding program in Sweden has been fully overseen by the ASVH. Today the ASVH, which is also a registry, supports the development of the Swedish Warmblood.

In the last century, two stallions that have had the most influence on the modern Swedish Warmblood type were Humanist, born in 1916 in Trakehnen, Germany, and imported to Sweden in 1927, and Utrillo, born in 1962 in Hanover, Germany, and later imported to Sweden. Combined, these two stallions are responsible for much of what has made the Swedish Warmblood famous. The internationally renowned stallion, Gaspari, born in 1949 in Sweden (sired by Parad, son of Humanist), is probably the most famous Swedish sire. Gaspari was widely sought after in his day and produced many Olympic horses in several different countries.

There are currently about 5,000 mares bred in Sweden every year, resulting in approximately 3,500 Swedish Warmblood foals born annually just within Sweden. From this number, ASVH still manages to stay in the top ten in global stud book rankings for dressage and jumping.

In the United States

Dr. Jan Philipsson of Sweden was the first to promote Swedish Warmbloods in North America, and in the late 1970s, Anne Gribbons became the first representative for ASVH in North America. By 1981, there were enough Swedish Warmbloods in North America to hold the first ASVH inspection there, and increased interest led the ASVH to appoint more representatives in North America. In 1994, the Swedish Warmblood Association of North America (SWANA) was formed and became a sub-organization under the direction of ASVH.

Highly versatile, Swedish Warmbloods have a competitive spirit in eventing. *Courtesy Carol Reid*

SWANA continues the traditions of ASVH, employing its breeding committee for inspections to maintain consistency of the breed. Yearly inspections by ASVH representatives are now held in several locations in North America. Approximately 150 horses are registered annually in the United States, and the future of the Swedish Warmblood horse in North America looks bright.

As a Performance Horse

In numbers, this is a small breed compared with other European breeds, yet Swedish Warmblood horses are competing well in the world. Mostly recognized as world-class dressage horses, more Swedish Warmblood competitive jumpers are taking the stage. Large numbers of these horses are reaching the Federation Equestre Internationale (FEI, the governing body for international competition) levels in competition every year, a direct result of centuries of skillful management.

Olympic statistics provide the most striking proof of excellent performances by Swedish Warmblood horses on the international scene. Ever since the equestrian sports were introduced into the Olympic Games by Swedish horseman Clarence von Rosen in 1912, Swedish horses have been very successful, especially in dressage and three-day eventing. In total, Swedish horses have captured no less than seven individual gold medals in dressage and four in three-day eventing.

So far, there have been few Olympic Games or World Championships without Swedish Warmblood horses in the top ten. A Swedish team became the European Champions in three-day eventing in 1983. In the 1988 Seoul Olympic Games, thirteen Swedish Warmbloods competed in dressage, and six won medals.

Swedish teams in single-horse carriage driving have dominated the sport globally in the last few years. Also, a driving team of Swedish Warmbloods won the gold medal in the Four-In-Hand Combined Driving event at the World Equestrian Games 1990 and the World Championships in 2000.

Show jumpers bred in Sweden today compete with success and have taken team silver medals in both the European Championship 2001 and the World Equestrian Games 2002. Swedish Warmblood, H&M Butterfly Flip was third in the World Cup finals in Las Vegas 2003.

Breeding Program

To meet the needs of competition and recreational riders, the ASVH breeding program has developed into what is perhaps the most sophisticated of its kind in the world. It has an efficient selection system utilizing modern genetic principles rather than closed book breeding. The three cornerstones of the program are the stud book, selection procedure, and progeny testing of the stallions.

In contrast to most other riding breeds of Europe, the Swedish Warmblood has a unique tradition of a consolidated type specifically developed for the purpose of riding. Thus the breeding result is very predictable. The stud book is also open to

This superlative-looking stallion is a good example of the Swedish Warmblood. *Courtesy Carol Reid*

acceptance of carefully selected individuals of other breeds. No matter what the breed—Thoroughbreds, Hanoverians, Trakehners, or Anglo Normans—the individual must serve the purpose to preserve the desired type and performance qualities.

Since 1983, the ASVH has extended its services to North America, which now has its own mares, foals, and stallions recorded in their own part of the stud book. Mares and stallions are listed under their dams until approved for breeding, at which time they receive their registration number.

Registry Overview

ASVH is a performance-based sport horse breeding program. Its goal is to produce noble, correct, durable, warmblood horses with rideability, performance-minded temperaments and good gaits and/or jumping ability that can compete successfully at the international level in both dressage and jumping.

The Swedish Warmblood Horse breeding standard of today is the result of selective breeding for more than a century. The current breeding program is a progressive mixture of tradition, experience, and scientific approaches aiming at a continuous improvement of the breed for all disciplines of riding.

In order to give the best service to American and Canadian breeders and owners, the association performs an inspection tour of North America on an annual basis. Some of the most experienced and knowledgeable judges are used for this purpose, and their advice is invaluable for keeping high standards of breeding in North America.

Breeders have unique scientific tools at their disposal for selecting the appropriate horses for breeding. Data collected from the Three-Year-Old Test, the Quality Test, and the Stallion Performance Test (SPT), along with competition results, are computed into the BLUP index (best linear unbiased prediction) of each potential breeding horse. These indices are published on the internet.

The stud book contains about five thousand mares, which are entered after having a foal by an approved stallion that has been judged. Foals by licensed Swedish Warmblood stallions out of registered Thoroughbred mares, as well as those of several other warmblood breeds with four known generations, can be registered.

There are approximately 145 living licensed stallions in Sweden and 35 in North America. Every year around two hundred pre-selected three-year-olds are tested in Sweden for soundness, gaits, jumping, and rideability, after which ten or twenty are chosen. In North America, similar inspections are held annually throughout the continent.

Stallions are continually evaluated based on their offspring's performance. In Sweden this is done through so-called quality tests like stallion approvals and through the recording of the offspring's show performance. Approximately fifteen thousand horses have participated in Quality testing, and the average score for all stallions is 100. Scores are given for conformation, gaits (dressage), jumping, and temperament. The overall score is computed and published as soon as a stallion has had fifteen of his get (offspring) tested.

Quality test scores are, in most instances, well correlated to the ranking by the offspring's show performance. The scores are calculated as BLUP, which nowadays, in the Swedish breeding evaluation, refers to Quality testing. The Quality testing is not performed in North America for geographic reasons and is substituted by the Three-Year-Test, which is suitable for North America and was introduced in the year 2002.

All horses to be registered must be DNA tested, as must their biological parents. Qualified horses can be branded with the ASVH crown logo, but it is optional.

Standards

Swedish Warmbloods come in all colors, but mostly chestnut and bay. Buckskins and palominos are rare. Most horses stand between 15.3 and 16.3 hands, with the average being about 16.2 hands. The breeding goal of ASVH uses conformation, gaits, and jumping ability as its criteria, regardless of size and color.

A horse of international quality is one that is noble, correct, and sound. It excels in its competitive temperament, rideability, and movement and/or jumping ability. Considering the breed's principal qualities, it is a highly versatile horse that has been shown successfully and distinguishes itself in all major equestrian disciplines: dressage, jumping, three-day eventing, and carriage driving.

The character of the Swedish Warmblood is friendly and sensitive, yet also competitive. It shows a positive attitude, but does demand a certain amount of "horse sense" from its rider. If treated right, the Swedish Warmblood will try its best, whether at a local, lower-level show, or in the Olympics.

Stallions: There are no specific defects present in the Swedish Warmblood, but there are, and have been for many years, strict guidelines to ensure that no stallions with osteochondrosis (OCD) are allowed to breed. Stallions with other potential genetic defects, such as testicular hernias, are prevented from breeding as well.

The relatively new, revised selection program for breeding stallions focuses on selecting talents in either jumping or gaits, thereby keeping up with modern demands for more specialized horses.

Three-year-old stallions undergo a three-day SPT that includes a veterinary inspection, judging for conformation, free jumping, and gaits under their own rider. They are graded for type, head, neck and body extremities, walk, and trot. Approved stallions receive a one-year breeding permit. Other stallions are judged on further criteria and are awarded breeding allowances accordingly. Owners can decide whether the stallion should continue to be tested for dressage or jumping. Dressage stallions are shown in gaits and jumping stallions are shown jumping.

For each stallion, a separate index for its performance in dressage and in jumping is computed. Approved stallions are presented on the day of keuring and at ASVH stallions show. All entering stallions have their pedigree carefully evaluated by the inspection committee, and this information is incorporated in the overall impression of the horse.

Mares: Mares are judged in-hand when three years old and judged on conformation, free canter,

Swedish Warmbloods are dynamic performance horses. This one is doing the extended trot. *Courtesy Carol Reid*

free jumping, and a simple riding test. The riding test is optional, but in order to receive a diploma, the horse must be shown under saddle. The test serves as a training goal for the young horse and is also a valuable tool in selecting young mares for breeding. The best mares in dressage and jumping qualify to go to the Sport and Breeding Championships held in Flyinge, the Swedish National Stud.

At four and five years of age, the mare is examined through the Quality Test. It is judged on health, conformation, gaits under a rider, and either jumping under a rider or free jumping. Rideability and temperament are also evaluated. The owner receives valuable advice from veterinarians and judges on the horse's future potential and suitability for either dressage or jumping disciplines, as well as information on how to proceed with its training.

Five-year-old mares that have had a foal are especially welcomed to be shown at the Quality Test, which is ultimately a performance test for mares. The best mares qualify for the Sport and Breeding Championships.

Credit: Swedish Warmblood Association of North America

THOROUGHBRED

A British stallion racehorse. Thoroughbreds are lithe, supple, and built for distance. *Ron Mesaros*

The Jockey Club
821 Corporate Drive
Lexington, Kentucky 40503
www.jockeyclub.com

The Thoroughbred is a brilliant and versatile breed, renowned for its ability to carry speed over a variety of distances. Although primarily associated with racing, the Thoroughbred is also popular and ideally suited for many disciplines beyond the racetrack. With courage, determination, and will, coupled with fluid coordination and balance, the Thoroughbred is highly prized by horse people in the non-racing Olympic equestrian disciplines of eventing, show jumping, and dressage. The breed also makes ideal hunters, polo mounts, police horses, and recreational horses. Due to its physical prowess, the Thoroughbred has been used to create new breeds and upgrade others, but its forte has always been racing and athletic performance.

Editors Note: *The Principal Rules and Requirements of The American Stud Book* contains the official rules for Thoroughbred breeding and registration in North America. The Jockey Club recommends that owners and breeders consult the online edition of *The Principal Rules and Requirements of The American Stud Book*, available at http://www.jockeyclub.com/registry.asp?section=3, for the most current rules of the stud book.

History

The Thoroughbred's ancestry traces back more than three hundred years to three foundation stallions—the Darley Arabian, the Godolphin Arabian, and the Byerly Turk. Named for their respective owners, Thomas Darley, Lord Godolphin, and Capt. Robert Byerley, these stallions were imported to England in the late 1600s and early 1700s. Ancestry of all Thoroughbreds today can be traced through the male line to one or more of these three Arabian stallions that lived more than two centuries ago.

The Byerly Turk lived from 1680 to 1696. At the siege of Buda in Hungary, Captain Byerley captured him from the Turks, and the horse became known as the Byerly Turk. In spite of his name, he was probably an Arabian. Captain Byerley reportedly rode the stallion at the Battle of the Boyne in 1690 and later brought him to Britain. Although not bred to many mares, he distinguished himself as a sire and carried the captain's name into Thoroughbred history. (Due to a printer's error, the Byerly Turk's name was registered in the General Stud Book without the final "e.") The Byerly Turk founded a line of Thoroughbreds, the most distinguished of which was Herod, a descendant that proved to be a very successful sire himself.

The Darley Arabian lived from 1700 to 1733. He was bought by Thomas Darley in Aleppo, Syria, in 1704. He was the second of the three foundation stallions to be imported to England, being sent by Darley from Syria to Yorkshire, England, where he was bred to numerous mares. The most successful matings were with Betty Leeds, which resulted in two very important colts, Flying Childers and Bartlet's Childers. Approximately 90 percent of all Thoroughbreds today are descended through Flying Childers and his great-great grandson, Eclipse. As such, the Darley Arabian is the most important of the three foundation stallions in terms of his lasting influence on the Thoroughbred breed.

The Godolphin Arabian (also called Barb) lived from 1724 to 1753. He was foaled in Yemen and given by the Bey of Tunis to the king of France as a gift. Apparently something went amiss, as one story tells of the horse being relegated to pulling a lowly water cart in Paris. The carthorse was admired and bought by an Englishman named Edward Coke, who brought him to England. Coke subsequently presented him to the Earl of Godolphin, at whose stud he was bred to several distinguished mares. He sired the champion mare Aelima, that was imported to Maryland in 1750. Mated to the mare, Roxana, the Godolphin Arabian sired Lath, the greatest racehorse in England after Flying Childers. Another mating of these two produced Cade, the sire of the great Matchem that carried on the line of the Godolphin Arabian. In 1850, it was remarked that "the blood of the Godolphin Arabian is in every stable in England."

Out of some two hundred Oriental horses imported to England between 1660 and 1750, only the direct descendants of these three foundation stallions contributed to the Thoroughbred's greatness. All three originated in the Middle East and were bred to Britain's native sprinting mares, which were very probably Scottish Galloways, with the resultant foals being the first Thoroughbreds, per se. The breed was noticed for its ability to carry weight with sustained speed over extended distances. These qualities brought a new dimension to horse racing, a sport then supported by the burgeoning English aristocracy. So began a selective process of breeding the best stallions to the best mares, with the proof of superiority and excellence being established on the racetrack.

Descendents of Foundation Stallions

Although the three Arabian sires were the progenitors of the Thoroughbred as it is known today, a number of generations were required to create horses that could consistently pass on the distinguishing characteristics of the breed.

Herod: A descendent that fixed the influence of the Byerly Turk as a foundation sire was Herod, foaled in 1758. He was owned by the Duke of Cumberland, the third son of King George II, who was an important breeder of horses at Newmarket and in Hanover. Although Herod was not an

Fillies at a morning workout. Thoroughbreds have great stamina and courage. *Darlene Wohlart/equinephotography.com*

outstanding racehorse, he did prove to be a superlative sire. His descendants were extremely important in the development of the Thoroughbred throughout Europe and North America.

Eclipse: In 1764, there was a great eclipse, and this astronomical event became the name of the horse that would become a star in the history of the Thoroughbred. Eclipse began racing in 1769 at age five and ran away from the competition in his first race at Epsom. It was at this race where the famous Denis O'Kelly remarked, "Eclipse first, the rest nowhere." Eclipse won eighteen races in his career and was never whipped or spurred. The list of Eclipse's distinguished descendants is virtually endless, and he is the reason for the predominance of the Darley Arabian line over the other two foundation stallions' lines.

Matchem: Most racehorses are noted for their speed, but speed sometimes comes at the price of an excitable temperament, yet this was not the case with the horse Matchem. Foaled in 1748, he was the grandson of the Godolphin Arabian. Besides speed, he passed on an excellent disposition. The horse, Snap, a grandson of the Darley Arabian, was compared to the gentle Matchem: "Snap for speed and Matchem for truth and daylight." When considering Matchem's blood heirs, there can be found many even-tempered, yet fast horses. Matchem's offspring had a particular influence on American horses after his owner's son, Edward Fenwick, immigrated to South Carolina in 1755 and brought ten of Matchem's descendants to America. Brutus, one of Matchem's sons, dominated racing in South Carolina for some time.

The Thoroughbred is a bold horse with a refined head and intelligent eyes. *Kay Holloway*

Significant American Thoroughbreds

Bulle Rock: An event of central importance in the history of American horseracing was the importation of Bulle Rock to Virginia in 1730 by Samuel Gist. A son of the Darley Arabian, Bulle Rock is remembered as the first Thoroughbred to reach U.S. shores. He was twenty-one years old when he arrived and had been a successful racehorse in Britain in his youth. By 1800, Bulle Rock had been followed by a succession of 338 other imported Thoroughbreds.

Monkey, Janus, and Fearnought: Of the sixty-three identifiable Thoroughbred imports before the American Revolution, the most important were Monkey, Janus, and Fearnought. Monkey was imported in 1747 at the age of twenty-two and sired some three hundred colts in Virginia. Janus was imported as a ten-year-old by Mordecai Booth in 1756 and had a profound influence on the Quarter Horse. John Baylor imported Fearnought in 1756 as a nine-year-old. Fearnought had a stud fee that was five times the amount charged for other good sires and was the most important Thoroughbred sire in the United States until Diomed.

Diomed: Among the most important horses imported after the American Revolution was Diomed, foaled in 1777. A great racehorse in his youth, he was the winner of the first Epson Derby in England in 1780, but his career later floundered.

An American, Col. John Hoomes, bought him in 1798 and Diomed sired some of the most famous horses in American turf history, including Sir Archie.

Messenger: In May 1788, another Thoroughbred was imported from England that put his stamp on the future of American racing. This horse was Messenger, and he first stood at stud in Philadelphia. After having been sold to Henry Astor of New York and later to Cornelius Van Ranst, he sired a number of superior racehorses. His greatest descendant was Rysdyk's Hambletonian, his great-grandson that became the foundation sire of the Standardbred breed.

Sir Archie: Sir Archie became a singularly important influence in Thoroughbred history. Foaled in Virginia, he became what most experts consider to be the first great Thoroughbred stallion bred in America. At the age of four, he became one of the greatest runners of his day, excelling in four mile heats. William Ransom Johnson, the "Napoleon of the Turf," once owned Sir Archie and described him as "the best horse I ever saw." After no more challengers could be found, Sir Archie's racing career ended and he went to stud. In twenty-three years at stud from 1833, he sired many magnificent horses and was also the great grandsire of Lexington.

Lexington: Foaled in 1850, Lexington was a United States champion race horse who became the most successful sire during the second half of the nineteenth century. Lexington became the leading sire in North America sixteen times. Nine of the first fifteen Travers Stakes were won by one of his sons or daughters. Lexington sired three Preakness Stakes winners and also sired Cincinnati, General Ulysses S. Grant's favorite horse. Cincinnati was depicted in numerous statues of Grant that remain to this day. Lexington was part of the first group of horses inducted into the National Museum of Racing and Hall of Fame in 1955. The Belmont Lexington Stakes runs every year at Belmont Park in honor of Lexington, as does the Lexington Stakes at Keeneland Race Course.

U.S. Racing History

Although there are records of horseracing on Long Island as far back as 1665, the introduction of organized Thoroughbred racing to North America is traditionally credited to Governor Samuel Ogle of Maryland, at whose behest racing "between pedigreed horses in the English style" was first staged at Annapolis in 1745.

As the United States developed, so did Thoroughbred racing, spreading across the nation from coast to coast. Today, the volume of racing in the United States far outweighs that of any other country, and American bloodlines are the most sought after in the world.

What began as a pastime and sporting amusement for the wealthy has now become a worldwide multibillion dollar industry whose economic impact is widely felt at regional and national levels. According to the study entitled, "The Economic Impact of the Horse Industry on the United States," issued in 2005 by Deloitte Consulting, the Thoroughbred industry in the United States has a $33.6 billion total effect on the gross domestic product (GDP) and creates over five hundred thousand fulltime jobs.

Racing

With Thoroughbreds pounding down the stretch, racing is the most popular test of equine speed and a great moment in sport. Although most Thoroughbreds in the Northern Hemisphere are born in the spring, regardless of the actual date, January 1 is their official birthday. The youngsters spend their formative months playing with other colts and fillies and growing in size and spirit. Some yearlings are auctioned at such places as the Keeneland Thoroughbred Racing and Sales in Lexington, Kentucky. The record price paid for a Thoroughbred yearling is more than $13 million.

Having spent its first year developing size and power, the young Thoroughbred begins training as a yearling. It learns to accept a saddle and bridle and a rider on its back, and ultimately to break from a starting gate and run around a track. Leading a horse around a training track to develop wind and muscle is called "ponying." Whether on a farm or at a track, Thoroughbreds are galloped in morning workouts to keep them in racing trim.

Although jockeys are generally small, they must have the strength and courage necessary to guide a horse thundering down the track at top speed. Leading jockeys have quick reflexes, a finely developed sense of timing, and, above all, a mastery of turf strategy. They express "a cool hand with a hot horse."

Jockeys sat upright until the end of the 1800s, when Tod Sloan developed the exaggerated forward-seat position. Placing the rider's weight over the horse's center of gravity not only greatly reduces wind resistance, but more importantly it also keeps a rider in better balance with a horse at high speeds.

To ensure that each horse will carry the precise assigned weight, jockeys and their equipment weigh out before and weigh in after a race. Weight is an ever-present factor in a jockey's life, as few weigh more than 114 pounds, and those who have difficulty with excess poundage must diet constantly. Like coats of arms, the distinctive colors and designs on their shirts and caps, known as "silks," are a way to identify horse and rider. The racing saddle also is small, weighing approximately two pounds. The difference between assigned weight and the rider's actual poundage is made up by lead bars carried in saddle cloth pockets. Some types of races require more accomplished horses to carry more weight as a handicap.

Famous Races

Winning the Triple Crown race series is one of the most elusive and coveted achievements in all of sports. The Triple Crown consists of three races within a five-week span and only three-year-old horses are eligible, meaning a Thoroughbred has only one shot at winning the Triple Crown. Through 2008, only eleven horses had won the Triple Crown, with the horse Affirmed in 1978 being the last to accomplish the feat.

The first race of the Triple Crown is the Kentucky Derby held on the first Saturday in May at Churchill Downs in Louisville, Kentucky. It has been run for more than 130 years and is widely considered the premier race in the United States, with up to twenty Thoroughbreds running 1.25 miles. White carnations were the Derby's original official flowers, but when they were not delivered in 1903, one owner's wife made a blanket of roses; since then the race came to be known as the Run for the Roses. The stallion Secretariat set the record for the fastest time (1:59.4) when he won the Kentucky Derby in 1973.

Two weeks later is the 1.1875-mile Preakness Stakes at Pimlico Race Course in Baltimore, Maryland. The last race in the Triple Crown follows three weeks later and is the Belmont Stakes in Elmont, New York. It is dubbed the Test of the Champion, because one lap around Belmont Park's huge 1.5-mile oval track is the longest distance most of its entrants will ever race.

In addition to the "classic" races for three-year-olds each spring, Thoroughbred racing has had a championship day since 1984, which is held in the fall and known as the Breeders' Cup World Championships. Similar to the National Football League's Super Bowl or Major League Baseball's World Series, the Breeders' Cup is North America's richest day of racing, offering more than $25 million in prize money in fourteen championship races. National pride is also on the line because the event annually attracts many of the best horses, jockeys, and trainers from around the world.

Twentieth Century Champions

Any list of the greatest racehorses of the twentieth century must include Man O'War. Foaled in 1917, Man O'War is still regarded by many as the greatest of American racehorses. He finished first in all but one of his twenty-one starts, often winning in record time and by wide margins.

Count Fleet won the Triple Crown in 1943 capped by a twenty-three-length victory in the Belmont Stakes in 1948. Citation followed Whirlaway as the second Triple Crown winner for the famed Calumet Farm and, at six, became the first Thoroughbred to reach $1 million in career race earnings. Native Dancer won twenty-one of his twenty-two starts from 1952–1954, his only loss coming by just a head in the Kentucky Derby. Kelso was the only horse in history to be voted Horse of the Year five times, from 1960–1964. In 1973, Secretariat became the first horse in a quarter century to win the Triple Crown, capped by an astounding thirty-one-length victory in the Belmont Stakes. His image graced the covers of *Time, Newsweek,* and *Sports Illustrated* magazines.

Forego was awarded a record eight Eclipse Awards, including Horse of the Year and Champion Handicap Horse in 1974, 1975, and 1976, as well as Champion Sprinter in 1974.

In 1977, Seattle Slew became the first undefeated winner of the Triple Crown and was named Horse of the Year. The following year, Slew firmly established himself as one of the greatest champions of the twentieth century by defeating 1978 Triple Crown winner, Affirmed, in the Marlboro Cup Invitational Handicap in what was the first ever meeting of two Triple Crown winners.

In racing's greatest ongoing rivalry, Affirmed and Alydar waged war through 1977 and 1978. Affirmed won seven of their ten meetings, including all three Triple Crown races, but most were extraordinarily close finishes.

In recent years, four Thoroughbreds—John Henry, Alysheba, Cigar, and Curlin—have set the all-time record for career earnings. The ultimate rags-to-riches story, John Henry dominated U.S. turf racing in the early part of the 1980s. Purchased as a yearling in 1976 for just $1,100, John Henry earned $6,597,947 on the track and was named Horse of the Year in both 1981 and 1984.

Dubbed as America's horse after capturing the first two legs of the Triple Crown in 1987, Alysheba was named Horse of the Year in 1988 following his dramatic victory in the Breeders' Cup Classic at Churchill Downs. He retired with earnings of $6,679,242.

Mare and foal. Thoroughbreds have been used to create and upgrade other breeds. *Darlene Wohlart/equinephotography.com*

During one phase of his career over three seasons, 1994–1996, Cigar won sixteen consecutive races, matching the then modern record of Citation. He traveled to Dubai to win the inaugural running of the Dubai World Cup, and his career earnings were around $10 million.

Cigar's earnings record stood through the conclusion of the twentieth century, but was eclipsed in 2008 by Curlin, classic winner of the Preakness Stakes and Breeders' Cup Classic at age three, whose four-year-old season was highlighted by a dominant performance in the Dubai World Cup. Curlin retired with eleven wins from sixteen starts and earnings of $10,501,800.

Registries

Key to the selective breeding process is the integrity of the breed's records. In early days, English Thoroughbred breeding records were sparse and frequently incomplete, it being the custom, among other things, not to name a horse until it had proven its outstanding ability. It was left to James Weatherby, through his own research and by consolidation of a number of privately kept pedigree records, to publish the first volume of the General Stud Book. He did this in 1791, listing the pedigrees of 387 mares, each of which could be traced back to three stallions: Eclipse, a direct descendent of the Darley Arabian; Matchem, a grandson of the

Landscape of a Thoroughbred farm in Kentucky's bluegrass country. *Kay Holloway*

Godolphin Arabian; and Herod, whose great-great grandsire was the Byerly Turk. The General Stud Book is still published in England by Weatherby and Sons, secretaries to the English Jockey Club.

Several years later, as racing proliferated in North America, the need for a pedigree registry of U.S.-bred Thoroughbreds similar to the General Stud Book became apparent. Colonel Sanders D. Bruce, a Kentuckian who had spent a lifetime researching the pedigrees of American Thoroughbreds, published the first volume of The American Stud Book in 1873. Bruce closely followed the pattern of the first General Stud Book, producing six volumes of the register until 1896, when The Jockey Club assumed responsibility for the project. The Jockey Club, a U.S. Thoroughbred organization, was established in 1894 and today is the governing body for all matters pertaining to Thoroughbred registration in North America.

When The Jockey Club published its first volume of the stud book, the foal crop was about three thousand; by 1986, it had exceeded fifty-one thousand, and these days, the annual registered foal crop encompasses approximately thirty-five thousand foals. The Jockey Club's database holds the names of more than 4 million Thoroughbreds tracing back to the mid 1700s. The American Stud Book includes all Thoroughbreds foaled in the United States, Canada, and Puerto Rico, as well as Thoroughbreds imported into these countries from nations around the world that maintain similar Thoroughbred registries. The system also handles daily results of electronically transmitted pedigree and racing data from areas throughout North America as well as from the United Kingdom, Ireland, France, Australia, Japan, and other leading Thoroughbred racing countries around the world.

Registration Criteria

Beginning in 2001, The Jockey Club replaced conventional blood-typing with DNA typing for parentage verification as a requirement for registration in the stud book. Besides DNA typing, registration requires that a foal satisfy all of the rules for registration as set forth in the "Principal Rules and Requirements" section of The American Stud Book.

The rules require, among other things, the following:

- A foal's pedigree authentically traces in all its lines to horses recorded in either The American Stud Book, or a foreign stud book approved by The Jockey Club and the International Stud Book Committee;
- The foal is the result of a stallion's live, natural cover of a broodmare; and a natural gestation takes place in, and delivery is from, the body of the same broodmare in which the foal was conceived. Any foal resulting from, or produced by, the processes of artificial insemination, embryo transfer or transplant, cloning, or any other form of genetic manipulation is not eligible for registration.

When owners submit their name choices for registered foals, The Jockey Club checks each name for phonetic similarity against more than 430,000 names already in active use and for compliance with the rules of naming the horses.

Breed Characteristics

The Thoroughbred stands a little over 16 hands on average, though "average" is a key word, since there are many over or under this height.

Coat colors in Thoroughbreds may be bay, dark bay/brown, chestnut, black, gray/roan, white, or palomino. White markings are frequently seen on both the face and legs.

Conformation is based on practical application of what the Thoroughbred body is supposed to do: carry more than 1,000 pounds of body weight over a variety of distances, traveling at speeds of 35 to 40 miles per hour, and yet still have the strength and suppleness to respond to the changes of pace or direction of racing conditions.

The Thoroughbred's Arabian ancestry is revealed in its refined head. It should be correctly proportioned to the rest of the body, displaying a good, flat forehead with widely spaced, intelligent eyes. Carried relatively low, the head sits on a neck that is somewhat longer and lighter than in other breeds.

The withers are high and well defined, leading to an evenly curved back. The shoulder is deep, well muscled, and extremely sloped. The heart girth is deep and relatively narrow.

The legs are clean and long with pronounced tendons. From the point of the shoulder, the forearm should show adequate muscling that tapers toward a clean-looking knee, which, in turn, tapers into the full width of the cannon. The cannon should be short and comparatively flat, with tendons distinctly set out and clean. The pastern should be neither too long nor too short and should be set at an angle that is a little less than 45 degrees to the vertical. When viewed from behind or in front, the legs should be straight and move smoothly in unison through one plane.

The bone structure of the upper hind leg makes room for long, strong muscling. The thighbone is long and the angle it makes with the hipbone is wide. The powerful muscling of the hip and thigh continues to the gaskin that is set low. The trailing edge of the hind cannon should follow a natural perpendicular line to the point of the buttock.

The Thoroughbred's conformation enables it to reach speeds exceeding 40 miles per hour. Its rear legs act as springs as they bend and straighten during running. This tremendous spring power helps thrust the horse forward as its front legs provide pull. The head and long neck also help to make running smooth and rhythmic. The neck moves in unison with the forelegs, aiding the horse in its forward motion and extending the time that it literally is airborne.

Thoroughbreds are also equipped with the most athletic feet in the world. Their hooves have a unique structure that gives it built-in cushioning to withstand the equivalent of one hundred times the force of gravity on each hoof, which is the force exerted when a Thoroughbred is running at full speed.

Credit: The Jockey Club

TRAKEHNER

A three-year-old stallion. Though a large horse, the Trakahener is refined and balanced. *Unbridled Photography*

American Trakehner Association
1536 West Church Street
Newark, Ohio 43055
www.americantrakehner.com

It has been said that the Trakehner has every-thing everybody is looking for in a performance horse, and indeed, the breed's list of attributes cer-tainly leads one to believe it. Trakehners have size, bone, and correctness of conformation, yet are extremely "breedy" and beautiful. They are athletic, with magnificent movement that is comfortable, balanced, and free. Best of all, they have an ideal temperament—keen and alert, yet level-headed and able to take intense work. The breed's popu-larity is growing at an astounding rate.

The correct name for the breed is the East Prussian Warmblood Horse of Trakehner Origin.

It is one of the oldest European warmblood breeds with a history that reaches back more than four hundred years. Its foundation is the main stud farm established in Trakehnen, East Prussia, in 1732. The breed's name is derived from this world-famous farm and the bloodlines can be traced back to this source.

A significant number of Trakehner-bred horses are now competing in performance arenas and gaining national and international recognition. As the list of Trakehner accomplishments grows, so does the list of breeders, riders, and friends who are charmed by the beauty and talent these horses have to offer. Trakehner enthusiasts firmly believe that their breed is the horse of the future in the Western Hemisphere.

History

Trakehner breeding began with a small local East Prussian horse, the Schwaike, which had phenomenal endurance and versatility. For many years it was crossed with various larger imported stallions to provide mounts for warfare, general transportation, and agricultural work.

In the early eighteenth century, King Friedrich Wilhelm I of Prussia, the father of Friedrich the Great, began to see the need for a new type of cavalry mount for the Prussian army. War tactics had changed and now required a lighter, more comfortable horse with more endurance and speed than the heavier horses previously needed to carry armor and haul heavy equipment. The king wanted horses for his officers to ride that were attractive enough to make them proud, solid enough to stay sound, and had a comfortable, ground-covering trot that would enable them to travel quickly and efficiently. He chose the best horses from seven of his royal breeding farms and in 1732, moved them to the new royal stud at Trakehnen, where he began selectively breeding them and where the Trakehner breed evolved.

When Count Lindenau took over the stud management in 1787, he instituted even stricter selections, eliminating two-thirds of the stallions

and one-third of the broodmares. He also allowed private breeders to bring their mares to be serviced by the royal stallions. Later, during the twenty years from 1817 to 1837, select English Thoroughbred and Arabian stallions were purchased and added to the breed, a practice that is still followed today under strict approval conditions by the German Trakehner Verband.

The first stud book of Trakehnen was published in 1877. Through the latter part of the 1800s and up to World War II, the Trakehner was a most successful breed, excelling as a military and endurance horse as well as proving its versatility by doing light draft work in the fields.

As a performance horse, the Trakehner also made its mark. In 1924, 1928, and 1936, Trakehners won three gold medals, two silver medals, and a bronze medal in the Olympics (Dressage and Three-Day Eventing). In 1936, a German Trakehner won the Prix des Nations. Between 1921 and 1936, the Great Pardubice Steeplechase (next to the English Grand National, the most difficult steeplechase in the world) was won a total of nine times by East Prussian horses.

The breed easily recovered from its population being halved during World War I. But in October 1944, as World War II was in its final stages and the Soviets were closing in on the area around Trakehnen, orders came to evacuate the horses from the Stud. About eight hundred of the best horses were hastily transferred, but unfortunately they did not go far enough west. Most of them eventually fell to Russian forces and were shipped to Russia. Private breeders and their horses were not allowed to leave until January 1945, when the Russians had broken through the German lines.

What followed was a horror story that went down in history as "The Trek." Mostly women, children, and the elderly fled with some eight hundred horses. It was the dead of winter and the snow was deep. The horse feed ran out and they had to scavenge along the way. For two and a half months and 600 miles, the group fled the pursuing Soviet troops and strafing of Soviet planes. They escaped

A supremely beautiful horse, the Trakehaner is solid and stylish. This is a stallion. *Abramova Kseniya/Shutterstock*

across the treacherous expanse of ice and knee-deep water of the frozen Baltic Sea. Of the eight hundred beautiful horses, only one hundred pitiful skeletons limped into West Germany, carrying open wounds from shrapnel and burlap bags frozen to their feet because they could not stop to have their lost or worn-out shoes replaced. Only the hardiest had survived.

Only a few hundred Trakehner Horses of the original eighty thousand in East Prussia were available by the time the rebuilding began. Though almost one thousand horses had actually reached the safety of West Germany, most of them were

eventually lost to the breed due to the hard times. Those that were left were located and accounted for with the new Verband.

The next decade was spent rebuilding and re-establishing the breed. After 1945, the Trakehner breed was developed (according to the principals of maintaining a pure breed) at its primary German breeding location in Trakehnen using the East Prussian warmblood horses of Trakehner origin that remained after World War II. In 1947, the West German Association of Breeders and Friends of the Warmblood Horse of Trakehner Origin, otherwise known as the Trakehner Verband, was founded, replacing the East Prussian Stud Book Society, which could not function outside its homeland at the time.

The late 1940s and early 1950s saw a scarcity of Trakehners in competition as breeders struggled to rebuild their stock after the devastation of the war. By the 1950s, Trakehners were beginning again to win at dressage in international competitions. In 1950, the German Federal Government joined the state of Lower Saxony in support of a small breeding farm near the large stud at Hunnersruck. Through the late 1980s this corporation—the business arm of the Trakehner Verband—owned and managed stud farms at Hunnersruck, Rantzau, and Birkhausen. At each of these, it carried on selective breeding with its own mares as well as those belonging to private breeders. They used, and still use, Thoroughbreds and Arabians to improve and refine the breed.

Since then, Trakehners have experienced a comeback at the Olympic Games that culminated in the 1984 Olympics with a team gold and individual silver medal in show jumping by Abdullah, a Trakehner who competed for the United States. He also won the World Cup the following year. Another Trakehner, Amiego, out of the same dam as Abdullah, won the bronze in the 1987 Pan Am Games. Also in 1987, the Trakehner gelding, Livius, was a successful member of the United States Team.

Breed Development

At the beginning, the breed was a stocky, strong, native animal that needed size and refinement. The really important and decisive development of the breed occurred in the early 1800s when top-quality English Thoroughbred and Arabian blood began to be introduced in small quantities. The goal of the breeding programs then was directed toward breeding a better endurance horse that would prove itself not only highly efficient as a riding horse during wartime but also as a working horse on East Prussian farms during times of peace. The object ultimately was to add the size, nerve, spirit, and endurance of the Thoroughbred to the bulk, stability, and nobility of the native breed.

Further refinement in the breed came with the addition of Arabian blood. It is this carefully controlled addition of "full" blood that has given the Trakehner its characteristic breediness and refinement—the elegance and beauty that gives it the edge in stiff competition and sets it apart from other European warmblood breeds.

It is significant that, while the Trakehner still adds only Thoroughbred and Arabian blood to its pedigrees, most of the other European warmblood breeds use Trakehner stallions as improvers in addition to their Thoroughbred and Arabian breeding. This is because in Trakehners, the desired refinement is already present.

The Trakehner of today is a large horse, standing generally between 16 and 17 hands. The breed is characterized by great substance and bone, yet displays surprising refinement, perhaps more so than any other European warmblood breed. It is a superb performance horse with natural elegance and balance. It excels in dressage because of its elastic way of moving—the light, springy, "floating trot," and the soft, balanced canter, made possible by a deep, sloping shoulder and a correct, moderately long back and pasterns. With its characteristic, powerful hindquarters, and strong joints and muscles, the breed also produces outstanding jumpers. However, perhaps the most outstanding attribute of the Trakehner is its temperament. It is keen, alert, and intelligent, yet stable, accepting, and anxious to please.

One of the most interesting and important annual equine events in modern Germany is the stallion testing and approval program, a procedure that originated for the Trakehner in East Prussia in 1926. Trakehners are tested and approved at a special function before breeding is allowed by the Trakehner Verband. This approval is acknowledged to be the strictest of any in the country.

For stallions, the philosophy behind these approvals is this: in order to be an effective, prepotent, and successful sire, a stallion must display the most correct conformation, paces, and temperament possible and these features must all be natural. Approximately one hundred young stallions are selected out of hundreds applying for certification and for three days, they are carefully examined by an official commission. Only the very best are approved and each year out of approximately one hundred assembled, twenty to twenty-five are given this treasured honor. Within the next two years, the newly approved young stallions must undergo government training and performance testing. By these methods, it is assured that only the very finest stallions of the breed are preserved as breeding stock.

Broodmares are also evaluated before they are entered into the Stud Book. Very rarely is there an approved breeding stallion whose dam's marks are not somewhat above average, indicating that these painstaking evaluations are the reason that the Trakehner has remained the superior breed it is today. Careful selection has retained the qualities that are valued and desired by breeders and trainers alike.

All over the world, Trakehner Horses continue to excel in most disciplines of equine competition, although since World War II when they were driven from their East Prussian homeland, their primary breeding area has been Germany. The full-bred German Trakehner of today is clearly recognizable by its famous brand—the double moose antler on the left hindquarter—a brand that has been used since the original days in East Prussia.

In North America

The Trakehner was first introduced into North America in significant numbers only in the late 1950s, being imported first into Canada and later to the United States. In 1957, Gerda Friedrichs, a German-born breeder who emigrated to Canada, began importing West German Trakehner stock to institute her own breeding program in North America. The get of three of her stallions—Antares, Prusso, and Tscherkess—have made major contributions to the bloodlines still found in the Western Hemisphere today.

In 1974, the American Trakehner Association (ATA) was incorporated. It eventually unified with the North American Trakehner Association (NATA) established in 1977, the same year stallion inspections began. These inspections now include a representative of the Trakehner Verband and are much the same as those in Germany. In 1979, the German Trakehner Verband signed an Agreement of Cooperation between the two associations where the Verband assured its help and support in establishing goals and breed preservation practices. The ATA was granted the right to use the double moose antler brand—the brand used in East Prussia—for their full-bred horses, but with a distinguishing mark underneath it to identify the horses were foaled in North America.

The Trakehner scene in North America is one of tremendous growth and enthusiasm.

Breed Specifics

Trakehners should not be saddle broke until they are about three years old. Though they grow rapidly, they tend to mature more slowly than their full-blooded cousins. Also they carry so much body that they don't need the extra weight of the rider until fairly well grown. Once they are saddle broke, training progresses easily and quickly because of another shining attribute of this breed—its temperament. The Trakehner is keen, alert, extremely intelligent, and quick to learn, yet patient, accepting, and able to take concentrated work without "blowing up," enabling it to excel in dressage as well as jumping.

The registry is based on bloodlines and registration candidates must have at least 50 percent Trakehner blood to be considered. Foal evaluation is optional and their certificates are issued based on documented bloodlines, not inspection scores. All fillies, colts, and gelded weanlings are entered into the appropriate registry book. Qualifications for the Original Stud Book or approved breeding entries are made when the mares are presented for inspection at three years of age or older and stallions are presented for inspection at two years of age or older.

The Trakehner has a light, floating trot and fluid movement. This is a young gelding.
Bob Tarr

There are four registration books: the Official Appendix Book, the Official Registry Book, the Preliminary Stud Book, and the Official Stud Book. Each has a different requirement for eligibility. Also there are five divisions of the Official Registry Book: Purebred Trakehner, Anglo-Trakehner (cross with a Thoroughbred or Anglo-Trakehner mare), Arab-Trakehner, Part-Trakehner (cross to a mare other than Trakehner, Throughbred, or Arabian), and Imported Trakehner (pure Trakehners imported into the Western Hemisphere). Any horse qualifying for one of these divisions can be registered without any inspection for conformation or performance.

All horses must be DNA-typed. Colts require a veterinary exam for soundness and freedom from obvious congenital defects. They are also required to have radiographs as well as a personal inspection by the Inspection Committee to qualify for the Official Stud Book. Only about two out of one huundred colts are approved.

The recommended minimum size requirements for stallions at two-and-a-half years old are 15.3 hands, but the average is about 16.2 hands. They must have a heart girth of 72 inches and a cannon bone of 7.5 inches. They must have a truly masculine, dramatic and powerful appearance.

The recommended minimum size for mares is 15.1 hands (preferably between 15.1 and 16.1 hands) with a heart girth of 70 inches and a cannon bone that approaches 7.5 inches. Mares do not jump. They should have a feminine, motherly expression.

Stallion breeding registration (after approval) is final after stallions complete their performance test requirements. They are judged on athletic ability, conformation, willing attitude, and a rigorous performance test. Stallions four years old and older are required to have an Under Saddle demonstration.

Similar to the process in Germany, stallions are ridden in a group with other stallions and are expected to perform the walk, trot, and canter. They must also free jump three obstacles.

Standards for these inspections include obedience, willingness to work, and elegant, flowing, and elastic movements, which are the dominant characteristics of the Trakehner breed. The overall impression should be one of freedom, harmony, and balance. This selection process helps to preserve the true Trakehner type and provides an objective evaluation, insuring that only the best are bred.

Breeding Goals

The ATA uses the Verband bylaws to establish its breeding goals, which include a riding sport horse of Trakehner type that is talented for many uses. Selection criteria are the following:

I: Pedigree

The breed is based on the warmblood horses of Trakehner origin created in East Prussia, which carry high percentages of Thoroughbred and Arabian as well as Shagya Arabian and Anglo-Arab genes.

II: Outward Appearance

Colors: All colors allowed.

Size: The objective is a height of 160 cm to 170 cm (15.3 hands to 16.3 hands).

Type: Embodying the most noble German riding horse breed, the horse is characterized primarily by Trakehner breed type. Desirable is the highly elegant appearance of a noble, harmonious riding horse with great lines and distinguished by its expression and striking features. Trakehner type is to be evident in a well-defined, expressive head, large eyes, well-shaped neck, sculpted muscles, and correct, clearly defined limbs. Breeding stallions and broodmares should also display the typical expression of their gender.

Undesirable type is a coarse, plump appearance, big head, indistinct outlines, undefined joints, and in breeding stock, lack of gender expression.

Conformation: Desirable is a large-lined and harmonious body that enables the horse to perform in the disciplines of equestrian sports. This includes a medium-long neck that tapers towards the head, good freedom in the throatlatch, and a large, sloping shoulder. There should be well-defined withers extending far into a back that is able to perform its function, meet the requirements for an athletic sport horse and allow for movement that combines swinging, thrust, and balance. There is a long, slightly sloping, powerfully muscled croup as well as a harmonious division of the body into forehand, mid-section, and hindquarters.

Also desirable is a well,defined foundation matching the body with correct, large joints, medium-long pasterns, and well-shaped hooves, promising long years of use. In addition, the foundation should include correctly positioned legs; that is, legs that are correct when seen from behind, forelegs that are straight when seen from the front, and hind legs that have well-coupled hocks set at an angle of approximately 150 degrees with each leg having a straight toe axis that forms an angle of about 45 to 50 degrees with the ground.

Undesirable traits are the following: an overall unharmonious body, particularly a short, heavy, low-set neck; a short, steep shoulder; short or undefined withers; a short or overly long, soft back; tight or convex loins; a short or straight croup with a high-set tail; no depth of barrel; tuck-in flanks with a short area behind the ribs; incorrect limbs, including small, narrow, or tied-in joints; weak cannon bones; short, steep, or overly long soft pasterns; and hooves that are too small, particularly with inwardly directed walls. Also undesirable are misalignments of the legs, particularly legs that toe in or toe out; wide base or narrow base; calf-kneed, open-angled, or scimitar-shaped legs, and cow-hocks or barrel legs.

III: Way of Going

Desirable are diligent, cadenced and ground-covering basic paces (walk—four-beat; trot—two-beat; canter—three-beat). The movement should be

Charm and nobility
are evident in the
Trakehner's refined
head. *Julie Moses*

elastic and energetic, developed from the hind-quarters, transmitted over a supple, swinging back to the forehand, which freely moves forward out of the shoulder. The direction of movement of the legs should be straight and forward.

At the walk, the movement should be supple, energetic, and elevated with clearly defined steps. At the trot and canter, there should be a clearly noticeable phase of suspension, with the movement being elastic, full of impulsion, and light-footed, carried with balance and natural elevation of the neck. Some knee action is desirable. Horses are examined in-hand as well as at liberty.

Undesirable are short, flat, and non-elastic movements with a tight back, irregular movements and heavy movements that fall onto the forehand.

Also undesirable are wobbling, rocking, paddling, winging, base-narrow, toeing-in, base-wide, or toeing-out movements.

Jumping: Desirable is an elastic, "scopey," and deliberate jumping technique that displays calmness and intelligence. The jumping sequence should clearly show a collecting (powerful and quick push-off at takeoff), a distinct, quick angling of the limbs (with the forearms being as horizontal as possible over the obstacle), a rounded back with noticeably projecting withers, and a neck that is bent downward while the hind legs open up ("bascule"). During the entire sequence, the flow of the movement and the rhythm of the canter should be maintained.

Undesirable is careless jumping and lack of aptitude, hanging legs, a high head over the obstacle connected with a hollow back in which the flow of movement and the rhythm of the canter are lost, being out-of-control, and hesitant jumping.

IV: Internal Characteristics

Internal Characteristics includes performance aptitude, character, temperament, and soundness. Desirable is an uncomplicated, friendly horse that is willing to work. It isn't nervous but reliable, which, in the way it appears and behaves, gives a wide-awake, intelligent impression and reveals a good character and a calm, even temperament. Also desirable is robust health, good mental and physical stress ability, natural fertility, and freedom from genetic flaws.

Undesirable are horses that are difficult to handle, are nervous, timid, or cowardly.

V: Summary

What is desired is a sound, large-framed, correct riding sport horse of Trakehner type with harmonious lines and talented in many ways, with impulsive, ground-covering, elastic movements. Good character, well balanced temperament, intelligence, willingness to work, endurance, and hardiness during work are to be particularly apparent characteristics of its innate traits.

The observer should immediately be aware of a striking, elegant presence. The combination of size, bone, and substance with a classic breediness, producing the unmistakable Trakehner type is clearly distinguishable from all other warmbloods. Charm and nobility are evident in the refined head, often slightly concave in profile, with its broad forehead, smallish muzzle, large, kind, wideset eyes, and solid jawbone. The throatlatch is clean and fine and the long, graceful neck is set into the shoulder at just the right angle to provide maximum balance.

The ideal Trakehner has a large, solid body, standing in a rectangular frame—compared to the square frame of the Thoroughbred, as an example—with a deep, sloping shoulder that allows for tremendous freedom of movement. The legs should be correct and the movement true and square. The pastern should have medium length—neither too short and upright nor too long and sloping—and the cannon bones should be relatively short, thus allowing the horse to stay sound through years of hard work. A back of medium length flows into large and powerful hindquarters with broad, solid hocks carried well under the animal as it travels. A deep barrel provides the necessary lung capacity and is closely coupled to a long, sloping croup.

It is the combination of the thrust from the quarters, the swinging back and the freedom of the shoulder that produces the Trakehner's famous floating trot. Its trot eats up the ground, is supremely comfortable, and is so light and springy that it actually looks as if the horse does not quite touch the ground as it strides. The ideal Trakehner is naturally balanced, so its canter is soft and flowing, and jumping comes easily from the strong quarters and the well-defined hocks that provide the necessary thrust.

Credit: American Trakehner Association

CONFORMATION ESSENTIALS

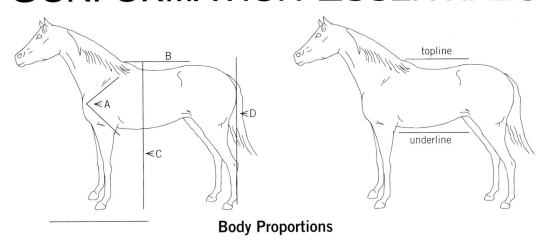

Body Proportions

A: Angle of the shoulder. B & C: Height is measured from a point horizontal with the highest point of withers (line B) straight down to the ground (line C). D: Proper alignment of the rear legs for most breeds should have the back of the cannon lying in a direct vertical line from the point of the buttock dropping down and perpendicular to the ground (line D).

This is the ideal conformation of a Thoroughbred-type race horse, which may not be identical to other breeds, such as a gaited breed or a draft horse. Other good riding breeds may differ from this description somewhat, but this is the general conformation common to most riding horses.

Feet: A horse's hooves must be able to withstand a great deal of pressure. At full speed, a 1,000-pound Thoroughbred will place the equivalent of one hundred times the force of gravity on each hoof with every stride, so it is essential that the foot be shaped properly to withstand this concussion and dissipate the shock of impact. Consider the proportion, substance, and size of the hoof. The underside of the hoof should have a round, slightly oval shape, with some depth. Look for balanced feet on both sides, or symmetry. Avoid misshapen, dished, or cracked feet.

Pasterns: The pastern should be at a 45-degree angle. Its length should be proportionate; a pastern

that is too long could indicate weakness and tendon strain, while if it is too short it may absorb too much concussion, thus stressing the bone structure.

Ankle: As with the pastern, the ankle joint size should be proportionate to the rest of the leg. Beware of spread or prominent sesamoids.

Cannon bones: Ideally, the cannon bone should be short and strong and have mass. The cannon bone bears the most weight of any bone in a horse's body. The bone should exit the lower knee or hock cleanly and be well-centered. From the front, the cannon bones should appear straight and be of the same length. Keep an eye out for splints under the knee on the front of the cannon bones.

Knee: Bones in and leading to the knee should line up in a balanced manner. They should not tilt for-ward (over at the knee, or buck-kneed) or back (back at the knee, or calf-kneed), or be severely offset to one side or the other when viewed from the front. It is best if the knees are set squarely on

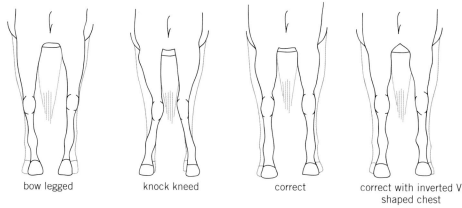

bow legged   knock kneed   correct   correct with inverted V
                                                                                   shaped chest

FRONTS

top of the cannon bones, not off to one side or another (offset knees).

Shoulder: The shoulder should have the same slope or angle as the pastern. The ideal slope of the shoulder is approximately 45 to 50 degrees. In general, the angle of the pastern will correspond with the angle of the shoulder. Stride length is largely determined by the conformation of the shoulder. The straighter the shoulder, the shorter the stride. Also, a straight shoulder absorbs concussion instead of dispensing it and puts stress on the bones of the leg and shoulder. Look for balance, symmetry, and good muscling. A straight line from the point of the shoulder should bisect the entire front leg all the way to the toe. Also, the width of the toes on the ground should be the same width as the legs' origin in the chest.

Neck: The neck should be sufficient in scope to provide adequate wind for the horse and be well tied in at the withers, without being too low, or "ewe necked." A horse with a well-muscled, well-proportioned neck has a longer, more rhythmic stride and can more easily maintain its balance when running. An easy, rhythmic stride will cause less fatigue. Fatigue can increase the chances of injury. In short, does the neck fit with the rest of the body?

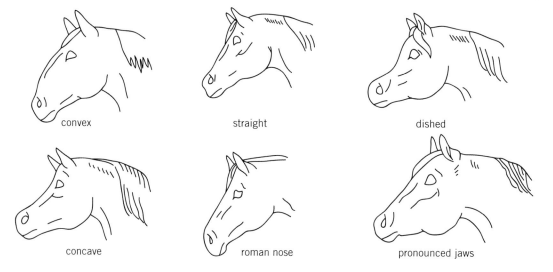

convex   straight   dished

concave   roman nose   pronounced jaws

Head: The head should be broad enough to permit adequate air passage. Generally, the distance from the back of the jaw to where the head ties into the neck should be about the size of a fist. Nostrils should be of adequate size. When people refer to an "attractive" head, they usually mean the head is short with well-set ears and has large bold eyes, a short distance from eye to muzzle, large nostrils, and a refined muzzle with a shallow mouth. In general, there is no physiological benefit to the horse having an attractive head, as any type head functions the same.

Back: The distance from the withers to the top of the croup or hips should match the length of the horse's neck from the poll to the withers. The length of the back is directly related to the slope of shoulder. The steeper the shoulder, the longer the back. A horse with a long back is usually not as well balanced as a short-backed one.

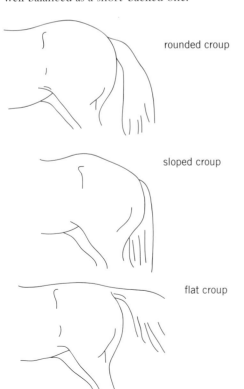

rounded croup

sloped croup

flat croup

Hips and buttocks: The croup or hip should have a gentle slope, not too steep or flat, and good width. The gaskin should depict strength and complement the muscles of the quarters. Note that much of the horse's athleticism and power comes from behind. Definition and development are key attributes.

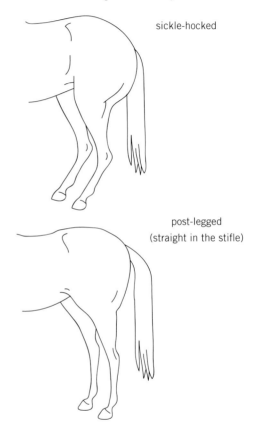

sickle-hocked

post-legged
(straight in the stifle)

Hocks: A horse's hocks should not be straight as a post, or curved so deeply as to be "sickle-hocked," but somewhere in between. From the rear, the hocks should appear to point straight at the viewer and should not turn in (cow hocks), turn out (open in the hocks) or be bow-legged. Ideally, if you dropped an imaginary plumb line from the point of the buttocks to the ground, it should run parallel to the cannon bone and be slightly behind the heel.

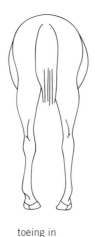

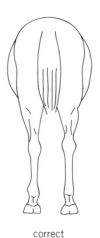

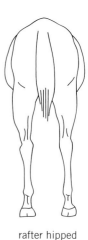

cow hocked   toeing in   correct   rafter hipped

REAR QUARTERS

Stance: Does the horse stand with hocks tucked up underneath the body (sickle-hocked), or behind the body like a German Shepherd? The horse should be standing balanced and straight. The same goes for the front legs.

Chest: A horse's chest should be broad and appear powerful. Narrow chested or slab-sided horses are said to lack power.

Conformation Essentials: Walking Stride

Front and rear view: The horse should move straight toward and away from the viewer. Observe whether the horse toes in or toes out as it walks.

Side view: Check for the overstep: Do the hind feet reach beyond the front hoof prints? Observe the horse's head. Be certain it does not bob unusually when walking, as this may indicate soreness or lameness.

Walk: Look for a smooth, long stride. Avoid yearlings that walk "wide" in front.

Unsoundness and Blemishes: Front Legs

An unsoundness is any defect in form or function that interferes with the usefulness of the horse. A blemish is an acquired physical defect that does not interfere with the usefulness of the horse, but may diminish its value.

Inbreeding

Inbreeding is the term utilized to describe breeding in which the same ancestor appears two or more times within the first four generations of pedigree. For example, if the same ancestor appears in the third generation and again in the fourth, the horse is referred to as being "inbred 3x4." The significance of inbreeding is that the ancestor to whom the particular horse is inbred will have greater influence, thus emphasizing certain characteristics. Most believe it is radical for a horse to be inbred closer than 3x3.

Outcross breeding is the opposite of inbreeding, in that there is no repeat presence within four or more generations. An outcross is believed to offer greater variety and avoid concentration of good or bad characteristics.

Credit:
Thoroughbred Owners and Breeders Association
P.O. Box 910668
Lexington
Kentucky 40591
www.toba.org
Copyright © 2008. All rights reserved.

Horse Colors

There are only two base colors in all horses: black and chestnut. All other colors are the work of other dilutions, modifiers, or white patterns.

True **black** horses do not fade from sun or weather conditions, while fading blacks do just that—fade.

Chestnut or **red** is sometimes referred to as **sorrel** depending on the breed or particular equine organization. Genetically speaking, both chestnut and sorrel come from the same gene no matter what shade of red they are. Chestnuts can vary in many shades from light to dark, but they will never carry black hairs, and the mane/tail and legs will (almost) always have a reddish tinge to them. Points can vary from flaxen mane/tail, which can appear almost white at times, to very dark (black or dark brown).

Bay is a dominant color with many varying shades. It is a red body color with black points (mane/tail and legs). Bay is really black based, but restricts the black hairs to the points.

Buckskin is a tan color with black points.

Palomino is a golden color with a white mane and tail.

Gray is a progressive color that can begin by looking like any other color. Since gray takes away color, it is a gradual process. Many gray horses go through a dapple stage, then a flea-bit stage, then eventually turn white. Any white horse that has pigmented or black-looking skin would be a gray.

A **white** horse is born white and never changes. Its skin is pink (non-pigmented). Its eyes can be any color except hazel. **Albino** is a complete de-pigmentation of all color, including red eyes.

Dun, also referred to as **dun factor**, is actually a dilution of the base color while leaving the points dark. Points include outlined ears and dorsal stripe as well as the legs, mane, and tail. Other markings a dun can have include leg bars, reverse face mask, cobwebbing, tipped ears, shoulder bars, mane/tail frosting, ventral stripe, ghost smiles, and other primitive markings.

Grullo (or **grulla** in feminine form) is gray with a black mane and tail. It is the dun dilution on a black base coat. The dilution turns the base coat to any shade of a steel-grayish color. It can be any version from a light, silver grullo, to a dark, seemingly black color. The mane and tail can hold a dark to light frosting also—anywhere from a dark bronze to an almost white overlay of hairs in the mane and along the sides of the tail.

Sooty is a modifier that affects both black- and red-based horses by darkening the whole color or just in particular areas. It can manifest as

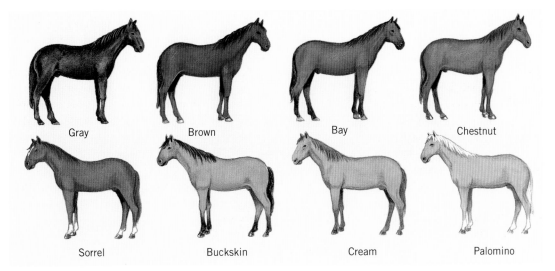

Gray   Brown   Bay   Chestnut

Sorrel   Buckskin   Cream   Palomino

darker-shaded dapples or uniform coat darkening, as well as a darkening in small spot or individual hair areas, or across the topline. Sooty buckskins (bay+creme+sooty) are often mistaken for grullos, especially when the sooty modifier causes a dark topline (referred to as countershading).

Creme horses look like they are off-white. **Cremello** is a double creme gene with a red base (chestnut), and these horses usually appear almost white, but can vary in shade to a creme color.

A double creme gene on a bay produces a **perlino** with the points being a few shades darker than the body. These horses appear more orange looking. On a black horse, a double creme gene will produce a **smoky creme**, which can appear to be a cremello. All double dilutes will have blue eyes.

Roan and **appaloosa** coloring are examples of white hairs mixed in with color, while **pinto** coloring is an example of colored spotting separated by white areas. (White patterns are super-imposed over any color on the horse.)

Credit: Michelle Clarke, Rancho Bayo

L to R: Coronet Band, Stocking, Sock, Pastern, Coronet

REGISTRY RESOURCES

Abaco Barb
Arkwild, Inc.
2829 Bird Avenue
Suite 5, PMB No. 170
Miami, Florida 33133
www.arkwild.org

Wild Horses of Abaco
P.O. Box AB 20979
Marsh Harbour, Abaco, Bahamas

Akhal-Teke
The Akhal-Teke Society of America, Inc.
P.O. Box 207
Sanford, North Carolina 27331
www.akhaltekesocietyofamerica.com

American Azteca
American Azteca Horse International Association
P.O. Box 1577
Rapid City, South Dakota 57709
www.americanazteca.com

American Bashkir Curly
American Bashkir Curly Registry
857 Beaver Road
Walton, Kentucky 41094
www.abcregistry.org

American Cream Draft
American Cream Draft Horse Association
193 Crossover Road
Bennington, Vermont 05201
www.acdha.org

American Creme Horse
American White and American Creme Horse Registry
90000 Edwards Road
Naper, Nebraska 68755
http://awachr.com/home

American Indian Horse
The American Indian Horse Registry
9028 State Park Road
Lockhart, Texas 78644
www.indianhorse.com

American Miniature Horse
American Miniature Horse Association
5601 South Interstate 35W
Alvarado, Texas 76009
www.amha.org

American Miniature Horse Registry
81 B Queenwood Road
Morton, Illinois 61550
www.shetlandminiature.com

American Paint Horse
American Paint Horse Association
P.O. Box 961023
Fort Worth, Texas 76161
www.apha.com

American Quarter Horse
American Quarter Horse Association
P.O. Box 200
Amarillo, Texas 79168
www.aqha.com

American Saddlebred
American Saddlebred Horse Association
4083 Iron Works Parkway
Lexington, Kentucky 40511
www.asha.net

American Sorraia Mustang
American Heritage Horse Association
26232 Shirttail Canyon Road
P.O. Box 27
Pringle, South Dakota 57773-0027
www.americanheritagehorse.org

American White Horse Horse
American White and American Creme Horse Registry
90000 Edwards Road
Naper, Nebraska 68755
http://awachr.com/home

Andalusian
International Andalusian and Lusitano Horse Association
101 Carnoustie North, Box 200
Birmingham, Alabama 35242
www.ialha.org

Anglo-Arabian
Arabian Horse Association
10805 E. Bethany Drive
Aurora, Colorado 80014
www.arabianhorses.org

Appaloosa
Appaloosa Horse Club
2720 West Pullman Road
Moscow, Idaho 83843
www.appaloosa.com

International Colored Appaloosa Association, Inc.
P.O. Box 99
Shipshewana, Indiana 46565
www.icaainc.com

AraAppaloosa
AraAppaloosa Foundation Breeders' International
Route 8, Box 317
Fairmont, West Virginia 26554

Arabian
Arabian Horse Association
10805 E. Bethany Drive
Aurora, Colorado 80014
www.arabianhorses.org

Banker Horse
Corolla Wild Horse Fund, Inc.
P.O. Box 361
1126 Old Schoolhouse Lane
Corolla, North Carolina 27927
www.corollawildhorses.com

Foundation for Shackleford Horses, Inc
306 Golden Farm Road
Beaufort, North Carolina 28516
www.shacklefordhorses.org

Belgian
The Belgian Draft Horse Corporation of America
125 Southwood Drive
P.O. Box 335
Wabash, Indiana 46992
www.belgiancorp.com

Belgian Warmblood
Belgian Warmblood Breeding Association
North American District
1979 CR 103
Georgetown, Texas 78626
www.belgianwarmblood.com

Brabant
American Brabant Association
2331A Oak Drive
Ijamsville, Maryland 21754
www.theamericanbrabantassociation.com

Brindle
International Buckskin Horse Association, Inc.
P.O. Box 268
Shelby, Indiana 46377
www.ibha.net

Brindle and Striped Equine International
11819 Pushka
Needville, Texas 77461
www.geocities.com/sbatteate/brindlehos

Buckskin
International Buckskin Horse Association, Inc.
P.O. Box 268
Shelby, Indiana 46377
www.ibha.net

Canadian
Société des Éleveurs de Chevaux Canadiens
Canadian Horse Breeders Association
59 rue Monfette Suite 108
Victoriaville, Quebec G6P 1J8 Canada
www.lechevalcanadien.ca

Carolina Marsh Tacky
Carolina Marsh Tacky Association
6685 Quarter Hoss Lane
Hollywood, South Carolina 29449
www.marshtacky.org

Equus Survival Trust
775 Flippin Road
Lowgap, North Carolina 27024
www.equus-survival-trust.org

Caspian Horse
Caspian Horse Society of the Americas
www.caspianhorse.com

Cerbat
Cerbat Society
Apache Trail Ranch
4970 South Kansas Settlement Road
Wilcox, Arizona 85643
www.anglefire.com/az/xochitl/cerbats.html

Chincoteague Pony
National Chincoteague Pony Association
2595 Jensen Road
Bellingham, Washington 98226
www.pony-chincoteague.com

Cleveland Bay
Cleveland Bay Horse Society of North America
P.O. Box 483
Goshen, New Hampshire 03752
www.clevelandbay.org

Clydesdale
Clydesdale Breeders of the USA
17346 Kelley Road
Pecatonica, Illinois 61063
www.clydesusa.com

Colonial Spanish
Horse of the Americas, Inc.
202 Forest Trail Road
Marshall, Texas 75670
www.horseoftheamericas.com

Colorado Ranger
Colorado Ranger Horse Association
1510 Greenhouse Lane
Wampum, Pennsylvania 16157
www.coloradoranger.com

Connemara
The American Connemara Pony Society
P.O. Box 100
Middlebrook, Virginia 24459
www.acps.org

Dales Pony
Dales Pony Society of America
32 Welsh Road
Lebanon, New Jersey 08833
www.dalesponies.com

Dales Pony Association of North America (Canada)
P.O. Box 733
Walkerton, Ontario
Canada, N0G 2V0
www.dalesponyassoc.com

Dartmoor Pony
American Dartmoor Pony Association
203 Kendall Oaks Drive
Boerne, Texas 78006

Dartmoor Pony Registry of America
295 Upper Ridgeview Road
Columbus, North Carolina 28722
www.dartmoorpony.com

Dole Horse
North American Dole Horse Registry
9650 46th Street NE
Doyon, North Dakota 58327
www.dolehorseusa.com

Donkey
American Donkey and Mule Society, Inc.
P.O. Box 1210
Lewisville, Texas 75067
www.lovelongears.com

Drum Horse
Gypsy Cob and Drum Horse Association, Inc.
1812 E. 100 N.
Danville, Indiana 46122
www.gcdha.com

Dutch Warmblood
The Dutch Warmblood Studbook in North America
P.O. Box 0
Sutherlin, Oregon 97479
www.kwpn-na.org

Exmoor Pony
Exmoor Pony Association International
P.O. Box 1517
Litchfield, Connecticut 06759
www.exmoorpony.com

Exmoor Pony Enthusiasts
P.O. Box 155
Ripley, Ontario N0G 2R0
Canada
http://exmoorenthusiasts.fortunecity.com

Canadian Livestock Records Corporation
2417 Holly Lane
Ottawa, Ontario K1V 0M7
Canada
www.clrc.ca

Falabella Blend Miniature Horse
Falabella Blend Registry
33222 N. Fairfield Road
Round Lake, Illinois 60073
www.falabellafmha.com

Falabella Miniature Horse
Falabella Miniature Horse Association
33222 N. Fairfield Road
Round Lake, Illinois 60073
www.falabellafmha.com

Fell Pony
Fell Pony Society and Conservancy of the Americas
775 Flippin Road
Lowgap, North Carolina 27024
www.fellpony.org

Fell Pony Society
Ion House, Great Asby
Appleby, Cumbria CA16 6HD
United Kingdom
www.fellponysociety.org

Florida Cracker Horse
Florida Cracker Horse Association, Inc.
2992 Lake Bradford Road South
Tallahassee, Florida 32310
www.floridacrackerhorses.com

Foundation Quarter Horse
Foundation Quarter Horse Registry
P.O. Box 230
Sterling, Colorado 80751
www.fqhr.net

Friesian
The Friesian Horse Society, Inc.
17670 Pioneer Trail
Plattsmouth, Nebraska 68048
www.friesianhorsesociety.com

Friesian Heritage Horse
Friesian Heritage Horse and Sporthorse International
133 E. De La Guerra, #159
Santa Barbara, California 93101
www.friesianheritage.com

Galiceno
Galiceno Horse Breeders
P.O. Box 219
Godley, Texas 76044
www.galiceno.homestead.com

Georgian Grande
International Georgian Grande Horse Registry, Inc.
P.O. Box 845
Piketon, Ohio 45661
www.georgiangrande.com

Gotland Pony
Gotland Russ Association of North America
811 Carpenter Hill Road
Medford, Oregon 97501
www.gotlandponies.org

Gypsy Cob
Gypsy Cob and Drum Horse Association, Inc.
1812 E. 100 N.
Danville, Indiana 46122
www.gcdha.com

Gypsy Vanner Horse
The Gypsy Vanner Horse Society
P.O. Box 177
Marlboro, New York 12542
www.gypsyvannerhorsesociety.org

Hackney Horse and Pony
American Hackney Horse Society
4059 Iron Works Parkway, A-3
Lexington, Kentucky 40511
www.hackneysociety.com

Haflinger
American Haflinger Registry
1686 East Waterloo Road
Akron, Ohio 44306
www.haflingerhorse.com

Half Arabian
Arabian Horse Association
10805 E. Bethany Drive
Aurora, Colorado 80014
www.arabianhorses.org

Hanoverian
The American Hanoverian Society
4067 Iron Works Parkway, Suite 1
Lexington, Kentucky 40511
www.hanoverian.org

Highland
Highland Pony Enthusiasts Club of America
1651 Barren Road
Oxford, Pennsylvania 19363
www.hpeca.org

Scottish Highland Pony Society of North America
P.O. Box 425
Boonville, California 95415
www.highland-pony.org

Holsteiner
The American Holsteiner Horse Association, Inc.
222 East Main Street, Suite 1
Georgetown, Kentucky 40324
www.holsteiner.com

Icelandic
United States Icelandic Horse Congress
4525 Hewitts Point Road
Oconomowoc, Wisconsin 53066
www.icelandics.org

Flugnir Icelandic Horse Association
1250 Waterville Road
Waterville, Minnesota 56096
www.flugnir.50megs.com

Irish Draught
Irish Draught Horse Society of North America
4037 Iron Works Parkway, No. 160
Lexington, Kentucky 40511
www.irishdraught.com

Kentucky Mountain Saddle Horse
Kentucky Mountain Saddle Horse Association
P.O. Box 1405
102 Finley Drive, Suite 108
Georgetown, Kentucky 40324
www.kmsha.com

Kiger Mesteño
Kiger Mesteño Association
11124 NE Halsey, Suite 591
Portland, Oregon 97220
www.kigermustangs.org

Lac La Croix Indian Pony
Lac La Croix Indian Pony Society
1–341 Clarkson Road
Castleton, Ontario K0K 1M0, Canada
www.rarebreedscanada.ca

Lipizzan
Lipizzan Association of North America
P.O. Box 1133
Anderson, Indiana 46015
www.lipizzan.org

Mangalarga Marchador
Mangalarga Marchador Horse Association of America
P.O. Box 770955
Ocala, Florida 34477
www.mmhaa.com

Missouri Fox Trotting Horse
Missouri Fox Trotting Horse Breed Association, Inc.
P.O. Box 1027
Ava, Missouri 65608
www.mfthba.com

Morab
International Morab Breeders' Association
International Morab Registry
24 Bauneg Beg Road
Sanford, Maine 04073
www.morab.com

Morgan
The American Morgan Horse Association, Inc.
122 Bostwick Road
Shelburne, Vermont 05482
www.morganhorse.com

Moriesian
Moriesian Horse Registry
1001 N. Russell Road
Snohomish, Washington 98290
www.moriesianhorseregistry.com

Mountain Pleasure Horse
Mountain Pleasure Horse Association
P.O. Box 112
Mount Olivet, Kentucky 41064
www.mtn-pleasure-horse.org

Mule
American Donkey and Mule Society, Inc.
P.O. Box 1210
Lewisville, Texas 75067
www.lovelongears.com

National Show Horse
National Show Horse Registry
10368 Bluegrass Parkway
Louisville, Kentucky 40299
www.nshregistry.org

National Spotted Saddle Horse
National Spotted Saddle Horse Association, Inc.
P.O. Box 898
Murfreesboro, Tennessee 37133
www.nssha.com

National Walking Horse
National Walking Horse Association
Kentucky Horse Park
4059 Iron Works Parkway, Suite 4
Lexington, Kentucky 40511
www.nwha.com

New Forest Pony
The New Forest Pony Association, Inc., and Registry of North America
P.O. Box 206, Pascoag, Rhode Island 02859
www.newforestpony.net

Newfoundland Pony
Newfoundland Pony Society
P.O. Box 8132
St. John's, Newfoundland and Labrador
A1B 3M9 Canada
www.newfoundlandpony.com

Nokota
Nokota Horse Conservancy
208 NW 1st Street
Linton, North Dakota 58552
www.nokotahorse.org

North American Spotted Draft
The North American Spotted Draft Horse Association
17549 U.S. Highway 20
Goshen, Indiana 46528
www.nasdha.net

Norwegian Fjord Horse
Norwegian Fjord Horse Registry
1203 Appian Drive
Webster, New York 14580
www.nfhr.com

Oldenburg
Oldenburg Horse Breeders' Society
150 Hammocks Drive
West Palm Beach, Florida 33413
www.oldenburghorse.com

Palomino
Palomino Horse Association, Inc.
Route 1, Box 125
Nelson, Missouri 65347
www.palominohorseassoc.com

Paso Fino
Paso Fino Horse Association, Inc.
101 North Collins
Plant City, Florida 33563
www.pfha.org

Percheron
Percheron Horse Association of America
P.O. Box 141, 10330 Quaker Road
Fredericktown, Ohio 43019
www.percheronhorse.org

Peruvian Horse
North American Peruvian Horse Association
3095 Burleson Retta Road, Suite B
Burleson, Texas 76028
www.napha.net

Pintabian
Pintabian Horse Registry, Inc.
P.O. Box 360
Karlstad, Minnesota 56732
www.pintabianregistry.com

Pinto Horse
Pinto Horse Association of America, Inc.
7330 NW 23rd Street
Bethany, Oklahoma 73008
www.pinto.org

Pinto Draft Horse
Pinto Draft Registry, Inc.
P.O. Box 738
Estancia, New Mexico 87016
www.pinto-draft-registry.com

Pony of the Americas
Pony of the Americas Club, Inc.
3828 South Emerson Avenue
Indianapolis, Indiana 46203
www.poac.org

Pryor Mountain Mustang
Pryor Mountain Mustang Breeders Association
P.O. Box 884
Lovell, Wyoming 82431
www.pryorhorses.com

Pura Raza Española
The Foundation for the Pure Spanish Horse
4001 Juan Tabo NE, Suite D
Albuquerque, New Mexico 87111
www.prehorse.org

Quarab
International Quarab Horse Association
P.O. Box 263
Hopkins, Michigan 49328
www.quarabs.org

Racking Horse
Racking Horse Breeders' Association of America
67 Horse Center Road
Decatur, Alabama 35603
www.rackinghorse.com

Rocky Mountain Horse
Rocky Mountain Horse Association
4037 Iron Works Parkway
Suite 160
Lexington, Kentucky 40511
www.rmhorse.com

Shetland Pony
The American Shetland Pony Club
81 B East Queenwood Road
Morton, Illinois 61550
www.shetlandminature.com

Shire
American Shire Horse Association
1211 Hill Harrell Road
Effingham, South Carolina 29541
www.shirehorse.org

Spanish Barb
Spanish Barb Breeders Association
P.O. Box 1628
Silver City, New Mexico 88062
www.spanishbarb.com

Spanish Mustang
Spanish Mustang Registry, Inc.
323 County Road 419
Chilton, Texas 76632
www.spanishmustang.org

Spanish–Norman
Spanish-Norman Horse Registry, Inc.
P.O. Box 985
Woodbury, Connecticut 06798
www.spanish-norman.com

Standardbred
U.S. Trotting Association
750 Michigan Avenue
Columbus, Ohio 43215
www.ustrotting.com

Standardbred Pleasure Horse Organization of Maine
SPHO-ME
45 Old Falls Road
Kennebunk, Maine 04043
www.sphomaine.net

Steens Mountain Kiger
Steens Mountain Kiger Registry
26450 Horsell Road
Bend, Oregon 97701
www.kigers.com/smkr

Suffolk
The American Suffolk Horse Association
4240 Goehring Road
Ledbetter, Texas 78946
www.suffolkpunch.com

Sulphur Springs Horse
SulphurSprings Horse Registry, Inc.
1245 South 6300 West
Cedar City, Utah 84720
www.sulphurspringshorseregistry.com

Bureau of Land Management
Utah State Office
440 West 200 South, Suite 500 Salt Lake City, Utah
84145-0155

Sulphur Herd Management Area
Contact: Cedar City Field Office
Chad Hunter
176 E. D. L. Sargent Drive
Cedar City, Utah 84720

Swedish Warmblood
Swedish Warmblood Association of North America
P.O. Box 788
Socorro, New Mexico 87801
www.swanaoffice.org

Tennessee Walking Horse
Tennessee Walking Horse Breeders' and Exhibitors'
Association
P.O. Box 286
Lewisburg, Tennessee 37091
www.twhbea.com

Thoroughbred
The Jockey Club
821 Corporate Drive, Lexington, Kentucky 40503
www.jockeyclub.com

Tiger Horse
The Tiger Horse Association
1604 Fescue Circle
Huddleston, Virginia 24104
www.tigerhorses.org

Trakehner
American Trakehner Association
1536 West Church Street
Newark, Ohio 43055
www.americantrakehner.com

United Kingdom Shetland Pony
Personal Ponies Ltd
The Shetland Register
23 Sergio Way
Hot Springs Village
Arkansas 71909
www.personalponies.org

Virginia Highlander
Virginia Highlander Horse Association
1463 Teas Road,
Sugar Grove
Virginia 24375
www.highlandfarm.iceryder.net

Welara Pony
American Welara Pony Registry
P.O. Box 3309
Landers
California 92285
www.welararegistry.com

Welsh Pony and Cob
Welsh Pony and Cob Society of America, Inc.
720 Green Street
Stephens City, Virginia 22655
www.welshpony.org

INDEX